Image and Brain

Image and Brain

The Resolution of the Imagery Debate

Stephen M. Kosslyn

A Bradford Book
The MIT Press
Cambridge, Massachusetts
London, England

This book was set in Palatino by Asco Trade Typesetting Ltd., Hong Kong and was printed and bound in the United States of America.

Library of Congress Cataloging-in-Publication Data

Kosslyn, Stephen Michael, 1948–
   Image and brain : the resolution of the imagery debate / Stephen M. Kosslyn.
     p.   cm.
   "A Bradford book."
   Includes bibliographical references.
   ISBN 0-262-11184-5
   1. Mental representation. 2. Imagery (Psychology) 3. Visual perception. I. Title.
BF367.K668   1994   93-29742
153.3′2—dc20   CIP

Contents

Preface

This book not only develops a theory of what visual mental imagery is and how it is related to visual perception, but it also explains how this theory developed. Perhaps it is only an urge toward cognitive dissonance reduction, but I have persevered and continued to try to resolve the "imagery debate" long after most of my colleagues have lost interest. And (perhaps more cognitive dissonance reduction?) this turns out to have been a good idea: by turning to the brain, this debate can be resolved to the satisfaction of most people, which is all one can ask.

I found this book exciting to write on the heels of *Wet Mind: The New Cognitive Neuroscience* (Kosslyn and Koenig 1992). *Wet Mind* is an overview of the emerging field of cognitive neuroscience, and by necessity does not delve deeply into any one topic. It was comforting to see that one piece of the larger story could be fleshed out while remaining "plug compatible" with the other parts of the theory (e.g., the parts concerned with memory and motor control). In addition, I finished writing this book at the same time I was reviewing page proofs for my book *Elements of Graph Design*. I was delighted to realize that some of the theory developed here had solid implications for visual display design.

In spite of the excitement I felt when writing this book, it had a difficult birth. It originally started as two separate books, one on high-level visual perception and one on imagery. But it became clear that the two topics were so closely interwoven that they could not easily be distinguished, at least as I conceived of them. By using a theory of visual perception as the foundation for a theory of imagery, I was suddenly confronted with a mountain (almost literally) of research reports to read. Without the gentle but firm prodding of Harry Stanton, I don't know how long I would have compulsively kept reading and writing.

But Harry, and then Teri Mendelsohn, convinced me that there would be no end to the work if I did not restrict the scope of my review. Thus, I have focused here on issues surrounding the nature of imagery representation per se. I have not systematically reviewed work on the role of imagery in learning or in reasoning; nor have I considered imagery in children, the elderly, or other special populations. I also restricted the scope of the material by excluding material on reading and on face recognition and identification; one could argue (as we did in *Wet Mind*) that such abilities ought not be excluded from a general discussion of high-level vision because they draw on processes that are used to identify objects. However, it seems clear that there are special aspects of both reading and face perception, and these topics are rather removed from the central concerns of this book. Even so, getting back to that mountain of articles, many excellent articles did not make it into these pages; there just wasn't time or space.

In addition to thanking Harry and Teri, I would also like to thank Irving Biederman, Charles Gross, Pierre Jolicoeur, Steven Pinker, Justine Sergent, and Michael Tye for taking the time to read an earlier draft and help me weed out errors, clarify the logic, and supply critical missing information. This book is far superior for their efforts, and I cannot thank them enough for letting me profit from their experience, knowledge of the literature, critical acumen, and just plain good sense. Probably to my detriment, I have not always taken their advice (some of the notes explain why), and I must take full responsibility for all flaws in the final version. I would also like to thank my many and varied collaborators (noted in the text), without whom the research summarized here would not have been carried out so well or so quickly. I am particularly grateful to Nat Alpert for his role in leading our PET group and taking the time and trouble to tutor me.

This book would not have been finished so soon if not for Adam Anderson, Christopher Chabris, Gregory DiGirolamo, Greg Horwitz, Anne Riffle, Lisa Shin, Amy Sussman, and William Thompson. Not only did they dig out articles I needed (sometimes in obscure places), but they often had the good judgment to bring me additional material to read. Moreover, Christopher Chabris, Shelia Kennison, and Lisa Shin provided valuable advice about the structure of the book and made useful editorial suggestions. Adam Anderson, Christopher Chabris, and William Thompson also did a superb job producing most of the artwork. And Gregory DiGirolamo and Anne Riffle performed yeoman service checking scores of specific queries I had about articles, helping me to reason through some sticky points, and generally managing the manuscript through its final phases.

I would also like to take this opportunity to thank Terry Allard and Susan Chipman of the Office of Naval Research, John Bruer of the James S. McDonnell Foundation, Alfred Fregly of the Air Force Office of Scientific Research, and Joseph Young of the National Science Foundation. They have been generous not only with their time and advice but also with their intellectual and emotional support. And, of course, I must acknowledge the financial support of their respective institutions, over many years. Without both their personal encouragement and the financial wherewithal to run my laboratory, this book would not have been written.

Finally, I also must thank my wife Robin and sons Justin, David, and Nathaniel for putting up with yet more cranky behavior and distant gazes. I cannot express how grateful I am to have such a supportive family.

Image and Brain

1 Resolving the Imagery Debates

Mental imagery has a long and checkered past, but research and discussion about it never seems to stay away for long. There is probably a good reason for this: Imagery is a basic form of cognition, and plays a central role in many human activities—ranging from navigation to memory to creative problem solving. One of the reasons I find imagery an exciting topic is that it is likely to be one of the first higher cognitive functions that will be firmly rooted in the brain. We are well on our way toward understanding how visual mental images arise from brain activity, and in this book I will describe how such information has illuminated the mechanisms that produce, maintain, interpret, and transform visual mental images.

This is the third book I have written on visual mental imagery, and the fourth that focuses heavily on it (see Kosslyn 1980, 1983; and Kosslyn and Koenig 1992). Thinking about what has changed during these years, I cannot help but see a sharply rising trajectory. In this book I want to show that there has indeed been dramatic progress. I begin with some very brief historical context (for more, see Kosslyn 1980; Paivio 1971; Richardson 1969; Shepard and Cooper 1982; and Tye 1991) and then trace one line of research.

Plato moved imagery to center stage with his famous wax tablet metaphor. He believed that mental images are like patterns etched in wax, and that individual differences could be understood in terms of properties of the wax, such as its temperature, purity, and so forth. The notion that information is represented as images was common throughout the history of philosophy, perhaps finding its heyday during the eighteenth century with the British Associationists. Imagery played a major role in theories of mental events up until psychology and philosophy parted ways; indeed, it held sway during the infancy of scientific psychology, when both Wilhelm Wundt and William James devoted much energy toward understanding it.

But imagery did not remain of central concern long after psychology became a topic of scientific inquiry. The early experimental psychologists were highly aware that they were starting a new science, and were intent that it be a genuine science; this apparently sometimes led them to be obsessed with methodological purity. As philosophers of science have noted, the scientific method rests on being able to distinguish among alternative hypotheses to everyone's satisfaction, which requires that the subject matter be publicly observable (for a classic version of this view, see Popper 1959). Mental images —like all mental events—are notoriously difficult to put on public display, and so the topic is sometimes greeted with raised eyebrows by scientists. But electrons, quarks, and black holes are also difficult to put on public display, and so this cannot be the only reason why imagery is not always regarded as a proper topic for scientific study.

One problem is that with mental images, unlike electrons and the like, psychologists could not even point to the tracks or the spoor left behind. Subatomic particles cause certain effects that can be measured, and these measurements are publicly observable. But how does one measure a mental image? This methodological problem was exacerbated by deeper conceptual problems; psychologists did not know how to characterize the nature of imagery. Clearly, mental images are not actual pictures in the head (there is no light up there, and besides, who would look at them?), but if not actual pictures, what?

These problems made imagery a ripe target for the behaviorists, who denied its very existence. All manner of mental events, and imagery in particular, were not generally considered proper subject matter for scientific psychology from roughly 1913, with Watson's famous article attacking imagery, to the early 1960s.

Imagery returned to the scene for a number of good reasons. First, the radical behaviorism of Watson and his ideological descendants ran out of steam. If that program had lived up to its early promise, scientists may never have strayed from its path. However, as many others have documented (e.g., see Gardner 1985), the radical behaviorist program fell short when applied to the most central human faculties, such as language and thought. Second, as the limits of behaviorism became clear, many researchers interested in "verbal learning" suddenly became cognitive psychologists. The transition often consisted of a shift from studying factors that affect acquisition to those that affect retention, but what of it; the important thing was that mental events were once again acceptable—indeed, essential—components of psychological theories. Third, the necessity for internal events was highlighted by Chomskian linguistics and, perhaps more importantly for the majority of psychologists, by the advent of artificial intelligence (AI; for a review of these developments, see Gardner 1985). It is clear that one needs to understand what goes on in a computer to alter its behavior, but one does not need to know the state of every circuit or piece of memory. Rather, one needs to understand the computer at a slightly more abstract level, at the level of its function—the level of information processing. Psychologists such as Newell, Shaw, and Simon (1958) realized that the language of information processing could be applied as easily to brains as to electronic machines. And so did philosophers, who attempted to buttress the conceptual foundations of the "new" approach (e.g., see Fodor 1968).

Just as imagery was swept out with the receding tide of the early mentalistic psychology of James, Wundt, and their followers, it was swept back in with the rise of cognitive psychology. Paivio in particular deserves enormous credit for spearheading the return of theorizing about imagery during the 1960s. Paivio began his research squarely in the tradition of verbal learning, and quickly discovered that one's ability to learn a set of words was predicted well by how easily one could visualize their referents (e.g., see Paivio 1971). He forced hard-nosed experimental psychologists to take imagery seriously by playing by the rules; he showed that factors affecting imagery accounted for empirical results. This work opened the way for more daring investigations (including some by Paivio himself; see Paivio 1986).

Perhaps the most dramatic example of the new wave of research on imagery is that of Shepard, Cooper, and their colleagues (see Cooper and Shepard 1973; Shepard and Cooper 1982). This research demonstrated conclusively that complex properties of imagery could be studied scientifically—and lent credence to the existence not only of mental images but also of complex operations that could transform them in various ways. For example, these researchers showed that people can mentally rotate objects in images, and that this rotation operation is incremental: People require progressively more time for every additional amount that they must mentally rotate an imaged object. Indeed, these researchers demonstrated that "mentally rotating" an object moves it along a trajectory, showing that one could "catch the image on the fly": They computed the rate of rotation and asked subjects to imagine a pattern rotating, and then presented a stimulus perceptually that should line up or not line up with the image. The presence of the imaged object at a specific orientation was neatly demonstrated by showing that subjects could compare the imaged object to the perceived stimulus fastest if the two were aligned than if additional rotation were necessary (see Cooper 1976; Metzler and Shepard 1974). Similar experiments demonstrated that people can "mentally fold" objects in images and otherwise transform them (e.g., Shepard and Feng 1972). These experiments gave life to the idea that images are internal representations that "stand in" for (re-present) the corresponding objects.

THE IMAGERY DEBATES

The systematic results obtained in imagery experiments convinced researchers that there was something to the claim that humans have "mental images." But this term is notoriously ambiguous, and most interest in psychology has focused on only one facet of imagery—its role in information processing, not its phenomenology or role in emotional life. In this book we will focus on the nature of the internal events that underlie the experience of "seeing with the mind's eye"; we shall not consider the qualities of the experience itself. The term "image" will refer to the internal representation that is used in information processing, not the experience itself. The experience of imagery is a sign that the underlying brain events are taking place, and hence plays an invaluable role in the research—but is not in its own right the present topic of study (for discussions of such research, see Kaufmann 1981, 1983; Marks 1983).

Theories about the role of imagery in information processing took a leap forward when researchers began to think about how one could program a computer to produce specific types of behavior. To program a computer to mimic imagery, one must specify an image representation with particular properties; a representation is a type of code, a way of specifying information. This approach forces one to think clearly about the nature of such representations. As this method became increasingly popular, researchers soon realized that there were many ways to program a computer to mimic imagery. And this soon resulted in a series of debates about the nature of mental imagery representations.

I use the term *debates* rather than *debate* because the so-called imagery debate actually developed into a series of discussions, and each of them had a different focus. Researchers have worked through two phases of this continuing debate and are now in the third (and, I hope, final) phase. In the first phase, the focus was tightly constrained by concepts of alternative types of mental representations that might underlie imagery. This phase consisted of an interplay of philosophical exchanges and empirical research; indeed, professional philosophers played a key role in the discussions (e.g., see Block 1981). In the second phase, the focus shifted to the nature of the empirical results collected during the first phase, and the arguments concerned possible methodological problems with the experiments. And in the third phase, researchers have responded to the possible methodological and conceptual problems with the earlier purely behavioral research by turning to facts about brain function.

Although it may not always have been clear at the time, these debates have resulted in genuine progress; indeed, some of the key issues now appear to be settled.[1] To see how there has been progress, it will be useful to consider each phase of the debate in more detail.

Phase 1: Alternative Mental Representations

There are many ways to specify information in a computer, such as in lists, trees, or images. This observation led researchers to consider how information is represented in the mind when one experiences visual mental imagery. A theory of such "mental activity" is a theory of what the brain does—not at the level of individual neurons, but rather at the level of what ensembles of neurons accomplish. Thus, a given type of mental representation corresponds to a particular method used by the brain to store information. The situation is analogous to the computer: One can talk about a "list" even though there is no physical list in the machine; rather, the machine specifies the information in a way that functions as a list. The properties of representations are necessarily defined in the context of a processing system, which includes both representations and processes that can interpret and manipulate them; functional properties of a representation are only conferred if the appropriate processes are available in a system. For example, if there were no processes that could iterate through items in succession, a list could not be ordered in that system.

As Marr (1982) argued so effectively, different representations make different information easily accessed and used in a processing system. For example, consider the difference between the pattern A and the description "two symmetrical diagonal lines that meet at the top and are joined roughly halfway down by a horizontal line." Both the pattern and the description are representations, and they both are representations of the same thing. However, the first one would be easier to use to determine whether the pattern has an enclosed region, and if so what shape it is. The difference between these two kinds of representations corresponds to the difference between a *depictive* and a *propositional* representation. During the first phase of the debate, researchers argued about whether images correspond to one or the other type of representation.[2] Before we can understand the issue, we must distinguish between the two types of representations in more detail.

A propositional representation is a "mental sentence" that specifies unambiguously the meaning of an assertion. Such a representation must contain a relation, which is often called a predicate. This relation ties together one or more entities, which are called arguments. To use the example from Kosslyn (1980), consider a scene in which a ball is sitting on a box. We can represent this scene propositionally with the notation "ON (BALL, BOX)." In this case, ON is the predicate, which ties together the arguments, BALL and BOX. I have chosen a somewhat clunky notion intentionally, to emphasize that a propositional representation is not a statement in a natural language (such as English), but rather is an abstract way to specify unambiguously the meanings of assertions (which often can be expressed by sentences in natural languages; e.g., see Anderson and Bower 1973). The basic elements of a propositional representation are symbols. In this example, ON is a symbol for a certain relation and BALL and BOX are symbols for certain entities. Symbols convey meaning by arbitrarily assigned associations; XYZ could have been used for any of them as easily as the symbols that were used.

A depictive representation is a type of picture, which specifies the locations and values of configurations of points in a space. For example, a drawing of a ball on a box would be a depictive representation. The space in which the points appear need not be physical, such as this page, but can be like an array in a computer, which specifies spatial relations purely functionally. That is, the physical locations in the computer of each point in an array are not themselves arranged into an array; it is only by virtue of how this information is "read" and processed that it comes to function as if it were arranged into an array (with some points being close, some far, some falling along a diagonal, and so on). In a depictive representation, each part of an object is represented by a pattern of points, and the spatial relations among these patterns in the functional space correspond to the spatial relations among the parts themselves. Depictive representations convey meaning via their resemblance to an object, with parts of the representation corresponding to parts of the object.[3] In this case, a "part" can be defined arbitrarily, cutting up the representation in any way; no matter how you cut it, the part will still correspond to a part of the object (for a more comprehensive treatment of the syntactic and semantic characteristics of the two types of representations, see Kosslyn 1984).

Even this simplified overview should make it clear that the two kinds of representations are very different. When a depictive representation is used, not only is the shape of the represented parts immediately available to appropriate processes, but so is the shape of empty space—and hence your ability to readily determine the shape of the enclosed space in the letter A. Moreover, one cannot represent a shape in a depictive representation without also specifying a size and orientation—but one can easily use a propositional representation to describe a shape without ever mentioning size or orientation. Furthermore, depictive representations do not represent predicates explicitly; instead, the relation between "arguments" emerges from the spatial positions of the depicted objects and parts. In this form of representation, the basic element is a point placed in a certain location, as opposed to an abstract symbol. In short, the two types of representations are clearly distinct, and imagery will have very different properties depending on which type (if either) is used.

Much confusion surrounded this phase of the imagery debates. The issue was not whether people experience visual mental images. All parties agreed that they do. The issue was not whether propositional representations are sometimes used in cognition. All parties agreed that they are. And the issue was not whether images are solely depictive representations. All parties agreed that for a depiction (a picture or mental image) to have meaning, it must be interpreted in a specific way, which involves a propositional component (see Fodor 1975; Rollins 1989; Tye 1991; Wittgenstein 1953). The issue was whether visual mental images rely on depictive representations (which are in turn interpreted by other processes), or whether they are purely propositional representations.

The opening salvo of the first phase of the imagery debates was fired by Pylyshyn in 1973. Pylyshyn attacked the very idea of depictive mental representations; he argued that visual mental images could not be depictive because there is no "little man" to look at them, no light to see by, and so forth. His initial attack rested on putative logical problems with the idea of depictive representations, and he asserted that all internal representations are propositional. According to Pylyshyn, the same types of representations are used in imagery and language—indeed, in all cognitive processing. He argued that the pictorial aspects of the experience of imagery have nothing to do with the nature of the representation that takes part in information processing. Pylyshyn claimed that the pictorial properties evident to introspection are "epiphenomenal"; these properties are like the heat of a flashlight's bulb, which plays no role in performing the function of the device, to shed light.

Pomerantz and I (Kosslyn and Pomerantz 1977) summarized each of Pylyshyn's arguments, and showed that they did not rule out the possibility that depictive mental representations are used during imagery (see also chapter 2 of Kosslyn 1980). Our article triggered a series of exchanges, and a number of others were drawn into the debate (for example, see the commentaries following the article by Kosslyn et al. 1979). This exercise seemed to have helped clarify the issues, but as far as I can tell convinced nobody. If one believed that all mental representations are propositional before reading the debate, one continued to do so afterward; if one believed that imagery relies in part on a distinct type of internal representation, different from that which underlies language, one continued to do so afterward.

The debate moved ahead, however, because of the results of experiments that were conducted to address the issue. These results shifted the focus of the debate to what the findings meant, away from discussions of introspections (e.g., why one cannot "see" all of a tiger's stripes in an image) and preconceptions (e.g., why only propositional representations can convey meaning). Many of these results were from experiments that were designed to focus on what I have called the *privileged properties* of depictive representations, which are not shared by propositional representations; all of these properties arise from the fact that a depiction is a set of points in a functional space. For example, experiments on "mental scanning" focused on the fact that depictive representations use "functional space" to represent actual space, whereas propositional representations do not. In the first paper on image scanning (Kosslyn 1973), I hypothesized that if visual mental images are patterns in a functional space, then more time should be required to shift attention farther distances across imaged objects; scanning was used as a kind of tape measure to show that distance is in fact embodied in the representation.[4] I asked subjects to close their eyes and visualize previously memorized drawings of objects. For example, subjects might close their eyes and visualize a boat with a motor on the left end, a porthole in the middle, and an anchor on the right end. Then, they would focus attention on one end of the object, say the one with the motor. Next, they would hear the name of a part (such as "porthole," or "anchor"—or "mast," which was not present), and were to "look" for the named part on the imaged object. The subjects were to press one button if they could "see" the named part and another if they could not. And in fact, the farther along the object the subjects had to scan from the initial point of focus to find a named part, the more time was required—even though the object was no longer present and the subjects' eyes were closed.

As soon became evident, the results from mental scanning experiments were not conclusive. Propositionalists immediately suggested that the results did not reflect the time to scan across objects in depictive images, but rather reflected the time to work down mental lists of propositions. According to this reasoning, the subjects memorized objects by formulating a series of linked propositions. And the representations of parts that are farther apart on an object would be farther apart on such a list—and hence more time would be required to search from the representation of one part on the list to the representations of increasingly distant other parts. These researchers also showed that networks of linked propositions could capture the spatial structure of complex objects. In this kind of theory, focusing attention on a part corresponds to selecting one argument or proposition in the structure, and scanning corresponds to iterating through the structure (e.g., see Anderson and Bower 1973).

My colleagues and I conducted many experiments to rule out such possible accounts for the scanning results. For example, Kosslyn, Ball, and Reiser (1978) independently varied the distance and the number of objects that subjects scanned over in an image, and showed that subjects required more time to scan greater distances per se (and also required a separate increment of time for each additional object scanned over). Thus, it is not simply the number of parts on the scanned object that determines scanning time. But even so, one could salvage a propositional theory by positing that "dummy" entries are added to a list or network to mark off distance, with more such nodes for greater distances. If so, then the farther the subject would have to scan, the more entries would need to be traversed.

It became clear that the "propositional theory" of imagery was a moving target, and the debate was not going to be settled by any single type of experiment. Part of the problem was that the two kinds of theories are not really cast at the same level of analysis. The depictive theory posited a rather specific type of representation with fixed properties, but the propositional theory posited a formalism that specifies a set of elements that can be combined to form any number of types of representations (ranging from lists to complex interlocking networks).

Even so, as additional experiments were conducted the propositional accounts became more varied and required additional assumptions, whereas the depictive accounts did not require revision. Thus, although no single experiment or type of experiment was conclusive, the weight of the evidence seemed to me (from a purely objective perspective, of course) to lean toward the depictive position. Nevertheless, the hard-core propositionalists staunchly defended their position.

I believe that the propositionalists were not simply being perverse, but rather had several reasons for maintaining their views. First, members of the AI community often think about mental events by analogy to programs written in the LISP programming language. LISP was designed to facilitate recursive search of lists of properties, and such lists correspond to propositional representations. The intuitions developed over years of working with computers transferred to thinking about biological information processing. Second, AI got off to a roaring start, at least in many people's minds if not in reality (see Dreyfus 1979). At the time of this phase of the imagery debates, most researchers in AI and the allied parts of psychology were impressed by how well AI seemed to be doing, and saw no reason to change. If an approach was working in one domain, it seemed reasonable to push it as far as it could go. Third, many researchers liked the apparent simplicity of a single-representation system. I say "apparent" because none of these researchers actually went so far as to implement a computer model that could mimic the observed results. Without such models, it was difficult to know whether such a system would really be very simple. Computer models of imagery by Baylor (1971), Moran (1973), and Farley (1974; for a review see Kosslyn 1980) mimicked selected aspects of imagery, but not those responsible for the results at the center of the debate. (Shwartz and I [Kosslyn and Shwartz 1977, 1978] did in fact implement a system that used depictive images to perform such tasks, thereby laying to rest the idea that such representations would require a "little man in the head" to "look" at them.) And finally, I noted that the eyes of many theoretically oriented researchers tended to glaze over when empirical results were being discussed. These researchers were not very impressed by laboratory findings and instead preferred to rely on their intuitions and logical arguments.

However, most cognitive psychologists tend to focus on data, and many of these researchers took pause when they considered whether the propositional theories provided compelling accounts for all of the empirical findings about imagery. For example, although it was possible to explain the mental rotation findings in terms of networks of propositions and lists of symbols (e.g., see Palmer 1975), such accounts were ad hoc and post hoc. Furthermore, the results that did support a propositional approach (such as those reported by Hinton 1979; Nickerson and Adams 1979; Pylyshyn 1979; and Stevens and Coupe 1978), did not undermine the claim that images rely on depictive representations—they simply showed that imagery also involves propositional representations. But that was never in dispute. Indeed, the imagery theory my colleagues and I developed could easily explain such results (e.g., see Kosslyn 1980, chapter 8). Moreover, the depictive view was leading to a host of nonintuitive (to many, at least) findings (for summaries, see Kosslyn 1980, 1983).

Phase 2: Methodological Problems?

As increasing numbers of empirical findings were reported that documented the effects of "privileged properties" of depictive representations, the focus of the exchanges shifted to these results. In the second phase of the imagery debates, the experiments themselves came under fire. Two kinds of potential methodological problems were debated, sometimes at the same time. First, Pylyshyn (1981) now suggested that the very act of asking subjects to use imagery may lead them to try to mimic what they would do in the corresponding perceptual situation. For example, asking people to scan imaged objects may lead them to mimic what they think they would do when scanning actual objects—and thus to wait longer before responding when a greater distance should have been scanned. He claimed that the task is actually performed using propositional representations, but the variations in response times are determined by another layer of (perhaps unconscious) processing that regulates the output appropriately. Pylyshyn argued that the *task demands* that led subjects to regulate their responses in this way are an inherent aspect of the way imagery tasks are defined.

Although my original imagery experiments (Kosslyn 1973) assiduously avoided using the term *scan* in the instructions, it is possible that the subjects unconsciously inferred that this was what was expected of them. Such possible task demands could be ruled out conclusively by designing imagery tasks that did not require imagery instructions. And such tasks were not long in coming. For instance, Finke and Pinker (1982, 1983; see also Pinker, Choate, and Finke 1984) designed image-scanning experiments in which they never asked the subjects to use imagery, or even told them that imagery might be helpful. In their tasks, the subjects briefly saw a set of randomly located dots, which were replaced by an arrow. The subjects were asked to decide whether the arrow, if it were placed in the same display as the dots, would point directly to one of the dots. The subjects did in fact report (after the experiment) that they had used imagery in this task. Finke and Pinker found that response times increased linearly with increasing distance between the arrow and dot, just as they had in the original scanning experiments; indeed, the rate of increase was very similar to that found in the original experiments. It is hard to see how these findings could have been produced by task demands, given that the tasks were not characterized as "imagery tasks."

The second kind of methodological attack was articulated by Intons-Peterson (1983), who argued that the experiments were flawed because the experimenters had unconsciously led the subjects to produce the expected results. According to this view, the subjects were trying to cooperate by producing the results they thought they were supposed to produce. Similar sorts of *experimenter expectancy effects* have been found in other areas of psychology (e.g., see Rosenthal 1976; Rosenthal and Jacobson 1992). Intons-Peterson (1983) conducted a study in which she explicitly manipulated the expectations of the experimenters, giving half of them one "predicted" pattern of results and the other half another "predicted" pattern of results. In this study, subjects scanned imaged displays in one part of the experiment and scanned actual displays in another part, and the "predictions" concerned the relative times in the two conditions. And in fact, the experimenters' expectations did influence the subjects' mean response times (but did not alter the relative effects of distance on scanning times in the two conditions).

In addition, other researchers reported evidence that subjects sometimes can infer how they are expected to perform in imagery tasks. Richman, Mitchell, and Reznick (1979) and Mitchell and Richman (1980) reported that their subjects could guess the results Kosslyn, Ball, and Reiser (1978) expected in one of their scanning tasks. However, Reed, Hock, and Lockhead (1983) showed that such guessing could not predict all features of image scanning, such as the fact that subjects required more time to scan curved or bent trajectories than straight ones. Furthermore, when Denis and Carfantan (1985) gave 148 subjects a questionnaire and asked them to predict the results of imagery experiments, they found that very few expected the obtained findings. Specifically, they asked, "When people are asked to inspect a mental image, is it generally the case that the time it takes to scan between any two points is proportional to the distance to be scanned?" and found that only 9.5% of the subjects responded "yes," whereas 58.8% responded "no" and 31.8% abstained. (Similar results were obtained when subjects were asked to anticipate the results of "mental rotation" and "mental zooming" experiments.) Regarding Richman, Mitchell, and Reznick's results, Denis and Carfantan wrote, "However, it may be the case that these experiments, which were designed to pin down the alleged role of demand characteristics in Kosslyn, Ball, and Reiser's (1978) experiments, were not themselves free from such demand effects" (p. 56).

Nevertheless, one could argue that experimenter expectancy effects do not require the conscious cooperation of the subjects; perhaps the subjects are only peripherally aware of these expectations, and hence cannot articulate them when asked. Such concerns are countered by a different approach to this issue. Jolicoeur and Kosslyn (1985) responded to Intons-Peterson's argument and results by showing that experimenter expectancies do not alter the time to scan per se, as measured by the increase in time to scan increasing distances across an imaged object. This was the important result, given that my colleagues and I had offered this aspect of the response times as the evidence that image representations embody spatial properties. Jolicoeur and I used a variant of Intons-Peterson's methodology, but now told different experimenters to expect different effects of distance. For example, in one experiment we told the experimenters that subjects would have trouble scanning between close objects on an imaged map because they would be grouped as a single perceptual unit (according to the Gestalt law of proximity), and would have trouble scanning between far objects because more distance needed to be traversed—and thus we expected fastest times for intermediate distances (producing a U-shaped function). We told other experimenters that we expected the increase in time with distance to be sharper for colored maps than black-and-white ones, because the colored ones purportedly had more information; and told yet other experimenters the opposite prediction, because the colored maps were purportedly more vivid. In all cases, the times to scan increased linearly with increasing distance and the experimenter expectancies did not affect the rate of scan. In one case we went so far as to tell the experimenter that the results could not possibly have been correct, that we had very good reason to expect nonlinear increases in scanning time with distance, and sent him back to do the experiment "right."[5] This replication produced the same results as before. We found no effects of experimenter expectations on the slopes of the increases in response times with distance, and this critical aspect of the results cannot be ascribed to such effects.

The limits of such demand characteristics became clear when some researchers intentionally exaggerated them and observed the consequences. These researchers went so far as to tell the subjects to expect to take more time to scan shorter distances than longer distances. Even here, the subjects required more time to scan increasing distance (Goldston, Hinrichs, and Richman 1985). The subjects did vary their rate of scan depending on the instructions, but I would have been surprised otherwise (what good would imagery be if one did not have some control over it?). Given the results, I could not see how one could argue that the increase in time to scan farther distances is due to demand characteristics.

This research showed that imagery is highly constrained. The subjects apparently can control some aspects of processing, such as the speed of scanning, but not others; in particular, they could not eliminate the effects of distance on the time to shift attention across an imaged object. The enduring effects reflect inherent properties of the representation and processes that operate on it; these properties are apparent even when there are no potentially contaminating task demands and even when experimenter expectancy effects lead subjects to have contrary expectations.

Nevertheless, the second phase of the imagery debates ended with a fizzle, with no clear consensus on a resolution. Many found it difficult to rule out the possibility that unconscious motives and beliefs govern subjects' behavior in imagery experiments. Instead, most researchers apparently got tired of the issues and moved on to other topics. Perhaps because I had put so much effort into this work, I was not as willing to move on as were others. It is clear that the brain is a machine, and it works in a specific way and not in other ways; there is a "fact to the matter." If we are doing science, then there should be a way to convince everyone else that some theories are incorrect and others are approximately correct.[6] At this point, we were still trying to pour the foundations: Until we could agree that one theory of how images are represented is worth building on, we could not really move ahead to other central questions, such as how images are formed and used. There is no sense in building on a foundation of sand.

Phase 3: Beyond Behavioral Results

Part of the reason why the imagery debate stalled was that behavioral data typically can be easily explained by more than one theory. Anderson (1978) went so far as to prove that one can always formulate a propositional theory to mimic a depictive one. His proof rests on the pervasive possibility of *structure-process trade-offs*. For example, let us return again to the image-scanning findings. A depictive theory posits a depictive representation (the structure) and an incremental scanning operation that shifts attention across the representation (the process). A propositional theory posits a list or network of propositions (the structure) and an iterative list search operation (the process). The two mechanisms can produce the same results because the difference in the structure is compensated for by a difference in the process that operates on it. There are often many ways to modify a structure or process to make one type of mechanism mimic another. For example, as noted earlier, one can posit "dummy nodes" in the structure to explain the effects of the amount of metric distance that is scanned, or one could just as easily posit that the speed of the iterative search process varies, taking more time when a longer "distance" is specified between two entities. Anderson proved that one can always play fast and loose in this way, making two theories mimic each other even though they posit different representations.[7]

Anderson's paper was greeted with a range of responses. To some, it appeared to raise major problems and was discouraging; to others it appeared irrelevant;[8] and to others it appeared plainly wrong (e.g., see commentaries on Kosslyn et al. 1979, as well as Hayes-Roth 1979 and Pylyshyn 1979). Anderson pointed out, however, that there is at least one clear way out of the quandary: nail down the properties of the structure or process by appeal to something other than behavioral data per se. Once the structure or process is specified, the other will then be highly constrained. He suggested that facts about the brain might provide critical constraints, preventing one from arbitrarily varying properties of a theory.

My colleagues and I have adopted this tack, with some success. Our research was inspired in large part by findings in monkey neuroanatomy and neurophysiology, starting with the discovery that there are many visual areas in the monkey cortex (at least 32 [see Felleman and Van Essen 1991], with additional ones still to be found [e.g., Boussaoud, Desimone, and Ungerleider 1991]). Moreover, roughly half of these visual areas are *retinotopically mapped*. That is, the neurons in the cortical area are organized to preserve the structure (roughly) of the retina. These areas represent information depictively in the most literal sense; there is no need to talk about an abstract functional space akin to that defined by an array in a computer.

This existence of retinotopically mapped visual areas was originally suggested by the existence of "blind spots" that soldiers experienced when specific parts of their brains were damaged; surgeons noticed that these spots could obliterate different parts of the visual field, depending on the location of the wound (see Polyak 1957). The strong demonstration that the cortex itself is spatially organized did not occur until researchers began to record from neurons and mapped their receptive fields (a neuron's receptive field is the part of the visual field in which a stimulus will be registered by the neuron). These researchers found that contiguous stimuli fell into receptive fields of contiguous —or almost contiguous—neurons (see Daniel and Whitteridge 1961).

Tootell et al. (1982) provided dramatic evidence of the spatial structure of certain cortical regions. They first trained a monkey to stare at the center of the pattern illustrated in figure 1.1, which had flashing lights staggered along it. They then injected the animal with 2-deoxyglucose, as the animal stared at the display. The more active a neuron was as the animal viewed the pattern, the more of this radioactively tagged sugar it took up. Shortly thereafter, the animal was sacrificed and the amount of radioactivity was measured across the cortex. The results are illustrated in figure 1.1. As is evident, an image of the pattern was projected into area V1, the first cortical area to receive input from the eyes (also known as primary visual cortex, striate cortex, OC, and area 17). In the image the pattern was magnified at its center (which follows from the greater representation given to the foveal areas of the retina in this area) and otherwise distorted, but its spatial structure is clearly evident.[9] Although V1 is the largest visual area in the macaque, it is not the only one that is retinotopically organized and was not the only one to show the pattern in the animals they studied.

Fox et al. (1986) used positron emission tomography (PET) to demonstrate that area V1 is retinotopically mapped in humans. They asked subjects to look at a disk covered with alternating black and red checks, or to look at rings that were progressively larger and spared larger regions in their centers, which also were covered with alternating black and red checks. A sample stimulus is illustrated in figure 1.2. The subjects stared straight ahead in all cases, so that the larger rings stimulated increasingly peripheral parts of the retina. The experimenters injected the subjects with a small amount of radioactive water

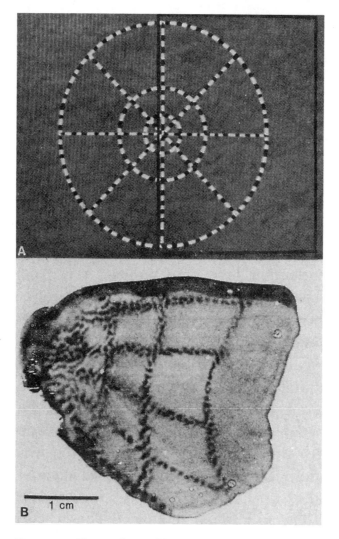

Figure 1.1 The stimulus used by Tootell et al. (top) and portions of area V1 that were particularly active in one hemisphere when the monkey viewed the stimulus (dark stripes, bottom). The results illustrate the retinotopic organization of area V1 in the macaque monkey. (Copyright 1982 by the AAAS. Reprinted from Tootell et al. 1982, with permission.)

(containing ^{15}O, a radioactive isotope of oxygen that has a half-life of about 2 minutes). The harder a portion of the brain works during a task, the more blood is required—and the more blood that is used, the more radioactive water is transported. Thus, more radioactivity in a small region indicates that more blood was present, and hence that more metabolic activity took place. As is discussed in chapter 2, these data are used to construct a three-dimensional image of cerebral blood flow.

Area V1 in human beings is located in the medial part of the back of the brain. As illustrated in figure 1.3, Fox and his colleagues showed that the fovea provides input to the most posterior region, with increasingly peripheral parts of the retina providing input to more anterior parts.

Figure 1.2 An example of the stimuli used by Fox et al. (1986) to study retinotopic mapping in human visual cortex. The size varied so that different parts of retinotopically mapped areas would be stimulated. (Reprinted from Fox et al. 1985, with permission.)

Another important discovery shaped the brain-based approach to studying mental imagery my colleagues and I have adopted: Almost every visual area in the monkey that sends fibers to another visual area also receives fibers from that area. And the fibers running upstream and downstream are of comparable sizes (e.g., see Desimone and Ungerleider 1989; Felleman and Van Essen 1991; Rockland and Pandya 1979; Van Essen 1985). An enormous amount of information apparently runs backward in the system. Although the precise function of these backward (efferent) pathways is not known, it seems clear that these fibers modulate processing of lower-level areas. For example, it has been convincingly demonstrated in monkeys that neural activity is modulated by the animal's goals and intentions (e.g., see Wurtz, Richmond, and Newsome 1984). Indeed, Sandell and Schiller (1982) found that if area V2, which sends efferent fibers to area V1, is cooled to the point where it is functionally deactivated, the responses of fully 32% of the cells in area V1 are affected, with most of them responding less vigorously to visual stimulation. In addition, the feedback connections from at least some prestriate areas to V1 also appear to be topographically organized (Tigges, Spatz, and Tigges 1973; Weller and Kaas 1983; Wong-Riley 1978).

These neuroanatomical features suggested to us that stored visual information might be capable of evoking a pattern of activity in at least some of the retinotopically mapped areas—which would produce a mental image. This general idea has been raised repeatedly (e.g., see Damasio 1989; Damasio et al. 1990; Farah 1989a; Harth, Unnikrishnan, and Pandya 1987; Hebb 1968;

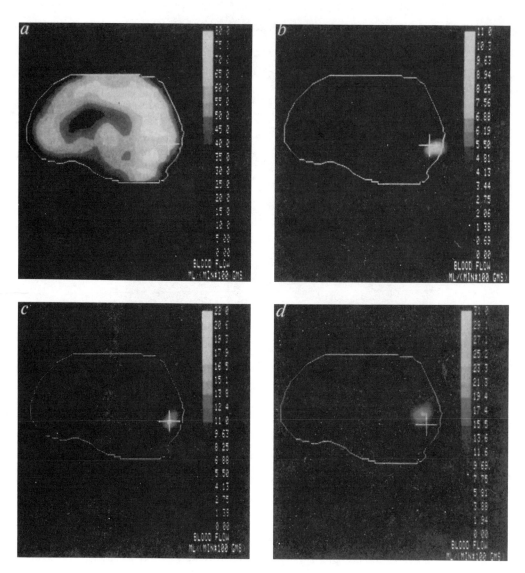

Figure 1.3 Results of Fox et al. 1986, showing that area V1 is retinotopically mapped in humans. The more peripheral parts of the retina project to more anterior portions of the calcarine cortex, as is illustrated in the scans: at the upper left is the resting state; the upper right panel shows response to macular stimulation (mean visual angle of 0.7°); the lower left, response to perimacular stimulation (mean 3.5°); lower right, response to peripheral stimulation (mean 10.5°). (Reprinted from Fox et al. 1986, with permission.)

Kosslyn 1987; Kunzendorf 1990; Merzenich and Kaas 1980). Indeed, similar ideas have been proposed at least since the nineteenth century (see Park and Kosslyn 1990; Kunzendorf 1990).

And in fact, as I shall review in chapter 3, numerous researchers have demonstrated that parts of the brain used in visual perception are also involved in visual mental imagery. Two types of studies have been conducted. First, researchers have tested patients with brain damage; these patients sometimes have imagery deficits that parallel their perception deficits (for reviews, see Farah 1988; Kosslyn and Koenig 1992, chapter 4). For example, Bisiach and his colleagues (e.g., Bisiach and Luzzatti 1978; Bisiach, Luzzatti, and Perani 1979; see also Meador et al. 1987) found that patients with "unilateral visual neglect" not only ignore objects on one side of space during perception, but also ignore objects on that side during visual mental imagery. For example, if asked to close their eyes and visualize a familiar scene and describe what they "see," these patients will not mention objects on the side that they ignore in perception. However, if asked to switch perspectives in their image, so that they are "looking back" toward the previous vantage point, they will ignore objects previously mentioned and describe objects previously ignored (e.g., see Bisiach and Luzzatti 1978). Second, researchers have measured brain activity while subjects use visual mental imagery to perform tasks, and found activation in brain areas used in visual perception. For example, Farah, Peronnet, Gonon, and Girard (1988) recorded evoked potentials while subjects used visual imagery to perform a task, and found activation in the posterior scalp; Goldenberg, Podreka, Uhl, Steiner, Willmes, and Deecke (1989) monitored blood flow with single photon emission computed tomography (SPECT), and found activation in the occipital lobe; and Roland and Friberg (1985) monitored blood flow with the xenon-133 regional cerebral blood flow (rCBF) technique, and found that the posterior part of the brain is active during visual mental imagery.[10] (These methods are described in chapter 2.)

However, all previous research on the brain basis of visual mental imagery relied on methods that have relatively poor spatial resolution. My colleagues and I (Kosslyn, Alpert, Thompson, Maljkovic, Weise, Chabris, Hamilton, and Buonanno 1993) used PET to discover whether visual mental imagery involves topographically organized visual cortex. We asked subjects to *close their eyes* and listen to the names of letters of the alphabet. They were to visualize the standard uppercase version of each letter, and then to judge one of its properties. For example, we asked whether the letter had any curved lines (e.g., which is true for *B* and *C*, but not true for *A* and *E*). On one set of trials, the subjects were asked to form their images as if the letters were being seen at a very small size (i.e., so that they seemed to subtend a small visual angle). The letters were to be as small as possible while still remaining "visible." On another set of trials, the subjects were to form their images as if the letters were being seen at a much larger size, as large as possible while still remaining entirely "visible." The image was retained at the appropriate size for three seconds before the query was presented. As usual, we found that subjects generally required more time for the smaller images (replicating

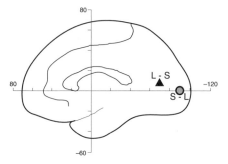

Figure 1.4 Results of a PET-scanning experiment in which subjects closed their eyes and visualized letters at small sizes or at large sizes. The triangle labeled L-S indicates the focus of activity when blood flow evoked by small images was subtracted from blood flow evoked by large images; the circle labeled S-L indicates the focus of activity when blood flow evoked by large images was subtracted from blood flow evoked by small images. Each tick mark specifies 20 mm relative to the anterior commissure. (Adapted from Kosslyn, Alpert, Thompson, Maljkovic, Weise, Chabris, Hamilton, Rauch, and Buonanno 1993.)

Kosslyn 1975), which was behavioral evidence that they were following the instructions.[11]

We reasoned that when the letter was imaged at a small size, neurons in a small region within a topographically mapped area would have to work harder to preserve fine-grained spatial variation, compared to when the letter was imaged at a large size. When the image was large, this small region might be empty or a single segment might pass through it. On the other hand, when the image was large, regions of a topographically mapped area that represent more peripheral stimuli should be active that were not active when the image was small. Thus, we could use the same task as its own control, comparing the selective effects of forming images at relatively large versus small sizes.

As illustrated in figure 1.4, even though the subjects performed this task with their eyes closed, area V1 was activated. But more interesting, the *anterior part* of this area—which represents parafoveal input—was more active when the subjects visualized the letters at the large size, compared to when they visualized the letters at the small size. And the *posterior part* of this area—which represents foveal input—was more active when the subjects visualized the letters at the small size, compared to when they visualized the letters at the large size. This result was as expected, given the topography of area V1 in humans.

Moreover, the precise loci of the differences in activation for large versus small images are about where one would expect to find them if V1 were in fact activated. The stimuli used by Fox et al. (1986) subtended means of 0.7, 3.5, and 10.5 degrees of visual angle. Steven Petersen was kind enough to translate the published coordinates for the centroids of activation into the Talairach and Tournoux (1988) coordinates that we used; using these coordinates, the centroids for the three progressively larger sizes were -83.7, -77.7, and -74.18 mm posterior to the anterior commissure (AC, the locus where the crosshairs meet in figure 1.4), respectively. In our imagery experiment, the letters imaged at the small size selectively activated a region 88 mm posterior to the AC. Given the results reported by Fox et al. 1985, this finding would imply that subjects imaged the small letters at a fraction of a degree of visual angle. This inference is plausible: this size corresponds to the angle subtended by typed letters on a page held at normal reading distance.

The letters imaged as large as possible selectively activated a region 69 mm posterior to the AC. The subjects were told to visualize the letters "as large as possible while still remaining entirely visible." In my earlier experiments (Kosslyn 1978), I estimated the "visual angle" subtended by imaged objects with such instructions. In these experiments, subjects visualized objects and imagined "walking toward them" until the object just seemed to "overflow" the image (i.e., its edges became blurred). At this point, they estimated the distance to the object (in various ways, such as by positioning a tripod away from a wall), which allowed me to compute the visual angle subtended by the imaged object at the point of overflow. The estimated angle was about $12.5°$ for line drawings of animals, but this estimate varied from about $16.5°$ to $20.5°$ for black rectangles (depending on the precise instructions and procedure). The mapping of the visual field to different parts of area V1 can be approximated by a logarithmic scale (outside of the more central regions; e.g., see Schwartz 1977; Van Essen, Newsome, and Maunsell 1984; see also Cavanagh 1984). Thus, the 69 mm location that was selectively activated by the large images is within the region one would expect, given the resolution limits of the technique and the Fox et al. (1985) finding of a centroid at -74.18 mm when their stimuli subtended a mean of $10.5°$ of visual angle.[12]

For present purposes, all that is important is that imagery relies on topographically organized regions of cortex, which support depictive representations. Hence I do not want to press the issue of whether area V1 per se was activated here. It is important to note that in the monkey the fovea is represented in contiguous portions of several areas (V1, V2, V3, and V4; see Van Essen 1985) at the occipital pole. The activation we observed could have been from the human analog of any of these areas. Indeed, neurons in at least one of these areas, V4, have been shown to be modulated by nonvisual input (e.g., see Haenny, Maunsell, and Schiller 1988; Moran and Desimone 1985). In addition, given the resolution limits of PET, it is possible that the large images activated another topographically organized area near area V1. In general, one must be cautious about making strong claims about localization as established by PET, if for no other reason than that the results are obtained by averaging over subjects; it is well known that there are large individual differences in the size and positions of specific anatomical areas, especially primary visual cortex (e.g., see Rademacher et al., in press).

Nevertheless, it is worth noting that several functional magnetic resonance imaging (fMRI) studies have now produced converging evidence that area V1 is in fact activated during visual mental imagery. Specifically, Le Bihan et al. (1993) report activation in V1 when subjects are asked to visualize just-seen flashing square patterns of diodes, and Menon et al. (1993) report (small) activation in V1 when subjects visualize a scene and visualize navigating through it and when they imagine familiar objects (such as fruit and vegetables). Similarly, in a collaboration with Belliveau we have found activation in V1 in some subjects when they visualize letters with their eyes closed.

At first glance, these findings suggest that imagery does rely on depictive representations, given that such representations occur in topographically organized cortex. But what would a critic say? The obvious comeback is that the effect is purely epiphenomenal. Perhaps area V1 gets engorged with blood during imagery because when higher-level (propositionally based) visual areas operate, they "automatically" stimulate lower-level areas via the feedback connections. But, according to this view, the lower-level activity we observed would play no role in information processing.

Given that one could interpret the PET results this way, it is comforting that there is a way around this problem. Namely, if the activity in V1 were epiphenomenal, then damaging this area should not affect imagery. In contrast, if the damaged area serves as the spatial medium in which depictive images occur, then when it is reduced, the possible scope of imaged objects should thereby be restricted. If this occurs, one cannot assert that area V1 utilizes purely propositional representations.

Thus, it is important that damage to the occipital lobe, including area V1, impairs visual mental imagery. Farah, Soso, and Dasheiff (1992) recently asked a patient to indicate the visual angle subtended by objects in her mental images before and after brain surgery. This patient had the occipital lobe in one hemisphere removed. And in fact, removing one occipital lobe drastically reduced the visual angle at which objects could be visualized. Indeed, the angle shrank to a roughly half of its previous size along the horizontal axis! (In one experiment, using relatively complex images of common objects, there was a postoperative decrease of approximately 60%, but this decrease could not be isolated to the horizontal axis; in a second experiment, using a horizontal or vertical ruler as the stimulus, a 40% decrease was observed along the horizontal axis per se.) Farah, Soso, and Dasheiff showed that this result was unlikely to be due to experimenter expectancy effects; even when told that "patients like her" have trouble visualizing color, she was still within normal limits at using imagery to recall colors of objects (when the colors were not verbally associated with the objects; e.g, the color of the skin of a pineapple). By self-report, her images apparently were complete, but apparently were crammed into a smaller visual angle than normal.

In short, we have good evidence that imagery is not purely propositional, but rather relies on depictive representations. Area V1 and nearby visual areas are spatially organized, and—as will be discussed in more detail in chapter 9—visual mental images rely on such structures.

RESOLVING THE IMAGERY DEBATES

Are the imagery debates now resolved? Unfortunately, no. At the heart of the debates lie two issues. I have so far focused on the narrow one, delimiting the properties of the representation itself. But there is a broader, perhaps more compelling issue. Pylyshyn's first paper on imagery was entitled "What the mind's eye tells the mind's brain: A critique of mental imagery." As the title implies, one of his concerns was that there may be an infinite regress: if something is interpreting the image, what inside that something must be interpreting its interpretation of the image, and so on? His concern was that depictive images can only represent information if the appropriate kind of processes are available, which he felt was implausible. Shwartz and I (Kosslyn and Shwartz 1977, 1978) developed computer simulation models to show that this was not an in-principle problem; if computers could use depictive representations, there could not have been a reason why such infinite regresses must, in principle, occur. But Shwartz and I formulated our models in ignorance of facts about the brain; we relied primarily on empirical results and on logical analyses when designing the architecture of our model. One could argue that such a model does not speak to the issue; the fact that a computer can be programmed to use depictive representations does not necessarily imply that such an ability falls within the purview of the mind. If the mental machinery does not exist to use depictive mental images, then—by definition—they are epiphenomenal.

Thus, in order to resolve the imagery debates one must not only make a compelling case that imagery relies on depictive representations, but also must show how such representations *arise* and are *used* within the context of the processing system as a whole. The imagery debate, then, can only be resolved by a relatively thorough understanding of imagery. The remainder of this book focuses on this broader aim, to understand how depictive imagery representations are produced in the brain and used by neural mechanisms in the service of memory and other cognitive processes.

Plan of the Book

The organization of this book reflects a fundamental assumption, which is defended in chapter 3: specifically, visual mental imagery and visual perception share common mechanisms. It is now common to think of imagery as a by-product of mechanisms that are also used in visual object identification; mechanistic proposals along these lines date at least back to Bain (1885; see James's chapter on imagery in his *Principles of Psychology*, 1891). But I will argue that imagery is not merely a parasite, piggybacking on perception. Rather, imagery is an integral part of how perception operates. This idea has become popular in—of all places—some corners of AI. Thus, in this book I shall provide an integrated theory of visual object identification and visual mental imagery.

Chapter 2 To settle the debates, one must show how depictive mental images arise and are used.[13] My goal is to specify a set of mechanical components that constitute a processing system, to pull the imagery system apart at its joints, as it were. But how can one discover its joints, the boundaries that delimit distinct processing subsystems? This chapter outlines the cognitive neuroscience approach taken in the book. I summarize my fundamental assumptions about computational systems and neural information processing; I also summarize the primary methodologies that have been used in the field, and briefly note the relative strengths and weaknesses of each. This discussion provides a strong motivation for the converging evidence approach adopted in this book.

Chapter 3   In this chapter I argue that a single theory should be developed to understand the later phases of visual perception and visual mental imagery. This approach is conducive to theorizing about imagery in part because it is much easier to understand visual perception than to understand imagery. If mechanisms subserving visual object identification also underlie imagery, then one can build on the wealth of knowledge about perception, its computational properties, and its neural substrate when theorizing about imagery. After reviewing evidence that imagery and perception share common processes, I provide a taxonomy of the major perceptual abilities that must be explained by any theory; much of the discussion in the ensuing chapters is directed at understanding some of these specific abilities. Following this, I introduce the "protomodel," the basic processing framework, that will guide the investigations throughout the rest of the book.

Chapter 4   This is the first of four chapters that focus on perceptual processes; in these chapters I consider how the visual system solves specific classes of "problems" that any visual system like ours must solve if we are to recognize and identify objects as we do. The proposed solutions rest on decomposing visual processing into sets of "processing subsystems" (black boxes). This and the following three chapters are devoted to developing a theory of subsystems; each of these chapters focuses on progressively more difficult problems. The "solutions" for the more difficult problems build on those offered in the previous chapters. The questions in chapter 4 focus on how we humans can identify objects when they are in different parts of the visual field or appear at different distances (and so project images of different visual angles on the retina). I begin here to flesh out the protomodel, and show how imagery is indeed a critical part of perception per se.

Chapter 5   In this chapter I discuss the problem of how people can identify objects when an object is rotated or seen from an unusual vantage point, so that not all its parts are visible. This problem can be addressed only by augmenting the theory, fleshing out the kinds of events that must take place in various processing streams. In so doing, additional properties of imagery come to the fore.

Chapter 6   The previous analysis is here extended to address how people can identify objects when the input is degraded; for example, as occurs when another object partially occludes an object. I will argue that the processes that underlie imagery play an important role in such circumstances.

Chapter 7 Many objects, such as a human form or bicycle, can project many different input images, depending on how the parts are arranged. This chapter centers on the problem of how people identify objects when they project novel shapes. The solution I propose implies the existence of additional component processing systems and implies that objects are represented in memory in specific ways.

Chapter 8 Before moving more strongly into imagery proper, it is necessary to ensure that the theory is solidly grounded. Hence, after summarizing the theory, I present a PET study that tests key predictions, review how the theory explains (at a coarse level of analysis) five classes of our abilities to identify objects in different circumstances, and review the literature on picture naming. The theory not only allows us to understand subtle differences in the time required to name pictures in various conditions, but also helps us to understand behavioral deficits following brain damage.

Chapter 9 In this chapter I show how the subsystems inferred for object recognition and identification are used to generate and maintain visual mental images. In so doing, I distinguish among four distinct ways in which images may be generated, which rely on different parts of the brain; these distinctions illuminate the complex patterns of cerebral lateralization that have been reported in the literature. The results from additional PET studies of imagery are also discussed; these PET results provide strong support for the claim that the same subsystems are used in high-level visual perception and visual mental imagery, and thereby move us closer to a resolution of the imagery debates.

Chapter 10 Once an object or scene is visualized, it may be inspected and transformed. I argue here that image inspection and transformation not only work together, but also share some of the same underlying processes. Image transformations are particularly interesting because they are somewhat paradoxical: Objects rotate through trajectories, grow or shrink incrementally, and so on—even though there is no necessary reason why they must pass through intermediate positions. In this chapter I explore the relation between the motor system and the visual system, and suggest that some image transformations involve specific types of interactions between the two systems.

Chapter 11 This chapter begins with a summary of how the perceptual subsystems give rise to our imagery abilities, and then I describe how the present theory subsumes the critical distinctions made by the earlier version of the theory (Kosslyn 1980), which allows the new version to account for all of the phenomena explained by the previous one. I then describe a test of the theory as a whole that focuses purely on the claims about function; this test also provides insights into the nature of individual differences in imagery. The book ends end with a look toward the future, and some thoughts about ways in which a theory such as the present one can illuminate other aspects of cognition.

2   Carving a System at Its Joints

At the end of the previous chapter we were left with the puzzle of how mental images arise and are used. To solve this puzzle, one must specify the architecture of the system in which images arise and are used, which requires delineating its major components and the ways in which they interact. To eliminate any whiff of mysticism, the components must be characterized mechanically; we need to see how particular kinds of inputs are converted to particular kinds of outputs. I call the "black boxes" that perform such input/output mappings *processing subsystems*. I assume that each processing subsystem corresponds to a neural network or to several related neural networks. "Related" neural networks, in this sense, work together to produce an output from an input.

There are many sorts of explanations one could seek for our visual abilities. In the present project, the ultimate goal is to understand visual processing so well that one could program a computer to mimic the brain. As stated, this goal is patently beyond reach; we simply do not know enough to mimic every aspect of what the brain is doing during even the simplest acts—let alone during something as complex as vision or mental imagery. Thus, I am forced to be more modest in the immediate goal: I seek to understand the components of visual processing and the principles that govern their interactions well enough to mimic such processing on a computer at a relatively coarse level. My goal is to pull the bird apart at the joints, not to describe the musculature, vasculature, and neural enervation of the limbs themselves. I want to make the case that specific subsystems exist, not that they use specific algorithms.

PROCESSING SUBSYSTEMS

A processing subsystem is characterized in terms of its function; it corresponds to a network or set of networks that maps an input to an output. Processing subsystems can be characterized more precisely as performing *computations*. A computation is a *systematic mapping between interpretable inputs and outputs*. To clarify the concept, consider a simple example: When the input is 2 + 2, the computation produces the output 4; when the input is 3 + 2, the computation produces the output 5, and so on. The input can be interpreted as specifying quantities and a relation between them, and the output can be interpreted as specifying a quantity. The mapping between input and output is systematic; it can be described by a function. Thus, the mapping is a computation, addition.

Computation need not involve numbers. For example, the input and output might be interpreted as words. In this case, one input might be *cat, ape, boy*, and the corresponding output *ape, boy, cat*, and another input *fox, bird, dog*, and the corresponding output were *bird, dog, fox*, and so on. The mapping could be described as reordering the inputs so that words starting with letters near the beginning of the alphabet are placed before those starting with letters toward the end of the alphabet. Thus, this mapping is a computation, alphabetization.

Any mechanism can compute, provided that the input and output are interpretable and there is a systematic mapping between input and output. For example, a computation could be performed by a strainer, if one had a bowl of lumpy flour and a way of interpreting lumps in the flour as conveying information. Lumps of specific sizes could be interpreted as numbers, with relatively large ones corresponding to smaller numbers and relatively small ones to larger numbers. If so, then pouring the flour through the strainer could allow it to map an interpretable input to an interpretable output in a systematic way, and hence to perform a computation. For instance, a largish size lump might be interpreted as 2, and when two of these go in, the only interpretable small lump coming out might correspond to 4. In this case, the strainer would be performing addition. If we interpreted the sizes of lumps differently, it might perform division, alphabetization, and so forth. What a system computes depends on how the inputs and outputs are interpreted.

Processing subsystems can be likened to a strainer, taking an input pattern and converting it to an output pattern. As was illustrated by the analogy, what is computed is determined in part by how the input and output are interpreted. In the brain, the interpretation of visual input depends, ultimately, on its relation to physical properties of objects in the world. Similarly, the interpretation of output (e.g., commands to move one's eyes) depends, ultimately, on its effect on action. In the following chapters, I will characterize each processing subsystem by specifying the input a set of neurons receives, the operation they perform on the input, and the output they produce (which then typically serves as input to other processing subsystems).

In this book I assume that computations are performed by "neural networks" (also known as "parallel distributed processing systems" or "connectionist systems," see Anderson, Pellionisz, and Rosenfeld 1990; Churchland and Sejnowski 1992; Grossberg 1988; McClelland and Rumelhart 1986; Rumelhart and McClelland 1986). Models of such networks accept a binary vector (string of 1's and 0's) as input, and produce another binary vector as output. Perhaps the most basic principle underlying the operation of neural networks is that of *constraint satisfaction*. Although the inputs to subsystems may often be noisy (i.e., some values of elements may be determined randomly), they function effectively because networks attempt to reconcile all aspects of the input with a single interpretation. Consider the following metaphor: During one phase of my life, my wife and I moved a lot. When moving into a new house, we had to decide where to put our furniture. In the bedroom had to go the bed, a couch, two end tables, and a small table. Each piece of furniture had some weak constraints associated with it (weak, because in and of themselves they did not dictate exactly how the piece must be placed). For example, the headboard of our bed was old and needed to be against a wall, so the bed could not be placed free standing; the couch was missing a rear leg (it rested on three telephone books), and hence could not be positioned so that one could see it from behind; the table had to go in front of the couch; and the end tables had to go next to the bed. Even though each of these constraints was weak, a remarkable thing happened as soon as the bed was positioned: There usually was only a single way to arrange the rest of the furniture while respecting each of the constraints. The bed took up one wall, and only one other wall was long enough for the couch, the table had to go in front of the couch, and so on. Although satisfying each constraint individually was easy, it was no mean feat to satisfy the entire set at once.

My colleagues and I have used network models in a somewhat unconventional way. We do not take the networks seriously as realistic models of the internal workings of individual subsystems, but rather treat them as devices that perform a specific type of input/output mapping. We use the networks to determine under what circumstances (e.g., with which patterns of connectivity among the units) a given input/output mapping can be accomplished effectively. To measure how well a network performs, we simply train it for a fixed number of trials and then measure the error (the squared value between what it produces and what it should produce, if it were operating perfectly).

To assess the ease of establishing specific input/output mappings, we have used the simple feedforward, backward error propagation technique (see Rumelhart and McClelland 1986). To review briefly, the units in such models can be divided into three types: input, "hidden," and output. The input to the network is a pattern of activity over the input units, a vector. Each input unit is connected to one or more hidden units, and the strength of each connection is adjusted during training. Connections with strong positive (excitatory) weights pass more activation to the receiving unit than connections with weaker weights. Similarly, connections with strong negative (inhibitory) weights inhibit the receiving unit from being activated more than connections with weaker negative weights. Each hidden unit is activated in proportion to the total activation reaching it from the input units. However, the output from each hidden unit is not linearly related to its total input, but rather is filtered by a logistic function, so that small increments of activation have less effect if the total amount is relatively small or relatively large. Each hidden unit in turn is connected to one or more output units, which are like the hidden units but receive their input from the hidden units rather than from the input units directly. If an output unit receives a total amount of activation over some threshold, it is "on." In general, each output unit corresponds to a single response. For example, if a set of shapes is presented in the input (which may be an array, representing shapes by patterns of "on" and "off" units), each output unit might correspond to the name of an individual shape.

These networks typically are trained so that they "learn" to perform a specific input/output mapping. At the outset, very small, random weights are placed on the connections. Thus, the network begins by performing randomly. For example, when presented with one shape, it might respond by having no output unit turn on. On each trial, a "teacher" compares the output with the expected output. If a given output unit were off and should have been on, the difference between its current value and 1 (the expected value) is computed, and the weights on all of the connections leading to that output unit are adjusted to reduce the disparity between what was observed and what was expected. In this example, the positive weights would be increased, and the negative ones reduced (made less negative). This process is performed incrementally, so that other associations built into the network (e.g., to other input shapes) are not obliterated. (For a very introductory treatment of these networks and this training technique, see chapter 2 of Kosslyn and Koenig 1992.)

Although feedforward network models of this type capture certain coarse properties of neural networks in the brain, they are poor models of actual neural processing. For example, unlike actual neural networks, they require a teacher, units within a level do not influence each other, with training the same connection can change from excitatory to inhibitory or vice versa, they do not embody the recurrent connections endemic to neural networks, and so on. Nevertheless, the input/output mappings performed by these models are of interest because they capture key features of the corresponding mappings performed by groups of neurons. For example, I find it remarkable that Zipser and Andersen (1988) were able to reconstruct the shapes of receptive fields of neurons in area 7a (in the parietal lobe) by examining the "receptive fields" (regions of the input that maximally activate a given hidden unit) of simulated networks. Similarly, Lehky and Sejnowski (1988) trained a network to compute shape from variations in shading. The hidden units of their networks developed properties like those of neurons in visual cortex, with some units appearing to be tuned for different orientations. In addition, they found that some output units spontaneously became sensitive to the termini of lines, developing strong "end-stopped inhibition"—mimicking "end-stopped" complex cells in visual cortex (see Hubel and Wiesel 1962). This finding is fascinating because the existence of such cells was something of a mystery; the world is not filled with line termini. And the fact that no cells had been found that are tuned for curvature was also a mystery, given that the natural environment is characterized by curved objects. Lehky and Sejnowski's finding suggests that "end-stopping" may be a consequence of processes that compute curvature (see also Dobbins, Zucker, and Cynader 1987). Such findings, then, suggest that the mapping accomplished by feedforward, backward error propagation models do indeed reflect key aspects of the corresponding mappings accomplished in the brain.[1]

Weak Modularity

Because the present goal is to delineate processing subsystems, it is critical to have a good idea of what we are seeking. It will be useful to contrast the sorts of components sought here with the "modules" posited by Fodor (1983). For Fodor, a module is a kind of cognitive reflex; it is a self-contained black box that does the same thing to an input regardless of what else is going on in the system. A module is not "cognitively penetrable"; outputs from one module cannot affect the inner workings of another module. Fodor did not try to characterize components within the visual system, but rather treated the entire visual system as a module. Although his characterization may have utility at very coarse levels of analysis, it stands little chance of being an apt description of the component processes that underlie visual processing (nor would Fodor have argued that it should). Rather, such components appear to be only weakly modular. This assumption is based on the following observations.

Penetrability   As noted in chapter 1, one of the most striking aspects of the visual system is the fact that almost every area that sends projections to another area in turn receives projections from that area. Feedback is the rule, and the projections do not simply gate the output of the sending network. Rather, in most cases feedback appears to modulate actual internal processing (e.g., see Rockland and Pandya 1979; Shepherd 1988; Van Essen and Maunsell 1983).

The crosstalk among components suggests that it is useful to adopt Simon's (1981) conception of *nearly decomposable subsystems*. The idea can be illustrated with a metaphor (which I have freely adapted from one used by Simon). Imagine that there is a large warehouse that is subdivided into rooms, and each room in turn is subdivided into cubicles. The rooms are separated by relatively thick walls, and the cubicles by relatively thin walls. As you can imagine, it is not easy to make the employees happy in such a rabbit warren. As a concession to the workers, each of the cubicles has its own thermostat, and the workers are free to set the temperature as they wish. One cubicle houses someone who sets his thermostat to 53°; another, someone who sets her thermostat to 82°, and so on. At the end of each winter day, the heat is turned off and the building begins to cool. If we measure the temperature in the cubicles 5 minutes after closing time, they appear to be independent; each has its own temperature. But consider what happens when we return to measure the temperature several hours later: Now the cubicles in a room have roughly the same temperature, but the rooms still have different overall temperatures. And when we return several hours later still, now even the rooms are approximately the same temperature. The system is best understood as having nearly decomposable subsystems. At a coarse level of analysis, the subsystems operate independently; the interactions among them are weak, and are only evident when sensitive measures are used.

Functional Interdependence   Processing subsystems can be characterized at multiple levels of scale, with coarse subsystems specifying the joint activity of a number of finer-grained subsystems that work together to accomplish an input/output mapping. In some cases, two or more coarse subsystems may draw on the same component process. I assume that a relatively specialized processing subsystem may contribute to the operation of more than one more coarsely characterized processing subsystem. For example, visual area MT contains neurons that respond selectively to motion, which has led many to conclude that a process that encodes motion is implemented in this area (as will be discussed in chapter 6). The outputs from this area project to area V4, which has a preponderance of cells that respond selectively to wavelength; this and other properties of the neurons have led many to infer that V4 is involved in processing color (e.g., see DeYoe and Van Essen 1988). Color is one cue we used to discriminate figure from ground. The connections from area MT to area V4 make sense if motion is also used to perform figure/ground segregation. MT also has connections to the posterior parietal lobe, which make sense if motion is used to track objects (which the parietal lobe appears to be involved in; see Allman, Miezin, and McGuinness 1985; Van Essen 1985, 1987).

Some subsystems may be like letters in a crossword puzzle that are used in two words. This sort of arrangement could arise if brain structures that evolved for one purpose later were recruited in the service of another (see Darwin 1859). This sort of functional interdependence implies that two or more subsystems (e.g., involved in figure/ground segregation and in visual tracking, respectively) may be mutually constrained. If the shared component subsystem is degraded (due to drugs, brain damage, old age, etc.), it will affect all of the subsystems that utilize it. Moreover, if the subsystem has just been used in one context, it may be primed to be used in another. Thus, the state of one subsystem (characterized at a relatively coarse level) can affect the inner workings of another, violating Fodor's notions of strong modularity.

Incremental Transitions   Subsystems that work together to accomplish a particular computation or set of computations should be "plug compatible"— the output from one should provide useful input to at least one other. This assumption suggests that some individual computations, although distinct, may be intimately related. Indeed, the abundance of recurrent connections in the brain suggests that lines between some subsystems are only weakly drawn.

Anatomical Localization   The subsystems I characterize need not always correspond to a group of neurons that are in contiguous parts of the brain, but I suspect that at least some portions of the networks usually are localized to discrete sites in the brain. My reasoning is as follows: First, nearby neurons receive similar inputs and project similar outputs, and subsystems are defined in part by the inputs they receive and the outputs they project. Second, nearby neurons typically are richly interconnected in the cortex (indeed, the majority of cortical connections are short), which affords them ample opportunity for fast, local interaction. Such interaction is particularly useful if the neurons are cooperating to carry out a single operation, in which case the interactions facilitate precise mapping of input to output. As an analogy, cities sprang up in part because local proximity facilitates communication. With the advent of the information age, we see some of these forces lessening, but this is only possible because of telephones, electronic mail, fax machines, and other high-speed long-distance communication. The brain is a relatively slow machine, and such long-distance communication is not as rich as local communication; neuronal cities appear to be a good idea. Indeed, Jacobs and Jordan (1992) report that networks with predominantly short connections can self-organize into modules more easily than networks with longer connections. Such properties may be fortunate, given Cherniak's (1990) compelling arguments that physical constraints dictate that most connections must be short.

Nevertheless, it is important to note that not all of the neurons that compose a subsystem need to be in the same anatomical location. Damasio (1989, 1990) suggests that what is localized are *convergence zones*. These are regions where input serves to trigger associative responses, including feedback to augment the input itself. All other parts of neural networks may be intertwined—and may share common neural substrates (for a similar view, see also Harth, Unnikrishnan, and Pandya 1987). From my perspective, this idea makes good sense both physiologically and anatomically. Hence, when I later speak of subsystems as if they are implemented in a particular site in the brain, this should be understood as shorthand for speaking of these critical portions of the networks. I do not assume that all of a network is necessarily localized to a given region of the brain. PET scanning and the like will tell us about the very active central core of a network, but may well miss more diffuse activation elsewhere.

Overlapping Implementation   The assumption that subsystems are implemented at least in part in localized tissue does not imply that neural loci are dedicated to only a single type of processing. Different processing subsystems may be implemented in partly overlapping neural regions. For example, color and shape are probably extracted in interdigitated portions of area V2 (Livingstone and Hubel 1987, as well as in other areas, such as V4; see Desimone and Ungerleider 1989). Moreover, at least in some cases the same neurons may participate in computing more than one type of information (e.g., Marder 1988), and under some circumstances a neuron can even switch which network it contributes to depending on a variety of factors (see Hooper and Moulins 1989). When one subsystem works hard, the tissue will become highly oxygenated; in addition, if neurons are driven too long, various waste products may build up, impairing their function. If the same tissue is used to implement two or more subsystems, such effects that arise during the operation of one will affect the others.

Note that this breakdown of strong modularity does *not* imply that a subsystem computes more than one function. Rather, I conceive of the set of input/output mappings performed by a network as the function it computes;

indeed, an "extensional" definition of a function is simply a list of all of the input/output pairings it produces. We can always conceive of a subsystem as computing a single function, but it sometimes may be difficult to characterize that function using common sense or natural languages. For example, color and shape information, although obviously distinct in our sensoria, may be conflated at some stages of neural information processing. There is no reason why our common sense intuitions about function, based on our subjective experience of interacting with objects in the world, should reflect the details of neural information processing.

Interactions among Subsystems

It is clear that interactions among subsystems are affected by complex neuromodulatory events (e.g., see Kandel, Schwartz, and Jessell 1991). However, for my purposes I need only make two general assumptions.

Concurrent Processing   During normal cognition, each of the subsystems is always operating; there is no central executive that turns a subsystem on and off selectively in real time. This assumption has two facets. First, each network does not "wait" for the preceding networks in a sequence to finish before beginning to engage in processing. The subsystems constantly map whatever input they receive to the corresponding output. Thus, subsystems often operate on partial or degraded inputs, and produce partial or degraded outputs for the next subsystem in line. This sort of processing forms a series of cascades (McClelland 1979). Second, subsystems are sometimes organized into separate parallel streams. As we shall see with patient R. V. (in chapter 8), more than one combination of subsystems sometimes can perform a task. Because they are all operating at the same time, the behavior will be determined by whatever combination of subsystems runs to completion first.

Cooperative Computation   The use of recurrent feedback lies at the heart of "cooperative computation." Cooperative computation occurs when a subsystem later in a sequence assists a subsystem earlier in the sequence. As a later subsystem begins to produce a consistent input/output mapping, it may provide more consistent feedback to an earlier subsystem—helping it to accomplish a consistent mapping. It seems plausible that the reciprocal connections in the visual system evolved primarily for this purpose, which is pervasive, rather than for use in imagery per se.

Cooperative computation is an example of constraint satisfaction at work, but at a coarser level of analysis: Now a set of subsystems—not the neurons in a single network—attempts to settle into a mutually consistent overall pattern of activity. Given that subsystems may not be sharply differentiated, it is not surprising that principles that apply to processing within an individual subsystem also apply to interactions among subsystems.[2]

FORMULATING THEORIES OF PROCESSING SUBSYSTEMS

How does one formulate theories of which specific information processing operations (i.e., input/output mappings) are carried out by distinct subsystems? Our perceptual, cognitive, and motor abilities appear to be produced by a confluence of different mechanisms working together (e.g., see Kosslyn and Koenig 1992). These mechanisms are generative; they can produce an infinite number of cognitions and behaviors. The nature of such mechanisms often is not intuitively obvious, any more than the workings of a complex computer program are intuitively obvious. Hence, it is unlikely that common sense will often help us to characterize such components of neural information processing.[3]

One of the primary methods I use to formulate hypotheses about the existence of distinct subsystems is computational efficiency. According to the *principle of division of labor* (Kosslyn and Koenig 1992), two distinct subsystems are likely to exist if the mappings they perform are accomplished more efficiently by separate networks than by a single network. Qualitatively distinct input/output mappings interfere with each other in the same network because the same set of connections (each with a specific strength) is forced to accomplish different mappings. Not only do computational considerations suggest that the brain has adopted this principle, but so does neuroanatomy.[4]

The present approach owes much to the work of David Marr (e.g., see Marr 1982). Marr did more than offer a particular theory, develop in detail the general idea that brain function could be understood as computation, and provide some good examples of the computational approach. Marr tried to systematize what he was doing, laying the foundations for a new science. One of his most important ideas is the concept of a *theory of the computation*. Rather than use intuition as the sole guide for formulating theories of the componential structure of the visual system, Marr provided a detailed argument for each component. This argument is a theory of why a specific computation or group of related computations should be performed by a system that has certain abilities. I will use a modified form of his reasoning to hypothesize the existence of specific processing subsystems, and so it is worth considering this idea in some detail.

It is useful to regard a theory of what is computed by a processing subsystem as having four aspects, which can be best understood in the context of a specific case. (I will present only the sketchiest version of this example, which has been further elaborated since Marr's death; the following is intended not to describe the depth of Marr's theory, but simply to make the general ideas concrete.)

1. *Specify the goal of a computation.* For example, a fundamental ability of the visual system is to segregate figure from ground. That is, the brain isolates a particular part of the input that is likely to correspond to an object (a figure), distinct from other objects (the ground). We can view figure/ground segregation as the goal of a computation or computations. Marr sometimes spoke of this phase as identifying the "problem to be solved" by the system.

2. *Characterize the problem itself.* This depends on the goal and on what information is available in the input. In this example, the question is which aspects of the input can be used to isolate figures. Marr characterized the input as an array of intensity values, which could be modeled by a matrix with a number in each cell. He noticed that edges could be used to isolate objects, and characterized the output as a map that indicated where the edges of objects are located. Hence, the problem is to delineate the edges of an object when given only an array of local intensity values.

3. *Characterize the operation necessary to derive the output from the input.* Marr observed that there is a property of the input that serves as a cue for edges: rapid changes in intensity. However, such changes often indicate texture (e.g., grain in wood) or other non-edge information. Marr then noticed that edges result in sharp changes in intensity at different levels of scale. That is, if one blurs the image, edges are present at each level of blur, whereas texture differences are not. Thus, Marr defined the operation as locating places where intensity changes rapidly at different levels of scale, and then connecting these locations to indicate edges. The first step in this operation could be characterized precisely as finding "zero crossings" in the second derivative of the function relating position and location. Zero crossings indicate locations where the second derivative of this function changes sign, which indicates a rapid shift in the level of intensity. Contiguous zero crossings could then be connected up to form small oriented bars, blobs, and so on.

4. *Specify the "assumptions" that must be met for appropriate output to be produced on the basis of the input.* Philosophers and mathematicians have discovered that problems of induction cannot be solved unless they are restricted in specific ways beforehand (e.g., Goodman 1983). Although this point is usually discussed in the context of learning (e.g., Pinker 1988), it also applies to the problem of identifying an object on the basis of the visual input. Any given image on one retina in principle could have arisen from an infinite number of objects. For example, a square could depict a square piece of wood, one side of a box with sides of the same length, an infinite number of different trapezoids that are tilted in depth, and so forth. Marr recognized this inherent ambiguity, and assumed that certain "assumptions" must be made by a system if a computation is to succeed. He included these "assumptions" as part of a theory of a computation. For example, one must assume that actual objects reflect light in order for the zero-crossing technique to specify edges. If this assumption is violated, we may detect edges when none are actually present. Indeed, photographs work because they violate this assumption, which fools us into seeing objects that are not there.

The reason I've put quotes around the word "assumption" is that Marr did not mean that the computation actively makes assumptions the way a person would; rather, he meant that any computation has boundary conditions that must be respected if it is to operate appropriately. If the input conditions fall outside an acceptable range, the output from the computation will be misleading.

According to Marr, a computation is virtually dictated by the various requirements on it. Indeed, he said that a theory of what is computed "corresponds to a theorem in mathematics" (Marr and Nishihara 1978, 16): Given a specific goal, specific input to work with, and specific "assumptions" about the world, Marr hoped that there often might be only one set of computations that would allow a system to produce the requisite output.

Marr's Method Reconsidered

Although many others were converging on similar ideas (e.g., Grossberg 1988; Nakayama and Loomis 1974), Marr was the first to systematize the idea of a theory of a computation. This idea was an enormous advance over much of the previous work in neuroscience, which tended to minimize theory, and over most of the previous work in artificial intelligence, which tended not to rest on careful analyses of a problem. Nevertheless, although the approach I have adopted here rests in part on Marr's ideas, it differs from his professed philosophy in key ways (for a more extended discussion, see Kosslyn and Maljkovic 1990).[5]

According to Marr (1982), theories of the computation are at the top of a three-level hierarchy. A theory of a computation specifies *what* is computed. The next level down is a theory of the algorithm, which specifies *how* a computation is computed. The theory of the algorithm specifies an explicit set of steps that will guarantee a given output when provided with a given input. Typically, many different algorithms can carry out any computation. Marr treated the theory of the computation as paramount because it characterizes the problem that must be solved by a system—and until one understands what a system does in specific circumstances, one cannot specify the details of how the system works. Marr placed the algorithm at a lower level of the hierarchy because it does not characterize a problem, but rather specifies a possible solution to a problem that is characterized at the more abstract level. Finally, at the third level one specifies how the algorithm is actually implemented in the brain.

My approach arose following a meditation on two difficulties with Marr's approach. First, the distinction between the theory of the computation and the algorithm (*what* versus *how*) is not clear. For example, consider the operation of addition. At first glance, it appears to be a computation; indeed, Marr uses addition as a paradigm example of the distinction between *what* and *how*. Addition can be characterized completely independently of the other levels of analysis. We can specify the function without indicating whether one is adding using arabic numerals, roman numerals, or tick marks, and without indicating whether one is adding in one's head, with an abacus, or with a computer. It seems clear that addition defines a computation, which is indeed independent of the lower levels of analysis. Furthermore, one of the lower levels of analysis seems clearly to pertain to the level of the algorithm and another to the level of the implementation.

However, when we take a second look, we see that this clarity is more apparent than real. Consider another function, multiplication. Multiplication also seems to define a computation. Just as with addition, the multiplication computation can be carried out using various algorithms. But one way we can multiply is by converting numbers to logarithms and adding the exponents, and hence addition is part of an algorithm. And now consider a joint probability. Again, at first glance, this seems like a clear case of a *what* that is computed, but multiplication is part of the algorithm.

It should be clear that the notion of *what* versus *how* is relative to where one stands. Addition is a what or a how, depending on whether we focus on it or multiplication; multiplication is a what or a how, depending on whether we focus on it or joint probability, and so forth. I do not see a principled way to decide which level of abstraction should be treated as *the* level of the computation and which should be treated as *the* level of the algorithm. Instead, there appear to be computations defined at different levels of coarseness, and algorithms correspond to a combination of computations defined at a more fine-grained level of analysis than the computation of interest. The more fine-grained a computation, the simpler the process that produces the requisite output when given the input. (I leave the notion of "simplicity" to intuition at this point, although technical definitions are possible; e.g., see Leeuwenberg and van der Helm 1991).

One could argue, however, that the proper distinction is between characterizations that require one to specify the nature of the representation versus characterizations that do not require one to specify representations.[6] We can speak of multiplication as adding a number to itself a certain number of times without saying anything about how numbers are represented, and we can speak of adding without specifying how it actually works.

However, even this distinction between the level of the computation (what and how, representation-free) and the level of the algorithm and representation is problematic. For example, Marr was very sensitive to the fact that different ways of representing information make different operations more or less easy to perform. He argued that visual representations must make explicit important properties about the world, be stable over various perturbations of the input, be sensitive to critical aspects of the input, and so on (see Marr 1982, pp. 20–21, 297–298). The problem is that different computations are more or less feasible depending on what representations are available in a system. Consider again the operation of multiplication. This computation is much easier if quantities are represented using the arabic representation than the roman one; arabic numbers make explicit powers of ten, whereas roman numbers do not. Indeed, if certain types of representation are not possible in a system, certain computations become infeasible. Marr was aware of this interdependency. In fact, in a colloquium at Harvard University in 1979, Marr specified the representation as part of the theory of the computation; he later changed his mind and specified the representation at the level of the algorithm (see Marr 1982, p. 23).[7]

The second, and perhaps more fundamental, concern I have about Marr's scheme focuses on the separation between working at a computational level (at any level of coarseness) and working at the level of the implementation. Marr sometimes seemed to say that one could work at the computational level without concern for the level of the implementation. But mental processes are nothing more—or less—than descriptions of specific brain function. The brain does more than regulate the heart, consume glucose, and so forth: To say that a process specifies zero-crossings is to describe the operation of some part or parts of the brain. Insight into how such processing occurs cannot help but be forthcoming if one discovers the critical parts of the brain, charts the relevant connections, discovers the sensitivities of relevant neurons, and so forth. Thus, it seems odd to formulate a theory of what is computed without considering relevant neurophysiological and neuroanatomical facts. Surely properties of the brain itself have something to do with how it works.

In fact, I do not think that Marr actually kept the levels so distinct when formulating theories. At the end of his book Marr warns us that

> there is no real recipe for this type of research—even though I have sometimes suggested that there is—any more than there is a straightforward procedure for discovering things in any other branch of science. Indeed, part of the fun is that we never really know where the next key is going to come from—a piece of daily experience, the report of a neurological deficit, a theorem about three-dimensional geometry, a psychophysical finding in hyperacuity, a neurophysiological observation, or the careful analysis of a representational problem. All these kinds of information have played important roles in establishing the framework that I have described, and they will presumably continue to contribute to its advancement in an interesting and unpredictable way. (Marr 1982, p. 331)

I recall one of Marr's lab meetings, held shortly after he returned from a lengthy absence. While away he had read many papers on the neuroanatomy and neurophysiology of the monkey brain, and he reported to us details about the numbers of neurons in different parts of the cortex. He was puzzled about why there were so many in one case and so few in another, and clearly was turning over various possible reasons in his mind. Marr knew about the properties of on-center/off-surround cells in visual cortex before he formulated his theory of edge detection, and surely used such information when formulating his theory of the computation.

The Cognitive Neuroscience Triangle

Rather than a hierarchy, the Marrian approach may be better reconstructed as the triangle in figure 2.1. At the top of the triangle is *abilities*. There is nothing to explain until we know what a system can do. By "abilities" I do not mean simply overt behavior; I mean things the organism can do.[8] I would prefer to use the term *competence* here, but it has already been endowed with a specific technical meaning by Chomsky (1965). Depending on the abilities

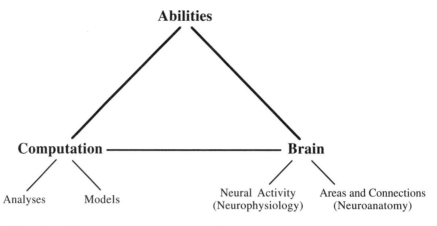

Figure 2.1 The cognitive neuroscience triangle.

exhibited by a system, different "problems" are posed. For example, if the visual system does not segregate figure from ground purely on the basis of sensory input, a different kind of theory would be needed than that offered by Marr. The two bottom vertices are labeled *computation* and *brain*. These vertices represent a particular kind of account, which arises from two kinds of considerations: The goal is not only to understand how sets of computations could produce the observed abilities, but to understand how the brain could perform such computations. Thus, the two kinds of considerations work together in theorizing. Just as Marr probably used the receptive field properties of neurons in visual cortex to guide his thinking about edge detection, I will use properties of brain to guide theorizing about imagery and related processing.

An important feature of the triangle is that each consideration interacts directly with the others; the three kinds of concerns feed back in every direction. I will start with relatively crude characterizations in all three domains, and then begin to cycle around the triangle when refining the theory—further specifying the system's abilities and then considering the implications for the underlying computations, which in turn leads to additional questions about the neural substrate. And as additional information about the neural substrate is found, the computational analysis is modified and additional abilities are considered, which often leads to an experiment to test a prediction, and so on. I go back and forth between the different sorts of facts and analyses, allowing them to mutually inform each other. The effort does not depend on working out a detailed analysis of what is computed before proceeding; I start coarse from all ends at once, and converge on more precise characterizations as the pieces are put together.

In short, I exploit the concept of constraint satisfaction in three ways. First, I attempt to make the theory mutually consistent with the observed system abilities, computational analyses, and facts about the neural substrate. Second, I assume that the individual networks operate via constraint satisfaction: They take an input and map it to the output that is most consistent with all of the characteristics of the input. This is a standard feature of neural network models. Third, I posit processing subsystems that are mutually consistent with each other; these subsystems work together to produce the observed abilities. That is, given that one specific subsystem is posited, that is a constraint on what else must be posited. And not all subsystems are equally constraining. To return to the furniture metaphor, I will spend a lot of time placing beds. Once there are grounds for positing a few specific subsystems, this will lead to hypotheses about other subsystems that may be present. I describe experiments that test specific predictions along the way; Allen Newell, in his 1987 William James Lectures at Harvard University, called these experiments "sanity checks," which ensure that one has not strayed too far off the path. In addition, when faced with plausible alternatives, my colleagues and I sometimes conducted experiments to discriminate between them.

METHODOLOGICAL CONSIDERATIONS

The theory developed in this book is grounded in much empirical research. This research relies primarily on six types of methods (there are many more, but most do not figure prominently in the relevant literatures). Four of the methods are used in studies of humans and two rely on animal models. Each of these methods has its strengths and weaknesses, and no individual finding should be taken as definitive. My strategy is to seek converging evidence from as many different sources as possible. If the same inference follows from very different types of studies, it seems unlikely that the results were a consequence of methodological quirks. Although space limitations prevent a detailed critique of each method, it is worth pausing briefly to consider each one's major strengths and weakness before we rely on it.

Using humans as subjects has at least three major advantages over nonhumans. First, by studying humans, one can observe the entire range of human abilities—which are not all present in monkeys or other animals. Second, rather than spending upward of 6 months training the subject to perform the task, one simply gives the subject a set of instructions. Third, there is no issue about whether one can generalize from the subjects to humans. However, there are several drawbacks to testing humans. For example, humans devise their own strategies and tricks for performing tasks, which cannot always be anticipated in advance; ethical concerns preclude extended single-cell recordings, except when medically justified; human neuroanatomy is not as well understood as nonhuman primate neuroanatomy; and even among humans, individual and group differences may make generalization difficult. Thus, there is a role for both human and animal studies.

Response Times and Error Rates

Human subjects are asked to perform a specific task, and their response times and error rates are recorded.

Major Strengths   These experiments are easy to carry out. Moreover, they can be modified and followed up quickly. In addition, task design has become very sophisticated, allowing researchers to consider elementary information processes (e.g., see Puff 1982).

Major Weaknesses   The previous chapter illustrated a major problem with response time and error rate measures from humans. In a nutshell, these data often are too underconstraining; there are many theories that are consistent with a pattern of response times or error rates. This problem arises in part because of structure-process trade-offs, as discussed earlier. However, this problem diminishes as one considers larger and larger sets of data. With a sufficiently large data set, some have argued that it is difficult to formulate even a single theory that can explain all of the details (e.g., Newell 1990).

Another problem, however, is that it often is unclear what is the appropriate psychological scale: Should it be simple response times, or the logarithms of the times? Error rates or the arc-sin transformed error rates? These issues have yet to be resolved conclusively (e.g., see Luce 1986). I will not use response times to try to distinguish individual processing stages (see Sternberg 1969), and thus will sidestep many of the potential problems with using such data (e.g., see McClelland 1979).

Divided-Visual-Field Studies

The left part of each retina projects to the left cerebral hemisphere, and the right part projects to the right hemisphere. If a visual stimulus appears briefly to the left or right side (so briefly that the subject cannot move his or her eyes), its image will strike only a single hemiretina (in both eyes) and the stimulus will be initially processed in one or the other hemisphere. When normal subjects are tested in divided-visual-field studies, the logic is that the subject should be faster and/or more accurate if the stimulus is presented initially to the hemisphere that is specialized for the appropriate processing. If it is presented to the other hemisphere, not only should that hemisphere require more time (if it is indeed less efficient at that sort of processing), but time is required to cross the corpus callosum (the major fiber track that connects the hemispheres) to the other hemisphere. Moreover, it is possible that information is degraded when it is sent across the callosum (see Springer and Deutsch 1985). For brevity, I shall speak of the effects of showing a stimulus in one visual field as presenting a stimulus to the left or right hemisphere. However, keep in mind that the stimulus is only presented *initially* to a single hemisphere; within 15 ms or so, information has reached both hemispheres.

Divided-visual-field studies are of interest for two reasons. First, if one ability is performed more effectively when stimuli are presented to the left hemisphere, and another is performed more effectively when stimuli are presented to the right hemisphere, this is good evidence that the two abilities are not carried out by the identical subsystems. Second, such data can provide one form of evidence regarding the anatomical localization of a subsystem.

Major Strengths   The strengths of the method are largely practical: The experiments are easy to design and carry out. In addition, however, the method has the advantage of being applied to intact, healthy subjects. Thus, it avoids the problems of inference that exist if split-brain subjects are tested or if brain-damaged subjects are tested (see below).

Major Weaknesses   There are several problems with the logic of these studies. Perhaps critically, it is possible that differences in processing specialization can be overwhelmed by differences in attention. Indeed, I will argue in chapter 9 that much—if not most—visual lateralization corresponds to attentional biases, with the left hemisphere's tending to attend to smaller regions of space than the right. However, these biases can be upset, and even reversed, by task demands (for similar concerns, see Peterzell, Harvey, and Hardyck 1989). Schwartz and Kirsner (1982) argue that attentional effects may have an even larger role in determining the outcomes of divided-visual-field experiments, not only affecting perceptual encoding but also affecting postperceptual processes.

If such claims are correct, then we should not be surprised that divided-visual-field studies with normal subjects are very fragile; these results are notoriously difficult to replicate (e.g., see White 1969, 1972). Only if the task demands, as explicit and implicit in the instructions and the nature of the task itself, are just right will default biases be revealed. Sergent and Hellige (1986) and Hellige and Sergent (1986) review evidence that many types of factors can affect the outcomes of divided-visual-field experiments. And these biases themselves apparently can vary from person to person; Levy et al. (1983) present evidence that people differ in the characteristic "level of arousal" of the hemispheres, which could influence the way attention is allocated. These ruminations lead me to conclude that results from divided-visual-field tasks with normal subjects should be used only as convergent evidence in combination with results from other techniques.

The divided-visual-field method has been used not only with normal subjects, but also with people who have had the corpus callosum severed for medical reasons. A primary strength of this approach is that the input is restricted to a single hemisphere, which often produces large differences in performance when stimuli are presented in different visual fields. However, another set of problems must be considered. First, these subjects do not have normal brains. Their corpora callosa were severed to treat severe epilepsy. This is a treatment of last resort—the patients had this disorder for years, it was severe, and it did not respond to conventional drug therapy. Second, even if their brains were normal at the outset, they obviously are not after surgery. The normal brain is an integrated system. When parts of it are isolated, they may not operate as they did before. Third, it is also possible that the same kinds of attentional effects that occur in normal brains also can mask functional specialization in split-brain patients. Nevertheless, such patients are of interest to study because their brains reveal what sorts of functions *can* be performed by distinct subsystems; if two abilities are accomplished better by opposite hemispheres, then at least one distinct subsystem is used to carry out each ability.

Deficits Following Brain Damage

Brain damage disrupts one's information processing and consequent behavior. Some researchers study patients who have had strokes, injury, brain surgery, or disease, and try to infer the nature of information processing by observing selective deficits.

Major Strengths   In many cases, counterintuitive patterns of deficits follow brain damage, which suggest interesting hypotheses about the nature of normal processing. For example, some patients have difficulty naming fruits and vegetables, but little else (e.g., see Hart, Berndt, and Caramazza 1985; Shallice 1988). Such patients are relatively rare, but in large cities a surprising number of patients with brain damage are available for study. Moreover, with modern magnetic resonance imaging it is now possible to localize lesions very precisely, which holds promise for relating specific brain loci to specific functions.

Major Weaknesses   It is tempting to infer a direct mapping between a dysfunction and the processing carried out by the damaged structures. This was the tradition established by the founders of behavioral neurology, such as Broca and Wernicke. Unfortunately, drawing inferences about normal information processing from dysfunction and lesion location is not so straightforward. Because this methodology is so prevalent, and I will address much data of this sort in subsequent chapters, it is worth dwelling on the weaknesses of this approach for a moment. Kosslyn and Van Kleeck (1990) and Kosslyn and Intriligator (1992) consider these issues in greater detail, as does Farah (1993; see also the associated commentaries); for an alternative perspective, see Caramazza (1992) and Shallice (1988).

Some researchers infer the existence of processing subsystems by observing patterns of *dissociations* and *associations* among deficits (see Caramazza 1986; Shallice 1988). A dissociation occurs when one patient can perform task X by not task Y; a so-called double dissociation occurs when two patients have opposite dissociations (one can perform task X but not Y and vice versa for the other). An association occurs if difficulty in performing task X is always accompanied by difficulty in performing task Y. When two tasks dissociate (especially when they double dissociate), the researcher infers that at least one distinct subsystem must be recruited by each task (Teuber 1955); when two tasks associate, the researcher infers that at least one subsystem is shared by them.

However, damage does not alter the performance of subsystems in isolation. In order to induce a theory from dysfunctions, researchers typically assume, implicitly or explicitly, that brain damage results in only a local modification of the cognitive system, with nondamaged parts of the system remaining fundamentally equivalent to those of normal subjects (see Caramazza 1984, 1986, 1992). But processing and behavioral dysfunctions can arise for a number of other reasons (see also Caplan 1981; Glassman 1978; Gregory 1961; Lenneberg 1975; Shallice 1988; Von Eckardt Klein 1978). First, undamaged subsystems might be used in new ways following brain damage. If so, then processing and behavioral aberrations would reflect in part the new uses of the intact subsystems, not simply the missing subsystem. Consider an analogy: A dog has a tumor in his front left leg, and so has to have it amputated. Following the operation, the three remaining legs do not operate as they did before. Not only does the leg on the damaged side step twice as often, but the others move more slowly to take more of the burden. In this case, old functions are not modified, but the limbs are used in new ways.

Second, subsystems might be modified. Returning to our hapless dog, the remaining front leg might become much more muscular, and hence be less agile than before when used to scratch behind the ears.

Third, it is possible that new neural networks develop following damage. In terms of the dog metaphor, the dog might learn a way of half-crawling when faced with steep inclines. This addition to his repertoire would produce odd behavioral aberrations, such walking more awkwardly as an incline steepens, prior to dropping into the new locomotory mode.

Fourth, old strategies might be used in new contexts. A strategy consists of a set of subsystems working together to accomplish a task. Typically, there is more than one set that could accomplish a given task. Our dog might discover that a hop-skip-and-jump motion previously used just for fun was now just the thing for swimming. Or that nodding his head could be used to help him lever his way up steep stairs. Some strategy changes may be "automatic," and not depend on any conscious decision by the patient. Alternatively, some strategies depend on deliberate planning.

Fifth, in some situations dissociations that should be present may not be, because damaged subsystems interact to mask the effects (see Weiskrantz 1968). Perhaps our dog was lucky enough not to need the leg amputated, but instead only had some muscle removed. Unfortunately, other legs were also affected, and muscle had to be removed from them too. Thus, the various weaknesses might result in a gait that is generally slower, but not qualitatively different from a normal one.

Sixth, most brain-damaged people are slowed down; damage disrupts cortico-subcortical feedback loops that are essential for alertness. And such activation is essential for information processing throughout the brain. This notion is to be distinguished from Von Monakow's (1914/1969) idea of *diaschisis*. Nondamaged regions may suffer a kind of shock when they lose their normal inputs from the damaged area, which causes them to perform poorly and produce symptoms. This effect typically is transient, whereas the deficits I note here are not. A reduction in activation can produce numerous impairments. The more interesting ones occur if more complex processing, which presumably requires more activation, is affected while less complex processing is not (for a detailed discussion of such effects, see chapter 10 of Shallice

1988). After the muscle was removed from his legs, our dog may walk more or less normally, but he can no longer run or jump normally (which does not imply that his running or jumping abilities per se were disrupted).

Thus, subsystems remote from the point of damage may actually be at the root of a dysfunction. If damage in any part of the brain reduces overall activation, a subsystem in a remote region can be impaired. This is a particularly vexing problem because it foils any direct attempt to correlate lesion locus with the locus of subsystems that are critical for normal processing: the fact that an ability is disrupted following brain damage does not imply that the lesioned area is responsible for that ability. To use Gregory's (1966) classic example, if one removes a resistor from a radio and it squawks, this does not mean that the resistor is a squawk suppressor. Fortunately, PET scanning offers a way to observe the extent of such impaired function, as we shall discuss when we consider a specific case study in chapter 8.

It should now be easy to see why one cannot use dissociations and associations as rock-steady evidence for the existence of processing components. Dissociations can arise not only because individual subsystems have been disrupted, but also because of interactions among the undamaged subsystems. In addition, Wood (1982) showed that under certain circumstances different "lesions" of a single neural network can produce double dissociations; in his models, different "lesions" left different input/output mappings intact while others were impaired. Thus, even finding a double dissociation (Teuber 1955), with one patient having a deficit along with an intact ability and vice versa for another patient, does not necessarily implicate separate subsystems. Shallice (1988) argues that the logic of double dissociation is valid if certain assumptions and conditions are met, but he emphasizes that one must take great care in interpreting such data.

But what about associations, when two abilities are impaired in tandem? It is tempting to infer that associations show that at least one subsystem is shared in two tasks. Unfortunately, it is clear that performance of two relatively difficult tasks can be disrupted due to general activation decreases. Associations also can arise following various compensations. Furthermore, associated deficits could merely indicate that different functions are implemented in the same or nearby tissue. For example, the blob and interblob structures in area V1 (which appear to process color and form, respectively; see Livingstone and Hubel 1987) are likely to be damaged by a single lesion. (See Shallice, 1988, for a compelling critique of the logic of using associations among deficits following brain damage to draw inferences about normal processing.)

The upshot, then, is that it would be very difficult to induce the nature of processing subsystems solely by observing the effects of brain damage on behavior. Nevertheless, it is important to note that the logic *does* work in the other direction: if a region of cortex that is responsible for a specific kind of processing is damaged, then that processing should be disrupted. Thus, although we cannot easily use dissociations and associations to *induce* processing systems in a simple way, we can use such data to *test* such theories. If we fail to find a predicted dissociation or association, we have something to worry about.

Brain Activation

Another set of methods involves having a person perform a task and measuring brain activity at specific sites. There are a number of such techniques, each of which has its own strengths and weaknesses. I first will briefly describe key features of the more popular techniques and note specific strengths and weaknesses, and then will turn to strengths and weaknesses of activation studies in general.

EEG, ERP, and MEG   There are several interrelated methods that rely on recording electrical activity from scalp electrodes. These techniques include electroencephalography (EEG), in which the power at different frequency bands is computed, and event-related potentials (ERP), in which the amplitude of an electrical response to a stimulus is observed over time. In general, the strengths of these methods are that they have good temporal resolution and are noninvasive and inexpensive. One major weakness is that it is difficult to infer the locus of the neural generator. Not only do electric currents travel across the brain and across the scalp, but they are also distorted when they pass through the skull. Indeed, the skull has a different thickness at different places, and so the distortion is not homogeneous.

These techniques must be distinguished from magnetoencephalography (MEG), in which magnetic fields are recorded. These fields do not travel across the cortex or scalp and are not distorted by bone. Moreover, it is possible to isolate the dipole that gives rise to a specific field. Hence, MEG has both good temporal and spatial resolution. The main drawback of this technique, aside from cost (one needs a magnetically shielded room, as well as expensive detectors), is that the alignment of the neurons does not allow one to record from gyri. Nevertheless, the technique is very useful for studying events in sulci.

^{133}Xe rCBF and SPECT ^{133}Xe regional cerebral blood flow (rCBF) depends on having subjects inhale ^{133}Xe (an inert radioactive gas) while they are performing a cognitive task. Regions of the brain that work harder exchange blood more rapidly than regions that are not so active. As more blood arrives, the amount of radioactivity changes, and the total amount over the scan period is observed. The strengths of this method are that it is relatively inexpensive, easy to administer, and available in large hospitals. A major weakness of the method is its intrinsically poor spatial resolution, which is a result of the low-energy gamma ray emission of ^{133}Xe. Moreover, although three-dimensional studies are possible, most available equipment only allows one to know about activity at the scalp. Finally, it has very poor temporal resolution; the subject must engage in a task for at least 5 minutes per image.

Single photon emission tomography (SPECT) involves injecting a radio-active marker that is taken up with nutrients into the brain, but not broken down in the brain. The isotopes are relatively long-lasting. Thus, a single detector can be shifted around the person's head repeatedly, registering the arrival of individual photons, so that a three-dimensional image can be reconstructed. The strengths of this technique are that it produces a three-dimensional image, it is relatively inexpensive, and it is available in large hospitals. The weaknesses include poor spatial and temporal resolution (the subjects must perform a task during the entire uptake period, typically about 5 minutes). In addition, the isotopes typically have long half-lives, and so one cannot record multiple images in the same session (often sessions must be 1 week apart). Moreover, relatively large doses of isotopes are necessary to detect differences in local brain activity when subjects perform a task. Using the FDA-approved dosages, my colleagues and I were unable to use this technique to detect left-hemisphere activation while subjects repeated back rapidly spoken sentences. In Vienna, in contrast, subjects commonly are given much larger doses and effects of cognitive activity are recorded.

PET Positron emission tomography (PET) is like SPECT, except that photons are recorded using coincidence detection and that allows improvement in resolution, sensitivity, and the ability to calculate quantitative effects. Two methods are used to study cognitive processes. In one method, the subjects are injected with 2-deoxy-D-glucose labeled with F-18 (FDG), which allows one to assess local cerebral metabolism. FDG is taken up into the brain along with sugar, but is not broken down and hence is trapped in the tissue, marking the amount of nutrients taken up in different loci. This technique has very poor temporal resolution; it requires about 40 minutes for FDG to be lodged in the brain. The more common method for studying cognitive processes allows one to assess cerebral blood flow (which is linked to metabolism). The subjects are injected with water or inhale carbon dioxide in which some of the oxygen atoms are ^{15}O. This radioactive isotope of oxygen has a half-life of about 2 minutes, and an image can be obtained in as little as 40 seconds. When the radioactive oxygen decays, a positron is emitted and travels up to 2 mm before undergoing an annihilation reaction. Two photons are thereby produced that travel in opposite directions along a line (preserving parity). The PET camera records the near-simultaneous arrival thereby determining the line along which the photons were produced. A three-dimensional image is built up using these measured lines of interaction. One strength of this technique is that a relatively high-resolution (in theory 2 mm, in practice in the range of about 4–7 mm) image can be constructed, in relatively little time. In addition, because of the brief half-life of ^{15}O and the relatively low levels of radiation that are necessary, many scans can be performed in a single session; our group collects as many as eight, at which point the subject typically is beginning to tire. Moreover, an enormous amount of technology has been developed to normalize scans from different people and map them into high-resolution magnetic resonance images (MRI) of the structure of their brains. The major weaknesses are that it is very expensive, invasive, and relies on relatively exotic equipment.

fMRI   Finally, the newest member of the tool box is functional magnetic resonance imaging (fMRI). Unlike standard MRI, which produces structural images that can be used instead of x-ray photographs, fMRI provides information about blood flow and oxygen use. A large "reference" magnetic field is produced, which aligns some of the atoms in the brain. Another field is then produced along a different axis; this field is pulsed at a radio frequency, which imparts energy to those protons that resonate with it. When that pulse is terminated, those atoms release the energy that was imparted by the radio pulse. This electromagnetic wave sweeps across a coil, which generates a current; these currents are amplified and used to reconstruct the image. The extent to which these atoms will resonate with a given frequency depends on the other atoms in a molecule, and thus one can detect the presence of specific molecules in specific locations. For fMRI, this technique is used to detect where additional oxygen has been transported in the brain by observing the effects of the iron in deoxygenated hemoglobin on the resonance of hydrogen protons, and hence can be used to track blood flow. This technique is very promising; MRI has superb spatial and temporal resolution, is noninvasive, and is relatively available and inexpensive. At present, however, it is not as sensitive to signal as PET. However, by the time this book is published, these problems may well have been solved and this may be the technique of choice for studying cognitive activation in the brain.

Major General Strengths   The beauty of brain scanning is that one can observe neural activity in an awake, behaving human being. These techniques are more robust than divided-visual-field studies, do not require the assumptions that must be made in studies of response times and errors, and avoid the difficulties of studying effects of brain damage. The scanning techniques all are designed to indicate where in the brain activity occurs while one performs a specific task. But one could ask, Who cares about where a process occurs in the brain? There are at least two reasons why it is useful to discover where processing occurs in the brain. First, if two subsystems are implemented in different places, this is prima facie evidence that they are in fact distinct. Second, once one has characterized an area in a specific way, one then has a strong hint as to what sort of processing is taking place when that area is active in a novel task. To the extent that we are successful in localizing subsystems, we can test complex predictions of a theory by observing the overall configuration of activity that is engendered when one performs specific tasks. I will present an illustration of this strategy in chapter 8.

Major General Weaknesses   Three major classes of potential problems must be considered when evaluating results from brain scanning. First, it is not clear how to interpret evidence of greater activation in a specific locus. We cannot tell whether the activation indicates excitatory processes or inhibitory processes. We cannot tell whether the activation arises in a location or is an indirect consequence of another location, which releases inhibition. Moreover, it is not clear that more blood flow always occurs when there is more processing: If one is very efficient at a specific kind of processing, the neural substrate may require relatively little additional nutrients or oxygen.

Second, most contemporary brain-scanning techniques rest on averaging data across subjects. The individual scans typically are normalized to a standard stereotactic space (usually that defined by one of the Talairach atlases, most recently that by Talairach and Tournoux [1988]). But brains differ enormously, in both the relative locations and sizes of specific regions. Thus, averaging data from different brains decreases the level of resolution one can obtain.

Third, among the most vexing problems concern the use of subtraction methodologies; most contemporary brain-scanning studies involve subtracting two or more images. The brain is always doing something; it is never simply "off." Thus one must compare the effects of a specific task to some other effects. In many studies, the effects of performing a given task are compared to a "resting baseline." The subject is simply asked to relax and think of nothing in particular. But of course, the subject will be thinking of something—and the investigator has no control over what this may be. (This is a very real problem in studies of imagery, given that subjects may daydream when told to relax with their eyes closed; hence, subtracting activation from this baseline condition may remove the contribution of the imagery processes one wants to study in a test condition.) Thus, most contemporary studies of brain activation compare activity in two tasks, which are designed to differ in a specific way. However, there is no guarantee that one really understands how two tasks differ.

Indeed, we may have something to learn from history (e.g., see Boring 1950). At the turn of the century researchers subtracted response times in one task from those in another, aiming to estimate the time to carry out the operation that was not shared by the two tasks. A critical problem with this method came to be known as the "fallacy of pure insertion": the method assumed that the subjects used the same strategy in both versions of the task, so that the processing used for the simpler one was embedded in the processing used for the more complex one. However, sometimes the subjects adopted different strategies for the different versions—hence the subtraction did not implicate a specific process. The same problem exists in activation studies when researchers subtract blood flow engendered in one task from that engendered by another; we cannot be certain that the residual reflects the processing we assume it does because we cannot control exactly how subjects perform the tasks. Moreover, when an additional component process is added, it may provide feedback to other processes and thereby alter processing that occurred in the baseline task (for a discussion of such problems, and evidence that they do occur, see Sergent et al. 1992).

In addition, even if these problems with subtractions were not present, there are others. For example, if one does not find a difference in blood flow between two tasks one cannot know whether a given process was present in both or in neither; "automatic" processes, such as those involved in naming, may be difficult to study using such techniques. In addition, problems may arise because increases in blood flow with neural activation cannot be linear: the vessels can expand only so far. Hence, it is not clear that subtracting blood flow when both conditions (the test and baseline) engender great activity is comparable to subtracting blood flow when both conditions do not cause great activity.

Finally, we know that at least in some cases different processes are implemented in the same or interleaved tissue (e.g., see Livingstone and Hubel 1987). Given the resolution limits of contemporary brain scanning, in many situations we would be unable to distinguish the two kinds of activation if two tasks relied on different types of processing and the blood flow in one were subtracted from the other. (For additional discussion about problems arising from the subtraction technique, as well as illuminating examples, see Sergent et al. 1992.)

Animal Brain Lesions

Some researchers remove parts of animals' brains and study the resulting changes in behavior.

Major Strengths   The major strength of animal lesion studies is control: the experimenter can make a lesion of a specified size at a specific location, which can be checked precisely after the study.

Major Weaknesses   These studies have all of the weaknesses of studies of humans with brain damage, as summarized above. In addition, animal brains are not human brains, and hence we must be cautious in generalizing from studies of animals to humans. Nevertheless, monkeys have very similar visual abilities to humans, which suggests that their visual systems may not be radically different (see De Valois et al. 1974; De Valois, Morgan, and Snodderly 1974). And in fact, many neurological features of the monkey visual system have been found to have human homologs (e.g., Levine 1982).

Animal Single-Cell Recording Studies

Microelectrodes can be inserted either within a neuron or between several neurons. Such studies correlate the response of the neuron, or neurons, with specific stimulus properties.

Major Strengths   This technique avoids the problems of disconnections, reduced activation levels, and possible compensations that plague ablation studies. One has control over the stimulus situation and hence can test hypotheses about the stimulus dimensions that are registered by neurons. Moreover, histology can reveal the precise locations of the electrodes, allowing one to draw inferences about possible roles of specific anatomical pathways.

Major Weaknesses   In addition to the problems of cross-species homology noted above, there are problems with this particular technique. One problem is that it is very difficult to know for sure what aspect of the stimulus is driving the cell. Moreover, one cannot try all logically possible stimuli; for all one knows, some as-yet-untested stimulus would provide the maximal response. In addition, it is not yet clear whether simple response rate or some modulation of response frequency conveys information (see Optican and Richmond 1987). Furthermore, cortical neurons have many, many inputs. It is very difficult to know which set of inputs is driving a particular neuron at a particular point in time; it is possible that it is activated as a by-product of some other set of neurons that is activated. See Van Essen (1985) for additional caveats regarding this methodology.

For present purposes, single-cell recording and lesion studies with animals are useful primarily as a way to develop hypotheses about human information processing. In order to discover whether these hypotheses are correct, one must study humans. However, I assume that it is better to have a hypothesis than not to have one; a hypothesis not only directs one's attention to specific aspects of data but also helps to one to formulate issues that can be addressed empirically. In the next chapter I will use facts about the neuroanatomy and neurophysiology of monkey brains to develop a set of hypotheses about major component processes used in imagery.

The Necessity of Converging Evidence

As should be clear from this brief discussion, no single method is ideal. These considerations suggest two general conclusions. First, they demand that one rely on converging evidence, obtained using multiple methodologies. Each of the methods has different potential problems, but—I wish to stress—these problems are *potential*: they do not necessarily account for any specific result. If one is led to the same conclusion from several different methods, one can be confident that the potential problems with any individual method are not leading one astray. In essence, I view individual results as weak constraints on a theory; the goal is to fit together as many such constraints as possible into a mutually consistent interpretation.

Second, Sir Arthur Eddington is reputed to have said, "Never trust an empirical finding that hasn't been confirmed by a theory." I would not go so far, but am struck by the number of ways in which spurious results (or non-results) can occur. Results are often easiest to interpret if one has a hypothesis in hand and is testing a specific prediction. For example, if the theory posits specific types of processing in the frontal lobes, then it is in dire straits if damage to this region does not impair such processing. If unexpected regions disrupt this processing (or are activated during brain scanning), such findings should be interpreted within the context of the theory and then this hypothesis should be tested directly. In this book such hypotheses will be constrained by the web of the entire theory, which will structure our interpretations of individual phenomena.

CONCLUSIONS

The goal is to specify processing subsystems, which are networks or sets of related networks that transform inputs to outputs. In order to infer the existence of specific processing subsystems, I have made seven assumptions about neural information processing: (1) Neurons compute; they systematically map interpretable inputs to outputs. (2) A unit of neural computation is the network, which maps an input vector to an output vector. The neurons that function as the core of a network tend to be implemented in nearby tissue. (3) The brain evolved so that qualitatively distinct input/output mappings tend to be accomplished by distinct networks. (4) Processing subsystems (which are implemented as one or more networks) are weakly modular: feedback affects the inner workings of subsystems, the same fine-grained network can be a member of more than one subsystem, very fine-grained networks cannot be easily differentiated, and different processing subsystems may be implemented in overlapping or shared tissue. (5) Concurrent processing is the rule: subsystems sometimes race each other, and subsystems produce output continuously—which allows subsystems later in a sequence to operate before prior subsystems have completed processing. (6) Later subsystems in a sequence send feedback to earlier subsystems, which helps the earlier ones to complete their computations. (7) There are many combinations of processes that will accomplish a given task.

The present approach is derived from Marr's notion of a "theory of the computation." I consider three factors simultaneously: the abilities of a system (its "competences," if you will), the neurophysiology and neuroanatomy of the underlying brain systems, and the types of computations that would allow that brain system to produce the observed abilities. The goal is to infer a set of processing subsystems that satisfies all three considerations.

3 High-level Vision

The study of visual perception is arguably the most successful area of experimental psychology. There has been steady progress over the past 100 years, and we now have a sophisticated understanding of the nature of many visual phenomena. Moreover, we now understand many features of the neural substrate of vision (e.g., see Desimone and Ungerleider 1989; Felleman and Van Essen 1991; Kaas 1986; Newsome and Maunsell 1987; Van Essen, Anderson and Felleman 1992). However, this progress has been uneven: we can describe the mechanisms of the retina in remarkably precise detail (e.g., Dowling 1987), but until recently we could only talk in generalities about the higher cortical processing responsible for visual memory.

Even today, "low-level" vision is understood much better than "high-level" vision. Low-level visual processing is driven purely by stimulus input. These processes use sensory input to locate edges, detect motion, register depth, and so on, and are relatively easy to study because their operation is tightly coupled to specific properties of the stimulus (such as the orientation and position of an object). In contrast, high-level visual processing relies on previously stored information about the properties of objects and events. By definition, the processes that produce and utilize visual mental images rely on such high-level mechanisms. During perception, these mechanisms typically operate on the output from low-level processes. However, this does not imply that they make their contributions relatively late in the sequence of activity that allows us to identify objects, navigate, reach toward a visible goal, and so forth. Rather, it appears that high-level processes affect all cortical processing of visual input, and perhaps even some of the subcortical processes that intervene between the retina and the cortex. High-level visual processes have deep and pervasive effects during perception. Indeed, in the following chapters I will argue that imagery plays an important role during ordinary perception.

Our knowledge about high-level visual processing has increased dramatically during the past decade, for at least two reasons. First, new techniques have allowed researchers to document increasing numbers of visual areas in the cortex and their interconnections in nonhuman primates (e.g., Desimone and Ungerleider 1989; Felleman and Van Essen 1991; Van Essen 1985), and sophisticated methodologies have allowed the physiological properties of neurons in these areas to be studied in awake behaving monkeys (e.g., see Kaas 1986; Newsome and Maunsell 1987, for reviews) and human beings (e.g., Posner et al. 1988). Second, the ready availability of powerful computers and new "neural network" formalisms have provided the tools for understanding the function of patterns of neural activity (e.g., Anderson, Pellionisz, and Rosenfeld 1990; Grossberg 1988; Rumelhart and McClelland 1986).

Such research is producing an emerging picture of the structure of high-level visual processing. The remainder of this book sketches out that picture as I see it. I will not consider the inner workings of the individual networks in great detail, but rather will concentrate on identifying processing subsystems and the ways in which they interact. The subsystems identified here will be treated, for the most part, as "black boxes" that perform specific tasks. As noted in the previous chapter, the goal, so to speak, is to carve the system at its joints.

IMAGERY AND PERCEPTION

Perception is much easier to study than mental imagery, in large part because the phenomena are more easily characterized. One cannot begin to theorize in earnest until one knows a considerable amount about what needs to be explained. Moreover, good animal models have been developed for perception, but such models have yet to be developed for imagery. However, recent neuropsychological findings, some of which were described at the end of chapter 1, have revealed that mechanisms of visual perception are also used in visual mental imagery. This is most fortunate because it suggests that if we can develop a theory of high-level visual perception, we gain considerable leverage in understanding imagery.

The idea that imagery and perception share the same underlying mechanisms has been voiced repeatedly at least since the time of Aristotle, and was part and parcel of the original scientific psychologies of Wundt and James. But only recently has this claim become widely accepted.[1] Comprehensive reviews of the literature have been written recently, and I will not reiterate all of the details here. For reviews of the behavioral results, see Finke (1985, 1986, 1989, 1990), Finke and Shepard (1986), Shepard and Cooper (1982), and Hampson and Morris (1990); for reviews of the neuropsychological results, see Farah (1988), Kosslyn and Koenig (1992, chapter 4), and Kosslyn and Shin (in press). To give the reader some sense of the key findings, I will briefly summarize a few representative examples below.

Behavioral Findings

Researchers have tried to demonstrate that imagery and perception share common mechanisms at least since the beginning of this century. For example, in 1910 Perky asked subjects to visualize objects while pictures were being presented, and found that imagery appeared to interfere with visual perception. Perky, unfortunately, did not use the proper controls (e.g., for the difficulty of performing any two tasks at the same time), and it was not until the 1960s that the problems with her early research were ameliorated. Segal and her collaborators (e.g., Segal and Fusella 1970), for example, used signal detection methodology to show that maintaining a visual image impairs visual perception more than auditory perception, but maintaining an auditory image has the reverse effects. Given such results, it is not surprising that people sometimes confuse their images for percepts and vice versa. Finke, Johnson, and Shyi (1988), Intraub and Hoffman (1992), and Johnson and Raye (1981) have shown that in some circumstances people have difficulty remembering whether they had actually seen something or merely imagined that they were seeing it (Johnson and Raye call this discrimination "reality monitoring").

Perhaps the most compelling results in this tradition were reported by Craver-Lemley and Reeves (1987), who had subjects form images while they decided whether two line segments were perfectly aligned (a "vernier acuity" task). Craver-Lemley and Reeves found that accuracy fell from 80% to 65% when subjects formed images compared to when they did not. They found comparable effects when the subjects formed images of vertical or horizontal lines or a gray mist; however, moving the image away from the target almost eliminated the effect. Somewhat surprisingly, this sort of interference persisted for at least 4 seconds after the subjects were told to eliminate the image (but this may have been a little like asking one not to image a pink elephant; it is not clear exactly how quickly the subjects could eliminate the image). Elegant control conditions allowed Craver-Lemley and Reeves to make a good case that the results were not caused by peripheral factors, such as an increased pupil size, better or worse fixation, or changes in accommodation of the eye; moreover, the results were not due to changes in a decision criterion. It was clear that images were interfering with perception at a relatively "central" level of processing.

Imagery may also interfere with one's ability to perceive objects that are presented in visual noise. Peterson and Graham (1974) asked subjects to indicate which of two brief presentations contained a picture; in one presentation was a picture covered with visual noise, in the other was just visual noise. The subjects visualized the target object (such as a spoon on the floor with ants on it) on half the trials, and visualized an inappropriate object on the other half of the trials. Another group of subjects heard appropriate or inappropriate descriptions but was not asked to form images. Both groups also saw noncued pairs of stimuli, and were asked to indicate which had the picture and to name it. The subjects in the imagery group detected and named (a joint measure of performance was used) correctly cued objects more accurately than noncued objects, but detected and named incorrectly cued objects less accurately than noncued objects. The subjects in the control group also were more accurate with correctly cued objects, but they did not perform more poorly with incorrectly cued objects.

On the other hand, imagery can sometimes facilitate visual perception rather than interfere with it. For example, Farah (1985) used signal detection techniques to show that forming an image of a shape can actually enhance detection of that shape. Farah asked subjects to form an image of a *T* or an *H* and then to decide which of two intervals contained a faint letter (either one of the letters; they were not asked to identify the letter). The subjects could detect the letter better if they were forming an image of it than if they were imaging the other letter. Indeed, in a second experiment Farah had the subjects visualize a letter in one of two vertically stacked boxes, and then indicate in which of the boxes a letter appeared. She again found that images facilitated detection only for the same letter, and only if the image was in the location in which the letter appeared (for related work, see Finke 1986).

Before continuing, I should note that Rhodes and O'Leary (1985) failed to obtain evidence that imagery interferes with like-modality perception. They asked subjects to visualize square-wave gratings, and then to detect gratings. Although the detection thresholds were higher when subjects imaged than when they did not, the effect did not depend on whether or not the subjects formed the image in the same quadrant of the field where the target actually appeared. Kunen and May (1980) provide evidence that subjects do not include the fundamental frequency in their images, which may explain why imaged square waves were not an effective mask for same-frequency targets. In addition, Rhodes and O'Leary asked their subjects to visualize 15 bars, a task the subjects reported was "fairly difficult" (p. 386), and which I would judge to be nearly impossible. Indeed, they found that imagery produced an overall elevation in thresholds, which indicates that the imagery task required considerable effort. The authors conclude that their results make sense because the "pattern-processing mechanisms of the sort found in the primary visual cortex (e.g., location-specific, orientation-specific, width-specific mechanisms) do not appear to be activated during visual imagery." Given that my colleagues and I have PET results to the contrary, an alternative account of their results seems more likely to be correct.

Probably the most compelling evidence that imagery and like-modality perception share common mechanisms rests on counterintuitive phenomena, which subjects are unlikely to have experienced before (so that they cannot second-guess the experimenter and produce the results; see Intons-Peterson 1983). One of the original reports of this sort was reported by Finke and Schmidt (1977, 1978), who found that the McCullough effect (orientation-specific color aftereffects) could be induced via imagery. They asked subjects to visualize black horizontal or vertical bars on colored backgrounds (e.g., vertical bars on red, horizontal bars on green). When the subjects later viewed black horizontal and vertical bars on white backgrounds, they reported faint afterimages of the complementary color to that associated with the orientation, just as is found in the analogous perceptual task. However, the effect was not obtained when subjects imaged a colored background behind bars, rather than vice versa. In addition, Broerse and Crassini (1980) did not obtain the effect when the subjects were not forced to choose a color (the technique used by Finke and Schmidt), which may suggest that the effect is very small (see also Broerse 1981; Finke 1981). It is important to note, however, that Kunen and May (1980) did obtain consistent imagery-induced pattern-contingent aftereffects without using a forced-choice paradigm. But even when they have been obtained, the imagery effects are not entirely like the corresponding perceptual effects; for example, the imagery effect transfers from one eye to the other, but the actual McCullough effect does not (Kaufman, May, and Kunen 1981; see also Kunen and May 1980). Finke (1989) reviews this literature and concludes, "These differences call into question whether mental imagery really does involve the direct stimulation of bar detectors and other types of feature analyzers, as had been supposed. Instead, it seems more likely that the imagery-induced aftereffects are due to associations among visual features occurring at some higher level of the visual system" (p. 47). However, the stimuli used in these studies are complex, and failure to obtain some of the subtle perceptual effects could reflect our limited ability to use images of such stimuli. Kunzendorf (1990) summarizes additional evidence that visual mental imagery can, in some cases, actually activate (albeit slightly) the lowest-level parts of the sensory mechanisms, as indicated by imagery-induced afterimages and the like. To my mind, the fact that nonintuitive, psychophysical effects occur in imagery at all is impressive evidence that imagery and perception share modality-specific common mechanisms.

In addition, Freyd and Finke (1984) showed that an imaged "context" and a corresponding perceived context can have similar effects on a perceptual discrimination. They showed subjects crosses, formed by horizontal and vertical lines that were very similar in length. The subjects were to decide, as quickly as possible, whether the horizontal or vertical line was longer. The subjects performed this task faster if the cross appeared within a square. The subjects also performed this task faster if they did not see the square but instead imaged it (connecting up dots that delineated the corners of the square; the dots were removed right before the stimulus was presented). In contrast, no such facilitation was found when the subjects imaged an X of the same size as the square, and a smaller effect was found if subjects saw the dots but were not told to form images (although some may have done so spontaneously). Similar results were obtained when an X, or only the dots, were actually presented along with the cross. One could argue that visualizing the square had effects because it induced specific patterns of eye movements but even this account is not uninteresting; even here, the results would show that imagery taps into visual mechanisms.

Moreover, numerous researchers have reported that imagery can induce a variety of perceptual illusions (e.g., Berbaum and Chung 1981; Finke 1985; Okhuma 1986; Wallace 1984). For example, if subjects visualize arrowheads that point inward on the ends of one line, and arrowheads that point outward on the ends of another line, they apparently experience the Muller-Lyer illusion—with one line appearing longer than the other even though both were in fact the same length (but see Reisberg and Morris 1985, for some caveats). Finke and Shepard (1986) report numerous such findings, which converge in indicating that imagery uses "central" perceptual mechanisms.

Finally, there is good evidence that common processes are used to evaluate imaged and perceived patterns. For example, Podgorny and Shepard (1978) showed subjects block letters that were drawn in grids, or asked subjects to visualize the letters. Following this, a dot or dots were presented, and the subjects had to indicate whether the dot or dots fell on the letter. The subjects responded faster when the dots fell on intersections, when the figures were more compact, and so on, and the times varied in the same way in both the perception and imagery conditions. Bagnara et al. (1988) report convergent findings when they asked subjects to decide whether two letters were the same or different. They showed that the same factors affect the ease of distinguishing a visible letter from another and distinguishing an imaged letter from a visible letter. For example, in both cases the time to respond "different" decreased when letters shared fewer segments, and this decrease was comparable in the perception and imagery conditions.

Neuropsychological Results

In chapter 1 I briefly noted two classes of neuropsychological data that implicate common mechanisms in imagery and perception. This is such an important claim that I will provide more detailed support here. Although the PET experiment discussed in chapter 1 was the first to provide evidence that imagery selectively affects area V1, several previous studies showed that visual imagery recruits brain mechanisms used in visual perception. For example, Goldenberg, Podreka, Steiner, Willmes, Suess, and Deecke (1989) used SPECT to study which brain areas are activated when subjects use imagery to answer questions. In part because only a single photon is recorded at a time, SPECT has poorer resolution than PET. Goldenberg and his colleagues compared brain activity when subjects answered two types of questions. One type of question typically is answered by visualizing the object or objects (such as "Is the green of pine trees darker than the green of grass?"), and the other type typically is answered without using imagery (e.g., "Is the categorical imperative an ancient grammatical form?"). The imagery questions evoked increased blood flow in the occipital regions, relative to the other questions; the occipital lobes contain many areas that are used in visual perception.

However, it is important to note that Goldenberg, Podreka, Uhl, Steiner, Willmes, and Deecke (1989) and Uhl et al. (1990) obtained different results when they tested the same subjects in the same tasks but used SPECT (Goldenberg et al.) or examined cortical DC potentials (Uhl et al.). Goldenberg et al. found evidence for increased bilateral activity in the basal temporal lobes, as well as more activation in the right inferior temporal lobe. In contrast, the electrical recordings indicated occipital, parietal, and temporal activity, and more activation in the left hemisphere. These disparities are difficult to understand in part because the subjects had more practice prior to the Uhl et al. study, and in part because the techniques differ in their sensitivity; moreover, as noted in chapter 2, it is unclear how well electrical activity at the scalp reflects the localization of the underlying neural generators.

Roland and Friberg (1985) asked subjects to imagine that they were walking along a path through their neighborhood, first making a right turn, then a left, and so on. Before beginning the task, the subjects began to breathe ^{133}Xe, and Roland and Friberg compared the pattern of blood flow in this spatial imagery task with the pattern of blood flow evident when the subjects simply rested, with their eyes closed. They found that visual mental imagery resulted in large increases in blood flow in the superior occipital lobe, posterior superior parietal lobe, and posterior inferior temporal lobe. As we shall discuss shortly, there is evidence that each of these areas is used during high-level visual perception.

Other sorts of neuropsychological data have also indicated that imagery and perception share processing mechanisms. For example, Bisiach and his colleagues (e.g., Bisiach and Berti 1988; Bisiach and Luzzatti 1978; Bisiach, Luzzatti, and Perani 1979) studied unilateral visual neglect in imagery. Patients with this syndrome ignore ("neglect") the half of space contralateral to the lesion (usually the left side of space; right parietal lobe lesions are the most common cause of this syndrome). Neglect patients typically fail to copy half of objects, may fail to shave half of their faces and so on. The syndrome is particularly interesting because it is often accompanied by *anosognosia*—a lack of awareness of the deficit. And so the patient does not try to compensate for the problem (e.g., by moving his or her head or eyes appropriately). Bisiach and his colleagues showed that patients with this syndrome also fail to "see" the left half of objects in mental images, just as they do when they view the objects. For example, Bisiach, Luzzatti, and Perani (1979) asked such patients to view pairs of bloblike shapes, which could be identical or could differ on one side. The stimuli were presented as if they were moving behind a piece of cardboard with a vertical slit in its center, so that only a small portion was visible at a time. The subjects reported that to compare two shapes they built up an image of each as it moved past the slit. And in fact, the patients made many more errors when the stimuli differed on the neglected side than when they differed on the non-neglected side—even though all portions of the stimuli were originally presented in the central field, as they moved past the slit.

Similarly, Levine, Warach, and Farah (1985) describe patients with relatively fine-grained deficits in perception that were also present in their imagery. One patient had trouble recognizing objects in either perception or imagery, but could identify spatial relations in both cases, and vice versa for the other patient. The claim that imagery and like-modality perception share common structures is also supported by results such as those reported by Shuttleworth, Syring, and Allen (1982), who found that brain-damaged patients who cannot recognize faces often report that they also cannot visualize faces. Mehta, Newcombe, and De Haan (1992) describe a patient who had much more difficulty both identifying and visualizing living things than nonliving things, but could both read and visualize words.[2] Others (e.g., Beauvois and Saillant 1985; Damasio et al. 1980; De Renzi and Spinnler 1967) report that patients who had trouble distinguishing colors after suffering from brain damage also had trouble forming mental images that include color.

In short, we are on firm ground in assuming that visual imagery shares mechanisms with visual perception. My strategy will be to begin by characterizing high-level visual mechanisms used in visual perception, and to consider how various characteristics of imagery arise from this system.

THE PROBLEM OF OBJECT IDENTIFICATION: FIVE CLASSES OF ABILITIES

I earlier suggested that the puzzle of how objects are identified is easier than the puzzle of how mental images arise and are used, in part because our visual abilities are better understood. Unlike imagery, it is clear what vision is, and it is not very difficult to consider ways it can be used. Thus, I will start with vision, and hope to piggy-back a theory of imagery on a theory of high-level visual perception.

Although vision may be easier to fathom than imagery, it is, nevertheless, a remarkably challenging problem. I will focus on the mechanisms that allow us to identify objects. When one has identified a stimulus, one knows more about it than is apparent in the input per se. For example, as soon as one identifies an object as an apple, one knows that it has seeds inside, even though one cannot see the seeds. One also knows its name, what it can be used for, where to find it, and so on. The brain systems underlying object identification allow one to know more about a stimulus than is apparent in the immediate input. This is achieved by activating stored information that applies to the object.

Understanding how we identify objects visually would be hard enough if the world were inhabited only by two-dimensional line drawings that never varied. But this is a much more challenging problem: The world is a highly variable place, and yet we usually can easily identify novel versions of objects in novel circumstances. In this section I summarize the circumstances in which we can identify objects. I do so at a relatively general, qualitative level of analysis, but even these coarse descriptions of our abilities are sobering. It is no small feat to formulate a theory that is consistent with even the most general characterization of our abilities. We can identify objects in the following circumstances, each of which is illustrated in figure 3.1.

Different Locations and Distances (Visual Angles)

One typically can identify objects when their positions shift relative to each other or to oneself. This ability is relied upon so often that it is easily taken for granted. This ability has two major facets:

1. *Identifying objects when their input images subtend different visual angles.* The visual angle varies when we view objects at different distances, and when we view different-sized variants of objects.

2. *Identifying objects when their input images fall on different places on the retina.* We can identify an object when it is seen out of either corner of our eye,

Figure 3.1 This figure illustrates different circumstances in which we can identify objects, as discussed in the text (courtesy of Adam Anderson).

regardless of where its image fell when we first viewed it. The problem of understanding this ability has sometimes been called the "problem of stimulus equivalence across retinal translation" (Gross and Mishkin 1977); this ability is a puzzle because input images falling on different parts of the retina send information to different parts of many visual areas, but these images are nevertheless treated as equivalent.

These abilities, which involve identifying objects seen from different points of view, are often associated with the *perceptual constancies*. Although objects may project different images on the retina (such as occurs when a rectangular sheet of paper is rotated away from one, projecting a trapezoidal image), we do not see the shape changing; similarly, although they may project images of different sizes from different distances, we do not see the actual size changing. I will not dwell on the phenomenology of such constancies, but instead will focus on the functional properties of the system, that is, on the fact that it can access the appropriate memories under varying circumstances.

Shape Variations

If we could identify only specific individual objects that we had seen before, the mechanisms underlying object identification would be of limited use. Thus, it is not surprising that we can identify a range of novel shapes as corresponding to a given type of object. Generalization is part and parcel of our ability to identify objects; we typically can identify objects when their shapes do not exactly match the shapes of previously seen objects. Such generalization over shape variations occurs in a number of circumstances. This ability has the following major facets:

1. *Identifying objects when they are seen from different vantage points.* We can identify objects when they are rotated or seen from different vantage points, so that they project different shapes and different parts and characteristics are visible. For example, we can identify a car when it is seen from the side, the rear, or the front.

2. *Identifying objects when the shapes of their parts vary.* We can identify objects when the shapes of their parts vary. For example, we can identify chairs when they are king-sized, doll-sized, stuffed, or Shaker slim, with curved or straight arms, with tall, thin, or stubby backs, with wingtip backs, with massive sturdy legs or fragile spindle legs, or with narrow seats or broad seats.

3. *Identifying objects when the spatial relations among parts vary.* We identify a shape as a person when he or she is standing, squatting, sitting, hopping on one foot with one arm waving free, and so forth. This ability is extremely impressive, given the wide range in variations among the shapes projected by the different configurations of an object.

4. *Identifying objects that contain or do not contain optional parts or characteristics.* In addition, we can identify objects when they are missing certain parts or characteristics. For example, we identify chairs when they are missing arms, and dogs when they have no tails. Indeed, we can identify objects in black-and-white photographs. However, some parts or characteristics cannot be missing: a chair is not a chair without a seat, and a dog would not be a dog without a body. In addition, we also can identify objects—albeit often with some difficulty—when they include extra parts or characteristics (e.g., faces when they have beards or scars, and pencils when they have clips on them).

Impoverished Input

We do not always see objects under ideal circumstances. The problem of object identification would be much less challenging if we always saw objects on individual pedestals with optimal lighting. Instead, we often must exercise the following abilities:

1. *Identifying objects that are partially occluded.* We can identify objects when they are partly hidden behind another objects. Indeed, we can identify several different objects that are tossed into a bucket, so that no one of them is completely visible. We do not even need entire parts to use the visual information to help identify the object: I have observed that even a baby can identify its bottle when only the tip of its nipple protrudes from under a towel (but the bulge is clearly visible, and is the right size for the bottle).

2. *Identifying objects when the image is degraded.* We often see objects under poor viewing conditions. Images can be degraded because of poor lighting or atmospheric conditions. They also can be degraded because they are por-

trayed in line drawings or sketches, and only some contours are presented (and often texture is removed almost completely). We clearly did not evolve in an environment where identifying line drawings was important, and hence it is of great interest that we can easily identify line drawings.

3. *Identifying objects that are very close.* We only see about 2° of visual angle (roughly the width of your thumb viewed at arm's length) with high resolution in a single eye fixation. Thus, when an object is very close, the initial encoding is in a sense degraded because only a portion of the object can be seen clearly. We have the ability (which is a special case of our ability to identify objects at different distances) to identify objects that are so close that we need to make multiple eye movements to examine them. This ability raises two problems: First, how do we direct our eye movements so that we encode useful information effectively? Second, how do we integrate information encoded over the course of separate fixations?

Specific Instances

As if these abilities were not difficult enough to understand, we must consider them in the context of another ability: We do not always generalize, but instead sometimes register the differences among individual examples of an object. In particular, we have the following abilities.

1. *Identifying specific objects.* We often can identify a specific member of a class of objects, for example distinguishing between Sally's cat and the cat next door, one's own car and the others in the parking lot, and so forth. The visual system not only can ignore variations that are irrelevant for identifying an object as a member of a class, but also can turn around and make such variations relevant. We often can have our cake and eat it too.

2. *Identifying specific spatial relations.* We also can note whether the spot on our cat is in the same place as the one on Fred's cat, or whether the sofa has been moved to a new place in the living room. These abilities imply that we associate information about shape and location in memory. Furthermore, even though we can identify an object in a wide range of locations, we can also store information about the typical locations of objects.

Objects and Scenes

We rarely see an object in complete isolation. Usually, we are assaulted by a very rich stimulus montage in which many objects are present. In such circumstances we easily apprehend more than a single object; we do not identify only one object and then stop. This ability also has distinct facets.

1. *Identifying multiple objects in a single fixation.* We can identify more than a single object in a single fixation. This conclusion follows from Biederman, Mezzanotte, and Rabinowitz's (1982) finding that context affects identification even when scenes are presented for less time than is required to make an eye

movement. For this result to have occurred, subjects must have identified the context as well as the object itself.

2. *Identifying multiple objects "automatically."* We do not intentionally search for each individual object. Rather, the visual system "automatically" identifies more than a single object in a fixation. Context would not affect identification if one did not identify more than a single object reflexively.

These abilities pose a difficult challenge to any theorist, even working at the coarse level adopted here. The situation is complicated further by the evidence that faces and written words are special cases, which may involve mechanisms that typically are not used in other types of identification (e.g., see Farah 1990). I will not attempt to characterize the special mechanisms used in face perception or reading, but will sometimes note ways in which more general mechanisms are used in the two cases (see chapter 5 of Kosslyn and Koenig 1992 for a discussion of such mechanisms in reading). My strategy is to start simply, and build on a sturdy foundation, as described in the next section.

STARTING SMALL: THE ROLE OF A PROTOMODEL

In my earlier work on imagery I found it useful to begin with a minimalist theory, based on relatively few assumptions. In a field such as this, we simply do not know enough to specify a detailed theory from the start, and the effort spent on developing the details is likely to be wasted; thus, it makes sense to begin with a few central ideas, defend them, and build on these foundations. I called such a minimalist theory a *protomodel*. A protomodel embodies only the bare bones of a theory, and the goal of research is to discover whether these fundamental hypotheses are correct and, if so, how they should be augmented to develop a full-blown theory. One not only considers the key claims but also devises alternate ways to flesh out the protomodel, and thereby generates issues that can drive an empirical research program.[3]

The protomodel is rooted in fundamental facts about the anatomy and physiology of the primate visual system. I will begin with a very brief overview of the anatomical areas and connections, which play a major role in shaping the theory; additional information will be provided in the following chapters as it becomes relevant.

Basic Neuroanatomical Constraints

The first neural structure subserving vision is, of course, the retina. The light-sensitive cells at the back of the eye send input to ganglion cells, which in turn project input back into the brain (Dowling 1987). Although there are at least four classes of ganglion cells, two types have received much attention recently: the magnocellular (M) and parvocellular (P) cells. The larger M cells respond better to motion and transient stimulation, whereas the smaller P cells have better spatial resolution and respond to color (e.g., see DeYoe and Van Essen 1988; Knierim and Van Essen 1992; Livingstone and Hubel 1988; Schiller and Logothetis 1990; Schiller, Logothetis, and Charles 1990a, 1990b; Zeki and Shipp 1988). The two classes project to distinct layers within the lateral geniculate nucleus (LGN) of the thalamus, and for a time it appeared as if they were preserved as separate streams far into cortex (e.g., see Livingstone and Hubel 1988). However, subsequent research revealed that the two streams interact and do not correspond to entirely distinct functional divisions in cortex (e.g., DeYoe and Van Essen 1988; Schiller and Logothetis 1990; Schiller, Logothetis, and Charles 1990a, 1990b). Schiller and Logothetis (1990) suggest that the M cells extend the temporal resolution of the system, whereas the P cells extend the spatial resolution and wavelength sensitivity of the system.

The ganglion cells project to the cortex along two major pathways. The geniculostriate pathway synapses first on the LGN, and then to the first cortical visual area, V1 (also known as primary visual cortex, area 17, striate cortex, area OC, and sometimes simply—and misleadingly—"visual cortex"). The tectopulvinar pathway (also sometimes called the tectofugal pathway) synapses first on the superior colliculus, and then to the pulvinar (another nucleus on the thalamus), and then projects rather diffusely to cortex (see Kaas and Huerta 1988 for details of the anatomy and functions of these structures). Schneider (1969) and others have shown that the geniculostriate pathway plays a special role in object identification; if that pathway is cut, animals can no longer identify objects visually. In contrast, the tectopulvinar pathway plays a role in spatial orientation; if that pathway is cut, animals no longer orient properly when their whiskers are brushed.

Area V1 is the first cortical area that receives information directly from the LGN, but it is by no means the only cortical area involved in vision. At last count, some 32 areas in the macaque cortex were known to process visual information (Felleman and Van Essen 1991; Van Essen 1985; Van Essen et al. 1990). These areas are interconnected in orderly ways, although this story is far from complete (e.g., see Rockland and Virga 1989).

Figure 3.2 illustrates the areas and their connections as interpreted by Van Essen and his colleagues, and figure 3.3 presents the locations of these areas in the macaque monkey brain. Figure 3.4 presents the anatomy as interpreted by Distler et al. (1993). As is obvious, figures 3.2 and 3.4 differ in several ways. Note that not all of the areas in figure 3.2 are present in 3.4. figure 3.2 includes a few areas that are not, properly speaking, "visual areas" (such as HC, the hippocampus). In addition, in some cases, areas in figure 3.4 have been further subdivided in figure 3.2. In yet other instances, different notations are used (e.g., AIT in figure 3.2 appears to correspond to TE in figure 3.4).

Felleman and Van Essen (1991) estimate that each area is linked to about 15 other areas, and these connections are usually reciprocal; considerably

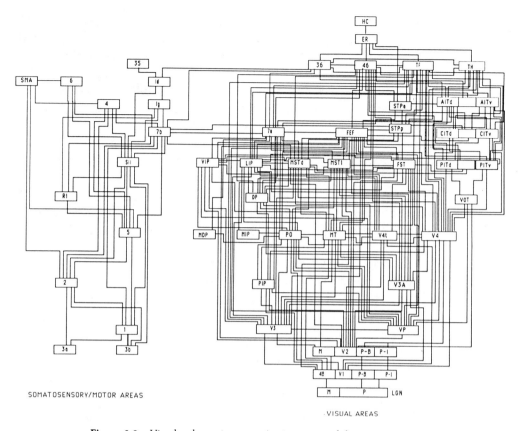

SOMATOSENSORY/MOTOR AREAS

·VISUAL AREAS

Figure 3.2 Visual and somatosensory/motor areas and their connections, as reconstructed by Van Essen et al. 1990 and discussed in Felleman and Van Essen (1991). (Reprinted from Van Essen et al. 1990, with permission.)

fewer connections are portrayed by Distler et al (1993). In the figures, Van Essen et al. indicate all connections in the same way, whereas Ungerleider et al. highlight the connections that are very strong; the dotted lines in figure 3.4 indicate pathways between areas that are only weakly connected. The filled arrowheads and open arrowheads of figure 3.4 specify afferent and efferent connections, respectively. In both figures, virtually every visual area that receives input (i.e., afferent fibers) from another area also projects information back to that area (via efferent fibers). Moreover, the two types of connections are of comparable size.[4] In addition, it has recently been found that some higher-level areas project directly back to much lower-level areas (e.g., area TE, in the inferior temporal lobe, projects directly to V1; see Douglas and Rockland 1992). Thus, the anatomy suggests that much information is flowing backward in the system.

In short, although our understanding of the detailed neuroanatomy of high-level vision is still in flux, we know a considerable amount about the structure of the system. Rather than attempt to resolve inconsistencies, I treat any areas or connections that are not evident in both figure 3.2 and figure 3.4 as controversial, and focus on those for which there is good agreement.

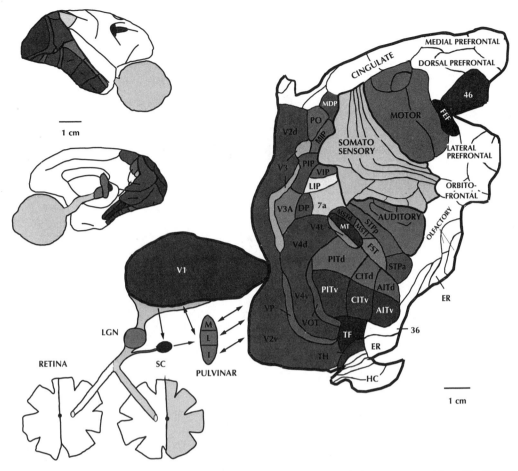

Figure 3.3 Illustration of the location of visual areas in the brain. (Reprinted from Van Essen et al. 1992, with permission. Copyright 1992 by the AAAS.)

It is worth noting again that some 15 of the visual areas, particularly those early in the processing sequence (i.e., fewer synapses removed from the eye), are spatially organized. As discussed in chapter 1, these areas roughly preserve the local geometry of the retina (with magnification factors and other distortions; see Van Essen 1985). The fact that imagery activates at least some of these topographically mapped areas is consistent with key features of the neurophysiology: As a general rule, the "higher" into the visual system one goes (as specified by number of synapses from V1), the looser is the topographic mapping; areas in the inferior temporal lobe (e.g., area TE) are not topographically mapped. Part of the reason for this is that the receptive fields of neurons in higher areas become very large (some subsuming over 100° of visual angle, as will be reviewed in later chapters); when receptive fields cover much of the field, they no longer can be said to be spatially organized. Thus, in order to depict the spatial structure of objects, lower-level areas would have to be used.

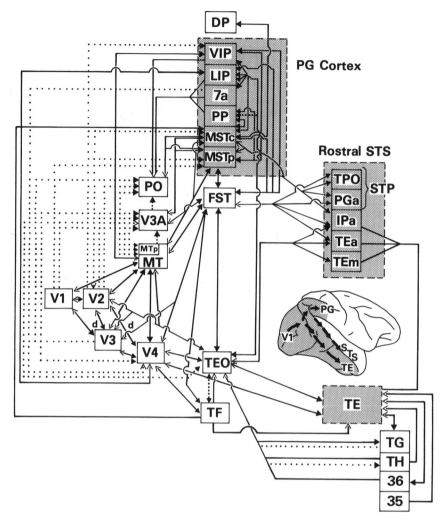

Figure 3.4 Visual areas and their connections, as reconstructed by Distler et al. (1993). (Reprinted with permission.)

Seven Subsystems

Reasoning about how to build a device that can identify objects in the circumstances outlined in the previous section and has the properties of the brain led me to carve high-level vision into the seven major components illustrated in figure 3.5. This protomodel defines a framework for the remainder of the book; I will further articulate different portions of the protomodel in the course of considering specific abilities of the system. At this juncture I will only hint at how the protomodel can account for some of our abilities. I first sketch out how the protomodel operates in visual object identification, and then consider visual mental imagery.

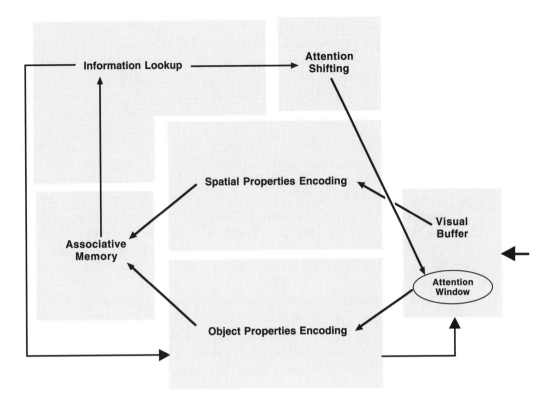

Figure 3.5 The protomodel.

The Protomodel in Visual Object Identification   When most people begin to think about the problem of object identification, the first mechanism they think of (and one of the first that was thought of historically; see Neisser 1967) is *template matching*. A template, in this sense, is a stored model of a shape. The idea is that one has in memory a template of each familiar shape, and when an object is seen its input image is compared to the templates; the template that overlaps the most with the image is selected as the best match.

This approach was quickly ruled out when researchers considered our ability to identify objects when their shapes vary. For example, say you stored an image of an open hand and matched input to it when later trying to identify hands. This procedure might work well if the hands you saw were always open. But what happens when you see a hand that is closed, gesturing with two fingers, and so forth? Imagine that you had a photograph of the different hands taken on transparent pieces of plastic, and placed them over the photo of an open hand. If you measured the degree of overlap, you would find that a hand balled into a fist barely overlaps the open hand—in fact, it overlaps a hand grenade better than a hand!

One approach to solving this problem is to store a separate template for each possible shape. The large number of necessary templates that are required by this scheme is not such a terrible flaw; as will be discussed in chapter 7, human memory has a truly awesome capacity to store information. A fundamental problem with this approach is that we see novel shapes all the time, and can identify them anyway. For example, you may never have seen a man squatting on one foot with both hands pointing to the sides of his neck, but you can identify the shape as a person nevertheless. As outlined in the previous section, we can identify objects in an astounding range of circumstances.

The workings of high-level visual mechanisms are apt to be very complex, and it is no wonder that they have proven difficult to fathom. Nevertheless, the depth of the problem was not obvious from the start; people find vision so easy that researchers initially expected it to be easy to program a computer to see. The reason vision is so easy for us is that we come equipped with an enormous amount of sophisticated machinery. These inborn abilities are ours for the using; we do not need to learn to see. The following components are key features of this innate architecture.

The Visual Buffer   Input from the eyes produces a configuration of activity in a set of topographically organized visual areas (in the occipital lobe) that are used to segregate figure from ground. I group these areas into a single functional structure, which I call the visual buffer. The spatial organization of this structure is useful for detecting edges and growing regions of homogenous value (see Marr 1982).

The Attention Window   The spatial organization of the visual buffer also allows an "attention window" to select the input from a contiguous set of points for detailed processing (for similar ideas, see Neisser 1967; Posner 1988; Treisman 1969; Treisman and Gelade 1980, Treisman and Souther 1985; Treisman and Gormican 1988). Our ability to covertly shift attention to different regions (e.g., Sperling 1960) may help us to identify objects when their images fall in different locations. The pattern in the attention window then is sent downstream to two major systems for future processing.

The Ventral System   The ventral system is a set of brain areas that runs from the occipital lobe down to the inferior temporal lobe, as is illustrated in figures 3.3 and 3.4. As illustrated at the bottom of figure 3.4, in the monkey this system includes areas V3, V4, TEO, TF, and TE. Cells in this area typically respond to properties of objects, such as shape, color, and texture. Cells in some of these areas are highly tuned, for example responding only when a face is seen in profile (for a review, see Desimone and Ungerleider 1989). Cells in the "higher" (further along the processing stream) areas of this system respond when an object is in a wide range of positions (i.e., they have large receptive fields), which presumably indicates that stimuli in a wide range of positions can be matched to stored information (see Gross and Mishkin 1977).

The Dorsal System By treating a wide range of locations as equivalent, the ventral system throws away information that is critical for reaching and navigation. Thus it is of interest that a second system preserves exactly this information. At the same time that information is being processed in the ventral system, it is also being processed in the dorsal system. This system is a set of brain areas that runs from the occipital lobe up to the parietal lobe; as illustrated at the top of figure 3.4, in the monkey it includes areas PO, 7a, LIP, and so forth. This system processes spatial properties, such as location and size (see Farah 1990; Haxby et al. 1991; Horwitz et al. 1992; Levine, 1982; Maunsell and Newsome 1987). Ungerleider and Mishkin (1982) call the ventral and dorsal systems the "what" and "where" systems, respectively (see also Mishkin and Ungerleider 1982; Mishkin, Ungerleider, and Macko 1983). Although this is a good mnemonic, it should soon be evident that this characterization does not clearly capture the distinction between the systems, and hence I will avoid these terms.

Researchers have used a wide range of methods to characterize the functional properties of the two systems. For example, Mishkin and Ungerleider (1982, following up on findings of Pohl 1973) studied monkeys who were trained to lift a lid covering one of two food containers placed in front of them. Only one of the lids concealed food, and the monkey had to learn which one. In one version of the task, each lid had a different pattern. For example, one lid had the outline of a plus, and the other had the outline of a square. The food would always be under one of the lids, which were switched from the right to the left side randomly from trial to trial. The monkey was fed only if it lifted the correct lid, which required learning to tell the patterns apart. Even if a monkey could perform this task well prior to surgery, this task becomes exceedingly difficult after the inferior temporal lobes are removed (the portion beneath the superior temporal sulcus).

In contrast, another version of the discrimination task is not greatly impaired when the inferior temporal lobes are removed, but is devastated if the parietal lobes are removed. In this task, both of the lids that conceal the food wells are painted gray, and the monkey must learn that the relative location of a small tower (a "landmark") is the relevant cue. The position of the tower is varied from trial to trial, and the food is always under the lid that is closer to the tower. Even if a monkey could perform this task well prior to surgery, this location task becomes exceedingly difficult after the parietal lobes are removed. These animals do not have a severe deficits in the pattern learning task (Pohl 1973; Ungerleider and Mishkin 1982).

Thus, there is a double dissociation: damage to the inferior temporal lobes more severely disrupts pattern discrimination than location discrimination, and vice versa for damage to the parietal lobes.

Moreover, when researchers insert microelectrodes in brain cells in the inferior temporal lobes, they have found that the neurons fire most vigorously when specific object properties are present in the input (such as color or shape; see Desimone and Schein 1987; Schwartz et al. 1983; Zeki 1978).

Indeed, some of these cells fire only when the animal sees a face, hairbrush, or hand (e.g., Desimone et al. 1984; Gross et al. 1981; Gross et al. 1984), and some will respond to a face only when the eyes are pointed in a certain direction (Perrett et al. 1985).

In contrast, neurons in the parietal lobes tend to be sensitive to location (as gated by eye position), size, and orientation (see Andersen 1987; Goldberg and Colby 1989; Hyvarinen 1982; Maunsell and Newsome 1987; Robinson, Goldberg, and Stanton 1978). These neurons have strikingly different properties from those in the inferior temporal lobes. These cells are not particularly sensitive to shape or color, in many cases do not respond preferentially to input falling on the fovea, and often are sensitive to direction of motion. Furthermore, Gross (1978) and Holmes and Gross (1984) report that monkeys with temporal lobe lesions can learn to discriminate between the same object presented at different orientations of 60° or more, presumably on the basis of the parietal lobes. Indeed, Eacott and Gaffan (1991) found that when the inferior parietal lobe was lesioned, monkeys had great difficulty discriminating between shapes that were rotated 180°; in contrast, these monkeys could discriminate between different shapes relatively well.

The ventral (object-properties encoding) system not only registers key properties of shapes but also encodes color and texture; this information is matched to that of objects stored in this structure (e.g., see Desimone et al. 1984; Desimone and Ungerleider 1989; Miller, Li, and Desimone 1991; Miyashita and Chang 1988). The anterior portions of the ventral system store information in a visual code, which cannot be accessed by input from other sensory modalities. The goal of this processing is to discover which stored object is most like the object being viewed. If a good match is obtained, the object is recognized; however, in some cases the input may not match any particular stored object very well.

It is useful to distinguish between *recognition* and *identification*. Recognition occurs when input matches a perceptual memory, and hence one knows that the object is familiar; identification occurs when input accesses representations in a multimodal, "conceptual" memory store, and one thereby has access to a wide range of knowledge about the object (its name, favorite habitat, sounds it makes when shaked, and so on). When an object is identified, one knows more about it than is apparent in the immediate sensory input. The ventral system does not contain the kinds of memory representations necessary for identification, but rather is best viewed as helping to organize the input into familiar packets.

The dorsal (spatial-properties-encoding) system appears to encode information that is used primarily to guide actions, such as reaching and moving one's eyes; indeed, the majority of the neurons in the posterior parietal lobe either register the consequences of a movement, such as current eye position, or discharge immediately prior to a movement (e.g., Andersen, Essick, and Siegel 1985; Lynch et al. 1977). In addition, this pathway allows one to use spatial properties for other purposes, such as categorizing the locations of objects or of the parts or characteristics of objects (as will be discussed in chapter 7).

Although much of the empirical support for this distinction between the two cortical visual systems comes from animal models, there is strong converging evidence from studies with humans. One type of evidence comes from studies of patients with focal brain damage, who display different types of deficits depending on the locus of the lesion. As Farah (1990), Levine (1982), and Kosslyn and Koenig (1992, chapter 3) review, when the occipital-temporal area is damaged, the patient often has trouble recognizing or identifying objects; in contrast, when the occipital-parietal area is damaged, the patient often has trouble encoding spatial information (see also De Renzi 1982; Goodale et al. 1991; Newcombe, Ratcliff, and Damasio 1987).

Another type of evidence for the distinction between the two cortical visual systems in humans comes from PET studies, which have revealed activation in inferior temporal regions when recognition tasks are being performed (Kosslyn, Alpert, Thompson, Chabris, Rauch and Anderson 1993; Sergent, Ohta, and MacDonald 1992; Zeki et al. 1991) and activation in parietal regions when spatial tasks are being performed (e.g., Corbetta et al. 1990; Haxby et al. 1991; Kosslyn, Alpert, Thompson, Chabris, Rauch, and Anderson 1993).

Associative Memory   The outputs from the ventral (object properties) and dorsal (spatial properties) encoding systems come together at an associative memory (which appears to be implemented in part in the posterior, superior temporal lobes), where they are matched to stored information. Associative memory contains not only associations between perceptual representations, but also more abstract "conceptual" information (names, categories, parts of speech, and so forth). Information in associative memory can be accessed by input from all sensory systems; once one has accessed the appropriate information, the object has been identified.

In many circumstances, the match in visual memory (in the ventral system) is good enough to select the appropriate representation in associative memory, especially in conjunction with information about the size, orientation, and location of the object that is sent to associative memory by the dorsal system. However, in some circumstances the input to the ventral system does not match a visual memory very well; for example, if one sees a dog on its back with its legs splayed to the side, the overall shape may not match one stored in visual memory. In such cases perhaps only one part or characteristic could be matched to a stored representation. If so, then additional information must be collected.

Information Lookup   When the input does not initially implicate a specific object, more information must be collected. In such circumstances, we do not look around randomly to collect additional information. Rather, the stored information that is partially activated by the input guides further encoding (e.g., see Gregory 1966; Neisser 1967, 1976). One actively seeks new information that will determine whether the best-matching object is in fact present. This use of stored information is called *top-down processing*. The first step is to look up relevant information in associative memory. As will be discussed, there is evidence that dorsolateral prefrontal cortex plays a critical role in this process (e.g., Damasio 1985a; Goldman-Rakic 1987; Luria 1980).

Attention Shifting   Finally, in top-down search one not only must access stored information but also must engage mechanisms that actually shift attention to a location where an informative part or characteristic (e.g., distinctive mark) should be located. The frontal eye fields (area 8), posterior parietal lobe (area 7a, in particular), pulvinar, and superior colliculus play critical roles in this process (e.g., see Posner and Petersen 1990). Attention shifting has two components: one that actually shifts the body, head, eyes, and/or attention window to focus on a specific location, and another that, at the same time, "primes" the representation of the sought property, making it easier to encode.

After attention has been shifted, the portion of the object at the attended location is encoded and matched to representations of objects, parts, and properties in the ventral system; at the same time, the spatial properties of this portion of the object are extracted in the dorsal system. The object and spatial properties that are thereby registered in associative memory may then be sufficient to identify the object. If not, this cycle is repeated, possibly using a different representation to guide search.

The Protomodel in Visual Mental Imagery   A visual mental image is a pattern of activation in the visual buffer that is not caused by immediate sensory input. The components of the protomodel have the same properties when they are used to "inspect" an object that is visualized instead of perceived. For example, if asked whether Snoopy the dog has pointed ears, people report visualizing the cartoon and "looking" at the dog's ears. The shape of the ears is matched to stored shapes in the ventral system, and the size, location, and orientation of the ears is registered by the dorsal system— just as would occur if the dog were being perceived. Once a pattern of activity is evoked in the visual buffer, it is processed the same way, regardless of whether it was evoked by input from the eyes (perception) or from memory (imagery).

But this is not to say that the system has exactly the same properties in imagery and perception. Imagery has at least three major differences from perception: First, mental images fade rapidly, unlike percepts (i.e., representations formed on the basis of visual input while one is perceiving an object). In perception, the world serves as an external store. One can be leisurely when looking around, but not when looking within; imaged objects fade too quickly to be inspected thoroughly. Second, mental images are created from stored information; the external world does not dictate the contents of one's imagery at any specific time. Mental images arise under a variety of contexts, and may not have any resemblance to the on-line perceptual representations. Third, images, unlike the perceptions of normal people, are remarkably malleable. One can image objects twisting, turning, bending, and so on—but perception is not (and should not be, for the sake of one's survival) so cooperative. In the course of this book, I shall expand and further develop these observations, but let us now briefly consider how the protomodel addresses each in turn.

The claim that the visual buffer is shared by imagery and perception allows us to explain the fact that images fade quickly. In perception, one does not want a representation to linger after one has shifted one's eyes. This property is to be distinguished from saccadic suppression, where input is actively suppressed when the eye is moved. The point here is that the input from a previous fixation should not linger; because the visual buffer is retinotopically mapped, such persistence would result in a smeared mess after a few eye, head, or body movements, as new input was mixed with the inputs from previous fixations. Thus, it is a good idea for the visual buffer to have the equivalent of "fast-fade phosphor." But this property, which is so useful in perception, has not-so-useful consequences in imagery: the image fades quickly, and effort is required to maintain it.

How are visual mental images formed? In some cases, one may have just seen an object, and can retain the image briefly. But in most cases the image is *generated* on the basis of information in memory. Images can be generated by exactly the same mechanisms that are used to prime the ventral system so that it can easily encode a sought part or characteristic during top-down search. For imagery, a visual memory representation is primed so much that it in turn primes the lower areas, forming the image. The fact that objects can be recognized guarantees that visual information must be stored in memory. In chapter 1 I suggested that visual memories can be activated to form mental images, using the efferent connections from areas "higher" in the processing stream to topographically organized areas. The areas that appear to play a role in storing visual information in the inferior temporal lobe in monkeys are not topographically organized (or have only a very rough topographic organization at best; see Van Essen et al. 1990). Thus, imagery may be necessary to "unpack" the stored visual information, laying out the geometric relations inherent in a shape. This is accomplished, I have suggested, by projecting information backward in the system—using the efferent connections—to evoke a pattern of activity in the visual buffer.

This sort of mechanism will explain how images of individual shapes are generated, but this is not all there is to image generation. We also can build up an image from several previously encoded representations (e.g., of Abraham Lincoln shaking Lenin's hand). In such situations, the system could operate just as it does when top-down processing is engaged during perception. The information lookup subsystem would access the location of a to-be-imaged part or characteristic in associative memory, and the attention shifting subsystem would shift the attention window accordingly. Only now, instead of encoding a new part or characteristic after the attention window has been shifted to a new location, one would visualize the part or characteristic at that location. This idea allows us to understand why progressively more time is required to form images of objects with greater numbers of parts (see chapter 6 of Kosslyn 1980).[5]

Finally, if mental images are patterns of activity in the visual buffer that are not fixed to perceptual input, then there is no reason why they cannot be transformed. In chapter 10, I will argue that the mapping function from the stored memory to the visual buffer can be altered, so that the projection in the visual buffer shifts. Images fade quickly; the initial pattern in an image is not fixed and hence can be rearranged rather easily. And once rearranged, the new object properties and spatial properties can be encoded and the object reinterpreted. Thus, once one mentally rotates the letter N 90° clockwise, one can "see" that a new letter has been formed.

It seems clear that this protomodel has promise of helping us to understand the mechanisms of high-level visual perception and imagery. However, it is too impoverished to provide mechanistic accounts for most of our visual capabilities; rather, it serves primarily to define a framework, a skeleton that must be fleshed out to do much real work. I begin this task in earnest in the next chapter.

CONCLUSIONS

Visual mental imagery shares processing mechanisms with high-level visual perception, and so a theory of high-level visual perception can provide the foundations for a theory of visual mental imagery. In order to develop a theory of the processing subsystems used in both imagery and perception, I first will consider five classes of visual perceptual abilities. The goal of the following four chapters is to infer the subsystems that confer our ability to identify objects (1) in different locations and at different distances; (2) with different, sometimes novel, shapes; (3) when the input is impoverished; (4) as specific exemplars, including ones that are not typical for the category; and, (5) when we see objects embedded in scenes. Each of these abilities corresponds to a set of more specialized abilities.

I begin with a coarse decomposition of the high-level visual system into seven subsystems, which can be summarized as follows: (1) The visual buffer is a spatially organized structure in the occipital lobe that provides the input to the rest of the high-level visual system; images (both perceptual and mental) are patterns of activation in this structure. (2) The attention window selects the configuration of activity in one region of the visual buffer for further processing. (3) Information in the attention window is sent to two cortical visual systems. The ventral system (in the inferior temporal lobes) encodes object properties, such as shape, color, and texture; stored representations of such information can also be activated to prime the system to encode an expected property or to generate a mental image. (4) At the same time the ventral system is operating, the dorsal system (in the posterior parietal lobes) encodes spatial properties, such as location, size, and orientation. (5) Information about object properties and spatial properties come together in an associative memory (which probably relies on tissue in the posterior, superior temporal regions). If the input does not implicate a single representation, the best-matching representation is used to guide a search. (6) To initiate this search an information lookup subsystem (in dorsolateral prefrontal cortex) accesses information about a distinctive part or characteristic of the most-activated object in associative memory (e.g., a spot on the head of one's cat. (7) Finally, attention shifting subsystems (in frontal, parietal, and subcortical areas) use the representation of the location of this part or characteristic to direct the attention window to the appropriate location; at the same time, the ventral system is primed for the sought part or characteristic. New information is then encoded and matched to stored information and the cycle is repeated until the object is identified.

According to the theory, these components play similar roles in visual mental imagery. The priming mechanism can activate a stored representation so much that an image is formed, and numerous images can be juxtaposed by shifting attention to the appropriate location in the visual buffer before forming the image. Once the imaged objects are formed, they can be "inspected" using the same internal processing that is used during perception.

4 Identifying Objects in Different Locations

Perhaps the most basic type of generalization during object identification is the ability to identify objects when their positions shift relative to one another or to oneself. This ability is so basic that it may not seem puzzling. And yet, stimuli that fall on different parts of the retina are processed by different parts of many visual areas; how is it that we treat them as equivalent? Indeed, humans typically recognize a picture as easily in a new location as in its original location (Biederman and Cooper 1991c). The insights we gain by considering this question will provide us with the foundations for understanding how people can identify objects seen at different distances, which causes them to subtend different visual angles. At the end of this chapter we will see how the inferences we have drawn about visual perception inform theories of visual mental imagery.

IDENTIFYING OBJECTS IN DIFFERENT POSITIONS IN THE VISUAL FIELD

Many mechanisms could allow a system to identify objects in different positions in the visual field. We can organize the alternatives along a continuum. At one extreme, the system creates a duplicate representation of an object for each location in the field; this process occurs when an object is initially encoded. When the object is seen subsequently, it will thus match a stored representation, no matter where the image falls on the retina. The theory of word reading developed by McClelland and Rumelhart (1981) posits a mechanism of this sort; they include duplicate sets of feature detectors and letter detectors at each location where a letter can appear. These representations thus preserve information about the location of the stimulus as well as its shape.

At the other extreme of the continuum, only one representation is stored. In this case, no matter where an image falls on the retina, it is converted to a standard representation before being compared to stored representations. The standard representation might be object-centered, specifying the parts of an object relative to the object itself (e.g., Feldman 1985; Hinton 1981; Hummel and Biederman 1992; Marr 1982). Hence, stimuli that appear in a wide range of positions are treated as equivalent; the representation strips away information about location in the field. In this case, a separate system is required to register location.

Various intermediate mechanisms also are possible, which posit more than a single representation but fewer than one for every possible location. For example, two representations might be stored, with one in each hemisphere (subserving the contralateral visual field). Or four representations might be stored, one in each hemisphere for the upper field and one for the lower field, and so forth.

There is a trade-off between the amount of storage and difficulty of processing; moving along the continuum, as the amount of storage increases, the difficulty of processing decreases. At the first extreme, one must store many more representations, but processing is straightforward. At the other extreme, although storage is minimized, processing must be more sophisticated: Not only must the object be converted to a standard form, but additional processing is necessary to represent information about location.

Gross and Mishkin (1977) suggest that the brain adopted a mechanism that falls near the second pole of the continuum; this mechanism includes a system that discards information about location when encoding an object's form for recognition, but also includes a second system that preserves location for reaching, navigation, and so forth. Thus the specialization of the inferior temporal lobe for processing of object properties, and the complementary specialization of the parietal lobe for processing spatial properties; this is a good example of the principle of division of labor (see chapter 2; see also chapter 2 of Kosslyn and Koenig 1992). And in fact, neurons in the inferior temporal lobe, which apparently encode shape, color, and texture, respond similarly when stimuli are placed within a wide range of positions in the visual field (e.g., Schwartz et al. 1984).

It is useful to recast Gross and Mishkin's idea in terms of input/output mappings. The input is an object that can appear in a variety of locations, and the output is a representation of the identity of the object and its location. A task is difficult when it is difficult to map the input onto the desired output, and one way to cope with difficult mappings is to divide them into a number of relatively simple mappings. If so, then the division of labor between the inferior temporal lobe and the parietal lobes makes good sense computationally. Rueckl, Cave, and Kosslyn (1989) explored this idea more formally.

Is the Division of Labor Computationally Efficient?

My colleagues and I developed two types of feedforward "neural network" models to explore the computational properties of Gross and Mishkin's (1977) proposal. One type included only a single system, which encoded both identity and location; in contrast, the other type incorporated a bifurcated system, with one subsystem that encoded identity and another that encoded location. We used the output error (i.e., the squared disparity between correct and observed output) after a fixed number of training trials as a measure of the

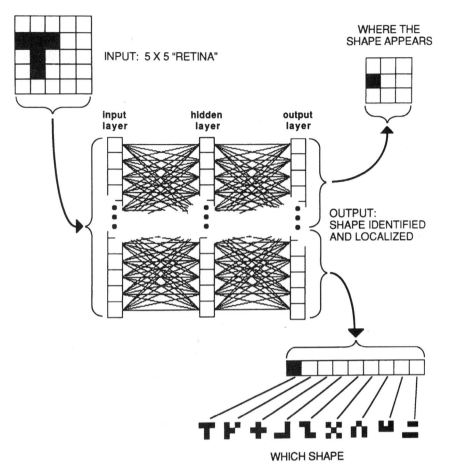

Figure 4.1 The architecture of Rueckl, Cave, and Kosslyn's network models that encoded the identity and location of stimuli. (Reprinted from Rueckl, Cave, and Kosslyn 1989, with permission.)

relative difficulty of establishing an input/output mapping. In addition, by analyzing the patterns of weights on connections to and from the hidden units, we could ascertain how the mappings were actually performed.

Our hypothesis was that, all else being equal, the bifurcated system would establish the mappings more readily. All networks had the same input layer, which was an array of 25 units. As is illustrated in figure 4.1, the 25 input units were organized into a 5 × 5 matrix, and patterns were represented by selectively activating specific input units. We devised 9 patterns by selectively filling in cells of a 3 × 3 grid. These patterns were presented in 9 distinct locations in the 5 × 5 grid, producing a total of 81 input stimuli.

All networks also had the same output layer, which consisted of 18 units. Nine of these units were dedicated to representing the individual shapes, and nine were dedicated to representing the individual locations. Thus, on any given trial only two output units should be active: the one representing the shape's identity and the one representing its present location in the matrix.

Identifying Objects in Different Locations

The networks varied only in the structure and size of the hidden layer. In all cases, each hidden unit received input from (i.e., was connected to) each input unit. The unsplit network had 18 hidden units, each of which sent input to all 18 output units. In the split network, the hidden layer was effectively sliced down the middle. Half of these units were connected only to the *where* output units, and half were connected only to the *what* output units. The split network, then, functioned as two separate systems, with half computing the mapping of the input to the *what* outputs and half computing the mapping of the input to the *where* outputs.

Counter to our expectations, the unsplit network established the mapping more easily. Fortunately, Kyle Cave looked more carefully at the outputs and noticed that although the unsplit network was better at establishing the mapping for the identity task, the split network performed as well as the unsplit model in the location task.

Why did the split network classify location as well as the unsplit network, but classify identity more poorly than the unsplit network? This result makes sense if the two classifications are not equally difficult. The mapping necessary in the location task is straightforward; indeed, it is "linearly separable": a distinct feature of the input could be directly identified with a specific output. A network without hidden units could establish a direct connection between each location and the required output classification of location. In contrast, there was no single feature that could be used to classify the shapes when they appeared in different positions. And in fact, the identity task was more difficult for both networks.

At first blush, the results were disappointing; we expected the division-of-labor strategy to be better than the single-system strategy. Upon reflection, however, we realized that the idea of division of labor does not imply anything about how resources should be allocated within each partition. The split network may have been hobbled by too few resources to establish the identity mapping; nine dedicated hidden units may not have been enough.

To investigate this possibility, we varied the relative number of hidden units that were allocated to mapping identity and location in a split network. And in fact, the performance of the split network varied greatly depending on the internal organization. Provided that enough hidden units were devoted to the identity problem, and the location problem was not starved to death, the split networks were indeed superior to the unsplit ones.

How Mapping Was Achieved: Receptive and Projective Fields   In these networks, the hidden units were used to map the input onto identity and location outputs. As discussed in chapter 2, these mappings are accomplished by adjusting the weights on the connections coming to and leading from the hidden units. By analyzing the patterns of weights on connections to and from the hidden units, we could ascertain how the mappings were actually performed. That is, by examining which connections from the input layer contributed heavily to the activation state of a given hidden unit, we could determine which aspects of the input were particularly important for that unit. This is called an analysis of *receptive fields*, by analogy to the relation between a neuron and the area of space in which a stimulus can drive it. The receptive field of a hidden unit consists of those input units that have strong weights on their connections to the hidden unit (and hence will influence it strongly when stimulated by an input). Similarly, by examining which connections from a hidden unit contributed heavily to the activation state of the output units, we could determine which combinations of input properties (as registered by the hidden unit) were important for specific responses. This is called an analysis of *projective fields*. The projective field of a hidden unit consists of those output units that have strong weights on their connections from that hidden unit.

As noted in chapter 2, Zipser and Andersen (1988) analyzed a network that was trained to locate points in space, and found that the hidden units developed receptive fields that resembled those of neurons in area 7a of the parietal lobe (the nature of these fields will be discussed in chapter 6, when we consider properties of the dorsal system in detail). Similarly, Lehky and Sejnowski (1988) performed these analyses on a network that learned to specify shape when given input about the shading of a surface, and discovered that the receptive fields resembled those of neurons in area V1. Moreover, the projective fields from hidden units sent information to output units about the orientation of the principal curvatures, whether they were convex or concave, and the relative magnitude of the curve.

In a way, this use of network models is like performing a multiple-regression analysis in which one seeks to discover which independent variables account for variation in a dependent variable. But in this case one does not specify the independent variables in advance; the goal is to discover them. The analysis of receptive and projective fields provides information about what aspects of the input were used by a network to accomplish a particular input/output mapping, and provides hints about how the brain may accomplish a similar mapping.

We examined the receptive fields of the what/where unsplit networks, which were free to develop the mapping in any way that was useful, and found that some hidden units had strong positive weights from input units that were arranged into horizontal, vertical, or diagonal bars in the input array. These units apparently served as "feature detectors." Other hidden units had strong positive weights on contiguous regions of the input array, and still others responded to a region along a border of the input array. The network was not simply storing templates of each object and then matching them to input; rather, it analyzed the features of the input and identified objects by the sets of features that were present. Neurons in inferior temporal cortex have been identified that appear to register similar types of features, as will be reviewed in the following chapter.

These findings were intriguing because, like the corresponding cells found in inferior temporal cortex, some of these different types of receptive fields spanned large regions of the array. These units responded to input over a wide region, and may have developed such large receptive fields for the same reason that shape-dependent neurons in the ventral system have large receptive fields. However, not all of the networks' receptive fields had this property, and the networks could not have worked if they relied only on those receptive fields that were very large. These sorts of large receptive fields may be part of the solution, but they cannot be the entire story.

When we examined the projective fields, we discovered that most of the hidden units in the unsplit network participated in both mappings (they had large weights on the connections to both types of output units). The split networks, of course, were explicitly designed so that this could not occur. To quantify this observation, we correlated the sums of the absolute values of the weights to the identity and location output units. If individual hidden units in the unsplit networks had become specialized for one type of output, then units with strong weights on connections to identity output units should have weak weights on connections to location output units, and vice versa. Thus, the correlation between the weights on connections to identity and location output units should approach -1.00. However, the actual correlation was $-.31$. In unsplit networks, only a small amount of specialization occurs, which presumably is why the appropriately divided split networks perform better.[1]

Conclusions from the Simulations   Identifying an object and specifying a location are logically independent, and hence it seemed unlikely that efficient input/output mappings for the two tasks would share connections in a network; indeed, the opportunity to share connections seemed likely to cause interference. Thus, we expected the two types of mappings to be accomplished more easily by two mechanisms than by one. This expectation was borne out, but only if there were enough processing resources to establish the individual mappings. The most efficient split network had 3.5 times more hidden units for the identity mapping than for the location mapping. These results are consistent with a feature of the gross neuroanatomy: many more neurons compute object properties in the inferior temporal lobe than compute spatial properties in the parietal lobe (c.f. Van Essen 1985). Encoding shape is, apparently, more difficult than encoding location—even when the shapes vary only in two dimensions.[2]

It is worth emphasizing that I use network models in a somewhat unusual way: I am not interested in learning per se, nor do I regard these simulated networks as realistic models of actual neural networks (with each unit corresponding to an individual neuron). Rather, the models are cast at a more abstract level; they are a way to assess the relative ease of performing certain kinds of input/output mappings. One could think of this approach as a way of assessing the relative "computational complexity" of computations in systems with different functional organizations; the more error after a fixed number of training trials, the more complex the computation performed by that structure. As I noted earlier, the ease of establishing mappings in these networks is of interest because we have reason to believe that similar mappings are established by the brain (given, for example, Zipser and Andersen's [1988] and Lehky and Sejnowski's [1988] findings).

Having said this, one can question whether we have learned anything from the toy problem put to the network. The brain certainly does not perform the mapping performed by the models; it does not identify a small set of two-dimensional patterns in a small number of locations. However, one could reconstrue the result to make it more plausible. The network does not "know" how the human user interprets the outputs; from its point of view (so to speak), the outputs could correspond not to identity but to the presence of key features. Thus, the appropriately divided split network operated better because it segregated the mapping of features of the input that are useful for encoding shape from those that are useful for encoding location. The important general point is that to the extent that two input/output mappings are logically distinct (i.e., one can be specified entirely independently of the other), interference occurs if the same hidden units are used for both mappings.

The Visual Buffer

Think again about the problem at hand. There are really two versions of it. We have so far been discussing the problem of how one identifies objects when their input images fall in different regions of the retina *and* one must process the input fully in each region. Another version of the problem probably arises more frequently, namely how one identifies an object when its image initially falls on different regions of the retina but one can move one's eyes to fixate on the object. If one moves one's eyes, so that objects are fixated upon no matter where they are in the field, the problem becomes trivial. Once one has shifted one's eyes, the same sensory information can be encoded when the object is numerous different locations.

The solution to this version of the mapping problem suggests a solution to the more challenging problem that occurs when one cannot move one's eyes (e.g., when one only catches a glimpse of an object from a moving vehicle or in a divided-visual-field experiment). The computer models included an array, which preserves the spatial layout of the perceived environment. This array allowed the networks to develop some large "hard-wired" receptive fields; but these alone would not have encoded the distinct stimuli (other, "special purpose" connections were also present). Nevertheless, if the brain contains such a spatial structure, it may have solved the harder version of the problem by analogy to how it solved the easier version. Just as one can move one's eyes to fixate on different parts of the actual environment, one may be able to shift internally the focus of attention—which would be like an internal eye movement, allowing one to focus on patterns in different regions of the internal array. The mechanism I have in mind would be exactly the sort that Skinner (1978) railed against; he felt that cognitivism solved no problems because it simply "moved the world into the head." But in fact, if certain properties of the world are internalized, are embodied by properties of our brains, many problems might be solved relatively easily (for a related view, see Shepard 1987). As summarized in the previous chapter, I call the internal array the *visual buffer*, and the internal locus of attention the *attention window*.

As presently conceived, a representation in the visual buffer is similar to Marr's (1982) "2.5 D Sketch." Following Marr, I assume that the distance and orientation of points in the visual field are explicitly represented in this structure.[3] I also assume that the edge information computed by low-level processes is explicitly represented in the visual buffer. In addition, I assume that the visual buffer actively organizes regions of similar values (colors, intensities) into perceptual units.[4]

Marr's "principle of least commitment" is particularly important for processing that occurs relatively early; if too much information is discarded, a later computation may be impossible. The spatial layout of the visual buffer is useful because it allows representations within the buffer to contain an enormous amount of implicit information about spatial properties; such information can be used for numerous purposes downstream. For example, one may want to observe relative lengths, aspect ratios, or areas of different portions of an object. In addition, a spatial structure can represent many properties of shape independently of location, which facilitates separate processing of the two types of information. As noted in chapter 3, the concept of a visual buffer is consistent with key properties of the brain's neuroanatomy.

Anatomical Localization   I have characterized high-level processes as those that make use of stored information about objects and events, in contrast to low-level visual processes, which are driven purely by the stimulus input.[5] Hence, the visual buffer corresponds to a set of retinotopically mapped areas in which knowledge about objects and events affects processing. These areas constitute a functionally characterized structure; they need not be anatomically contiguous. There are many candidate visual areas that may be components of this functional structure (see Allman and Kaas 1976; Cowey 1985; Desimone and Ungerleider 1989; Felleman and Van Essen 1991; Van Essen 1985; Zeki and Shipp 1988), including areas V1, V2, V3, V3A, and V4.

Based on findings from nonhuman primates, it is tempting to place the boundary between low-level and high-level vision somewhere between areas V1 and V4. For example, consider the findings of Moran and Desimone (1985). They identified stimuli that selectively caused individual neurons in areas V1, V4 and IT to respond, and mapped out their receptive fields. They then taught the monkey that it would be reinforced (with sugar water) only when it responded to a stimulus in one quadrant of a cell's receptive field. After training, Moran and Desimone found that cells in V4 and IT only continued to respond when the stimulus fell within the attended quadrant. The neurons began to fire when the stimulus appeared anywhere in the receptive field, but this activity was rapidly squelched if the stimulus appeared outside the favored area. Cells in V1 were not affected by training.

In contrast, the PET results my colleagues and I have obtained in imagery experiments (see chapter 1) suggest that the visual buffer includes area V1 in humans. This inference is buttressed by fMRI results from individual subjects. Imagery appears to affect the lowest-level cortical visual processing. These findings are sobering from the point of view of visual processing: One's knowledge and beliefs apparently can affect visual processing almost from the start.

Spitzer, Desimone, and Moran (1988) also report evidence that knowledge and beliefs modulate visual processing in a spatially organized area. They examined the activity of neurons in V4 in the monkey during orientation and color discrimination tasks. Cells in this area typically are tuned to respond to selected orientations and wavelengths. They found that as a discrimination was made more subtle, making the task more difficult, the cells responded more vigorously. Presumably higher (downstream) areas were involved in tuning the cells in V4 to be more sensitive when more precise information was needed; the cells in V4 themselves do not "understand" the task, and hence do not "know" how precise the output needs to be.

Taking another tack, Haenny, Maunsell, and Schiller (1988) trained monkeys to make a discrimination between patterns of stripes (gratings) at different orientations. The animals first were given a cue for an orientation, and then a series of gratings was presented. These gratings were at different orientations, and the monkey had to release a switch when a grating appeared at the same orientation as the original cue. The cue was given either visually or tactually (the animal felt a grooved plate, which was kept out of sight). Approximately 57% of the neurons recorded in V4 responded differently when different orientations were cued. For present purposes, the most important finding was the discovery that the tactile cue was as effective as the visual one—even though the neurons did not respond when the monkeys felt the grooved plate but were not performing the orientation-matching task. Thus, knowledge about the cue affected a visual area appropriately, even when the stimulus was initially encoded in another modality. Without question, knowledge of objects and events affects processing in area V4.

The Attention Window

For the proposed solution to the "problem of stimulus equivalence across retinal translation" to be viable, there must also be a mobile attention mechanism, which could shift focus to different regions within the visual buffer. There is, in fact, considerable evidence that such a mechanism exists.

Attention, as I will use the term, is the *selective aspect of processing*. Apparently, there is more information available in the visual buffer than can be passed downstream, and hence the transmission capacity must be selectively allocated; some information can be passed along, but other information must be filtered out. The attention window is a mechanism that selects a pattern in the visual buffer and passes it to the further reaches of the system. From the point of view of most of the high-level vision system, the only important portion of the visual buffer is that subsumed by the attention window. Thus, properties of the attention window place constraints on what can be accomplished by all subsequent processing subsystems (for similar ideas, see Eriksen and Yeh 1985; Koch and Ullman 1985; Nakayama 1990; Neisser 1967, 1976; Olshausen, Anderson, and Van Essen 1992; Posner 1978, 1988; Treisman

1969; Treisman and Gelade 1980; Treisman and Souther 1985; Treisman and Gormican 1988).

The attention window may not only be born of necessity, because of information processing capacity limitations, but may also play an essential organizational role in the system. As noted in the previous chapter, many results suggest that object properties are processed separately from spatial properties (for reviews, see Desimone and Ungerleider 1989; Levine 1982; Maunsell and Newsome 1987; Ungerleider and Mishkin 1982). If so, then there must be a mechanism that splits the two kinds of information and yet keeps them coordinated; we need information about shape to program the position of our hand as we reach to grasp a specific object, and hence information about shape and location must be coordinated (see Goodale and Milner 1992). The attention window serves these functions because it samples from a specific region of the visual buffer (and hence its outputs are yoked in time) and its contents are sent to both the dorsal and ventral systems (for a related view, see Treisman and Gelade 1980).

In addition, consider the difficulties faced by a system without an attention window. For example, Feldman (1985) dedicates a different detector to each feature and combination of features, and samples over the entire field continuously. A problem with this approach, as noted by Feldman, is that properties of two objects become conflated: there is no way to know which properties belong to which object. In addition, there simply are too many possible representations of location to duplicate the entire set of detectors for each one (as was done by McClelland and Rumelhart [1986] in their model of reading). The problem of coordinating object properties and spatial properties is made easier if one selects a single region for further processing; by sampling from only one region at a time, properties can be more easily conjoined. This advantage may not always be important, particularly when the stimuli are relatively simple or the spatial relations are simple and well-defined. Moreover, as I shall address in chapter 6, this mechanism does not completely solve the problem of how the system "binds" object properties and spatial properties together.

The claim that the attention window can be shifted incrementally receives support from the classic findings of Sperling (1960). Sperling showed subjects arrays of letters for very brief amounts of time, and then presented a high or low tone. The tone cued the subject to report the top or bottom row of the display. Even though subjects could only report a few of the letters when no cue was provided, they were virtually perfect when cued to attend to a particular row. Thus, the subjects could internally shift their attention (the tones were provided after the stimulus was removed), and could focus on a specific row and then scan across the letters in that row. Given that the entire display subtended a maximum horizontal extent (for displays with 4 letters per row) of only about 3.5° of visual angle, the attention window must be capable of being placed at rather precise locations; it is not constrained to select an entire quadrant of the field.[6]

Convergent evidence for an adjustable attention window was provided by Eriksen and Hoffman (1974), who showed that subjects can detect a target faster if its location is cued just before a display is presented than if its location is not cued; the cue apparently allowed subjects to shift attention to the cued location. Because cues occurred at most 150 ms before the targets, and an eye movement requires at least 200 ms, the attention shift must have been accomplished covertly—and presumably corresponds to moving the attention window to the cued location. Many other researchers have found evidence for such covert attention shifting (e.g., Eriksen and Yeh 1985; Hoffman 1979; Inhoff et al. 1989; Jonides 1980, 1983; Posner 1978; Prinzmetal and Banks 1983; Shulman, Remington, and McLean 1979; Tsal 1983; Wurtz, Goldberg, and Robinson 1980).[7]

Eriksen and Hoffman's interpretation of their findings receives particularly compelling support from a study of Pollatsek, Rayner, and Collins (1984). They asked subjects to fixate on a point initially, and then to name objects in line drawings that were placed either 5° or 10° from fixation; the subjects had to make an eye movement to name the objects. The subjects could name the objects faster when the picture was presented parafoveally than when they initially were shown a rectangle that changed into a picture as soon as they fixated upon it. This "preview benefit" makes sense if the subjects could shift the attention window before being able to move their eyes. Indeed, Saarinen and Julesz (1991) estimate that only about 30 to 50 ms are required to shift covert attention. In addition, Pollatsek, Rayner, and Collins found greater facilitation if the subject previewed the same drawing, as opposed to another one of the object seen from a different point of view—which suggests that the subject could initially begin to encode the physical shape per se. In another experiment, they showed that the preview facilitation depends on visual similarity, not semantic similarity. In fact, if the preview was visually dissimilar to the target, the subject was actually inhibited (relative to previewing a rectangle), which suggests that he or she was midstream in encoding the initial shape when the switch occurred.[8]

Similarly, Pollatsek, Rayner, and Henderson (1990) showed subjects two objects parafoveally, and replaced one with a checkerboard when a subject shifted his or her gaze. The remaining object either switched locations or remained in its initial location. Switching the location of the object typically did reduce the "preview effect," as one would expect if the attention window was in the incorrect location after the switch. Nevertheless, there was a preview effect even when the locations were switched. The authors argue that "covert attention" was shifted prior to moving one's gaze. Consistent with this view, Henderson, Pollatsek, and Rayner (1989) found little or no preview effect unless the subject was about to fixate on an object.

Operation of the Attention Window The attention window selects a region within the visual buffer for detailed processing. More precisely, the subsystem selects which set of neural outputs will be gated and which will be allowed to send outputs further downstream (see Anderson and Van Essen 1987 for a neurally plausible algorithm that could accomplish this function). And in fact, many researchers have shown that humans cannot attend to more than one region of space (i.e., one set of contiguous locations) at a single time (e.g., see Downing and Pinker 1985; Eriksen and Yeh 1985; Hoffman and Nelson 1981; Jonides 1983; LaBerge 1983; LaBerge and Brown 1986; Larsen and Bundesen 1978; Posner, Nissen, and Ogden 1978; Posner, Snyder, and Davidson 1980; Treisman and Gelade 1980). Some of the evidence comes from a now-standard paradigm developed by Posner and his colleagues (e.g., Posner 1978; Posner, Nissen, and Ogden 1978; Posner, Snyder, and Davidson 1980). Subjects fixate on a central point and see a cue that a stimulus will be presented to the left or right of the fixation point (e.g., the cue could be a rectangle on one side or an arrow pointing to one side). The stimulus is a small dot, and the subjects simply respond as quickly as possible when it appears. The subjects respond faster when the stimulus appears in the cued location than when no cue is provided, and respond slowest when they are cued to one location but the stimulus appears in another.[9]

Although this result indicates that attention selects one region for privileged processing, it does not implicate any particular mechanism. Posner likened attention to a spotlight that is focused on the cued location and shifted as necessary. When the cue is invalid, the spotlight needs to be shifted—which requires more time than when the cue is valid and the spotlight does not need to be shifted. This interpretation, however, has been challenged by several alternatives (for a review, see Sereno and Kosslyn 1991).

According to one theory, the results reflect a gradient of attention, not a moving spotlight. Attention is greatest at a single point, and drops off gradually from that point. Thus, when attention is focused at the cued location, more time is required when the stimulus appears in another location because of decreased attention at that spot. Downing and Pinker (1985) showed that the facilitatory effects of cuing drop off with increased distance from the cue (see also LaBerge and Brown 1986).[10]

Another theory posits that attention acts to select an entire segment of the visual field. Although Hughes and Zimba (1985) originally reported that responses were facilitated for all stimuli within the same hemifield, Hughes and Zimba (1987) provided evidence that individual quadrants of the field are activated. Many of the visual cortical areas represent only contralateral input above or below the horizontal meridian. However, Klein and McCormick (1989) argued that Hughes and Zimba's results were probably due to they way they cued the stimuli, and their findings could be explained if the scope and location of attention can be varied.

In any event, all these theories are consistent with the concept of an attention window; the theories can be conceptualized as differing in the presumed size and method of shifting the window. The spotlight theory posits a relatively small window that is shifted continuously; the gradient theory can be regarded as defining a probability distribution, describing the probability that a relatively large window is covering a region at any one point in time;

and the quadrant-selection theory can be construed as positing a relatively large window that is shifted among a relatively small set of discrete locations. The other differences among the theories appear to be matters of emphasis (e.g., in the importance of the drop-off of attention away from the central point of focus).

Evidence in favor of something like an attention window comes from the findings of Moran and Desimone (1985) discussed earlier. They found that attention has great spatial selectivity even within a visual area, and hence the attention window is not constrained to select the output from an entire visual area or hemifield. Moran and Desimone found that the responses of cells in areas V4 and IT are greatest to stimuli at the location where an animal is attending; the cells are inhibited when stimuli fall in nonattended locations within the cells' receptive fields. These findings suggest that attention is restricted neither to discrete locations nor to a fixed scope. We can think of the "receptive field" of an IT cell as corresponding to the range of locations of the attention window that will feed input to that cell (for additional evidence that attention alters receptive field properties of individual neurons, see Sato 1988).

In this light, Hughes and Zimba's (1985, 1987) findings (if not an artifact of their method, as argued by Klein and McCormick 1989) may suggest that the ease with which the attention window can be adjusted depends on whether regions within the same hemifield, or quadrant, are being selected. Alternatively, their findings may indicate that dots can be registered by preattentive mechanisms (Neisser 1967), and these mechanisms operate over restricted regions of the field. Hughes and Zimba required subjects simply to detect a dot, which is very different from classifying an oriented colored shape, as Moran and Desimone required. Preattentive processes must indicate the presence of an object outside the field of attention, if only to help one decide where to attend next; if one only registered what was being attended, one would not be able to notice important changes in the environment (cf. Neisser 1967). Consistent with this notion, Fisher, Bridgeman, and Biederman (1990) found that there was no effect of cuing or the number of alternatives in a simple dot-detection task.[11]

Anatomical Localization   The attention window operates within the visual buffer, and hence is localized in the same parts of the brain as the visual buffer. It is possible that the pulvinar plays a critical role in delineating the location and scope of the attention window by inhibiting certain regions within the visual buffer or outputs from those regions. The pulvinar has reciprocal connections with V4, IT, and the posterior parietal lobe (e.g., see Robinson and Petersen 1992); such connections may help it to regulate the output from the lower-level areas to the higher-level ones. In addition, the pulvinar projects to layers 1, 2, and 3 of V1, and layers 1, 3, and 4 of V2, V4, and IT (Benevento and Rezak 1976; Ogren and Hendrickson 1977; Rezak and Benevento 1979); Rezak and Benevento (1979) claim that these projections are excitatory, but do not report whether there are inhibitory interneurons. Layer 4 is the "input layer," and it is of interest that the pulvinar can itself provide input to higher-level visual areas; as will be discussed in chapter 9, one form of imagery may depend on such attentional inputs.

The role of the pulvinar in spatial attention also receives support from single-cell recording studies. For example, Petersen, Robinson, and Keys (1985) found increased activity in neurons of the pulvinar that project to the portion of cortex that represents the region "within the attentional beam." In contrast, neurons in the pulvinar that project to other regions of cortex had little or no response. However, this finding must be tempered with the fact that the effect only occurred in neurons in the dorsomedial pulvinar (which projects to the posterior parietal lobe), and not those in the inferior or lateral pulvinar—which project to V1 and visual areas in the ventral system. However, Petersen, Robinson, and Keys used a simple detection task that did not require analysis of object properties, which may explain why the other portions of the pulvinar were not involved.

Stimulus-based Attention Shifting

In order to encode the appearance of an object in detail, the attention window must be positioned to surround its representation in the visual buffer. But how is the attention window—or the eyes, for that matter—shifted to focus on the location of an object? One method must involve what I will call the *stimulus-based attention-shifting subsystem*. This subsystem reflexively moves attention to the location of a salient stimulus; salient objects differ relatively sharply from their surroundings—they often, but not always, are relatively large, brightly colored, or moving. When such an object is seen out of the corner of one's eye (i.e., is registered by low-level, preattentive mechanisms), attention must be shifted to see it more clearly. This sort of bottom-up attention-shifting mechanism must exist, otherwise attention would always be directed either at random or in accordance with what one expects to see; it obviously is adaptive to fixate quickly on objects that may be of particular importance, especially if one does not expect to see them. Figure 4.2 illustrates the stimulus-based attention-shifting subsystem in the context of the system as a whole.

Consider again the case in which one identifies objects in different locations by moving one's eyes. How does one know where to move one's eyes to focus on the object? Schneider (1969) showed that the two subcortical visual pathways convey different types of information in the golden hamster; the geniculostriate pathway conveys information about shape, and the tecto-pulvinar pathway conveys information about orientation. The tectopulvinar pathway appears to play a critical role in bottom-up attentional focusing. Good evidence for this comes from a study reported by Rafal et al. (1990), who studied brain-damaged patients. These people had "homonymous hemianopia"; they were blind in one visual field (not one eye, but one half of space). Rafal et al. were able to infer that the blindness was caused by damage

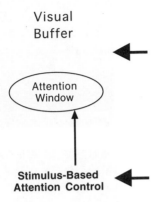

Visual
Buffer

Attention
Window

**Stimulus-Based
Attention Control**

Figure 4.2   The stimulus-based attention subsystem illustrated in relation to the visual buffer and attention window.

to the geniculostriate pathway or areas that receive input from it. Thus, any residual vision in the blind field would be due to the operation of the tecto-pulvinar pathway. And in fact, if a cue was flashed into the blind field, the subjects required more time to shift attention to a target in the good field; apparently the cue drew their attention into the blind field, and they required time to reorient. Weiskrantz (1986) reviews evidence that some of these kinds of patients can "see" movement and visually register other kinds of spatial information even though they are otherwise blind (for a particularly gripping case study, see Kolb's (1990) description of the visual consequences of his own stroke).

In short, the stimulus-based attention-shifting subsystem leads one to respond to a stimulus by moving the body, head, eyes, and/or attention window so that one fixates on a potentially important object. Once the object is attended, it is processed in the same way, regardless of where its representation happens to fall in the visual buffer.

Anatomical Localization   The superior colliculus, which is a critical component of the tectopulvinar pathway, plays a key role in this subsystem (e.g., Jay and Sparks 1984; Sprague 1991). However, Keating and Gooley (1988) show that there are two routes whereby saccades can be induced by activity in the occipital lobe. One route is mediated by the superior colliculus, and the other is mediated by the frontal eye fields (also known as area 8). In some tasks, these two routes apparently can substitute for one another (e.g., see Schiller, Sandell, and Maunsell 1987). In addition, the right frontal and parietal lobes apparently can play a role in setting one to expect a stimulus, so that attention is more easily drawn to the stimulus once it appears; Pardo, Fox, and Raichle (1991) found selective activation in the right frontal and parietal lobes in a vigilance task. The same regions were active when subjects were attending to visual stimuli or to somatosensory stimuli (for additional structures that may play a role in implementing this subsystem, see Posner and Petersen 1990).

Summary: Identifying Objects in Different Positions in the Visual Field

The brain apparently solves the problem of identifying objects seen in different locations as follows: First, an object is represented as a spatial pattern of activity in the visual buffer. The representation is the same (in the critical respects—we will return to this hedge in the following chapter) in different locations of the buffer. Second, the stimulus-based attention-shifting subsystem reflexively positions the attention window in the visual buffer, so that it surrounds a salient configuration of activity (which arises when an object has a clearly different color, intensity, size, or movement than its background). This shifting operation may involve moving the body, head, eyes, and/or attention window; the attention window can be shifted covertly, allowing one to attend to objects seen out of the corner of one's eye. Third, once the attention window selects a configuration of activity in the visual buffer, it sends information to two separate systems, one that encodes object properties (shape, color, texture) and one that encodes spatial properties (location, size, and orientation). I will discuss the encoding process itself in more detail in the next chapter, but for now it is enough to say that these three properties of the visual system lie at the heart of our ability to identify objects when they appear in different locations.

IDENTIFYING OBJECTS AT DIFFERENT DISTANCES

We readily identify objects when we see them from different distances. This is impressive because the visual angle subtended by the object—and the size of the input image—changes dramatically when it is viewed at different distances. This problem can be solved in part if the scope of the attention window in the visual buffer can be altered.

Incremental Adjustment

The present conception of the attention window implies not only that its location can be shifted incrementally, but also that its size can be adjusted incrementally. This hypothesis receives support from the results of numerous experiments. For example, Eriksen and St. James (1986) showed subjects letters that were arranged around a circle, and asked the subjects to search for one of two targets. Eriksen and St. James cued 1, 2, 3, or 4 adjacent locations about the circle. They also varied the amount of time following the cue before the stimuli were presented, which presumably gave the subjects more or less time to adjust the scope of attention. Furthermore, they included a target in a noncued location, which served as a distractor; the subjects were to ignore the target if it did not appear in one of the cued locations. Critically, they also varied the distance between the distractors and the cued locations. The logic of the experiment was that if subjects had enough time to adjust attention after the cue, they should not be affected by distractors that were relatively far from the cued locations.

The results were as expected if the attention window began by being focused over the entire circle and then was constricted incrementally until it focused on the cued location. If the stimuli were presented only a brief time after the cue, distractors that were even three positions away interfered with the task. But if the stimuli were presented after a longer interval following the cue, the subjects could restrict attention to smaller regions and distractors at greater distances did not interfere; at the longest delay, only the target location was in focus and even distractors adjacent to the target location did not interfere.

Cave and Kosslyn (1989) used another method to test the claim that the scope of attention is adjusted incrementally. We reasoned that the time to encode a shape should depend in part on the size of the region being attended prior to seeing that shape. Thus, on 75% of the trials the sizes of two successive stimuli were the same, but on 25% of the trials they were different. In this experiment, the shapes were a rectangle and a diamond, and the subjects simply decided whether the sides of each stimulus were of equal length (half the time they were, half the time they were not). As predicted, the subjects required more time to make this judgment when there were greater disparities between the expected and observed sizes; indeed, the response times increased linearly with increasing size disparity. When an unexpected size appeared, the subjects apparently had to adjust the attention window to surround the region occupied by the stimulus. This finding dovetails with those of Larsen and Bundesen (1978), who used a similar technique.

In short, we have ample evidence that the scope of the attention window can be altered incrementally, allowing one to focus on different sized regions of the visual buffer. Once the attention window is properly scaled, the material within it is sent to the ventral and dorsal systems.

Additional Properties of the Visual Buffer

The claim that the scope of the attention window can be adjusted brings to mind the spotlight theory, but this is probably misleading. The visual buffer itself appears to represent information at multiple scales, and the attention window is adjusted by selecting a level of scale within the buffer. The visual buffer can be conceptualized as a pyramid, with a single number at the top that specifies the average intensity level represented across the entire structure, and a number at each individual location in the buffer at the bottom, each of which specifies a local intensity; intermediate heights correspond to intermediate amounts of averaging over local regions in the buffer (see Burt and Adelson 1983; Nakayama 1990; Sakitt and Barlow 1982; Rosenfeld 1985). As was noted in chapter 2, Marr (1982) posited a multiscale representation in his theory of how edges are detected; if sets of zero crossings (i.e., locations of maximal changes in intensity) appear at multiple levels of resolution, they are likely to indicate an edge and not texture or the like. A multiscale representation is also useful for computing depth from stereo and a host of other low-level computations (e.g., see Adelson et al. 1984; Burt and Adelson 1983; Marr 1982; Rosenfeld 1985). The neural hardware appears to be available to represent images at different scales (see De Valois and De Valois 1988; Wilson and Bergen 1979).

The multiscaled property of the visual buffer is important in part because it leads the attention window to have a scope-resolution trade-off: the larger the region monitored, the poorer the resolution within the region.[12] If so, then when an object is far away, and so the attention window is set to a small size, one may have increased acuity—which would partially compensate for any decrease in the quality of the image. Shulman and Wilson (1987) report one of the most direct tests of a scope-resolution trade-off. They asked subjects to observe large letters that were composed of smaller letters (modeled after those of Navon 1977). For example, the letter *T* was composed by stacking copies of small versions of the letter *H* to form the stem, and then arranging small versions of *H* at the top of the stem to form the crossbar. The subjects were asked to identify or categorize either the composite letter or the smaller letter (*T* or *H*, in this example). To help subjects "lock onto" the appropriate level, two stimuli were presented in rapid succession on each trial. However, on some trials a sine-wave grating (i.e., equally wide black and white stripes that meld smoothly into one another) was superimposed over the second stimulus; the subjects were asked to indicate whether a grating had been presented after every trial. The contrast between the black and white stripes was adjusted so that this discrimination was not very easy.

The key to this experiment was that Shulman and Wilson varied the "spatial frequency" of the grating (i.e., the number of stripes within a fixed distance). Thus, if attending to the larger scope of the composite letter caused reduced resolution, then the subjects should have had more trouble detecting high spatial-frequency gratings (which have finer stripes) than they would have had after attending to the smaller letters. Similarly, if attention was restricted when subjects encoded the small letters, then detecting stripes that were so large that they fell outside this region should have been impaired; it has been documented repeatedly that presenting a large region of a grating makes it easier to detect gratings with low spatial frequencies, but not high spatial frequencies (Hoekstra et al. 1974; Savoy and McCann 1975; McCann, Savoy, and Hall 1978).

The results were straightforward: The subjects more accurately detected gratings with fine stripes if they had been attending to the small (local) letters, and more accurately detected gratings with thick stripes if they had been attending to the large (global) letters. Thus, we have direct evidence for the existence of a scope-resolution trade-off.[13]

Eriksen and his colleagues have reported a number of experiments that further document the scope-resolution trade-off predicted by the present conception of the attention window. Eriksen and Yeh (1985) and Eriksen and St. James (1986) develop a variant of the idea in which attention is likened to a zoom lens. Consistent with the present notion, they posit that as attention is distributed over a larger area, sensitivity decreases within the area. Eriksen and Yeh showed subjects arrays of eight letters arranged around a circle, and asked them to search for one of two target letters. They varied the probability that the target would fall in the cued location or one diametrically opposite it. They found that subjects could encode targets remote from the cue more easily when there was a greater probability that the target could appear in that location. These results indicated that subjects distribute attention over a larger region when there is a high probability that the target will be presented in diametrically opposed locations. They suggest that, "Analogically speaking, when attention is in the focus mode, the 'internal eyeball' essentially has tunnel vision" (p. 591). They report a control experiment that showed that subjects were not "time sharing" their attention between different locations, nor were they dividing attention between two separate locations.

Numerous other results in the literature are consistent with the present claim. For example, Egeth (1977) describes an experiment by Egeth and Shwartz in which subjects expected a target within a $3.8°$ circle or a $12°$ circle. The task was to distinguish a *T* from an *L* or a *T* from a *T* tilted $45°$. As we would expect, subjects required more time to make the discrimination if they distributed their attention over the wider area; a similar result is reported by Beck and Ambler (1973). Jolicoeur and his colleagues (e.g., Jolicoeur and Ingleton 1991; Jolicoeur, Ullman, and Mackay 1991; McCormick and Jolicoeur 1991) have also provided much evidence that is consistent with such a mechanism. They asked subjects to determine whether dots fell on the same or different curved lines. Subjects apparently adjust the size of the attention window so as to have the necessary level of resolution and yet take in as great a scope as possible. In my terms, Jolicoeur and colleagues showed that the way the attention window is adjusted can be manipulated by altering the distance along a curve between two dots and the distance between a target curve and distractor curves.[14]

Before finishing this section, I must note that LaBerge (1983) reports data that, at first blush, appear inconsistent with the present conception. He asked subjects to attend to a single location, and found that performance suffered progressively more when the target was presented progressively farther from the target location. Well and good. But he also found that subjects could focus on an entire five-letter word and process it more quickly than a single letter. This result is difficult to interpret, however, because of possible context effects that occur when more than one letter is presented at the same time, which facilitate encoding (see chapter 5 of Kosslyn and Koenig 1992). Such context effects might alter the sensitivity of encoding; we must keep in mind the finding of Spitzer, Desimone and Moran (1988) that cells in area V4 responded more vigorously when a more difficult discrimination was required (see also Eriksen and St. James 1986, for methodological difficulties in inferring properties of the attention window from the LaBerge experiments). The scope-resolution trade-off can be documented if all else is kept equivalent; however, it is possible that the sensitivity of sampling within the attention window can vary, depending on what information is required to perform the task.

Finally, there are two situations in which adjusting the attention window to subsume an object in the visual buffer will not solve the problem of recognizing objects at different distances. First, if the object is so far away that key parts and characteristics are obscure, one cannot recognize it under any circumstances. And second, if the object is so close that only a small portion is seen clearly, one may not be able to encode distinguishing properties. Indeed, if it is too close, one typically will have to make multiple eye movements to encode the object. Two problems arise when multiple eye movements are necessary: How are the eyes moved so that one encodes the object effectively? And how is a sequence of encodings integrated so that one can identify a single object?

It would be foolhardy to attempt to offer solutions for these problems given the inferences I have drawn so far. Rather, solutions for both of them will "drop out" of inferences I shall draw for other reasons in the next two chapters. Thus, I will defer these problems for now but will return to them after we have drawn additional inferences about the system as we consider additional abilities.

Summary: Identifying Objects at Different Distances

Our ability to identify objects when they are seen at different distances arises in part because the scope of the attention window can be adjusted; one can scale the attention window so that a representation in the visual buffer is subsumed within it, and similar input is sent to the ventral system. However, if an object is very close, one must move one's eyes over it and must integrate the input from the sequence of encodings. This special case of the problem of identifying objects at different distances will be taken up later, after I discuss the motivation for drawing additional inferences about the nature of the processing system.

IMAGERY AND PERCEPTION

In this chapter I have been led to make three major claims about the architecture of high-level vision: I posit a multiscaled, spatially organized visual buffer, an adjustable attention window that selects a region of the visual buffer (and allows material within this region to be processed in detail downstream), and a stimulus-based attention-shifting subsystem. Each of these components of the system has an impact on the nature of imagery.

The Visual Buffer in Imagery

The visual buffer corresponds to neurons in a set of retinotopically mapped areas. PET findings suggest that visual mental images correspond to configurations of activity in at least some retinotopically mapped areas of cortex. This is an important finding because properties of the visual buffer that are evident in visual perception also should affect visual imagery in corresponding ways. This appears to be true.

Resolution   The visual buffer has a fixed resolution, presumably in part because the eyes have only a limited resolving power and the buffer evolved to process input from the eyes. The resolution limits of the visual buffer may reflect the phenomenon of "spatial summation." Visual neurons average input over a certain area. This averaging process is equivalent to introducing a "grain" in the buffer, and all representations should be affected by this grain.

Some of my early experiments (first described in my Ph.D. thesis in 1974) documented resolution limits in visual mental images. In these experiments, the subjects were led to visualize objects at large or small sizes (i.e., so that they seemed to subtend large or small visual angles). After the object (typically an animal) was visualized, the subjects heard the name of a possible property (e.g., "whiskers"); their task was to "look" at the object in the image and decide whether they could "see" the property. If so, they pressed one button; if not, they pressed another. The subjects required more time to perform this task when the objects were visualized at a small size. In fact, many subjects reported that they had to "zoom in" to "see" the properties of objects visualized at a small size. In addition, Kosslyn and Alper (1977) showed that subjects recalled objects that were visualized at large (but not overflowing) sizes better than those visualized at small sizes.

Visual Angle   If the visual buffer is used in both perception and imagery, then imaged objects should have a maximum extent: The visual buffer evolved to process input from the eyes, and the eyes subtend only a limited visual angle; hence, the visual buffer itself presumably has a circumscribed spatial extent, which would constrain visual mental images as well as visual percepts.

I tested this idea (Kosslyn 1978) by asking subjects to visualize objects off in the distance, and to imagine that they were "walking toward" each one. The subjects visualized different-sized objects, one at a time. They claimed that the objects seemed to "loom larger" as they visualized approaching them. The subjects were asked to focus their gaze at the center of each object, and to "stop the mental walk" at the point where the edges of an object started to "overflow," not all being clearly "visible" at the same time. At this point, the subjects estimated their apparent distance from the object (e.g., by positioning a tripod away from a blank wall at the distance that the object appeared). The results were remarkably consistent: The larger the object, the farther away it seemed at the point of overflow. Hubbard and Baird (1988) subsequently replicated these results. In addition, I found that the visual angle subtended by the object was relatively constant at the point of overflow (although this angle varied for different types of materials, which differed in how sharply their boundaries were defined, in how recently they had been seen, and other factors that presumably affected the image). Moreover, as one would expect if the angle were constrained by the spatial extent of the visual buffer, the best predictor of the "distance" at which an imaged object began to overflow was the single greatest extent (typically a diagonal) through the object, not its height, width, or area.

The inference that the extent of the visual buffer affects imagery and perception the same way is further supported by another of my 1978 experiments. In this experiment the subjects performed the "walk to the point of overflow" task with black rectangles. In one condition, they visualized the rectangles; in another condition, they viewed rectangles that were mounted on a wall. In the imagery condition they imagined walking as described above, whereas in the perception condition they performed the task while actually viewing the stimuli. The results from the imagery and perception conditions were virtually identical. This finding is strong evidence that the same factors affected performance in the two versions of the task, as expected if the critical variable was the extent of the visual buffer.

However, Hubbard and Baird (1988) report findings that they claim challenge my interpretation. First, they measured the time the subjects required to "mentally walk" to the point of overflow; although the subjects did take more time to "walk" farther distances, these times did not increase linearly with distance. However, as Hubbard and Baird point out, the subjects need not have "moved" at a constant rate—and need not even have moved continuously; it is possible that they deleted the initial image and regenerated an image of the object as it would appear at a closer distance (performed a "blink transformation," to use my term). The subjects apparently sometimes reported such processing (as was also observed by Finke and Shepard 1986). Second, Hubbard and Baird also asked subjects to estimate the distance to the perceived "vanishing point" in images. They found that larger objects subtended larger angles at the vanishing point than did smaller objects. Hubbard, Kall, and Baird (1989) argue that subjects could estimate distances properly, and hence the subjects were not systematically underestimating the distance for large objects. Hubbard and Baird suggest that the "grain" of the visual buffer varies, and was finer for smaller objects. Given the results of Spitzer, Desimone, and Moran (1988), which showed that attention does indeed modulate the sensitivity of neurons in area V4, it is possible that the grain of the visual buffer may change depending on task demands, at least slightly. However, there is no need to posit this effect to explain Hubbard and Baird's results. At typical viewing distances, more parts or characteristics may be evident on larger objects. If the subjects included more details in their images of larger objects, they may have required more time to move them to the vanishing point than to move smaller objects. If so, then images of larger objects would have more time to decay, and would be more likely to be gone before actually reaching the vanishing point. Such an account can explain why the large objects were "closer" than they should have been when the image vanished without assuming that the resolution of the visual buffer changes (although it may well have that capacity, to some degree).[15]

Maintenance   If the visual buffer is used in imagery and perception, then properties of this structure in perception could explain why objects are so difficult to maintain over time in mental images. As noted in the previous chapter, because the visual buffer is retinotopically mapped, the representations within it change every time one moves one's eyes. Hence, the representations should "fade" quickly during perception. Humans can make an eye movement in about 250 ms, which implies that a configuration of activity in the visual buffer should not persist longer than about a quarter of a second. This effect is to be distinguished from saccadic suppression (i.e., input is terminated while the eye is in transit). However, saccadic suppression could also contribute to the rapid decay of mental images: subjects often move their eyes during image generation (for reasons that will be discussed in chapter 9), and these eye movements may suppress mental images in the visual buffer.

Attention Window

The attention window apparently operates the same way in imagery and perception. For example, Podgorny and Shepard (1983) provide evidence that the process of attending to perceived and imaged patterns is subject to a scope-resolution trade-off. They asked subjects to view or to visualize patterns of filled cells in 3 × 3 grids. A dot or dots was then presented, and the subjects decided whether the dot or dots fell on the figure. Podgorny and Shepard systematically varied how compact the patterns were (as indexed by the square root of the area divided by the perimeter), and found that the subjects required less time for more compact figures. The same result was obtained both in perception and in imagery; indeed, the responses times for the 12 probes were highly correlated between the imagery and perception conditions, $r = .92$. These data indicate that the smaller the area the subject had to attend to, the easier it was to detect the probe dots.

Image Scanning   Properties of the attention window also help us to understand an additional facet of imagery, image scanning. As discussed in chapter 1, image scanning occurs when one shifts attention over an imaged object or scene, which is often a prerequisite to "inspecting" it. Recall that one of the apparent paradoxes that Pylyshyn levied against depictive theories of imagery was that there are no eyes to scan mental images (nor is there any light for them to see by, even if such eyes were present). Our meditation on the ability to recognize objects in different locations offers a simple way out of this conundrum: If visual mental images are patterns of activity in the visual buffer, as the PET results suggest, then they can be scanned by shifting the attention window. If so, then some of the scanning findings are easy to understand.

However, this cannot be all there is to it: Kosslyn (1978, 1980) found that people can scan to parts of objects that are not immediately "visible" in a mental image—and that scanning "off screen" is just as fast as scanning the same distance between two "visible" parts. This finding may suggest that although scanning relatively short distances may be accomplished by moving the attention window, scanning relatively long distances may involve another mechanism. In this case, the imaged pattern may be translated across the visual buffer, so that different portions fall under the attention window. Provided that one can add new material at the leading edge, one could scan indefinitely without "bumping into the edge" of the visual buffer. This mechanism leads us to expect the same rate of scanning whether one scans between two relatively far "visible" points or the same distance "off screen." This proposal is also consistent with the fact that the retinotopically mapped areas are neither homogeneous nor isotropic—and yet the time to scan over an imaged object increases linearly with the distance scanned. If the attention window were moving, these properties would require complex changes in the rate of shifting with distance (for additional discussion of reasons for positing two scanning mechanisms, see Pinker 1980).

Stimulus-based Attention Shifting

The stimulus-based attention-shifting subsystem shifts the body, head, eyes and/or attention window so that one is focused on a stimulus that is relatively distinct from its surroundings. This subsystem is driven by low-level input from the eyes, and hence is not used in imagery. However, it may nevertheless have relevance for a discussion of imagery. When first hearing the claim that perception and imagery are intimately intertwined, many ask, "Then how do we tell them apart"? One answer is that we sometimes do not. This was the point of the original imagery/perception interference experiments reported by Perky (1910). Moreover, such confusions are a bugaboo for those concerned with the accuracy of eyewitness testimony (see Loftus 1979). But this is not the entire answer; we usually can distinguish mental images from percepts. We do not live in a dream world. Several cues may help us distinguish imagery from perception.

First, the stimulus-based attention-shifting subsystem operates only during perception; thus, if our attention is suddenly grabbed by an object or event, we are not engaged in imagery. This may not be true during dreams, however: During waking imagery, one always knows the identity of the objects one is imaging; during dreaming, this apparently is not always true. Moreover, the "rules" of dreaming allow objects to appear in unusual contexts, so it is conceivable that one's mental attention is "grabbed" during dreaming in a way that is reminiscent of the way it is captured during perception. I have no evidence one way or the other that the same subsystem is used when attention is shifted by stimulus properties during perception and during dreaming, but I tend to doubt it: The connections from the eye to the superior colliculus, which appear critical for the attention-shifting subsystem, are unlikely to be evoked during imagery.

Second, stimulus-based attention shifting may help one to distinguish between imagery and perception in part because it is "automatic" during perception, whereas attention shifting is not automatic in imagery. Johnson and Raye (1981) and Intraub and Hoffman (1992) suggest that images can be distinguished from percepts in part on the basis of the types of processes that are used. Perception typically involves fast "automatic" processes, whereas imagery involves at least some slower, more "controlled" processes. Indeed, images that are created incidentally in the course of performing a task are more likely later to be mistaken for percepts than images that were created intentionally (Durso and Johnson 1980; Intraub and Hoffman 1992). Similarly, Finke, Johnson, and Shyi (1988) found that subjects were less likely to mistake a remembered image for a percept if the imagery task was difficult than if it was relatively easy, presumably because the subjects were more aware of controlling the processing during the difficult task.

In this context, it is of interest to consider a patient described by Coslett (1988). This patient had a right frontal-parietal lesion, and neglected objects to her left side in imagery. She initially had also neglected objects on this side in perception, but this deficit quickly resolved even though she continued to neglect objects to the left side in her mental images. As discussed in the previous chapter, neglect usually appears to affect imagery and perception in similar ways. In Coslett's patient, the dissociation between imagery and perception may reflect the operation of the stimulus-based attention-shifting subsystem: In perception the attention window may have been repositioned via the stimulus-based attention shifting subsystem, which was not available in imagery. The patient performed normally in the Posner endogenous cuing task, where a square or darkened field cues the subject as to the likely location of a probe. Similarly, she could perform a "pop-out" task normally (spotting the different character in a field of another character (Treisman and Souther 1985); this task also would appear to be based on stimulus-driven attention shifting. The deficit apparently involved using stored information to shift the attention window. This inference is consistent with the fact that the lesion apparently extended into parts of the frontal lobe that are known to be involved in shifting attention (see chapter 7).

A third factor that allows us to discriminate mental images from percepts is the duration of the stimulus; imaged objects fade very quickly, whereas percepts exist as long as one is looking at an object (under normal viewing conditions; if one's gaze is fixed on an object by special contact lens or the like, the object will fade—e.g., see Ditchburn and Ginsborg 1952).

A fourth way we distinguish the two is based on the fact that images are limited by the information encoded in memory. If one did not study an object carefully, the information necessary to evoke a vivid mental image may be lacking. In contrast, one usually can garner more information about an object during perception just by looking more carefully at it.

A fifth cue is that we have control over objects in images, but the world is rarely so cooperative. As will be discussed chapter 10, we can rotate, expand, distend, and otherwise transform imaged objects at will. Thus, if one can perform such operations, this is evidence that one is imaging rather than perceiving.

Scope-resolution Trade-off

Finally, the existence of a scope-resolution trade-off during perceptual encoding implies that a stored visual representation of the overall shape envelope will have relatively low resolution. Such a representation may be adequate for generating images in a task such as deciding whether an object is higher than it is wide, but would be inadequate if one needed to "see" details. Given that people can in fact "see" details on imaged objects (see chapter 7 of Kosslyn 1980), the scope-resolution trade-off implies that (a) people store not only the general shape envelope but also representations of smaller portions of objects, and (b) additional information can be added to an imaged object as needed. We shall consider the implications of these observations further in chapter 9.

CONCLUSIONS

I have characterized three components of high-level visual processing. The visual buffer is a multiscaled spatially organized structure that corresponds to a set of retinotopically mapped areas in the occipital lobe; these areas are used to segregate figure from ground during perception. The visual buffer contains much more information than can be processed at the same time, and hence an attention window selects one portion for thorough processing. The attention window may depend critically on the pulvinar nucleus of the thalamus. The scope and location of the attention window in the visual buffer can be adjusted; the scope is altered by selecting different portions of a multiscaled representation in the visual buffer. The attention window is adjusted in part by a stimulus-based attention-shifting subsystem. This subsystem appears to rely critically on the superior colliculus. The output from the attention window is sent to a recognition system in the temporal lobes, which allows shapes to be matched when their images fall at different sizes or in different locations in the visual buffer. The visual buffer and the attention window play similar roles in imagery and perception, and the properties of each affect both sorts of processes. The stimulus-based attention-shifting subsystem apparently is not used in imagery, which may be one way to distinguish between imagery and perception.

This chapter raises almost as many questions as it answers. To understand the abilities considered here in greater detail, we must consider additional properties of the mechanisms. In chapter 5 I will argue that imagery is a part of perception itself, not simply a parasite on mechanisms that exist for other purposes.

5 Identifying Objects When Different Portions Are Visible

People can identify a chair when seen from the front, side, back, or various angles in between. This ability is remarkable because the image projected by the chair onto the retina varies widely in each case. The most direct solution to this problem is simply to store a separate representation for each vantage point, and we probably do this at least some of the time (e.g., see Tarr and Pinker 1989, 1990). But this cannot be the entire solution: We can identify objects in novel positions, when we have not previously had the opportunity to store a corresponding representation (Jolicoeur 1990a). Imagery appears to play a particularly important role in this aspect of our visual abilities.

IDENTIFYING OBJECTS SEEN FROM DIFFERENT VANTAGE POINTS

Consider again the problem of identifying objects seen from different vantage points. This problem can be framed in terms of a many : one mapping. Namely, how are numerous input images mapped to the same output? This is a difficult problem: Depending on how the object is oriented, different patterns of activation will be evoked in the visual buffer.

The Necessity of Intermediate Processing Steps

The neuroanatomy of the visual system suggests that there are numerous processing subsystems that intervene between initial encoding in the visual buffer and object identification. The apparent success of neural network models, such as that of Rueckl, Cave, and Kosslyn (1989) discussed in the previous chapter, is misleading. For example, in Rueckl, Cave, and Kosslyn's model, each input shape was always identical, was always the same size and orientation, was two-dimensional, and always appeared in one of a fixed number of locations. This model could not solve the problem at hand, nor many of the other problems to be discussed in this book. It would be very difficult to map the actual range of possible inputs in the visual buffer directly to the proper representations of object identity; indeed, it is unclear whether such a one-shot mapping is even possible.

A better approach is to rely on the strategy of division of labor, breaking a very complex mapping problem down into a set of simpler problems. Rather than mapping an input pattern corresponding to an entire object directly to a single representation of the object, it is easier to map the pattern to a set of features that are stable when the object is seen from a given point of view, and then map these features to stored object representations. This general idea has had appeal for many years (e.g., Neisser 1967), and recently it has begun to become clear how such a sequence of relatively small steps may operate.

It may be worth pausing to consider an argument for a division-of-labor strategy that also raises another interpretation of the findings from the network models described in chapter 4. This argument hinges on an analysis of the evolution of the visual system. The evolution of the eye is a good example (e.g., see chapter 4 of Dawkins 1987). The best current guess is that the eye began as a light-sensitive patch of skin on some water-dwelling animal. A genetic variation (i.e., a mutation or reshuffling of alleles) resulted in a dimple at such a patch, which caused greater directional sensitivity for that patch. This increased directional sensitivity helped the animal find food, avoid predators, and so on—and so the animal had relatively many surviving offspring and that genetic variation was propagated. Another genetic variation caused the hole to narrow, which allowed it to focus an image on the light-sensitive patch beneath, just as is done in lensless pinhole cameras. However, the light would be rather dim. In addition, as long as there was an open hole, muck could enter and obscure the light. Thus, when a genetic variation produced a thin piece of transparent skin over the dimple, those animals had an advantage. And of course the more transparent the skin, the better, and so animals with clearer skins over the dimple had more surviving offspring. When another genetic variation produced a thickening of the skin that was over center of the dimple, creating a lens, this allowed the image to be focused while at the same time letting in more light—which was even more useful, and hence was propagated. And so forth, until a sophisticated eye evolved. At each stage during the evolutionary sequence, the system was useful in its then-current state; there were no intermediate stages that were not intrinsically useful. This is very unlike what happens when one builds most machines; until they are finished, they are useless.

By analogy, it is not difficult to imagine that in an early stage of evolution a primitive brain performed a simple what/where mapping of the sort performed by the network computer models. Even today, frogs identify flies by noting a dark spot of a certain size moving at a certain rate; they do not perform complex shape analyses (Lettvin et al. 1959). Similarly, it may have been useful for some earlier organism if primitive object identification and location encoding were accomplished by separate systems; our network models showed that it is easier to encode both sorts of information at the same time in an appropriately divided system than in a single system.

Once this organizational structure was laid down, it was the foundation for further development; later organisms did not start over, but rather built upon what was available in a previous nervous system. If so, then the division of labor into the ventral and dorsal systems of primates may have evolved partly as a consequence of the requirements of more primitive organisms.

This reasoning further supports my working hypothesis that the ventral system is composed of numerous subsystems. However, the primary motivation for this hypothesis is that it would be very difficult, if not impossible, to model our visual abilities with direct mappings from input patterns to representations of identity. As a first approximation, my colleagues and I have found that many of these abilities can begin to be understood if the ventral system is divided into two subsystems.

PREPROCESSING SUBSYSTEM

Bottom-up processing in the visual buffer organizes the input image into regions of common color, texture, or intensity, and also detects edges. These processes often do not entirely segregate objects; edges, for example, may be represented by sets of disconnected fragments. Thus, to be useful, these elements are organized into higher-order perceptual units. According to the present theory, sets of elements that signal some types of higher-order perceptual units are extracted from the input image and are then passed downstream for matching to stored representations.[1] The computations necessary to extract such sets of elements are qualitatively distinct from those considered previously or those that compare an input to stored representations, which leads me to hypothesize that this process is accomplished by a distinct subsystem. In this section I develop the theory of a *preprocessing subsystem*, which accepts an image as input (from the attention window) and extracts specific types of properties on the input image. This subsystem is illustrated in the context of the subsystems discussed in chapter 4 in figure 5.1.

Not all perceptual units will be useful for recognizing objects, particularly when they are seen from different points of view. For example, shadows may not help one recognize many objects. However, other perceptual units may

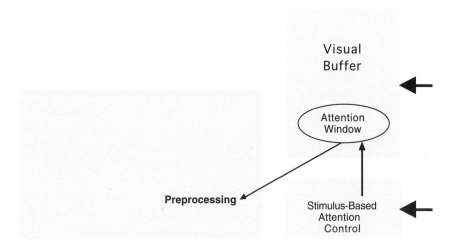

Figure 5.1 The preprocessing subsystem illustrated in the context of the subsystems discussed previously.

often provide cues as to the object being viewed. Some criteria must exist that allow a set of stimuli to be treated as equivalent. These criteria need not consist of sets of necessary and sufficient conditions, which must be satisfied by all members of the group; rather, they may be a Wittgensteinian set of partially overlapping features (see Wittgenstein 1953). That is, many subsets of the total number of possible features could be mapped to the same output, with each projection (i.e., input image arising from a specific point of view) of an object providing a different subset of the total number of possible features. However, there must be some overlap between the subsets, otherwise the mapping would be entirely arbitrary and novel views could not be recognized (a classic example of such an arbitrary mapping is a strike in baseball, which is defined in terms of swings of the bat or pitches that pass over the plate). The first question, then, is what sorts of features are likely to be present when an object is seen from multiple points of view.

Fortunately, many able researchers have considered the problem of how we are able to identify objects that project different input images, and we now have the beginnings of an solution to this problem. I have drawn heavily on the work of Lowe (1985 1987a, b), partly because he was the first to formalize a particular approach and partly because he built an impressive working computer vision system that demonstrated the usefulness of his ideas. I have, however, modified his views in light of subsequent insights by Biederman (1987), Edelman, Ullman, and Flash (1990), and Ullman (1989). Moreover, I have not adopted the details of Lowe's algorithms, which were written for computers, not brains.

Lowe set out to build a computer vision system that could identify objects in very noisy contexts, such as disposable razors jumbled into a bucket. His system first extracted edges on an image using standard edge-detection techniques (some of which were derived from Marr's algorithms, briefly discussed in chapter 2). These techniques are not perfect, but they often succeed in detecting isolated fragments even if they fail to join contiguous fragments into a single edge. Lowe noticed that certain aspects of an object's input image remain relatively constant under scale changes, rotation, and translation. He called these *nonaccidental properties*. For example, a straight edge of an object tends to project collinear fragments, and a curved edge tends to project fragments that fall along a smooth function, no matter how the object is aligned. Furthermore, parallel edges of an object tend to project roughly parallel sets of fragments, no matter how the object is positioned. Similarly, intersections of edges tend to project coterminating lines, parts that are close together tend to project lines that are close in the image, and symmetrical parts tend to project symmetrical patterns. Biederman (1987) provides a good summary of the properties identified by Lowe, which are illustrated in figure 5.2. Zemel and Hinton (1991) showed that unsupervised networks (i.e., without a "teacher") could learn to extract such properties.[2]

When a nonaccidental property is present, it is unlikely to have arisen from chance. Lowe (1987a) developed a Bayesian method for estimating the probability that a given nonaccidental property in an image is due to chance.

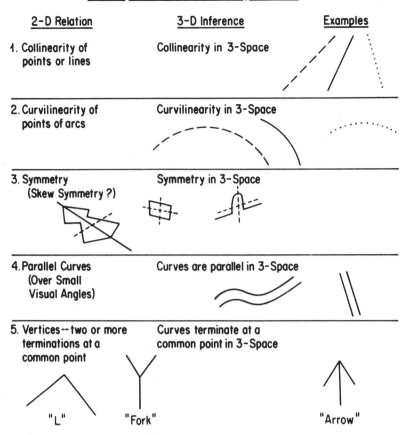

Figure 5.2 Examples of Lowe's nonaccidental properties. (Reprinted from Biederman 1985, with permission.)

By analogy, imagine throwing a bunch of match sticks down on a tabletop over and over, noting each time the number of match sticks that line up, whether such lines are parallel within specific tolerances, and so on. By such a method one can derive a set of baseline statistics, which can then be used when evaluating the properties in an image. This approach allows one to characterize nonaccidental properties quantitatively.

In Lowe's system, the nonaccidental properties (and representations of their relative locations) are extracted from an input image and sent downstream for further processing (as will be discussed in more detail shortly).[3] However, as Lowe notes, in some circumstances the nonaccidental properties are not sufficient to implicate a specific object. For example, a pen and a mechanical pencil may have identical nonaccidental properties. In such circumstances, one may match the image itself; the image is not a set of nonaccidental properties, but rather a representation of the distribution of various properties (such as intensity and color) on a surface. Thus, I infer that the preprocessing subsystem sends as output both the extracted nonaccidental properties and the image itself. The simplest way to do so, it would seem (although this has yet

Identifying Objects When Different Portions Are Visible

to be demonstrated), would be to dedicate a separate input "channel" for the nonaccidental properties. In this case, the nonaccidental properties would be a subset of the vector that represents the input; this vector would also specify color and texture as well as the shape itself.

Evidence for the Use of Nonaccidental Properties

Biederman and Blickle (1985) and Biederman et al. (1985) describe a series of experiments in which subjects were asked to name pictures, some of which were degraded in specific ways. In a typical experiment, Biederman and Blickle (1985) asked subjects to name drawings like those illustrated in figure 5.3. The left column shows the intact versions of the objects, and the interesting comparison is between the middle and right columns. Although the same amount of contour has been deleted in both cases, the locations of the deleted contours are different. In the middle column, all of the nonaccidental properties have been left intact; indeed, the fragments line up along smoothly fitting functions. In contrast, in the right column, the nonaccidental properties themselves have been deleted. Not only do the deletions disrupt collinearity but they also obscure intersections and symmetries. In addition, one is led to complete fragments improperly, forming misleading "virtual" lines.[4]

The results were dramatic. The subjects had an extremely difficult time naming the objects when the nonaccidental properties were disrupted. Furthermore, presenting the names of the drawings before the naming task did not help; the subjects simply could not use this input to access the appropriate stored representations. In contrast to this abysmal performance, subjects could identify drawings like those in the middle column relatively easily. The subjects were increasingly accurate with longer exposures, and were virtually perfect when the pictures were presented for five seconds. When the pictures were presented briefly, however, performance degraded—but never got as bad as performance when the nonaccidental properties were deleted.

In other experiments Biederman and his colleagues asked subjects to name pictures when different amounts of the contour were removed and the pictures were presented for different amounts of time. In general, the subjects named pictures faster when more nonaccidental properties were available and when pictures were presented for more time. With very long exposure durations, accuracy was not affected very much by the percent of contour deletion. In addition, more time was generally required when vertices were deleted than when middle portions of segments were deleted; this is interesting in part because Attneave (1954) long ago pointed out that vertices are high-information regions of pictures.

In addition, in a series of experiments Biederman and Cooper have used a "repetition priming" paradigm to study the recognition process. Subjects are asked to name pictured objects aloud, and then are asked to name the objects a second time. Subjects typically name objects faster the second time they see them, but especially so if the picture has the same shape (not just the same name) in both cases (Biederman and Cooper 1991a). For example, there was

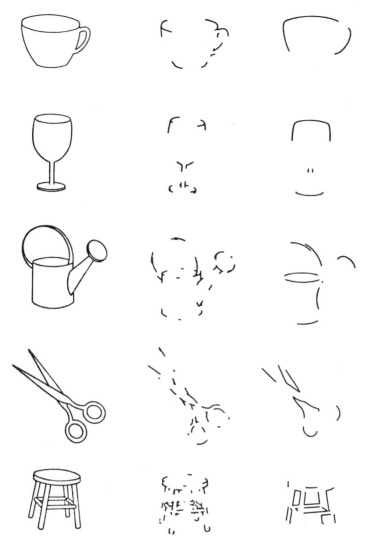

Figure 5.3 Illustrations of the stimuli used by Biederman and his colleagues to study the psychological reality of nonaccidental properties. (Reprinted from Biederman 1985, with permission.)

greater facilitation for two upright pianos than for one upright and one grand piano, even though both were named as "piano." Biederman and his colleagues take the amount of such priming as a measure of the degree to which the same specific visual memory representation is used in the two cases.

Biederman and Cooper (1991a) prepared pairs of pictures by removing every other edge and vertex of each part, and then removed the complementary portions of the contours to produce another version of the picture (so that a complete picture would be formed by overlaying them); each version was missing about 50% of its contour. Subjects named the object in one version, and then were shown either the original or complementary version and asked to name the object again. In this case, the subjects speeded up on the second trial the same amount for the original and complementary versions of the pictures. This result suggests to me that a number of different combinations of nonaccidental properties can address a visual memory, and do so equally well (of course, some sets of nonaccidental properties could be less effective). In many circumstances, it does not matter which set of constraints is present in the input; as long as enough appropriate nonaccidental properties are present, the representation is activated.

Clinical Evidence Some of the visual dysfunctions observed following brain damage are consistent with the claim that the preprocessing subsystem can be selectively damaged, limiting the number of nonaccidental properties that can be extracted. A good recent example of such dysfunction was described by Riddoch and Humphreys (1987) and Humphreys and Riddoch (1987). They studied a patient who could not identify an object by attending to its entire shape, but could identify it if he looked at one part at a time and identified the parts individually (Luria 1980 also describes similar cases, as do many others; for a review, see Farah 1990). This patient had trouble not only naming line drawings and objects but also determining whether a shape corresponds to an object and identifying overlapping figures.

However, this patient could judge whether a silhouette corresponds to an object better than he could judge whether a line drawing corresponds to an object. In addition, he was able to determine whether two simultaneously present drawings depict the same object, even when they were depicted as seen from some different points of view. Furthermore, he could draw reasonably well, and could identify many individual features of objects (such as an elephant's legs).

Humphreys and Riddoch (1987) explain their patient's problems as reflecting "integrative agnosia," which they characterize as difficulty in integrating separate parts. They point out that their patient was successful if a task could be accomplished in a piecemeal fashion, such as by comparing individual parts of shapes. The patient's deficits were not related to the size of the object per se, and so cannot be ascribed to a problem in adjusting the attention window. Instead, they can be easily understood as a deficiency in the number of nonaccidental properties that can be extracted, leading him to adopt piecemeal strategies. By focusing on relatively small regions (i.e., surrounding them in the attention window), the preprocessing subsystem would need to extract fewer nonaccidental properties.

This interpretation also explains the difference between silhouettes and line drawings, if line drawings include additional nonaccidental properties that tax the preprocessing subsystem but are not distinctive for a given object. If the preprocessing subsystem can only extract a few nonaccidental properties, it will suffer if it extracts redundant or extraneous ones at the expense of distinctive ones. It has no idea of which nonaccidental properties will prove important downstream; it operates reflexively, purely on the basis of the stimulus input.

The preprocessing subsystem is likely to incorporate separate subsystems (which correspond to "channels") that process separately color and shape. It is well known that color perception can be selectively impaired following brain damage (e.g., see De Renzi 1982). In addition, PET results have shown that different areas encode shape and color (e.g., see Corbetta et al. 1990; Zeki 1992; Zeki et al. 1991). Moreover, even the subsystem that encodes shape features may be decomposed into separate subsystems. Kosslyn, Hamilton, and Bernstein (1993) describe a patient who had selective difficulty encoding curvature. In one experiment, subjects were shown a "standard" curved line and five other curved lines, and were asked to indicate which of the alternatives matched the standard. This patient required more time to match curved lines (both when the standard and alternatives were present at the same time and when the standard was presented first) than corresponding angular lines, and this difference was greater than that for a control group. Similarly, he required relatively more time to determine whether an X mark drawn with curved lines was on or off a curved blob than whether an X mark drawn with straight lines was on or off an angular shape, and required more time to name curved objects in pictures and even to read a paragraph printed in a curved type font (relative to a type font with less curves). These results may suggest that the preprocessing subsystem includes distinct mechanisms for different types of shape information.

The patient we studied who had difficulty encoding curvature was unable to identify individual people's faces (he was a *prosopagnosic*). This co-occurrence of the two deficits in this patient may suggest that one must organize patterns of subtle curvatures to distinguish among individual faces.[5] Indeed, Levine and Calvanio (1989) describe another prosopagnosic patient who could not perform tasks requiring perceptual organization (particularly those involving visual closure, as is needed to identify a fragmented drawing), which led them to conclude that the patient had a "loss of configural processing." If "configural processing" corresponds to extracting nonaccidental properties that extend over relatively large visual angles, such as fragmented contours, this deficit could reflect an impaired preprocessing subsystem.

Observations reported by Gaffan and Heywood (1993) underline the importance of considering such preprocessing abilities. Many researchers have reported that brain-damaged patients can have selective deficits for naming pictures of living things, compared to nonliving things. This sort of selective deficit has been taken to reflect damage to a part of "semantic memory" (e.g., Farah and McClelland 1991; Farah, McMullen, and Meyer 1991; Damasio 1990; Warrington and Shallice 1984). However, Gaffan and Heywood found that normal people have more trouble identifying pictures of living things than nonliving things when the pictures are presented in a tachistoscope, and monkeys have more trouble learning to discriminate between such categories. Apparently it is more difficult to distinguish among various living things perceptually than it is to distinguish among various nonliving things. This difficulty may arise because living things have a preponderance of curved lines, which require more effort to extract. Alternatively, living things may tend to be more similar to each other than nonliving things, and hence encoding them will be more easily disrupted by impairments of the preprocessing subsystem. One should not infer a higher-level cause for a deficit before ruling out lower-level difficulties.

Recognizing Objects in Different Locations, Revisited

The concept of nonaccidental properties also allows us to understand the problems considered in the previous chapter in more depth. A kink I did not previously consider concerns the structure of the visual buffer. The retinotopically organized areas that compose the visual buffer are neither homogeneous nor isotropic. They all have greater representation of the fovea, and distort the local geometry in other ways (such as by stretching out the horizontal axis). Thus, an input image that is projected from different parts of the field will not result in the identical representation in the visual buffer. It is not clear whether this is really a problem, however, because some of the distortions in these areas appear actually to help preserve aspects of the shape of the objects (e.g., see Cavanagh 1981, 1982, 1984; Johnston 1986; Schwartz 1984).[6] But if some distortions in the representation of shape persist, they would pose a problem: I earlier assumed that the attention window could be shifted to any given location within the visual buffer and send essentially the same representation downstream. But the same representation will not be present when the image falls in different parts of the visual buffer; it is neither homogeneous nor isotropic. However, if nonaccidental properties are extracted by the preprocessing subsystem, then the same sets of nonaccidental properties may be extracted from the image, in spite of the local distortions caused by inhomogeneities of the structure of the visual buffer.

"Signal" Properties

Although nonaccidental properties are powerful, they are not the only kind of information we use to recognize objects. Indeed, because nonaccidental properties capture what is constant over various perspectives, they are relatively coarse—which is a drawback when one wants to discriminate between very similar objects (such as your pen versus that of a co-worker). Moreover, many natural objects, such as trees, animals, and fruit, cannot be described easily using nonaccidental properties. These sorts of observations led J. J. Gibson (1950, 1966, 1979) to focus on properties of surfaces and texture gradients, rather than properties of edges. In my own view, depending on what kinds of objects one needs to distinguish among, one relies on different kinds of information. I will call characteristics that serve to distinguish objects, but which are not nonaccidental properties, *signal properties*.

Numerous research findings suggest that the preprocessing subsystem extracts signal properties using two types of principles. First, the preprocessing subsystem extracts sets of elementary perceptual units, which are organized by bottom-up processing in the visual buffer itself. Nonaccidental properties correspond to sets of edges that are provided as input to the preprocessing subsystem. In addition, the preprocessing subsystem can extract sets of other sorts of perceptual units that are formed in the visual buffer. These units include regions of homogeneous color and texture, as well as sets of contiguous elements (obeying the Gestalt laws of similarity, proximity, good continuation, and so on; e.g., see Kaufman 1974).[7]

Second, the preprocessing subsystem can be "tuned" via top-down training, causing it to extract specific units from the input image; configurations of such units delineate a distinguishing characteristic of the object. If one must distinguish one's office chair from those of colleagues, an oddly shaped blotch on its cushion may be critical. The preprocessing networks apparently can be trained to register and extract such "ad hoc" properties. This training may involve feedback from higher areas, via the efferent connections, which modifies the preprocessing subsystem so that it more easily extracts properties that have proven useful for recognition. Once one has noticed an important distinguishing characteristic (such as the shape of a colored region, a pattern of light intensity, and so on), it may be a key feature of the stored representation of the object (i.e., its presence would exhibit a disproportionate influence on the output from visual memory). Thus, it would be useful to be able to detect such a characteristic when it is present, and new "detectors" could be trained in the preprocessing subsystem. I assume that just as shapes are specified by sets of nonaccidental properties, distinguishing characteristics typically are specified by sets of more primitive signal properties. By adjusting the attention window appropriately, signal properties could be registered from a wide range of positions and distances.

Biederman and Shiffrar (1987) studied an intriguing example of the use of signal properties. They asked subjects to judge the gender of day-old chicks, which is important because the females lay the eggs. The externally visible genitalia of male and female baby chicks are very similar. Biederman and Shiffrar found that subjects could evaluate the sex of day-old chicks once they learn to attend to the shape (convex versus concave or flat) of a particular cloacal structure. These amateurs were not as fluent as experts, however; an expert can glance at the structure and immediately see the difference—without necessarily being aware of the decision criteria. Apparently the experts have "feature detectors" for the key characteristics, and do not need to deliberate on the perceptual distinctions. It would have been of interest to overtrain the amateurs, and discover whether they eventually behaved "automatically"—and came to forget how they were doing so.[8]

Some signal properties may be evident when an object is viewed from multiple perspectives (such as those that specify a tiger's stripes); alternatively, there may enough such properties so that at least some are visible from different points of view (such as those that specify a splotch on a chair's cushion and a scuff on its back). In either case, such properties would help us to recognize objects when seen from different perspectives.[9]

Anatomical Localization

It is reasonable to assume that the preprocessing subsystem is implemented in the occipital-temporal area, if only because we assume that the visual buffer is localized in the occipital lobe and that object properties are processed in the inferior temporal lobe. The preprocessing subsystem is the bridge between the attention window and a visual memory. And in fact, damage to the occipital-temporal area can produce deficits of the sort described earlier (e.g., see De Renzi 1982; Farah 1990).

This putative localization is also consistent with PET results reported by Petersen et al. (1988). For present purposes, the most interesting comparison is between two of their simplest tasks. In one, the subjects stared at a fixation point (a small +). Petersen et al. assumed that this task would activate low-level visual processing, but the stimulus is so impoverished that relatively little processing would occur. In the other task, the subjects passively looked at words. Because the words had four letters, the preprocessing subsystem should have been much more active here than in the first task. Thus, it is of interest that the occipital-temporal area was selectively activated during the second task, relative to the first, particularly on the right side.

In addition, area V4 in the macaque is often cited as a possible "color area." On the order of 60% of the cells in this area are wavelength sensitive (Desimone et al. 1985; Van Essen 1985; Zeki 1983). In humans, acquired achromotopsia (i.e., color blindness resulting from brain damage) often follows damage to the inferior medial portions of the occipital-temporal boundary (Damasio 1985b). In addition, recent PET-scanning studies by Zeki et al. (1991) and by Corbetta et al. (1990) have shown that an area of the human brain exists that is selectively activated during color perception (in the vicinity of the fusiform and lingual gyri); this region may be homologous to area V4 in monkeys. However, Bogousslavsky et al. (1987) describe a patient with bilateral damage to the lingual gyrus who did not have difficulty encoding color; thus, the fusiform gyrus may be the critical area for this ability. This region may carry out at least part of the functions accomplished by the preprocessing subsystem.

Notice also that some neurons in area V4 could implement part of the visual buffer, which would make the transition from one sort of processing to another particularly easy. The anatomically defined areas are not likely to correspond to complete processing subsystems, nor need one area contribute to only a single subsystem (recall the discussion of weak modularity in chapter 2).

The hypothesis that area V4 may in part implement the preprocessing subsystem is consistent with results from ablation studies in monkeys (e.g., see Heywood and Cowey 1987). If the posterior portion of the inferior temporal lobe is ablated, monkeys appear to have difficulty making discriminations per se. Their performance declines when redundant cues are removed or when irrelevant cues are added to the stimuli (e.g., see Gross 1973; Mishkin 1972;

Wilson and Kaufman 1969). In contrast, monkeys with more anterior lesions are affected by factors that appear to influence memory per se (as will be discussed shortly).

PATTERN ACTIVATION SUBSYSTEM

Part of the solution to the problem of how we identify objects from different points of view is the existence of nonaccidental properties, many of which will be evident in different projections of an object. Another part of the solution rests on the ways that nonaccidental and signal properties are matched against stored visual representations of objects. Much of the power of a set of nonaccidental properties arises from what Lowe (1987a) called the *viewpoint consistency constraint*. The interpretation of the nonaccidental properties and their relative positions must be consistent with seeing a shape from a single point of view. This is such a powerful constraint that one does not need to segregate figure completely from ground prior to accessing memory; to begin comparing input to stored representations, all one needs to do is extract the nonaccidental properties and their relative locations.[10] Indeed, Lowe showed that images of multiple, partially overlapping objects can be entered into a high-level vision system at the same time, and the viewpoint consistency constraint will pull out sets of nonaccidental properties that belong to the same object.[11]

The output from the preprocessing subsystem must be matched in another subsystem, which I call the *pattern activation subsystem*. This subsystem stores visual representations of patterns, each of which includes a set of nonaccidental and signal properties. In a sense, these properties are a representation's "address"; this subsystem matches the input properties to those associated with all stored representations (in parallel).[12] The stored representation that is most consistent with the set of input properties is most strongly activated. I will argue that when the input properties are not sufficient to discriminate among similar objects, a mental image is generated and compared to stored patterns (using a top-down procedure, as will be discussed shortly). The output of the pattern activation subsystem is a *pattern code*, which specifies the best-fitting match as well as a measure of how well the input matched that shape. I will argue shortly that the output does not specify left-right orientation or size (these spatial properties are extracted and represented in the dorsal system). Figure 5.4 illustrates the pattern activation subsystem in the context of the system as a whole.

As briefly noted in chapter 3, there is evidence that visual memories are stored in the inferior temporal lobes (as will be discussed in more detail shortly). This region is not used to store other types of representations, such as those used to understand speech, to guide movement, and so forth. The existence of such a distinct visual memory structure is consistent with the principle of division of labor. This principle implies that complex input/output mappings are accomplished best by a series of processes: When very

Identifying Objects When Different Portions Are Visible

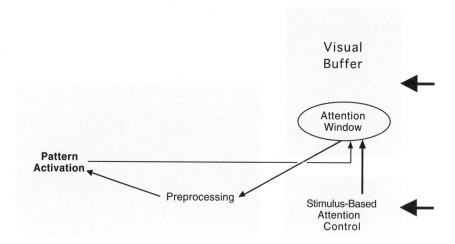

Figure 5.4 The pattern activation subsystem illustrated in the context of the subsystems discussed previously.

dissimilar inputs are to be mapped to the same output, the mapping can be accomplished more efficiently if an initial process reduces the variation in inputs to be mapped to the same output. In this case, interposing a distinct visual memory between the output from the preprocessing subsystem and associative memory simplifies the problem of establishing the mapping necessary to identify an object. If a single memory representation were used for inputs in all modalities, the input/output mapping would be very complex. My conceptualization of a distinct visual memory structure is similar to the theory of "perceptual representation systems" of Tulving and Schacter (1990), which has been further elaborated by Cooper et al. (1992), Schacter, Cooper, and Delaney (1990), and Schacter et al. (1991).

The visual memory structure probably stores information in a distinct format (i.e., type of code). Consider the following reasoning: As was noted earlier, to distinguish among similar shapes, one may need to compare properties of a stored image to the input. One cannot know in advance what properties will be useful. Indeed, in some cases the properties may need to be computed from the stored information (e.g., I am told that aspect ratios of dogs' faces are important in distinguishing a prizewinner from an "also ran"). Thus, it is important to store information that will allow one to recover a wide range of properties; these properties need not be explicit in the representation, but must be able to be reconstructed from it. Ideally, this information will allow one to reconstruct the image itself: Not only are there an infinite number of propositions one can assert about an object (Goodman 1983), but also one must note the spatial relations among these properties. Storing a representation that specifies enough information to reconstruct an image, then, would respect Marr's (1982) "principle of least commitment."

Long-term visual memories are probably stored as "population codes," with each neuron participating in many representations (e.g., see Desimone and Ungerleider 1989; Rolls 1987; Young and Yamane 1992). Indeed, Fujita et al. (1992) present evidence that the anterior portion of the inferior temporal lobe in monkeys (which appears to store visual memories, as discussed below) is organized into repeated sets of columns. Fujita et al. modified stimuli that drove each neuron until they could not increase its response rate; in most cases, these "optimal" stimuli were meaningless patterns that did not resemble any actual object (see p. 345 of their article; for another example of how similar sorts of meaningless stimuli activate neurons in this area, see also Gallant, Braun, and Van Essen 1993).[13] They found that nearby cells showed "maximal or nearly maximal responses to the same stimuli" (p. 343); neurons that were tuned for similar patterns tended to cluster together. As expected, in some cases there were sharp discontinuities for nearby neurons, which presumably reflected a transition across the boundary between columns. Fujita et al. estimate that there are between 1,000 and 2,000 columns in the macaque monkey, which may register different features. Presumably, the long-term representation of an image would be a feature vector across such columns. For lack of a better term, I will refer to such representations as *compressed image* representations to highlight both the lack of topography and the inclusion of sufficient information to reconstruct an image.

Matching Input to Stored Patterns

I have so far discussed only the first phase of matching in the pattern activation subsystem, when inputs from the preprocessing subsystem are matched bottom-up to properties of stored representations; representations are activated to the extent that their properties match those of the input configuration. In many cases, more than one representation will be activated to some degree. In such circumstances, "winner-take-all" networks have been offered as computational mechanisms to select the best-matching representation (e.g., Feldman 1985; Koch and Ullman 1985). In a winner-take-all network, each representation inhibits each other representation, and the amount of inhibition a representation imposes is directly proportional to how strongly it is activated. Thus, the most strongly activated representation will suppress the others (see also McClelland and Rumelhart 1981). Note that a winner-take-all network does not require that each representation be implemented as a single "grandmother" cell. If visual memories are stored as population codes, a winner-take-all architecture would imply inhibition among the coalitions of neurons that compose different representations.

Provided that enough nonaccidental and signal properties are visible, a winner-take-all mechanism will allow the system to recognize objects when they are seen from novel points of view. A problem here, however, is that when fewer distinguishing properties are visible, they place weaker constraints on what the object must be. For example, if the edges that indicate a pen's clip are lost, it will be difficult to use the remaining nonaccidental and signal properties to distinguish between a pen and pencil. This problem is exacerbated if one is trying to identify a particular member of a category, such as one's own pen rather than somebody else's. Indeed, in many cases patterns of nonaccidental properties are insufficient to identify members of a class even if all nonaccidental properties can be recovered. By definition, nonaccidental properties are impoverished relative to the image itself; they are the properties of the image that are likely to remain constant under different viewing conditions.

In some situations in which the nonaccidental properties are not sufficient, there may be enough signal properties to recognize the object. The pattern activation subsystem operates via a process of constraint satisfaction. It does not matter which particular input properties are matched to those of the stored objects; all that matters is the number that are matched. Thus, one sometimes can recognize an object even when only a few properties are visible if those properties are distinctive enough (such as the color and shape of the nipple on the end of a baby bottle). But signal properties are not always visible from different perspectives. If one cannot see enough distinguishing properties —nonaccidental or signal—then the object will not be initially recognized.

Image-based Matching Similar considerations led Lowe to implement a second phase of processing. He found that when nonaccidental properties do not strongly implicate a single object, it is useful to activate a stored "model" of the best-matching shape. Activating a stored model (which corresponds to the compressed image representation I posit) generates an image in the input array (the visual buffer, in my terms). This generated image is then compared to the input image itself, and the object is recognized if the image generated from memory matches the input image. The images generated here are none other than mental images; if Lowe is correct, then the ability to form visual mental images plays a key role in object recognition. Other researchers in computer vision are adopting similar views, which are inspired in part by the neural underpinnings of natural vision (e.g., see Mumford 1991, 1992, 1993).

In Lowe's system, the size and orientation of the generated image are adjusted until the best possible match to the input image is achieved. I assume that the representation in the pattern activation subsystem does not specify size (which is encoded by the dorsal system). Indeed, when Biederman and Cooper (1992) asked subjects to name objects twice, they found equivalent priming for the second presentation when an object's size was changed as when it was the original size. This finding suggests that the visual memory representation does not specify size. Similarly, Cooper et al. (1992) asked subjects to examine novel objects, and then asked them to decide whether objects were possible or impossible. Half of these test stimuli had been shown originally, and half were new; and half of the familiar stimuli were presented at the same size as originally and half were presented at a new size. Cooper et al. (1992) found equivalent priming regardless of whether the size was changed from the original size. As will be developed in the following chapters, I argue that a representation of size is conjoined with a representation of shape in associative memory. During image-based matching, the representation of size in associative memory is used to alter the mapping function from the pattern activation subsystem to the visual buffer, thereby changing the size of the image projected into the buffer. I will defer further discussion of such processing until chapter 10.

The generated image will not always correspond to the input image (if it did, then the criteria used to select which image to generate would be so good that there would be no need to generate the image). If the initial generated image does not match the input to a desired degree, that representation would be inhibited (and hence would cease to inhibit the other representations), and the representation that now matches the input best would be activated and the process repeated.

Although I am very impressed with Lowe's system, I do not mean to imply that it is an accurate model of human processing. In particular, his system generates a complete image that is used as a template; I am not proposing that human imagery operates this way. I doubt that a template-like image is fully generated and then compared to the input. Rather, a better way to conceive of this imagery-feedback process involves the concept of vector completion. Some neural network models contain recurrent connections, so that the states of units farther along in the processing stream feed back to affect the states of input or earlier hidden units (see Rumelhart and McClelland 1986). If the input is noisy, such feedback may actually fill in missing elements. This process is called vector completion. Imagery may play a similar role here: The generated image is information that will complete missing portions of the input. Thus, also unlike Lowe's system, in humans imagery feedback does not "wait" for bottom-up matching to be completed. Rather, as soon as one stored representation is activated strongly enough to inhibit the others, it begins to send imagery feedback. This conceptualization hinges on the concept of cooperative computation, wherein each visual area provides feedback to earlier ones to assist them in their computations. The state of each area must be consistent with the states of the other areas engaged in carrying out a computation or set of related computations. In this sense, imagery serves to augment the input to the visual buffer, allowing the representation there to be consistent with the representation downstream.[14] Although this process typically does not produce a fully formed image, it can do so if it is driven strongly enough by the activated representation.

The recognition process depends not only on a specification of the best-matching representation, but also on information about the degree to which a stored representation matches the input. Information about the degree of goodness of fit is useful when information reaches associative memory, particularly for regulating generalization. That is, part of the problem of generalization is to keep it within acceptable limits; one does not want to identify a fox as a dog. Generalization can be held in check by requiring a certain degree of matching before the best-matching representation in the pattern activation subsystem fully activates the corresponding representation in associative memory. Using information about the goodness of fit to regulate the degree of generalization has an added benefit: Depending on the context, the system can adjust an acceptability criterion, so that different levels of matching are acceptable (i.e., will activate the appropriate information in associative memory). Clearly, if we expect to see an object, we examine it less assiduously than if we do not expect to see it (Gregory 1966; Potter 1966).

Hence, I hypothesize that the output from the pattern activation subsystem indicates not only which stored representation best matches the input, but also how well it uniquely matches. The "strength" of the output would reflect the degree to which the best-matching representation uniquely "captures the variance" in the input; to the extent that a single representation is consistent with the pattern of input, that representation will produce a strong output.

Evidence for Imagery Feedback   Cave and Kosslyn (1989) performed a simple experiment to discover whether a stored representation of a pattern produces feedback that fills in the input image, and thereby facilitates encoding, during human object recognition. This experiment rested on a variant of the method we used to demonstrate that the scope of attention is adjusted incrementally (see page 95). Based on Lowe's ideas, we expected an image to be activated and used to augment the input when the nonaccidental properties are not sufficient. Thus, subjects were shown a rectangle or a diamond, and decided whether the sides of each stimulus were of equal length (not whether the shape was a rectangle or diamond). In this experiment, however, the two stimuli were superimposed; one was drawn in heavy black lines, and one was drawn in lighter narrow lines. The subjects were to evaluate the figure drawn in narrow lines. Examples of the stimuli are presented in figure 5.5. On 75%

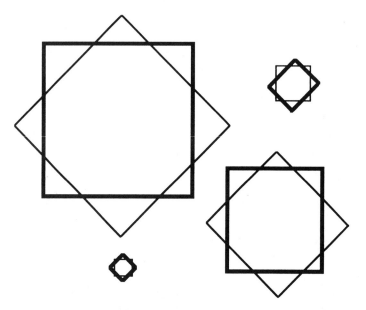

Figure 5.5   Examples of stimuli used by Cave and Kosslyn (1989). (Copyright 1989 by the American Psychological Association. Reprinted from Cave and Kosslyn 1989 by permission of the publisher).

of the trials the sizes of two successive target stimuli were the same, but on 25% of the trials they were different. Furthermore, on half of the trials, the second figure was the same as the first and on half the trials it was different.

We presented overlapping figures to muddy the waters, making it difficult to use the nonaccidental properties alone to identify the target figure. We reasoned that one way subjects could "pull out" the target figure is by matching a stored shape to the input. Given that the subject had no way of knowing in advance which shape would be probed, we expected that a representation of the just-seen shape would be used; such a representation had just been activated, and so would be most available. If so, then we expected the subjects to require less time to evaluate the same shape on the succeeding trial, and this was in fact found. But the more interesting results are shown in figure 5.6.

Figure 5.6 illustrates the time to evaluate the second figure in a pair when it appeared at different sizes relative to the first. The top line summarizes the results when the second stimulus was different from the first. This slope is very similar to that found when individual stimuli (not overlapping ones) were presented, as was described in chapter 4. The bottom line summarizes the results when the second stimulus was the same as the first. In both cases, the time to evaluate the second figure increased linearly with the difference between its size and that of the first figure. However, when the second

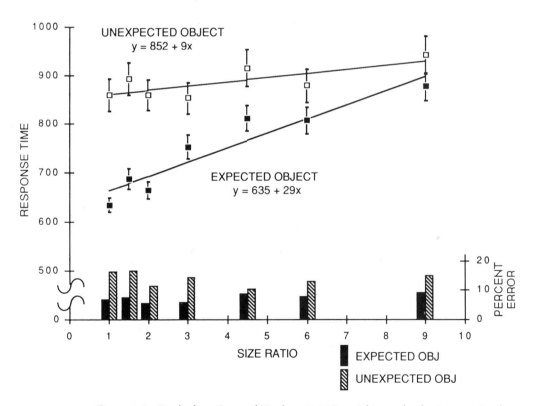

Figure 5.6 Results from Cave and Kosslyn 1989. (Copyright 1989 by the American Psychological Association. Reprinted by permission of the publisher.)

Identifying Objects When Different Portions Are Visible

stimulus was the same as the first and was close in size to the first, the subjects could evaluate it relatively quickly. But the larger the difference in size, the smaller the advantage of evaluating the same, compared to different, stimuli on two successive trials. Apparently, the represented size of the stored shape had to be adjusted to make the match to the input, which was a relatively slow process.

In chapter 4, results like those at the top of the figure were taken to indicate that the scope of the attention window was incrementally adjusted when a stimulus appeared at a new size. In the Cave and Kosslyn experiment summarized there, response times increased with size disparity whether or not the second stimulus was the same as the first. This adjustment time is much faster than the time to rescale a stored shape representation for comparison to the input. The dramatic difference in slopes is evidence that different processes were at work; subjects were not simply adjusting the attention window in both situations. Indeed, one of the interesting features of the results of the experiment just discussed is that the slope of the function at the bottom of figure 5.6 is about what would be expected if subjects adjusted the mapping function from the pattern activation subsystem to the visual buffer as they would when changing the size of a visual mental image (see Cave and Kosslyn 1989).

The results of this experiment make sense if the attention window is adjusted to surround the input image in the visual buffer to encode the stimulus bottom-up; at the same time, stored information is activated, and imagery feedback is projected back into the visual buffer to augment the input. Because the subjects knew that the stimulus would be one of two forms, they could activate an image as soon as a stimulus was presented. Furthermore, because a shape was very likely to be the same size as the previous one, the image was generated at that size. Hence, the greater the disparity in represented sizes, the more time was taken to adjust the mapping function from the pattern activation subsystem so that the imagery feedback could augment the input image. If the expected object was in fact present, this process allowed the subjects to encode the shape faster than when that activated material did not successfully augment the input (when a different object was presented) and bottom-up processing had to run to completion. However, as more time was spent adjusting the mapping function, this advantage diminished. This inter pretation is consistent with many other similar findings in the literature (e.g., Bundesen and Larsen 1975, 1981; Howard and Kerst 1978; Larsen and Bundesen 1978; Sekuler and Nash 1972; see the review and discussion in chapter 8 of Kosslyn 1980).

The same mechanisms will also explain comparable findings that occur when the orientations of successive stimuli are varied. Koriat, Norman, and Kimchi (1991) showed Israeli subjects four Hebrew letters sequentially, and asked the subjects to press one of four keys to report the identity of each letter. The letters appeared at different orientations. They found that the time to identify a letter was affected by the orientation of the previous letter only when the same letter appeared twice in succession. On these trials, the subjects responded increasingly slowly when there were larger disparities in the orientations of the two letters. However, analogous to what Cave and I found when we examined the effects of size disparity, Koriat, Norman, and Kimchi found that even though the times increased with greater orientation disparity when a letter appeared immediately after it had just appeared, the times were still faster than when the preceding letter was different. Again, the representation of the previous letter may have been primed, allowing an image representation to be activated and rotated (i.e., the mapping function adjusted) quickly when that letter appeared again—which facilitated recognition. When a different letter appeared, it did not benefit from such priming, and more bottom-up processing was necessary.[15]

Besner (1983) describes an experiment in which imagery feedback apparently was used on only some of the trials; it is important to ensure that the present theory can explain why imagery processes were important in some cases but not others. Besner showed people pairs of complex angular bloblike stimuli, one next to the other, and asked if they were the same or different. Each of the stimuli in a pair was one of three sizes, and all possible pairs of disparities were presented (in his first two experiments, which I am discussing now). Besner reports that when the subjects had to discriminate between a form and the same form that was upside down, they required more time to evaluate pairs that had more disparate sizes. In addition, the "same" and "different" trials had the same increases in time with size disparity. In contrast, when the discrimination was between different shapes, Besner found much smaller effects of size disparity for "different" trials (replicating an earlier finding of Besner and Coltheart 1976).[16]

I assume that the subjects perform this task by encoding the stimuli successively (e.g., first the figure on the left, and then the one on the right). If the nonaccidental properties are similar, the judgment is not made immediately and there is time for the imagery feedback process to occur. In this case, a representation of the first stimulus is activated and used to augment the input image of the second figure; the mapping function is adjusted so that the feedback properly augments the input image. If this process is successful, then the second figure should be quickly encoded. Indeed, the figure should seem to "snap into focus" very quickly—which itself may be used as a sign that it matches the other stimulus in the pair. If so, then the similarity of the targets and distractors will be critical: If the distractors are relatively similar to the targets, they cannot be compared using only nonaccidental properties. Use of the viewpoint consistency constraint would cause upside-down blobs to match representations of right-side-up blobs reasonably well (but not perfectly because the patterns are likely to be perceptually organized differently in the two cases; see below). Hence, we find evidence that stored image representations were activated, scaled, and used to augment the input image. (In chapter 9 I will develop the theory of how the image is generated, and in chapter 10 I will develop the theory of how the transformation process occurs.) In contrast, if the distractors were not very similar, then they could be rejected quickly. Presumably, at least some of the stimuli in different-objects pairs were sufficiently dissimilar to be rejected based on the initial matching process.

Introspectively, the claim that imagery is used in object recognition may seem peculiar. We are not aware of generating images when we recognize objects. In most instances, this process may be so rapid that we are unaware that stored information has augmented the input. Moreover, as I noted earlier, this process typically may not run to completion, producing a distinct mental image. In most cases, it succeeds in filling out the input image and we will simply see the object.

But what about when the activated image does not match the input? In such circumstances, the imagery-feedback process should produce one of two results. On the one hand, if the perceptual input is degraded (as happens when one sees something out of the corner of one's eye), the imagery feedback may alter what one sees. An anecdote illustrates this result: I was once searching for an automatic pencil, and "saw" it off to one side; what I saw was in fact a pen, but at first glance I apparently erroneously "completed" the input to see a pencil. On the other hand, if the perceptual input is strong (the object is foveated and not obscured), then it will overwhelm the imagery feedback; the strong perceptual input will override the state of the visual buffer imposed by the activated image representation, and hence one will not be aware of the image.

It is worth pausing to consider what at first glance seems to be a more straightforward mechanism than that incorporated into Lowe's system. Why not simply match the input bottom-up to the stored image when the non-accidental properties are too weak to make a necessary discrimination? Some kind of representation of the image must be encoded into memory (as a "model"), otherwise one could not later reconstruct it. Matching the compressed images themselves is a simple template operation, and falls prey to all of the problems with such approaches; the image varies too much from instance to instance (which is a primary motivation for the idea of nonaccidental properties). However, Huttenlocher and Ullman (1987) developed a variant of Lowe's approach in which stored patterns can be deformed (within limits) to provide the best alignment with the input, and Ullman (1989) and Edelman, Ullman, and Flash (1990) have shown that this technique has utility in computer vision. This sort of "deformable template" matching is likely to be of limited use in the brain, however, because the cortical areas that store visual memories are not organized topographically (e.g., see Van Essen 1985; Desimone and Ungerleider 1989). The spatial information apparently is stored in a compressed form, as is done in computer graphics programs. None but the most primitive graphics systems actually store a bitmap of an image; rather, a more abstract code is stored, which can later be used to reconstruct the image. Such representations do not make explicit each visual dimension; for example, a single entry in the code might indicate a conjunction of features. And if the local geometry of a shape is not accessible in the higher-level visual image representations, then it would be difficult to generalize over variations in geometric properties of the object when the input is compared to, and does not exactly match, such a stored representation. Activating a compressed image representation and allowing the feedback to produce an image in the visual buffer makes accessible the local geometry, which is only implicit in the stored representation.

Object-Centered versus Viewer-Centered Representations

Consider again the problem of how we identify objects seen from different perspectives. Its solution hinges in part on the way objects are represented in visual memory (in the pattern activation subsystem). There are two oft-discussed methods for representing information in memory so that a system can recognize objects when they are seen from different points of view. On the one hand, as advocated by Marr (1982), objects could be identified by matching the input to three-dimensional, object-centered representations of stored shapes. In an object-centered representation, parts are related to the object itself and are independent of any point of view (e.g., a dolphin's fin is dorsal, regardless of how it is leaping or swimming). A three-dimensional representation will include all the parts of an object, and thus parts encoded from any given point of view will match some of those stored in the representation. Hence, this type of representation would allow the system to generalize over multiple points of view.

On the other hand, one could store a separate representation of each view or shape. Ullman and Barsi (1990) proved that at most six images would need to be stored to allow one to reconstruct how an object appears from any point of view, and Edelman and Bulthoff (1991) and Bulthoff and Edelman (1992) showed that human beings can interpolate across different stored representations when recognizing nonsense patterns (such as bent-paper-clip-like forms) seen from different points of view.[17] Depending on what particular stored representations were present, a specific novel shape would be more or less similar to a stored one—which would make generalization more or less easy.

Marr's views have been extremely influential in some corners of the cognitive science community, and many theories of high-level vision posit that the input is matched to stored object-centered representations (e.g., Biederman 1987; Brooks 1981; Feldman 1985; Hinton 1981; Hummel and Biederman 1992; Palmer 1983; Pentland 1986). Even Lowe assumed that the representations stored in memory are object-centered, although a viewer-centered process was used to access them (which relied on the viewpoint consistency constraint). Huttenlocher and Ullman (1987) and Ullman (1989) provide exceptions to this approach. But the evidence for object-centered representations is weak, and there is good evidence that stored visual representations preserve some viewer-centered properties. In my view, neither extreme is likely to be correct; it is useful, however, to consider the extreme alternatives.

Evidence for Viewer-Centered Representations   Desimone et al. (1984), Perrett et al. (1989), Perrett, Smith, Mistlin, et al. (1985), and Perrett, Smith,

Potter et al. (1985) describe neurons in the ventral system that are tuned for different views of the head and body. For example, Perrett, Smith, Potter, et al. (1985) recorded from neurons in the superior temporal sulcus (STS, which defines the upper boundary of the inferior temporal lobe, often called area IT),[18] and found that about 10% to 11% of these cells respond selectively to static views of the head. They found that some of these cells were tuned to respond only when the head was in specific orientations or the eyes were gazing in specific directions. About 69% of the cells that responded selectively to one class of object (the face or head) responded best when the object was seen from a particular point of view. Indeed, some cells responded maximally to a single profile (e.g., a face seen from the left side). These results are difficult to explain if viewer-centered representations are not stored.[19]

But what about the fact that other neurons in these areas have been found to generalize over changes in visual angle subtended, position, and orientation (e.g., Bruce, Desimone, and Gross 1981; Hasselmo et al. 1989; Perrett, Rolls, and Caan 1982; Perrett, Smith, Potter et al. 1985; Rolls 1987; Rolls and Baylis 1986)? For example, Perrett, Smith, Potter, et al. (1985) found that about one quarter of the cells that responded preferentially to faces were relatively insensitive to viewpoint. Similarly, although Yamane, Kaji, and Kawano (1988) also report some remarkably specific responses for such "face cells" (e.g., one cell purportedly detected "the combination of the degree that the forehead is covered with hair and the distance from eyes to mouth," p. 213), they also report that 41 of the 86 cells that responded to faces also responded to a green dot, and 24 of the 86 responded to a square or ellipse.

At least in some cases, these cells are probably responding on the basis of a single attribute of the stimulus that is visible in all of the different conditions (e.g., see Bruce, Desimone, and Gross 1981; Fujita et al. 1992; Tanaka et al. 1991). In other cases, generalization over visual angle and location may reflect the operation of the attention window (as described in the previous chapter), and generalization over orientation may indicate that the input is matched to stored information in accordance with the viewpoint consistency constraint.

In short, the existence of neurons that generalize over variations in shape, visual angle, location, or orientation does not imply that the underlying *representation* is object-centered; it could be viewer-centered, but the input is encoded by adjusting the attention window and matched to stored representations using the viewpoint consistency constraint. Similarly, the fact that the inferior temporal lobe appears to be necessary for a monkey to recognize objects when the animal must compare objects of different sizes, from different viewing angles, or under different lighting conditions (see Weiskrantz 1990) does not necessarily imply that this structure stores object-centered representations; rather, these findings may simply indicate that this structure is critically involved in the representation of objects and/or in the operation of the viewpoint consistency constraint during the matching process.

Although object-centered representations require that relatively little information must be stored, considerably more processing is necessary to encode them than to encode viewer-centered representations. Patterns of activation in retinotopic maps are viewer-centered; they depict an input image as it falls on the retina when one sees an object from a particular point of view. Thus, the input representations are viewer-centered. It is not trivial to derive object-centered representations from such input; indeed, to my knowledge no successful computer vision system has been built that performs this transform reliably over a wide variety of different objects. However, a number of viewer-centered representations would be needed to store the information in a single object-centered representation. Thus, we are faced with a trade-off; the virtues of storing fewer object-centered representations must be evaluated against the drawbacks of creating them.

The drawbacks of using viewer-centered representations for recognition have proven not to be severe. The capacity of our visual memories is truly staggering; it is so large that it has yet to be estimated. For example, Shepard (1967) showed subjects 612 pictures for about 6 seconds each, and then asked them to select the previously shown objects from pairs of alternatives. The subjects were correct on fully 98% of the trials (see also Nickerson 1965, 1968; Standing, Conezio, and Haber 1970). Perhaps the most staggering results are reported by Standing (1973), who showed some of his subjects 10,000 arbitrarily selected pictures for 5 seconds each. Standing distinguished between "normal" and "vivid" pictures; a typical picture of a dog was judged normal, but a picture of a dog with a pipe in its mouth was vivid, and an ordinary picture of an airplane was normal, but a crashed plane was vivid. His findings showed that there is no apparent upper bound on human memory for pictures, even normal pictures. Moreover, with immediate recall, Standing estimated that if 1 million vivid pictures were shown, 986,300 would be recognized if one were tested immediately afterward; even after a delay, he estimates that 731,400 would be recalled. And this is when subjects only saw each picture once, for 5 seconds, with an interstimulus interval of 600 ms.

Moreover, Standing collected response times when subjects decided whether they recognized pictures; the results suggested the truly astounding conclusion that subjects could search 51,180 pictures per second in long-term memory! It is clear that we must have many different representations in visual memory, if only because of the discriminations we can make; given that we can identify specific examples (e.g., your cat versus the one next door), the corresponding information must be stored in memory. Thus, it is comforting that so many representations can be searched so quickly.[20]

Rock (1973) reported findings that strongly suggest that humans store viewer-centered representations. He showed subjects novel bloblike patterns at a particular orientation. Later he tested the subjects by showing them the patterns at the same orientations or different orientations. If subjects were unaware that the orientation had been changed, they could not recognize the pattern. A variation of the method produced particularly striking results. On half the trials, subjects tilted their heads so that the misoriented images were now aligned on the retina the same way as originally. But even now, the subjects did not recognize these patterns unless they knew about the rotation. Clearly, we often encode patterns relative to a frame of reference that is not fixed on the pattern itself (see also Blum 1973; Corballis, Zbrodoff, and Roldan 1976; Humphreys 1983, 1984; Humphreys and Quinlan 1987, 1988; Jolicoeur 1990a; McMullen and Jolicoeur 1990; Palmer 1980, 1982, 1985; Rock and DiVita 1987; Rock, DiVita, and Barbeito 1981).

Tarr and Pinker (1989, 1990) provide additional evidence that viewer-centered representations are stored. They asked subjects to memorize ideogram-like line patterns, and later to determine whether stimuli were members of the memorized set. The stimuli could be presented at the same orientation as originally studied or at a new orientation. Tarr and Pinker found that identification times increased when stimuli were presented at new orientations; this result is similar to the now-classic mental rotation findings of Shepard and Cooper (1982), who showed that people require more time to "mentally rotate" a stimulus greater amounts. A particularly interesting aspect of Tarr and Pinker's findings is that the increase in time was predicted by the angular disparity between the stimulus and the nearest familiar orientation. However, Tarr and Pinker found that this rotation effect was transient. After subjects had seen a stimulus at an orientation even once, they no longer required more time when they subsequently saw the stimulus at that orientation.

Tarr and Pinker's findings nicely extended earlier results of Jolicoeur and his colleagues and other researchers (e.g., Maki 1986; Shwartz 1981; for an excellent review of this literature, see Jolicoeur 1990a). When subjects were asked to name a pictured object or letter of the alphabet, they required more time when the stimulus was tilted progressively farther from the standard upright. The increase in time to name objects at different orientations (for the range of orientations from 0° to 120°) can be similar to what is found when visual mental images are rotated (see Jolicoeur 1985, 1990a) or can be smaller (Jolicoeur 1988). Indeed, it is clear that one does not simply mentally rotate misoriented pictures to the upright before naming them: unlike mental rotation slopes (see Shepard and Cooper 1982), naming times typically display an M pattern; the subjects are faster for upside down orientations than for rotations of 120°

In some of these naming studies (e.g., Corballis and Nagourney 1978; Corballis, Zbrodoff, Shetzer, and Butler 1978; Young, Palef, and Logan 1980; see Jolicoeur 1990a for a review), no effects of orientation were obtained; but all of these studies incorporated practice trials with the same stimuli used in the test trials. This methodological detail is critical because even when effects of orientation were obtained, they were present primarily on the initial trials; after practice, the effect was greatly diminished.[21] However, this effect of practice did not transfer to new items. Thus, what was learned was specific to a set of stimuli and was not a general-purpose procedure. The initial effect of orientation, and the fact that practice greatly diminishes this effect only for the items that were named, strike me as critical findings—and lead me not to posit the kind of "frame-independent" representation advocated by Corballis (1988a).

At first glance, these sorts of findings appear to be evidence that pictures are stored using viewer-centered representations. In this case, the input would consist of viewer-centered representations, which are matched directly against stored viewer-centered representations. However, this notion does not explain the findings of Jolicoeur and Milliken (1989). Even when their subjects initially named objects in *upright* orientations, they showed a great a reduction in the effects of orientation when subsequently naming the objects at novel orientations. Indeed, this reduction was as large as when the subjects initially saw the objects misoriented!

In addition, if the brain stores viewer-centered representations, we might expect good memory for left-right orientation. But people are notoriously poor at this task. For example, Nickerson and Adams (1979) found that most people cannot recall which direction Abraham Lincoln faces on a penny (see also Madigan and Rouse 1974). However, Standing, Conezio, and Haber (1970) showed that we do store some information about left-right orientation, at least within a relatively brief time after having seen pictures. But this information need not be stored as part of the shape representation used in recognition; it could be stored in associative memory as a kind of "tag." This hypothesis would explain why people can recall shape even when they cannot recall left-right orientation (e.g., Frederickson and Bartlett 1987; Standing, Conezio, and Haber 1970); if the representation were fully viewer-centered, orientation would be stored intrinsically with shape. In addition, Biederman and Cooper (1991c) have shown that when people are asked to name previously seen pictures of objects, the prior experience of naming facilitates subsequent naming of mirror-reversed pictures as much as it does subsequent naming of the originals. And Cooper et al. (1992) found equivalent priming when left-right direction was varied in their object-decision task (see also Bradshaw, Bradley, and Patterson 1976; Corballis and Beale 1976, 1983; Klatzky and Stoy 1974).[22]

Computationally, it makes sense not to store information about left-right orientation as part of a representation of shape: Not only must objects be identified when seen from different points of view, but there are no natural objects that can be identified only if they are discriminated from mirror-reversed shapes. Thus, as Corballis and Beale (1976) and Gross and Bornstein (1978) point out, it would be most efficient for the brain simply to ignore left-right orientation when representing shape.

So, we are faced with a puzzle: How can we reconcile the fact that people are sensitive to variations in planar orientation with the fact that they are insensitive to variations in left-right orientation? And how do we explain the effects of practice on the time to identify objects at different orientations—especially the equivalent effects of showing subjects misoriented or upright pictures initially?

Consider the following possibility. Perhaps the properties of stored objects are organized as seen from a particular point of view, but the matching process relies on the viewpoint consistency constraint. The viewpoint consistency constraint can be implemented so that a stored image will be matched equally easily to itself and its mirror reflection. But the use of such a matching process would not necessarily match input patterns to rotated versions of the pattern stored in memory. The reason why is straightforward. As Rock (1973) showed, the way the input is organized into perceptual units depends in part on how a stimulus is oriented in the plane. Such perceptual units define the components of nonaccidental and signal properties. For example, when shown a Star of David, people tend to organize it into two overlapping triangles. But, with effort, they can "break up" some of the lines and symmetries to reorganize it into a central octagon and six small triangles; until they break it up, the configuration of nonaccidental properties that define the octagon is not present. The processes in the visual buffer that organize forms are affected by the gravitational upright, other environmental cues, position on the retina, and the way the body is oriented (see Corballis 1988a, 1988b; Hinton and Parsons 1988; Howard 1982; McMullen and Jolicoeur 1990; Parker, Poston, and Gulledge 1983; Rock 1973; Takano 1989; Templeton 1973).[23]

Depending on the nature of the perceptual units that are the input to the preprocessing subsystem, different (although overlapping) sets of nonaccidental and signal properties will be extracted. Thus, altering the orientation of an object can change the nature of the input that is matched to stored representations. Depending on how a figure is organized, the input may or may not match the information stored in the pattern activation subsystem. For example, Cooper, Schacter, and Moore (1991) asked subjects to view pictures of novel objects, and then briefly presented these objects intermixed with additional novel objects; half of the objects could exist in the the world and half were Escher-like drawings of impossible objects. The subjects were asked to decide whether each object was possible. The researchers found that the subjects could evaluate possible objects that had been seen initially faster than new objects, but such priming was eliminated when the stimuli were presented in novel orientations in the picture plane. Moreover, there was no priming at all for impossible objects—presumably because they could not be organized effectively into perceptual units and stored (for reviews of related findings, see Cooper and Schacter 1992; Schacter, Chiu, and Ochsner 1993). Thus, matching via the viewpoint consistency constraint is limited; this process will only operate well within a limited range of orientations, when the figure is perceptually organized the same way as the corresponding representation in memory.

This conceptualization also allows us to understand the effects of practice. As Jolicoeur (1990a) points out, the most straightforward account for these results is that the subjects encode new characteristics of the pictures that can be recognized at different orientations. One could organize new units that will delineate sets of nonaccidental properties that can be recognized at different orientations. This process might require "breaking up" an initial set of nonaccidental properties by focusing on only a portion of an edge or a part of a symmetric region. For example, rather than encode the entire shape of a dog, which will be perceptually organized differently at different orientations, one could encode the parts separately, which will tend to be organized the same way when seen at different orientations (e.g., the head is a simple enough shape that it is not open to too many alternative organizations). Such representations would the allow one to look for specific parts or characteristics during subsequent naming trials (in the following chapter I will discuss how one might be able to search for parts per se). These proposals appear to be similar to those of Takano (1989), who showed that subjects often use mental rotation to identify misoriented objects, but can be led to use "orientation-free" information; however, this strategy requires additional effort (see also Corballis 1988b).

The present theory is consistent with Jolicoeur and Landau's (1984) finding that orientation effects persist over repeated presentations if the stimuli are presented only very briefly and followed by a mask; in such circumstances, subjects may not have enough time to organize additional perceptual units that can be recognized at different orientations. Moreover, McMullen and Farah (1991) found that the effects of orientation on naming time are eliminated with practice for symmetrical, but not asymmetrical, pictures (within the range of practice they used). Presumably symmetrical figures not only have fewer properties to encode, but the mirrored parts of symmetrical figures (with the strong horizontal axis between them) are easier to organize into units that can be recognized at any orientation. Tarr and Pinker (1989) review the literature on effects of tilt on recognition time, and note that most of the studies that find no such difference included stimuli that could be recognized on the basis of such cues.[24]

Similarly, Tarr and Pinker's (1989) subjects had to discriminate among very similar ideogram-like patterns; the distractors differed subtly from those in the memorized set. Thus, the pattern of nonaccidental properties per se was unlikely to implicate a specific object, and so an image presumably was generated. But on subsequent trials, the subjects may have studied the figures more carefully, and encoded specific portions of the figures (such as the region where two sticks joined a third) that would distinguish them.[25]

The present theory also allows us to understand the dip in response times when the stimuli are upside down. There are two facets of this result that need to be explained. First, why are times faster than would be expected if rotation were used? The answer to this question may hinge on the fact that the usual gravitational axis is preserved when an object is upside down, and hence many of the parts will be perceptually organized the same way. Thus, the input is more likely to match the corresponding properties of the appropriate stored representation than when the normal gravitational axis is not preserved. If so, then on some percentage of the trials, rotation would not be required.[26] Second, why are the times still greater than when an object is viewed at the standard upright? The gravitational upright is only one factor that influences how regions are organized. It seems plausible that some portions of objects are not organized the same way when viewed in the context of an upside-down figure. If so, then the input would not match the stored memories as effectively as when the figure is upright—and thus more time is required for the winner-take-all mechanism to settle down. In addition, as noted above, in this situation rotation might be required on some percentage of the trials.

In short, I am proposing that the operation of the viewpoint consistency constraint during matching must be understood in the context of the effects of orientation on perceptual organization. Depending on the orientation, a pattern is organized into different perceptual units, and subsequent matching is between properties of such units. The viewpoint consistency constraint allows flexibility when matching, but this process will be successful only to the degree that the stored representation and the input have been organized in the same way. If the match is not good enough, then an image is generated, which reconstructs the pattern and allows it to augment—if possible—the input image in the visual buffer.

Before continuing, we must consider a result that appears to fly in the face of this theory. Farah and Hammond (1988) tested the ability of a patient with a large right-hemisphere frontal-temporal-parietal lesion to name misoriented objects and to perform mental rotation. They examined his performance on three mental rotation tasks, all of which required him to distinguish left-right orientation (the tasks were judging the direction of an uppercase letter *L*, the Ratcliff [1979] "mannequin" mental rotation task, and a similar task involving "little people" who were holding an object in the left or right hand). Their patient performed these tasks very poorly. In contrast, this patient could name misoriented numbers perfectly, could reinterpret letters as if they were seen from a different orientation 86% of the time, could identify the parts of an *L* perfectly even when it was misoriented, and could identify drawings 78% of the time when they were upright or upside down (two other tasks were administered, but they are less relevant to the present issue). When tested 7 months later, the patient could identify upright drawings 94% of the time, but still named upside-down ones correctly on 78% of the trials. These findings suggested to Farah and Hammond that mental rotation does not play a role in normal object identification.

There are several problems with this inference, however. First, upside-down pictures may not always require mental rotation, even on the first trial; as noted above, such a picture may be perceptually organized in a way that allows the input to be matched to the appropriate stored representation (via that viewpoint consistency constraint). In addition, "mental flipping"—a different kind of transformation—could substitute for mental rotation in this special case. It is unfortunate that the pictures were always presented either upright or fully upside down. Second, Farah and Hammond did not measure response times, and hence it is possible that their patient did have a deficit in the naming task—but it was reflected in his response times. Indeed, the usual effects of orientation on naming appear in response times (Jolicoeur 1990a), and only small effects, if any, are present in accuracy data. Moreover, without measuring response times it is impossible to know whether there were speed-accuracy trade-offs in the data. Indeed, Farah and Hammond comment that the patient may have answered impulsively when he thought a judgment was easy. Given that he could make the mirror-reversal judgments perfectly when the mental rotation stimuli were upright, he may have underestimated the difficulty of making this judgment when the stimuli were rotated. By the same token, it is of interest that the patient did seem to have more difficulty naming the inverted pictures than the upright pictures after 7 months. It is possible that his relatively high error rates for upright pictures during the initial testing session were due to a speed-accuracy trade-off, because he was overconfident. Third, the mental rotation tasks required making mirror-reversed/normal judgments, whereas the identification tasks required naming the object. It is possible that more of the stimulus needs to be rotated when parts must be compared to make the mirror-reversed/normal judgment than when an object must be identified. If so, then these mental rotation tasks would be more difficult than the picture naming tasks. As I discussed in chapter 2, brain-damaged patients are generally slowed down; thus, it is not surprising that they may fail at more difficult tasks but succeed at simpler ones. However, Farah and Hammond argue effectively that difficulty per se cannot explain the results; indeed, they found that normal control subjects made more errors when asked to name rotated pictures that were presented very briefly than when asked to name upright pictures—even though their patient did not make more errors in the initial session. However, as they acknowledge, their mental rotation tasks may have been difficult in a way having nothing to do with the type of rotation necessary to name misoriented pictures.

In summary, although Farah and Hammond's results are interesting and give us reason to take pause, they cannot be regarded as conclusive evidence against Jolicoeur's proposal nor against the present theory.

Evidence for Object-Centered Representations   It is also possible that, under some circumstances, one can organize input into object-centered representations. This inference was supported by the results of an experiment by Jolicoeur and Kosslyn (1983). We asked subjects to study a set of treelike stick figures, one at a time. Each of these stimuli had a large dowel as the major axis with smaller asymmetric dowels protruding at different angles, which in turn had tertiary dowels protruding from them. After a stimulus was studied it was removed, and shortly thereafter the subjects rated the similarity of that figure and another. The trick was that we systematically varied the similarity of the distractor and the target in different ways. Some distractors were in fact simply rotated versions of the study figure, and thus had the same object-centered descriptions. Other distractors had secondary and tertiary limbs in the same places in space as the study figure, but the major axis was oriented differently; thus, these figures had similar viewer-centered descriptions as the study figures, but different object-centered descriptions.

Therefore, by performing multidimensional scaling of the similarity ratings data, we could determine what sort of stored information was being compared to the input. We also varied the instructions given to the subjects in order to influence the kind of information that would be encoded. When subjects were told to study the three-dimensional structure of the objects, we found increased perceived similarity when the distractors had similar object-centered descriptions as the targets. Such similarity was particularly apparent when subjects were asked to rate similarity of the structures of the objects per se. But even in this extreme condition, viewer-centered similarity still influenced the ratings, as evident in both the reconstructed scaling solutions and in the time to make the various judgments. In contrast, when subjects were asked to remember what the objects looked like from a particular point of view, there was no evidence that they also encoded object-centered information.

We can conclude, then, that subjects typically store viewer-centered information, but in some circumstances can also store object-centered information (cf. Corballis and Beale 1976, 1983). Such object-centered information may not be stored as representations in the ventral system; rather, such information may correspond to "routines" that one can follow to locate distinguishing parts or characteristics when an object is in any orientation (see Ullman 1984). For example, one can find the dorsal fin of a leaping porpoise by locating the nose, finding the convex surface (its back), and tracing along that surface until reaching the fin; this procedure will work no matter how the animal is positioned in mid-leap. Such a routine would be stored in associative memory and would require effort to devise, store, and later execute—which is consistent with Jolicoeur and Kosslyn's finding that object-centered information could be encoded only with additional effort, when people knew it would be useful for a later task (for a similar view, see Takano 1989).

The finding that object-centered representations are encoded only with additional effort is consistent with the observation that a storage-processing trade-off occurs for viewer-centered and object-centered comparisons: additional processing is required to produce object-centered representations of the input, and the system typically may simply store numerous viewer-centered representations in order to avoid this additional processing. A new viewer-centered representation would be stored whenever an input did not match a stored representation very well; Kosslyn and Koenig (1992) suggest that perceptual representations are stored reflexively if they do not match representations already in memory.

The present theory implies that one typically cannot recognize an object the first time it is seen from a novel point of view if one cannot encode enough nonaccidental and signal properties or if the image does not match one generated from a stored representation. An interpretation (in associative memory) would be associated with such a new encoding only after the object is identified by other means (e.g., it moves so that another view is evident, someone names it, etc.). In short, I suggest that objects typically may have more than a single representation in the pattern activation subsystem.

Anatomical Localization

The pattern activation subsystem is apparently localized in the inferior temporal lobe of monkeys. Dean and Weiskrantz (1974), for example, showed that the deficit suffered by animals with a lesion in IT was due to a loss of memory per se. They had animals with IT lesions, superior temporal lesions, or no lesions learn a large number of discriminations (30) prior to the operation, and compared performance postoperatively to performance with novel discrimination problems. Scores on the first trial (and the first 20 trials) showed no evidence of retention for the animals with IT lesions, compared to the normal animals and the animals with superior temporal lesions. In contrast, even early during the course of relearning, the normal animals and the animals with superior temporal lesions performed better with familiar problems than with novel ones. This difference was not eliminated over time as learning progressed, which is as would be expected if the memory itself were obliterated (see also Iversen and Weiskrantz 1964).

Consistent with the proposals offered in the previous chapter, cells in IT have very large receptive fields, which allow them to respond over large regions of space (Desimone et al. 1984; Gross et al. 1981; Gross et al. 1984). In addition, these cells virtually always include the fovea in their receptive fields (i.e., they respond to stimuli whose images fall on the fovea), and the sensitivity of the cells to stimuli that do not fall on the fovea typically drops off irregularly with distance in different directions. Furthermore, neurons in the ventral system have similar patterns of activation when the same input image is at different locations and at different sizes on the retina (e.g., Schwartz et al. 1984). These findings are consistent with the claim that changing the location or scale of the attention window allows similar representations to be passed downstream when an object appears at different locations or sizes. Presumably the stimulus-based attention-shifting subsystem, which operates reflexively, can adjust the attention window even when the animal is not fully conscious (as was the case in these experiments).

Van Essen et al. (1990) report that the inferior temporal lobe consists of at least four distinct areas (and there is some evidence for six such areas), not all of which must be involved in the same type of processing. At least some of the areas in IT appear to serve as a modality-specific visual memory structure, perhaps with different areas playing a critical role in short-term (e.g., Miyashita and Chang 1988) and long-term (e.g., Martin-Elkins, George, and Horel 1989) memory.

Weiskrantz and Saunders (1984) provided evidence that is consistent with the claim that the inferior temporal lobe is critical for the viewpoint consistency constraint to operate normally. They trained monkeys to distinguish "target" objects from foils (which varied on every trial; the target object did not appear with only one foil). Later, target objects were transformed occasionally by altering their size, orientation, or lighting (and hence shadow configuration). They found that lesions in prestriate cortex (in "posterior inferotemporal" cortex) or in anterior IT disrupted the ability to recognize objects when they appeared at different sizes or orientations. In addition, the animals with anterior lesions to IT had particular difficulty learning the discriminations even before the objects were transformed, which is again consistent with the claim that this area plays a critical role in storing visual information. However, these results may not speak directly to the operation of the viewpoint consistency constraint; it is possible that the damage simply reduced the percentage of nonaccidental and signal properties that could be encoded. When an object is rotated, some properties that were initially visible will no longer be present, and other properties that were not visible will be revealed. To encode enough familiar properties to recognize the object, a greater percentage of the total will need to be encoded when the object is transformed in a novel way than when it is not transformed. Similarly, changing the size makes some properties that previously were salient no longer salient, and vice versa; thus one must encode more than the most highly salient properties when the size is changed.[27]

In addition, D. Gaffan, S. Harrison, and E. A. Gaffan (1986) and Gross (1978) found that monkeys with lesions in IT could discriminate normal from mirror-reversed figures virtually as easily as control monkeys.[28] This task requires encoding left-right orientation per se, which I claim is not performed in the ventral system. This finding is consistent with the observation that matching in accordance with the viewpoint consistency constraint obscures information about left-right orientation—if it is stored at all in the ventral system. Rather, processing in the dorsal system is necessary to make such judgments (as will be elaborated in the following chapter). In this case, then, lesions did not affect performance because the lesioned areas did not help the normal monkey.

Fuster and Jervey (1982) and Miyashita and Chang (1988) conducted single-cell recording experiments that provided additional evidence that at least part of IT stores short-term visual memories. For example, Miyashita and Chang trained monkeys to discriminate among novel patterns (fractal shapes), which were presented sequentially. One pattern was presented and removed, and then a test pattern was presented; the monkey had to retain a representation of the first pattern in order to decide whether the second matched it. Miyashita and Chang found the usual increased activity of IT cells during visual perception, and also found neurons in IT that were active during the retention interval itself. Different neurons were active during the retention interval for different initial stimuli. The paper does not, unfortunately, indicate the precise relations between the neurons that were activated during perception and during retention, nor does it provide precise comparisons of patterns of neural activation for patterns that are more or less similar (as determined by discrimination errors, or even human similarity ratings of the sort that have been used so successfully in multidimensional scaling studies, e.g., Henle 1969; see also Shepard 1980).

Similarly, Miller, Li, and Desimone (1991) showed monkeys a series of pictures of common objects, and trained them to release a bar when a sample object was repeated. In one experiment, they recorded from 146 neurons in the anterior part of IT, and found that "nearly half responded selectively not only to particular test items but also according to whether the test items matched the sample item held in memory" (p. 1377). Specifically, fully 85% of the neurons responded selectively to specific stimuli and 48% responded differently when the stimulus matched the sample. Also of interest is the finding that 15% of the neurons had a disproportionately large difference in response for a matching stimulus when it was the one that they responded to optimally. However, for nearly all the neurons, they responded *less* to a matching stimulus than to a nonmatching one. This decrement was evident even with six intervening items. The authors note that they sometimes found high activity immediately after the sample was presented, which is consistent with findings reported by Fuster and Jervey (1982) and Miyashita and Chang (1988). However, these responses decreased when the test stimuli were presented. Miller, Li, and Desimone note that if the decreases across neurons are averaged, the pattern of responses could distinguish 90% of the targets from the distractors—which was very similar to the actual behavioral responses.

Miller, Li, and Desimone also investigated the effects of how familiar the animal was with the stimuli. They showed the monkeys 20 novel objects, all of which served as sample and matching stimuli (but not as nonmatching distractors). A new set of objects was used for each cell. The sample was shown after either 4 or 35 intervening trials. Each sample was presented 10 to 20 times in each session. They found that many neurons decreased their responses as the targets became more familiar, reaching a stable level after about 6 to 8 trials. But these neurons still responded at levels greater than the resting baseline, even with 35 intervening trials. Indeed, the cells responded selectively after 140 intervening trials! Similar results have been reported for some of the cells in STS that respond selectively to faces (Rolls et al. 1989).

Miller, Li, and Desimone suggest that the selective decrements reflect a "focusing of activation" during the retention interval, with an increasingly selective subpopulation of neurons encoding the stimulus. It seems also possible that the results reflect the effects of repetition per se, not matching; in this case, they would reflect a type of stimulus-specific habituation. In any event, it is clear that the selective responses of the neurons depend on their storing information in memory.

Sakai and Miyashita (1991) used a different task to examine activity when a monkey was cued to retrieve a learned stimulus from visual long-term memory. They generated 24 nonsense "Fourier descriptor" shapes (some of which were vaguely snowflake-like, some with sharp points, others with only rounded curves, etc.) and randomly created pairs of the stimuli. They trained two monkeys to memorize the pairs. The monkeys saw one stimulus and were then to choose the proper associate from a pair of stimuli; the pair included the associate and a member of another pair. The monkeys received a reward if they quickly chose the associate for the cued pair. After the monkeys had memorized the pairs (and performed between 70% and 100% correct during the testing session), Sakai and Miyashita recorded from the anterior portions of the inferior temporal lobes. They recorded from 577 isolated neurons, and found that 91 responded selectively during the cue period. The cells varied in how sharply tuned they were to the stimuli; 32 of the 91 responded to only one picture, and 59 responded to more than two pictures. When cells responded to two or more pictures during the cue period, they responded more strongly to the associated pictures than to random pairs. Another type of neuron had picture-selective activity during the interstimulus interval. Sakai and Miyashita report that one cell produced the highest response when shown a single picture; when the associate was used as a cue, this cell responded only weakly—but then it responded vigorously during the delay period. Indeed, it actually increased its activity over the course of the delay, "anticipating" the choices; such activity may underlie the kind of priming that can generate mental images. In addition, a similar but weaker response occurred for the associate of the "second-best cue-optimal picture." Eleven of the 91 neurons produced more picture-selective activation during the interstimulus interval than they did when cued. These findings, then, indicate that the anterior portions of the inferior temporal lobe are involved in accessing visual memories.

However, it is important to note that data have been reported that purportedly challenge the idea that memories are stored in IT (e.g., see Dean 1976).[29] For example, E. A. Gaffan, S. Harrison, and D. Gaffan (1986) observed that the strongest available evidence for the role of IT in visual memory came from studies of concurrent learning, where several discriminations must be learned at the same time. IT lesions greatly impair performance in this task, even if it was mastered prior to the lesion. In contrast, IT lesions do not appear to disrupt visual memory when discriminations are learned consecutively (see Mishkin 1972). E. A. Gaffan, S. Harrison, and D. Gaffan (1986) found that monkeys with IT lesions could learn concurrent discriminations if given enough practice, which raised the issue of whether IT in fact stores visual memories. However, they noted that monkeys with lesions in IT appeared to use a restricted set of visual features to make the discriminations (as was noted earlier by others such as Butter and Gekoski, 1966, and Iversen and Weiskrantz 1967); this may be a hint as to what was going on in this task.

In my view, E. A. Gaffan, S. Harrison, and D. Gaffan's results do not bear on the issue of whether IT is a visual memory structure; rather, they speak to Mishkin, Malamut, and Bachevalier's (1984) distinction between a "habit" system and a "cognitive" system. The cognitive system involves internal representations that can be accessed in multiple contexts, whereas the habit system involves representations that are accessed only by specific stimuli and in turn produce specific responses. The habit system relies on anatomical connections that run from prestriate cortex (e.g., Saint-Cyr, Ungerleider, and Desimone 1990), which presumably implements the preprocessing subsystem I discussed earlier, to the neostriatum, and from there to motor cortices (via the thalamus; see Mishkin and Appenzeller 1987). Provided that this pathway is intact, monkeys with lesions to IT can learn concurrent discriminations— but they cannot learn a delayed nonmatching-to-sample task (Malamut, Saunders, and Mishkin 1984). The delayed nonmatching-to-sample task requires remembering a previously seen sample and then selecting the novel object from a pair that also includes that sample; hence, this task requires visual memory. In contrast, if the concurrent discrimination task is administered at a rate of only one trial every 24 hours (and so it presumably is difficult to encode "cognitive" memory representations of the objects), then damage to the tail of the caudate (part of the neostriatum, which is central to the habit system) disrupts performance. Such lesions do not disrupt performance of the delayed nonmatching-to-sample task (Wang, Aigner, and Mishkin 1990).

In short, the stimulus-response associations established by this "habit" system probably can be used to perform the discrimination tasks used by E. A. Gaffan, S. Harrison, and D. Gaffan (1986) because the same object was always the target in any given pair. In fact, after IT was removed, the animals persisted in early preferences for one stimulus in a pair, whereas normal monkeys did not have such a bias. In addition, Iwai (1985) reports findings that suggest that monkeys with IT lesions make extensive use of size and flux cues when learning discriminations, whereas normal animals do not. These cues might be registered by the spared dorsal system (see Livingstone and Hubel 1988), which could underlie the animal's successful performance after many trials. These alternative strategies apparently are not as effective as the normal one, as witnessed by less effective performance even after animals with IT lesions are extensively retrained (e.g., Laursen 1982).[30]

In addition, Heywood and Cowey (1992) report that lesioning the superior temporal sulcus of monkeys, an area rich in neurons that respond to faces, in some cases produces no deficit or only a "mild" deficit in the ability to recognize faces; when such deficits were present for faces, they also were present when the animals had to discriminate forms and colors. Although a discussion of processing underlying face recognition per se would lead us too far afield, these particular findings might challenge the claim that IT is a visual memory, and hence are worth considering in some detail. Heywood and Cowey's tasks and results are as follows:

1. The animals were shown a sample alphanumeric stimulus, and were trained to select it from a set of nine stimuli that differed in shape and color; the lesioned animals were like control subjects if the same target stimulus was used from trial to trial and the distractors were varied or if the target was varied and the distractors remained the same. In contrast, when novel stimuli were used and the target and distractors were changed from trial to trial, the lesioned animals did have a significant deficit (this technique would prevent them from learning cue-based strategies, as note above).

2. The animals were shown a sample stimulus, and then two more stimuli appeared along with it, one to either side. The animals were to touch the stimulus that was different from the central one. Both faces and objects were used in this task (but only one type of stimuli were used within a block of trials). The STS-lesioned animals were "mildly, but not significantly impaired." The "operated animals were impaired during the early postoperative sessions, but reached a normal level of performance, i.e., they would have shown a significant group difference if errors to criterion had been measured. However, this was true for both objects and faces" (p. 34). The experimenters then introduced a novel series of faces, with the faces portrayed from different

points of view. The animals had to match the same face across different perspectives; the lesioned animals and control animals performed comparably.

3. The animals saw a sample stimulus, which was removed and then presented along with a novel stimulus; the animals had to select the new stimulus (this was a standard "delayed-nonmatching-to-sample" task). The lesioned and control animals performed comparably. The same stimuli used in the first and second tasks were also used here; it is of interest that the lesioned monkeys performed *more poorly* with these familiar stimuli than with a novel set—which may suggest that they had encoded cues to make the prior decisions that were no longer useful. The authors administered the novel stimuli for 1,000 trials of the second task postoperatively prior to this task, but this still may have been less experience than the animals had with the "familiar" stimuli preoperatively. Heywood and Cowey note, "Overall, STS animals performed more poorly than unoperated controls but not significantly so" (p. 34). Moreover, "When a new set of faces from E. K. Warrington's Face Recognition Test were used and animals were tested to a criterion of 90% correct, STS animals were significantly impaired" (p. 34). Heywood and Cowey conclude, "The overall results indicate a mild impairment in form discrimination following STS lesions which is not specific to faces" (p. 34).

4. Monkeys were shown pairs of faces, one familiar and one novel; the animals were to select the novel face. Sixteen faces of each type were used until the animals reached a criterion level of performance. The lesioned animals performed as well as the control animals.

5. Each of four faces was associated with a specific level of reward: 1, 2, 3, or 4 peanuts. The animal then was shown pairs of faces, and was to choose the one previously associated with the larger reward. Testing continued until a criterion level of performance was reached; only two animals in each group could learn this task, but these lesioned and control animals performed comparably.

6. The animals were given pairs of faces, with the same faces always appearing in the same pair, and chose the one that was consistently associated with a reward (this was a "concurrent learning" paradigm). Four faces were used, each of which appeared in 3 conditions—a front, left profile, and right profile view. Not surprisingly, given the discussion about the possible role of the habit system in such tasks (see above), the lesioned animals performed as well as the control animals.

7. Finally, the animals were shown pairs of faces, one with the eyes looking ahead and one with the eyes averted; the animals were to choose the face with the eyes averted. The STS lesioned animals were highly impaired at this task, compared to the control animals.

On the basis of this set of results, Heywood and Cowey suggest that STS is not involved in recognition, but rather in "the perception of facial expression and bearing." However, their conclusions are not entirely warranted. Not only could the habit system contribute to performance in tasks in which the animals could learn specific cues to identify targets, but also the lesions did not disrupt all of the regions of IT that contain face cells; hence, other areas might compensate for the damaged region. E. T. Rolls, in a commentary directly following Heywood and Cowey's article, notes that there are large numbers of neurons that respond to faces in inferior temporal areas such as TE2 and TE3, and hence a deficit in face perception might not be expected unless those areas were also lesioned. Moreover, at most, only about 20% of the neurons in STS are selective for faces (e.g., Baylis, Rolls, and Leonard 1987); the other 80% are presumably sensitive to other types of stimuli. Hence, we should expect deficits for other types of stimuli when faces are disrupted following lesions of this area (see also Hasselmo, Rolls, and Baylis 1989).

Finally, although IT is a viable candidate for storing visual memories, it is not the only such candidate. I must note that the ventral-medial portion of the frontal lobe may also play a role in storing visual memories. Bachevalier and Mishkin (1986) showed that ablation of this area impairs visual recognition in monkeys. However, this finding may not address the locus of storage; Goldman-Rakic (1987) has found that dorsolateral prefrontal cortex is involved in a visual "working memory" that may be useful in some types of visual recognition, and it is possible that Bachevalier and Mishkin's lesions indirectly affected this area (see chapter 2). Nevertheless, it is possible that IT plays a key role in encoding visual representations and preparing them to be stored elsewhere, but that the visual memories are not actually stored in IT. It is also possible that different aspects of visual memory are stored in the different loci. The idea that memories are stored in the subsystems that encode them is consistent with the hypothesis that IT stores visual memories, and the sum of the data taken together strongly suggest that IT plays a critical role in matching visual input to visual memories.

However, we must always be cautious about generalizing from the monkey findings to human beings. Indeed, Haxby et al. (1991) used PET to study picture processing in humans. They asked their subjects to observe a face, and then to match it to two other faces. The faces were similar, and the lighting was changed in the photographs—making this a very challenging task. Relative to a baseline (three empty squares), Haxby et al. found selective activation in the occipital-temporal region, and none in the inferior temporal lobe proper. However, the task used by Haxby et al. involved comparison, and did not necessarily involve recognition; moreover, it involved faces, which may be special kinds of stimuli (e.g., see Young and Ellis 1989). Thus, we must be cautious here as well.

Indeed, Sergent, Ohta, and MacDonald (1992) obtained different results when subjects identified objects and faces. In one baseline condition, the subjects viewed sine-wave gratings, and decided whether they were horizontal or vertical. These patterns of blood flow were subtracted from those engendered in another task, in which the subjects judged whether pictures depicted living or nonliving objects. The researchers found selective activation for object identification in the following regions of the left-hemisphere:

inferior temporal gyrus, fusiform gyrus, middle temporal gyrus, middle occipital gyrus, superior parietal lobe, and supramarginal gyrus; they also found selective activation of the right supramarginal gyrus and the gyrus rectus. In addition, Sergent, Ohta, and MacDonald asked subjects to decide whether a face was a man or a woman, and used this as a baseline for another condition in which the subjects decided whether a face was an actor. The face identification task activated several areas that were not activated in the object identification task (the medial anterior temporal gyrus and temporal pole bilaterally, the right parahippocampal gyrus, right fusiform gyrus, and the right lingual gyrus); indeed, only the left fusiform, left middle temporal, and gyrus rectus were activated in both face identification and object identification.

Additional relevant findings were reported by Sergent, Zuck, Lévesque, and MacDonald (1992), who tested subjects in four conditions: a passive fixation point; viewing pictures of common objects and deciding whether they were living or nonliving; viewing uppercase letters and deciding whether they faced normally or were mirror-reversed (which they called a "letter-spatial" task); and viewing the same letters, but deciding whether they rhyme with "ee." The relevant results for present purposes focus on the object-categorization task. Compared to the fixation point, the object-categorization task activated left areas 17 and 18, left and right area 19, the left and right fusiform gyrus, and the left cerebellum (the cerebellum may have been activated because the control task did not include a motor component). Comparing the results to the other tasks, Sergent et al. also found that the left area 18 and the left and right fusiform gyrus were activated in the object-categorization task and not the others. They also found significantly more activation during the object-categorization task in the left lingual gyrus and in the left fusiform gyrus. In addition, when the activation from the letter-spatial task was subtracted, there was greater activation in the left middle temporal gyrus.

Corbetta et al. (1990) also found activation of the left middle temporal gyrus in a shape recognition task (to be described in detail in the following chapter); similarly, in a PET study designed to test key aspects of the present theory, which will be described in chapter 8, my colleagues and I found selective activation in the middle temporal gyrus and fusiform gyrus when subjects identified pictures. Thus, the middle temporal and fusiform gyri are good candidates for anatomical regions that implement the pattern activation subsystem in humans.[31] Finally, Sergent, Ohta, and MacDonald's finding that the gyrus rectus, in the orbital frontal region, was activated in both object and face identification is also intriguing, given Bachevalier and Mishkin's (1986) finding noted above; it is possible that this region also plays a role in storing visual memories.

All of these conjectures are consistent with results recently described by Biederman et al. (1992). Biederman et al. administered their standard name-priming task to patients who were missing the anterior potion of one temporal lobe. The stimuli were presented in the left or right visual field, directly to either the damaged or to the intact hemisphere. The same amount of priming occurred in this task when stimuli were presented initially to the damaged hemisphere as when they were presented initially to the intact hemisphere. Similarly, in another task the subjects saw pairs of pictures presented sequentially and determined whether they were the same or different. Again, there were no effects of which hemisphere received the input initially. Unless callosal transfer was completely efficient, these data suggest that visual memories are not stored or matched in the anterior portions of the temporal lobes, which is consistent with the more posterior activation observed in the PET studies summarized above (see also Milner 1967).

Summary: Identifying Objects from Different Vantage Points

Three mechanisms allow us to recognize objects from different vantage points. First, nonaccidental and signal properties are extracted from an input image; the nonaccidental properties are particularly useful because the same ones tend to be evident from multiple points of view. Second, these properties and their relative positions are matched to stored visual memories via the viewpoint consistency constraint. An object representation is activated to the extent that input is consistent with seeing that object from a single point of view. The most strongly activated representation inhibits the others. Third, as the input is matched, the representation of the best-matching object sends feedback to the visual buffer. The mapping function from this representation to the visual buffer is adjusted until the feedback can augment the input pattern as well as possible. This adjustment process alters the size, location, and orientation of the region covered by the imagery feedback. If it fails to match, another mental image is generated based on a close competitor. (If this fails to correspond to the input image, more drastic steps are taken, as is discussed in the following chapter.) Once the object is recognized, a pattern code is sent to associative memory, where it activates the appropriate representations and the object is identified; in the following chapter we shall consider this phase of the identification process in more detail.

IMAGERY AND PERCEPTION

The hypotheses I have developed in this chapter suggest that imagery plays an essential role in normal perception. The central idea is that when the input to the pattern activation subsystem activates a representation sufficiently strongly, a representation of the most likely candidate is activated and imagery feedback is sent to the visual buffer. The mapping function of this feedback is adjusted to maximally augment the input image. According to the present theory, mental images are produced when a compressed image representation is activated so strongly that the feedback it provides is strong enough to impose a configuration of activity in the visual buffer, rather than simply augmenting an input image that is already present. In this section I consider these proposals in enough detail to argue that they are worth building upon in later chapters.

Image Activation

I hypothesize that mental images arise when representations in the pattern activation subsystem are activated and impose a configuration of activity in the visual buffer (for similar ideas, see Mumford, 1993). This configuration of activity in the visual buffer is the image proper. The information in the pattern activation subsystem corresponds to the "literal files" of Kosslyn (1980), which are part of the *deep representation* used to generate images (I will flesh out the remaining parts of the deep representation in the following chapter). And the pattern in the visual buffer is the *surface representation*.

This theory rests on the idea that efferent connections allow higher-level areas to impose a state on lower-level areas. It would easy to gloss over some potential problems with this idea, but it is better to air them and consider their implications. One problem with this idea is that the pattern of efferent connections do not simply mirror the corresponding pattern of connections made by the afferent (input) pathways (Rockland and Virga 1989). Rather, the efferent connections are more diffuse than the afferent ones. For example, Zeki and Shipp (1988) note that areas MT (V5, in their parlance) and V4 both project back to V2, with MT projecting back primarily to the "thick stripes," which are the primary source of its input, but also projecting back to the "thin stripes" and "interstripes" (these stripes are identified by specific types of staining, and neurons in the different types of stripes have been shown to have different properties; see Livingstone and Hubel 1988). Similarly, although area V4 projects back primarily to the thin stripes and interstripes, it also sends efferent fibers to the thick stripes.[32] Rockland and Virga (1989) point out that such divergence could arise because of processing in the higher-order area (V2, in their study), perhaps through relatively long-range lateral connections (see also Rockland in press). If so, then each higher-level neuron might receive input from multiple lower-level neurons, and the diffuse feedback projections would in fact be point-to-point to these input neurons. But even here, such diffuse efferent connections suggest that if information is stored in high-level visual areas, reconstructing the original image will not be a trivial computation.

Now to turn a sow's ear into a silk purse. This problem may actually suggest a mechanism whereby images are created: Perhaps the back projections operate using coarse coding, rather than a 1:1 mapping (see Hinton, McClelland, and Rumelhart 1986). That is, rather than attempt to reconstruct the precise point-for-point pattern of activation by storing each individual point value, the high-level visual areas may store relative strengths of inputs from larger regions. When these representations are activated, they would project back to overlapping regions in the visual buffer. And the degree of overlap would determine the value of each specific point, producing a higher-resolution spatial representation. Such coarse coding schemes are very efficient; for example, the relative outputs of the three types of cones in the retina code a huge number of colors.[33]

In addition, this scheme offers hope of solving another problem, namely, how is a spatial representation reconstructed from a nonspatial one? Area IT is not organized into precise topographic maps (although some parts have a hint of a loose topographic organization; see Van Essen et al. 1990). Indeed, the relevant parts of IT appear to have a columnar organization (see Fujita et al. 1992), and shapes are represented as feature vectors defined over these columns. How can such representations engender a topographic pattern upstream? One answer: coarse coding.

Images could also be constructed using something like the sophisticated computational scheme recently described by Stucki and Pollack (1992), who proposed a fractal-based reconstructive memory mechanism for image activation. Stucki and Pollack's system stores visual memories as a small set of linear functions (contractive affine transforms) over a metric space. The image itself is reconstructed via an attractor, and the trajectory of a single point through the abstract space can specify the imaged pattern. Stucki and Pollack describe a neural network architecture that performs these computations. One of the interesting aspects of their system is that the mapping function can easily alter the location, orientation, and size of the image. Indeed, one image can be continuously transformed into another simply by linear extrapolation between their underlying representations.

Another potential problem arises if the connections between areas are merely reciprocal. If so, then to generate an image, the system would need to chain through all of the areas that lead up to the areas that store visual information. Not only does such a scheme seem awkward, it also appears to make the inverse mapping problem more difficult (offering even more opportunities for the topography to become obscured). Thus it is of interest that Rockland, Saleem, and Tanaka (1992) report that feedback connections from high-level visual areas TEO and V4 are widely distributed to various earlier areas; indeed, Douglas and Rockland (1992) report direct connections from TE (at the anterior end of IT) to V1! There appear to be direct cortico-cortical connections from the higher-level areas to the lower-level ones, which would facilitate the task of forming a mental image. These connections apparently are not as dense as the reciprocal ones (and are relatively diffuse), however, and hence may play an ancillary role (perhaps serving as "attractors" in the visual buffer, causing the proper pattern of activation to reach equilibrium).

In addition, imagery may hinge on information that is sent via the thalamus. Virtually every visual area is connected via the thalamus (which is a subcortical structure that has often been likened to a relay station; e.g., for a review, see Mumford 1991). The cortical areas project long axons from the deep layers to the thalamus, and some of the input coming back from the thalamus terminates in layer 4 of cortex, the same layer that input from other cortical areas enters. This sort of connection must be contrasted with the efferent feedback cortico-cortico connections—which rarely if ever terminate in layer 4 (Rockland and Pandya 1979). Rather, the efferent pathways terminate in the superficial or deep layers of cortex. This distinction between the two kinds of connections may suggest that two sorts of feedback exist, one that modulates processing (via the thalamus) and one that supplements it (via the cortico-cortico connections; cf. Mumford 1991, 1992). Both sorts of information may be used during image generation. In fact, as will be discussed in chapter 9, my colleagues and I have found that the thalamus is activated during some types of imagery.

According to the present proposal, imagery is a natural by-product of "cooperative computation" in systems in cascade (McClelland 1979). That is, each area does not wait to finish processing an input before producing an output. Rather, the neurons are active as soon as input arrives, and produce output immediately. Thus, partial mappings may be sent to other areas, like water falling in cascades. Higher-level areas in turn project information backward to facilitate lower-level processing; the areas "cooperate." This mechanism presumably underlies one kind of priming, which facilitates the speed of recognizing a picture. Such priming would occur when high-level areas provide input to lower-level ones that makes them especially sensitive to specific types of input. Indeed, Fuster (1990) found that neurons in IT responded more vigorously if they were tuned to a color that an animal was seeking in a target. Similarly, Spitzer, Desimone, and Moran (1988) found that color-tuned neurons in area V4 respond more vigorously when a color discrimination is more difficult, and orientation-tuned neurons in this area respond more vigorously when an orientation discrimination is more difficult. As noted earlier, the animals' abilities to discriminate actually improved in the conditions when the neurons responded more vigorously, which may imply that the sampling rate was increased to promote more precise encoding. Consistent with these results, Sanocki (1991) found that visual primes actually enhanced his human subjects' ability to discriminate between similarly shaped targets and foils—even though the primes contained only properties that were shared by both shapes. The priming apparently increased the sensitivity of the matching process.[34]

In my view, imagery arises following a great amount of priming, so much that lower-level areas are forced into a new state as a consequence of the information flowing into them from higher-level areas, even with no appropriate bottom-up input. Thus, although priming may increase the sensitivity of matching in the pattern activation subsystem, it may also bias certain kinds of judgments—if imagery lowers the thresholds of neurons in the visual buffer to the point where they fire spontaneously. And in fact, Farah (1989b) found that imagery lowers one's criterion (beta, in signal-detection parlance) for detecting signals within the boundaries of an imaged shape. In chapter 9, I will describe direct tests of the claim that the mechanisms responsible for modality-specific priming also underlie image generation.

In addition, if visual representations are organized as seen from a particular point of view, then people should visualize objects seen from a familiar point of view more easily than objects seen from other points of view. In fact, Steven Shwartz and I examined this issue many years ago and found that people could not visualize objects immediately as if they were seen at novel orientations; rather, they visualized the objects as they had initially seen them, and then incrementally rotated them to the target orientation. Pinker, Stromswold, and Beck (1984) also found this.

Image Inspection

According to the present theory, imagery feedback augments input images, thereby facilitating encoding. This process typically operates "on line," operating as input activates stored representations. However, in some situations the imagery process can be initiated prior to the input; in such cases, it may allow a complex pattern to be recognized very quickly. Nielsen and Smith (1973) provide good evidence that mental images can be used in this way. They asked subjects to visualize schematic faces that contained five features; on each trial, the subjects encoded a face, visualized it, and then decided whether a new face was the same or different. One group of subjects retained the image for 1 second, and another group retained the image for 10 seconds. Nielsen and Smith specified that either three, four, or all five facial features were relevant for making the same-different decision. Another group of subjects read descriptions of faces at the outset, rather than encoding pictures. Subjects who used imagery could evaluate "same" faces equally easily, regardless of how many features had to be inspected. In contrast, subjects who used descriptions required more time as more features were included. In addition, the subjects in the imagery group required more time in general for the longer delay, which is not surprising given that the image would have to be refreshed prior to being matched to the input. In contrast, the group receiving descriptions actually required less time with the longer delay, and showed a smaller effect of increased numbers of features with the longer delay; clearly, these subjects were somehow organizing the features during the delay—perhaps by visualizing the face. Kosslyn (1980, pp. 265–268) presents a more detailed description of the results, and accounts for the details; these accounts are subsumed neatly by the version of the theory developed in this book (see chapter 11).

In addition, I have claimed that people typically encode viewer-centered coordinates in perception; if so, then we should expect people typically to use viewer-centered coordinates in imagery. It is clear that images depict objects as seen from a single point of view. If this were not true, mental rotation would not be necessary. In fact, one of the reasons Shepard and Metzler's (1971) original mental rotation experiment had such a large impact was that the then-current approaches to visual representation emphasized object-centered representations, and the rotation results were clearly not predicted by such approaches. Additional support for the claim that imagery utilizes viewer-centered coordinates has been provided by Franklin and Tversky (1990). The subjects in these experiments had to indicate which object was in a specific location or had to indicate the location of a specific object. When the subjects were explicitly asked to use imagery (experiment 3), Franklin and Tversky found that not all directions from the viewer were equally accessible. Rather, the subjects could evaluate imaged objects that were above and below them as easily as those that were in front of them, but found it more difficult to evaluate objects imaged behind them or to their sides. Similar results were obtained even when imagery was not explicitly required, except that the salience of objects in front of the subjects decreased. In other experiments, Franklin and Tversky asked the subjects to imagine themselves reclining, which altered the results (although not always entirely in the expected ways); for present purposes, the critical finding was that not all directions relative to the body are equally accessible in an image: imagined scenes are not organized using object-centered coordinates. Similarly, Hintzman, O'Dell, and Arndt (1981) found that subjects could evaluate objects imaged to be in front of them faster than those behind them, but in their task the subjects had the most difficulty with objects to one side or the other.

One important implication of these findings is that subjects do not image themselves in the center of a three-dimensional scene. If they did, then they should have been able to "turn" to "see" objects to the side more easily than objects behind them. If images are configurations of activity in the visual buffer, as I have claimed, then people will be able to visualize only a limited region (at most about 40° of visual angle with good resolution; see Kosslyn 1978), and must generate new images when they shift perspective. In this case, if the shift is large enough, the subjects presumably perform a *blink scan* (Kosslyn 1980): they delete the initial image and form a new image of the sought material. And depending on how the material is stored in long-term memory, it will be more or less easily visualized. In the following chapter I argue that descriptions of spatial relations are used in perception and in imagery; the representations of left and right may be very similar in such descriptions, making it relatively difficult to access them and hence to form images in those relative locations.

Image Maintenance

I earlier suggested that the "fast-fade" characteristic of the visual buffer arises from properties of the neural substrate. There may be a second reason for this characteristic. I assume that mental images arise because stored visual memory representations are activated, and these same representations are used during object recognition. This makes sense because the representations that produce images must be based on perceptual encodings; how else could they come to be stored? (Even an image of a novel scene or object must be based on previously viewed objects.) And I have argued that these representations are not stored solely for their use in imagery, but also play a vital role in object recognition. If so, then there could be a logjam in the pattern activation subsystem if representations activated during imagery were still fully activated when information flowed in from the visual buffer. This is a problem because the winner-take-all mechanism I suggest operates whenever a representation is activated in the pattern activation subsystem—whether during imagery or perception. Hence, one could not recognize an object if an image of a different object were being generated at the same time (particularly if the stimulus is only briefly seen and the input is somewhat degraded, and thus the input will not be "stronger" than the imagery-induced activation). In fact, as discussed in chapter 3, imagery can interfere with like-modality perception.

Thus, images may fade quickly because the compressed image representations can only be activated very briefly at any one time, which would free up the pattern activation subsystem so that a new representation could be activated (bottom-up by an input image or by a mental image that was just being generated). Indeed, I have heard many people describe their images as being "like a flashed picture."

These reflections suggest that we are mistaken in viewing the capacity limits of imagery as unfortunate. Although they impose severe limitations on our ability to use imagery, they may in fact be critically important for our being able to use imagery at all.

Image Transformations

A critical aspect of Lowe's model is that a "mental" image is adjusted to make the best possible match to an input image. Although I reject the strong view that images serve as templates during recognition, I have argued that the mapping function from a stored representation to the visual buffer can be adjusted so that the imagery feedback can cover different sizes, locations, and orientations in the visual buffer. This same process can also adjust these aspects of mental images. Indeed, the ability to adjust the size, location, and even shape of an imaged object lies at the heart of many of the functions of imagery. We often use imagery as a kind of mental simulation, "looking with the mind's eye" to anticipate the possible consequences of some action or event. But how does such processing proceed? In chapter 10 I shall posit a subsystem that alters the contents of images in the visual buffer, but I defer further discussion of this aspect of the theory until we consider in detail how image transformations arise.

CONCLUSIONS

In this chapter I broke the ventral system into two finer-grained subsystems. The preprocessing subsystem extracts nonaccidental properties and signal properties (some of which were learned when they turned out, via experience, to be useful for discriminating among objects). These properties are heavily weighted in the pattern activation subsystem. The pattern activation subsystem stores compressed images that are accessed by sets of nonaccidental and signal properties. Such bottom-up recognition is achieved via a process of constraint satisfaction: the representation of the object whose properties best match those in the input pattern is most strongly activated and hence most strongly inhibits the other representations. The matching process respects the viewpoint consistency constraint; to be activated, a representation must be consistent with seeing the input properties from a single point of view. If the representation that is most activated is sufficiently strongly activated, it produces an output—which specifies a code for that particular object and indicates how well the input matched the stored representation.

However, as bottom-up processing proceeds, a second phase of processing commences. When the input has activated one representation strongly enough to inhibit the others, that representation sends feedback to the visual buffer; if appropriate, this feedback augments the input image, filling it out so that it is encoded more quickly. The mapping function from the representation to the visual buffer is adjusted until the feedback best completes the input image. This process adjusts the mapping function by altering the size, location, and orientation of the region it covers in the visual buffer. If the feedback does complete the input image, this is an indication that the object has been recognized; if it does not, the activated representation is inhibited, and the now-most-activated representation produces imagery feedback and the process is repeated.

According to this theory, then, the processes that underlie mental imagery play a major role in normal perception. Images are generated using the efferent connections among visual areas, perhaps exploiting "coarse coding" to impose patterns of activation in the visual buffer. In addition, visual mental images are represented in viewer-centered coordinates, as are most representations in the pattern activation subsystem. And the fast-fading properties of imagery in part may be a necessary consequence of ensuring that recognizing an object or activating a mental image does not block the recognition process by inhibiting representations in the pattern activation subsystem.

However, I have glossed over an important aspect of processing: What happens if an initial match is not good enough, even following imagery feedback? In some circumstances one will have to use additional information to implicate a specific object. In the following chapter we consider such additional types of information that can be used in recognition and identification. These mechanisms also play a vital role when images are built up from separately stored representations, as occurs when one visualizes a novel scene.

6 Identifying Objects in Degraded Images

In ordinary viewing conditions, the perceptual input is rarely ideal. In some situations, an object is degraded overall, so that it cannot be seen clearly (e.g., if seen at a distance on a foggy day); in other situations, an object is partially occluded, so that only some portions are visible. Such difficulties are typically overcome by encoding nonaccidental and signal properties and matching them (via a constraint satisfaction process) to stored representations, as discussed in the previous chapter. The power of such a process is enhanced if the viewpoint consistency constraint is respected, which greatly reduces the number of possible alternative interpretations.

A key part of this solution to the problem of degraded input follows from my assumptions about the visual buffer. As Marr (1982) pointed out, different representations make different information explicit and accessible. The spatial organization of the visual buffer is useful because it makes geometric properties of the input readily accessible, including location and shape properties. Depictive representations in the visual buffer can be easily used to determine which disconnected portions of an occluded contour are continuous, and allow the preprocessing subsystem to recover nonaccidental properties. But if enough distinguishing properties (nonaccidental and signal) cannot be recovered by the preprocessing subsystem, the constraint satisfaction process in the pattern activation subsystem will fail.

When an object cannot be identified on the basis of information about shape, other types of information will play a critical role. The logic of constraint satisfaction dictates that, as a general rule, the more relevant information the better. Thus, my strategy for investigating how this problem is solved is to look for sources of additional information. What other kinds of information does the visual system extract? We shall consider four types of information: motion, parts, spatial properties, and shapes of specific exemplars.

MOTION

Motion plays a critical role in two distinct types of processes. First, it helps to delineate an object itself, providing another cue as to the location of edges and regions. The Gestalt psychologists formulated the "law of common fate," which states that stimuli that move in the same way are grouped into the same perceptual unit. Thus, even if the input image is so degraded that the contours are not visible when the object is motionless, they may become immediately apparent as soon as the object moves. Johansson (1950, 1973, 1975) probably provided the most compelling demonstration of this phenomenon by attaching lights to people's joints and observing them in the dark. When the people were motionless, it was not clear how the segments were organized; but as soon as they moved, it was obvious which lights belonged to the same segment. Indeed, Ullman (1979) and others have shown that motion alone can delineate the three-dimensional structure of an object.

Second, motion cues can be used to recognize an object. Indeed, in his experiments in which lights were attached to people's joints, Johansson found that observers could use motion cues to classify a figure as a man or woman. Moreover, Cutting and Kozlowski (1977; and also Cutting and Proffitt 1981) showed that people can use such motion cues to identify specific individuals. Cutting (1978) showed that observers can use as few as six points of light to determine whether a person is carrying a light or heavy load. It is clear that many objects have distinctive patterns of motion, such as a falling leaf, a pouncing cat, and a swooping bat (see also Cutting 1982).

Such observations suggest that motion information is entered into the pattern activation subsystem along with the output from the preprocessing subsystem. Such motion cues can allow us to recognize objects in even highly degraded images, provided that their patterns of motion can be discerned and are distinctive. Thus, I am led to infer that the pattern activation subsystem does not simply store static images but also stores information about motion.

Motion Relations Encoding Subsystem

My reasoning thus far suggests that motion information is extracted from the input and has the same status for recognition as nonaccidental and signal properties. The computations necessary to specify motion vectors are logically distinct from those discussed so far. Indeed, Krumhansl (1984) provided evidence that motion and form information are encoded by separate systems. She showed subjects rotating or stationary patterns (dots arranged into a rectangle or ellipse), which were sometimes accompanied by a stationary or rotating field of random dots. A stationary mask always followed the display. Krumhansl asked the subjects to report both the form and its direction of motion. She found that performance on the two measures was independent, which suggests that the preprocessing subsystem is not used to encode both sorts of information. Consistent with this observation, Albright (1992) found that many directionally selective neurons in area MT respond the same way independently of the form of the particular shape that is moving.

Thus, I am led to infer a *motion relations encoding subsystem*, which codes distinctive aspects of motion fields and operates in parallel with the preprocessing subsystem. It seems clear that the brain is "wired" to code certain "standard" properties of motion fields, which indicate whether one is moving through a field or an object is moving relative to one (e.g., Andersen 1989;

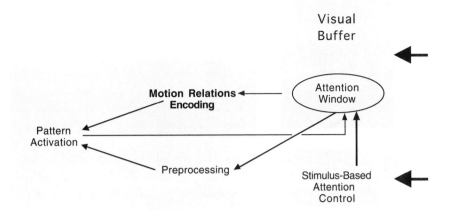

Figure 6.1 The motion relations encoding subsystem illustrated in the context of the subsystems discussed previously.

Boussaoud, Ungerleider, and Desimone 1990; Gross et al. 1984; Nakayama 1985). The Gestalt law of common fate describes the consequences of such processing. In addition, it seems likely that the motion relations encoding subsystem can become tuned via experience. A former gymnast will literally see different things when watching that sport than will someone who has never seen it before; the former gymnast has become adept at noticing specific patterns of movement. Although a novice can be instructed where to look to encode the critical aspects of an event, this effortful, strategic process is quite different than the automatic, effortless encoding of the expert. The tuning process presumably rests on the kind of training that builds novel signal property detectors in the preprocessing subsystem. The motion relations encoding subsystem is illustrated in figure 6.1 in the context of the subsystems discussed in previous chapters.[1]

Anatomical Localization   Neurons in several areas of the brain are tuned to patterns of motion. Some of these neurons are probably involved in registering motion at the level of the visual buffer, others at the level of the motion relations encoding subsystem, and yet others at the level of the pattern activation subsystem. I assume that if a neuron is sensitive to multiple types of input in different modalities, as are some of those in area STS in the monkey, then the neuron is not implementing the motion relations subsystem. Some of those neurons, for example, respond selectively to different patterns of gait (e.g., Gross et al. 1984). Similarly, although neurons in V1 in monkeys are sensitive to the direction of motion (e.g., Dow 1974; Hubel and Wiesel 1968), the neurons also respond to other sources of input (such as edges). V1 is an area that implements the visual buffer.

However, neurons in area MT in the middle superior-posterior temporal lobe and in nearby (more superior) area MST are clearly involved in encoding motion relations per se; these cells are tuned to the direction and rate of motion (Allman et al. 1985). It is likely that neurons in areas MT and MST implement part of the motion relations encoding subsystem (in monkeys) because they are sensitive not simply to isolated movements but rather to specific patterns of motion (such as expansion versus contraction of a field of dots; see Saito et al. 1986; Andersen 1987; Maunsell and Newsome 1987; Movshon et al. 1986; Snowden 1992). In particular, area MT has been shown to play a special role in such processing (Allman and Kaas 1971; Dubner and Zeki 1971; Maunsell and Newsome 1987; Zeki 1978). Neurons in this area are tuned to stimuli that move in a specific direction and may be tuned to other properties of motion, such as speed (Allman, Miezin, and McGuinness 1985). These areas may also partly implement subsystems that are used in motor control (recall the assumption of weak modularity); for example, some neurons in MT provide information that is used to guide smooth-pursuit eye movements during visual tracking (e.g., Newsome 1985).

PET-scanning experiments by Zeki et al. (1991) have shown that a region of the human brain, near the occipital-parietal-temporal junction, is activated when one tracks moving stimuli. However, Corbetta et al. (1990) found that a slightly different region was activated by motion in a different task, but this region was also on the lateral, posterior surface of the brain.[2] Moreover, when patients have brain damage in this area, they may have deficits in motion perception (e.g., Zihl, Von Cramon, and Mai 1983; Vaina 1989). Vaina (1989) found that the right parietal lobe, and not the temporal lobe, is critical for motion encoding (but keep in mind the possibility of indirect effects of lesions); patients with left-hemisphere damage did not display marked deficits in motion encoding (see also De Renzi 1982).

Turning back to monkeys, where the details of the neuroanatomy and neurophysiology are clearer (and, recall that the monkey visual system appears to be very similar to the human visual system), it is of interest to note that area MT and area V4 are not connected with afferent or efferent fibers; their interconnections are between corresponding layers. In addition, Baizer, Ungerleider, and Desimone (1991) found area V4 to be one of the only two areas that receive strong projections from both the ventral and dorsal streams (the other was the anterior part of the superior temporal sulcus). Neurons in area V4 are tuned to color and orientation (see Nakayama 1985; Zeki 1983); this retinotopically mapped area probably plays a role in figure-ground segregation. If so, then it is no accident that motion information feeds directly into area V4, and that this area feeds directly into an area (MT) that processes motion information. Common fate no doubt interacts with other stimulus properties when figure is segregated from ground.

In addition to providing input to V4, area MT also sends information to the dorsal system, which makes sense because motion indicates location. Indeed, without registering motion, it would be very difficult to update changes in locations. Thus, the motion relations encoding subsystem is a good example of one form of weak modularity; although it plays a critical role in encoding object properties, it also plays a role in encoding spatial properties. I include the motion relations encoding subsystem in the ventral system because of its role in object recognition, but an argument could be made that it belongs in the dorsal system.

PARTS AND WHOLES

In some situations, we recognize some of an object's parts or its distinctive characteristics (e.g., surface texture) even though we cannot recognize an entire object. And we use this information to help us infer the identity of the object. However, although we talk easily of objects and parts, the line between them is not clear. Is a face an object or a part? In some sense, it is both. Furthermore, what about an eye? As Marr (1982) argued, most shapes can be hierarchically decomposed; parts themselves have parts. For example, a person has arms, legs, a head, and so on; the arm has an upper arm, forearm, and hand; the hand has four fingers and a thumb; the thumb has two joints and a nail. There is no one level of the "part" and another of the "object." Depending on what the attention window is focused on, different patterns will be matched to stored representations.

In most situations, any given input will match more than one stored pattern, if only because of the hierarchical structure of objects. A hand, for example, matches not only a hand but also fingers, fingernails, and so on. Given that the output should specify a single pattern, there must be a mechanism for selecting among the candidates. In the previous chapter I suggested that a winner-take-all mechanism selects the best-matching representation; this mechanism presumably operates across different levels of scale. If so, then representations of larger patterns would inhibit representations of smaller ones when one is viewing a larger pattern. Such hierarchical inhibition would not need to be built explicitly into the system. Rather, it would emerge from a matching process in which the best-matching pattern is the one that, in a sense, accounts for the most variance in the input. The larger the stored pattern, the more input properties can be matched at the same time. And the better a represented pattern matches the input, the more strongly it is activated; the more strongly it is activated, the better it inhibits other, less strongly activated representations. (See Hummel and Biederman 1992 for a model that incorporates a related mechanism.)

This proposal is consistent with Navon's (1977) finding of a "global precedence effect." When subjects were asked to view large letters composed of smaller ones (e.g., an S made up of sets of the letter H), they could identify the larger form faster than the smaller ones. In addition, when the responses to the larger and smaller letters were in conflict, there was interference from the identity of the larger letter if the subject was judging the small letter, but not vice versa. However, this global precedence effect is mitigated if the pattern is very large (Kinchla and Wolfe 1979) or distorted (Hoffman 1980). If the pattern is very large, it may not be subsumed entirely by the attention window—and hence the input will not match the stored representation of the larger letter as well as that of the component letters (see Navon and Norman 1983, for evidence that effects of size are caused by eccentricity). Similarly, if the overall letter is distorted, it may not match a representation of the larger letter very well, and so the representation of the smaller component letter will "win."

However, a number of other factors sometimes affect the order in which the global pattern and local parts are encoded (including familiarity, spatial uncertainty, and how long a stimulus is presented; e.g., see Boer and Keuss 1982; Hoffman 1980; Hughes et al. 1984; Kimchi and Palmer 1985; Pomerantz 1983; Ward 1982; for a review, see Kimchi 1992). In addition, Earhard (1990) provides evidence that outer portions of forms are encoded prior to inner portions, but also shows that this effect can be eliminated by presenting the two kinds of targets in separate blocks of trials. The outer portions may be more evident if the attention window is set to subsume the entire shape, whereas the scope-resolution trade-off would require that it be set to a smaller size to encode inner components. It seems clear that people have at least some strategic control over how a stimulus is encoded, which is consistent with the idea that the effect reflects the operation of the attention window (which, as will be discussed, I assume is under strategic control).

Loftus, Nelson, and Kallman (1983) provided a different kind of evidence that people initially encode a global shape and then seek specific details in subsequent encodings. The subjects studied a scene and then selected it from a pair of pictures. On some trials the distractor differed from the studied stimulus by a detail (e.g., the presence of a tape measure versus a pack of cigarettes), whereas on other trials it differed by a more "holistic" property (the scene was photographed from a different angle or was left-right reversed, so the relative locations of the objects and general shape envelope changed; the two methods were used in different experiments). The experimenters varied the amount of time the subjects had to study the original stimuli. At the low end, only 250 ms were allowed, which is about the time necessary to make an eye movement; at the high end, the subjects had 1 or $1\frac{1}{2}$ seconds to study the pictures (in different experiments). Following a brief exposure, the subjects were more accurate when discriminating the scene from the distractors that had different global shapes; this is as expected if they initially encode global shapes. Following a longer exposure, the subjects actually became more accurate with the different-detail distractors. These results are as expected if the subjects initially encoded the global shape, but then encoded representations of parts and characteristics. This inference is consistent with results reported by Loftus and Mackworth (1978), who observed patterns of eye movements when subjects examined pictures and found that later eye movements in a sequence appeared to seek out particularly informative details.

Perceptual Parsing

In order to encode parts, they must somehow be delineated in the input image. Properties of stimuli that allow figure to be separated from ground often will also define parts of an object (if the object is viewed with high enough resolution). In the previous discussion I only vaguely considered how perceptual units are parsed. I noted that nonaccidental and signal properties are registered only after the input image has been organized into at least some perceptual units. One of the interesting features of Lowe's system is that figure-ground segregation need not be accomplished entirely on the basis of bottom-up processing. Rather, imagery feedback could help one to organize the perceptual input. Such processing would be particularly useful when the visual buffer contains a mosaic of projections from different objects that partially overlap, each of which often contains parts, which also partially overlap.

However, such feedback matching cannot be essential for all figure-ground segregation: We can encode novel shapes, which do not have a corresponding image stored in memory. Moreover, how would one encode an image into memory in the first place if one must have a prior image representation to parse the input? Input images apparently can be segregated on the basis of the input per se, even when edges alone cannot parse figure from ground. The parsing process relies on constraint satisfaction, with a variety of weakly constraining information converging on a single interpretation. In this case, different types of information are used together to define an image. For example, regions of homogeneous value (of color, texture, or intensity) can be used in conjunction with information about edges to define perceptual units.

Mumford et al. (1987) provide evidence that figure-ground segregation is achieved by a constraint satisfaction process. We asked subjects to study a set of black, multipoint, angular polygons, and then used each member of the set as a "target" in a series of discrimination trials. During these test trials, the subjects were shown a series of polygons and determined whether each was the target. As illustrated in figure 6.2, these test stimuli were degraded in two ways, either by blurring the transition at the edges, making the ramp from light to dark more or less steep, or by adding noise to the interior and exterior of the figure (by increasing the variability of the pixel values, keeping the mean values of figure and ground constant). We expected the first manipulation to affect processes that delineate edges, and the second to affect processes that delineate regions. Every combination of the two kinds of manipulations was examined, and we observed how quickly and accurately subjects could evaluate these stimuli.

The important finding was that the two manipulations did not affect the response times independently. Instead, the effect of degrading the stimulus one way depended on how much it was also degraded the other way. This result was expected if the system uses both sorts of information, about edges and regions, to segregate figure from ground. Thus, we had evidence that figure-ground segregation proceeds in part via grouping regions and extracting nonaccidental properties. Carpenter, Grossberg, and Mehanian (1989) describe an algorithm that displays the kinds of properties we found in our data.[3]

Such results lead us to expect that many of the same factors that serve to define objects as a whole also define parts. Such bottom-up processing will also parse regions corresponding to parts. Oddly enough, however, there is

Figure 6.2 Stimuli used by Mumford et al. (1987). (Reprinted with permission.)

relatively little evidence that people store distinct parts of objects. Consider, for example, what I previously took to be good evidence for such processing, results reported by Reed and Johnsen (1975). They asked subjects to study patterns, such as a Star of David, and later asked them to decide whether fragments corresponded to parts of the previously studied patterns. They found that some fragments were much easier to recognize than others. For example, if shown a Star of David, a triangle was much easier to recognize later than a parallelogram, although both are embedded in the star. The star purportedly was encoded as two overlapping triangles, and hence a triangle presented later matched a stored part; a parallelogram presented later did not match a stored part and had to be compared piecemeal against a number of stored parts—therefore it was much more difficult to evaluate.

The problem with this and similar findings is that "good" parts also correspond to sets of nonaccidental properties that are produced by bottom-up parsing, and "bad" parts require disrupting these nonaccidental properties. The results could simply show that the sets of nonaccidental properties were stored, and patterns that contain those properties are easy to recognize whereas patterns that cut across those properties are not easy to recognize. So, for example, a triangle consists of sets of collinear segments that meet at vertices and define a symmetrical region. All of these nonaccidental properties are present in the star itself. In contrast, the sides of a parallelogram are isolated portions of collinear segments of the star, and hence, nonaccidental properties that are produced by the original parse must be disrupted to find it. Moreover, the segments of the parallelogram are members of different symmetrical regions, and so removing them violates this nonaccidental property. In short, the results can be explained purely in terms of the ease of matching nonaccidental properties of a part to those of the overall pattern. We do not have to assume that the parts are stored as such (see also Bower and Glass 1976; Palmer 1977).

Perhaps the best evidence that parts are actually stored comes from single-cell recordings of neurons in the inferior temporal lobe. Perrett et al. (1985) found cells in STS that not only responded preferentially to eyes but also responded equally vigorously whether the eyes were seen through a slit or as part of a face. These neurons appeared to be sensitive to the parts per se. In contrast, the entire pattern seemed to be registered by other cells, which did not respond to the eyes alone but did respond well when the entire head was viewed. Thus, these data suggest that the pattern is represented at multiple scales; at one scale the parts are represented, whereas at another they are embedded in an overall pattern.

The Role of Parts in Recognition   The hypothesis that parts are stored individually has led many researchers to assume that all shapes can be specified in terms of sets of parts; the idea of an "alphabet of shape" goes back to the beginnings of computer vision (e.g., Selfridge 1959; see chapter 3 of Neisser 1967), and has been a common component of many theories. Most recently, Biederman (1987), Brooks (1981), Koenderink and van Doorn (1982), and Pentland (1986, 1987, 1989) have repopularized the idea. Biederman, for example, posits a set of "geons" (geometrical ions) that represents a range of simple shape variations. Each geon corresponds to an elementary shape (e.g., a brick, a cylinder, a curved cylinder), and all shapes are represented by combinations of geons. Biederman uses Lowe's ideas about nonaccidental properties, and claims that each geon is accessed via a set of such properties. Lowe (1987a, b) himself, on the other hand, sees no need for such representations; in his system the nonaccidental properties access object representations directly.

Biederman and Cooper (1991a) report findings that they have taken as evidence that objects are recognized via recognizing their parts. In one experiment, they showed subjects drawings in which portions of the contour were deleted, like those illustrated in figure 6.3, and asked them to name the objects. The subjects later were shown the original contour-deleted drawings or drawings in which the missing segments were presented but the original ones were

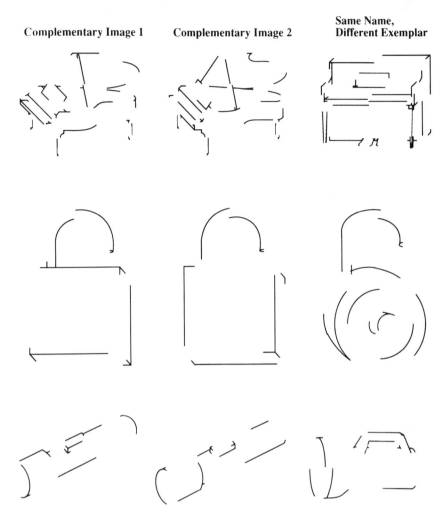

Complementary Image 1   **Complementary Image 2**   **Same Name, Different Exemplar**

Figure 6.3 Stimuli used by Biederman and Cooper (1991a). (Reprinted with permission.)

deleted. The interesting finding was that the facilitation in naming speed on the second presentation was unaffected by switching the segments. In another experiment, Biederman and Cooper asked subjects to name drawings that were missing entire component parts, and then asked the subjects to name the same drawings or ones where the same object was presented but the previously visible parts were removed and the previously missing parts were provided. They found greater facilitation in naming if the same parts were present, which they took as evidence that subjects encoded the parts in the course of recognizing the objects. (Note, however, that even if we take these results at face value, they do not offer evidence for any particular theory of how parts are represented.)

Comparing the results from the two experiments, contour deletion versus part deletion, I note that Biederman and Cooper found no more priming when the drawings had the same components than when they had different partial contours. This is odd if only some parts were recognized when parts were deleted, but all of the parts were recognized when partial contours were presented. These findings taken together are consistent with the claim that the subjects encode a representation of the global shape of the stimulus in all cases. The stimuli have the same global shapes when different portions of the contours are deleted, but have different global shapes when different parts are deleted.

Alternatively, the fact that there was less priming with complementary parts than with the identical parts may indicate that the subjects did in fact encode and recognize parts. However, such a result would not necessarily imply that subjects encode parts as a prerequisite for recognizing objects normally. Perhaps parts are used only if the stimulus is so degraded that the overall shape does not match a stored representation. When there are not enough input properties in the degraded pictures to activate the object-level visual representation in the pattern activation subsystem, representations of parts are activated instead—with the best-matching one "winning." I assume that as soon as one part or object is recognized, the next most strongly activated representation is "released," which allows one to recognize multiple parts or objects in rapid succession (I will review evidence for this claim in the following chapter). In Biederman and Cooper's (1991a) task, the presence of specific parts was sufficient to identify the object. This task is particularly easy because the subjects are given the names of all of the objects in advance, which lowers the thresholds for those objects in associative memory (see below).

Cave and Kosslyn (1993) performed a number of experiments to determine whether objects are always identified by encoding the parts individually. We showed subjects a series of line drawings of common objects and asked them to say each object's name aloud, as quickly and accurately as possible; each drawing was presented in free view, and remained visible until the subject had named the object. We recorded response times and error rates. Because the objects were depicted from typical perspectives, subjects presumably could recognize them by matching the patterns directly to an object-level representation in the pattern activation subsystem.

The drawings were presented in six conditions: They were intact, missing a part, or disrupted. Four types of disruptions were produced by cutting up the objects in two ways and arranging these fragments in two ways (thereby producing four combinations). Specifically, as illustrated in figure 6.4, the objects were cut at the natural parse boundaries of constituent parts (as determined by subject ratings), or at arbitrary locations that violated natural parse boundaries. The pieces were then exploded outward, which maintained their relative spatial positions, or were scrambled, which disrupted the spatial relations.

If objects are recognized by first matching parts, then disrupting the parts should impair naming. As is evident in figure 6.4, when the parts are disrupted but their spatial relations are preserved, one can visually "fill in" the missing contour (presumably via a kind of "vector completion" operation, as described

Natural-
disconnected

Natural-
scrambled

Unnatural-
disconnected

Unnatural-
scrambled

Parts-
removed

Whole-
object

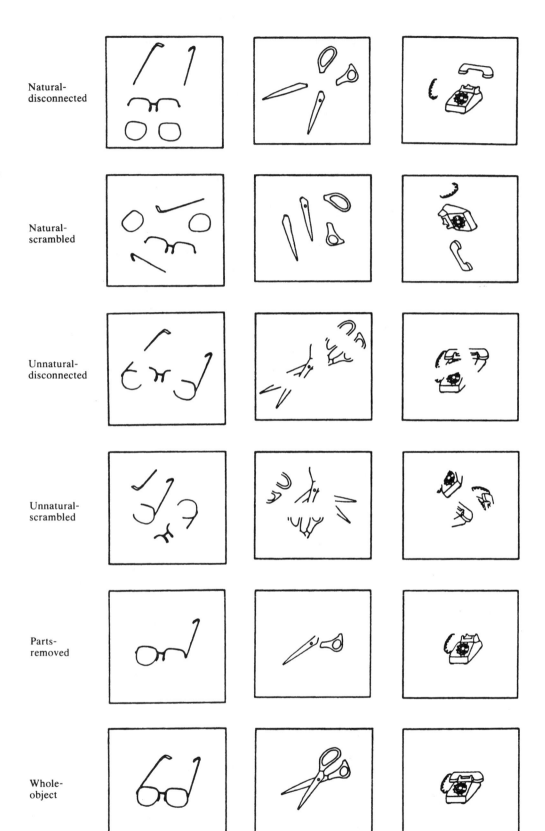

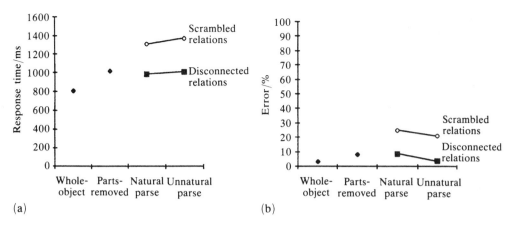

(a)   (b)

Figure 6.5 Results of the Cave and Kosslyn (1993) experiment, when parts were rotated arbitrarily. (Reprinted with permission.)

in the previous chapter). Thus, it may not matter how the parts are parsed. This objection cannot be raised for the scrambled conditions, where one cannot visually complete the missing contour. Parts-based theories predict that subjects should be impaired when the parts are disrupted here, relative to when they are intact and hence more easily recognized.

In contrast, if objects are recognized by matching nonaccidental and signal properties to a stored pattern of the overall shape, and not via representations of parts, then we expected that scrambling the fragments should impair recognition; scrambling the fragments disrupts matching via the viewpoint consistency constraint. However, as long as the spatial relations are preserved, the input properties will still be in the correct relative positions. Thus, if the overall pattern is matched, then chopping up the object at arbitrary places should have the same effect as dividing it at natural part boundaries; although such drawings define a stretched version of the object, the pattern activation subsystem should generalize over such relatively minor distortions.

The results are illustrated in figure 6.5. We were very surprised to discover that there was no effect of how the object was cut up; times and errors increased for scrambled objects, but to the same degree when they were parsed into parts or parsed arbitrarily.

The first experiment we conducted had a confounding: Only when pieces were scrambled were they also misoriented. To remove this confounding and to replicate the result, we repaired the stimuli by translating pieces in the scrambled conditions but not rotating them. The times and errors obtained here are illustrated in figure 6.6. The first thing to notice is that we did in fact replicate the earlier result: There was no effect of how the objects were parsed, but there was a big effect of their spatial organization. The second thing to notice is that rotating the pieces in the scrambled conditions of the

Figure 6.4 Stimuli used by Cave and Kosslyn (1993). (Reprinted with permission.)

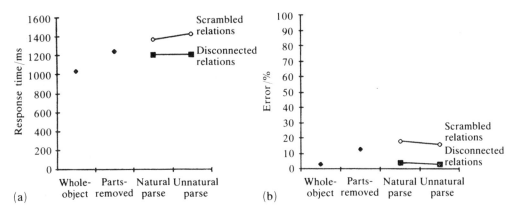

Figure 6.6 Results of the Cave and Kosslyn experiment when parts had their original orientations. (Reprinted with permission.)

first experiment apparently did make a difference: The error rates were lower when parts were translated without rotation.

These results provide strong support for the importance of the viewpoint consistency constraint: The fragments had to be consistent with seeing an object from a single point of view in order for subjects to identify the object easily. But the results run counter to the idea that objects are represented in terms of elementary shapes; it simply did not matter how the objects were divided into pieces. If the input could be matched to the overall shape directly, the representations of parts did not play a role in the identification process.

As noted earlier, one interpretation of Biederman and Cooper's (1991a) results is that if an image is degraded, so that a representation of the overall shape will not be matched, then representations of parts are matched. Cave and I investigated an implication of this idea. We presented the stimuli very briefly (200 ms), followed by a mask. The brief presentation and mask degrade the representation, which we expected to impair bottom-up encoding. In this case, one may either recognize individual parts bottom-up, or seek them out to confirm a hypothesis (as was outlined in chapter 3 and will be developed in detail in the next chapter). These results are presented in figure 6.7. As expected, in this condition the subjects made more errors when the objects were parsed arbitrarily than when they were parsed along natural part boundaries (error rates were too high to take response times seriously).

In short, the weight of the evidence suggests that people first attempt to match the overall pattern that corresponds to an object, and do not always match representations of parts. If the image is degraded, however, so that the overall pattern cannot be matched, then they will match the input to representations of individual parts. Parts are likely to have been encoded and stored previously, and hence are available for matching, in a number of circumstances. One is especially likely to parse parts when an object is relatively close at hand, so that its parts are viewed with high resolution and discontinuities in perceptual qualities are visible. Furthermore, when objects are

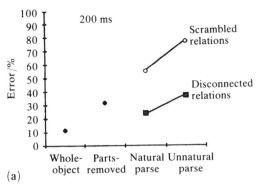

Figure 6.7 Results of the Cave and Kosslyn experiment when the pictures were presented for only 200 ms. (Reprinted with permission.)

nearby, one often examines them over the course of multiple eye fixations. In this case, images of different parts may fall on the fovea at different points in time, and one is forced to encode the parts individually. In addition, one is likely to fixate on parts, rather than arbitrary portions of an object, if parts have distinctive stimulus attributes—and hence the stimulus-based attention-shifting subsystem will draw attention to them. Overt attention shifts are not necessary to encode parts individually; they can be encoded within a single eye fixation if one shifts attention covertly (see Sperling 1960). One is also likely to encode parts when objects are seen in circumstances that preclude matching the entire pattern, and so parts are the largest perceptual units. Finally, one will of course encode parts if they are seen in isolation.

In addition, in some situations distinctive characteristics, such as a pineapple's texture or a fire engine's color, may be recognized when the shape is not. These distinctive characteristics (which are specified as sets of signal properties extracted by the preprocessing subsystem) play the same role in recognition as parts per se, and I shall treat them in the same way. Like parts, they can be recognized individually and provide cues as to the identify of the object.

Although I have assumed that the pattern activation subsystem includes a representation of overall shape and representations of parts and distinctive characteristics, I do not mean to imply that the representations of overall shape have no internal structure. A compressed-image representation has an internal organization. Cooper et al. (1992), Schacter, Cooper, and Delaney (1990), and Schacter et al. (1991) have shown that priming occurs with novel visual patterns only when the patterns could correspond to possible objects; no priming occurs with impossible, Escher-like patterns. Schacter and I (in preparation) obtained the same result when the stimuli were presented very briefly in one visual field so that the subjects were forced to encode only a single representation (presumably of the shape as a whole). Such findings imply that the representations of overall shape are themselves structured, and that the shapes are structured according to more general principles about how objects in the world are constructed.

Identifying Objects in Degraded Images

SPATIAL PROPERTIES

In some circumstances, one uses spatial properties, such as the size or location of an object, to identify the object. For example, a distinguishing property of a black house cat, versus a panther, is its size; and that odd thing on somebody's head is probably a hat, simply by dint of its location. When the input is degraded, one may use not only motion and parts, but also spatial information to identify an object. Indeed, spatial information may play an important role in helping one to identify parts, which in turn are used to identify the object. Because the dorsal system operates before the input has been identified, it presumably treats objects and parts in the same way; it encodes spatial properties of perceptual units, and does not "know" whether they correspond to objects or parts.

However, to be useful for identification, spatial properties must characterize the object or part, not the image itself. One needs to know how large the cat is, or where the hat is in relation to the head—not how large the image is or where it falls on the retina. Recall that the visual buffer corresponds to a set of retinotopically mapped areas of cortex; in each area, adjacent—or almost adjacent—neurons receive input from adjacent receptors on the retina An image is specified relative to the retina and hence changes every time one moves one's head or eyes. Thus, there must be a mechanism that converts the spatial coordinates in the visual buffer to a different type, as is discussed in the following section.

Spatiotopic Mapping Subsystem

The *spatiotopic mapping subsystem* I posit converts the retinotopic coordinates of the visual buffer to more stable coordinates that are based on parts of the body or external objects. This subsystem specifies a location, size, and orientation for each parsed unit in three dimensions. All of these types of information can help one to identify objects in degraded images. Figure 6.8 illustrates this subsystem in the context of the system as a whole.

Reference Systems   Location must be specified relative to something, and different reference systems are more or less useful for different tasks. For example, if one wants to determine whether a painting is a subtly inaccurate fake, objects and parts can be located relative to each other, to the frame, or to a specific point on the canvas. In contrast, if one wants to reach for an object, its location should be specified relative to one's body. Depending on the situation, then, it may be appropriate to locate an object relative to the viewer or relative to another object.

Reference systems can be characterized relative to a number of dimensions. To note the most commonly used distinctions, objects can be located relative to the retina (*retinotopic* coordinates) or to an anchor point in space (*spatiotopic* coordinates). If spatiotopic coordinates are used, they can be specified relative to the body (*body-centered* coordinates) or to another object (*allocentric*

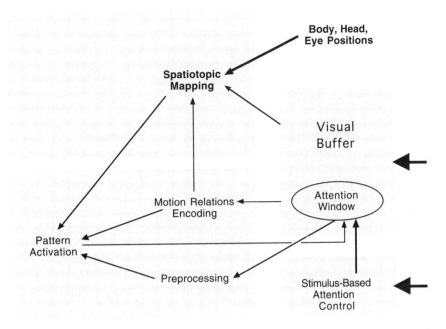

Figure 6.8 The spatiotopic mapping subsystem in relation to the subsystems discussed previously.

coordinates). If body-centered coordinates are used, they can be head-based (*craniotopic*) or body-based. If allocentric coordinates are used, they can be specified relative to the viewer (*viewer-centered*) or relative to the object itself (*object-centered*); in contrast, retinotopic and body-centered coordinates are, by definition, always viewer-centered because they specify location relative to one's point of view.

In all cases location can be specified with different parameters, such as those used in Cartesian coordinates (along X, Y, and Z dimensions) or polar coordinates (a radius and planar and depth angle from an origin). In addition, coordinates can be embedded in processes that guide action (*implicit* coordinates) or matched to stored representations of location, such as occurs during recognition (*explicit* coordinates). In either case, *local* coordinates can be used to specify parts relative to one another, with many separate origins forming an interlocking coordinate system, or *global* coordinates can be used to specify location relative to a single origin.

Furthermore, the reference system is to some extent dependent on how shape is represented; the shape of objects and parts can be specified in 2, 3, or 2.5 dimensions (a 2.5-dimensional representation is like a bas relief; it specifies only the part of the third dimension that projects from the object to the viewer). Two- and 2.5-dimensional representations are necessarily viewer-centered, whereas 3-dimensional representations can be either viewer-centered or object-centered.

It should be obvious that there are a large number of possible types of reference systems. Surprisingly little research has been conducted on the

Identifying Objects in Degraded Images

precise types of reference systems we use for specific types of tasks (although such research appears to be on the rise; e.g., see Franklin and Tversky 1990). It is clear, however, that retinotopic representations are not useful if one wants to reach for an object, look at a specific location on an object, or distinguish the sizes or locations of objects; other types of reference systems are necessary.

A Distinct Subsystem   The observation that the brain transforms retinotopic coordinates to other types of coordinates does not imply the existence of a distinct subsystem. One could argue that the subsystems that encode spatial information into memory or that use it to guide movements perform this transformation in addition to their other duties. I hypothesize a distinct spatiotopic mapping subsystem for the following reasons.

First, a separate spatiotopic mapping subsystem simplifies the tasks of other subsystems that encode spatial relations into memory or that use spatial information to guide movement. In general, the more varied the inputs that must be mapped onto the same output, the more difficult the mapping. Thus, intermediate computations are desirable if they simplify the individual input/output mappings. The spatiotopic mapping subsystem eliminates considerable variability in the mapping by eliminating effects of where an image falls on the retina. Thus, including such a subsystem is computationally efficient.

Second, some sort of nonretinal coordinates are needed to compute all useful representations of spatial information. Thus, an initial transform from retinotopic to body-centered coordinates not only simplifies later computations but also eliminates needless duplication of effort that would occur if this computation were performed separately by each spatial relations encoding subsystem.

Third, and most speculatively, primitive organisms needed to represent location relative to the body to approach food and mates and avoid predators, even if their ability to remember locations was not particularly impressive. Thus, one could argue that mapping to body-based coordinates evolved before the more sophisticated processes that transform and use these coordinates for object identification. And the later, more sophisticated, system could not disrupt what was present from earlier phases of evolution, and hence was added onto the prior structure.

I argue that the spatiotopic mapping subsystem produces explicit representations of coordinates. Such a general-purpose "map" could be accessed by a number of different subsystems, such as those used in navigation, in encoding spatial information into memory, and in transforming images (as will be discussed in chapter 10). Indeed, Nemire and Bridgeman (1987) found similar location errors in a manual pointing task and in a multiple-saccade eye fixation task, which they argue is evidence that the same map of space is used in pointing and directing eye movements.

The spatiotopic mapping subsystem may compute location on the basis of other types of coordinates and need not be physically organized spatially (as are retinotopically mapped areas). Andersen, Essick, and Siegel (1985) found cells in area 7a of the parietal lobe that respond to location on the retina as gated by eye position. This representation is presumably useful if head-centered coordinates play a major role in directing eye position. Zipser and Andersen (1988) found that neural network models could compute head-centered information when given eye position and location on the retina as inputs, and the hidden units developed receptive fields very much like those found in neurons in area 7a.

Some have argued that what I call the spatiotopic mapping subsystem in fact corresponds to two distinct subsystems, one that computes locations in near space (using body-based coordinates) and one that computes locations in far space (using allocentric coordinates). In fact, selective deficits following brain damage suggest that different processing is required to use the two sorts of information (e.g., see Bisiach, Capitani, and Porta 1985; Butters, Soeldner, and Fedio 1972, Rizzolatti, Gentilucci, and Matelli 1985; for a review of recent findings, see Sakata and Kusunoki 1992). For example, Rizzolatti, Matelli, and Pavesi (1983) found that lesions of area 6 (premotor cortex) of the monkey caused visual neglect in near space but not far space; in contrast, lesions of area 8 (the frontal eye fields) had the reverse effects (see also Rizzolatti and Berti 1990). Consistent with these results, Rizzolatti et al. (1981) found neurons in area 6 that respond to visual and somatosensory stimuli. Approximately half of these neurons responded to stimuli that were within reach of the hand, and the other half responded to stimuli near the animal's skin. The visual receptive fields of many of these "bimodal" (visual-somatosensory) neurons remained in registration with the tactile receptive fields even when the animal moved its eyes (Gentilucci et al. 1983; see also Graziano and Gross 1992a, b). Another set of neurons, in area 8, responded to stimuli farther than an arm's reach.

I have previously used such evidence as grounds for hypothesizing two distinct subsystems, and the evidence certainly suggests that different subsystems contribute to the different types of performance. However, it is not clear whether the dissociations following brain damage or the single-cell recording results show that the spatiotopic mapping system itself is further articulated. Note that area 6 and area 8 are in the frontal lobes; I will shortly argue that the spatiotopic mapping subsystem is implemented in the parietal lobes. Moreover, both area 6 and area 8 are involved in motor control; this function is distinct from actually representing a map of the environment. The so-called near-space map (in area 6) may have functions analogous to those of the tectofugal pathway, which is involved not in forming representations of stimuli but rather in guiding orienting responses (see Schneider 1969). The areas that register properties of nearby space may be part of an "implicit" memory system, as opposed to the "explicit" representations in the spatio-topic mapping subsystem. This notion is consistent with the fact that at least three somatopically organized maps of "immediate extrapersonal space" in the monkey brain are implemented in areas that play critical roles in motor control (the putamen, area 6, and area 7b in the posterior parietal lobe; for a summary, see Gross and Graziano 1992a, b). These areas form a tightly linked (mono-synaptically connected) network. Similarly, the map in area 8 may be used specifically to guide eye movements and attention.

It would be difficult to obtain compelling evidence that two separate representations of space exist, as distinguished from evidence that two systems use spatial information in different ways—one that guides orienting and body movements (perhaps dependent on area 6) and one that represents spatial information for recognition, space exploration, and large-scale navigation (perhaps involving area 8). Thus, I will leave this issue open, but for now will assume that the same (admittedly coarsely characterized) spatiotopic mapping subsystem computes all visual nonretinotopic coordinates. In any case, my focus is on the representation of allocentric coordinates of objects and parts, not on the representation of location relative to the body. For present purposes, specifying a single subsystem will be sufficient.

Location, Size, and Orientation   The dorsal system must encode the sizes of objects and parts. A three-dimensional representation of the size of a part or object is critical if one is to avoiding hitting it during navigation. In addition, the size of an object or part may help one to identify it, as noted earlier. Although we can identify an object when it projects images at different visual angles (essentially ignoring the visual angle for this purpose), we also encode its size. At a conceptual level, there are reasons to suspect that a system that registers location would also register size. Size is, after all, the number of small locations an object occupies. Thus, it is not surprising that neurons in some areas of the dorsal system respond selectively to changes in stimulus size (Maunsell and Newsome 1987).[4]

Parallel arguments lead us to expect the dorsal system also to encode orientation: to shift attention, reach, or navigate effectively, one needs to know an object's orientation. Indeed, there is a simple correspondence between orientation and location—if location is specified at multiple levels of scale, orientation is specified implicitly. For example, the orientation of a line can be specified by the relative locations of its ends. In general, the orientation of an object can be recovered by breaking it into parts and noting their relative locations. I do not mean to imply that this is how orientation is actually represented; it is not. The visual system appears to treat orientation as a "primitive" property; neurons at many levels of the visual system are tuned for orientation. Rather, it is clear that the two spatial properties, orientation and location, are conceptually related and would be useful for similar tasks.

Levels of Resolution   The visual buffer represents input at multiple scales of resolution (see chapter 4), and the input will be grouped into units at each scale. It is clear that we can represent location at multiple scales. For example, we can represent the location of a needle precisely enough to allow us to reach right to it, and we can also represent the location of an entire person (ignoring the locations of the fingers and so on) well enough to allow us to avoid hitting him or her while driving. These observations lead to the question of whether locations at more than one level of resolution are computed simultaneously by the spatiotopic mapping subsystem.

Three possibilities present themselves. The subsystem could compute (1) the location only of the object or part currently being attended; (2) the location of every parsed region at every scale; or (3) the locations of all of the parsed regions that are at the level of resolution at which one is attending.

The first possibility can be eliminated simply by the fact of preattentive processing. In order to direct attention to objects that are not currently the object of attention, we must represent the locations of objects outside the field of attention. Moreover, to navigate properly, one needs to be aware not only of objects one is attending to but also of objects that might be in the way if one moved in a certain direction. Some neurons in the posterior parietal lobe actually show smaller responses to attended targets than to unattended ones (Steinmetz, Connor, and MacLeod 1992). Indeed, we can search numerous locations simultaneously, looking for the location of a target (Sagi and Julesz 1985). It is difficult to imagine how an organism could survive without this ability; without a preattentive representation that something is at a particular location, one would only be able to direct eye movements haphazardly or according to a previously stored action pattern.

The second and third possibilities cannot be evaluated so easily. However, the reasoning that led me to posit an attention window can be applied here. Recall that selective attention may reflect in part the existence of limited-capacity data transmission lines; only so much information can be transmitted by the anatomical connections. If such limits constrain data flow to the dorsal system, then the choice is to eliminate some locations within each level of resolution or to eliminate entire levels of resolution.

Consider the problem of picking up a needle. One needs to select the location among locations of other similar-sized objects; one does not even consider picking up a coffee cup nearby. This observation leads me to expect that the system will select a single, or relatively few, levels of resolution in which to compute locations of perceptual groups. The results of Shulman and Wilson (1987)—in which subjects detected high- or low-spatial-frequency gratings after having attended to a global letter or local components of it (see chapter 4)—as well as those of many others, indicate that people can in fact attend to a given level of resolution, but they do not indicate whether all locations at that level are computed (see also Atkinson and Braddick 1989). This clearly is an empirical issue, and one that is open as of this writing.

Finally, it is of interest that damage to the right parietal lobe can disrupt one's awareness of the left side of space (i.e., produce unilateral visual neglect with anosognosia) but leave intact one's ability to recognize objects in the neglected field. Berti and Rizzolatti (1992) found that objects presented in the neglected field could prime encoding of other objects in the same category even though the patients were unaware of having seen the priming stimuli.[5] This finding suggests that some information about object properties is encoded even at unattended scales or outside the attention window; again, the mere fact that preattentive processing occurs suggests that this must be the case. However, such processing is not as complete and does not appear to involve very high-resolution representations, as does that which occurs when one attends to a stimulus.[6]

Anatomical Localization The spatiotopic mapping subsystem is implemented in the posterior parietal lobes. Andersen (1989) notes that the posterior parietal lobes of monkeys can be divided into a number of architectonically distinct areas. Area 7a contains neurons that are tuned to particular locations in space and that are involved in fixation (e.g., Andersen, Essick, and Siegel 1985); area 7b contains neurons that respond when the animal reaches toward something or manipulates it (e.g., Mountcastle et al. 1975); area LIP contains neurons that appear to play a role in saccadic eye movements (e.g., Gnadt and Andersen 1988); and area MST is involved in smooth-pursuit eye movements (e.g., Sakata, Shibutani, and Kawano 1983). All of these areas appear to work together, integrating sensory information about spatial layout with motor information.

Although a variety of areas within the posterior parietal lobe probably are involved in encoding spatiotopic information, area 7a seems particularly likely to play a role in this process. Not only do the neurons in this area have properties that would allow them to convert retinotopic coordinates to spatiotopic ones (Zipser and Andersen 1988), but this area has rich connections to the "higher-order" parts of the brain that presumably would use such information. In particular, area 7a projects strongly to the frontal and temporal lobes, and also to the anterior cingulate gyrus (which may play a critical role in attention; see Posner and Driver 1992; Posner and Petersen 1990). Area 7a also projects strongly to area 46, near the principal sulcus, which appears to be a short-term memory structure for spatial location (Goldman-Rakic 1987, 1992).

Consistent with the claim that the spatiotopic mapping subsystem is implemented in the posterior parietal lobe, damage to these structures in humans can disrupt reaching directly to a target location in the periphery, often only in the visual field contralateral to the side of unilateral damage (e.g., see Ratcliff and Davies-Jones 1972). Although the spatiotopic mapping subsystem appears to be duplicated bilaterally, the right hemisphere seems to play a special role in its function. Mesulam (1981) argues compellingly that the right parietal lobe computes a representation of both halves of space, and Corbetta et al. (1993) present PET evidence that the right hemisphere has a separate representation for each visual field whereas the left has only a single representation.

The observation that the spatiotopic mapping subsystem relies heavily on a single cerebral hemisphere makes sense from a computational perspective. A single map of space would allow one to navigate and search through the environment more easily than two separate maps, one per hemisphere, that must be coordinated. Moreover, I will argue in the next chapter that the right hemisphere in particular plays a special role in computing the kind of coordinates that are used to guide movement; having a map of the nearby environment would be convenient for this computation.

The inference that this subsystem encodes more than location per se is consistent with numerous findings. For example, Gross (1978) and Holmes and Gross (1984) found that monkeys can discriminate between patterns presented at different orientations even with anterior, posterior, or complete lesions of the inferior temporal lobes. Although this result does not necessarily implicate the dorsal system, it indicates that an object's orientation is not represented in the ventral system (which makes sense if this system is insensitive to spatial properties, which vary from instance to instance).

The spatiotopic mapping subsystem plays a critical role in characterizing the three-dimensional extent of an object, which would help one to identify objects in degraded images. This function of the subsystem allows us to grapple with a potential problem: there is ample evidence that right parietal lobe lesions in humans disrupt the ability to identify degraded or unconventional depictions of objects (e.g., Newcombe and Russell 1969; Warrington and Taylor 1973, 1978; Warrington and James 1967, 1988, 1991). On the face of things, this deficit might seem to contradict the notion that the parietal lobe encodes spatial properties and the inferior temporal lobe (or whatever its homolog turns out to be in humans) encodes object properties.

For example, Warrington and James (1988) report three case studies of patients who suffered posterior right-hemisphere damage. As we would expect, given that the ventral system was intact, these patients could identify intact objects seen from conventional points of view and retrieve various attributes of those objects from memory. (Judging from the illustrations in the article, all of the objects in Warrington and James's "visual semantic knowledge" tests were intact and seen from canonical points of view.) But they had great difficulty identifying objects in impoverished images (e.g., seen as foreshortened silhouettes) or objects seen from unconventional views.

In chapter 2, I argued that it is difficult to interpret effects of lesions; perhaps this finding is due to an indirect effect of the dorsal lesion—perhaps diaschisis occurred (Von Monakow 1914/1969) and nondamaged regions suffered a kind of shock when they lost their normal inputs from the damaged area. However, the patients seemed otherwise quite intact. All of them had normal acuity, could discriminate simple shapes, had intact color vision, and could determine whether a fragmented letter (an X or O) was present in a noisy background (as opposed to no figure; this task requires effective perceptual organization and effective encoding by the preprocessing subsystem I posit). As expected given the locus of the lesion, these patients had a deficit in spatial localization. They saw two squares, one with a dot in the center and one with a dot that was slightly off center; they had great difficulty pointing to the square that had the off-center dot. This result is consistent with the hypothesis that they could not encode metric spatial information effectively. In contrast, the patients could point to a spot of light that appeared in one of five distinct positions on the horizontal meridian (all in the right visual field), which is consistent with their being able to encode classes of locations (which do not rely on fine-grained spatial information, as will be discussed in the following chapter).

There is considerable evidence that the dorsal system computes information about depth. For example, damage to the parietal lobes, particularly on the right side, can disrupt depth perception (e.g., Carmon and Bechtoldt 1969; Durnford and Kimura 1971).[7] If the parietal lobes implement a subsystem that encodes location, size, and orientation in three dimensions, then we would expect patients with damaged parietal lobes to have difficulty using such information. Such spatial properties may be particularly important when one sees a picture of an object as it appears from an unusual point of view or as a foreshortened silhouette. The spatiotopic mapping subsystem presumably uses many sources of information to compute such properties, including shading and foreshortening. If this subsystem is disrupted or its connections are disrupted, this type of information will not be available for recognition.

Three-dimensional information is probably not specified in detail in the ventral system; we do not always need this information to recognize objects, as witnessed by the simple fact that we can recognize line drawings. (In fact, Lowe's system uses two-dimensional representations as input.) But when the input is impoverished, or an object is seen from an unusual view, the surface layout in depth may play an important role in recognition. This information may be supplied to the pattern activation subsystem via the dorsal system. As mentioned earlier, Baizer, Ungerleider, and Desimone (1991) found strong anatomical projections in monkeys from both the ventral and dorsal streams to the anterior part of the superior temporal sulcus (which defines the upper bank of IT); the human analog to this area could be the locus where information about three-dimensional extent is provided to the pattern activation subsystem. Alternatively, Harries and Perrett (1991) found precise connections from the posterior parietal lobe to the superior temporal sulcus. But more than that, they used single cell recording to identify cells in IT that responded selectively to faces. These cells were stained, and were found to fall into clumps. And it was these clumps that were especially well connected to the parietal lobe. Such connections might facilitate coordinating the corresponding representations that are computed in the two systems, and it is clear that three-dimensional information is very useful for encoding faces. Finally, connections via the thalamus might allow communication between the dorsal and ventral systems (cf. Mumford 1991, 1992).

Resolving an Inconsistency The inference that the spatiotopic mapping subsystem is implemented in the posterior parietal lobe, in the human analog of area 7a, leads to another potential quandary. In chapter 4 I argued that the segregation of object-properties and spatial-properties processing allows the system to ignore location when recognizing shape. Gross and Mishkin (1977) cite the very large receptive fields of neurons in area IT as support for this hypothesis; these neurons encode object properties when a stimulus appears in a wide range of positions in the visual field. The problem is that the neurons in area 7a have equally large receptive fields (e.g., Motter and Mountcastle 1981)—and yet we are inferring that these neurons encode location.

The fact that both types of neurons have large receptive fields does not indicate that neither can encode location precisely. Large overlapping receptive fields could, in principle, encode location via coarse coding. As noted earlier, the classic example of coarse coding is color vision, where three types of cones have overlapping distributions of sensitivity to different wavelengths; the overlap in their sensitivities allows the three types of cones to encode a wide range of colors. Thus, the question becomes, are there properties of IT neurons that impair using coarse coding to register location, and—conversely—are there properties of area 7a neurons that promote using coarse coding to register location?

O'Reilly et al. (1990) reviewed the literature on the response profiles of neurons in the two areas. We found one salient difference between the two types of neurons that seemed likely to be relevant. Namely, IT neurons virtually always respond most vigorously when the input image of a stimulus falls on the fovea. In contrast, neurons in area 7a typically do not respond most vigorously when the input image strikes the fovea; rather, about 40% of these neurons exhibit "foveal sparing"—they do not respond when the image falls on the fovea. Some of the neurons in area 7a respond most vigorously to stimuli when the image falls on one edge of the receptive field, others respond most vigorously when the input image falls in one quadrant, and so on.

We conjectured that the receptive field properties of neurons in area 7a might be conducive to using coarse coding to represent location, whereas the receptive field properties of IT neurons would not promote such encoding. (For evidence that coarse coding does in fact take place in the brain, albeit in another area, see Malonek and Spitzer 1989). Coarse coding of location would depend on differences in the mixture of outputs of neurons that register location, and hence would be less effective if virtually all neurons respond most vigorously to stimuli at the same location (i.e., the fovea).

We tested this idea by constructing network models that received a point in an array as input, and specified the X and Y coordinates of the point as output. We systematically varied the receptive field properties of input units. That is, we defined the regions of the stimulus array so that some more strongly influenced the level of activation of each input unit. When a dot fell in a location of the stimulus array, it affected a given input unit in proportion to the weight on the connection from that location to the unit. We "hard-wired" the weights so that input units had different types of receptive fields; recall that the "receptive field" of a unit is defined by the inputs that affect it most strongly (see chapter 4).

In these models, we systematically varied the number of input units that had IT-type receptive fields, which are most sensitive to stimulation at the "fovea" (the center of the stimulus array, in the models). We then observed how easily the different models could achieve the mapping, in this case to a Cartesian representation of location. As expected, if the input units all had maximal responses at the center of the field, the network models had difficulty mapping a dot in an array to X and Y coordinates. And the more receptive fields that were constructed to be most sensitive to inputs off the center, the more effectively the network encoded the location of the dot (although the benefit of including more such units diminished after most of the units had this property).

These results eliminate the apparent paradox. The critical factor is the response properties of the neurons in IT and 7a, not simply the size of their receptive fields. If the vast majority of neurons respond most vigorously to stimuli at the center, as occurs in IT, then the overlap in their outputs cannot be used to compute location very effectively. In contrast, if there is variation in the location where neurons respond most vigorously, then the overlap in their outputs can be used effectively to compute location.

In summary, I argue that certain minimal functions must be performed by a subsystem that intervenes between the retinotopic input from the visual buffer and subsystems that encode spatial relations into memory. These functions include computing a representation of location, size, and orientation for each parsed unit in spatiotopic coordinates at one or more levels of resolution. This information can then be used to help identify an object in a degraded image.

TWO VISUAL MEMORY STRUCTURES

Information about motion, parts, and spatial properties of objects and parts all may play a role in helping us to identify objects when their images are degraded. This process can be further aided if the ventral system is better able to make use of fragmentary cues. One way in which it could do so is by detecting specific exemplars as well as members of a category. Specific exemplars often have idiosyncratic distinguishing characteristics (e.g., patterns of surface markings), which will not help one to identify all members of a category, but will help one to identify that exemplar.

Consider the problem of how to build a system that could identify an object as a member of a class, such as dogs, and also could identify an object as a specific exemplar, such as Fido. For purposes of categorizing, one wants to throw away the information that distinguishes one object in the class from another. But it is this very information that is critical for identifying the specific example. The two mappings are incompatible, which leads me to hypothesize that separate subsystems encode the two types of information. Moreover, empirical evidence suggests that an *exemplar pattern activation subsystem* encodes specific examples of a type of stimulus (e.g., Rover, not dogs in general), whereas a *category pattern activation subsystem* encodes classes of objects.

Empirical Evidence

Marsolek, Kosslyn, and Squire (1992) report four experiments that tested the hypothesis that separate subsystems store visual memories for categories and specific exemplars. We showed subjects a set of words and asked them to rate how much they liked each one. This was an orienting task. We then presented a three-letter stem (such as "CAS") and asked the subjects to say the first word that came to mind that would complete these letters into a word (such as "CASTLE" or "CASKET"). Subjects often completed the stems to form words on the initial orienting list, even though they were not asked to memorize those words or to recall them; this phenomenon is one form of priming. This task, in a sense, speaks directly to the problem of identifying objects in degraded images; the subjects use fragments to access an appropriate representation in memory.

When the stems are presented in free view (in the center of a screen or on a page), this "stem-completion" priming paradigm has been shown to be largely modality specific and even case specific (e.g., Graf, Shimamura, and Squire 1985; Jacoby and Dallas 1981; Kirsner, Milech, and Standen 1983; Roediger and Blaxton 1987). That is, if subjects heard the words during the orientation phase, they showed much less priming when later presented with word stems than if they had seen the words initially; similarly, if they saw the words initially in lowercase, they showed much less priming if the stems were later shown in uppercase than if they were shown in lowercase.

Categorizing shapes would be particularly useful for language; such categories would be easily named. Probably the least controversial claim in neuropsychology is that the left hemisphere is critical in language production and comprehension (in right-handed males, at any rate). Another uncontroversial claim in neuropsychology is that the right hemisphere plays a special role in navigation. Information about the specific shapes of objects has obvious importance in navigation; one needs to know more than that an object is a table to know how to move around it—one also needs to know its specific shape. Such considerations led us to conjecture that the left hemisphere might be more adept at storing categorical visual information about shape, and the right might be more adept at storing specific exemplars. If we found such a dissociation, we would have evidence that two subsystems exist for storing information about shape.[8]

Thus, we lateralized the stems in a standard stem-completion task. That is, the subjects stared at a central fixation point, and saw a word stem briefly in one visual field. This input was seen initially by only one cerebral hemisphere. The subject was to say the first word that came to mind that would complete the stem. As expected, if subjects read words that could complete the stems during the orienting task, we found more priming than if the subjects heard these words. Moreover, all of this additional priming was in the right hemisphere. In addition, if the subjects saw the stems in the same case as the original words, there was more priming than if they saw the words in a different case. And again, this additional priming was restricted to the right hemisphere. These data provide good support for the idea that the right hemisphere plays a special role in the representation of specific exemplars.

In addition, Marsolek (1992) used a visual pattern categorization task to show that the left hemisphere is in fact better than the right at storing information about visual categories. He asked subjects to learn simple patterns of lines. A family of six similar patterns was created by shifting the locations of individual parts of a prototypical pattern; eight sets of stimuli were created, each of which corresponded to a member of a category. The subjects were better able to determine the category of the previously unseen prototypes when the stimuli were shown initially to the left hemisphere than when they were shown to the right. This finding is consistent with the possibility that the left hemisphere actually stores prototypes as a means of representing categories.

In addition, Vitkovitch and Underwood (1991) lateralized pictures of objects and nonobjects that were created by combining parts of actual objects in novel ways (see Kroll and Potter 1984), and found that subjects could determine that a picture was an object better if it was presented initially to the left hemisphere. This sort of implicit memory task involves accessing stored categorical representations of objects, and hence the left-hemisphere advantage is as expected. Vitkovitch and Underwood did not find any hemispheric difference for nonobjects, which presumably would not have matched any representation in either pattern activation subsystem. The nonobjects required more time in general, which is as expected if they failed to match representations in the pattern activation subsystems very well and a second encoding cycle was used.

Furthermore, Sergent, Ohta, and MacDonald (1992) found predominantly left-hemisphere activation in a PET study when subjects categorized objects as living or nonliving. Part of this activation was in the left, but not the right, middle temporal gyrus. Similarly, in a PET study my colleagues and I conducted (to be summarized in chapter 8), we also found primarily left-hemisphere activation in the left middle temporal gyrus when subjects decided whether words named pictures of objects. This area is one candidate for implementing the category pattern activation subsystem (see also Damasio, Damasio, and Van Hoesen 1982).

The claim that the right hemisphere is more adept at storing specific exemplars of shapes and the left hemisphere is more adept at storing categories of shapes (perhaps as represented by prototypes) is consistent with numerous other findings. For example, Bryden and Allard (1976) reported that the right hemisphere encodes script better than left, but the left encodes standard fonts better than the right (but see Umilta, Sava, and Salmaso 1980, for ambiguous results). This finding might also indicate, however, that the right-hemisphere preprocessing subsystem more effectively encodes subtle variations in shape (such an account was suggested by Bryden and Allard themselves, 1976). Milner (1968) reported a selective deficit in memory for pictures in patients who had had their anterior right temporal lobes removed (for treatment of otherwise intractable epilepsy); the tasks always involved matching specific exemplars, and so this result is consistent with the idea that the exemplar pattern activation subsystem is implemented primarily in the right hemisphere. In addition, Nebes (1971) tested split-brain patients and found that their right hemispheres could match an arc to a circle more accurately than their left hemispheres; Hatta (1977) essentially repeated this study with normal subjects, and reported similar results. Although both researchers interpreted this finding in terms of part-whole relations, it is equally consistent with the idea that the right hemisphere stores a more precise representation of a particular circle. However, neither researcher reported response times, making it difficult to interpret their findings with confidence.

I also must note that other results have been reported that are not consistent with this distinction. For example, Simion et al. (1980, experiments 3 and 4) found that subjects could judge two differently shaped versions of the same geometric figure (e.g., triangles) as the same faster when the stimuli were presented initially to the right hemisphere. Similarly, Sergent et al. (1992) found no visual field difference when the subjects who participated in their PET experiment also performed the same object categorization task in a divided-visual-field paradigm. I would have predicted that the left hemisphere should be faster in these categorization tasks.

In many cases, it is relatively easy to explain such counterevidence; it is well known that divided-visual-field effects with normal subjects depend critically on a host of variables (e.g., see Hellige and Sergent 1986; Sergent 1982b; Sergent and Hellige 1986). For example, in order to keep the paradigm as similar as possible to the one used in the PET study, Sergent, Ohta, and MacDonald (1992) presented their stimuli for one second, and subjects had to maintain fixation on a central point during this period (fixation was monitored); in this case, it is possible that the attention window could shift to the stimulus equally effectively in either visual field (see my discussion of the findings of Pollatsek and his colleagues on p. 89). In addition, Sergent, Ohta, and MacDonald (1992) report very fast decision times (with means of 774 and 764 ms for left- and right-visual-field presentations, respectively); these times are remarkable in part because the stimuli were presented relatively far into the periphery (5° to the left or right of fixation). It is possible that the intensity was so high that many low-level neurons provided input to higher-level processes, which eliminated any differences in encoding efficiency. Indeed, as will be described in the following chapter, Kosslyn et al. (1992) used computer models to show that the sheer amount of input could in principle eliminate some types of hemispheric differences in performance.

Similar factors can explain other results that at first glance appear to contradict the present theory. For example, Sergent and Lorber (1983) asked subjects to categorize pictures of animals at different sizes and lateral orientations, but they also presented stimuli at high levels of intensity. This factor might explain why the subjects evaluated the pictures equally quickly in the two visual fields. In contrast, when they presented the stimuli for a relatively brief interval (50 ms) and at a relatively low level of illumination, the subjects performed better when the stimuli were presented initially to the right hemisphere. Given the task, which required categorizing different shapes in the same way, I would have expected a left-hemisphere superiority. This result is also easy to explain: if the contrast is low, the right hemisphere may encode the stimulus pattern itself more effectively (see Sergent 1982a, assuming that "low energy" displays have low contrast). This facilitation in encoding the stimulus may have overshadowed any hemispheric difference in matching input to stored representations. Furthermore, if the variants were highly familiar, each could be recognized in the exemplar pattern activation subsystem and then categorized at the level of associative memory; if the initial recognition process is very fast, both operations could require less time than recognition in the category pattern activation subsystem alone.

The importance of stimulus conditions may also explain why Biederman and Cooper (1991b) found no evidence that the right hemisphere was primed more than the left when pictures were named a second time, although there was priming in general from having named them before. The mean naming time for these pictures was approximately 720 ms. This is remarkably fast, given that the pictures were presented 2.4° to the left or right of fixation (and subtended a maximum of 4.8° of visual angle). Indeed, very few studies report naming times this fast when pictures are presented in the central visual field in free view (for a review, see Kosslyn and Chabris 1990). Biederman and Cooper presented the pictures on a video display terminal without a filter, which we have found can obscure lateralization effects in divided-visual-field experiments (Kosslyn et al. 1989). Indeed, if the pictures were presented with high contrast, as Biederman (personal communication) reports that they were, then this finding may parallel Sergent and Lorber's (1983) findings with high-intensity pictures. I return to this issue in chapter 7.

The Role of Differences in Receptive Field Sizes

I began this section with the observation that two recognition tasks, recognizing a stimulus as a specific individual and recognizing it as a member of a category, have incompatible requirements; information that is needed to recognize the individual must be discarded to classify it as a member of the category. Similar reasoning led Rueckl, Cave, and Kosslyn (1989) to expect a split network model to perform better than an unsplit one when shape and location had to be encoded at the same time. Thus, it is not a surprise that Marsolek (1992) found that a network model performed categorization and exemplar-identification mappings best when organized into two separate streams, one for each task. This is evidence that the two types of mappings are in fact qualitatively distinct and may be encoded by different subsystems.

Jacobs and Kosslyn (in press) and Kosslyn and Jacobs (in press) extended this line of research one step further to consider cerebral lateralization. We reasoned that higher-resolution encodings would be needed to recognize a stimulus as a specific exemplar than would be needed to recognize it as a member of a broad category. As was illustrated by the models constructed by O'Reilly et al., discussed above, larger, overlapping receptive fields can produce higher-resolution representations than smaller, less overlapping receptive fields. Jacobs and I investigated how networks categorize shapes versus how they identify exemplars when the input is filtered through relatively large or small receptive fields.

Prototype   Exemplars

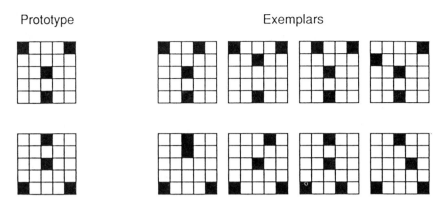

Figure 6.9 Prototypes and exemplars used by Jacobs and Kosslyn (in press). Reprinted with permission.

We designed eight shapes, half of which were from one category and half from another. We defined each category by a prototype pattern, which was formed by filling cells in a 5 × 5 grid. The individual exemplars for each category were produced by selecting one filled cell of the prototype and moving it one cell left, right, up, or down. Figure 6.9 illustrates the prototypes and four exemplars from each category. Some networks specified the category of a stimulus, and other networks specified the identity of the individual exemplars. And in fact, the networks encoded individual exemplars better when the input was filtered by large, overlapping receptive fields, and categorized sets of stimuli better when the input was filtered by small, less overlapping receptive fields. In another set of experiments, we did not fix the receptive field properties in advance, but rather allowed the networks to develop receptive fields spontaneously. After training, we analyzed the receptive field properties of the hidden units and found that networks that classified the shapes into two categories developed smaller receptive fields than those that named the individual exemplars.

The results suggest that the right hemisphere may monitor outputs from neurons with larger receptive fields than does the left hemisphere. This idea allows us to explain a variety of research results. For example, Jonsson and Hellige (1986) showed subjects pairs of letters and asked whether they had the identical shape. The letters were either sharply focused or blurred. When the letters were very blurred, the subjects had more difficulty making the same-different judgment when the stimuli were presented to the left hemisphere than when they were presented to the right hemisphere. This is as expected if the right hemisphere monitors outputs from neurons with large receptive fields, which would be less affected by blurring than outputs from neurons with small receptive fields. Similar findings have been reported by Michimata and Hellige (1987) and Sergent (1987).

The proposal that the right hemisphere monitors larger, overlapping receptive fields also can account for results in additional types of tasks. For example, Hellige and Webster (1979) asked subjects to identify letters that were embedded in an overlapping masking pattern. When these stimuli were lateralized, subjects identified more letters when the stimuli were presented initially to the right hemisphere. Hellige and Webster suggest that the right hemisphere is more efficient at "extracting relevant visual features" of letters. Presumably this process is enhanced by the higher resolution conferred by the larger overlapping receptive fields.

As will be discussed in the next chapter in detail, it is probably misleading to interpret these results as showing that the hemispheres have greater or fewer hard-wired connections to neurons with different-sized receptive fields. Rather, the hemispheres may differ in their attentional biases, which lead them to process outputs from neurons with different-sized receptive fields by default. Such attentional biases can eventually lead to structural lateralization if different sorts of information come to be encoded in the two hemispheres, which later causes each to be able to match different sorts of information more effectively. However, as I shall discuss in the following chapter, such attentional biases can be overcome by task demands, which would disrupt the typical patterns of hemispheric performance in visual tasks.

The consequences of differences in receptive field sizes are not the same in all situations. In some, such differences will not affect performance, whereas in others the consequences will depend on the nature of the stimuli. If one must only detect the presence or absence of a pattern, the sizes of receptive fields should be irrelevant. For example, if one is asked to discriminate between black-and-white stripes and a homogeneous gray field, all that is needed is a great disparity in the outputs of any two neurons; if such a disparity is found, the field is not homogeneous gray. And in fact, the hemispheres have the same sensitivity to different spatial frequencies in a simple detection task (see Kitterle 1991; Kitterle, Christman, and Hellige 1990; Kitterle and Selig 1991).

In contrast, if alternative targets can be distinguished using local features, one should focus on a relatively small region of space. I have suggested that only a limited number of outputs from the visual buffer can be monitored at once (these are allocated by the attention window). If small receptive fields are distributed over a relatively large region, they will not overlap very much— and hence coarse coding cannot be used effectively. However, if one can focus on a small region and monitor outputs from small, but overlapping receptive fields, one should have very high resolution within that region. To take perhaps the simplest example, if one must distinguish between thin stripes (i.e., high-spatial-frequency gratings patterns), one will perform better by focusing on just the size of the stripes—which will be more effective with the left hemisphere, if small overlapping receptive field are monitored. In contrast, if one must distinguish among thick stripes, monitoring the outputs of larger overlapping receptive fields would be more effective. In this case, monitoring smaller receptive fields in the left hemisphere would help one distinguish smaller stripes better than larger receptive fields in the right hemisphere, and vice versa for larger receptive fields. And in fact this is exactly what is found when subjects must identify or compare striped patterns (see Christman,

Kitterle, and Hellige 1991; Kitterle 1991; Kitterle, Christman, and Hellige 1990; Kitterle and Selig 1991). These hemispheric differences may reflect "default" attentional biases.

Similarly, Kitterle, Hellige, and Christman (1992) asked subjects to classify bars on the basis of whether they were thin (3 cycles per degree of visual angle) or wide (1 cycle per degree) or on the basis of whether the edges were fuzzy or sharp (the researchers cast the distinction between the tasks in terms of encoding the "fundamental frequency" versus the harmonics). They found that the subjects classified the width of the bars better if the stimuli were presented initially to the right hemisphere, and the fuzziness of the bars better if the stimuli were presented initially to the left hemisphere. Again, this result can be understood in terms of the receptive field hypothesis: To classify width, the subjects would need to monitor larger regions of space, and hence outputs from neurons with large overlapping fields would be better; to classify fuzziness, high resolution in a small region is necessary, and hence outputs from neurons with small overlapping fields would be better.

Christman, Kitterle, and Hellige (1991) also report evidence that these hemispheric differences depend in part on relative spatial frequencies (i.e., the width of the black and white stripes in the grating). They asked subjects to discriminate between a two-component baseline grating and a three-component variant that was created by adding a 2-cycle-per-degree pattern onto the baseline pattern. The experimenters found that adding this component to a lower-spatial-frequency baseline shifted performance away from a right-hemisphere advantage, and adding the same component to a higher-spatial-frequency baseline shifted performance toward a right-hemisphere advantage. These results are consistent with the hypothesis that the hemispheric effects depend on attention; by looking for the added component, the subjects may have had to monitor outputs from larger or smaller receptive fields than those that best encoded the baseline pattern.

The claim that the hemispheres differ in their default attentional biases also leads us to expect hemispheric differences in categorization of targets in hierarchical stimuli. For example, Sergent (1987) showed subjects lateralized versions of the Navon (1977) hierarchical stimuli; these stimuli consist of a large letter (the global level) that is composed of smaller versions of another letter (the local level). The subjects were to determine whether a target letter is present, at one level or the other. Typically, only two targets are used in the course of an entire experiment and the stimuli are always presented in exactly the same place in the left or right visual field; thus, outputs from small receptive fields could facilitate encoding local features and outputs from larger receptive fields could facilitate encoding global features. As expected if subjects relied on default attentional biases, Sergent found that subjects could encode the global (larger) pattern better when the stimuli were presented initially to the right hemisphere, and could encode local (smaller) pattern better when the stimuli were presented initially to the left hemisphere.[9]

Similarly, Delis, Robertson, and Efron (1986); Robertson and Delis (1986); and Robertson, Lamb, and Knight (1988) have used the Navon figures to

Identifying Objects in Degraded Images

study perceptual encoding in brain-damaged patients. They report that patients with right-hemisphere damage have difficulty encoding the global shape, whereas patients with left-hemisphere damage have difficulty encoding constituent parts. Moreover, Robertson, Lamb, and Knight (1988) provide evidence that it is damage to the temporal lobes, and not the parietal lobes, that produces this deficit (at least for the left-hemisphere-damaged patients; the right-hemisphere damaged patients could not be divided into the appropriate groups). Specifically, the patients with damage to the left superior temporal gyrus (which may well have also affected the middle temporal gyrus) showed a strong bias toward encoding the global patterns, whereas the patients with damage to the inferior parietal lobule showed no such bias. However, patients with damage to the left inferior parietal lobule had difficulty allocating attention selectively to one level or the other. The results suggest that at least two processes are at work when patterns are encoded at different levels of scale—one that involves attentional allocation in the parietal lobes, and one that involves specialization for encoding different levels of scale in the temporal lobe. Such specialization may develop with practice if attention is consistently allocated to outputs of neurons with relatively large or small receptive fields. If a certain type of stimuli are typically encoded primarily in one hemisphere, their representations presumably become more effective in that hemisphere (e.g., see Kosslyn, Sokolov, and Chen 1989).

In addition, Delis, Kramer, and Kiefner (1988) found that a split-brain patient could recognize and draw higher-level (more global) shapes better when he used his left hand (which is controlled primarily by the right hemisphere) to respond, whereas he could recognize and draw smaller, component shapes better when he used his right hand (controlled primarily by the left hemisphere) to respond. It may or may not be of interest that, judging from data presented in tabular form in this article, the patient had a tendency for such a difference even prior to the surgery.

Finally, I must note that the divided-visual-field results have sometimes been difficult to replicate (for a review, see Van Kleeck 1989; see also Brown and Kosslyn, in press). Although Van Kleeck's (1989) metanalysis revealed that Sergent's (1987) findings were consistent across the reported studies, the fragility is as expected if the effect depends on how one sets one's attention. Specifically, I assume that the visual buffer represents the input at multiple scales of resolution (see chapter 4), and the attention window operates at a single level of scale. The scales differ by the average sizes of the receptive fields being monitored; nevertheless, there will be a range of receptive field sizes within each level. According to the present theory, the hemispheres by default monitor the outputs from neurons with relatively large or small receptive fields within a level of scale. If one is focused on the wrong scale, the hemispheric differences may not be evident. For example, if one is focused on too coarse a scale, the receptive fields generally may be so large and separated that they may obscure the shape of the component letters of hierarchical stimuli. Neurons with large receptive fields average the spatial variation within them, and coarse coding of shape will be impossible if the shape is too small relative to the overlap of the fields. If the sizes of the large and small letters differ enough, there may not be a single scale that will allow one to encode both levels easily. These factors, then, will also encourage the system to seek distinctive properties when classifying few targets of different sizes.

We will return to these issues in the following chapter, when we consider the ways in which spatial relations representations are encoded and the possible role of attending to neurons with different-sized receptive fields in this process. The important conclusion here is that there is converging evidence that the pattern activation subsystem can be further decomposed into an exemplar pattern activation subsystem and a category pattern activation subsystem. These two subsystems are presented in figure 6.10 in the context of the subsystems discussed in previous chapters.

Anatomical Localization

Milner (1968) long ago showed that patients who had the right anterior temporal lobe removed had a selective deficit for recognizing specific faces, which is consistent with the claim that the exemplar pattern activation subsystem is more effective in the right hemisphere temporal lobe. In contrast, I have been unable to find results of experiments in which unilateral temporal lobectomy patients had to recognize visual categories (e.g., they were shown different versions of the same type of drawing at study and at test). However,

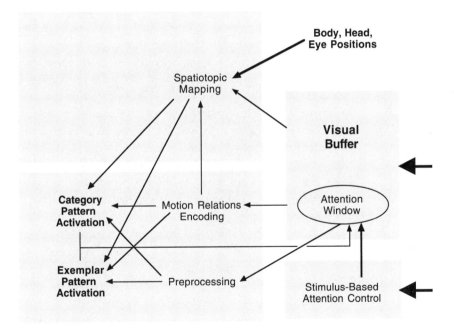

Figure 6.10 The division of the pattern activation subsystem into two more specialized subsystems, one that encodes categories (perhaps represented as prototypes) and one that encodes specific exemplars. The subsystems are illustrated in the context of the subsystems discussed previously.

Identifying Objects in Degraded Images

Marsolek (1992) found that people categorize new instances of novel patterns better when the stimuli are presented initially to the left hemisphere; this finding is consistent with the claim that the category pattern activation subsystem is more effective in the left hemisphere.

Summary: Identifying Objects in Degraded Input Images

We identify objects in degraded input images by exploiting constraint satisfaction processes. When images are degraded, information that otherwise might be of little import in object identification becomes paramount. We use motion, parts, spatial properties of objects and parts, and shapes of exemplars and categories (perhaps represented as prototypes) to identify objects. All of this information is encoded in the ventral and dorsal systems, and then is sent to associative memory. It is in associative memory that these various types of information converge to implicate a specific object. We will consider the operation of associative memory in more detail in the next chapter.

IMAGERY AND PERCEPTION

The subsystems I have posited here play major roles in visual mental imagery. For example, the distinction between category and exemplar pattern activation subsystems predicts that we can visualize both prototypes (e.g., of a dog) and specific examples. This distinction allows us to understand a finding reported by David and Cutting (1992), who showed pictures of objects to subjects in the left or right visual field. In one task, the subjects decided whether the pictured object is larger than a cat (in real life). Kosslyn et al. (1977) had shown that subjects use imagery in this task, provided that the objects are close in size. And in fact, the subjects required less time if the pictures were shown initially to the right hemisphere; this task would appear to require a precise representation of size, and so may draw upon spatial information associated with (via associative memory) representations in the exemplar pattern activation subsystem. In contrast, David and Cutting found that subjects could evaluate whether a pictured object was living or nonliving faster if it was shown initially to the left hemisphere. Indeed, Cutting (1990) draws a distinction between left and right hemispheric function very much like the one proposed here.

Similarly, the other subsystems play roles in recognizing patterns in imaged objects or scenes. One can visualize a race and "see" when a particular horse started to falter, visualize a room and "see" the size and position of a chair, and so on. But more than this, the dorsal system plays an essential role in the process of generating multipart images. For example, such images may be used to retrieve spatial information when one navigates without visual cues (see Loarer and Savoyant 1991). To see how the dorsal system is used to generate images, we will need to consider the information lookup and top-down search subsystems in more detail. Thus, I shall defer any more discussion of imagery until the following chapter.

CONCLUSIONS

A combination of computational analyses, computer simulation modeling, and neuropsychological results converged to implicate three additional processing subsystems. The motion relations encoding subsystem codes specific types of motion relations; these relations are "standard" patterns that are "wired in" or patterns that have been discovered to be distinctive. The output from this subsystem is sent to the ventral system for recognition and to the dorsal system for tracking. In the dorsal system, the spatiotopic mapping subsystem converts spatial properties from retinotopic coordinates to spatiotopic coordinates. Finally, the pattern activation subsystem was divided into two more specialized subsystems. The category pattern activation subsystem classifies a stimulus as a member of a visual category, and the exemplar pattern activation subsystem registers that it is a particular instance.

The processes discussed so far will allow one to identify objects in moderately degraded input images. If an image is highly degraded, however, one may only be able to form a rough guess as to the identity of the object following the initial encoding, and may need to seek additional information to confirm this guess. I discuss this sort of top-down hypothesis testing in the following chapter.

7 Identifying Contorted Objects

Perhaps the most difficult problem in object identification occurs when an object is contorted in a novel way so that its shape is dissimilar to any familiar shape associated with the object (such as might occur when a cat is sleeping in an unusual position or a bicycle has tumbled to the ground). If an object is rigid or in a typical posture, and is seen from a familiar point of view, a direct match often can be made to a pattern stored in the ventral system. When only a poor match is made, other sorts of information—motion, parts, distinctive characteristics, and spatial properties—can help one to identify an object. In this chapter I will argue that we use a specific kind of spatial information, in conjunction with representations of parts, to identify objects in unusual shape configurations. This chapter further fills out the picture that has emerged in the previous chapters.

The logic of computational analysis leads us to look for properties of the input that are preserved across the different shapes an object can assume. One such property is the identity of the parts. For example, even though the projected shape changes radically when a hand clenches and stretches, no new fingers or joints are added. Even if there is no match to an object, the input may match patterns that correspond to parts of the object; the pattern activation subsystems do not "know" whether a pattern corresponds to an object or a part, they just match patterns. If the system can identify the parts, it has strong clues as to the identity of the object (Biederman 1987; Hoffman and Richards 1985; Koenderink and van Doorn 1982; Pentland 1986, 1987, 1989; Vaina and Zlateva 1990).

Notice also that an object is more than the sum of its parts; the arrangement of the parts is often a critical feature of the object's identity (see Attneave 1974; Biederman 1987; Hoffman and Richards 1985). Hence it is important to note that the spatial relations among the parts of contorted objects do not change, provided that the spatial relations are described at a relatively abstract level: the joints remain connected to each other in the same way, regardless of how the hand is configured. Thus, if the system can identify the parts and compute relatively abstract spatial relations among them, it can describe the structure of an object regardless of how it is configured. It is clear that people can in fact identify an object even when they see only a portion at a time, and hence are forced to integrate the parts and their locations in memory; this ability is dramatically illustrated by our ability to identify a moving object when we see it through a hole in a piece of paper that is placed over it (e.g., Rock, 1981).[1]

But in some circumstances, the visible parts and their spatial relations are not enough to allow one to identify an object at first glance. In such circumstances, the system goes into a problem-solving mode, which is relatively laborious. The relation between imagery and perception comes to the fore when we consider this top-down hypothesis testing mode. Indeed, such visual problem solving involves virtually all imagery processes. In this chapter I describe the subsystems that are used to encode spatial relations and those that are used in such visual problem solving. I concentrate here on perception, and flesh out the implications for imagery in chapters 9 and 10.

CATEGORICAL VERSUS COORDINATE SPATIAL RELATIONS

The spatiotopic mapping subsystem performs a coordinate transformation; it does not compute different types of spatial relations. To use location to identify the thing on someone's head as a hat, one must know that it is *on* the head. I distinguish between two distinct classes of spatial relations representations, which have very different roles in information processing.

Consider first another one of our abilities: Most people can walk around a familiar room in the dark without bumping into the furniture (very often, anyway; see Rieser et al. 1990). Human beings are reasonably good at reaching or moving to a familiar location even when visual feedback is not available (see also Goodale, Pelisson, and Prablanc 1986; Loarer and Savoyant 1991). Furthermore, like Tolman's (1948) rats, we can navigate to a goal along novel routes. Such examples illustrate not only that we can store information that is useful for guiding movements, but also that we do not store actual sequences of motor commands. Rather, we store locations as sets of coordinates, which can be continually updated to reflect our present position. As noted earlier, Nemire and Bridgeman (1987) found very similar localization errors in a manual pointing task and a multiple-saccade eye fixation task, which they argue is evidence that the same map of space is in fact used in pointing and directing eye movements. To be retained over time, such spatial information must be encoded into memory. The spatiotopic mapping subsystem only performs a coordinate transformation; it does not specify motor-based coordinates nor does it store information. Hence, there is good reason to posit an additional subsystem. I hypothesize a *coordinate spatial relations encoding subsystem*, which encodes spatial information in a way that is useful for guiding action.

A critical aspect of the representations encoded by the coordinate spatial relations encoding subsystem is that they specify metric spatial relations. To move properly, one needs to know exactly where an object is located. Given my inferences about the kinds of spatial information that are computed by the spatiotopic mapping subsystem, I am led to hypothesize that the coordinate spatial relations encoding subsystem not only computes metric relations between distinct parsed regions, but also computes metric measures of size and orientation. Furthermore, my earlier line of reasoning leads me to posit that these representations characterize objects and parts, depending on the level of resolution; such relatively early encoding processes do not "know" whether a parsed region is an object or part. Thus, the coordinate spatial relations encoding subsystem computes metric information about location, size, and orientation for both objects and parts.

However, very few—if any—types of objects must be discriminated based purely on the metric spatial relations among their parts. Rather, to identify a stimulus as a member of a category, such as a dog or bike, one needs to ignore the precise spatial arrangements among parts—which vary for different exemplars. This requirement may be one reason why we organize parts using relations such as connected/disconnected, inside/outside, left/right, above/below and so forth (e.g., see Stevens and Coupe 1978; for a similar view, see Biederman 1987). Each of these spatial relations treats as equivalent a large class of relative positions; members of each class need share only one characteristic of their position. For example, one object can be *above* another regardless of their relative positions on the horizontal axis. Because these representations define such equivalence classes, I call them *categorical spatial relations*.

Representations of metric spatial relations are qualitatively distinct from representations of categorical spatial relations. A metric representation is "dense"; that is, an indefinite number of intermediate cases fall between any two relations (see Goodman 1968). In contrast, a categorical relation is discrete, not dense; for example, there is no range of intermediate values between *on* and *off* or between *above, level,* and *below*. Although in some cases a categorical spatial relation can subsume a range of coordinates (e.g., *near* and *far*), many categorical relations do not have corresponding metric relations; for example, there is no metric analog to left/right, above/below, inside/outside, and so on. Indeed, many categorical relations are independent of specific distances (e.g., *left of* and *above* imply nothing about distance). The categories specified by categorical relations treat as equivalent a very large number of specific relations. In addition, note that when one specifies a metric distance with a label, such as "two inches from," one is specifying a particular kind of category: it contains only one member (note that it may be impossible ever to specify this member precisely, because the scale is dense, but that is another matter).

In addition, categorical spatial relations differ qualitatively from one another; for example, *above* is not a finer characterization or different version of *left of*. The categories represented can be relatively general (e.g., *connected to*) or specific; for example, a categorical relation could specify a "connected by a hinge" relation, such as that between the forearm and upper arm. But in all cases categorical spatial relations representations capture general properties of a relation without specifying the position in detail (e.g., "connected by a hinge" without specifying the precise angle).

Hence, the two kinds of information are conceptually distinct, and different mappings are necessary to derive them from input. Recall that subsystems are characterized by the input/output mapping they perform; the greater the difference between two mappings, the more likely it is that separate subsystems perform them. Because metric spatial relations are distinct in this way from categorical spatial relations, I hypothesize that the mappings are computed by different subsystems. The *categorical spatial relations encoding subsystem* produces a "spatial code" that specifies a categorical relation between two or more objects, parts, or characteristics, or specifies the size or orientation of a single object, part, or characteristic. These spatial codes, unlike the coordinates produced by the coordinate spatial relations encoding subsystem, are propositional representations.

In many cases, the categories developed by the categorical spatial relations encoding subsystem may depend on the task at hand. However, I can state in principle that these categories cannot be restricted to topological spatial relations. Topological relations remain constant over the various configurations of semirigid objects; parts remain connected or disconnected, and they remain inside or outside the object. From a computational point of view, however, topological relations per se are too weak; they fail to draw many important distinctions. For example, a teacup and a phonograph record have identical topological descriptions because each has a single hole. To provide useful descriptions of how parts are arranged, the categorical spatial relations encoding subsystem must compute more restrictive abstract relations, which capture general properties of the spatial structure without making commitments to the specific topographic properties that are likely to change from instance to instance. The relation of the coordinate spatial relations encoding subsystem and the categorical spatial relations encoding subsystem to other subsystems is illustrated in figure 7.1.

Empirical Tests

Kosslyn et al. (1989) reported a series of experiments that provide support for the existence of distinct subsystems that encode categorical and coordinate spatial relations. The logic of these experiments rested on uncontroversial findings in neuropsychology. First, language is processed more effectively in the left cerebral hemisphere (in right-handed people—and in most lefties too, for that matter; see Springer and Deutsch 1985). As noted when we considered the categorical pattern activation subsystem in the previous chapter, language relies on categorical representations; such representations underlie not only word meanings but also individual phonemes and syntactic classes. Thus, although my colleagues and I believe that both subsystems are implemented to some degree in both hemispheres, we conjectured that the categorical spatial relations encoding subsystem might be more effective in the left cerebral hemisphere. Second, there is good neuropsychological evidence that navigation depends on processing in the right cerebral hemisphere (e.g., De Renzi 1982). As was argued earlier, effective navigation depends on

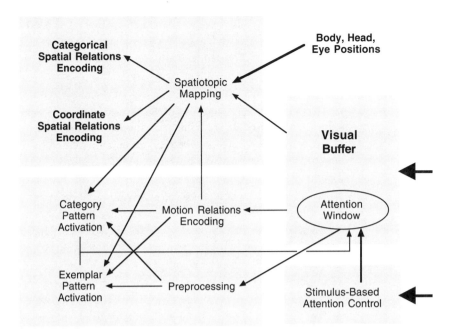

Figure 7.1 The categorical and coordinate spatial relations encoding subsystems in relation to the subsystems discussed previously.

coordinate spatial relations representations.[2] Thus, we conjectured that the coordinate spatial relations encoding subsystem might be more effective in the right hemisphere.[3]

The logic of the experiments rested on a simple fact of neuroanatomy. As it happens, the retina is actually part of the brain that has been pushed forward. Indeed, Dowling (1987) calls the retina "an approachable part of the brain." Furthermore, the left part of each retina can be thought of as an extension of the left cerebral hemisphere, and the right part of each retina as an extension of the right cerebral hemisphere. Thus, as noted in chapter 2, if an input image falls on only one hemiretina, one cerebral hemisphere will receive the input initially. We assumed, as have many others (see Beaumont 1982; Bryden 1982; Springer and Deutsch 1985), that if the input is presented initially to the hemisphere that is more effective at processing the task, the subject will be able to respond more quickly than if the input is presented initially to the hemisphere that is less effective at performing the task.

For present purposes, we did not care very much about cerebral lateralization per se. Our hypotheses about hemispheric specialization were important because they provided a way to document the existence of two distinct processing subsystems, each of which computes a particular type of representation of spatial relations. If only a single subsystem were used to encode all spatial relations, then it should operate better in one hemisphere or equally effectively in both hemispheres. This possibility can be ruled out by a dissociation between categorical and coordinate relations, with one hemisphere computing one type better and the other computing the other type better. Such a dissociation is evidence that distinct neural networks (in different halves of the brain) are used to compute representations of the two kinds of spatial relations.

The first experiment conducted by Kosslyn et al. (1989) required subjects to evaluate *on* versus *off* or a specific metric distance. *On* and *off* clearly are categorical spatial relations; recall that the hallmark of such relations is that a range of positions are grouped together and treated as equivalent. For example, a cat is *on* a mat no matter where it curls up on it; for purposes of assigning the relation, the differences in location on the mat are ignored. In contrast, if we asked whether the cat was within four inches of the edge of the mat, metric relations must be computed to make the judgment.

The first experiment used analogs of these two tasks. The subjects decided whether a dot was on or off the contour of a line drawing of a blob or whether a dot was within 1 cm of the contour. We asked the subjects to stare at a fixation point directly in front of them and then to evaluate stimuli that were presented to the left or right side of fixation. The stimuli were visible for less time than is needed to move the eyes (less than 200 ms), thereby ensuring that the input was perceived initially by only one cerebral hemisphere.

As expected, the subjects evaluated whether a dot was on or off a blob faster when the stimuli were presented initially to the left hemisphere, but evaluated distance faster when the stimuli were presented initially to the right hemisphere. This result is illustrated in figure 7.2. Thus, we had preliminary evidence that supports the psychological reality of two distinct ways of representing spatial relations.

As evident in the figure, however, there was a trend for slower response times in the on/off task; in addition, the subjects made more errors in this task. These results raised an alternative interpretation of the results: The left hemisphere simply might be superior at more difficult tasks. Thus, we designed

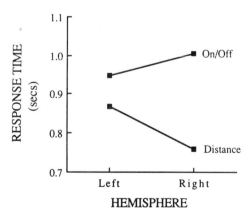

Figure 7.2 Results of an experiment in which subjects judged whether a dot was on or off a blob or whether it was within 1 cm of it. (Copyright 1989 by the American Psychological Association. Reprinted from Kosslyn et al. 1989 by permission of the publisher.)

a second experiment, which also provided additional evidence for the generality of the distinction.

The subjects in the second experiment saw a plus and a minus symbol, and judged either whether the plus was left of the minus or whether the two characters were more than an inch apart. We chose the various distances between characters with an eye toward making the two tasks of comparable difficulty. Exactly the same stimuli, pairs of plus and minus symbols, were presented in both tasks. As before, the stimuli were presented briefly to one side or the other of fixation, ensuring that only one hemisphere perceived the input initially.

As is illustrated in figure 7.3, the results were as expected. We again found a dissociation between the two tasks, with faster performance of the categorical task when stimuli were presented initially to the left hemisphere and faster performance of the distance task when stimuli were presented initially to the right hemisphere. However, although the overall difference in difficulty between the tasks was not statistically significant, there was still a trend for the left hemisphere to be better at the more difficult task.

Thus, Kosslyn et al. (1989) conducted another experiment. In this experiment we examined yet another categorical spatial relation, above/below. We used a paradigm introduced by Hellige and Michimata (1989), in which the subjects decide whether a dot is above or below a short horizontal line or whether a dot is within a specific distance of the line. In our version of the task, subjects decided whether the dot was within half an inch of the line. We selected the dot locations to make the discrimination difficult, hoping to eliminate the previous confounding between left-hemisphere superiority in the categorical task and superior overall performance.

As before, we found that presenting the stimuli initially to the left or right hemisphere had different effects for the two tasks, as is illustrated in figure 7.4. These results nicely replicated those reported by Hellige and Michimata,

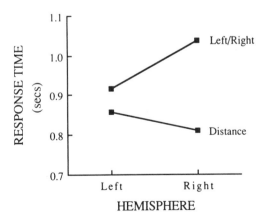

Figure 7.3 Results of an experiment in which subjects judged whether a plus was left or right of a minus or whether it was within 1 inch of it. (Copyright 1989 by the American Psychological Association. Reprinted from Kosslyn et al. 1989 by permission of the publisher.)

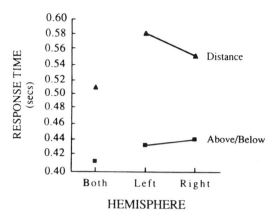

Figure 7.4 Results of an experiment in which subjects judged whether a dot was above or below a line or whether it was within 1/2 inch of it. (Copyright 1989 by the American Psychological Association. Reprinted from Kosslyn et al. 1989 by permission of the publisher).

and provide additional evidence for the distinction between the two subsystems. Furthermore, we succeeded in making the distance judgment more difficult than the categorical judgment, thereby eliminating the possibility that the hemispheric advantages simply reflect overall task difficulty. Rybash and Hoyer (1992) have since replicated this result for the coordinate task, but found only the tiniest difference (in the expected direction) for the categorical task.

My colleagues and I (Kosslyn, Gitelman, Alpert, and Thompson, in preparation) used Hellige and Michimata's tasks in a PET scanning experiment to produce another type of support for the distinction between categorical and coordinate spatial relations representations. In the baseline trials, we asked subjects first to view a series of horizontal bars, half of which had a dot above the bar and half of which had a dot below the bar. The subjects simply pressed a pedal when they saw a stimulus, alternating response feet over trials. The subjects also participated in two test conditions. In one, they decided whether the dot was above or below the bar. In the other test condition, they decided whether the dot was within half an inch of the bar (they were shown what this criterion distance looked like on the screen before the task); the order of the two test conditions was counterbalanced over subjects. Compared to the baseline task, we found a strong asymmetry in cerebral blood flow when subjects made the metric judgment. As predicted, the right inferior parietal lobe was much more active than the left. In contrast, we found greater activity in the left hemisphere when subjects made the categorical judgment. However, although significant in the parietal lobes, this asymmetry was larger in the frontal lobe. The relatively weak parietal asymmetry is consistent with the results of the divided-visual-field experiment illustrated in figure 7.4.

Convergent Evidence The results, then, provide evidence for the existence of separate subsystems that encode categorical and coordinate spatial relations. When the results of these and other similar experiments are compared, we consistently found that subjects could evaluate categorical relations better when stimuli were initially presented to the left hemisphere (although often by very small amounts), whereas they could evaluate distance better when stimuli were initially presented to the right hemisphere.[4] This finding was obtained for the categorical relations on/off, left/right, and above/below and for distances relative to 1 cm, 1/2 inch, and 1 inch. The results were not due to differences in the difficulty of performing the different judgments.

These conclusions are buttressed by clever experiments with focal-lesion patients reported by Laeng (1993). Laeng reasoned that if categorical spatial relations representations are computed primarily in the posterior left hemisphere, then damage to this area should cause the patient to become insensitive to changes in categorical relations among objects; in contrast, if coordinate spatial relations representations are computed primarily in the posterior right hemisphere, then damage to this area should cause the patient to become insensitive to changes in the metric relations among objects. Laeng tested 62 patients, half with left-hemisphere damage and half with right-hemisphere damage, and a group of similar, but neurologically intact, control subjects. He asked the subjects to perform two tasks. On each trial of the "identity task," he presented a drawing of one or more versions of the same object (e.g., a large cat to the left of a small cat); after a short delay, the patients were asked to decide whether another drawing was the same or different. The different drawings either had altered categorical spatial relations (e.g., if the large cat initially was shown on the left, it was now on the right), or the metric distance was varied. As expected, patients with left-hemisphere damage had more difficulty when categorical spatial relations were altered, whereas the patients with right-hemisphere damage had more difficulty when the metric distance was altered. The patients had the same numbers of overall errors, but they were of different types. These effects were largest for patients with damage to the parietal lobes per se. It is of interest that the same results were obtained when a single object was varied (by reversing its direction or altering its extent on the horizontal or vertical axis) as when the relations among objects were varied; this result is consistent with my claim that the spatial relations encoding subsystems also encode spatial properties of individual objects, parts, or characteristics that correspond to perceptual units in the usual buffer.

In Laeng's other task, the subjects saw a drawing and then were shown two variations—one that had altered categorical relations and one that had altered metric relations. They were asked to indicate which of the two "looked more similar" to the standard. Although both lesion groups tended to choose the categorical transformation as most similar to the standard, the left-hemisphere-damaged patients found the categorical variants more similar than did the right-hemisphere-damaged patients or the control subjects, and the right-hemisphere-damaged patients indicated that the categorical variants were more similar less often than control subjects. Moreover, when only the patients with parietal damage were examined, the right-hemisphere-damaged patients made more coordinate choices, whereas the left-hemisphere-damaged patients made categorical choices. A nice twist to this study was that the patients were given tests of aphasia, and those results were not related to performance in the spatial relations tasks.[5]

Other findings in the neuropsychological literature are consistent with the distinction between the two spatial relations encoding subsystems. For example, Umilta et al. (1974) asked normal subjects to judge the orientations of narrow rectangles. In one experiment, the rectangles were at vertical, horizontal, and 45° diagonal orientations. The subjects were to press a bar if the stimulus was at either of two specified orientations, and to refrain from pressing the bar if it was at another orientation. These subjects performed better when the stimuli were presented initially to the left hemisphere. In another experiment, the rectangles were presented at other oblique orientations (15°, 30°, 45°, and 60° from the vertical); these subjects performed better when the stimuli were presented initially to the right hemisphere (see also White 1971). I posit that the categorical spatial relations encoding subsystem computes orientation as well as location, and vertical, horizontal, and 45° orientations are likely to be easily categorized; hence, the left-hemisphere advantage for these orientations makes sense. Similarly, it is unlikely that the other orientations would be easily categorized, and hence they would be computed via the coordinate spatial relations encoding subsystem.[6]

Along the same lines, Hock, Kronseder, and Sissons (1981) asked subjects to judge figures as same or different when they were at different orientations. The right hemisphere showed orientation dependence whereas the left did not. This result is consistent with the claim that the left hemisphere computes categorical spatial relations that are invariant over orientation (e.g., "connected to"). Examining another categorical spatial relation, Servos and Peters (1990) showed that subjects could decide whether part of a display was in front of another part better when the stimuli were presented initially to the left hemisphere. (See also Olson and Bialystok 1983; for reviews of other results that are consistent with the categorical/coordinate distinction, see Davidoff 1982; Servos and Peters 1990).

In addition, many reports in the clinical literature are consistent with the distinction between the two spatial relations encoding subsystems. For example, Goldenberg (1989), Hannay, Varney, and Benton (1976), Taylor and Warrington (1973), and Warrington and Rabin (1970) all found that right-hemisphere damage disrupts a patient's ability to encode the precise position of a dot more than does left-hemisphere damage. Although Ratcliff and Davies-Jones (1972) failed to find this effect, it was replicated subsequently by Hannay, Varney, and Benton (1976), who used a more difficult version of Ratcliff and Davies-Jones's task. Similarly, De Renzi, Faglioni, and Scotti (1971) found that patients with damage to the posterior right hemisphere had difficulty pointing a rod in the same orientation as a sample rod; these orientations were not easily categorized, and so coordinate spatial relations representations presumably were required to perform this task. The patients with damage to the posterior right hemisphere not only did more poorly than control subjects but also did more poorly than patients with damage to the anterior right hemisphere or to the anterior or posterior left hemisphere.

Moreover, Ratcliff and Newcombe (1973) found that patients with posterior right hemisphere lesions were dramatically impaired (relative to other brain-damaged patients and control subjects) at learning a stylus maze task; the pathways were formed by connecting points (intersections of grooves) in a 9 × 9 array (see figure 1 of their paper) and hence were complex enough to discourage use of categorical spatial relations representations. Similarly, Mehta and Newcombe (1991) found that right-hemisphere damaged patients had difficulty determining whether two angles were the same, whereas left-hemisphere damaged patients performed this task normally.

On the other hand, left-hemisphere damage in the region of the angular gyrus sometimes results in Gerstmann's syndrome (e.g., see Critchley 1953; De Renzi 1982), one aspect of which is disruption of the ability to distinguish left from right. Levine, Mani, and Calvanio (1988) describe one such case in which the patient could not judge left from right but could point accurately to a target; this patient exhibited a clean dissociation between categorical and coordinate spatial relations processing. Similarly, Luria (1980) describes patients with left occipital-parietal lesions who could not determine categorical spatial relations such as *on top of* versus *under*. In short, right-hemisphere damage can disrupt one's ability to localize objects precisely, whereas left-hemisphere damage can disrupt one's ability to categorize spatial relations.

It is also important to note that many tasks can be performed using either type of spatial relations representation, and patients with unilateral lesions may not show selective deficits in these tasks. For example, De Renzi, Faglioni, and Scotti (1971) asked subjects to observe six geometric shapes on cards that were arranged into two rows of three. The shapes were covered, and the subjects were shown a copy of each shape and asked to point to the location of the corresponding card. Although patients with posterior lesions performed more poorly than patients with anterior lesions, there was no difference between patients with left- and right-hemisphere damage. This task clearly could be performed using either type of spatial relations representation, given that the row and the position in the row are easily categorized.

Similarly, Ratcliff and Newcombe (1973) found no difference between left- and right-hemisphere damaged patients at learning to walk along a pathway through a maze; only patients with bilateral posterior lesions were impaired in this task. The fact that unilateral damage did not impair performance can be easily explained: These pathways were produced by connecting points in a 3 × 3 array (see their figure 2), which was sufficiently simple that either type of representation could be used to encode the necessary spatial relations.

Finally, it is also important to note that all tasks are carried out by more than a single subsystem, and different hemispheres may be more adept at carrying out specific processes. Hence, in some cases damage to either hemisphere can disrupt task performance. For example, Mehta and Newcombe (1991), extending the earlier findings of Mehta, Newcombe, and Damasio (1987), report that left-hemisphere-damaged patients had difficulty in a task that requires encoding line orientation (Benton, Varney, and Hamsher 1978). In this task, the subject examined two oriented line segments and selected the corresponding segments from an array of oriented lines. The lines in the array were like spokes extending out from a circle, progressively tilted in 18° increments. Thus, the orientations would be difficult to categorize, and we would expect that the right hemisphere should have been required for this discrimination (in fact, the left-hemisphere-damaged patients were no worse than the right-hemisphere-damaged patients).[7] Following Mehta, Newcombe, and Damasio (1987), Mehta and Newcombe suggest that "the intervention of the LH [left hemisphere] is necessary in handling extraneous and/or distracting visual information." They suggest that such processing is necessary in this task "to disentangle the target two lines of given slope from the decoys in the array" (p. 164). Indeed, Corkin (1979), Russo and Vignolo (1967), Teuber and Weinstein (1956), Van Kleeck and Kosslyn (1989), and others have shown that the left hemisphere is critically involved in detecting target figures when they are embedded in other patterns. These results are consistent with my proposal (developed in the previous chapter and further developed below) that the left hemisphere is more adept at using outputs from neurons with relatively small receptive fields; such input may be necessary to select among nearby patterns, which is a prerequisite to encoding their orientation.[8]

Effects of Practice   Kosslyn et al. (1989) also found that after much practice the left hemisphere apparently became adept at encoding distance. This result was also replicated by Rybash and Hoyer (1992).[9] The subjects did not simply learn the appropriate verbal labels; they had those to begin with, or they could not have understood the instructions and produced the appropriate responses. Furthermore, verbal labels were used in both tasks, and hence could not account for differences between them. The left hemisphere apparently developed a new categorical spatial relation during the course of the task. This representation is preverbal. Indeed, this kind of perceptual category logically must come before a label can be applied. (This is also true when metric distances are to be labeled; at some point in processing a category must be formed, even if it is a very narrow one based on an approximation to an analog measurement.)

Perhaps more telling, the notion that verbal mediation is used to represent categorical spatial relations is inconsistent with the often weak left-hemisphere superiority in the categorical spatial relations tasks. The left hemisphere is superior at naming, and should have been much better at such judgments if verbal mediation were used. Please note, however, that we obtained statistical interactions between task and hemisphere in all of the divided-visual-field experiments, which is sufficient to argue for the distinction between the two subsystems (see Hellige 1983).

The claim that the left hemisphere develops new categorical spatial relations representations as needed helps to explain conflicting findings on dot localization. Kimura (1969) found in several experiments that subjects encoded dot location better when the dots were presented initially to the right hemisphere.

However, this finding has not always been replicated (e.g., see Bryden 1976). One possible reason why not is that differences in the precision of the discrimination and in the amount of practice can lead subjects to form new categorical representations more or less easily. With enough practice, categorical spatial relations can be used to describe position in terms of nested quadrants (by dividing the field into quarters and each quarter into quarters, and so on, as needed); location could in principle be described concisely with relations such as *upper left, lower right, upper right*.

The results, then, suggest that it is probably an error to conceive of categorical spatial relations representations as static. At first glance, it may seem obvious that categorical spatial relations representations develop over time, if only because the relation left/right is not mastered until age 7 or later by most people. However, the observation that different categorical relations are mastered at different ages does not imply that categorical spatial relations are ever learned; they might simply emerge when the necessary neural substrate is developed. Hence, it is of interest that the results from Kosslyn et al.'s (1989) experiment 3 suggest that at least some categorical spatial relations representations develop with practice.

It seems impossible to determine in principle which spatial relations will necessarily be computed by the coordinate spatial relations encoding subsystem. For example, with enough practice, "1 inch apart" might become a categorical relation. Depending on the requirements of frequently encountered tasks, specific relations will or will not be categorized. Nevertheless, although I do expect variation from individual to individual, profession to profession, and culture to culture, members of the same cultures should share a common set of experiences that promote a common set of categorical spatial relations representations.

Computer Models

Kosslyn et al. (1992) built network models that computed categorical and coordinate spatial relations representations. These models served two purposes. First, they provided a different sort of evidence that the two kinds of spatial relations subsystems are in fact distinct. Second, they demonstrated that a simple mechanism is sufficient to produce the observed hemispheric specialization.

We trained a three-layer feedforward network to compute above/below. The input to the network was a set of 32 units, which was treated as a column. Only three units received input, two of which were always contiguous; these units modeled a "bar," and the other unit was a "dot." The relative locations of the three units were varied from trial to trial, with the bar (pair of contiguous units) appearing in four different locations. We trained this network to evaluate whether the dot (single unit) was above or below the bar (the two units), which is a categorical spatial relation, or whether the dot was within four units of the "bar," which is a coordinate task because a precise distance, not an equivalence class, is specified. The output consisted of two units for each task, which indicated *above* and *below* for the categorical task, and *inside the criterion* and *outside the criterion* for the coordinate task.

As usual, we observed the amount of error after a fixed number of training trials, using this measure as an index of how well the network performed the necessary mapping. In these experiments, we adopted the method developed by Rueckl, Cave, and Kosslyn (1989), and compared performance in a network in which all of the hidden units were connected to both categorical and coordinate (metric) output units with performance in a network in which these connections were segregated into two groups. In this split network, half of the connections from the hidden units projected to the output units for the categorical task and half projected to the output units for the coordinate task.

Following the logic of Rueckl, Cave, and Kosslyn, we expected the split network to perform the necessary mapping better than the unsplit one if the computations are in fact distinct. By splitting processing into two streams, we prevented patterns of weights that accomplish one input/output mapping from interfering with those that accomplish the other mapping. And in fact, provided that they were large enough, the split networks were more effective.

We worried that split networks in general might perform better. Thus, we implemented another set of models that performed two metric judgments. In this case, the split networks performed worse than the unsplit ones—which is exactly as we expected, given that the two mappings are similar and can exploit a common set of connections in the net.

A Computational Mechanism   The distinction between categorical and coordinate spatial relations arose in part from the inference that coordinate spatial relations are used in action control, whereas categorical spatial relations are used in object identification. In particular, we observed that action control depends on precise representation of spatial location. The most effective way to represent spatial location precisely uses coarse coding to exploit the overlap among rather coarse representations of location (Hinton, McClelland, and Rumelhart 1986).

We speculated that differences in the use of coarse coding may underlie the hemispheric differences in computing the two types of spatial relations. The right hemisphere may preferentially process input from low-level visual neurons that have relatively large receptive fields; these receptive fields receive input from relatively large regions of space, and these receptive fields would also have a large degree of overlap. We expected these broadly tuned receptive fields to promote effective coarse coding, which might explain the right hemisphere's superior ability to encode precise location. In contrast, the left hemisphere may preferentially process input from low-level visual neurons that have relatively small receptive fields; and these receptive fields would not overlap very much when one is attending to a relatively large region of space. In this case, sets of these relatively small, nonoverlapping receptive fields could be used to delineate pockets of space, such as the regions that are above or below a reference point, left or right of a reference point, and so on. (Indeed, if the receptive fields did not overlap at all, such mappings would be "linearly separable"—these mappings are so straightforward that they can be accomplished by direct connections from the input units to the output units, without need of a hidden layer; see Rumelhart and McClelland 1986.)

The outputs from neurons with large receptive fields would be useful in preattentive processing. Such processes, almost by definition, must monitor a wide range of visual angle. As noted earlier, preattentive processing plays a crucial role in controlling actions; one needs to look at or reach to an object with reasonably high precision, even if it is seen out of the corner of one's eye. Livingstone (personal communication) has suggested that the magnocellular ganglia (see Livingstone and Hubel 1987) may project preferentially to the right hemisphere; or, perhaps this hemisphere preferentially uses such information. These neurons have relatively large receptive fields, and are probably involved in preattentive processing.

The outputs of neurons with relatively large, overlapping receptive fields also can produce the necessary precision to guide an initial movement—even if a target is seen out of the corner of one's eye. Thus it is of interest that Fisk and Goodale (1988; see also Goodale 1988) found that right-hemisphere–damaged patients have difficulty in the initial phases of reaching toward a visual target, but not in the final phases.

These hypotheses rest on several steps of reasoning, and there is ample opportunity for the logic to have jumped the rails. Thus, these hypotheses are ideal candidates for computer simulation modeling. We used network models to test these hypotheses in two ways. First, we examined the receptive fields that were developed by the hidden units of different networks after the networks were trained to encode categorical or coordinate relations. As before, we examined which input units most strongly influenced each hidden unit, and treated the area of the input array that was most strongly connected to the hidden unit as its receptive field.

Second, we tested the hypotheses by "hard-wiring" networks in advance, so that the input units had relatively large or small receptive fields. In this case, we set the weights on connections from the stimulus array at the outset and did not allow them to be modified during training. We then simply observed how effectively networks with relatively large, overlapping receptive fields performed the two kinds of mappings compared to networks with relatively small, nonoverlapping receptive fields.

The results were straightforward: As predicted, the networks that were trained to perform the categorical task spontaneously developed smaller receptive fields than those that performed the coordinate task. Moreover, when we fixed the sizes of the receptive fields in advance, the networks with large receptive fields performed the coordinate task better than networks with fixed small receptive field sizes, and there was a tendency for the opposite pattern in the categorical task. These results are similar to those from the corresponding experiments with human subjects (as summarized above).

In addition, we showed that the effects of receptive field size could be eliminated if enough input units were provided. This finding is important because Sergent (1991a) found that the hemispheric differences occur only when the bar-and-dot stimuli are presented with low contrast. Presumably, when the stimuli are presented with high contrast, more low-level neurons contribute input to the higher-level subsystems. In this case, even the minimal overlap of the small receptive fields may be enough to encode metric location effectively in the left hemisphere, and there might be so many active neurons that one or more is available to delineate discrete pockets of space in the right hemisphere. Judging from the very fast response times she obtained, this account would also explain why Sergent (1991a, b) failed to obtain hemispheric differences in a complex spatial evaluation task with split-brain patients.[10]

Testing a Prediction

Kosslyn, Anderson, Hillger, and Hamilton (in press) tested a prediction of the hypothesis that the right hemisphere receives proportionally more input from neurons that have relatively large receptive fields than does the left hemisphere. We showed subjects pairs of short lines, which were either left-pointing or right-pointing diagonals. The subjects were asked to decide, as quickly and accurately as possible, whether the two segments in a pair had the same orientation. We presented the members of each pair in succession, and usually lateralized them to the same visual field. The key to this experiment was that on half the trials the lines in a pair were presented in nearby locations (roughly 1° of visual angle apart), and on the other half of the trials the lines were presented in relatively distant locations (8° of visual angle apart).

We reasoned that if the right hemisphere typically processes outputs from relatively large receptive fields, then it would be less affected than the left hemisphere by the distance between the stimulus segments. This logic hinges on the idea that the first member of each pair primes the second, and such priming is less effective if different neurons encode the two stimuli. As illustrated in figure 7.5, the results were as expected: We found that the subjects evaluated lines that were in distant locations more quickly when the lines were shown initially to the right hemisphere (i.e., in the left visual field) than to the left, but had a tendency to evaluate nearby lines more quickly if they were presented initially to the left hemisphere.[11]

We next considered the possibility that these results reflect differences in how attention is allocated. Specifically, perhaps the left hemisphere is better than the right at adjusting attention so that one focuses on specific regions of space. Van Kleeck and Kosslyn (1989) provide support for this conjecture. We showed subjects line drawings, and then lateralized possible parts of the figures and asked the subjects to decide whether the parts had been embedded in the original drawing. The subjects in this experiment who performed above chance levels could identify "unnatural" parses of a figure (e.g., a hexagon embedded in a Star of David) better when they were presented to the left hemisphere than when they were presented to the right. This finding suggested to us that the left hemisphere can "override" bottom-up parsing better than the right hemisphere. (In addition, the subjects performed better when

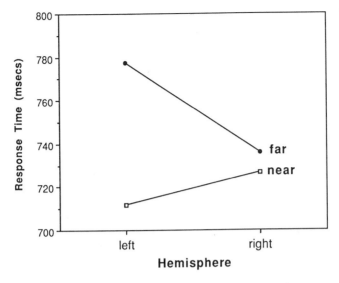

Figure 7.5 Results of an experiment in which successive line segments were presented to the left or right hemisphere; the segments were either in relatively nearby locations or in relatively far locations. (Reprinted from Kosslyn, Anderson, Hillger, and Hamilton (in press), with permission.)

"natural parses" were presented initially to the right hemisphere, which may indicate that parts were stored better or that nonaccidental properties were encoded better in the right hemisphere.)

If so, then perhaps because the line segments used in the task were relatively short (subtending slightly less than 1° of visual angle), the subjects may have tried to focus on the stimuli to encode them more effectively—and the left hemisphere was more adept at making this adjustment. Thus, the left hemisphere would encode more outputs from neurons with relatively small (but overlapping, to obtain high resolution) receptive fields than would the right hemisphere, but this would reflect a strategy (or attention bias)—not hard-wired differences in projections from neurons with different-sized receptive fields. We tested this alternative hypothesis in a second experiment.

The subjects in this experiment participated in two sets of trials, one of which was a replication of the first experiment and one of which used the same task except that the line segments were moved farther toward the periphery. If the hemispheres are hard-wired to monitor outputs from lower-level neurons with different-sized receptive fields, then we expected the right hemisphere to be better for both near and far pairs: Shifting the stimuli toward the periphery would not affect input to low-level visual neurons with relatively large receptive fields, but would filter the input to neurons with relatively small receptive fields—and hence would impair left-hemisphere processing. On the other hand, if the left hemisphere is better at selectively allocating attention, then we expected it more effectively to allocate attention to the periphery. In this task, the stimuli were difficult to encode, and subjects presumably tried to allocate attention to the periphery to facilitate encoding. In so doing, the left hemisphere would now focus on the outputs of lower-level neurons with relatively large receptive fields. Thus, the attention theory led us to expect this experiment to turn the results from the first experiment on their ear: The left hemisphere should be better than the right at encoding widely separated pairs of segments.

The results were clear-cut: As in the first experiment, when subjects saw the stimuli relatively close to the center of the screen, they evaluated two line segments that were relatively far apart faster when the stimuli were presented initially to the right hemisphere than when they were presented initially to the left. In sharp contrast, when the stimuli were toward the periphery, the subjects evaluated two line segments that were relatively far apart faster when they were presented to the left hemisphere than when they were presented to the right—exactly the opposite of the previous findings.

The results just summarized were from the first set of stimuli a subject evaluated. Half of the subjects first saw the stimuli when the lines were relatively close to the center of the screen, and half first saw the stimuli when the lines were toward the periphery. After evaluating one set, they evaluated the remaining set. We reasoned that if the results reflect differences in hard-wired receptive fields, then it should not matter whether subjects had just received another type of trials. But if the results reflect the hemispheres' abilities to allocate attention, then we expected an effect of the "set" established by the locations of the previous stimuli. Such effects were in fact found. The subjects now treated both near and far pairs as relatively close together (responding faster when stimuli were presented to the left hemisphere) if they had previously seen stimuli that were positioned toward the periphery, or as relatively far apart (responding faster when stimuli were presented to the right hemisphere) if they had previously seen the stimuli that were close to the center of the screen.

The results taken together eliminate the hypothesis that the brain is hard-wired so that low-level visual neurons with larger receptive fields project preferentially to the right hemisphere and low-level visual neurons with smaller receptive fields project preferentially to the left hemisphere. Rather, the results are most consistent with the view that the left hemisphere can adjust attention more flexibly than the right hemisphere. However, results reported in the literature (as summarized in the previous chapter and below) suggest that the right hemisphere habitually attends to a coarser spatial scale than the left, which may explain why coordinate spatial relations are computed more effectively in the right hemisphere whereas categorical spatial relations tend to be computed more effectively in the left hemisphere. If this attentional bias is relatively consistent over time, then practice effects will result in the hemispheric differences in efficiency we observed in our studies of spatial relations encoding.[12]

In summary, the results of the divided-visual-field experiments, patient studies, and neural network models lead to two conclusions. First, we have

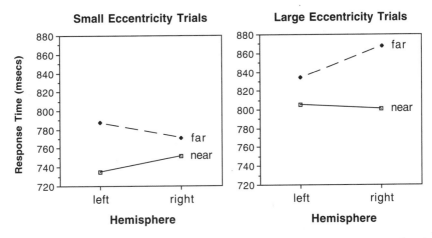

Figure 7.6 Results of an experiment in which successive line segments were presented to the left or right hemisphere. The stimuli were relatively near the center of the screen ("small eccentricity trials") or toward the periphery ("large eccentricity trials"), and were relatively near or far apart. (Reprinted from Kosslyn, Anderson, Hillger, and Hamilton, in press, with permission.)

good convergent evidence that categorical and coordinate spatial relations are encoded by distinct subsystems. Not only did the experiments show hemispheric dissociation for the two types of computations, but the network models also provided evidence that the two kinds of spatial relations are conceptually distinct. Second, network models illustrated a simple mechanism that can explain why the two types of processing are lateralized. Empirical results with humans supported the key assumption of the models, namely that the different subsystems tap input units with different-sized receptive fields. However, these results suggest that the hemispheric differences probably reflect the effects of habitual attentional biases rather than hard-wired structural differences.[13]

Complementary Dorsal and Ventral Representations

The distinction between categorical and coordinate representations in the dorsal system is analogous to that between category and exemplar representations in the ventral system. It is important, however, to keep in mind the distinction between object properties and spatial properties. The ventral system does not represent spatial relations per se. If the ventral system could explicitly represent spatial relations, why would ablation of the parietal lobes severely disrupt an animal's ability to learn spatial discriminations and make spatial judgments?[14] Furthermore, the results of the O'Reilly et al. computer simulations of receptive field properties provided good reasons why spatial relations are not explicitly represented in IT. Although the results obtained by Perrett and co-workers show that some neurons in IT are sensitive to the specific position of the eyes in a stimulus, they do not implicate distinct spatial relations representations per se. The results only indicate that some cells have sharper generalization gradients than others.

Nevertheless, the properties of the two kinds of spatial representations appear to parallel those of the two kinds of shape representations. My colleagues and I reasoned that information about specific examples plays a special role in navigation and reaching: one walks around a table differently if it is round instead of square, and reaches for a mug differently depending on the exact shape of the handle. These differences are not simply a matter of how we name or categorize the shape; we walk differently around tables with different-shaped elliptical tops. Thus, it seemed that representations of specific exemplars should be particularly useful when coordinate spatial relations are used. In contrast, information about categories is relevant when one uses categorical spatial relations. If one is organizing the parts of an object into a structural description, one wants the general type of the part (a hand, a forearm, etc.), not whose it is.

These observations led Jacobs and Kosslyn (in press) and Kosslyn and Jacobs (in press) to construct networks that encoded both the shapes of and spatial relations among stimuli. We wanted to discover whether the dorsal and ventral systems could be lateralized in compatible ways merely because of the sizes of the receptive fields that provided the inputs. In general, when large overlapping receptive fields filtered the input, networks were better able to encode coordinate spatial relations and shape exemplars; when small non-overlapping receptive fields filtered the input, networks were better able to encode categorical spatial relations and categories of shapes. Moreover, even without fixing receptive field properties in advance, networks that performed the two tasks spontaneously developed different-sized receptive fields; those that encoded exemplars or metric information developed larger receptive fields than those that encoded shape or spatial categories.

In addition, in other simulation experiments we paired networks so that they had to share the same input layer: In this case, networks computed their mappings fastest when one encoded categorical spatial relations and the other encoded shape categories, or when one encoded coordinate spatial relations and the other encoded shape exemplars. Other combinations of networks were not as effective. Analyses revealed that, in general, when the two categorical tasks were performed together, the receptive fields became small, whereas when the coordinate and exemplar tasks were performed together, the receptive fields became large. When the two tasks were not so coordinated, the receptive fields developed to a moderate size.

Thus, it is possible that the dorsal and ventral systems become lateralized in compatible ways because they tend to process outputs from the same lower-level neurons, which have relatively large or small receptive fields. This is a very simple idea, and it is surprising how much follows from it.

Two Types of Categorical Spatial Relations Computations

I must note that categorical spatial relations may be computed in more than one way. Ullman (1984) argued persuasively on computational grounds that some categorical spatial relations must be computed using serial processes ("visual routines," as he called them). In particular, he showed that such processes are necessary to decide whether a dot is inside or outside a convoluted blob. Ullman's algorithm involved tracing along the contour of the blob, and then "painting" its interior. Jolicoeur and his colleagues (e.g., Jolicoeur, Ullman, and MacKay 1986; Jolicoeur and Ingleton 1991; McCormick and Jolicoeur 1991) conducted a series of experiments in which they demonstrated that people do in fact scan along the contour of lines to determine whether two X marks are on the same segment; the farther apart the X marks, the more time the subjects needed to make the judgment. The time to scan was relative to the figure, and not determined by visual angle, which is consistent with the idea that the rate of scanning is under strategic control (as I shall discuss in chapter 10).

In contrast, when subjects are asked to decide whether a dot is above or below a line, they require *less* time when the dot is farther away (Kosslyn et al. 1989). In general, such relative position judgments become easier as the distance between two objects increases (obeying the Weber/Fechner law; see Schiffman 1982), which is the opposite of what would be expected if serial attention shifting were required. Thus, we have good evidence that attention shifts are used to compute spatial relations in some situations but not others. I assume that such processing is accomplished by the same mechanisms that shift attention during top-down search, as will be described shortly. In contrast, the categorical relations encoding subsystem as presently conceived is a network that computes categorical relations reflexively; it does not involve control processes that shift the attention window along a contour. Indeed, our network models found it easier to categorize a dot as above or below a bar when the dot was farther from the bar.

I hypothesize that the serial type of algorithm is useful when the stimulus is sufficiently complex or subtends a small enough visual angle that high spatial resolution is necessary to discern its structure. In addition, in some circumstances the two types of processes may work together. In this case, a visual routine would direct one to locate the relevant portions of a figure, and the categorical spatial relations encoding subsystem would then categorize their spatial relation. These conjectures allow us to understand recent PET results reported by Sergent et al. (1992). They asked subjects to decide whether uppercase letters (B, C, D, F, G, J, K, L, N, P, R, and Z) faced left or right, which should require encoding categorical spatial relations between selected segments of the letters. I assume that the description of a letter in associative memory specifies how segments are connected (e.g., for B, something like "a vertical line on the left, with two half-circles, one above the other, joining it at the right"). For example, a letter may include a vertical "spine" (e.g., B, D, F, L, K, P, R) or an open segment (e.g., C, G), and the direction of the letter can be determined by finding the spine or open segment and noting the relative position of the other segments.

Sergent et al. found bilateral activation in the inferior parietal lobule (when the results were compared to those from an object-categorization task, which did not require encoding spatial relations). The right-hemisphere activation was more dorsal than the left-hemisphere activation, which may suggest that the spatiotopic mapping subsystem was activated in the right hemisphere and the categorical spatial relations encoding subsystem was activated in the left hemisphere (which categorized the segments once they were isolated). In addition, Sergent et al. found greater activation in the left pulvinar, which is of interest because the pulvinar apparently plays a role in engaging attention (as will be discussed shortly), as would be necessary to isolate the segments prior to categorizing them. The left pulvinar may be engaged when one seeks high-resolution information, and hence will monitor the outputs from neurons with relatively small receptive fields.[15]

Resolving a Potential Paradox

Much of the present work is based on Ungerleider and Mishkin's (1982) distinction between the ventral and dorsal systems. One piece of evidence for this distinction was the fact that monkeys with IT lesions could not learn to distinguish among shapes but could encode spatial relations. But this finding is puzzling: How could such an animal encode spatial properties (and hence perform the location task), but not be able to distinguish between stimuli as different as a set of stripes and a checkerboard? Stripes define fewer locations than checks, have a different orientation, and are a different size. The spatial properties of the black regions should have been sufficient to allow the monkeys to make the discrimination, even without their temporal lobes.

The problem hinges on an ambiguity in the notion of "encoding." In discussing the temporal-lobe-lesioned monkeys' failure in the pattern discrimination task some years ago, Alan Cowey suggested that the monkeys may be interested in turning the lids over, and hence might attend only to the location of the to-be-grasped edge of each lid. If so, then they would not register the locations of the dark regions of the patterns, and would not be in a position to use spatial properties of the patterns to make the discrimination.

This idea suggests that the animals may not encode the locations of parts of patterns unless they visually attend to them directly. It is possible that the animals attend to one spatial scale ("spatial frequency"), and filter out information that is available at other scales. If so, then when they attend to the lid as a whole, the locations of the dark regions are not registered. As noted in chapter 4, there is in fact evidence that one can set one's attention to specific levels of scale (e.g., see Shulman and Wilson 1987; Shulman et al. 1986). Such an account could explain why animals do not register symbols placed on the lids (e.g., a + versus a square). However, in order to reach properly, the animal would have to encode not just the entire lid, but more specifically the edge that will be grasped. Stripes and checks would be visible at this level of resolution. Indeed, for one lid the animal presumably would grasp at least one stripe (or part of whatever pattern is on the lid), versus no stripes (or part of another pattern) for the other lid. Thus, it is worth considering another possible solution to this conundrum.

What if monkeys do not encode categorical spatial relations reflexively, the way humans appear to do? The human brain is much bigger than the monkey brain (roughly 16 times larger than a macaque's), and all that extra tissue is likely to be doing something. In this case, perhaps the animals encode coordinate spatial relations to guide action (reaching, eye movements, and navigation) but these representations are not available for use in object identification. It is of interest in this context to speculate about the role of categorical spatial relations in language, and vice versa.

Anatomical Localization

The spatial relations encoding subsystems are probably implemented in the posterior parietal lobes. This hypothesis is consistent with a large body of literature that implicates the posterior parietal lobe in movement control (e.g., see Andersen 1987; Hyvarinen 1982). Indeed, the first single-cell recordings from neurons in area 7 of the parietal lobe suggested that some were "command cells" (Mountcastle, et al. 1975). These neurons fire prior to an intentional movement. (Subsequent research has shown that these neurons may be involved in monitoring movements, but my point still stands; see Andersen 1987.)

In addition, I have argued that the coordinate spatial relations encoding subsystem is typically more effective in the right posterior parietal lobe. This hypothesis is supported primarily by two forms of converging evidence. First, as noted above, normal subjects evaluate metric spatial relations better if the stimuli are presented in the left visual field (and hence are seen initially by the right hemisphere) than if they are presented in the right visual field. Second, patients with posterior right-hemisphere lesions have greater difficulty encoding coordinate spatial relations than categorical spatial relations and vice versa for patients with posterior left-hemisphere lesions (e.g., De Renzi 1982; Laeng 1993). Of course, we must be careful in inferring from such results that the parietal lobes perform this function (see chapter 2), but we would have had difficulty defending the hypothesis if these results were not obtained.

I also hypothesize that the categorical spatial relations encoding subsystem may be more effective in the left posterior parietal lobe (at least in right-handed males). This hypothesis is consistent with the research on cerebral lateralization summarized above, in normal subjects and in brain-damaged patients. However, this evidence is not as strong as the evidence for right-hemisphere superiority in encoding coordinate spatial relations.

The present view, then, is a bit at odds with that of Biederman and Cooper (1992) and Goodale and Milner (1992), who emphasize the role of the dorsal system in motor processing and minimize its role in object identification. Although coordinate spatial relations are clearly most relevant for motor control, categorical spatial relations are used primarily in visual identification. Indeed, Goodale et al. (1991) may have provided additional evidence for this distinction. They describe a patient who can orient her hand so that a card fits properly through a slot, but cannot categorize the orientation of the slot. The patient suffered from carbon monoxide poisoning, and thus did not have a focal lesion. However, MRI revealed damage in the lateral occipital cortex (in the ventral system) and in the parasagittal occipital-parietal area (in or abutting the dorsal system, depending on the precise locus). Goodale et al. interpret her deficits in terms of the ventral damage, but it is also possible that the categorical spatial relations encoding subsystem was damaged, and that this is why she cannot classify orientation correctly. This patient is also of interest because she can orient her hand properly when she visualizes the target—which is yet further evidence that perception and imagery share common mechanisms.

ASSOCIATIVE MEMORY

I ended my earlier book *Image and Mind* with the idea that thinking of "memory" as a distinct function is a little like thinking of the "first 2 feet back from the front bumper" as part of a car. If one knew everything about the car's body, steering system, cooling system, and so forth one would automatically know about the first 2 feet back from the bumper. The idea was that "memory" may be an inherent part of different perceptual and output systems, and if one knew everything about them there might be little left to say about a memory faculty.

In retrospect, this idea was only partly correct. Squire (1987) provides an extensive review of the neuropsychology of memory, which led me to two conclusions, one of which is consistent with my car analogy and one of which is not. Consistent with the analogy, much of memory is a product of local processing. Indeed, it appears that representations are stored along with the processes that compute them in the first place. For example, it is common to find that damage to the parietal lobes disrupts memory for space in addition to impairing spatial cognition (e.g., see De Renzi 1982; Squire 1987). However, inconsistent with my earlier view, there is now overwhelming evidence that specialized parts of the limbic system have specific roles in memory per se. Indeed, the hippocampus seems to be dedicated to setting up associations in memory (see chapter 8 of Kosslyn and Koenig 1992).

We humans clearly have the capacity to store associations among various types of information. The mere fact that we can recall where furniture belongs in a room or where objects are on our desk demonstrates that we store associations between object properties and spatial properties. Moreover, location information must be associated with shape information in memory whenever one has learned to navigate in a particular place. A landmark is an object that is associated with a specific location. Learning spatial layouts and routes depends critically on storing such associations.

Moreover, we "bind" objects not to specific locations in the field but to other objects or parts. This claim was supported by results of Kahneman, Treisman, and Gibbs (1992). In one experiment they showed subjects two letters, each in a separate box on the screen. The letters were shown only briefly, and after they were removed the boxes moved in different directions. As soon as the boxes stopped, a new letter appeared in each box and the subject was cued to report the letter in one of the boxes. The subjects could encode the letter faster if it was the same one that was presented in that box at the outset. The actual location of the boxes was not critical; it was which box, not its location, that promoted the priming. Apparently the letters and boxes had become associated, and hence activating the representation of one primed the representation of the other. Kahneman, Treisman, and Gibbs showed that these representations can accumulate associations into a single "file" over time. This claim was supported by an experiment in which the subjects saw four boxes; each box contained a horizontal or vertical line, which soon disappeared and the boxes moved in different directions. When the boxes stopped, a line appeared within each. The subjects were asked to decide whether a plus sign appeared in the final display. The interesting result was that subjects required more time to respond "no" if a box that previously had a horizontal line now had a vertical one (or vice versa). Apparently, the representation of the box included the orientation of the previous line, which was conjoined to the representation of the new line.[16]

I will argue that a distinct structure, which I call *associative memory*, stores such associations. The contents of associative memory are more abstract than those of the modality-specific pattern activation subsystems; associative memory not only stores associations among individual perceptual representations, but also organizes "conceptual" information that may not be directly derived from the senses (e.g., mathematical truths, meanings of abstract terms, and so on). Figure 7.7 illustrates the relation of associative memory to the subsystems posited so far.

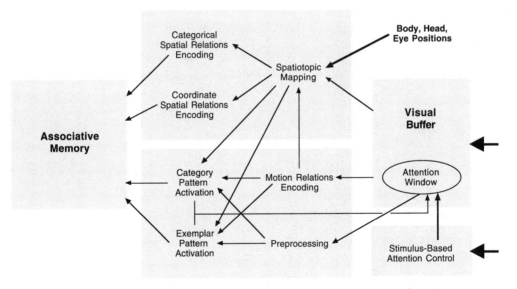

Figure 7.7 Associative memory and its relations to the subsystems in the ventral and dorsal system.

Identifying Contorted Objects

One type of representation in associative memory is particularly useful for identifying contorted objects. Such representations describe parts of objects or scenes and their spatial relations. This type of representation is called a *structural description,* and many researchers in computer vision have argued for its utility in object identification (e.g., Feldman 1985; Latto, Mumford, and Shah 1984; Marr 1982; Riseman and Hanson 1978; Winston 1975). The virtue of such a description is that it remains the same as long as the same parts are used and the same abstract spatial relations among them are maintained, which would be true for a playful cat in its various contortions. I argued earlier that the pattern activation subsystems do not contain such representations (in part because they do not support the right kind of generalization over geometric variation), but it is clear that the "compressed image" representations I proposed for visual memory will not always be satisfactory; if an object is contorted in a novel way, so that the shape is not similar to one previously seen, the input will not match such a representation. In such situations, one may have no choice but to encode and compare structural descriptions.

If one can recognize the individual parts of an object and compute categorical spatial relations among them, a structural description can be constructed. This structural description must be constructed after ventral and dorsal processing has taken place, and the structural description of the stimulus can then be matched to stored structural descriptions. Kahneman and Treisman (1984) suggest that "object files" accumulate evidence about the identity of an object over multiple eye fixations; stored structural descriptions of objects in associative memory may be a special case of such representations.

Connections Versus Tokens

The pattern activation subsystems store modality-specific visual representations; they cannot represent nonvisual information. Thus, there must be another memory structure to store nonvisual representations of properties of objects. However, this structure must receive visual input: The very idea of identification (as opposed to recognition) requires that nonvisual information (including an object's name, categories, etc.) be accessed by visual input. Moreover, this structure must receive input from other sensory modalities: One can identify objects when they are heard, felt, or—in some cases— smelled. Once one identifies an object, the same range of associated information becomes available; one can say its name, recount facts about its origins, and so forth. Such observations lead me to posit a subsystem at a relatively late phase of processing that receives input from multiple sensory modalities and stores associations among facts about objects.

In reasoning about the nature of a system that associates diverse sorts of information in memory, I began by considering two broad classes of mechanisms. On the one hand, pointers could organize *tokens* of representations that are stored in a separate structure. A token stands for a particular *type* in the way that a postcard picture of the Mona Lisa stands for the Mona Lisa; each type can have many tokens, which can be incorporated into many specific representations. The tokens representing perceptual information have "meaning" only by referring back to the type. That is, the tokens are place-holders, referring to the corresponding type; hence, they become meaningful only by being decoded by the appropriate input mechanism. For example, a visual representation of a shape in a pattern activation subsystem would be associated with a token for that shape in associative memory; this token would later be decoded when it activates a pattern of neurons in IT.

On the other hand, there may not be a set of tokens that reside in a distinct associative memory structure; the associations might be set up directly between other types of representations, with no intermediate token structure. This approach has simplicity in its favor. Unfortunately, this approach probably would not allow one to build a mechanism that has the right abilities; I do not believe that there is any way that direct connections can allow a system to do what our associative memories can do. My arguments against the second alternative are as follows.

First, this approach does not provide a means for specifying different types of relations among the stored information. It is unclear how simple direct linkages could specify that a cat *is* a certain shape, *has* a certain toy, *makes* a certain sound, and *likes* a certain food. The alternative is to have indirect links between representations of the specified properties, which make connections to intervening representations of relations. For example, a representation of *cat* would be associated with a representation of *likes*, which in turn would be associated with a representation of *food*. This system will work if each relation is used for only a single object or a single property. But this is rarely, if ever, the case; objects typically have partially overlapping properties. For example, a cat and a bird may both like the same toy, but eat different food. If the representation of *cat* and *bird* both have connections to a representation of *eats*, then the system will break down; there is no way to keep track of which connection from *eats*—to the representation of *meat* or *seeds*—to follow after getting there. The solution is to have tokens of the relations, with a different one for each association (cf. Valiant 1988).

Second, direct connections pose problems for the representation of abstract information. Associative memory specifies more than associations between observable properties. For example, after one has identified a person, one can recall information about such abstract characteristics as whether he or she is honest, sincere, and trustworthy, and hence such information must be represented in associative memory. There are many layers of abstraction between input or output representations and representations of abstract concepts. A virtue of a token-based system is that one can construct elaborate structures of the sort that are necessary to build abstract concepts (e.g., see Lakoff 1987). If a system has the ability to construct abstract concepts, it presumably has the ability to set up associations using token structures.

Third, as Mishkin and Appenzeller (1987) point out, we sometimes want to think about bread without associating it with butter. It is difficult to regulate the pattern of associations if there are direct connections between different representations, if only because one does not know what is being associated until it is activated. The problem is that there is too little structure in the associations in a direct-connection system; it is difficult to segregate associations of different sorts so that only relevant ones are pursued. In the direct-connection system, there are only links leading away from a representation; these links cannot be labeled, because this too would be an association, and hence would require another connection, which in turn would require another association (and hence connection) to be labeled, and so on.

In sum, these arguments suggest that associative memory is best considered as a distinct structure that contains tokens; these tokens are organized to specify different types of associations. Such associations cannot be conveyed simply by a set of connections among representations in different parts of the brain. Among other things, I assume that associative memory contains descriptions of how parts of objects are arranged.[17]

The Binding Problem

A critical step in identifying contorted objects, I have claimed, is associating representations of parts and categorical spatial relations. It is clear that information from the ventral and dorsal systems comes together in the brain, in at least two places. First, as noted earlier, Baizer, Ungerleider, and Desimone (1991) describe projections from both streams to the anterior part of the superior temporal sulcus. This area in turn sends projections into the limbic system, which plays a pivotal role in establishing the appropriate associations (see chapter 8 of Kosslyn and Koenig 1992). Second, Goldman-Rakic (1987, 1992) and Wilson, O'Scalaidhe, and Goldman-Rakic (1993) have shown that the dorsolateral prefrontal lobes receive projections from the dorsal and ventral systems. The dorsal system projects to area 46. If this area is ablated, the animal cannot move its eyes to the location previously occupied by a dot; in contrast, it can move its eyes to the location of a visible dot. Area 46 is topographically organized; damage affects memory for location to the contralateral side, and damage can selectively disrupt memory for locations within different portions of the visual field (see Goldman-Rakic 1987, 1992). In addition, the ventral system (the inferior temporal lobe, in the monkey) projects to a more orbital region of the frontal lobe (beneath and slightly posterior to area 46). This area appears to represent shape information for brief periods of time, and is a shape analog to area 46 (Goldman-Rakic 1987; Wilson, Scalaidhe, and Goldman-Rakic 1993).

The assumption that object properties (such as the shapes of parts) and spatial properties (such as categorical spatial relations) are encoded in separate systems leads to a problem: How does one conjoin the proper representations from each system? For example, if one sees a medium-sized ball next to a small box, with both on top of a large box, how are the representations of location properly paired with the representations of shape? Indeed, how are the representations of the different sizes conjoined with the individual representations of shape? This is called the *binding problem*.

One possible solution to this problem has been proposed by Gray and Singer (1989; see also Gray et al. 1989), as well as by many others (e.g., Crick and Koch 1990; Hummel and Biederman 1992; Mumford 1991). Gray and Singer recorded responses from neurons in different locations in the cat's visual cortex, and found that responses to the same stimulus oscillated in phase together (at around 40 Hz). It seems possible that such oscillations could "tag" associated representations in different regions of the brain; the inputs to associative memory would be conjoined if the patterns of neural activity were oscillating in the same way. If this theory turns out to be incorrect, then some other aspect of the corresponding representations must signal their kinship.

The inference that corresponding representations in the dorsal and ventral systems have a common "neural tag" is also consistent with the neuroanatomy. Recall that Harries and Perrett (1991) found precise connections from the posterior parietal lobe to the superior temporal sulcus (the superior boundary of the inferior temporal lobe). Moreover, they found that cells in this area that responded selectively to faces fell into clumps, and these clumps were especially strongly connected to the parietal lobe. As I suggested in the previous chapter, such connections might facilitate coordinating the corresponding representations that are computed in the two systems.

Indeed, Humphrey and Weiskrantz (1969) and Ungerleider, Ganz, and Pribram (1977) report that size constancy is disrupted following lesions of prestriate and IT cortex. In chapter 5 I suggested that these lesions may have impaired the animal's ability to exploit the viewpoint consistency constraint. The present reasoning suggests another possible interpretation: Size constancy requires that one encode the actual size of an object based on its visual angle and distance. The fact that prestriate and IT lesions affected this spatial property may suggest that the characterization of the shape of an object plays a critical role in computing its actual size. Such a computation would require connections between the spatial properties and object properties systems.[18]

Processing in Associative Memory

During object identification, the goal of processing in associative memory is to select the stored representation that corresponds to the stimulus; the representation that has properties most like those of the stimulus will become most activated—and if the representation is activated strongly enough, the object is identified. Each object, part, and object property corresponds to a pattern code that is produced by the pattern activation subsystems; this code is a kind of name, indicating what pattern has been recognized as well as how good the match is (see chapter 5). Similarly, each type of categorical spatial relation corresponds to a spatial code that is produced by the categorical spatial relations encoding subsystems. (The output from the coordinate spatial relations encoding subsystem is a set of motor-based coordinates, not a proposition.) I hypothesize that object and spatial properties are matched in

Identifying Contorted Objects

parallel to those associated with stored representations of objects. An object will be identified only when there is a good match between the input properties and the properties associated with the object in memory.

However, this kind of consistency with the input is not enough: some aspects of the input must also be distinctive to a specific object; one must be able to disconfirm the hypothesis that another object is being viewed. As noted earlier, a simple mechanism for implementing such processing was suggested by Feldman (1985). The representation of each object can be thought of as a node in a network, and these nodes are mutually inhibitory. A set of properties is associated with each node, and a node becomes more activated as more of its associated properties match those of the input. And the more activated a node, the more it inhibits the other nodes. This kind of arrangement can produce a winner-take-all mechanism, where only one node can be fully active at any one time. Thus, there is no need to posit an intelligent decision-making process that weighs the inputs and compares the various stored representations; the connections among representations alone can do the job. Note that I do not mean that "nodes" necessarily correspond to individual cells, which are physically connected by inhibitory axons; rather, a population of cells can serve to represent an object and its properties, and this population can inhibit populations of cells representing other objects.

Depending on where one looks, one will encode a different series of parts and characteristics; indeed, if the object is contorted oddly, some parts and characteristics may not even be visible. Moreover, some members of a class of objects have additional optional parts and characteristics or have missing parts and characteristics. For example, chairs may or may not have arms, and dogs may or may not have tails. Wittgenstein (1953) pointed out that members of a category often do not share a set of necessary and sufficient features. Rather, members are related by a kind of family resemblance, with some members sharing some features and other members sharing others. Thus, one cannot identify an object when it projects a novel shape simply by defining an acceptable range of variation from a standard shape and treating as equivalent all shapes within that range.

One possible solution to these problems is to require that only a subset of an object's parts, characteristics, and their spatial relations be encoded, and allow different subsets to be used in different instances. In this case the system would treat each input property as evidence, and an object would be identified when enough evidence had accumulated—regardless of which pieces of evidence were found. For example, to a first approximation we might identify a chair whenever we found three of its properties (a back, seat, and legs; arms, seat, and legs; arms, cushion, and back; etc.). However, simply counting the number or percentage of properties would not be satisfactory: different properties are more or less diagnostic. For example, a stool also has a seat and legs; thus, to identify a chair, as opposed to a stool, it is much more important to encode a seat and a back than to encode a seat and legs.

This reasoning suggests that a "distinctiveness weight" is assigned to each stored property. Every time an input property matches a stored property, the weight associated with that property is added to the hopper; an object can be identified only when enough weights have accumulated to exceed a threshold, regardless of which properties contributed the weights. This system allows many different combinations of properties to implicate a given object. For example, say that a chair is characterized by a seat (very important, very high weight), a back (fairly important, high weight), legs (important, medium weight), arms (not very important, low weight), and so on. One could identify a wide variety of chairs if the threshold is set so that it is exceeded if one encodes a seat and two or more of any of the other properties (see Smith and Medin 1981).

The weight associated with each property can be set simply by increasing it every time the property is used (although not necessarily an equal amount each time), which is easily accomplished using virtually all of the learning algorithms employed in parallel distributed processing systems. By definition, distinctive properties are those that distinguish an object from other similar objects. Thus, distinctive properties should be used disproportionately often to identify an object, and hence their weights will become larger.

Finally, consider now the fact that to a farmer gathering his cows at dusk, a passing shadow may be identified as a cow. This ability requires that thresholds be altered by context and that certain kinds of information be treated as criterial in particular contexts; depending on the task, some information in associative memory will be relevant and some will not. Less information will be needed to identify a highly contorted object, such as a sleeping cat can be, if one is expecting to find that object in that context.

Context also must be able to affect specific classes of representations, not just specific individual representations. For example, if one is shown a face and asked to name the person, many possible identifications of the input (e.g., "face," "man") must be inhibited. One seeks a particular sort of classification. Thus, there must be a mechanism whereby associative memory can be set to allow only certain types of representations to be activated (or, rather, to remain activated; other types may be activated initially but then are inhibited). In order to inhibit certain classes of representations, there must be some way to index those representations; this index might be explicit (e.g., a property indicating level of specificity), implicit (e.g., implied by the number of superordinates), or both.

Level of Hierarchy.   Objects can be named at many levels of hierarchy. Does one name a fruit a Delicious apple, an apple, or just a fruit? The present theory leads us to expect objects typically to be identified at a particular level of hierarchy. For example, without careful scrutiny, the defining characteristics of a Delicious apple may not be encoded into the exemplar pattern activation subsystem; the nonaccidental and signal properties (for most people) will characterize apples, but not a specific type. Similarly, the spatial properties of apples are sufficiently similar that they will not distinguish among the various types. On the other hand, the object and spatial properties of different types of fruit (watermelons, bananas, etc.) are sufficiently different that there probably is no representation of *fruit* in the categorical pattern activation subsystem. Thus, this subsystem will match at an intermediate level of hierarchy, *apple*.

Rosch et al. (1976) showed that pictures typically are named at an intermediate level, which they called the *basic level*. They characterized the basic level in a number of ways. The most pertinent for present purposes is that it is the most general level of hierarchy at which objects still have similar shapes. That is, if one plotted the overlap in the shapes of members of the category defined at each level of hierarchy, one would find an elbow in the curve; for example, Delicious apples overlap with each other very highly, as do apples in general, but not so fruit (which includes bananas, watermelons, kiwis, and so on). The elbow is at *apple*, which is the basic level.

Identifying objects at the basic level is a good idea if only because it activates the maximum number of properties that almost certainly apply to the stimulus. However, the basic level has this virtue only if the stimulus is typical of the category. For example, if one sees a penguin, categorizing it as a bird is not very helpful; penguins lack many properties of birds (e.g., they do not sing or fly) and have other properties that are not shared by birds in general (which adapt them for swimming underwater). In these cases, the shape of the bird is sufficiently different from the typical members of a category that it would be likely to have a distinct representation in the category pattern activation subsystem. Indeed, such "outliers" often have unusual sizes and orientations (a penguin is large for a bird and walks at an unusual orientation for a bird), and thus distinctive information is also provided by the dorsal system.

If so, then people should name typical objects at a basic level, but often should name atypical ones at a level subordinate to the basic level; for atypical objects, one cannot go quite as far up the hierarchy and still apply all of the properties to the object. And this is exactly what Jolicoeur, Gluck, and Kosslyn (1984) found. For example, people often named an ostrich as an ostrich, not a bird, but named a sparrow as a bird. We called the level of hierarchy at which a representation provides the maximum likely properties the *entry level*.

In addition, one also can provide proper names for some familiar objects. That is, one can name the dog that lives next door as *Fido*, as opposed to *cocker spaniel, dog, mammal*, and so on. It is clear that there must be separate representations in associative memory for categories (such as *bird* or *penguin*) and exemplars (such as one's pet bird); information that applies to a specific exemplar need not apply to all objects in that category. These representations are activated by pattern codes from the exemplar pattern activation subsystem. In addition, there is a special class of exemplars that always retain exactly the same shape, such as statues and paintings; not only will the exemplar pattern activation subsystem play a key role in identifying such objects, but the coordinate spatial relations encoding subsystem may also be able to help one to identify such objects if their parts or characteristics are always in precisely the same location.[19]

Anatomical Localization

At first glance, because the hippocampus has been shown to be critical for establishing new associations in memory (e.g., Mishkin and Appenzeller 1987; Squire 1987), it might seem like a good candidate for implementing associative memory. However, although the hippocampus may set up the neural equivalent of "pointers," linking representations that are stored in different loci, it does not store them indefinitely. For example, the famous patient H. M. had his hippocampus and amygdala removed from both hemispheres, and could not learn new facts thereafter (e.g., Milner, Corkin, and Teuber 1968). However, he did have intact recall of previously learned information, provided that it was learned a year or two prior to the operation. It is unlikely that the hippocampus implements the associative memory structure itself; the long-term associations are stored elsewhere.

The argument that tokens must be organized into a structure in associative memory does not imply that this structure must have a distinct anatomical localization. It is possible that the tokens themselves are stored in the subsystems that generate the types. In this case, associative memory itself would be distributed throughout the brain. However, there is reason to suspect that associative memory relies on specific tissue in the superior, posterior temporal lobes and the temporal-parietal-occipital junction area.

First, area STP (short for superior temporal polysensory) in the monkey is located in the posterior superior temporal lobe (e.g., see Bruce, Desimone, and Gross 1981, 1986; Hikosaka et al. 1988). Although this area is not specified in parcellations of the human brain, it is intriguing because it may be related to Wernicke's area (in the posterior superior temporal lobe of the human brain). Wernicke's area is involved in representing information used in language comprehension, and may be involved in implementing associative memory (e.g., see Hecaen and Albert 1978). Cells in STP receive converging input from visual, auditory, and somesthetic systems (from IT, from superior temporal auditory cortex, and from posterior parietal cortex), and over half of them respond to input in more than one modality. In addition, cells in area STP apparently play a role in directing attention shifts. For example, Colby and Miller (1986) found that the responses of some cells in STP are time-locked to the initiation of a saccade. This finding is consistent with the notion that these cells are part of an associative memory system, and—as will be discussed shortly—that stored information has a role in controlling where the eyes will move (see also Bruce, Desimone, and Gross 1986).

Like most very high-level areas, STP is not topographically organized. Bruce, Desimone, and Gross (1981) report that 45% of the cells in this area that respond to visual stimuli are tuned to higher-order properties of stimuli (e.g., some responded selectively to faces); that the cells in this area have very large receptive fields (most being over 150° of visual angle); that responses are equivalent across the receptive field (unlike neurons in IT, which typically respond better to foveal input); that many cells respond best when stimuli move in a specific direction or manner; and that most respond best to moving stimuli. Some of these cells respond best to a complex combination of visual and auditory input. Moreover, these cells are not sensitive to size, orientation, or color. (Perrett et al. [1985] note that some of the face-specific cells they studied may have been located in STP; they do not indicate whether these particular cells were tuned for faces seen from particular viewpoints or tended to generalize broadly.)

Also important for present purposes are connections to area STP from AIT (the anterior part of IT) and 7a (in the parietal lobe, via the hippocampus). These connections may have a role in bringing together the outputs from the ventral and dorsal systems, which in turn are stored in a long-term associative memory. As will be discussed shortly, the connection between STP and the frontal lobes may be important if STP does in fact have a role in storing visual information in long-term associative memory.

All of these properties of cells in STP are consistent with the claim that the area receives input that has already undergone modality-specific processing. Although it has been shown that these cells respond to both shape and movement, to my knowledge no one has yet examined conjunctions of shape and location; if the present idea is correct, such cells would be expected in this area. In this vein, Perrett et al. (1989) report that some cells in the bottom bank of STS (in area TEa), which is near STP, appear to be tuned for the object that a monkey is reaching for or walking toward. These cells do not respond to the position of a person's arm or body per se, but only the position in relation to a target object. These neurons appear be activated only if the monkey associates the position of the eyes or arm to the location where a specific object exists. The fact that these neurons are situated near area STP is another reason to suspect that this area is involved in the implementation of associative memory.

The hypothesis that structures in the posterior superior temporal lobe play a key role in implementing an associative memory structure in humans is consistent with much clinical literature. Most of this literature, however, has focused on the mechanisms underlying the acquisition of new memories, which involves subcortical structures underlying the anterior medial portions of the temporal lobe (see Mishkin and Appenzeller 1987; Squire 1987; Squire, Knowlton, and Musen 1993). Relatively little research has been conducted to isolate the anatomical bases of remote retrograde amnesia (i.e., disrupted memory for events in the far past, which had been stored in memory prior to the injury). One reason for this is that this syndrome is rare, which may suggest that associative memory is not stored in a single locus in the brain.

However, it is worth noting that De Renzi, Scotti, and Spinnler (1969), Warrington and Taylor (1978) and others provide evidence that left posterior lesions disrupt associative memory in humans. For example, Warrington and Taylor (1978) showed patients sets of three objects; in each set were two objects that have the same function but look different (such as two desk chairs) and one object that had a slightly different function (e.g., a wheelchair). One member of the pair of objects that had the same function was removed (e.g., one of the desk chairs), and the two objects with dissimilar functions were presented as a pair (e.g., a desk chair and wheelchair); the patient was given the object that had been removed and was asked to indicate which member of the pair had the same function. The patients with posterior left-hemisphere damage were impaired on this task, relative to a control group, but patients with left anterior or right anterior damage were not. However, patients with right posterior lesions also were impaired, but Warrington and Taylor argue that this deficit was in fact due to their problems in perceptually encoding the stimuli (see their pp. 699–700). The left posterior lesions were in occipital, parietal, temporal, temporal-parietal or occipital-parietal regions; but even if they had been precisely localized, this would not necessarily implicate the damaged structure as the seat of the impaired function (see chapter 2). In the following chapter I use PET data to argue that associative memory relies on tissue in the posterior superior temporal lobe and adjoining regions.

In addition, the phenomenon of source amnesia is usually associated with frontal lobe lesions (e.g., see Schacter, Harbluk, and McLachlan 1984). Patients with this disorder have difficulty remembering the context in which a fact was learned. However, it seems unlikely that this is the locus of stored memories; damage to the frontal lobes does not produce dense amnesia. Rather, this deficit may reflect either an impairment in the retrieval process, as discussed in the following section.

SUBSYSTEMS USED IN TOP-DOWN HYPOTHESIS TESTING

At first glance, only a few parts, characteristics (e.g., one may recognize a certain texture), and their spatial relations may be encoded, especially if an object is seen out of the corner of one's eye or if only one portion is focused upon. Thus, the initial input may not be sufficient to identify an object. In such situations, one will have to look again, encoding additional parts, characteristics, and their spatial relations. The fovea subtends only about 2° of visual angle, and one can see only a limited amount with high resolution in any given fixation. This limitation sometimes requires one to make multiple eye fixations when encoding additional information about an object.

Only two kinds of information can be used to direct attention to a new location. First, as noted in chapter 4, properties of the stimulus input can draw one's attention to a specific location; a sudden movement or a change in intensity is especially likely to have this effect. Second, knowledge, belief, and expectation can direct one's attention to a specific location. We are not passive receptacles of information during vision; we typically do not simply wait for more input and decide what we are seeing. Rather, it has long been known that humans formulate hypotheses about the stimulus on the basis of initial input and use those hypotheses to guide the collection of additional information (e.g., Gregory 1970; Neisser 1967, 1976).

Such "top-down" influences on attention are immediately obvious when one observes the pattern of eye movements made during object identification (e.g., Loftus 1972, 1983; Stark and Ellis 1981; Yarbus 1967). People typically examine high-information parts of pictures, systematically shifting between them; for example, the eyes, nose, and mouth are the targets of the vast majority of eye fixations when subjects examine a picture of a face. It is of interest that some patients with damaged frontal lobes do not display such systematic eye movements (e.g., Luria 1980; Tyler 1969).

Two sorts of top-down control strategies appear to underlie the patterns of eye movements that occur when people cannot identify an object at first glance. First, in some cases top-down attentional control is driven by a specific hypothesis, such as that one is viewing a cat and hence should look for whiskers at the front of its face. Second, in some cases, the subjects do not appear to be testing a specific hypothesis, but instead engage in systematic search strategies (cf. Luria 1980). If the input is weakly consistent with many possible objects, a good strategy is to scan the object systematically looking for more information. The highest-information parts of objects often are along its outer contour, and hence top-down mechanisms might simply lead one to scan along the object's boundary. Even this sort of top-down control is better than waiting for changes in the stimulus to guide eye movements, or engaging in a totally random search.

If one representation becomes more activated than others as object and spatial properties enter associative memory, this representation can be treated as a hypothesis to be tested. In such circumstances, the properties of the activated representation are themselves activated and the system can seek to determine whether appropriate properties are in fact present. As noted earlier, it is useful to assign distinctiveness weights to properties stored in associative memory. These weights can also be regarded as strengths, especially if they are incrementally increased every time a property proves useful for identifying the object; the greater the weight, the more activated the property is when the representation of the object is activated. Thus, once a representation of one object is activated more than are the representations of other objects, the properties associated with this most strongly activated representation are themselves activated in proportion to their distinctiveness—making the representations of more distinctive properties easier to access.

Although the associative memory subsystem, in essence, formulates a hypothesis and serves up the distinctive properties of the hypothesized object, that is all it does. Other subsystems must use that information to direct attention to the location where a specific property should be if the hypothesis is correct. In the following I focus on how a hypothesis about a specific object is tested, which is the more interesting case (the systematic scanning, default strategy draws on the same mechanisms, except that it is the same for all inputs, and so is less interesting).

Coordinate Property Lookup Subsystem

A perceptual hypothesis is necessarily based on one's knowledge about the possible range of objects one might be seeing; one uses partial information to guide search, seeking to discover whether properties of the hypothesized object are in fact present. In the previous section I offered proposals about how such a hypothesis can be formulated without appeal to any external agent or intelligent arbiter. We now turn to the second part of the process, when the hypothesis is actually tested by seeking further information.

The protomodel I developed in chapter 3 specifies an *information lookup subsystem* that accesses representations in associative memory. In the following I will further articulate this subsystem, now delineating three separate subsystems. These subsystems are apparently used in several functions, including language, reasoning, and navigation, and so are not proper components of a distinct top-down search component; there is no dedicated "top-down hypothesis-testing system" as such; I do not expect to find a part of the brain that carries out top-down hypothesis testing. Rather, the subsystems that accomplish this end are grouped together merely for expository purposes.

Recall that when the outputs from the ventral and dorsal systems (pattern codes, spatial codes, and coordinates) enter associative memory, the representations of some objects are satisfied better than others, and the stored properties associated with the most strongly activated representation are activated. Furthermore, more distinctive properties are activated more strongly than less distinctive properties; by "distinctive properties" I mean those that serve to discriminate among similar objects. An efficient hypothesis-testing system would begin by seeking particularly distinctive properties. For example, say the input was most consistent with properties of a cat. In the past, cats had to be discriminated from other small animals, such as poodles and squirrels, and representations of properties that facilitated this discrimination became stronger. A property such as "has four legs" would not help one to make these discriminations, and so would not be used very often, whereas a property such as "has pointed ears at the sides of the head" would be helpful. Thus, it would be most useful to look for the ears before bothering with the legs. If the right kind of ears were found in the right place, this would be additional evidence favoring the hypothesis that the stimulus was a cat—and disconfirming a hypothesis that it was a poodle.

Some distinctive properties are not defined solely by shape. A cat's whiskers lying on the barber's floor probably would not look much different from a poodle's. The size and location are what makes them distinctive. In order to test a hypothesis one must know where to look for the property and must be able to register that it is in fact at the right location. Thus, hypothesis testing often may involve a combination of object and spatial properties.

I argued that spatial properties are stored in two ways, using representations of categorical or coordinate spatial relations. If location is stored in motor-based coordinates, only one transformation is needed to map input representations of locations (accessed in associative memory) to output instructions (for attention-shifting mechanisms). This transformation converts the spatial coordinates to instructions about how far to move the body, head, eyes, and/or attention window. Coordinate representations differ quantitatively; they specify distance along each of two or three dimensions. In contrast, categorical representations come in a variety of stripes, and each is qualitatively distinct; for example, *on, left of, connected to,* and *above* do not specify distances along quantitative dimensions (they do not characterize values on "prothetic" scales). The categorical property lookup subsystem must interpret all the types of categorical relations in associative memory, and hence must perform different operations from the coordinate property lookup subsystem. In addition, if location is stored using a categorical spatial relation, the representation must be converted to a range of coordinates. A categorical representation alone does not specify where to shift one's attention to find the property in the particular instance being viewed; indeed, the virtue of categorical relations is that they treat a range of positions as equivalent. Because the different types of stored spatial relations constitute different inputs, and results of accessing them constitute different outputs, there are different input/output mappings. Furthermore, the coordinate mapping must preserve the very kind of information that is discarded in the categorical mapping, and the categorical mappings may be sensitive to distinctions that are irrelevant in the coordinate mappings. Thus, the mappings are likely to interfere with each other in the same network. Such considerations lead me to hypothesize that there are two distinct property lookup subsystems.

The *coordinate property lookup subsystem* accesses parts and distinctive characteristics that are associated with coordinate spatial relations representations. Part of the argument I offered for the existence of coordinate spatial relations representations assumed that they could be stored: I noted that coordinate representations are useful for navigating in the dark. Such coordinates would also help one search for properties of familiar rigid objects. For example, the Mona Lisa always has her cryptic smile in exactly the same place; if one sees a painting out of the corner of one's eye and suspects that it is the Mona Lisa, all one need do is look at that place and see if the mouth smiles that smile. Because individual pictures never vary, it is useful to store coordinate representations of the locations of distinctive properties. These representations later can be used to direct one to the appropriate location during hypothesis testing. Figure 7.8 illustrates this subsystem in relation to the others posited in previous pages.

Recall that the coordinate representations are motor-based; they can be used to direct the eyes and limbs toward a specific place in space. The coordinate property lookup subsystem must not make a commitment to a specific use of the coordinates, but rather must provide coordinate spatial relations to all other subsystems that can use them. One can look at a specific location, or point with the right hand, left hand, or even a foot (see chapter 7 of Kosslyn and Koenig 1992). I am led, then, to infer that other subsystems use the output from the coordinate property lookup subsystem to compute exactly how to shift attention to a specific location; these subsystems will be discussed shortly.

Anatomical Localization   The frontal lobe plays a critical role in generating and testing hypotheses (e.g., see Brody and Pribram 1978; Damasio 1985a; Goldman-Rakic 1987; Luria 1980), particularly parts of dorsolateral prefrontal

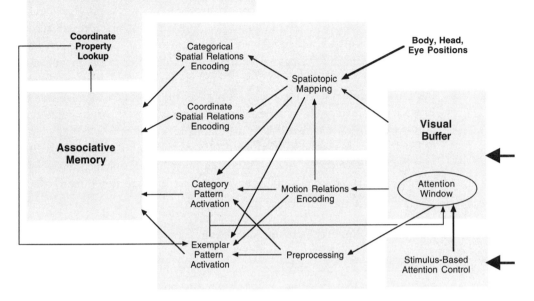

Figure 7.8 The coordinate property lookup subsystem in relation to the subsystems discussed previously.

cortex. For example, in PET studies part of dorsolateral prefrontal cortex has been found to be active when subjects actively seek specific information in memory. Petersen et al. (1988) asked subjects to produce a verb for each noun they read (e.g., "hammer" might elicit "pound"), and also asked them simply to read words aloud. The patterns of blood flow from the second task reflected encoding and response processes. Hence, by subtracting these patterns from those induced by the use-generation task, what was left over presumably was due to processes that actively sought information in memory. When Petersen et al. thereby isolated the contribution of processes that access associative memory, they found selective activation in the dorsolateral prefrontal cortex. This region was more activated on the left side, however, which may reflect the fact that words were being accessed (and language generally is processed more effectively in the left hemisphere); stored coordinates of the sort discussed here were not being accessed, and so we must be cautious about interpreting the details of this finding.

For present purposes, the important feature of the results of Petersen et al. (1988) is that the activated region was relatively near area 8, the "frontal eye fields," which plays a role in directing saccades; cells in this area are active prior to a saccade (e.g., see Crowne 1983). Moreover, area 8 (also called FEF) is adjacent to area 46, which Goldman-Rakic and her colleagues have shown is a short-term memory structure for spatial location (see figures 3.2 and 3.3 for additional information about these areas). Information about where objects, parts, and characteristics are located is critical for directing attention, and hence it is convenient that area 46 is so close to area 8. Furthermore, the superior longitudinal fasciculus (a fasciculus is a large bundle of fibers that travels a relatively long distance to join two parts of cortex) provides direct connections between the frontal lobes and parietal lobes, which would allow information accessed and used in the frontal lobes to direct mechanisms that play critical roles in how attention is allocated. In addition, the arcuate fasciculus joins the posterior superior temporal lobe to the posterior inferior frontal lobe. This connection could allow information about a stimulus stored in associative memory to be accessed by the frontal lobes, in part to guide eye movements, as will be discussed in the following section.

Finally, I earlier reviewed evidence that coordinate spatial relations are encoded more effectively in the right hemisphere. I have assumed that these representations are stored, and it is possible that they are stored more effectively in the right hemisphere.

Categorical Property Lookup Subsystem

I also hypothesize that a distinct *categorical property lookup subsystem* exists. I have assumed that attention can be directed to only a single location at any one time.[20] This observation has led many to assume that a winner-take-all network must be used to direct attention (e.g., Koch and Ullman 1985). If the attention-shifting subsystem receives two different inputs, the worst solution would be to average them; one would then be looking somewhere between two potentially useful locations. Rather, one must select one hypothesis to be tested at a time. I have assumed that the object representation that is most consistent with the input is most highly activated. I also assume that more distinctive properties of objects are themselves more active and that the two property lookup subsystems access the appropriate active representations. But how are they managed?

Consider the following analogy (derived from the Pandemonium model of Selfridge 1959; see also chapter 3 of Neisser 1967). Each stored property shouts its name as it becomes more active. Properties that are associated with categorical spatial relations shout in a male voice, and those associated with coordinates shout in a female voice. The more distinctive a property is, the louder it shouts. The lookup subsystems have ears, with each listening for its kind of voice. The more confident a subsystem is that it is hearing a distinctive part or characteristic, the more strongly it inhibits the other lookup subsystem. Thus, the lookup subsystem that "hears" the most strongly activated property actually sends its output to the subsystems that shift attention.[21] Thus, we can think of the property lookup subsystems as detectors that operate in parallel and mutually inhibit each other in proportion to their degree of activation.

Anatomical Localization   The reasoning that led me to hypothesize that the coordinate property lookup subsystem is implemented in the dorsolateral prefrontal cortex also leads me to hypothesize that the categorical property lookup subsystem is implemented in this region. However, the fact that these representations are encoded more effectively in the left hemisphere leads me to suggest that they are stored and accessed more effectively in this hemisphere. The finding of Petersen et al. that there is more activation in left dorsolateral prefrontal cortex when subjects retrieve possible uses of named objects is consistent with this conjecture.

Categorical–Coordinate Conversion Subsystem

Categorical spatial relations delineate a range of relative positions, but a property is to be located at a particular location in an image; if stored categorical spatial relations representations are to guide top-down search, they must guide one to look at a particular location for the specified property. Thus, a subsystem must convert categorical relations to coordinates. This subsystem also must learn to decode new categorical spatial relations representations. When the categorical spatial relations encoding subsystem develops a new category, these representations can be stored and subsequently accessed; thus, when new categories are developed, another subsystem must be modified to interpret them as a prerequisite for shifting attention to the specified location.

These tasks—acquiring category conversions and converting categories to coordinates—are very different from the task of looking up a representation in associative memory. The categorical property lookup subsystem takes as input representations in associative memory and sends those representations to other parts of the system. Because this output can be used in many different ways (e.g., language and reasoning), it is not transformed for any particular purpose by the lookup subsystem. Using my usual criterion of likely interference in mappings within a single network, I thus am led to hypothesize a distinct *categorical–coordinate conversion subsystem* to convert categorical spatial relations representations to a range of coordinates. The relations between the categorical property lookup and categorical-coordinate conversion subsystems and the other subsystems posited so far are illustrated in figure 7.9.

When Rex Flynn, Jonathan Amsterdam, and I built our first computer simulation models of high-level vision within this framework (in 1986), we were surprised by how difficult it was to derive a set of coordinates from a categorical spatial relation. We found that the input to the categorical–coordinate conversion subsystem must include information from the coordinate property lookup subsystem (coordinate information about the size, distance, and orientation of the object currently being viewed). We also found that it must include information that allows the object to be assigned to a reference frame, so that one can identify its front and back (categorical spatial relations ultimately must be anchored to some such reference frame). We used the taper of the overall shape envelope as a heuristic for identifying the front of an object,

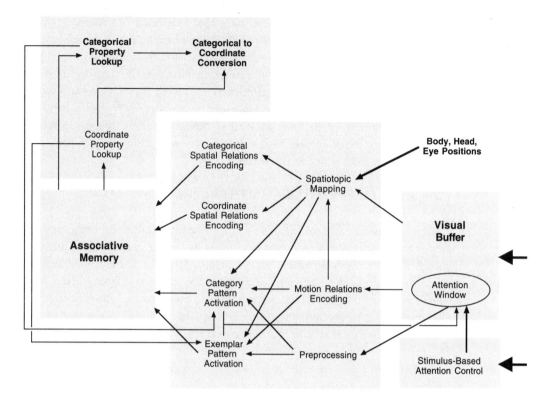

Figure 7.9 The categorical property lookup and categorical–coordinate conversion subsystems in relation to the subsystems discussed previously.

which appeared to work well for the animals and inanimate objects we examined; for example, the distance between the head and front paws of a fox is greater than the distance between its rear end and rear paws, and this is true in most circumstances. A number of such heuristics may be used, and different ones may be used for different objects.

Because categorical spatial relations correspond to a range of locations, one cannot use them to shift attention directly to the correct location. The best one can do is get within striking range. For some tasks, this may be sufficient, whereas for others one may want to focus on a precise location. For example, if one wants to determine whether someone is wearing a long-sleeved shirt (Joe always does, even on very hot days, so this is a good cue when seeing him from behind), precise positioning of attention is not necessary; but if one wants to toss him a paperclip, one needs to fixate attention on his hand rather precisely. The architecture developed so far suggests two different ways of adjusting attention precisely. First, once a range of locations is computed on the basis of stored categorical spatial relations representations, this range can be compared to the locations of parts that have been encoded via the coordinate spatial relations encoding subsystem. The system can then simply select the part that is located closest to the center of the range of locations and shift attention to that location. This method has the virtue that it always causes one to attend to a part rather than a region of space between parts.

The drawback with this method of specifying location is that a considerable amount of computation is necessary before one gets started. An alternative method has two phases. The categorical–coordinate conversion subsystem can simply send the specifications of the center of the region it computes to the attention-shifting subsystems, which would be relatively fast. But this method is sloppy, positioning attention only within the general region of the sought part. If need be, at this point one can "zero in" on the proper location. That is, in a second phase, the coordinates of the parts can be used by the attention-shifting subsystems to shift the body, head, eye, and attention window so that one is focused on the nearest part or characteristic (that corresponds to a perceptual unit in the visual buffer); these coordinates would also be used to scale the scope of the attention window so that it is properly calibrated to detect the appropriate units at each phase of processing. Fisk and Goodale (1988) provide evidence that many movements do in fact have two components of the sort described here.

Anatomical Localization   I have no theory as to where the categorical–coordinate conversion subsystem is implemented. If we assume that subsystems tend to be near the subsystems that send them input, then either the frontal or parietal lobe would be appropriate. However, functional distance is what is important, not actual physical proximity; direct connections by fasciculi are presumably almost as effective as local cortico-cortical connections. Thus, parts of the parietal lobe are closer, in this sense, to parts of the frontal lobe than to physically less distant parts of the temporal lobe.

Attention Shifting

The size and distance of an object must be considered when computing how far to shift the body, head, eyes, and attention window; one shifts the point of focus a certain visual angle, which depends on both factors. Somewhere in the brain the direction and degree that attention must be shifted is computed, and somewhere mechanisms must actually shift the body, head, eyes, and attention window, as appropriate. For present purposes, it is sufficient to group these various functions under a coarsely defined *attention-shifting sub-system*. (Recall that I am trying to outline a solution to the problem of identifying contorted objects, with the ultimate aim of using these inferences to develop a theory of visual mental imagery; I am not so ambitious as to try to specify the details of the entire high-level visual system!)

This subsystem receives input from either the coordinate property lookup subsystem or the categorical–coordinate conversion subsystem. The input consists of motor-based coordinates of the sort that can be used to compute the target of a movement. These coordinates are body-centered (or head-centered, for an eye movement); the attention-shifting subsystem must shift attention from the current point of view, and hence requires input in viewer-centered coordinates.

Subsystems within the attention-shifting subsystem must perform coordinate transformations. First, to shift attention, it needs to compute the inverse of the mapping function used by the spatiotopic mapping subsystem. This transformation need not be very precise if feedback is used to adjust the location of the attention window. All it must do is shift attention close to the sought part or characteristic. Second, it must also compute planar projections from three-dimensional representations, which is required to shift from coordinates that specify locations in space to specifications of locations relative to one's current point of view.[22]

Posner and his colleagues have studied attention using an approach that is very similar to that taken here. They have decomposed the attention-shifting subsystem into three finer-grained subsystems. Posner et al. (1987) hypothesize a subsystem that *disengages* attention from the current locus of fixation, another that *shifts* attention to a new position, and a third that *engages* attention at the new position. These inferences are based in large part on observed dysfunctions in attentional tasks by brain-damaged patients. For example, patients were given the standard Posner orienting task, in which subjects receive a cue that a signal will appear to the left or right of fixation. The cue is valid most of the time, but not always. Thus, if a patient has difficulty disengaging attention, it will be evident on invalid trials, when the probe in fact appears in the noncued location. Patients with damage to the parietal lobes do not fare well in this condition of the task. Posner et al. found no difference between patients who had lesions in the left parietal lobe and patients who had lesions in the right parietal lobe; in both cases, the patients had trouble when the expected cue was in the contralateral field (the one subserved by the damaged hemisphere), but there was no difference in the severity of the deficit for the different lesion loci (see also Posner et al. 1984). Findings like these suggested to Posner and his colleagues that the disengage subsystem is implemented (at least in part) in the parietal lobes (I will have more to say about the anatomical bases of the subsystems shortly). Similarly, patients with damage to the thalamus had difficulty taking advantage of a valid cue, which suggested to Posner and his colleagues that this structure is involved in engaging attention. And finally, patients with damage to the superior colliculus had difficulty shifting attention in general (i.e., using the cues), which suggested that the shift process relies on this structure (see also Sprague 1991).

Hence, there is good reason to decompose the attention-shifting subsystem into these three finer-grained subsystems, as is noted in figure 7.10. Not only is there empirical support for the decomposition, but it also makes sense computationally. Each subsystem clearly has a different function, and different input/output mappings are required in each case. First, before being able to shift attention, one must disengage the current focus; this operation requires inhibiting the processes that select some region of the visual field (or the visual buffer). Second, actually shifting the focus of attention is qualitatively

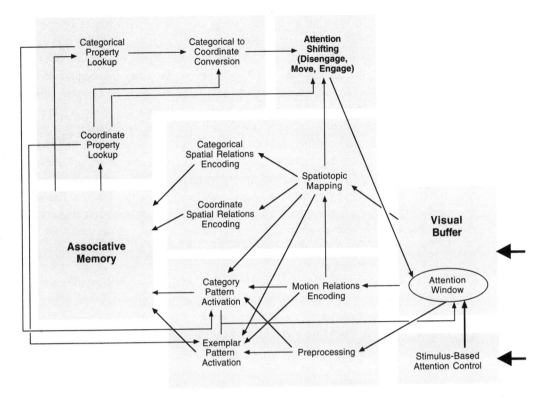

Figure 7.10 The attention-shifting subsystems in relation to the subsystems discussed previously.

distinct from this operation: One needs to select a new region of contiguous locations for further processing. Third, the process of reengaging attention requires gating a new set of cells in the visual buffer. Because these operations are logically distinct, the mapping from input to output would be very complex if only a single subsystem performed all three functions. I have assumed that the brain respects the principle of division-of-labor and that each subsystem performs sets of similar input/output mappings.

Priming Representations of Expected Shapes and Characteristics Shifting attention involves more than simply changing the location where stimuli are encoded. One can also set oneself to encode a specific shape or characteristic. The visual system seems to be constructed in a way that facilitates recognition when top-down hypothesis testing is required. There is an ample literature that demonstrates that people encode shapes more quickly if primed (e.g., see Biederman and Cooper 1991a, 1991c, 1992; Cave and Squire 1992; Rosch et al. 1976). In this case, stored information may bias the system to recognize specific properties. Context can create such biases (e.g., as when a farmer is set to see cows when gathering them at dusk), which allow one to encode information relatively quickly and with less effort than would otherwise be required (see Biederman and Cooper 1992).

This sort of priming is useful because it can reduce the amount of processing that must be performed in the pattern activation subsystems. That is, I assume that associative memory contains representations of pattern codes, spatial codes, and coordinates, which are the outputs from the ventral and dorsal systems. The lookup subsystems access representations of parts and distinguishing characteristics and their spatial properties at the same time. The lookup subsystem that "wins" would not only send the location specification to the attention-shifting subsystems (directly or indirectly, via the categorical–coordinate conversion subsystem) so that the locus of attention is shifted, but also would send the pattern code to the pattern activation subsystems—which would partially activate the appropriate representations and inhibit inappropriate ones (recall the findings of Fuster 1990, and Haenny, Maunsell, and Schiller 1988, which show priming of neurons in IT and V4).

Such a priming mechanism would play a key role in mental imagery allowing one to form mental images upon being given the name of the to-be-imaged object, which is understood via processing in associative memory; such processing in turn would affect the pattern activation subsystems, which are the only location where visual memories are stored. As noted before, this kind of feedback would be accomplished by the descending pathways in the visual system.

Anatomical Localization   Attention is subserved by a complex anatomical network (see Desimone 1992; Mesulam 1981, 1990; Posner and Driver 1992; Posner and Petersen 1990; Posner, Petersen, Fox, and Raichle 1988). The process of shifting the location of the focus of attention appears to involve at least five structures: the parietal lobes, the frontal eye fields (area 8), the superior colliculus, the anterior cingulate, and the pulvinar nucleus of the thalamus. Although Posner and his colleagues have offered localizations for each of their subsystems, they also note the possible roles of other structures (e.g., see Posner and Petersen 1990). Let us consider several possible anatomical bases of attention.

First, although the results of Posner and his colleagues provide evidence that the parietal lobes are involved in disengaging attention, these structures may also be involved in other aspects of attention. We can characterize the role of the parietal lobes in more detail by considering properties of neurons in different areas within it. Specifically, at least two areas within the parietal lobes of monkeys, LIP and 7b, are involved in attention, and these areas (and their human homologs) may not implement the same functions. According to Goodman and Andersen (1989), area LIP (lateral intraparietal area), unlike area 7a discussed earlier, has strong connections to the superior colliculus and area 8. Area LIP is adjacent to 7a and has strong connections to it, which is consistent with the idea that area 7a plays a critical role in implementing the spatiotopic mapping subsystem (see chapter 6). Eighty-five percent of the neurons in LIP respond when the animal makes a saccade, 59% responding before the saccade is made. When neurons in LIP are stimulated, they produce saccades that depend on initial eye position. These properties are consistent with the idea that the parietal lobes disengage attention from a present location in preparation for shifting it. However, these properties are also consistent with a role in controlling the shifting operation per se. Goodman and Andersen (1989) demonstrated that hidden units in a neural network model can also show such position-dependent responses, even when the network as a whole has been trained to produce head-centered coordinates.

In contrast, the response properties of some cells in area 7b of the parietal lobes depend on the expected consequences of an action (e.g., see Bushnell, Goldberg, and Robinson 1981; Lynch 1980; Lynch et al. 1977; Mountcastle 1978; Mountcastle et al. 1975; Wurtz, Goldberg, and Robinson 1980; Yin and Mountcastle 1977). These properties suggest that these neurons are "preparing to engage" at a new location. This role is not the same as disengaging attention from a previous location, and suggests that the parietal lobes cannot be identified solely with a single attentional subsystem.

Second, Posner and his colleagues note that the subsystem that actually moves attention appears to involve the superior colliculus (for details on the anatomy of this structure, see Kaas and Huerta 1988). Patients who suffer damage to this structure have a difficult time shifting attention to a cued location at all; it does not matter whether the cue is valid or not (see also Desimone et al. 1990). In addition, at least two other structures play roles in allowing one to shift attention: (1) The anterior cingulate is involved in preparing one to attend to the next step in a sequence (e.g., see Janer and Pardo 1991). This area appears to be active whenever one performs a task that requires a sequence of operations (see also Posner and Petersen 1990). (2) The frontal eye fields (area 8) in part govern where attention is shifted (note that the frontal eye fields are connected to the superior colliculus; see Crowne 1983). For example, Robinson and Fuchs (1969) stimulated cells in the frontal eye fields, and found that the eyes moved. However, the eyes moved the same way, regardless of where they were currently positioned. This finding may suggest that the frontal eye fields specify position retinotopically, and other areas perform the coordinate transform. And in fact, stimulation of cells in the cerebellum and the peripheral field of the superior colliculus produce eye movements whose direction and amplitude depend on the current eye position. However, Zipser and Andersen's (1988) computer simulation results suggest that we should not simply assume that area 8 specifies location in retinotopic coordinates; the population of units working together could specify location spatiotopically.

Third, as Posner and his colleagues proposed, the subsystem that engages attention appears to involve the thalamus. For example, Desimone et al. (1989) studied the pulvinar, a nucleus of the thalamus that is involved in attention (see Kaas and Huerta 1988). If one side of this structure is temporarily deactivated (with the GABA agonist muscimol) in awake behaving monkeys, the animals can no longer engage attention properly in the contralateral field; in particular, they have difficulty ignoring a distractor stimulus (for a review of this and related work, see Desimone 1992). LaBerge and Buchsbaum (1990) showed that such findings can be generalized to humans: In their PET study, the pulvinar was selectively activated during an attention task.

The thalamus has long been thought to be a kind of switching station, and hence it is of interest that it seems to be involved in engaging attention; in this case, attention can be thought of as switching off—and leaving on— specific regions of the visual buffer. Indeed, I earlier suggested that the attention window may function in large part by inhibiting regions surrounding the target region. LaBerge, Carter, and Brown (1992) develop three computational models of thalamic processes in attention that preserve this property but also enhance the contents of the attention window. In addition, I noted earlier that area MST is involved in smooth-pursuit eye movements (e.g., Sakata, Shibutani, and Kawano 1983); this sort of tracking involves another type of engaging attention.

It is worth emphasizing that attention involves other subsystems that are not part of an attention-shifting subsystem per se. For example, additional subsystems are involved in vigilance (which is not of interest in the present context; see Posner and Petersen 1990). And other subsystems are involved in priming, which is another form of attention. As noted earlier, this priming process presumably occurs at the same time that the attention window is being shifted to the location of an expected object, property, or part. Insight into the anatomical localization of such priming has been provided by Corbetta et al. (1991), who asked human subjects to perform attention tasks while they were being PET scanned. On each trial, the subjects saw 20 elements that had the same shape and color, all of which were moving in the same direction. Shortly thereafter, a second display was presented, and the shape, color, and/or speed of these stimuli could be different from those in the first display. The subject was to report whether the second display was the same as the first. On some trials, the subjects were to respond "different" only if there was a change in one particular stimulus dimension (color, shape, or motion); these trials required the subject to engage in selective attention. In contrast, on other trials they were to respond "different" if any of these dimensions changed; these trials required the subjects to engage in divided attention. Measures of cerebral blood flow while subjects passively looked at a fixation point were also collected and subsequently subtracted from measures of cerebral blood flow in each of the other conditions.

Selective attention to different dimensions did in fact result in activation in different regions. Specifically, when the subjects attended to shape, there was activation in the collateral sulcus (on the medial wall of the occipital lobe, inferior to the calcarine sulcus), fusiform, parahippocampal, calcarine/parietal-occipital sulcus intersection, and in the temporal cortex along the superior temporal sulcus. These results, particularly the increased flow in the fusiform gyrus and superior temporal sulcus, are about what one would expect if shape is processed in the ventral system. When the subjects attended to speed, a region deep in the inferior parietal lobule was selectively activated (the human analog to area MT?). For color, the collateral sulcus and dorsolateral occipital cortex were activated. It is of interest that there was very little activation in any of these areas in the divided attention condition, when the subject was not set to encode any specific stimulus dimension. Note also that attention affected other areas than those that have been found to be active when subjects encode color; the fusiform and lingual gyri (see Corbetta et al. 1990; Zeki 1992; Zeki et al. 1991) were not activated in this attention task.

The areas activated by this sort of attention, in my view, implement components of the preprocessing and pattern activation subsystems. Attention regulates their operation, either via priming or by gating the input to them. In contrast, other areas where Corbetta et al. (1991) found activation seem to subserve the process of allocating attention. Specifically, in the selective attention tasks (compared to the divided attention tasks), they found that the globus pallidus, caudate nucleus, posterior thalamus/colliculus, inferior premotor cortex, insular cortex, and lateral orbital frontal cortex were activated. The posterior thalamus may have corresponded to the pulvinar (see also LaBerge and Buchsbaum 1990); areas known to be involved in motor programming were also activated (portions of the basal ganglia and the premotor cortex). In addition, another set of areas was activated in the divided attention condition but not during selective attention, specifically the anterior cingulate gyrus and the right prefrontal cortex. Posner and Petersen (1990) suggest that the anterior cingulate is involved in sequential processing (in this case, perhaps checking the different stimulus attributes) and the right prefrontal cortex is involved in vigilance. In an earlier and not inconsistent formulation, Mesulam (1982) suggests that the anterior cingulate is involved in the motivational aspects of attention.

Clearly, attention is a complex process, which is likely to be accomplished by the workings of numerous subsystems; fortunately, the present project does not hinge on a detailed prior understanding of these mechanisms.

ACCUMULATION OF CONSTRAINTS IN THE VENTRAL SYSTEM

When one's eyes first alight on an object, one may not be so fortunate as to encode the global shape or even an entire part of the object. Rather, one may focus on a portion of it, which may match a stored representation well enough to provide a hypothesis but not well enough for full-blown recognition to occur. Hence, one must encode more information. At least in some cases, one may "get a better look" at the part or characteristic first encoded. As additional information is encoded, it not only provides further constraints on processing in associative memory (via information arriving from the ventral and dorsal streams) but also allows constraints to accumulate in the ventral system.

The mere fact that people can recognize objects seen through a moving pinhole (i.e., perform *anorthoscopic perception*) is evidence that information does accumulate in the visual memory structures over time (see Hochberg 1968, 1978; Morgan, Findlay, and Watt 1982; Rock 1981; Shimojo and Richards 1986). Figures can be seen even when subjects fixate on a slit in a mask and the picture moves behind the mask, which prevents "retinal painting" (e.g., see Morgan, Findlay, and Watt 1982). Indeed, subjects can even integrate three-dimensional information in this way (Klopfer 1985). The input at any point in time typically does not correspond to a specific part that can be recognized; rather, arbitrary segments are encoded. Arbitrary segments are not represented in associative memory, and associative memory representations are not in a visual format—and hence arbitrary segments cannot partially activate any given representation (recall my argument in chapter 5 about why a modality-specific visual memory exists). However, visual memories in the pattern activation subsystems are in the right format to allow generalization from arbitrary segments; this is one of the virtues of representations like the compressed image format I propose. Hence, in order to recognize a part of an object or the object itself when portions of it are encoded sequentially, the pattern activation subsystems must accumulate visual input over time.

In order to accumulate such information, one must somehow register where in the field the stimulus properties are located. That is, nonaccidental and signal properties are indexed by relative location, and such information must be registered even across eye movements. Festinger et al. (1967) argued that a copy of the efferent command to move one's eyes is used to integrate information over eye movements. Such commands are one source of information about the location, but cannot be the only one, given that one can recognize moving objects seen through a stationary slit (with no eye movements at all).

In the previous chapter I conjectured that the spatiotopic mapping subsystem computes the three-dimensional properties of parts and objects, and this information is sent to the ventral system, via connections noted by Harries and Perrett (1991), via connections documented by Baizer, Ungerleider, and Desimone (1991), or via the thalamus. It is also possible that this information reaches the ventral system indirectly, via connections from the frontal lobes (see Goldman-Rakic 1987). I am now suggesting that such input from the spatiotopic mapping subsystem also allows the ventral system to index the locations of material encoded over the course of time.

There is ample evidence that information collected over the course of separate eye movements (or attentional fixations) is integrated in a visual memory of the sort I posit, although such integration is not perfect and apparently does not index eye movements to absolute locations in space (e.g., see Hayhoe, Lachter, and Feldman 1991; Irwin 1991).[23] Thus, if the spatiotopic mapping subsystem is disrupted, it will be difficult to accumulate enough information to recognize degraded or unusual images of individual parts as well as the whole object.

This hypothesis is supported by numerous findings that patients with posterior right-hemisphere damage have difficulty identifying degraded pictures (such as the Gollin figures; e.g., see De Renzi and Spinnler 1966; Lansdell 1968; Newcombe and Russell 1969; Warrington and Taylor 1973, 1978; Warrington and James 1967, 1986, 1988, 1991). Similarly, Nebes (1972) cut geometric shapes and separated the parts (preserving their spatial relations), and showed the patterns to seven split-brain patients; after each stimulus, the subjects felt three shapes, and were to tap on the one that could be composed by bringing the fragments together. Nebes found that the left hand (and hence presumably the right hemisphere) was more accurate in this task in six of the seven patients.

Accumulation of such visual information over time could take place directly, in the pattern activation subsystems and/or indirectly, via the preprocessing subsystem. The pattern activation subsystems would retain information over time (as suggested by findings of Miller, Li, and Desimone, 1991, and Miyashita and Chang, 1988) and additional information would be "added to the pot" until a consistent output is achieved. Alternatively, information could be accumulated in the preprocessing subsystem, which builds up a collection of nonaccidental and signal properties; the entire set would be continuously sent to the pattern activation subsystems as it grows. In this case, the input from the dorsal system would add new material to missing portions of the contour, which would allow the preprocessing subsystem to extract nonaccidental and signal properties.

Summary: Identifying Contorted Objects

One identifies contorted objects by recognizing individual parts and distinguishing characteristics in the pattern activation subsystems, and computing the categorical spatial relations among them in the dorsal system. Such information flows downstream to associative memory, which accumulates inputs over time. A structural description of the object is thereby constructed and matched to stored structural descriptions. Each input serves as an additional constraint on this matching process, and the representation in associative memory that best matches the entire set of inputs becomes most highly activated.

In some situations, the initial input will not implicate a specific object representation, either because the parts and characteristics were not recognized with high confidence or because there simply was too little information. In these circumstances, additional parts or distinctive characteristics are sought. Four subsystems are involved in this process. Two property lookup subsystems access the most distinctive property of the most highly activated representation, which specifies where a part or characteristic is located on an object. The lookup subsystem that accesses the most activated part or characteristic will "win," and it will inhibit the other lookup subsystem. The coordinate property lookup subsystem seeks representations in which location is specified in motor-based (spatiotopic) coordinates; if it "wins," it passes the location specification to mechanisms that shift attention and the pattern code of the property to the pattern activation subsystems, which are thereby primed to encode that part or characteristic. The categorical property lookup subsystem accesses representations in which location is specified using categorical spatial relations. If it "wins," it passes the location specification to the categorical–coordinate conversion subsystem. The categorical–coordinate conversion subsystem uses input about the size and distance of the object (obtained via the coordinate property lookup subsystem) to convert the category to a range of coordinates. These coordinates are then passed to the mechanisms that shift attention to that location, and the pattern code of the property is sent to pattern activation subsystems to prime them for that part or characteristic.

Finally, the attention-shifting subsystem is divided into three components, which disengage the attention window, shift it, and engage it at a new location (shifting may require moving the body, head, eyes, and attention window). Once the attention window subsumes a new pattern in the visual buffer, new input enters the dorsal and ventral systems and is passed to associative memory. If the sought part or characteristic is in fact present, its representation is activated in a pattern activation subsystem. Similarly, if one "gets a better look" at a part or characteristic seen initially, or at the object as a whole, its representation is further activated in a pattern activation subsystem, which accumulates constraints over successive fixations. Depending on the context and the similarity of alternative possible objects, the output from the pattern activation subsystem may allow associative memory to converge on the identity of the object, or more parts or characteristics may need to be sought.

These same mechanisms are presumably used whenever the initial input does not allow one to identify an object. Not only would such top-down hypothesis testing be used when objects are so contorted that their inputs do not match stored representations very well, but the same mechanism would be used to direct successive eye movements when one is examining an object that is so close that its entire pattern cannot be represented in the high-resolution portions of the visual buffer. In the following chapter we will consider the various situations in which these mechanisms come to the fore.

IMAGERY AND PERCEPTION

The proposals I have developed in this chapter have several important implications for visual mental imagery. First, if the pattern activation subsystems store the shapes of objects and parts, plus other object properties (color, texture), then it should be possible to activate such information from memory to form mental images. Second, associative memory must play a critical role in mental imagery. This structure must index the visual memories per se, otherwise we could not explain how words could evoke specific images. Words must be understood in part by accessing stored associations, and those associations presumably include pattern codes and spatial codes. These codes correspond to the output from the perceptual subsystems that is produced when an object or part is encoded. When a property lookup subsystem provides the pattern code as input to the pattern activation subsystems, the code would match a representation in one of these subsystems better than one in the other (depending on whether the code is for a prototype or an exemplar). The pattern activation subsystem that includes the best-matching representation would inhibit the other (hence one would not form two different images at the same time), and would produce an image in the visual buffer.

Many types of neural network architectures have this kind of bidirectional structure (e.g., see Grossberg 1988; Hinton and Sejnowski 1986). However, it is possible that the code that is used to evoke an image is not the same as that produced by the pattern activation subsystems but is merely associated with it in memory. In any case, it is clear that the code used to evoke an image must be conjoined with other types of information in an associative memory structure.

In addition, the spatial relations encoding subsystems would be used during image inspection. For example, when one is asked whether an ape's ears protrude above the top of its head, the spatiotopic mapping and categorical relations subsystem would be used to "inspect" the pattern in the visual buffer. Furthermore, the claim that spatial relations are computed in two ways implies that two types of spatial relations are stored. If so, then there may be two ways of arranging objects, parts, or characteristics into an image—and hence there may be two different mechanisms that are used in generating visual mental images. Moreover, if the representations tend to be stored more effectively in the cerebral hemisphere that encoded them, then we are led to suspect that the left hemisphere will generate images better when categorical spatial relations are used to arrange objects, parts, or characteristics, whereas the right hemisphere will generate them better when coordinate spatial relations are used to arrange them. I will explore this idea in detail in chapter 9. Indeed, the machinery I have posited so far is almost all we need to understand most properties of visual mental imagery, including the bases of image generation, maintenance, inspection, and transformation.

The aspects of the theory developed in this chapter allow us to understand a counterintuitive dissociation between imagery and perception. Guariglia, Padovani, Pantano, and Pizzamiglio (1993) describe a patient who had no evidence of neglect in perception, but had neglect when visualizing familiar piazzas or a well-studied room. This patient also had moderately impaired face recognition, line orientation judgments, and constructional abilities, and performed the Raven's colored progressive matrices at the 15th percentile. In contrast, to Coslett's patient (described in chapter 4), this patient could visualize words without neglecting the left halves and could perform Bisiach, Luzzatti, and Perani's (1979) sequential discrimination task without neglecting part of the figures (this task was summarized in the previous chapter). Moreover, he could visualize colors and perform mental paper folding with a normal level of accuracy (although response times were not explicitly measured). Thus, the pattern of deficits probably did not reflect the ability of the stimulus-based attention shifting subsystem to direct attention during perception. And the problem did not seem to be in inspecting the image or shifting attention, nor did it appear to be a problem in image generation per se. Rather, as the authors suggest, the problem appeared to be in amalgamating images of separate objects into a three-dimensional scene.

This patient's lesion was in the right frontal lobe and anterior temporal lobe; a SPECT study revealed a wider region of hypoperfusion in the right frontal lobe, but the only remote hypoperfusion was in the left cerebellum. The right-hemisphere frontal lesion is consistent with a deficit in the coordinate property lookup subsystem, which is necessary both when the spatial relations are stored as coordinate representations and when such information is used to convert categorical spatial relations to specific loci in an image; in either case, stored coordinate spatial representations would be accessed when one visualized objects in particular locations in a scene or a room. But such representations would not be used to recall the shape of a single object (in the Bisiach et al. task) or a familiar written word (if the word is stored as a single unit).

Alternatively, the lesion location is also consistent with an impaired categorical-conversion subsystem, which may not have been necessary to form images of a specific shape or word (either because the word is stored as a single unit, or because even a moderately damaged categorical-coordinate conversion subsystem can perform the simple conversions necessary to arrange letters in a word, but not the complex relations necessary to arrange objects in a three-dimensional scene). These accounts are consistent with the report that the patient "misplaced some semantically relevant details from the left to the right side of one piazza" (p. 236). Such confusion might occur if stored coordinate spatial relations could not be accessed and so the patient was forced to use less-well-encoded categorical spatial relations or if the categorical-coordinate conversion subsystem were awry. The difficulties in judging line orientation and construction might also reflect difficulties in accessing stored coordinate spatial relations. (The authors used an earlier version of the present theory to account for these results, but suggested that the problem might be due in part to moving "the 'attention window' to select a number of items that belong to the image" [p. 236]; however, it is not clear to me why such difficulty would not also have affected the patient's ability to "read" visualized words. Given the precise language used, I wondered whether they had in mind a difficulty in using a property lookup subsystem to access descriptions in associative memory in the course of generating a multipart image. The accounts offered above obviate the need to posit an additional subsystem to match "a representation of external events and egocentric space," as suggested by the authors.)

CONCLUSIONS

A combination of computational analyses of system abilities, computer simulation modeling, and behavioral and neuropsychological results converged to implicate two subsystems that encode spatial properties: The categorical spatial relations encoding subsystem encodes representations of classes of positions (such as above, on, and connected to), sizes (such as large, medium, and small), and orientations (such as vertical, diagonal, and horizontal). The coordinate spatial relations encoding subsystem encodes representations of metric spatial properties; I assume that these coordinates are tailored to be used in guiding movements. The categorical and coordinate spatial relations encoding subsystems operate in parallel on the output of the spatiotopic mapping subsystem and provide input to associative memory.

In addition, I was led to posit four subsystems that are used in top-down hypothesis testing. The categorical property lookup subsystem accesses propositions in associative memory that use categorical spatial relations to specify where a part or distinctive characteristic is located on an object. Similarly, the coordinate property lookup subsystem accesses representations in associative memory that use coordinate spatial relations to specify where a part or distinctive characteristic is located on an object. The categorical-coordinate conversion subsystem converts a categorical spatial relations representation into a range of coordinates that apply to a specific image. And, finally, the attention-shifting subsystem accepts coordinates and shifts the focus of attention (the body, head, eyes, and attention window) to that location. The property lookup subsystems also prime the pattern activation subsystems so that they can more easily encode the expected part or characteristic. All of these subsystems play a role in both imagery and perception.

8 Identifying Objects: Normal and Damaged Brains

I have spent much time on visual perception per se, with the aim of developing the foundations of a theory of visual mental imagery. In this chapter I consider whether these foundations are in fact firm enough to build upon. It will be useful to begin by summarizing the theory as a whole, noting how the various subsystems interact. I then describe a test of predictions of the theory using PET scanning; these results provide the foundations for additional PET experiments investigating imagery, which are described in chapter 9. Following this, I return to the classes of visual abilities reviewed in chapter 3, and determine whether the theory lends insight into the mechanisms that produce these abilities. Next, the literature on time to name pictures is reviewed, and accounts are provided for these findings. This chapter concludes with a description of a single case study, and I show how the theory makes detailed predictions about the effects of brain damage on high-level visual perception. The theory is motivated in part on neural considerations, and so it is reasonable to expect it to illuminate such findings. If the theory appears coherent, is sufficient to provide accounts of the available data, and can make new and fruitful predictions, then it seems reasonable to take it seriously as the basis for an analysis of visual mental imagery.

THE WORKING SYSTEM: A SUMMARY

Consider how the system identifies a fox that is standing partly behind a barrier so that its rear legs and tail are occluded. Kosslyn et al. (1990) used such a stimulus to test a computer model of a version of the theory, and hence I can describe such processing rather precisely. For present purposes, imagine that this particular fox happens to be facing to the left. This is an interesting example because a fox looks rather like a dog, and occluding part of it will prevent the system from identifying it immediately.

High-level vision receives input from low-level mechanisms that register luminance, color, texture, motion, and depth. This information about the fox and the barrier is organized into perceptual units in the *visual buffer*. The presence of a new pattern leads the *stimulus-based attention-shifting subsystem* to shift the *attention window* to the appropriate part of the visual buffer; the eye, head, and body also shifts as necessary to allow the attention window to surround the pattern. The attention window inhibits information in other regions from being passed further into the system.

As a rule, the attention window always begins by surrounding a region of the visual buffer that has homogeneous properties (such as the same depth values, same color values, and so on). There is no set of cues that uniquely determines that a region contains an object, as opposed to several overlapping objects or a part. However, as a heuristic, an object is likely to correspond to a region in which the local information has similar distance, color, and texture. It is useful to begin with the overall shape of an object not only because it sometimes will match a stored pattern, but also because it establishes the lay of the land, the coordinates necessary to compute the locations of parts and distinguishing characteristics. In this case, let us say that the region selected includes the fox (which is reddish and furry, unlike the barrier) and part of the barrier. The contents of the attention window are sent to the *ventral system* and to the *dorsal system* for further processing.

The ventral system encodes object properties, and I propose that it includes four processing subsystems. The *preprocessing subsystem* extracts nonaccidental and signal properties on the input image. Nonaccidental properties are edges that are roughly parallel, intersecting, collinear, and so on; nonaccidental properties are unlikely to have arisen due to chance. Signal properties include colored and textured regions that distinguish the object. For the fox, the edges of the legs are roughly parallel, the edges that define the ears intersect, and so forth.

At the same time that the preprocessing subsystem is operating, the *motion relations encoding subsystem* is extracting motion patterns. The motion of a fox is different from that of many other animals, which would serve to narrow down the range of alternatives. (This subsystem was not implemented in our model, so let us suppose that the fox is standing stock-still.)[1]

The image and extracted properties are sent to the *pattern activation subsystems*. The process of matching the input to stored representations (i.e., "compressed images") respects the viewpoint consistency constraint. This constraint requires not only that the individual properties match but also that their relative positions be consistent with seeing an object from a single point of view. If this match is very good, and is much better for one particular pattern than for any other, the stimulus is recognized. In this example, the input image of a fox does not match any stored pattern very well in the *exemplar pattern activation subsystem* (it is an unfamiliar fox), but does match representations in the *category pattern activation subsystem* to a moderate degree. However, it matches the patterns corresponding to a dog and fox almost equally well, with a slightly better match to the fox (because of the distinctive color). Because the compressed image representation of the *fox* stored pattern is activated more than the others, it provides imagery feedback to the visual buffer to complete the input. This process engenders a pattern in the visual buffer, which is equivalent to a mental image representation. The mapping function is altered so that the image is rotated and translated (by another subsystem, to be discussed in chapter 11) until it matches the input image as well as possible. The overlap is moderately high, and so the category pattern activation subsystem sends a pattern code to *associative memory*; this code is a symbol for the fox pattern. It also sends an indication that the match was only fairly good.

At the same time that the ventral system is encoding object properties, the dorsal system is encoding a representation of location, size, and orientation for each of the perceptual units surrounded by the attention window. It also encodes such properties of other objects and parsed parts and characteristics in the visual buffer, allowing one to shift attention to these locations if need be; but representations of material outside the scope of the attention window are preattentive—they are not sent further downstream. In the example, because the attention window surrounded the entire fox, the resolution within it is not very high (recall that there is a scope-resolution trade-off: the larger the visual angle subtended, the less resolution can be achieved). Thus, the *spatiotopic mapping subsystem* computes the location, size, and orientation of the object as a whole. This information is sent to the ventral system to help integrate input over time and to supply specification of three-dimensional extent. At the same time, the spatiotopic mapping subsystem sends input to the *categorical spatial relations encoding subsystem* and to the *coordinate spatial relations encoding subsystem*.

The categorical spatial relations encoding subsystem encodes categorical spatial relations and categorizes size and orientation. For the fox, the stimulus (which corresponds to the overall shape) is in front of the viewer, is medium-large, and is oriented so that its major axis is horizontal. The coordinate spatial relations encoding subsystem encodes metric information about location, size, and orientation. In this case, the location, size, and orientation of the overall shape are specified in coordinates that can be used to program the eyes to focus on a given location, or the limbs to reach to that location. The output from both spatial relations encoding subsystems is sent to associative memory.

Associative memory receives inputs from both the ventral and dorsal systems. The input from the pattern activation subsystems may be sufficient for object identification if the stimulus is recognized with confidence (the match to a stored shape is very good), but in this example it is not. Thus, although the spatial properties encoded from the dorsal system are also consistent with those of a fox, and so this representation is activated more than it would be on the basis of the input from the ventral system alone, only a tentative identification can be made; the representation in associative memory of a fox is not activated above threshold. If the context had been different (e.g., one were riding through the English countryside on horseback, looking for a fox), this amount of activation may have been sufficient. But given no particular expectations, the threshold is set higher, and so *fox* is taken as a tentative identification.

This tentative identification serves as a hypothesis, which is tested by looking for the most distinctive of the properties (parts and characteristics, such as a particularly shaped spot) associated with the representation of the candidate object. The *categorical property lookup subsystem* and the *coordinate property lookup subsystem* attempt to access representations of the object's properties, and whichever one finds the strongest (most distinctive) representation inhibits the other. In this case, the head is the most distinctive part of a fox, and its location is represented using the categorical relation "at the front of the body." The categorical spatial relation and part are strongest because they have been used most often to distinguish foxes from similar objects; the categorical relation is general across all foxes, whereas a coordinate relation would be specific to a particular picture or statue of a fox. This is a live fox in an unusual situation; its precise posture has not been observed before and is not stored in either pattern activation subsystem (which would have registered a high match if it were) or in associative memory (which would have stored coordinates of parts). Similarly, the size and orientation of the head are accessed.

The categorical location specification is relative to the general shape envelope, and hence the system must compute where the "front" of the object is in the input image. This computation is performed by the *categorical–coordinate conversion subsystem*, which accesses information about the taper of the shape envelope, which is a heuristic for locating the front. The categorical–coordinate conversion subsystem also uses coordinate information about the size and distance of the shape to compute coordinates that are sent to the attention-shifting subsystems.

The *attention-shifting subsystem* disengages attention from its previous point of focus, shift the body, head, eyes, and/or attention window so that the attention window is centered on the input image of the specified portion of the object. In addition, the scope of the attention window is reduced, increasing its level of resolution; the categorical–coordinate conversion subsystem uses the categorical size representation in conjunction with information about the size and distance of the object to scale the attention window properly. In this example, the attention window is shifted to the left part of the overall shape envelope, and its scope is reduced to surround a medium-small part seen at the appropriate distance.

At the same time that the attention window is being shifted and rescaled, the pattern code representing identity of the sought part or characteristic is sent to the pattern activation subsystems. This input primes the sought representation (a visual memory of the shape of a prototypical fox's head), making it easier to match, and the primed representation inhibits representations of other shapes.

The system then engages in a second cycle, again encoding the object and spatial properties of the stimulus encompassed by the attention window. The new ventral and dorsal inputs are processed as described above, which in turn provide new inputs to associative memory. If either pattern activation subsystem succeeds in matching the part, and if the size, orientation, and location of the part specified by the dorsal subsystems are appropriate, then the input to associative memory is consistent with the properties of the candidate object. In this case, all of those requirements are met, and the *fox* representation in associative memory is activated above threshold.

However, if some other part or characteristic is encoded after the attention window has been shifted and rescaled, it will either be consistent or inconsistent with those of a fox. If it is not consistent with a fox, but is consistent with some other object, another representation in associative memory might become more active than the fox representation. In this case, the fox representation would be inhibited and a new hypothesis would be tested. This cycle is repeated as many times as necessary until the object has been identified.

A particularly dramatic example of this hypothesis-flipping phenomenon once happened to me. I was looking for a friend's black cat, and saw a plausible black lumpy shape out of the corner of my eye resting against the side of a couch. But when I looked for the head, I found a strap; when I looked again, I discovered it was a black handbag. This example sticks in my mind because my expectation was so thoroughly violated—usually, one is not so far off the mark.

Because the head is distinctive for a fox, the fact that this part is consistent with a fox shape—and inconsistent with a dog shape—is enough to activate the fox representation in associative memory past threshold in usual circumstances. However, the fox in our example is partially occluded behind a barrier. If less of the fox had protruded beyond the barrier, the initial match would have been even poorer, and locating a single part may not have been sufficient. In such a case one may need to engage in an additional cycle, checking for a second distinctive part or characteristic.

TESTING PREDICTIONS

At first blush, Warrington and James (1991) appear to report results that contradict a central principle of the theory. The theory posits that when one views objects that project unfamiliar shapes, property lookup subsystems in the frontal lobes look up a distinctive property in associative memory, which is used to direct attention. Warrington and James showed focal lesion patients objects seen from unconventional points of view, and asked them to identify each object (by naming, gesturing, or providing a description of its use). The subjects were also asked to select the silhouette of an object that was seen from an unusual point of view from among four silhouettes, the other three of which were object-like shapes but not objects. Although patients with posterior damage to the right hemisphere were impaired in these tasks (as discussed in chapter 6), relative to control subjects and patients with posterior damage to the left hemisphere, patients with unilateral anterior damage were not impaired.

The report that frontal lobe damage does not disrupt performance in this task must be tempered with the fact that Warrington and James did not report response times. If the frontal lobes are damaged, knowledge-guided search should be disrupted—which should slow down the time to name unfamiliar shapes. But random searching, or stimulus-based searching, eventually will allow one to encode the requisite information (albeit inefficiently)—which would produce longer times, not more errors. Alternatively, the results could indicate that search was as successful as possible even if no specific hypothesis was being tested; the input may have been so impoverished that subjects merely searched as systematically as possible, hoping to find a distinctive part or characteristic. As yet another possibility, the patients might actually have been impaired relative to a baseline condition in which normal objects were shown—but such a condition was not included in the study.

Kosslyn, Alpert, Thompson, Chabris, Rauch, and Anderson (1993) used PET scanning to discover whether the top-down hypothesis-testing subsystems are recruited, and additional information is encoded, when one views an object seen from a noncanonical point of view. Each subject participated in three sets of trials: baseline, canonical pictures, and noncanonical pictures. Each baseline trial consisted of a nonsense line drawing and the name of an object (presented auditorily); the subjects simply viewed the drawings and pressed a foot pedal upon hearing the name, alternating feet for successive responses. The drawings were created by modifying each canonical picture so that it was unrecognizable but still had the same number of pixels and subtended the same visual angle. The blood flow engendered by this task presumably reflects relatively low-level visual and auditory comprehension processes. These trials always were presented first, before the subjects knew what the objects looked like. Each object was used only once during the course of the entire experiment, and so the names used in the baseline task were not repeated later for any given subject; we tested three groups of subjects, which allowed each picture and name to be used equally often in each condition.

The other two conditions differed only in whether the pictures were objects seen from canonical or noncanonical perspectives. Each picture was presented along with a word. Half of the time the word named the picture, and half of the time it did not; the subjects determined whether the words named the pictures as quickly as possible. The canonical and noncanonical drawings subtended the same visual angles and had the same number of pixels, on average. The order of the canonical and noncanonical trials was fully counterbalanced. Figure 8.1 shows examples of the stimuli.

Consider first the results of subtracting blood flow in the canonical pictures condition from that in the noncanonical pictures condition. These results, illustrated in figure 8.2, tell us which areas had to work harder when noncanonical pictures were seen—and a second encoding cycle should have been used. The first step in top-down hypothesis testing is to access a distinctive property in associative memory. Hence, we expected activity in the dorsolateral prefrontal lobes, which may implement the property lookup subsystems. And in fact, there was more activity in this area. Indeed, there was massive activation in the left hemisphere, which may reflect the operation of the categorical property lookup subsystem in particular (and perhaps also the categorical–coordinate conversion subsystem; this area includes area 46, which in the monkey implements a working memory for spatial information

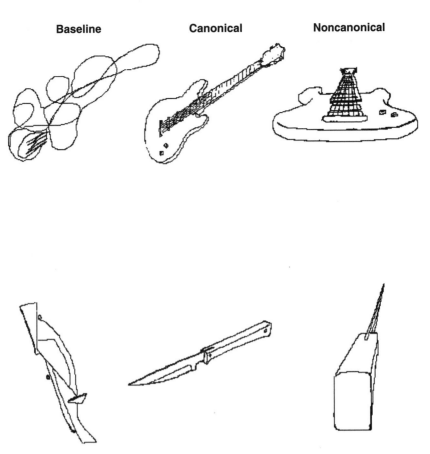

Figure 8.1 Stimuli used in the Kosslyn, Alpert, Thompson, Chabris, Rauch and Anderson PET study of picture identification (Reprinted from Kosslyn et al., (1993), with permission.)

[Goldman-Rakic 1987]). Because the drawings were novel, subjects would not be able to use coordinate spatial relations representations to direct their attention to distinguishing characteristics, and hence we expected the categorical property lookup subsystem to locate an appropriate representation of a property; this subsystem may be more effective in the left cerebral hemisphere. We also expected activation in the right dorsolateral prefrontal lobe, given that coordinate information must be accessed to perform the conversion from categorical spatial relations representations—and such activation was in fact present.

The next step is to shift attention to the location of the part or distinguishing characteristic. As expected, we found increased activity in the left superior parietal lobe, which may play a role in the disengage process. However, we did not find activity in area 8, the anterior cingulate, the thalamus, or the superior colliculus—which may suggest that these areas were also active in the canonical condition (the pictures were in free view and subjects presumably scanned them). We will consider this possibility shortly.

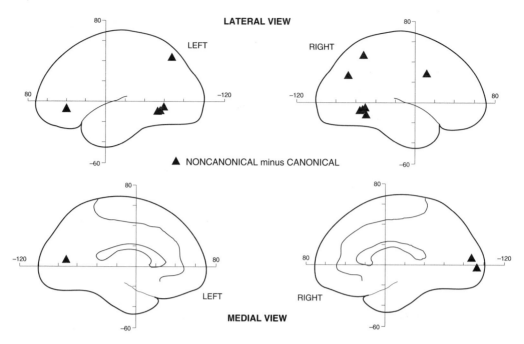

Figure 8.2 PET-scanning results (loci of strongest activation in activated areas) when people evaluated names for noncanonical pictures. The images were created by subtracting blood flow in a condition in which subjects evaluated names for canonical pictures from blood flow in a condition in which they evaluated names for noncanonical pictures. (Reprinted from Kosslyn, Alpert, Thompson, Chabris et al. (1993), with permission.)

Next, we expected additional activity in the visual buffer if additional parts or characteristics were encoded. As predicted, we found more activity in area 17 and area 18. However, although area 18 was activated bilaterally, area 17 was activated only in the right hemisphere.

We also expected more processing in the ventral system if additional parts or characteristics had to be encoded. And we did in fact find additional bilateral activation in the noncanonical task in the inferior temporal lobe and middle temporal gyrus, and additional right-hemisphere activation in the fusiform gyrus. Some of these areas may reflect activation of the preprocessing subsystem and others activation of the pattern activation subsystems, but these data do not allow us to identify the precise functions of the activated areas.

According to the theory, while additional parts and characteristics are encoded in the ventral system, their spatial relations are encoded in the dorsal system. As predicted, we found increased activity in the right inferior parietal lobe. This activation presumably reflects the operation of the spatiotopic mapping subsystem, which is expected if this subsystem plays a key role in computing depth information from shading, perspective, and other cues (see chapter 6). This finding is consistent with Warrington and James's (1991) demonstration that damage to this region impairs a patient's ability to identify objects seen from unusual perspectives. However, we did not find left-hemisphere activation that could be identified with the categorical spatial relations encoding subsystem; again, it may be that such activation was also present when subjects evaluated objects seen from canonical points of view, and hence was eliminated by the subtraction.

Finally, the ventral and dorsal streams project to associative memory. We found bilateral activation in area 19 and in the right angular gyrus (note that area 19 is extremely large; the activation we found here was in the more dorsal portion). Associative memory may rely on both of these structures. We expected more activity in associative memory when parts must be accessed and subsequently encoded over time, but it is not clear why this effect should have been more pronounced in the right hemisphere. Sergent, Ohta, and MacDonald (1992) also report activation in area 19 in an object categorization task, when blood flow in a line gratings classification task was used as the baseline. They did not detect activation in this area when they subtracted blood flow in a gender discrimination task from blood flow in a face identification task, which is as expected if both tasks tap associative memory. Indeed, when they subtracted blood flow in the gratings task from blood flow in the gender discrimination task, Sergent, Ohta, and MacDonald again found activation in area 19. Similarly, Sergent et al. (1992) found activation in area 19 when subjects decided whether pictured objects were living or nonliving. We also found activation in the precentral gyrus, which is difficult to interpret.

These results, then, are highly consistent with our predictions. However, we made many predictions, and one must wonder how likely such results would be to occur by chance alone. We computed the probability of this pattern of activity due to chance alone, taking into account spatial correlations within hypothesized regions. Using very conservative criteria, we estimate the chance occurrence of the pattern of increased activity for the noncanonical views, relative to the canonical views, as about $p = .00006$.

The design of our experiment also allowed us to test a second type of prediction. According to the theory, the subsystems operate concurrently in cascade; they do not wait for instructions to begin, and thus operate on partial information. If these assumptions are correct, then we expected activation of the entire system even when objects are viewed from canonical perspectives. That is, the system should not wait to discover whether it has recognized and identified a stimulus with high confidence before beginning to collect additional information about it; the subsystems do not operate as discrete stages (see chapter 2), even though for simplicity I sometimes have talked as if they do. But even so, as was demonstrated in the previous analysis, the theory predicts that the top-down hypothesis-testing mechanisms do not operate as much for canonical pictures as they do when they are actually needed, for noncanonical pictures; once an object has been identified, processing is terminated, readying the system for the next stimulus.

Figure 8.3 provides the results of subtracting blood flow evoked in the baseline condition from the blood flow in canonical picture condition. I first

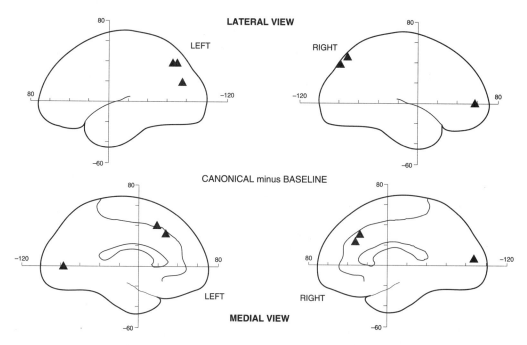

Figure 8.3 PET-scanning results (loci of strongest activation in activated areas) when people evaluated names for canonical pictures. The images were created by subtracting blood flow in a condition in which subjects saw nonsensense patterns and heard names from blood flow in a condition in which they evaluated canonical pictures. (Reprinted from Kosslyn, Alpert, Thompson, Chabris et al., with permission.)

consider the areas that should be active in bottom-up perceptual encoding, and then turn to those that are used in top-down hypothesis testing.

According to the theory, if a familiar type of object is seen from a common point of view, it should be recognized immediately in the category pattern activation subsystem, which is implemented primarily in the left hemisphere. To our surprise, we did not find significant activation in the ventral system, although there were trends for the left middle temporal gyrus and the left fusiform gyrus to be activated. Just as people can see faces in clouds, it is possible that subjects interpreted the nonsense patterns in the baseline condition—and hence this activation was subtracted out.

We also expected spatial properties to be encoded, and found activation in the dorsal system. Specifically, the left inferior parietal lobe was active, which is consistent with the fact that categorical spatial relations are encoded reflexively—as has been demonstrated in Stroop experiments (e.g., see Clark and Brownell 1975). We did not find selective activation in the right parietal lobe, which may implement the spatiotopic mapping subsystem. This is not surprising; this subsystem should have been active also during the baseline condition, and hence the resulting blood flow would have been subtracted from that in the canonical pictures condition.

The object properties and spatial properties encoding streams feed into associative memory, and hence we expected activation in this structure when one identifies objects. And we did in fact find bilateral activation in area 19. We did not find activation in the angular gyrus, however.

Now consider the regions that purportedly implement processing subsystems used in top-down hypothesis testing. First, we did in fact find right-hemisphere activation of dorsolateral prefrontal cortex, which may be involved in accessing information from associative memory. Second, we found bilateral activation of area 8 (FEF) and right-hemisphere activation of the anterior cingulate, both of which play a role in directing attention to specific loci. Thus, our failure to find activation in these areas in our analysis of the noncanonical pictures condition apparently was a consequence of the subtraction we used; such activation was also present in the task we used as the baseline for that comparison. In addition, we found more blood flow in both superior parietal lobes when subjects evaluated canonical pictures, relative to the baseline. We did not find activation in the pulvinar or superior colliculus, however, which may indicate that the baseline evoked the stimulus-based attention-shifting subsystem, leading the subjects to engage attention at one locus; if so, then the activation of these structures would have been removed by the subtraction.

Finally, we also found more activation in area 17 (left hemisphere) and area 18 (right hemisphere), which partly implement the visual buffer. This additional activation is remarkable because the baseline stimuli were visually complex and hence provided much input to the visual buffer. Nevertheless, if subjects encode additional information as a matter of course when identifying objects, then the visual buffer will be stimulated more than if they do not scan the stimulus. Thus, we had good evidence that the top-down processing subsystems were active even when subjects identified familiar objects seen from common points of view. This result is not surprising in this experiment, however, because the pictures were presented in free view and subtended 7° of visual angle. Moreover, the subjects heard names of objects, and hence may have searched for distinctive properties. These factors presumably led the subjects to scan over the pictures, and such scanning probably was not random, but rather was directed by the same processes that accomplish top-down hypothesis testing.[2]

We again estimated the probability that we would have obtained this pattern of results due to chance. On the basis of conservative criteria, the probability of obtaining the observed ensemble of areas due to chance is about one in one million.

In short, key predictions were borne out by the results. We found activity in the major structures that were hypothesized to implement key processes involved in these tasks. These findings are impressive because the hypotheses were based in large part on results from nonhuman primates, but they nevertheless provided a reasonably good guide for making predictions about information processing in the human brain. However, our predictions necessarily were vague because we did not know the precise homology between monkey and human brains; thus, there was plenty of leeway for "successful" prediction of localization. In the following chapter the predictions are tightened considerably by using the interpretation of the present results to formulate precise hypotheses for the pattern of cerebral activity that underlies visual mental imagery.

BASIC VISUAL ABILITIES

Many readers may have noticed that they would not identify objects equally easily in the various conditions considered in the previous chapters. A stimulus is easy or difficult to identify only by virtue of the properties of the processing system itself. A Martian might exhibit a very different pattern of relative difficulty, as might a computer vision system (as gauged by its processing time and errors). Variations in identification times reflect the nature of the underlying processing and must be explained by any viable theory of object identification. However, an account of relative response times is useless if the theory cannot also account for our most basic abilities. The time required to press a button or to say a name is not particularly interesting in its own right; such data only have interest in the context of a theory that addresses important real-world phenomena.

Thus, I will defer accounting for identification times until the following section, and begin with accounts of the five classes of visual abilities that were outlined in chapter 3. Many of these accounts, of course, have been offered in previous chapters. I will only briefly summarize the accounts offered previously and focus on accounts of abilities that were neglected or only mentioned in passing. To eliminate redundancy, I will note only those aspects of the system (as summarized above) that play key roles in conferring each specific ability.

Different Locations and Distances (Visual Angles)

The ability to identify objects when they are seen from different points of view was further differentiated into two capacities.

Identifying Objects When Their Input Images Subtend Different Visual Angles We can identify objects when they project input images that subtend different visual angles. One mechanism underlying this ability is the attention window, which can surround different-sized regions within the visual buffer. In addition, the spatiotopic mapping subsystem registers the actual size of an object, not its projected size, and hence spatial properties will be computed correctly regardless of the projected size. The preprocessing subsystem extracts nonaccidental and signal properties in the same way, regardless of the size of the input image. Such properties are compared to patterns stored in the pattern activation subsystems in accordance with the viewpoint consistency constraint. The matching process activates stored representations to the extent that they are consistent with seeing the input properties in those relative positions when the object is viewed from a single point of view; as long as enough distinguishing properties are present, it does not matter which particular properties are visible. The output from the pattern activation subsystems and spatial relations encoding subsystems converge on associative memory, as summarized above.

Identifying Objects When Their Input Images Fall on Different Places on the Retina We identify objects when they project images on different places on the retina. If the stimulus remains in view, the stimulus-based attention-shifting subsystem will shift the eyes, head, and/or body (as necessary) so that one is focused on the stimulus; processing then proceeds as summarized above. If the stimulus is available so briefly that one cannot make an eye movement, one encodes the input using the same mechanisms that allow us to identify objects that subtend different visual angles. The attention window shifts positions within the visual buffer and thereby provides input to the dorsal and ventral systems from different locations. Note, however, that depending on how an input image is projected into the visual buffer, different portions of an image fall in the periphery, and hence different parts will be degraded. This problem is dealt with in part by the use of nonaccidental properties (extracted by the preprocessing subsystem), which are robust under various types of degradation and transformation.

Shape Variations

More challenging were the problems that involve recognizing novel shapes. I considered four such problems, although two were noted only in passing.

Identifying Objects When They Are Seen from Different Vantage Points People identify objects when they are seen from different points of view, and hence project different input images. For familiar objects seen from familiar perspectives, this ability is accounted for by the storage of a number of viewer-centered representations of an object. However, in many instances a viewing perspective (and hence an input image) will not precisely match one of a stored representation. Our ability to generalize in such situations hinges in large part by the operation of the preprocessing and pattern activation subsystems. The viewpoint consistency constraint operates over sets of non-accidental and signal properties, and recognition can occur when many different combinations of such properties are visible. Input from the spatiotopic mapping subsystem, specifying the three-dimensional properties of objects and parts, also helps to constrain the recognition process. However, if only a poor match is made in the pattern activation subsystems, imagery feedback of the best-matching object will be generated and used to augment the input (with its size, location and orientation adjusted as necessary). If the shape of the input image is sufficiently novel, only a tentative match will be sent to associative memory, and the subsystems involved in top-down hypothesis testing will run to completion (as summarized above).

Identifying Objects When the Shapes of Their Parts Vary We can identify objects as members of a category when the shapes of their parts vary.

For example, chairs have differently shaped arms, backs, legs, and so on. If the different variants are represented in the exemplar pattern activation subsystem, a match will be made; this seems likely for atypical chairs (such as curved rocking chairs, Eames chairs, and so on). But even if the shape of the parts is novel, some variations in shape will not alter nonaccidental properties or their positions—and representations in the category pattern activation subsystem are accessed by these sorts of properties (which do not vary across members of the category). However, if representations of similarly shaped objects are stored, nonaccidental properties will not allow the pattern activation subsystems to match the input to a single stored representation. In this situation, imagery feedback is critical. If this process fails to provide a good match to a single stored representation, then the top-down hypothesis-testing process will run to completion. Indeed, if representations of similarly shaped parts are stored in the pattern activation subsystems, then several parts may need to be recognized before enough evidence has reached associative memory for identification.

Identifying Objects When the Spatial Relations among Parts Vary Chapter 7 focused on just this problem, and the summary of the system's operation provided at the beginning of this chapter also summarizes its operation when one views contorted objects.

Identifying Objects That Contain or Do Not Contain Optional Parts or Characteristics We can identify objects when they include or do not include optional parts or characteristics (such as arms for a chair). If the parts or characteristics are truly optional, and examples often occur with and without them, then separate representations of the different types may be stored in the exemplar pattern activation subsystem. But what about the first time one sees an object without a part or characteristics? If removing the part or characteristic alters the overall shape significantly, it may be impossible to recognize the object initially. In this case, individual parts and characteristics may be recognized, which may partially activate the representation of one object more strongly than those of other objects; this representation then serves as a hypothesis to be tested. This proposal leads us to expect that objects with missing parts should require more time to identify than intact objects, which is true (Biederman 1987; Cave and Kosslyn 1993). Similarly, adding an optional part (e.g., a hat on a person's head) also should slow down the matching process because a competing representation will initially inhibit the representation of the object (the head). Kosslyn, Clegg, Chabris, and Thompson (unpublished data) have confirmed this prediction.

Impoverished Input

A major challenge for any theory of visual object identification is to explain how we can identify objects even when the input is degraded. Degraded input arises in a number of ways.

Identifying Objects That Are Partially Occluded We can identify objects when they are partially occluded by other objects, sometimes even when the input image contains many partially overlapping objects. Because of the viewpoint consistency constraint, stored representations are activated to the extent that the input contains nonaccidental and signal properties in the proper spatial arrangement. However, only one representation can "win," even if there are multiple objects present in the input; without this characteristic of processing, the system would not necessarily converge on the representation of a single object. Thus, when more than one object is present, inhibition among their representations should allow only a single representation to be fully activated at a time. This representation projects imagery feedback to the visual buffer to augment the input and thereby facilitate encoding. As predicted by this theory, in most circumstances people can identify only one object at a time (if we assume that an "object" always includes a conjunction of "features"; see Treisman and Gelade 1980).

When objects are partially occluded, input from the motion relations encoding subsystem may be particularly important. The output from the motion relations encoding subsystem is entered into the pattern activation subsystems as another kind of constraint to be used in the matching process. But even so, in some circumstances only parts will be matched in the pattern activation subsystems, and thus top-down hypothesis testing will be required (as summarized earlier). If sought parts or characteristics are in the occluded region, more parts or characteristics will need to be considered. Thus, we expect retarded naming times when objects are partially occluded, as has in fact been observed (Kosslyn, Clegg, Chabris, and Thompson, unpublished).

Identifying Objects When the Image Is Degraded We can identify objects even when they are seen through a haze or the lighting varies arbitrarily (e.g., the object is under a tree, with dappled sunlight filtering through the branches). The mechanisms that allow us to identify partially occluded objects will also operate to good advantage in these situations. In addition, motion cues often will play a critical role, not only helping to organize the figure into the appropriate perceptual units, but also providing cues for matching the input to previously seen objects. In some circumstances, the lighting will alter the perceived color of objects. In this case, some of the object properties of the input may not match those stored in the pattern activation subsystem. As usual, when a nonoptimal match occurs, additional information must be sought (as summarized earlier).

Identifying Objects That Are Very Close We also can identify an object when it is so close to us that we cannot see it clearly in a single eye fixation, and hence must inspect it with multiple eye fixations. At each fixation, different information is sent to the ventral and dorsal systems. The ventral system attempts to match the input to stored patterns, which may correspond to overall shape envelopes or to representations of individual parts or characteristics; at the same time the dorsal system encodes the spatial properties of the input. The spatiotopic mapping subsystem indexes where one is looking, and this information is used to integrate the input from each fixation in the ventral system, forming a single pattern of activation. In addition, the two streams converge in associative memory, and a structural description is formed; the representation that is most consistent with the input becomes most highly activated. This leads to a systematic search of the object, as summarized earlier. As the eyes move, new information is accumulated in the pattern activation subsystems, as well as in associative memory, until the object is identified.

Specific Instances

In most ways, a system that overgeneralizes is as deficient as one that generalizes too little. It is clear that we can identify particular objects (e.g., one's own watch or wallet) and spatial relations (e.g., a tree that is a certain distance from a rock may serve as a landmark), curtailing generalization when appropriate.

Identifying Specific Objects   Our ability to identify specific objects can be understood in part because the exemplar pattern activation subsystem represents specific instances of objects. Thus, one can set the threshold in associative memory for a particular object very high, so that only a good match in this subsystem plus the appropriate spatial properties will satisfy it. If the initial match is not sufficient, the same processes that allow us to identify oddly contorted objects will be used here. In some cases, however, stored coordinates may guide top-down hypothesis testing. That is, if a picture or other rigid object is viewed, it is likely to have a distinct representation in associative memory. In such cases, coordinate spatial relations may be "stronger" than categorical relations, because they specify precise metric spatial properties that are always diagnostic of that specific object. Thus, one may sometimes use stored coordinate spatial relations to direct top-down search when viewing a specific exemplar.

Identifying Specific Spatial Relations   Our ability to identify specific spatial relations appears to be much poorer than our ability to identify individual objects (see Biederman 1987). To the extent that we can identify a specific size, orientation, or location, the coordinate spatial relations encoding subsystem must play a critical role. This subsystem encodes the coordinate spatial relations between objects, parts, or characteristics as well as metric spatial information about them. These representations can be stored in associative memory and compared to input that is encoded subsequently.

Objects and Scenes

I have focused primarily on the identification of individual objects, but we often see more than one object at a time and can identify more than one of them in a single glance.

Identifying Multiple Objects in a Single Fixation   Each representation in the pattern activation subsystems is activated to the extent that the appropriate nonaccidental and signal properties are present. I assume that the most strongly activated representation inhibits the others. Associative memory utilizes a similar winner-take-all mechanism, and hence only one object can be recognized or identified at a time. In both cases, I assume that shortly after the input has been matched, the representation stops inhibiting the other representations—allowing the next most activated representation to "win" and produce output. Thus, one can recognize and identify multiple objects in a single fixation but does so one at a time (see Treisman and Gelade 1980).

Identifying Multiple Objects "Automatically"   The visual system not only *can* identify more than a single object in a fixation, it typically appears to do so "automatically"; if this were not true, context would not affect identification (e.g., see Biederman, Mezzanotte, and Rabinowitz 1982; but also see Biederman et al. 1988 for situations in which context can have more complex effects). In chapter 2, I suggested that the subsystems operate in cascade and engage in cooperative computation, with each sending partial outputs to the next and receiving feedback from them. If so, then a subsystem has sent "interpretable" output when the feedback from the receiving subsystem meshes with the pattern of activation evoked by the present input to the sending subsystem. At this point, the two subsystems—the sending and receiving—are in danger of becoming "locked" together, mutually reinforcing each other indefinitely. Hence, it seems reasonable to suspect that there is a mechanism that "resets" a subsystem as soon as it has sent an interpretable output, allowing it to encode new information. The mechanism might be a form of adaptation, which would allow new input to disrupt a stable pattern of activation more easily with the passage of time. If so, then one consequence of this mechanism would be that when multiple objects are visible, more than one will be automatically encoded within a fixed period of time (see Olshausen, Anderson, and Van Essen 1992, for some similar ideas). However, figure 6 of Biederman et al. (1988) suggests that the time constant is on the order of 20 ms per object, which is fast for an adaptation effect.

In addition, Henderson, Pollatsek, and Rayner (1987) found that subjects can encode objects more easily if they have just fixated on a related object. Apparently when one object is identified, the representations of other related objects are primed. This sort of visual priming appears to be mediated by a *schema* in associative memory, which organizes objects into a familiar group (such as, but not limited to, a scene); this sort of schema is analogous to a structural description. When such a schema is activated by one constituent object, it presumably activates the visual representations of the other objects in the same way that a single object's parts can be primed after the entire object is seen—thereby facilitating subsequent encoding of these objects. Additional findings by Boyce, Pollatsek, and Rayner (1989) showed that such priming does not necessarily result from direct associations among the objects, but rather can arise via "episodic relatedness" (whether an object is plausible in a specific context; e.g., that a coffeemaker is commonly found in a kitchen); presumably, such information is stored in associative memory and could drive the kind of top-down priming I suggest here (for other reasons to posit such a priming process, see chapter 8 of Kosslyn and Koenig 1992).

In short, it is clear that the theory can address each of our basic visual abilities. However, these brief summaries may seem facile, for (at least) two reasons. First, the accounts are not precise; I have not specified the details of how each subsystem works. For example, Lowe (1987a), Ullman (1989), and others have expended much effort trying to describe exactly how an input representation of shape is matched to stored visual representations, which is only one facet of the mechanism I describe. As I noted in chapter 2, the present goal is to pull the bird apart by the joints, not to describe the musculature, vasculature, and neural enervation of the limbs themselves. I want to make the case that specific subsystems exist, not that they use specific algorithms. I sometimes have felt forced to suggest algorithms to show that my proposals are computationally feasible, but even here my goal was not to specify all of the details.

Second, the theory is complex, and there are many ways in which one might fudge an explanation for a phenomenon. Thus, it is important that my colleagues and I have implemented most of the theory as a computer simulation model, and we have tested the model in many of the situations summarized here (see Kosslyn et al. 1990). We have also developed more specialized models of specific aspects of the theory, as summarized in previous chapters. Moreover, the present accounts do generate testable predictions, both behavioral and neuropsychological, as has been pointed out in previous chapters. Thus, the theory not only serves as a framework for sharpening issues and for organizing the previous findings, but also can lead one to perform new and fruitful experiments.

NAMING TIMES

I have so far characterized performance only at the coarsest level. In reasoning about how to build a system that has the appropriate abilities, I was led to postulate a number of mechanisms that make predictions in their own right, some of which were tested explicitly. It is now of interest to push the theory and see how well it can account for the relatively subtle effects of a host of variables that produce differences in the time to name pictured objects. The theory was not formulated with all of these results in mind from the outset.[3] In what follows I first summarize the findings and then provide an account based on the theory. Some of these results have been mentioned before, but will be reiterated here (albeit briefly) for completeness. There appear to be three classes of findings, which primarily reflect processes that encode the stimulus, assign a name, and access the name to produce a response.

Encoding the Stimulus

The following findings bear primarily on processes that encode an object, and hence these results lead us to focus on properties of the ventral system.

Degraded Contours   Subjects require more time to name drawings when portions of the contours have been removed. Eliminating part of the contour is particularly disruptive when vertices are removed (Biederman and Blickle 1985). I discussed these results in chapter 5, when first considering the nature of nonaccidental properties. Degrading the contours can disrupt the encoding of nonaccidental and signal properties, and hence the input representations may not match those in the pattern activation subsystems very well—which will require allowing imagery feedback to augment the input fully and may require top-down hypothesis testing. Vertices are particularly high-information parts of contours, and so removing them has deleterious effects (cf. Attneave 1954). Indeed, if enough nonaccidental and signal properties are removed, an object cannot be recognized (see chapter 5).

Missing Parts   Subjects require more time to name objects when parts have been removed (Biederman, 1987; Cave and Kosslyn 1993; this is also suggested by comparing times on the first blocks of Experiment 2 of Biederman and Cooper 1991a and Biederman and Cooper 1992, but the stimuli were not comparable in other respects, such as visual angle subtended). As noted above, if the overall shape is disrupted, only parts may be recognized, and top-down processing required before the object is identified.

Disrupted Parts   Disrupting objects in arbitrary ways does not impair naming any more than disrupting objects at part boundaries (Cave and Kosslyn 1993), provided that the parts are still aligned properly. The input is matched to stored visual representations via the viewpoint consistency constraint. Thus, provided that the contours have the appropriate spatial arrangement, breaking up an object in an arbitrary way will not impair recognition any more than will breaking it up along part boundaries.

Disrupted Spatial Relations among Parts   Naming is greatly impaired if parts or arbitrarily determined fragments are in unusual positions (Cave and Kosslyn 1993). This sort of scrambling violates the viewpoint consistency constraint, and hence the initial input will not match a stored representation of an object in the pattern activation subsystems. However, individual parts typically can be matched, which will lead to a hypothesis to be tested. Such top-down hypothesis testing will be impaired because distinctive parts are not in their expected positions, and hence more time will be required to encode the necessary information to identify the object.

Differences in Projected Shape   Bartram (1974) asked subjects to name photographed objects, and observed increased speed when the objects were named on subsequent trials. Bartram (1974) found that subjects showed some improvement when a different object was later shown that had the same name (e.g., two clocks that looked different), but showed more improvement when the same object was later seen from a different point of view, and showed the most improvement when the exact same object was repeated. Bartram's use of photographs allowed the subjects to use surface cues, and thus it is important that Biederman and Cooper found the same results when the same line drawings or line drawings of objects with the same name (e.g., upright piano versus grand piano) were shown (and hence only shape could be used to recognize the object). Cave and Squire (1992) report similar results even when there was a 48-hour delay between the first and second presentation sessions.

All three sets of researchers interpret these findings as implying that two mechanisms, one visual and one nonvisual, are primed. This inference lines up with the present claim that the pattern activation subsystems are modality specific but associative memory is not. Thus, the representation of the identical shape is primed in both pattern activation subsystems and in associative memory, whereas a representation of a different shape with the same name is primed only in associative memory. Moreover, the representation of the same object seen from different points of view is only primed in the category pattern activation subsystem, and hence less overall priming occurs. The nonvisual priming could occur in accessing associative memory, retrieving the name, and/or producing the name. Priming could reflect changes in synaptic strengths in the relevant networks (see Kosslyn and Koenig 1992, chapter 8, for additional discussion of possible mechanisms underlying priming).

Differences in Color and Texture Ostergaard and Davidoff (1985) found that people name colored photographs of objects faster than black-and-white ones. When color is present, the input to the pattern activation subsystems contains more properties that constrain the matching process, and hence the appropriate representation is implicated more quickly (see also Davidoff and Ostergaard 1984; Seymour 1979). In contrast, Ostergaard and Davidoff (1985) found that recognition (as opposed to naming) is not facilitated by color, at least when there are very few alternatives and other cues are distinctive. In this task only three objects were used and subjects were told the names in advance. Presumably in this case the subjects could prime highly distinctive parts and characteristics, and identify the objects easily on the basis of minimal cues.

But the story cannot be quite so simple: Biederman and Ju (1988) report that subjects take the same amount of time to name an object in a color photograph as they do to name an object in a line drawing, even for objects whose color is partially diagnostic of their identity. Why have such seemingly contradictory results been obtained? First, Ostergaard and Davidoff used fruits and vegetables as stimuli; color is diagnostic for such stimuli, and many have similar shapes. In contrast, Biederman and Ju presented a wide variety of objects (such as a fork, a lock, a blow-dryer, a pipe, and a telephone). Color or texture might be important only if the to-be-discriminated objects are rather similar; if they are not similar, shape information alone may be enough to recognize the object with high confidence.

Second, Ostergaard and Davidoff compared color and black-and-white photographs, whereas Biederman and Ju compared color photographs to line drawings. The edges of objects may not be as clearly delineated in photographs as in line drawings, and so the addition of color may have been more important when subjects named the two types of photographs. In addition, Biederman and Ju's line drawings may have emphasized nonaccidental and signal properties, which facilitated processing—thereby obviating the advantage of color in the photographs.

Third, Biederman and Ju presented the pictures very briefly (for 50, 65, or 100 ms), whereas Ostergaard and Davidoff presented their stimuli in free view. Even when color would be useful, it may not be possible to use it effectively when pictures are presented only briefly. Biederman and Hilton (1987, cited in Biederman and Ju 1988) found that people take more time to name objects that are characterized in part by their texture than to name similar objects that are characterized by their shape per se, such as zebra versus horse, broom versus spoon, or file versus knife. This finding suggests that more time is required to encode more object properties.[4] If so, then the fact that color does not facilitate naming when objects are presented only briefly can be explained if shape tends to be encoded more easily (or prior to) other attributes.

These conjectures are consistent with the fact that Biederman and Ju's subjects typically tended to name color photographs faster than line drawings for the two longer exposure durations in their experiments II and III, when the pictures were presented at a relatively low intensity. The high intensity used in experiment I apparently made the color photographs harder to see (judging by the large increase in response times and error rates for the shortest duration, compared to when low intensity was used, and by subject self-reports; see p. 45). In addition, the same trend was present when subjects verified words against pictures for the "positive" trials of their experiments IV and V, when the words in fact matched. This trend was mostly due to cases where the distractors were similar to the targets—which would make additional cues, such as color, particularly useful. Although Biederman and Ju did not explicitly test these trends, the relevant interactions were not significant; however, Biederman and Ju used the conservative quasi-F statistic, which incorporates item variance in the error term, to evaluate significance; given the possible effects of intensity on the quality of the stimuli, it seems likely that there was considerable variability in the ease of seeing different items.

Differences in Orientation. Pictures require more time to name when they are tilted from the standard upright. Indeed, Jolicoeur (1985; for a review, see Jolicoeur 1990a) found a monotonic increase in naming time with the angular deviation of pictures from the standard upright orientation. However, this increase in time with angle was much less than that observed in typical mental rotation experiments in which mental images are manipulated (Cooper and

Identifying Objects: Normal and Damaged Brains

Shepard 1973; Shepard and Cooper 1982). Furthermore, although the effect was obtained the first time the pictures were seen, it was sharply attenuated with practice. This practice effect does not transfer to new objects; that is, even after subjects learn to name a set of objects in unfamiliar orientations, they cannot easily name novel objects in unfamiliar orientations.

Once a shape representation is encoded into the pattern activation subsystems, the viewpoint consistency constraint is used to match input regardless of its orientation. However, such matching requires that the input and stored pattern have the same organization. When objects are tilted, they may be perceptually organized differently from when they are seen vertically or tilted at a different angle. Thus, different representations are encoded for objects seen at different orientations. Before the pictures become familiar (and hence a new representation is stored), a high-confidence match cannot be made in visual memory, and imagery feedback is essential. The mental image is rotated until it matches the input. If a good match is made, the object is recognized. Presumably, more time is required to rotate greater amounts. (I will defer discussing the disparity in rotation times from those in typical imagery experiments until chapter 10.) After a stimulus has been encoded at a particular orientation, image rotation is no longer necessary for that orientation when the stimulus is seen subsequently; moreover, signal properties that are organized the same way at different orientations can be encoded, which decreases the probability that rotation will be needed when the object is seen at a novel orientation. New objects, however, will not benefit from these results of having become familiar with other objects in different orientations.

Differences in Size   As noted earlier, when subjects are asked to name or evaluate pictures on successive trials, the pictures become primed. Biederman and Cooper (1992), Cave and Squire (1992), and Cooper et al. (1992) all found that changing the size of the stimulus between trials has minimal, or nonexistent, effects on the amount of priming. This finding is consonant with the claim that the attention window surrounds an image in the visual buffer, and the configuration of activity is sent further into the system for analysis. As discussed in chapters 5 and 6, the same set of nonaccidental and signal properties is likely to be extracted when the image subtends different visual angles. To the extent that priming is not totally preserved, this presumably reflects differences in the signal properties that can be extracted under the viewing conditions.

In contrast, Biederman and Cooper (1992), Jolicoeur (1987) and Milliken and Jolicoeur (1992) find large effects of size in an old/new recognition paradigm. In this case, subjects are initially shown each object at one size and later see those objects at a same or different size, intermixed with new objects. The subjects are asked to ignore size when judging whether an object was presented previously. Both Jolicoeur (1987) and Biederman and Cooper (1992) find that subjects make these judgments much faster when they see the stimulus at the same size during the study phase and during the later test trials. Moreover, Milliken and Jolicoeur (1992) dissociated retinal size from perceived actual size, and showed that the result depends on perceived actual size.

The priming measure appears to tap residual activation of a modality-specific visual memory (see Biederman and Cooper 1992; Schacter, Chiu, and Ochsner 1993). In contrast, the old/new task presumably requires accessing "episodic" information about the context in which an object was seen; one is not asked whether one has *ever* seen the object, but rather whether it occurred during the study phase of the experiment. Such associations are stored in associative memory, and hence this structure must be accessed to perform the task. A representation of an object in associative memory specifies both its visual address (which corresponds to the pattern code produced by a pattern activation subsystem) and its size (and other properties). A representation of the actual size, not size on the retina, is stored. The representation in associative memory becomes increasingly activated (up to a threshold) as more of the associated information is present in the input. And the more activated it becomes, the more likely it is to inhibit other representations (i.e., to "win" during the winner-take-all process), and produce a response. Hence, in this sort of task, subjects will be faster when the test stimulus shares more properties—including size—with the original stimulus.

Differences in Location Biederman and Cooper (1991c) report that the same amount of name priming occurs when an object appears in the same location it occupied the first time it was presented and when it appears in a different location. This result can be explained in the same way as the fact that priming is preserved over variations in size. In this case, the location of the attention window is shifted (as well as the head and eyes, if possible) so that the same (or almost the same) representation is sent downstream from the different locations.

However, Kosslyn and Horwitz (1993) found that subjects do not always generalize completely across different locations. The subjects in this task saw objects in different locations on the screen, and then saw them intermixed with a set of new objects. The original objects were presented in the same or different locations during test, and the subjects were to indicate whether the objects had been shown originally or were new. In this situation, we found that subjects required more time to identify the previously seen objects when they were in novel locations, particularly if the objects were degraded in some way (e.g., presented very briefly, followed by a mask).

These findings can be explained analogously to my account for Jolicoeur's (1987) and Biederman and Cooper's (1992) findings when size was varied in an old/new recognition task. Again, associative memory must be accessed, and spatial information from the dorsal system will help to activate the appropriate representation (if it is congruent with what is stored). This benefit is likely to be most evident when the stimulus is degraded and so the shape does not match stored representations very well, as probably occurred when the stimuli were presented briefly and followed by a mask.

Differences in Left-Right Orientation   Biederman and Cooper (1991c) and Cooper et al. (1992) also report that the same amount of name priming occurs when an object is presented in the same left-right orientation as when it is presented in a different left-right orientation. Similarly, Klatzky and Stoy (1974) found that people could match mirror images as easily as identical images. These results are exactly as expected if the viewpoint consistency constraint is at the heart of the process whereby input is matched to stored visual memories. If so, then it should not matter how the object is oriented, provided that the parts are perceptually organized in the same way. Unlike differences in tilt, the same perceptual units should be formed when the object faces left or right—and hence matching according to the viewpoint consistency constraint will allow the same stored representation to be accessed in both cases.

Differences in Perspective   Pictured objects are named most quickly when viewed from a "canonical" point of view. The canonical point of view tends to be from a point above and to one side of the front of the object (Palmer, Rosch, and Chase 1981). Similarly, subjects name pictures more quickly when they are less foreshortened; when more extreme perspective effects alter the shape envelope, more time is required to produce the name (Humphrey and Jolicoeur 1988).

As noted in chapter 5, novel noncanonical views require extra processing. In addition, foreshortening has several consequences that will increase the time to identify the object. First, the spatiotopic mapping subsystem becomes more important for recognizing foreshortened objects; the reconstructed three-dimensional orientation may be critical for recognition. If foreshortening is severe, this subsystem may require additional time to compute the spatial properties of the object. Second, the canonical point of view is more likely to have been encoded previously, and hence the input from this perspective will best match the stored representation. Third, the canonical viewpoint typically is the one in which the most parts and characteristics are visible (although Humphrey and Jolicoeur controlled for the presence of key features), and thus more constraints can be encoded. Fourth, more distinguishing properties will be obscured with greater foreshortening, and hence the object will be difficult to recognize. Fifth, if the object is difficult to recognize at first glance, top-down processing will be required.

Palmer, Rosch, and Chase also asked subjects to visualize a pedestal that was oriented a specific way, and to see a pictured object as if it were on the pedestal. This procedure reduced the time the subjects needed to identify objects viewed from unusual perspectives, but not to identify objects seen from a canonical perspective. In this case, the imagery could not have primed the representation of the object itself (the object was not named in advance), but rather presumably helped one to shift attention to the location that would be occupied by the front of the object (I shall discuss similar "reference frame" results in chapter 10).

Similarity of Category Members   Objects are categorized more quickly when they must be distinguished from dissimilar categories than when they must be distinguished from similar categories. Snodgrass and McCullough (1986) told the subjects two categories in advance, either fruit versus animals or fruit versus vegetables. The subjects then saw a series of pictures and classified them into one of the categories. Context can set one's threshold in associative memory; hence, to distinguish a fruit from an animal, color, or texture alone may be sufficient, whereas much more information would be encoded to distinguish a fruit from a vegetable. Snodgrass and McCullough also presented the names of the objects, and report finding no difference for name categorization for the similar and dissimilar comparisons (when fruits were presented, which included the same items in both the similar and dissimilar discrimination contexts). However, part of the similarity effect may reflect the ease of accessing distinguishing information in associative memory. When Job, Rumiati, and Lotto (1992) controlled semantic similarity carefully, in addition to visual similarity, they found similar results when subjects received names instead of pictures. However, the effects of similarity were larger for pictures than for words, and hence visual processes were probably responsible for some of the results with pictures.

In addition, subjects name objects more quickly when their shapes are distinct from those of other objects within their category (Humphreys, Riddoch, and Quinlan 1988). Within the context of the present theory, this finding makes sense because a distinctive shape is likely to match only a single stored representation in the pattern activation subsystems, and hence the winner-take-all mechanism will produce a high-confidence match; in contrast, a shape similar to others will match more than one stored representation reasonably well, and so the initial output from a pattern activation subsystem may not be sufficient for identification.

Assigning a Name

Names are associated with visual properties only in associative memory. Thus, in order to assign a name to a picture, the outputs from the pattern activation subsystems and the dorsal subsystems must match properties of a representation of an object in associative memory.

Differences in Typicality   People name more typical examples of a category as members of the category more often than less typical members, and they also name more typical members with the category name more quickly than less typical members (Smith, Balzano, and Walker 1978; Jolicoeur, Gluck, and Kosslyn 1984; for a review, see Smith and Medin 1981). For example, a canary is named as a bird more often and more quickly than a swan is named as a bird.

These findings may in part be a consequence of the way shapes are stored in the pattern activation subsystems. If a previously seen object is very distinctive, it is likely to be stored as a separate representation in the exemplar pattern activation subsystem: Because it is distinctive, when first seen it did not match any other stored representations very well, and hence a new representation was encoded. In contrast, if an object is typical of a category, it is likely not to be stored as a separate representation; its image already corresponds to at least one stored pattern, and hence a new representation need not be encoded when it is seen.

Hence, typical shapes will tend to match a stored visual representation of the category. Such representations directly index information about the category in associative memory—which is associated with the name—whereas other representations do not. Atypical shapes, in contrast, may match a representation of a particular object (in the exemplar pattern activation subsystem) or a subtype of the class (in the category pattern activation subsystem) better than a representation of the category in question. Atypical shapes, by definition, have distinctive shape properties; for example, unlike typical birds, a penguin has an unusual vertical posture, flippers instead of wings, no visible legs, and so on. If the match is best to a more specific representation (e.g., penguin), then additional processing will be required to look up (in associative memory) or deduce (on the basis of information stored in associative memory) that a penguin is a bird, and thereby produce the name of the category (*bird*).

Differences in Level of Hierarchy   Subjects tend to name objects at the *basic level*. Rosch et al. (1976) characterized the basic level in a number of ways. For present purposes, the most important criterion is shape overlap: The basic level is the most inclusive level at which the members of a category have very similar shapes. For example, an orange would not be named navel orange or fruit, it would be named orange. All navel oranges have very similar shapes, but the shapes of oranges in general overlap only slightly less than shapes of naval oranges; in contrast, shapes of members of the category *fruit* (which includes bananas, grapes, kiwis, etc.) do not overlap very much. Thus, the basic level is orange. When subjects are given a name and then asked whether it is appropriate for a picture, they verify the names fastest when the names are at the basic level (see Rosch et al. 1976; Smith and Medin 1983).

But this result is not entirely general. As discussed in chapter 6, identifying objects at the basic level is a good idea because it often activates the maximum number of properties that almost certainly apply to the stimulus. However, Jolicoeur, Gluck, and Kosslyn (1984) noted that the basic level has this virtue only if the stimulus is typical of the category, and hence introduced the concept of the *entry level*. For example, if one sees a penguin, categorizing it as a bird is not very helpful; penguins lack many bird properties and have other, nonbirdlike properties (adapting them for swimming underwater). The entry level is as inclusive as possible while having as many properties as possible that are very likely to apply to a stimulus. So, if a shape is typical for a category, only those properties that apply to members of the category that share that shape will be activated; if a shape is atypical for a category, it is named at a more specific level, allowing more object-specific properties to be applied to it.

Given these considerations, it is not surprising that if an object is typical for its basic-level category, people tend to label it with that name. And people assign that category name more quickly for such objects than for atypical objects in the category. However, if the object is atypical, it is named fastest not at the basic level, but at a level subordinate to it. For example, a penguin usually is named as a penguin, not a bird, and is named more quickly as a penguin than as a bird (when the subjects are given a list of names in advance and told to use only those labels to name pictures; see Jolicoeur, Gluck, and Kosslyn 1984; see also Murphy and Brownell 1985).

The entry-level representation is accessed "automatically." If an object's shape is sufficiently different from that of the typical members of a category, there is likely to be a distinct representation of the object in the exemplar pattern activation subsystem. Moreover, these outliers often have unusual sizes and orientations, and hence distinctive information is also provided by the dorsal system. Thus, a penguin is recognized, identified, and named as such, and a canary is recognized, identified and named as a bird (for most people; for a bird expert, who makes many subtle distinctions among birds, even a canary may not be regarded as typical, and hence may be named as a canary). Also note that because the pattern activation subsystems store visual memories, they cannot represent abstract concepts such as *fruit*: the shapes do not overlap very much, and so the networks cannot generalize from one to the other; such generalization must be performed at a higher level of processing (in associative memory), which does not depend on shape per se.

But why do people require more time to name objects at a superordinate level or (for typical objects) a subordinate level? The constraint satisfaction process in associative memory produces a single name for an object, which is not at a superordinate level. Thus, a superordinate name must be inferred after the object is identified, which requires additional time. For example, once a stimulus is identified as a bird, an inference would be necessary to affirm that it is also an animal. Indeed, Jolicoeur, Gluck, and Kosslyn (1984) found that people required the same amount of time to make such an inference when they were shown a picture and when they were shown the entry-level name of the picture; the same process occurs once one enters associative memory, regardless of what information initially activated the entry-level representation of the object.

My account for the additional time to name objects at a subordinate level appeals to a different process: If an object is initially categorized at an intermediate level (e.g., *bird* or *apple*), then additional information must be encoded to determine whether it is a more specific type (e.g., a canary or a Delicious apple). For example, to determine that an apple is a Delicious apple, one might look for dimples on its bottom. This top-down hypothesis-testing process requires time.

Jolicoeur, Gluck, and Kosslyn (1984) tested a prediction of this theory. We asked people to decide whether a name was appropriate for a simultaneously presented picture. The name was either above or below the assumed entry-level name in hierarchy. For example, a picture of an apple might be paired with the name *fruit* or *Delicious apple*. We reasoned that if the picture is named at the entry level (i.e., *apple*, in this case), then the superordinate name can be verified merely by searching associative memory. In contrast, the subordinate name can only be verified by collecting more information about the object. For example, if one asks whether the object is a Delicious apple, and one first spontaneously names it apple (as people do), one must go back and look carefully at its aspect ratio and dimpled bottom to verify that it is indeed a Delicious apple, and not a McIntosh or some other kind of apple.

If so, then masking the picture shortly (75 ms) after it is presented should have dramatically different effects in the two cases. If the picture is masked when the name is a superordinate, this should not disrupt processing in associative memory. Once the entry-level representation has been activated over threshold, superordinate category names can be accessed directly (if they are associated with the object) or inferred (by some other subsystem accessing associative memory). However, if a picture is masked when the name is subordinate to the entry level, this should greatly disrupt an additional top-down encoding cycle. If one names a canary as a bird, and has to decide whether it is a canary, one will have difficulty checking whether it is yellow, a certain size, and so on if the picture is masked shortly after being presented. Jolicoeur, Gluck, and Kosslyn (1984) found exactly this pattern of results. Presenting a mask shortly after a picture was shown had very deleterious effects if the to-be-verified name was at the subordinate level, and minimal effects if the name was at the superordinate level.

Accessing the Name

The name of an object is one sort of information associated with it, and this representation must be accessed in order to initiate the processes that actually produce a response (see chapters 6 and 7 of Kosslyn and Koenig 1992). We next consider the factors that affect how easily the representation of the name can be accessed prior to making a response.

Differences in Name Frequency Subjects name pictures more quickly when the name itself has a higher frequency of occurrence in the language (Oldfield and Wingfield 1965). When names are used more frequently, I assume that their representations become more accessible in associative memory—as would occur if the appropriate weights were strengthened in a network (see Monsell 1991). Thus, these representations can be accessed more quickly than less frequently used ones. In addition, the effect of name frequency is larger if the object belongs to a heterogeneous category (e.g., *fruit*, which includes bananas, watermelons, grapes, etc.) than if it belongs to a homogeneous category (e.g., *shoes*); if objects in a category have dissimilar shapes, subjects not only can evaluate them faster in general (as noted above), but are especially fast for high-frequency names (Humphreys, Riddoch, and Quinlan 1988). In this case, the times are facilitated not simply because the distinctive shape results in a fast match in a pattern activation subsystem and the high frequency makes the name more accessible. If this were all there is to it, the effects of similarity and frequency would add, but they do not: The times for distinctive shapes with frequently occurring names are faster than would be expected due to the two factors (visual matching and name retrieval) in isolation. This result makes sense if one not only encounters the name frequently but also sees the object frequently, which strengthens the weights in the pattern activation subsystems, speeding this matching process as well as speeding the process of accessing the name in associative memory.

Differences in Age-of-Acquisition of Name   The effects of frequency are evident when subjects practice using a name repeatedly in the laboratory, and hence cannot be entirely due to another factor. However, the effects of the frequency of the word in the language may be an artifact of another variable, the age at which a word was learned. Morrison, Ellis, and Quinlan (1992) provide compelling evidence that the apparent relation between naming times and word frequency is due to the age at which the name was learned, which is correlated with the frequency of that word in the language (see also Carroll and White 1973; Lachman, Lachman, and Butterfield 1979, 341–343). Indeed, the age of acquisition is a better predictor of naming times than word frequency. For example, a zebra is named relatively quickly, despite its low frequency of occurrence. This finding can be explained in the same way as the effects of word frequency noted above if words learned early are represented by especially strong connections. However, if these words are not used frequently thereafter, their representations might decay or be subject to the effects of interference. Hence, additional factors may be at work. Specifically, words learned early may anchor *semantic fields*, which are organizational units in associative memory. The representations of the meanings of those words would form the core of a structured set of associations (e.g., zoo animals). Components of such structures would resist interference, and may be especially easy to access. To develop such a theory seriously, I would have to consider how semantic information is organized and used, which is too far afield from the present goal.

Familiarity   Subjects name familiar objects more quickly than unfamiliar ones (Jolicoeur 1985; Wingfield 1968). However, this effect is surprisingly small, and tends to be evident only when subjects name a picture for the first time (Jolicoeur 1985). It is possible that the names of unfamiliar objects are more difficult to access initially (because the relevant weights are not as strong in associative memory), but once primed become as easy to access as the names of familiar objects. Alternatively, the effect is highly reminiscent of the effect of orientation on naming time, which I explained by assuming that a new representation is encoded when the novel stimulus is first seen and that this representation is used subsequently. A new representation of a picture of an unfamiliar object would be encoded in the exemplar pattern activation subsystem, which would then be used to recognize the object on subsequent trials. Even though the representation may not be fully consolidated, its recent encoding may make it particularly easy to access.

Conclusions

The theory provides classes of explanations for each of the major empirical findings. These accounts are of interest in part because the theory was not designed with most of these data in mind; rather, the theory was initially intended primarily to account for the qualitative abilities that are obvious in the course of everyday behavior.

UNDERSTANDING DYSFUNCTION FOLLOWING BRAIN DAMAGE

The theory gains added credibility if it can provide accounts not only for the ways people identify objects normally, but also for the types of impairments that arise following brain damage. In a previous book, Kosslyn and Koenig (1992) showed how a theory much like this one could account for the classic visual neurological syndromes. Rather than repeating previous efforts, the goal of the present discussion is to show how the theory can help one to understand complex patterns of disruption. I will discuss a single case study. One virtue of considering case reports is that a case can be studied in detail, and the patterns of deficits can be counterintuitive and subtle; different patterns of behavior are produced depending on the precise locus of the damage and the way in which that person's brain compensated. Group studies, although essential (particularly for establishing correlations between function and lesion location), blur the subtle patterns of dysfunctions.

In chapter 2 I noted that behavioral dysfunctions following brain damage can result from complex changes in the dynamics of information processing. In this book I have considered patient studies only when I had a conception of what a specific part of the brain does. Given such a theory, one is led to expect deficits in tasks that require such processing when a contributing area is damaged. But the reverse logic does not hold; if one finds a deficit in a specific type of processing, this does not mean that the damaged area is responsible for such processing. As briefly discussed in chapter 2, the result could reflect disconnections, remote effects of disconnections, decreases in activation level, and/or various types of strategies. Kosslyn and Van Kleeck (1990) and Kosslyn and Intriligator (1992) consider these issues in greater detail, and the interested reader is referred to those articles for a more thorough treatment of the issues (for an opposing point of view, see also Caramazza 1992 and Shallice 1988). In this section, I illustrate how the present theory can illuminate the bases of a subtle and complex disorder following brain damage.

Disrupted Interactions among Subsystems: A Case Study

The following case study was reported by Kosslyn, Daly, McPeek, Alpert, Kennedy, and Caviness (in press), and focused on the relation between the processing of object properties and spatial properties. Logically, a shape is equivalent to a pattern formed by placing points at specific locations; a close look at any television screen is sufficient to convince anyone of this observation. Hence, at least in some situations, one should be able to use spatial processing to encode shapes. We reasoned that if the ventral, object-properties encoding system were impaired by brain damage, then a patient would be more likely to use the dorsal system to encode shapes. And depending on how shapes were encoded, different properties would affect the ease of evaluating them; our reasoning mirrors that of Gregory (1961), Sergent (1984), and many others.

Patient The patient, R. V., was a right-handed, bilingual male who was 39 years old at the time of testing. He had a B.A. and was working toward a Master's degree; he worked in technical training at a large computer company. R. V. suffered a left frontal infarct, and 6 months later presented with mild anomia and slight deficiencies in speech production. Caplan (personal communication) found that R. V. also had moderate problems in language comprehension. In addition, when tested 3 weeks after the stroke, R. V. named correctly only 40% of the line drawings of common objects in the Boston Naming Test. When tested 10 weeks after the stroke he named 72% of the items; about half of his errors occurred with pictures of animals. CT and MRI scans indicated that R. V. had a lesion in his left frontal lobe, with cortical damage near the region of the third convolution and extensive subcortical damage extending down to the head of the caudate. For present purposes, the most important aspect of the MRI scans was that fibers connecting the frontal lobe to posterior regions were probably disrupted (for more details, see Kosslyn, Daly, McPeek, Alpert, Kennedy, and Caviness, in press).

We used PET scanning to test an implication of the inference that R. V.'s lesion disconnected some of the input to the posterior regions of the brain; we expected the disconnection not to sever the flow of important information but rather to disrupt the usual "tonic" stimulation of the area, causing it to become sluggish. The scan was performed as the patient rested with his eyes open, performing no particular task. As expected, the results revealed hypoperfusion and hypometabolism that affected numerous remote parts of the brain, including areas that are known to be involved in vision in the occipital-temporal region. Thus, we had reason to suspect that R. V. would have impaired vision, even though the lesion did not directly damage the occipital or temporal lobes.

We also tested a group of eight control subjects; the control subjects were normal right-handed men who were about R. V.'s age and had comparable amounts of education.

Behavioral Testing   We developed a series of computer-administered tests to assess specific aspects of visual-spatial processing. The results of earlier testing showed that R. V. had difficulty naming pictures of common objects, but did not indicate whether this deficit reflected problems in visual processing or problems in accessing and/or producing names. To minimize such ambiguities, the tests we designed were as devoid of semantic content as possible.

We designed tests specifically to help us distinguish among seven possible consequences of the damage, not all of which are exclusive. These hypotheses were cast within the general framework of the theory developed in previous chapters. First, we had to consider the null hypothesis: Perhaps R. V. had normal vision, and his hypometabolism did not correspond to a "functional lesion." Second, such a functional lesion could exist, but perhaps all it did was to slow R. V.'s visual processing in general. If so, then we expected him to have difficulty on all of our tests. Third, the preprocessing subsystem may have been disrupted. We have tentatively identified such processing with lateral occipital-temporal cortex. This cortex was part of the hypometabolic area in R. V.'s brain. Hence, we considered the possibility that R. V. would not be able to encode edges and lines efficiently.

Fourth, given the left-hemisphere locus of the lesion, we hypothesized that R. V. might have specific difficulty encoding small regions of space. As reviewed in chapters 6 and 7, the left cerebral hemisphere apparently has a bias for encoding relatively local regions, whereas the right has a bias for encoding larger, more "global" regions (e.g., see Delis, Robertson, and Efron 1986; Robertson and Delis 1986; Robertson, Lamb, and Knight 1988; Van Kleeck 1989). Fifth, we considered the possibility that R. V. would have difficulty retaining information in the pattern activation subsystems; the region of hypometabolism extended into the portions of the temporal lobe that may be involved in representing visual memories (see chapter 6).[5]

Sixth, the damage might have limited R. V.'s ability to adjust his attention window to encompass large regions, which may have forced him to encode complex stimuli a part at a time. Recall that Moran and Desimone (1985) found neurons in areas V4 and IT that responded to restricted regions of their receptive fields after the animal had been trained to attend to those regions. If the damage disrupted processes that control the attention window, R. V. might not be able to attend to large regions effectively. Finally, we hypothesized that the hypometabolism might have slowed down processing in R. V.'s ventral system generally, which would give the dorsal system more time to complete processing. If so, then we expected R. V. to make decisions based on spatial properties in situations where normal subjects would use object properties.

Our tests were designed to distinguish among these seven alternatives. The first test was intended to establish that R. V. had a visual deficit in a nonsemantic visual matching task. On each trial, we showed the subjects a shape, removed it, and then asked them to decide whether another shape was the same or different. The shapes were black angular patterns, which were created

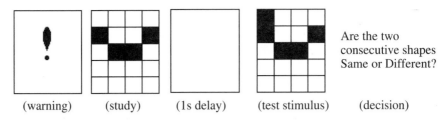

| (warning) | (study) | (1s delay) | (test stimulus) | (decision) |

Figure 8.4   Example of a trial sequence used in the tests of patient R. V. (Reprinted from Kosslyn, Daly, McPeek, Alpert, Kennedy, and Caviness, in press, with permission.)

by filling in specific cells in 4 × 5 grids; we created three kinds of patterns, which had one, two, or three perceptual units (bars or symmetrical forms). The trial sequence (with a three-segment stimulus) is illustrated in figure 8.4. As expected, R. V. required dramatically more time with the more complex shapes, whereas the control subjects did not.

Although this result demonstrated that R. V. did in fact have a visual deficit, it did not allow us to discriminate among the remaining six hypotheses. In our next test, we showed the subjects the same stimuli as in the previous test, but removed the internal grid lines and all of the perimeter of the grid except for brackets defining the four corners. We reasoned that if R. V. had a general visual impairment, he should still be impaired on this version of the test. In contrast, if he had difficulty encoding small regions or was overloaded by the additional grid lines, then his problem should be reduced or eliminated when the grid cells were removed. Similarly, without the grid lines he should have trouble encoding the shape as a set of discrete locations; if the previous results reflect such a strategy, then the effects of complexity should be eliminated when he could not encode discrete locations.

We now found not a hint of an effect of complexity on R. V.'s response times. It was clear that R. V. did not have a general visual deficit, nor did he have a general problem storing information in the pattern activation subsystems or comparing new input to stored patterns; similarly, he did not have a problem attending to large regions per se. However, the other hypotheses still were viable: Perhaps he was slower with the original stimuli because he had trouble encoding visual features, and the grid lines overloaded an impaired preprocessing subsystem. Or, R. V. may have had difficulty encoding sets of small regions. Alternatively, when the grid lines were present, his responses may have been based on encoding the sets of locations defined by the cells (in the dorsal system), and more time was required to encode more filled cells. Nevertheless, this process may have been completed before he encoded the shape (in the ventral system), and so his responses were based on the spatial encodings.

In contrast, in this test the control subjects required increasingly more time for the more complex stimuli. The control subjects may have worried that stimuli in brackets could differ by subtle shifts in the locations of segments within the brackets—and hence scanned the stimuli relatively carefully, which required more time when more units were present.

Identifying Objects: Normal and Damaged Brains

We next considered the possibility that the grid lines in our original test strained R. V.'s pattern activation subsystems. If this hypothesis was correct, then we did not expect any effects of grid lines when memory was not required. In contrast, we expected R. V. to have difficulty encoding patterns in grids even when memory was not required if (a) his preprocessing subsystem was overloaded by the additional visual features; (b) he had difficulty encoding sets of small regions; or (c) he based his response on encodings of the locations of the filled cells, and more time was required to encode more such locations.

On each of the trials in this test, the subjects saw one of the stimuli used in the first test, along with an X mark. They were asked simply to indicated whether the X fell on or off the shape. If R. V.'s deficit arose because he had difficulty remembering the first stimulus of a pair, then he should not have had more difficulty evaluating more complex patterns in this test. Alternatively, if his problem was a consequence of any of the three other possibilities noted above, then we again expected to find increased processing times for more complex patterns in grids.

R. V. did in fact require increasingly more time for more complex stimuli, whereas the control subjects required the same time for each type of stimulus. Given that there was no memory requirement in this task, R. V.'s problem could not be due solely to impaired memory. These results are reminiscent of similar findings reported by Luria (1959, 1980), who found that patients with lesions in the occipital-temporal area could not name pictures of objects that had random line fragments placed over them.

At this juncture, the results were consistent with three of the hypotheses we formulated at the outset: R. V. could have had an impaired preprocessing subsystem, and hence had difficulty encoding visual features; he could have had trouble encoding small regions of space; or he could have been using the locations of filled cells in the grid to encode the shapes into memory, and required more time to encode more locations. To check that we were on the right track, we considered the results of another test. We asked the subjects to perform the previous task, deciding whether an X was on or off a figure, but eliminated the grid lines. All three hypotheses predict that the deficit that was observed with the grid lines should now be eliminated, and this is exactly what happened. However, we now found that R. V. required the most time for the intermediate-level stimuli, which had two perceptual units.

This was a fortuitous result because it suggested that R. V. did not have trouble encoding visual features per se. If this were the root of his problem, he should have required more time for increasingly complex stimuli, or no increase in times if the stimuli were simple enough not to tax his preprocessing or pattern activation subsystems. The observed results were consistent with the hypothesis that when the grid lines were present, R. V. encoded sets of small regions, scanning from the top of the grid to the bottom. A close inspection of the stimuli revealed that most of the two-unit stimuli were presented toward the bottom of the grids; in contrast, the other stimuli were more centrally placed. Removing the grid lines may have led R. V. to scan the stimuli carefully from top to bottom. If so, then he would have had to scan farther on average when examining the two-unit stimuli because these stimuli tended to be lower in the stimulus frame.

We next considered in more detail the possibility that R. V.'s preprocessing subsystem was impaired. We noted that prior to the stroke, R. V. was an avid and fluent reader (which requires effective preprocessing); after the stroke, his reading had become very slow and awkward. This test was identical to the previous one, except that now we placed random line fragments over the stimuli. These fragments did not meet to form distinct cells, and hence did not provide the option to encode a pattern as a set of locations in a grid. These fragments should have made the test relatively difficult if the lines overloaded the preprocessing subsystem. But the noise fragments had no effect on R. V.'s or the control subjects' times or errors. These results allowed us to eliminate the simplest remaining hypothesis, that R. V. had an impaired preprocessing subsystem.

The following test was designed to investigate the hypothesis that R. V. had difficulty adjusting the attention window. We showed the subjects four gray blocks that were positioned at equal distances along the circumference of an invisible circle. On a given trial, the circle was either large or small. On half the trials of each type, an X mark appeared in two blocks on opposite sides of the circle, whereas on the other half of the trials only one X mark appeared. We asked the subjects to respond "yes" if both X marks were present, and "no" if only one was present. If the attention window was restricted to one level of size scale, then we expected R. V. to have impaired performance for one of the sizes of the circumference. We found no effects of the scope of the display on his performance.

Our remaining hypothesis was that R. V. encoded shapes in grids as sets of locations. It was possible that the result had nothing to do with storage, but rather with how he compared two successive stimuli. Thus, we eliminated the comparison phase of the task, but retained the memory component. In this test the subjects did not have to encode shapes at the time of test. Rather, they studied a shape in a grid, it was removed, and then an X mark appeared in the otherwise empty grid. The subjects were asked to decide whether the X mark would have fallen on the shape, if it were still in the grid. If R. V. stored the shapes as sets of filled locations, then we expected to find increased time with more complex patterns in this task. Indeed, because the task requires remembering which cells were filled, we expected the same results with the control subjects; this test encouraged them to "simulate" what we conjectured was R. V.'s usual performance, leading them to attend to specific cells in the grid.

As expected, both R. V. and the control subjects required more time for the more complex shapes. Unlike all of the previous tests in which patterns appeared in grids, the control subjects now required increasing amounts of time to evaluate increasingly complex patterns. R. V.'s strategy apparently was not outside the range of normal behavior; but he apparently used the spatial location strategy more generally than normal subjects.

In summary, our experiments allowed us to evaluate the seven hypotheses as follows:

First, the results ruled out the null hypothesis: R. V. clearly had a visual deficit (although it was rather subtle). Second, we showed that R. V. did not have impaired visual processing in general. He had normal response patterns when we removed the grid lines. Third, R. V. did not have an impaired preprocessing subsystem; his responses did not show an unusual pattern when random lines were placed over stimuli. Fourth, R. V. did not have specific difficulty when small regions of space had to be encoded.

Fifth, R. V. did not have a problem limited to visual memory per se; the deficit was present even when memory was not required. In addition, R. V. did not have difficulty (relative to the control subjects) comparing sequentially presented patterns when the grid lines were removed; the observed deficit was present only when grid lines were used. Thus, his pattern activation subsystems apparently were able to store and match patterns. Sixth, R. V. could attend to large regions of space. Seventh, although there may have been no specific impairment in the ventral system, our best account of R. V.'s performance was that this system was generally slowed down and so the dorsal system had more time to complete processing.[6] Hence, when grid lines allowed patterns of locations to be encoded easily, R. V.'s responses apparently were based on encodings of the locations of filled cells. This process required more time when more locations had to be encoded.

In sum, we had evidence that R. V. encoded shapes as sets of locations when the stimuli facilitated such encoding—but normal control subjects did not typically encode the stimuli in this way. These findings are easily interpreted as reflecting an "automatic compensation," like the changes in musculature and motions of the intact legs of the three-legged dog discussed in chapter 2. Our PET study of object identification, described earlier in this chapter, revealed that ventral and dorsal encodings occur in tandem in the normal brain; R. V. did not have to choose which sort of information to encode. Rather, apparently his response was based on whichever process finished first. The results are not easily interpreted as reflecting damage to isolated subsystems or disconnections among them. For example, if the preprocessing subsystem were damaged, we would have expected the same results with grids and when line fragments were randomly placed over shapes. Rather, the results are best understood in terms of a system of interacting components in which the normal patterns of interactions had been disrupted by damage.

The present approach is a departure from the usual neuropsychological study of brain-damaged patients, which aims to document dissociations and associations following brain damage (e.g., Caramazza 1984, 1986). My colleagues and I recognize that lesions are often relatively large, and sometimes have remote effects by de-enervating other parts of the brain. In our case study we found evidence of a system of functional impairments, which appears to reflect indirect effects of dysfunction in the occipital-temporal junction area. I acknowledge that this approach is more complex than the usual fare in neuropsychology, but this seems appropriate: The brain is a very complex organ.

CONCLUSIONS

The purpose of this chapter was to discover whether the theory of object perception developed earlier is worth being taken seriously as the foundation for a theory of visual mental imagery. The theory led us to predict the pattern of brain activity that occurs when people evaluate canonical and noncanonical pictures. Furthermore, it not only provides accounts (coarse ones, but accounts nonetheless) of key qualitative phenomena, but also provides insight into the relative amounts of time required to name pictured objects. In addition, the theory provides a useful framework for investigating the effects of brain damage on visual function; the theory allows us to think about a system of interacting components that can produce unusual behavior as a result of compensations, not simply on the basis of missing or disconnected components.

Probably the most important results discussed here, however, were the PET findings. This experiment provides us with a lever for studying imagery: If imagery really does utilize the same subsystems used in high-level perception, then the same brain areas should subserve the two activities. In the following chapter I describe a direct test of this prediction.

9 Generating and Maintaining Visual Images

I have argued in previous chapters that imagery plays a vital role in perception proper and have assumed that the mechanisms of high-level visual perception are also used in visual mental imagery. If this assumption is correct, then we should now be in a position to address the second facet of the imagery debate, namely the issue of what "looks at," produces, and "manipulates" imaged objects. It is now time to cash in the theory of perceptual processing and discover whether it adds genuine insight into the nature and functions of imagery.

Consider the following task: You are going to go camping with a friend's family, and are worrying about whether you can fit all of the gear into the trunk. So, you first visualize each item (the tent, the sleeping bags, the cooler, and so on), which would help you to remember each of the items that must be packed. You next visualize one of the items, say the tent, inside the trunk, and mentally manipulate it to "see" what position would leave the most room free in the trunk. Following this, you maintain this image—of the tent shoved into the left rear part of the trunk, say—and then add the sleeping bags, mentally moving them around until you "see" where they could be positioned to leave the most room free. You maintain this entire image, scanning over it, "looking" for openings for the cooler, and so on, and add the additional items to your image. When you finally find a way to pack all of the stuff into the trunk, you memorize that configuration. Thus, the next morning, you pile all of the stuff on the curb, and immediately pack it efficiently into the trunk, impressing all onlookers.

This task involves four classes of imagery abilities. It requires *image generation* (forming images of each item and the trunk), *image inspection* (observing the way the items fit in the trunk), *image maintenance* (retaining images of previously considered items), and *image transformation* (mentally moving the items around). It also illustrates one example of the role of imagery in reasoning (anticipating actual physical manipulations) and the role of imagery in learning (memorizing the end result, and possibly inducing some general principles, such as that oddly shaped items ought to go in corners). I assume that an imaged object can be encoded into the pattern activation subsystems in the same way that perceived stimuli can be stored; Kosslyn and Koenig (1992, chapters 4, 7, and 8) discuss how such a process may occur.

I will build on the inferences drawn in previous chapters to provide accounts of our image generation and image maintenance abilities in this chapter, and will consider image inspection and image transformations in the following chapter. I will not repeat what I have said in previous chapters except as needed. In chapter 11 I will summarize the role of each of the perceptual subsystems in imagery, and then will show how the present theory incorporates the central principles of the previous version (Kosslyn 1980). This is important because the previous version had considerable explanatory power, and I want to show that the principles that conferred this power are inherited by the present theory.

IMAGE GENERATION

Perhaps the most obvious fact about visual mental imagery is that we do not always have an image of any given object. Images come and go, and the particular image we have depends on the situation. The patterns of activity in the visual buffer that correspond to images are best viewed as short-term memory representations. Such representations are transient, and hence must be created on the basis of information stored in a more permanent form (or must be retained from on-line perceptual input).

It will be useful to begin by distinguishing among three general ways in which visual mental images are generated. First, one can recall a previously seen object or event. In this case, stored information may simply be activated. However, even this activation process is apt to be complex: one may see separate parts of an object individually (e.g., if the object moves from behind another object or if one is so close to it that multiple eye fixations are necessary), and so a set of distinct representations may be stored. If this occurs, then the generation process must integrate these representations. Second, one of the reasons that imagery is useful is that we can combine objects in novel ways. For example, one can imagine Charlie Chaplin riding a zebra, and "see" whether he would have been able to peer over the top of the zebra's head. A theory of imagery must explain how familiar components can be arranged in novel ways in images. Third, we also can visualize novel patterns that are not based on rearranging familiar components; we can "mentally draw" patterns that we have never actually seen. For example, people can imagine a bug leaving a path in its wake as it crawls one inch up a wall, and then turns left and crawls two inches, and then turns right and crawls two inches, and so on (see Bower 1972).

Image generation is not a simple process, which is probably one reason why the literature on this topic has grown dramatically in the past few years. Indeed, research on image generation has become controversial, in part because different researchers have reported conflicting results and in part because the theories have sometimes been overly restrictive (for a recent review, see Tippett 1992). In this section I show how the subsystems posited in earlier chapters lead to accounts for all three types of image generation.

Generating Single-Part Images

The problem of how we generate visual mental images of remembered objects or scenes can be usefully divided into two parts. First, we can ask how images of individual perceptual units are formed; and second, we can ask how images of two or more such units can be amalgamated to form a single object or scene. In this section we will consider the simplest part of the problem, how one visualizes individual perceptual units.

According to the present theory, image generation is an extension of the kind of attentional priming discussed in chapter 7. The representation of an object in associative memory is accessed (by a property lookup subsystem, which is engaged by other components of the system; see Kosslyn and Koenig 1992), and the "pattern code" associated with the object is activated, which in turn primes the modality-specific representation in the appropriate pattern activation subsystem. To form an image itself, the representation is primed so much that it sends feedback to earlier areas (see chapter 5). (It is possible that the pattern code does not operate bidirectionally, and another representation that is associated with it plays this role. For simplicity, however, I will refer to the representation that indexes stored visual memories as a pattern code.) This feedback engenders a configuration of activity in the visual buffer, which is the image proper. In essence, images are formed by the same processes that allow one to anticipate what one would see if a particular object or scene were present.

Rosch et al. (1976) provide evidence that imagery can prime one to encode specific shapes. They found that if one prepared for a picture of an object after hearing its basic-level name, one could determine whether two pictures of typical versions of the object were the same faster than if one did not prepare in advance or prepared when given the name of the superordinate category. Although Rosch et al. did not explicitly ask subjects to prepare by forming an image, it seems very likely that their instructions were interpreted in this way (see their p. 409). Rosch (1975) found analogous results with colors. The mechanisms that underlie such priming also would produce interactions between having perceived a color and then visualizing colored objects. Intons-Peterson and Roskos-Ewoldsen (1989) found that subjects could form images of colored objects more easily when the objects were visualized against the same color background. This result presumably reflects priming: The mechanisms that represent a specific color in an image were already activated, and hence their states would not have to be changed when one imposed a representation of a color on the visual buffer via imagery.

Kosslyn, Anderson, and Chiu (in preparation) obtained perhaps more direct evidence that the mechanisms that underlie visual priming are also used in visual imagery. We asked subjects to count the number of vowels in a list of words printed in lowercase type; this is a standard orienting task, which has been shown to produce priming when subjects later are asked to complete fragments to form words (e.g., see Schacter 1987). But instead of asking the subjects to produce words, we now asked them to produce images. Specifically, they heard the words and decided whether the first and last letters would be the same height if the words were printed in lowercase letters. For example, *near* has the letters the same height, as does *height*, but *far* does not. Half the words were on the original (exposure) list and half were not. The subjects later could visualize the words they saw on the exposure list faster than novel words.

In a second experiment, we repeated this task but now presented half the words on the exposure list in uppercase type and half in lowercase type. The subjects always generated images of words in lowercase type. If the results of the first experiment reflect processing in the pattern activation subsystem, then we expected priming only to affect images that look like the original stimulus. But our first analysis revealed no priming at all, even to same-case words. A more careful examination of the data revealed that some of the subjects did not pay attention to the words on the exposure list well enough and hence did not exhibit later priming. A regression analysis revealed that subjects who exhibited more priming in general also showed a larger amount of priming for same-case words than for different-case words. Indeed, when we removed the subjects who showed no priming at all and reanalyzed the data in an analysis of variance, we now found the expected interaction—with more priming when the imaged words were the same case as the studied ones.

We then asked another group of subjects to participate in the task and procedure of our second experiment, except that we asked these subjects to count the vowels of the words on the exposure list twice; we expected this greater exposure to produce more priming overall. In this experiment we did not find any response time differences in the imagery task, but did find large differences in error rates: As expected, subjects could visualize words in the same case as those in the exposure list better than words in the opposite case. Response time and accuracy trade off against each other; if we had emphasized accuracy more strongly in the instructions, the difference probably would have been evident in times rather than error rates.

Finally, we conducted a different kind of experiment to examine the flip side of the coin: whether imagery could prime perception. We asked subjects to study a set of pictures prior to the experiment proper. On each trial, they were asked to visualize one of these objects and to press a space bar when the image was complete. We then showed either the same object or a different object; in both cases, half the time the object was intact and half the times its parts were scrambled (e.g., the Statue of Liberty held its head in its hand, had an arm coming out its neck, etc.). The subjects were asked to determine whether the picture was "normal" or "abnormal." A second group of subjects did not form images prior to evaluating the pictures; rather, these subjects were asked to generate a sentence (and speak it aloud) that would place the object in a category, such as "The Statue of Liberty is a monument." This procedure was intended to activate associative memory without causing them to visualize the object, thereby controlling for the effects of thinking about the object or engaging in effortful processing. Subjects pressed the space bar when the sentence was generated.

As predicted, the subjects could evaluate the pictures faster when they generated an image of that object rather than some other object; the subjects were faster when their images matched the picture. Moreover, imagery priming resulted in faster performance than nonimagery priming, although the nonimagery primes were also more effective for the same object than a different object. However, the imagery task more effectively primed the picture of that object, relative to a picture of another object, than did the nonimagery task.

These results, then, provide strong evidence that imagery does indeed rely on mechanisms that produce priming in perception. Furthermore, the results provided evidence that the effect depends on the specific form of the imaged pattern, not solely on its identity. These results were as expected if images arise by activating representations in the pattern activation subsystems. Indeed, consistent with this view, Penfield and Rasmussen (1950) provided evidence that the ventral system does in fact play a key role in some types of image generation. They electrically stimulated discrete regions of the brain (as a prelude to surgery) and observed the patient's response. The most important result for present purposes concerns the temporal lobe: They found that patients sometimes reported vivid visual images when this structure was stimulated. This result is consistent with the claim that at least some forms of imagery arise when representations are activated in the pattern activation subsystems.

If images of individual remembered shapes (which may or may not include color, texture, or motion) are formed by activating representations in one of the pattern activation subsystems, then it is easy to explain why one can visualize a specific cup one has seen (activating a representation in the exemplar pattern activation subsystem) or can visualize a generic cup (activating a representation in the category pattern activation subsystem). However, in part because the efferent projections are not as precisely targeted as the afferent ones (see chapter 5), even images of specific exemplars may not be as vivid or sharp as input images of actual objects (indeed, this may be one of the cues that allow one to tell whether one has actually seen something or just imaged it).

Image generation must also involve associative memory; how else could a representation of a named object in a pattern activation subsystem come to be activated? In fact, we found some priming for different-case images, relative to novel words, although this priming was not as great as when subjects visualized words in the same case as the words on the exposure list. Such priming presumably arose when propositional representations were activated in associative memory. In addition, I have argued that the entry-level representation of an object is accessed most often in associative memory during perception, and hence it is not a surprise that subjects visualize basic-level objects faster than superordinate or subordinate objects (Hoffman, Denis, and Ziessler

Generating and Maintaining Visual Images

1983; see also Conway et al. 1991).[1] I assume that one usually images a prototypical shape of an object (see Cornoldi, De Beni, and Pra Baldi 1989) because the entry-level term corresponds to such a representation in the category pattern activation subsystem. Such images should be particularly easy to form because, in general, generic representations in the pattern activation subsystem are "stronger" (because they have been activated more often) than the representation of any specific object.

However, if this hypothesis is correct, then people should not visualize a prototype of the entry-level object in the following two circumstances: First, if one has had almost exclusive contact with a single exemplar of a category (e.g., one's own dog), this exemplar representation may be the strongest one that corresponds to the concept in associative memory, and hence will be used when one forms an image of that category. Second, if one is an expert in a domain, one may have encoded many more exemplars and made finer distinctions among them than is typical; indeed, the preprocessing subsystem may have become tuned so that a relatively wide range of information is encoded in this domain (recall our discussion in chapter 5 about chicken sexing). If so, then the representations of subordinate categories would be less similar than for a nonexpert, and generalization in the category pattern activation subsystem may occur at a lower level of hierarchy. For example, an expert on apples may have a separate category representation for Delicious, McIntosh, and Granny Smith apples, each of which would correspond to the representation of a prototype in the category pattern activation subsystem (specific examples of each could also be stored in the exemplar pattern activation subsystem). In this case, the strongest corresponding representation in associative memory will dictate which prototype is visualized.

The claim that one accesses the same representation in associative memory when one names an object and when one initiates the process of forming visual mental images leads to a simple prediction: If a representation in associative memory is "strong" (e.g., it is implemented by many redundant connections and/or strong weights on the connections), then subjects should identify the corresponding picture quickly and visualize it quickly. And in fact, Paivio et al. (1989) report just such a correlation. They asked subjects to form images of named objects and to press a button when the image was completed, and they measured these times. They also asked these subjects to name the corresponding pictures covertly, and to press a button when they had done so. These times were correlated, $r = .56$. The imagery times also were correlated, $r = .58$, with actual naming times (when the names were spoken and response times were recorded using a voice key) when other subjects named the objects. Presumably the factors that lead a given representation to be "strong" in one person tend to do so in others.

I find these correlations surprisingly high, given the number of other processes that must take place in each task. In the previous chapter I described many factors that affect naming, but not all of these variables affect image generation (such as those pertaining to encoding the object and producing the name); and I shortly will consider many factors that affect image generation (such as the method of adding parts) that do not affect naming. Paivio et al. report a factor analysis of the results and note that the naming and imagery tasks both load highly on a "referential processing" factor, which seems to refer to processes in associative memory (my term) that are common to the two activities.[2]

Other results indicate that processes in associative memory play a critical role in image generation, even when one images only a single perceptual unit. For example, Hubbard, Kall, and Baird (1989) report evidence that spatial information in associative memory is also used when people generate images. They asked subjects to visualize familiar objects and "nondescript rods" that were of different sizes, and to report how far away the imaged objects seemed. They found, as did Kosslyn (1978), that larger objects seemed farther away in the image. The larger objects were not proportionally farther away, however; rather, a power function (with an exponent less than 1) was a better fit to the data than a linear function (I earlier had found such linear functions when subjects were asked to imagine moving toward an imaged object until it seemed to "overflow"; I took these results to reflect spatial constraints imposed by the extent of the visual buffer itself). Hubbard, Kall, and Baird also asked subjects simply to recall how far away they typically saw familiar objects, and found very similar results. Hence, apparently the stored representation of typical viewing distance was used to adjust the mapping function from the pattern activation subsystem to the visual buffer. This inference dovetails nicely with the discussion in the previous chapter about the role of size in object recognition.

An alternative account of these results, however, stresses common constraints in imagery and perception. Specifically, if an object is seen at too great a distance, its details will be obscured. During perception one may be able to see the details of a relatively large object significantly more clearly when it is slightly closer than would be expected by a strict linear size/distance function. A similar process may occur when one later images the objects. Such a principle would influence how one visualizes even very simple objects, such as rods; if they are too "far away" in the image, their edges and surfaces will not be sharp—and hence they may be imaged slightly closer than would be expected if size and distance were linearly related.

In any event, these findings do not conflict with my earlier claim that one constraint on the visual angle subtended by an imaged object is the spatial extent of the visual buffer. This claim does not imply that other factors are not also at work when one generates images.

Generating Multipart Images

We must also understand how individually stored perceptual units can be integrated to form an image of a single object (or scene—but I shall focus on objects here). As was discussed in chapter 6, during perception one typically encodes the overall shape first. This representation is encoded by surrounding the input image in the visual buffer with the attention window. Hence, the representation suffers from a scope-resolution trade-off: individual portions of it will not be not very clear. As was discussed in chapter 4, at any one time the attention window subsumes material that extends over a specific visual angle, and the larger the angle, the lower the resolution of the encoded pattern. After encoding the overall shape, one then might inspect individual parts and characteristics of the object, which would be encoded one at a time, as well as the spatial relations among them. If so, then one subsequently must amalgamate several distinct representations to form a complete image of the object. In this case, one not only needs to activate stored visual memories, but also must activate stored representations of spatial relations and use those representations to arrange the component parts and characteristics appropriately.

In chapter 6 I inferred that as output from the ventral and dorsal systems reaches associative memory, a description of the stimulus is built up. To generate an image of a complex object or scene, this representation is accessed first; it specifies how the parts are arranged. The pattern codes associated with parts (or distinctive characteristics, such as a surface deformation, that are likely to be encoded as distinct perceptual units) are used to activate visual memory representations in a pattern activation subsystem, as described above. And the spatial relations are used to arrange the parts in the proper relative positions. This operation can be accomplished using exactly the same mechanisms that are used in top-down hypothesis testing during perception.

Specifically, multipart images could be formed in the following way. Computationally, it makes sense to form a *global* image of the pattern first (the "skeletal image" of Kosslyn 1980),[3] which can then be elaborated if need be. Because the global image suffers from a scope-resolution trade-off, additional representations must be activated and images formed at specific places if one needs high-resolution parts. For example, if asked to image a bear, and then asked whether it has curved front claws, most people report that the initial image did not contain that information. Instead, they started with a rather vague image of the overall shape, and added the part as necessary. And in fact, the strength of association between an object and a part predicts how much time people require to "see" a small part of an image object, just as it does when parts must be accessed in associative memory; in contrast, the size of the part is the best predictor when an image of the part can be "seen" on the initial image (see chapter 6 of Kosslyn 1980). I assume that "global precedence" is useful in both image generation and perceptual encoding, for the same reason: In both situations, having the "lay of the land" helps one to organize the details.

In imagery, once a global image is formed, the representations of parts and properties in associative memory are accessed (via the property lookup subsystems), exactly as they are during perceptual hypothesis testing; the strongest representation of a property/spatial relation pair "wins" and is used in subsequent processing. As before, the representation of a spatial relation can be used as input to the attention-shifting subsystems (either directly or via the categorical–coordinate conversion subsystem), which move the attention window to the part of the global image that needs to be elaborated.

The process of elaborating the global image requires first accessing the location of what I have called the *foundation part* (Kosslyn 1980), which is the portion of the shape that is indexed by the spatial relation associated with a to-be-imaged part or property. For example, if one wanted to image the head of a bear, its representation in associative memory would be looked up, which might specify its location as "attached at the top front of the global shape." This spatial relation representation in turn is used to direct the attention window to that location relative to the global image, exactly as occurs when one is seeking a part during perceptual top-down hypothesis testing.

However, in some cases the location of a part or property might not be indexed relative to the global image. For example, the "front claws" might be stored as "attached to the front of the front paws." Thus, one must locate the front paws before one can know where the claws belong. To locate the front paws, this representation must be looked up in associative memory, and its location (e.g., "bottom part of the front feet") accessed, which may require accessing yet other parts (to discover that the foot is at the bottom of the leg) until a direct reference to a portion of the global image is found. Each connected spatial relation must be kept activated (i.e., stored temporarily) until the reference to the global image is reached, at which point the list of spatial relations can used to direct the attention window to each part in turn; if a part or property is not indexed relative to the global image, such processing will also occur during hypothesis testing in perception. Phenomenologically, such a process would seem as if one were scanning over the object and, perhaps, zooming in at the requisite location. Clearly, it is better to relate parts and properties to the global image than to other parts or characteristics in the description of the shape in associative memory; if one builds detailed hierarchies of structural contingencies of the sort Marr (1982) suggests, it would be rather easy to exceed working memory capacity (i.e., limitations on how much information can be kept activated at the same time) when generating an image.

Once properly positioned, the attention window encodes a new pattern into the dorsal and ventral systems that matches the expected part or property (i.e., one recognizes and identifies the foundation part). At this point the attention window is adjusted as it would be when encoding the to-be-imaged part or property, and the appropriate representation in the pattern activation subsystems is activated to project feedback into the visual buffer, as would occur if it was augmenting the part or property at the size and location of the attention window. Like Lowe, I assume that the mapping function from the visual memories to the visual buffer can be adjusted so that the image appears at different sizes and locations (for a possible mechanism, see Stucki and Pollack 1992).

The mechanism just described makes a clear prediction: The more high-resolution parts that are included in an image, the more time should be required to generate the image. Kosslyn 1980 (chapter 6) summarizes much evidence that more complex shapes do in fact require more time to visualize and that the time to generate an image increases with increasing numbers of parts. Indeed, all of the data that could be accounted for by the previous version of the theory can be accounted for by the present one because the previous distinctions are preserved. Specifically, the previous version posited a PUT process that arranged parts into an image, which involved subprocesses that accessed stored *literal files* (which correspond to the representations in the pattern activation subsystems) and *propositional files* (which corresponded to representations in associative memory). The individual subprocesses included one called FIND, which was a top-down search mechanism; I now have supplemented such a mechanism (the property lookup and attention-shifting subsystems) with bottom-up perceptual encoding subsystems (dorsal and ventral processing). The PUT process also recruited a subprocess called PICTURE, which is now the function of activating a stored visual representation (in a pattern activation subsystem) to form an image. The FIND process was used to locate the foundation part, which was the location on the global image (or other part) where a new part should be placed; this information was used by PUT to guide the PICTURE process when forming an image of each successive part. The previous version of the theory posited an iterative process, with PUT evoking PICTURE and FIND for each individual part. The new version of the theory captures the key elements of the earlier one; the property lookup subsystems provide the necessary information for the attention-shifting subsystems to move the attention window to the foundation part and, once it is found (via dorsal and ventral processing), a new image is formed. As before, this process is iterative; it is repeated for each additional part or characteristic that is added to the image. In chapter 11 I will review the correspondences between the new version of the theory and the previous one in more detail.

Both the new and previous versions of the theory make a stronger prediction: Not only should more complex patterns require more time to visualize, because more parts should be added, but also parts should be added one at a time in a specific sequence. This prediction is somewhat at odds with the current vogue for parallel processing (e.g., Rumelhart and McClelland 1986). Kosslyn et al. (1988; see also Roth and Kosslyn 1988), tested this prediction. We used a variant of a task developed by Podgorny and Shepard (1978). Podgorny and Shepard asked people to visualize block letters in grids or in empty rectangles, and then after the image was formed to look at one or more dots in the same display. The subjects were to decide whether the dot or dots would have fallen on the letter if it were actually present as it appeared in the image. Half the time the dots would have been on the letter, and half the time they would have been off the letter. The response times in this task varied depending on the number of dots, their location, and the size of the image. Podgorny and Shepard compared these patterns of times with those from the corresponding perceptual task, in which the letter was physically present. They found very similar patterns of times in the imagery and perception tasks; for example, subjects were faster when dots fell at the intersections of segments than when they fell on individual limbs, were faster for more compact figures, and so on. These results led Podgorny and Shepard to argue that imagery and perception draw on the same attentional mechanisms, which monitor specific regions of space.

We modified Podgorny and Shepard's task in one critical way: We did not allow the subjects to finish forming the image before the probe mark was delivered. Specifically, we cued subjects which letter to visualize, and then presented a probe mark (an X mark or two X marks, depending on the experiment) half a second later. This was not enough time to finish forming the image before the X mark appeared. Thus, the subjects would have to generate the image on the spot, and we could study this process. Our idea was that we could "catch the process on the fly" by varying the locations of the X marks and measuring how long it took to evaluate them in different locations. Our first result of interest was that subjects did in fact require more time for more complex letters. Our second result was that the position of an X probe was critical. Prior to the experiment, we had observed a separate group of subjects when they copied the block letters into empty grids, and chose only those letters that were consistently drawn in specific way. We then placed some X probes on (or near, for the "no" probes) segments that were drawn early in the sequence, and the others on (or near) segments that were drawn late in the sequence. And in fact, we found that subjects in the experiment proper required more time to evaluate probes that were on or near segments that were drawn later in the sequence.

The variations in response times for different probe locations only occurred if the subjects were forced to generate the image on the spot. In another task we allowed the subjects to visualize the letters first, and only presented the probe after they had pressed a button when their image was complete. In this condition, the subjects could evaluate probes in different locations equally easily. Moreover, subjects could evaluate probes in different locations equally easily in a perception condition, when the probes were presented on light-gray letters; this result shows that the effect was not due to scanning. In short, we had good evidence that images of block letters were in fact created a segment at a time.

Categorical and Coordinate Spatial Relations in Image Generation

In chapter 7 I discussed two ways in which spatial relations can be encoded and stored: either as coordinates of the sort that are used to guide movements or as categories (such as above/below). If both types of representations are stored, it seems plausible that both types could be used to arrange parts or characteristics in images. In addition, my colleagues and I showed that coordinate spatial relations are encoded better in the right hemisphere, whereas categorical spatial relations are encoded better in the left (although this effect is not as robust as the lateralization of coordinate spatial relations; see Kosslyn, Chabris, Marsolek, and Koenig 1992). If representations are stored more effectively in the hemisphere that encodes them more effectively, then we might expect hemispheric differences in image generation. Specifically, the left hemisphere might be better than the right when categorical spatial relations are used to arrange parts into an image, but the right hemisphere might be better than the left when coordinates are used to arrange parts into an image.

Kosslyn, Maljkovic, Hamilton, Thompson, and Horwitz (1993) tested this prediction in a series of experiments using the divided-visual-field technique with normal subjects. In one experiment, subjects memorized descriptions of how segments were arranged to form a pattern, such as "a vertical line on the left, a horizontal line on the top, and a horizontal line halfway down." The subjects were given a 4 × 5 grid and asked to visualize the pattern that was described. The subjects associated each pattern with a digit, which was used later to cue the subjects to visualize that pattern. After memorizing the descriptions and associated digits, the subjects participated in a series of test trials. On each trial, they first focused on a dot placed at the center of a screen. A digit replaced this point, for half a second, and then an empty grid with a single X mark appeared in the left or right visual field. The subject was asked to decide whether the X mark would have covered the pattern previously paired with the digit, if that pattern were in the grid. When the grid was presented to the right of fixation, the left hemisphere encoded it first; when it was presented to the left of fixation, the right hemisphere encoded it first.

We expected the subjects to use categorical spatial relations to build up these images, and hence predicted that they would evaluate the probes more quickly when the stimuli were presented initially to the left hemisphere. This prediction was confirmed. In addition, the subjects required more time to image patterns with more segments. Furthermore, they required more time to evaluate X marks that fell on segments that were farther along the described sequence of segments; this result suggests that the subjects did in fact image the pattern a segment at a time.

These results were in sharp contrast to those from another experiment, in which subjects did not memorize descriptions at the outset. Rather, they saw a series of segments on a screen, one at a time, with the previous one being removed before another was presented. The segments were presented in different locations on the screen, and the subjects were asked to "glue the segments together" mentally, forming an overall pattern, and to remember these patterns. There was no grid, and so descriptions would not be very helpful (too many metric relations were critical to arrange the parts properly). Because the subjects had to remember the precise location of each segment, they presumably encoded coordinate spatial relations representations. As before, each pattern was associated with a digit, which was later used to name the pattern. These subjects performed the same experimental task as the subjects who first memorized descriptions of the patterns. They fixated on a dot, which was briefly replaced by a digit cue; they then saw an X in an enclosed region (defined by four brackets, indicating the corners of a grid) and decided whether it would fall on the cued pattern if it were within the brackets.

We expected the subjects to use coordinate spatial relations to build up these images, and hence predicted that they would evaluate the probes more quickly when the stimuli were presented initially to the right hemisphere. This prediction was confirmed. As before, the subjects required more time for more complex patterns and evaluated probes more slowly when they fell on segments that were later in the sequence; these results suggest that the subjects did indeed generate the images a segment at a time.

We next showed that we could induce these hemispheric differences simply by varying the stimulus materials, using the same instructions during the learning phase. The subjects saw block letters that were either in 4 × 5 grids or within sets of four brackets (the corners of an otherwise invisible grid). Examples of such stimuli are presented in figure 9.1. Each block letter was associated with a lowercase script cue. The task was the same as before: After memorizing the letters, the subjects saw a cue and an X mark within an otherwise empty grid or set of four brackets. The task was to decide whether the X mark would have covered the corresponding block letter had it been

Study stimulus   **Test stimulus**

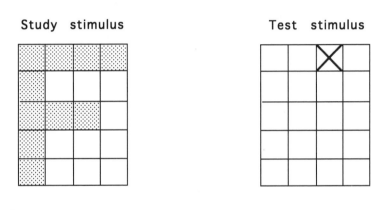

Study stimulus   **Test stimulus**

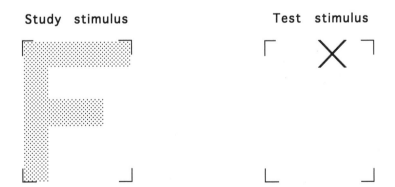

Figure 9.1   Examples of grids and brackets stimuli used to study image generation.

Generating and Maintaining Visual Images

present. We expected the grid lines to serve as a kind of crutch, which would allow subjects to encode the locations of segments using categorical spatial relations (e.g., for a *T*, one bar is "at the top," and another "descends down the middle"). In contrast, when given only the four brackets, the subjects would have to learn the precise metric positions of the segments, and so we expected them to use coordinate spatial relations representations when encoding—and later imaging—the letters.

When the stimuli were lateralized, we found a clear left-hemisphere advantage for the grids and a clear right-hemisphere advantage for the brackets. This result was replicated three times. As expected, the subjects required more time to evaluate **X** marks that fell on segments that typically are drawn later in the sequence of strokes. Given that Kosslyn et al. (1988) only found this effect of probe position when subjects were generating the image, and not when they were "inspecting" a pattern in a previously generated image, this is good evidence that the task did require image generation.

We conducted a series of six additional experiments to rule out various alternative accounts of these results. The left-hemisphere advantage could not be ascribed to the smaller regions defined by the grid cells nor to the requirement that an image be imposed over grid lines, and the right-hemisphere advantage could not be ascribed to the precision necessary to encode the **X** mark nor to the judgment itself. In short, we had good evidence that there are two ways to generate visual mental images of complex shapes: one in which categorical spatial representations are used to arrange parts, and one in which coordinate spatial relations representations are used to arrange parts. If categorical spatial relations are related to verbal material, then these findings support what I take to be Paivio's (1989) view, that the left hemisphere is better at imagery tasks that make contact with verbally related representations and the right hemisphere is better at imagery tasks that are entirely nonverbal.

Testing Critical Predictions: Perceptual Mechanisms and Image Generation

The theory is complex, which is appropriate given the complexity of the brain itself; indeed, what worries me is not its complexity but its simplicity. Nevertheless, the theory predicts a pattern of activation in a set of brain loci when one generates an image. Because I have hypothesized where specific subsystems are implemented in the brain, PET scanning is one appropriate way to test the theory.

A problem arises, however, because the theory does not specify the precise locus where activation should arise when a particular subsystem is at work. Not only must one be cautious in assuming that the localization of function in monkey brains will transfer directly to localization in human brains, but there are also a host of potential measurement problems—such as those associated with averaging over individual brains, resolution limitations, and so forth (see chapter 2). Thus, I can only predict that activation will occur within a set of rather large circumscribed areas. But this indeterminacy provides many opportunities to obtain results due to chance events. It would be best to have more precise predictions about the neural loci that should be activated during image generation.

One way to generate such precise predictions is by using the results of one experiment to provide the specific hypotheses for another. I posit that image generation draws on the same processes that underlie top-down hypothesis testing during perception. If so, then the same pattern of areas ought to be activated during both activities. This prediction is appealing because, on the surface, the two kinds of activities are not very similar; thus, we would not simply use a variant of a task to predict performance in the same task.

We administered the picture-identification task used by Kosslyn, Alpert, Thompson, Chabris, Rauch, and Anderson (1993) to study the neural bases of visual object identification (see chapter 8). Recall that the subjects saw a series of pictures of objects, each of which was accompanied by a spoken word. The subjects decided whether the words named the pictures. We now focus on two of the conditions. In one block of trials, the objects were portrayed from a canonical point of view, whereas in another block they were portrayed from a noncanonical (unusual) point of view. Recall that when we subtracted blood flow in the canonical condition from that in the noncanonical condition, we found additional activation in a specific set of areas; we had earlier hypothesized that these areas implement subsystems that are used to look up information in memory, shift attention, encode additional parts and characteristics, encode spatial properties of the parts and characteristics, and match this input to representations in associative memory.

The same subjects also participated in a variant of the grids image generation task described above, used previously by Kosslyn et al. (1988). This part of the study again included two conditions. In the baseline task, the subjects saw a fixation point (for 300 ms), replaced by a script letter (for 200 ms), and then saw a 4 × 5 grid that contained an X mark in one cell (for 200 ms). The subjects simply pressed a response pedal when they saw the X mark, alternating feet over trials. In the imagery task, the subjects first memorized the appearance of block uppercase letters in 4 × 5 grids; as before, they also associated each letter with a script letter. The subjects saw the same sequence of stimuli used in the baseline task. But now, on each trial the subjects were to read the cue and visualize the corresponding uppercase letter in the grid. They then were to decide whether the letter would have covered the X mark, if it had been present in the grid. The 200 ms between the script cue and the grid-with-X stimulus was not enough time to finish reading the cue and forming the image; hence, the subjects had to generate the image of the uppercase letter at the time the grid with the X appeared. By subtracting the blood flow in the baseline task from that in the imagery task, we should isolate those processes used to generate and evaluate the image.

We replicated the behavioral results from each task, the increased time for noncanonical pictures in the object-identification task, and the segment effect in the imagery task, which gave us confidence that the subjects did in fact follow the instructions.

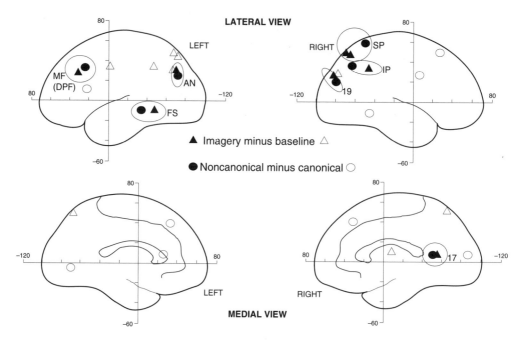

Figure 9.2 Results from two experiments that were administered to the same subjects. The circles indicate foci of activity that were evident when blood flow in the canonical pictures condition was subtracted from blood flow in the noncanonical pictures condition; the triangles indicate foci of activity that were evident when blood flow in the baseline condition was subtracted from blood flow in the imagery condition. The black symbols indicate areas activated by both types of processing. MF is the middle frontal area (also called dorsolateral prefrontal cortex), AN is the angular gyrus, FS the fusiform gyrus, SP superior parietal cortex, IP inferior parietal cortex, 19 area 19, 17 anterior area 17. (Reprinted from Kosslyn, Alpert, and Thompson 1993, with permission.)

The results are illustrated in figure 9.2. The circles indicate the locations of regions that were activated more by the noncanonical pictures than by the canonical pictures, and the triangles indicate areas that were activated more by the imagery task than by the imagery baseline task. The filled symbols indicate areas that were activated in common by top-down perceptual processing and image generation. As the theory predicts, we found common activation in the following areas:

• The left angular gyrus and right area 19, both of which we suggested earlier are involved in implementing associative memory (see chapter 7).

• The left dorsolateral prefrontal cortex, which is as expected if this area implements the categorical property lookup subsystem, which access information in associative memory.

• The right superior parietal lobe, which presumably is involved in shifting attention (specifically, in the disengage operation). Although area 8 was active in the perceptual task and the right thalamus was active in the imagery task, we did not find common activation of the superior colliculus, the pulvinar, or the anterior cingulate. As was discussed in chapter 7, this may indicate that the engage and shift processes were also used when the baseline stimuli were presented, which would not be surprising; if so, then we would have subtracted out evidence of these processes in our measures.

• Area 17 in the left hemisphere, which implements part of the visual buffer. This activation reflects the additional visual information encoded during a "second pass" in perception and the formation of images.

• The fusiform gyrus, bilaterally, which is a candidate for the human homolog of monkey inferior temporal cortex. This area presumably was involved in generating the image and in recognizing parts. The middle temporal gyrus was not activated in either task, which may suggest that it is involved in implementing the preprocessing subsystem; the subtractions presumably removed any activation due to such processing.

• The right inferior parietal lobe, which we hypothesize plays a critical role in encoding spatial relations representations. I claimed earlier that this area implements the spatiotopic mapping subsystem as well as the coordinate spatial relations encoding subsystem.[4]

As illustrated, we also found several other areas that were not activated by both tasks. This is not surprising, given the different processing requirements in the two cases.

These results are remarkable in several respects. Perhaps most important, we obtained parallel results in just those areas that are hypothesized to be involved in top-down hypothesis testing and image generation. The probability of obtaining such results due to chance is exceedingly small, under one in one million. In addition, these findings validate two of our overarching working assumptions, namely that imagery and perception share common neural mechanisms, and that these mechanisms can be decomposed into sets of component processing subsystems. In short, it is clear that the theory developed so far is on the right track.

Dorsal and Ventral Imagery

Consider what happens when you visualize a Christmas tree. Does the tree seem to have a specific color? A texture? Is illumination constant across it? Is the shape well defined, or does it just seem jagged at the edges? People often report that their images of objects have such properties. In contrast, consider what happens when you look at a tiled floor (such as is found in many bathrooms) and "see" a letter by attending to specific tiles. These two types of imagery appear very different. In one, object properties are activated; in the other, purely spatial properties are activated; when seeing patterns on arrays of tiles, one does not activate a specific visual memory (with color, texture, and other object properties).

This distinction between *visual-memory-based imagery* and *attention-based imagery* is consistent with findings reported by Levine, Warach, and Farah (1985). They studied one patient with lesions in the dorsal system and another patient with lesions in the ventral system. The patient with lesions in the dorsal system was unable to image locations, such as those used when navigating from one place to another, but was able to image shapes, such as common objects and faces. In contrast, the patient with lesions in the ventral system had the opposite pattern of disruptions. These findings suggested to the researchers that there is one kind of imagery based on object properties and another based on spatial properties (see also Farah, Hammond, Levine, and Calvanio 1988). As discussed in chapter 3, Farah (1986) had earlier reported results that suggest that at least some types of imagery engage attentional processes; if an image was formed at a location, this facilitated detecting that shape.

Uhl et al. (1990) report electrophysiological results that are nicely convergent with the findings of Levine, Warach, and Farah (1985). When subjects visualized a route on a map that they had memorized prior to the experiment, a DC shift was observed over the parietal lobes. Presumably, the map specified spatial information. In contrast, when the subjects imaged faces and colors, there was a sustained DC shift over the temporal lobe (in addition to the occipital lobe in both cases).

In the PET experiment described above, the grids were presented for only 200 ms. This feature of the design seemed likely to discourage the use of attention-based imagery. Attention-based images are generated the same way as visual-memory-based images (as described above), except that compressed image representations in the pattern activation subsystem are not activated; rather, one simply engages attention at each location, "painting" a pattern in the visual buffer. The process of shifting attention should require time. Hence, removing the grid so quickly may have discouraged the subjects from engaging attention in the appropriate rows and columns; instead, they may have formed visual-memory-based images.

We performed another PET experiment in which the grids were left in free view, which we conjectured should have encouraged an attention-based imagery strategy (indeed, look at figure 9.1 and note whether your image of the *F* included color and texture; given the situation, you may have instead attended to the appropriate rows and columns). This PET study also incorporated a different subtraction than one described above. One of the important findings of Podgorny and Shepard's (1978) study was that the results from the perception and imagery conditions were very similar; the response times varied in the same way when the number, size, and location of the dots was varied. This result is evidence that some of the same processes are used in both kinds of tasks. This finding led us to use a perception task as a control for the imagery task.

That is, we assumed that the imagery task has two major components: Subjects first must activate stored visual information to visualize part of an object, and only then can they "inspect" the imaged patterns for specific properties. Podgorny and Shepard's results suggested that the same "inspection" processes are used in imagery and perception in these tasks. Thus, by subtracting the blood flow in a perception baseline task from that in the imagery task, we could examine which brain loci are involved in generating visual mental images per se.

The perception task was like the imagery task, except that the subjects saw a single **X** mark in a grid along with a light-gray block letter; they simply indicated whether the **X** was on or off the letter. We also tested a second group of subjects to control for the effects of simply observing an empty grid. We worried that any differences between the imagery and perception tasks might be due to viewing high-spatial-frequency stimuli or scanning across sharp edges when the empty grids were present. The people in this control group participated in the perception task, but instead of the imagery trials they simply viewed grids with an **X** mark in a cell. To force the subjects to watch the grid, the **X** mark was removed after a variable amount of time, at which point the subject pressed a pedal and the stimulus was removed. We ensured that these people viewed the empty grids for the same length of time as the subjects in the imagery condition; the critical difference was that the subjects in the imagery condition visualized a letter in the grid, whereas these subjects did not.

The results are illustrated in figure 9.3. First, we did not find activation in the posterior portion of V1, as would be expected given the relatively small stimuli (they subtended about 3° of visual angle). This is not surprising,

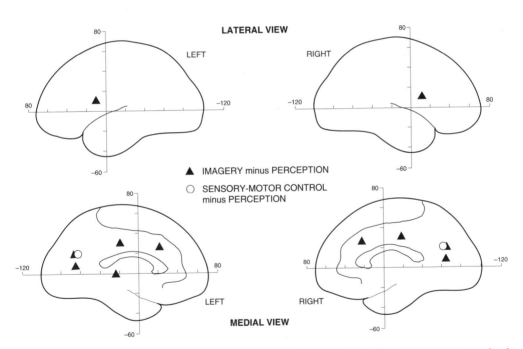

Figure 9.3 Results from an experiment in which subjects in the imagery group visualized letters in grids in free view and evaluated perceptual stimuli, and subjects in the sensory-motor control group viewed the grids for the same length of time and evaluated perceptual stimuli. (Reprinted from Kosslyn, Alpert, Thompson, Maljkovic, Weise, Chabris, Hamilton, Rauch, and Buonanno 1993, with permission.)

however, given that we subtracted the activation from a similar perceptual task. However, we did find activation of an area at the very anterior portion of area 17; this activation was along the midline of both hemispheres. This area could have been part of area 18, area 30, or another topographically mapped region that has yet to be characterized. It is of interest that we did not find activation in this area in the control group, when the subjects did not form images in the grids.

The second result to note is a negative one: There was no activation in the temporal lobe. This finding is as expected if visual memories are not activated in this task, but rather attentional imagery is used when the grids are available in free view.

Third, prefrontal lobe structures, specifically area 46, were activated bilaterally; these regions presumably implement the property lookup subsystems, which would be required to access a structural description and shift attention to the appropriate locations in the grid.

Fourth, the activated prefrontal region included area 8, and we found activation in the anterior cingulate; both of these areas are involved in shifting attention. We also found activation in the left pulvinar; the pulvinar has been identified with a process that engages attention at a specific site (e.g., LaBerge and Buchsbaum 1990; Posner et al. 1987; Posner and Petersen 1990). We expected these attentional structures to be more active during imagery than during the corresponding perceptual task because one engages attention only at the location of the probe in the perceptual task, but must also engage it when each new segment is added while when constructing the image. We also found unexpected activation in the posterior cingulate and the cuneus; it is possible that these structures also play a role in "fixing" attention to form an image.

Finally, we did not find greater activation in the posterior parietal lobes in the imagery task than in the perceptual task. The failure to find activation in the superior parietal lobe may indicate that subjects did not disengage attention but rather left it engaged, "painting" an image. Alternatively, it is possible that this operation was used to an equal degree in the imagery and perceptual tasks. Similarly, our failure to find activation in the inferior parietal lobe may indicate that subjects encoded spatial properties during both the imagery and perceptual tasks, and hence the subtraction removed these effects from the imagery task. And our failure to find activation in area 19 or the angular gyrus might indicate that associative memory was activated in both tasks.

Because the blood flow from the corresponding perceptual task was subtracted, none of the results can be ascribed to the process of encoding the probe mark, making the on/off decision, or generating the response (all of which were also involved in the perceptual task). In sharp contrast to these results, only the cuneus was activated more in the sensory-motor control task than in the perceptual control task; we have no good explanation for this result.

In summary, these results were consistent with the claim that the subjects used attention-based imagery to perform the task. Not only did we find activation in the pulvinar, area 8, and the anterior cingulate—none of which were activated in the other version of the task—but we did *not* find a hint of activation in the temporal lobe—which was activated in the other version of the task. We also found left-hemisphere activation in the area at the anterior portion of V1 and in the pulvinar, which is consistent with our results from divided-visual-field studies with these grid stimuli.

Functional Differences between the Two Types of Imagery   Consider what happens when you visualize your mother's face. Introspectively, such an image does not appear to be built up a part at a time, but rather seems to appear all at once. Such introspections are limited, however, in part because we may not easily be able to detect sequences that occur as quickly as those underlying image generation. Thus, it is worth considering the possibility that under some circumstances, patterns with parts at roughly the same level of resolution can be "chunked" into a single unit at the time they are encoded, and later activated all of a piece when one uses visual-memory-based imagery. For example, when imaging someone's face, you may not need to build up the image a part at a time, adding the nose, eyes, mouth, and so on, because normal faces are seen so often that a perceptual grouping process becomes built into the preprocessing subsystem. Hence a face might be encoded as a single unit, which can imaged as such.

In contrast, a pattern created during attention-based imagery cannot be formed by "shaping" the attention window to encompass a more complex region; attention apparently is restricted to a regular enclosed area (see Posner 1978). Thus, one must attend to the region of each segment individually and in sequence. This mechanism implies that the more complex the pattern, the more time will be required to form an attention-based image of it. In contrast, if one encodes the pattern as a single perceptual unit, the time to activate it should not depend on its complexity; the patterns of weights in a neural network operate in parallel to produce the output.

To test these hypotheses, Kosslyn and Anderson (in preparation) performed a variant of the grids-with-X task described above. We designed letters with patterns on them, as illustrated in figure 9.4, and asked one group of subjects to memorize these stimuli; another group memorized the standard stimuli, with no pattern imposed over the letters. The patterns were designed to lead the subjects to see the letters not simply as a set of segments, which could be encoded using attentional imagery, but rather as a single shape, which would be chunked and encoded in the ventral system. As before, the letters varied in complexity (from two segments, L, to five, G). The subjects saw a lowercase cue, and then an X mark. The subjects in the pattern condition were to determine whether the X probe would fall in a cell with a "split" or "solid" portion of the letter, if the figure were actually present in the grid. The probes could also fall off the form of the letter, on the white background, which we considered a solid-colored cell. In the standard letter condition, the subjects were to determine whether the X would fall on the "black" (on the letter) or "white" (off the letter) portion of the figure, if the figure were

Figure 9.4 Stimuli designed to encourage visual-memory-based imagery. The patterns were designed to lead the subjects to see the letters as a single shape, not just a collection of segments. (Reprinted from Kosslyn and Anderson, in preparation, with permission.)

actually present in the grid. As usual, the probes were on (for "yes" trials) or near (for "no" trials) segments that were typically drawn early or late in the sequence.

We replicated our usual results with the standard letters, finding clear effects of both probe location and complexity, as described earlier.[5] In contrast, the subjects who evaluated images of patterned letters evaluated the probes equally easily (regardless of the number of segments that would have to be drawn to reach the probe), and did not require more time for the more complex letters. These results were exactly as expected if the patterns led the subjects to organize each letter into a single visual memory representation.

To obtain convergent evidence, we designed a very different task to study whether visual-memory based images could be chunked into higher-order units and thereby visualized all of a piece. We began by asking the subjects to study 18 common advertisement logos or the corresponding letters and words in a Helvetica font; the logos were proportionally sized to match the width of the corresponding Helvetica version. Half of the stimuli varied in length from 2 to 4 letters (e.g., GE, TIME, LIFE) and half varied from 5 to 10 letters (e.g., MOBIL, COCA-COLA, LIFESAVERS). Half of the subjects studied the logos and half studied the corresponding letters and words in Helvetica type. During the task itself, the subjects closed their eyes and heard the names of the stimuli; they were to visualize each stimulus as it had been presented during the study session, and were to determine whether there had been more ink on its top or bottom half. That is, they were told to imagine the stimulus as if a horizontal line were drawn across it, at half the height of the tallest letter; they then heard the word "top" or "bottom," and decided whether there was more ink on that portion of the stimulus.

As predicted, the subjects who studied logos could visualize the short and long ones in comparable amounts of time, whereas those who studied the stimuli in Helvetica type required much more time for the longer ones. The logos were presumably encoded as single units in the exemplar pattern activation subsystem, whereas the stimuli written in a standard font were not. Hence, images of the logos could be formed by activating a single stored representation, whereas images of the letters and words in a standard font had to be constructed a letter at a time, as described above.[6]

This chunking process also allows us to understand findings reported by Intons-Peterson (1984, experiment 1). Intons-Peterson extended Nielsen and Smith's (1973) study (summarized in chapter 5) to investigate whether subjects could organize common and unusual features of schematic faces into templates. One group of subjects received trials in which they listened to a description of features of a schematic face and then saw a schematic face; the task was to decide whether the face contained the features on the list (which may have been a subset of the entire set of features on the face). A second group was asked to visualize a face that contained the features on the list, and then to use the image in the comparison task. A third group of subjects saw and memorized a schematic face on each trial, instead of memorizing features or forming images, and then compared the face to a test face presented subsequently. After each study stimulus, the subjects pressed a key to indicate when they were ready for the test face. The study faces included 1 to 6 common features and 0 to 6 unusual features (such as a dashed line for a mouth or two lines for a nose).

According to the examples provided in her article (on p. 702), Intons-Peterson always arranged the common features symmetrically and almost always arranged the unusual ones asymmetrically. Hence, I would expect chunking for the common features, and was initially surprised to discover that the preparation times increased for faces with more features, for both common and unusual features. I cannot put much weight in this finding, however, because (a) the descriptions were presented serially, which invited subjects to construct the images a piece at a time; (b) the preparation times were highly variable; (c) it is not clear that the manipulation of complexity necessarily reflects psychological complexity; for example, Intons-Peterson treated an oval with one off-center horizontal line "eyebrow" as less complex than an oval with two vertical parallel lines forming a "nose" in the center; (d) the subjects required an average of over three seconds to prepare for the test faces; these times are much longer than image generation times I have ever measured, which makes me suspect that the preparation times were not a good measure of image generation per se.

Nevertheless, once the images were generated, they could be reencoded and then regenerated as single units. The comparison times did provide evidence of chunking: When the subjects used imagery, Intons-Peterson found that the comparison times did not vary with the number of common features, but did increase with the number of unusual features in the asymmetric, difficult-to-organize faces. This result was obtained when the subjects imaged or compared faces with unusual features, which is as I expect if the same organizational principles dictate how images and percepts are organized. Indeed, similar results were obtained when subjects visualized faces on the basis of descriptions and when they retained information about previously seen faces in the perceptual condition. In contrast, the comparison times always increased with the number of features, common or unusual, when subjects memorized and used descriptions (for an earlier study with consistent results, see Intons-Peterson 1981).

Four Types of Image Generation?   The findings summarized here suggest that there are four distinct ways to form images: Images can be formed by using categorical or coordinate spatial relations representations to arrange components, and images of the individual components can be formed either by allocating attention or by activating visual memories. In many circumstances, one will not have an option about how to proceed. If one only encoded one sort of spatial relations representation, that places obvious constraints on how parts can be arranged. Similarly, if there is no visible structure to attend to (such as a tile floor), one will have difficulty using attention-based imagery to visualize a pattern. Nevertheless, it is striking that a single ability—image generation—can be so complex.

This proposal is consistent with the findings of Cornoldi, De Beni, and Pra Baldi (1989). They distinguish between *general, specific,* and *autobiographical* images. The distinction between general and specific images corresponds to my distinction between prototypical and exemplar images, and an autobiographical image is an image of a single episode in a person's life (which I take to be a special case of an exemplar image). Cornoldi, De Beni, and Pra Baldi found that specific images were rated as more vivid than the other two types, but that autobiographical images aided free recall of words better than the other types; they also found that subjects tended to require different amounts of time to form the different types of images, being fastest with general images, slower with specific images, and slowest with autobiographical images. The difference in time to form the different types of images would seem to line up with how often the representations are used. Presumably, one sees members of a category more often than any specific exemplar, and sees specific exemplars more often than those that appeared at a particular time and place. The same factors would tend to make autobiographical memories more distinctive retrieval cues.

Imaging Novel Arrangements of Familiar Objects

One of the reasons imagery is useful is that we can visualize objects with novel parts or characteristics or can visualize scenes we have never actually witnessed. For example, we can form an image of what furniture would look like in different parts of a room, or can visualize a contemporary President of the United States with his arm around George Washington, and so forth. When we read sentences or hear a description, a series of processes decodes the words, eventually activating specific representations in associative memory (for more discussion of such processing, see chapter 6 of Kosslyn and Koenig 1992). The descriptions correspond to names of objects and categorical spatial relations, and hence can access the representations in associative memory that are needed to image the components and position them properly. An image is constructed exactly as it is when categorical spatial relations are used to arrange parts of objects (one of the four circumstances described earlier). Except that in this case, objects themselves usually are imaged in relation to each other. The image of the first object is formed, and then the categorical relations specified in the description are used to shift the attention window to the location where the second object belongs. The mapping function from the pattern activation subsystems is altered appropriately, and the second image is formed, and so on.

Denis and Cocude (1989) showed that subjects could build up images of scenes on the basis of verbal descriptions of how objects are arranged, and then could scan between the objects in the image. The fact that scanning times increased with increasing distance not only showed that the subjects could scan such imaged scenes, but also showed that they could use verbal descriptions to place the component parts relatively accurately (see also Kosslyn et al. 1983). Denis and Cocude (1992) went on to show that the ease of generating the image depends on the coherence of the description. Their subjects imagined a circular map, with locations along the periphery. If the locations of objects (specified as numbers on a clock face) were described randomly, subjects needed to study the description more times before they could generate accurate images (as reflected in systematic scanning times) than if the locations were described moving clockwise around the circle. Denis and Cocude argue that the locations of the objects were easier to encode relative to a previous object on the circle than when absolute locations were necessary.

Glushko and Cooper (1978) showed that mental images formed on the basis of descriptions do in fact engage visual mechanisms. They constructed geometric patterns by juxtaposing triangles and squares, and varied the number of these components. The subjects were asked to recognize these patterns after being primed in two ways: they either saw a pattern or received a description of a pattern. If the prime and the test pattern were separated by three seconds, the subjects could recognize patterns with different numbers of parts equally quickly when primed with the picture or the description. Three seconds is ample time to form these sorts of images (see chapter 6 of Kosslyn 1980). When the subjects were given the description with shorter preparation times, so that they presumably could not finish generating the image, recognition times increased for more complex patterns. The image apparently could serve as a template, allowing rapid encoding of the corresponding pattern.

Presumably the same sequence of events occurs when an image of a novel pattern is specified not by a description one hears or reads, but rather by a thought. I assume that a thought corresponds to a set of activated representations in associative memory, which may be accompanied by an image (but the image itself must be "under interpretation" to have meaning; see chapter 11 of Kosslyn 1980).

Although the process described above often will be satisfactory, in some cases it may not. For example, to imagine Charlie Chaplin with his arm around George Washington, one may generate the images of the two gentlemen standing next to each other, and then may have to transform the Chaplin image so that his arm is properly placed. I will argue in the following chapter that this kind of transformation operation is not entirely distinct from the processes that underlie image generation.

Imaging Novel Patterns

People can "mentally draw," visualizing patterns that they have never seen and that are not simply new combinations of familiar components. This process is a special case of the attention-based imagery described above. Only in this case one does not shift the attention window to a sequence of discrete locations but rather moves it continuously, activating the path left in its swath. Presumably such image activation rests on the same connections from the pulvinar (which implements, at least in part, the engage component of the attention-shifting subsystems) to the visual buffer that are used when one "sees" patterns on a tile floor.

A Multiscaled Representation

Images are configurations of activity in the visual buffer. In the theory developed here I posit that the visual buffer is multiscaled, representing input at different levels of resolution. Hence, depending on what was stored, an image can later be generated at a particular level of resolution. My view is similar to that of Hebb (1968), who suggested that additional "cell assemblies" are activated when one forms a higher-resolution image. Inducing activity in area V1 would provide a high-resolution image, but less distinct images should be supported by patterns of activation in other topographically organized areas. I expect distinct visual areas to represent images at different levels of scale (cf. Van Essen 1985), and hence wish to emphasize that the visual buffer is not simply area V1. Because V1 is the largest topographically organized visual area, it is easiest to detect using PET and similar techniques—but it is not the only area that implements the visual buffer.

This property of the theory allows us to understand the findings of Kosslyn, Shin, and Mijovic (in preparation). We found that patients with visual field cuts (i.e., blindness in one visual field) can generate images that subtend the same visual angles as normal subjects. We tested 17 patients with focal lesions in the occipital lobe; on each trial, we asked them to visualize named objects as if the images were projected on a blank screen, and then to move a pointer to indicate the right and left sides of the imaged object. We measured these positions of the pointer and computed the angle subtended by the imaged object. Both brain-damaged and normal control subjects produced larger angles for larger objects, but there was no difference in the sizes of the angles produced by the two groups.

At first blush, these results may appear to contradict those of Farah, Soso, and Dasheiff (1992), who found that the horizontal extent of imaged objects was reduced by about half after their patient had one of her occipital lobes removed. However, their patient had the entire occipital lobe removed, not just V1. Our patients probably had functional extrastriate topographically organized areas that could be used in imagery. If portions of the images in such patients occur only in extrastriate cortex, then they should be vaguer than normal images. Hence, I predict that patients with damage to V1 should have lower-resolution images than control subjects on the side of the field cut, with increasingly lower resolution as more of the neural substrate of the visual buffer is damaged. This prediction has not been tested.

Consistent with these hypotheses, we did find a reduced imagery angle in a patient who had an entire hemisphere removed as a treatment for otherwise intractable epilepsy. Indeed, objects in his images subtended a mean of 11.25°, compared to 44° for the control subjects in this task (which involved forming images of common animals, without instructions to ensure that the edges were very sharp in the image; see Kosslyn 1978). We did not test this patient prior to surgery, unlike Farah et al., and so do not know the original size of his image angle; there are large individual differences in such angles in the normal population, and in fact this patient's angle was only about two standard deviations from the inferred population mean. Moreover, it is possible that the removal of so much cortex resulted in lower "activation levels" for the intact hemisphere (see chapter 2), and hence that less material could be generated into the image.

Anatomical Localization: Cerebral Lateralization

As noted earlier, the left or right hemisphere can play a special role in image generation, depending on the precise method used to generate an image. These results speak directly to a debate about the lateralization of image generation processes. This debate began when Farah (1984) reported a new analysis of case studies of patients who lost the ability to generate visual mental images following brain damage. She found that such a deficit was related to a lesion in the left posterior cerebral hemisphere. This result caused a stir because the common wisdom was that the right, not the left, hemisphere plays a critical role in imagery (e.g., see Bradshaw and Nettleton 1981; Ehrlichman and Barrett 1983; Ley 1979; Springer and Deutsch 1985; although others, such as Luria [1973, p. 145], had earlier made observations similar to Farah's). Shortly after this pioneering article, Farah et al. (1985) and Kosslyn et al. (1985) reported a series of experiments with split-brain patients that modified Farah's conclusions slightly. In particular, Kosslyn et al. (1985) found that the left hemisphere could perform imagery tasks that required adding high-resolution parts to an image (such as determining whether a specific animal's ears protrude above the top of its head) and also could perform imagery tasks that required only the global shape of an object (such as determining whether a specific object is higher than it is wide). In contrast, the right hemisphere was impaired when parts had to be added but was as good as the left hemisphere when only the overall shape was necessary. At the time, we interpreted our results with the split-brain patients as suggesting that the PUT process did not operate effectively in the right hemisphere; I now interpret them as reflecting a deficit in the ability to look up right-hemisphere-based spatial relations representations.

Until now, I have not been concerned with laterality per se, but have used it as a means of distinguishing distinct subsystems that encode different types of representations. However, the controversy in the literature on image generation concerns the locus of image generation processes, and hence it is important to reiterate that one cannot generalize confidently from the split-brain results to the normal brain (see chapter 2). Thus, it is important to consider this literature more generally.[7]

Left-Hemisphere Image Generation   Farah (1984, 1986) maintained that image generation is subserved primarily by the left hemisphere (see also Antrobus 1987). Consider a case study reported by Farah, Levine, and Calvanio (1988), which vividly illustrates an image-generation deficit in a patient, R. M., who had a left-posterior lesion. The researchers asked R. M. to evaluate statements that had previously been shown to require imagery (e.g., "A grapefruit is larger than an orange"), and statements that had been shown not to require imagery (e.g., "The U.S. government functions under a three-party system"; see Eddy and Glass 1981). This patient did in fact have more difficulty evaluating the imagery sentences than the nonimagery sentences. In addition, R. M. performed poorly in two imagery tasks that did not involve language comprehension (a coloring task and a drawing completion task), which appears to rule out Basso, Bisiach, and Luzzatti's (1980) idea that imagery deficits are caused by a disconnection of brain systems that process verbal information from those that process mental images.

One interesting facet of this study is that Farah, Levine, and Calvanio noted that R. M. was apparently not able to "relate separate parts of a visual representation" (p. 162). He could read letters but could not integrate words, and may have been able to image parts but not to integrate them into objects. This claim is, of course, consistent with the present analysis of image generation, and it is consistent with our earlier finding that split-brain patient J. W. could generate multipart images in his left, but not his right, hemisphere. However, R. M. also apparently had trouble imaging colors that belong to specific shapes, and so his deficit may best be characterized as one of integrating properties (parts and characteristics) of objects, not simply integrating parts.

Riddoch (1990) also describes a patient with a posterior left-hemisphere lesion who had difficulty using imagery. Her patient had difficulty judging from memory whether uppercase versions of named letters had any curved lines. However, he could not write letters when given their names, and hence may simply have not known which letters to image. The patient also had trouble drawing from memory, but this deficit does not necessarily reflect a problem in generating images per se; it is not clear what role imagery has in drawing—one might be able to draw purely on the basis of sets of motor coordinates that are formulated in the absence of imagery. Perhaps the strongest evidence for an imagery deficit was that this patient could not visually complete a drawing of an animal's body to determine the relative length of its tail. But it is possible that the patient had a disruption in associative memory that prevented him from associating the pattern code for the object (he could recognize pictures adequately) with its parts—an association I claim is necessary to form the appropriate image.

The idea that the left hemisphere plays a special role in integrating parts of images is also supported by results of Deleval, De Mol, and Noterman (1983). They describe a patient with posterior left hemisphere damage who apparently could not integrate the parts of an image together: "When I try to imagine a plant, an animal, an object, I can recall but one part, my inner vision is fleeting, fragmented; if I'm asked to imagine the head of a cow, I know that it has ears and horns, but I can't revisualize their respective places" (p. 71; translated by M. Farah and by O. Koenig).

Grossi et al. (1986) describe a patient with a lesion in the left occipital-temporal area who could copy pictures well but could not draw objects well from memory. Such a deficit could arise for many reasons, many of which have nothing to do with imagery (such as short-term memory limitations or problems in perceptual organization, which would not necessarily affect copying). The result is interesting, however, because this patient did not simply draw poorly, but tended to place parts in incorrect locations. Similarly, he could not describe familiar places (an ability that may often rely on imagery), although he could recognize them, and hence the stored representations must have been intact; these findings suggest that he did in fact have an image generation deficit. This patient could not draw faces of individual people, however, which may imply that he had only relatively low-resolution representations of them in his exemplar pattern activation subsystem, or that he did not encode coordinate spatial relations among the parts. Unless the face was scanned carefully, I have no reason to expect that these motor-based coordinates would be stored.

Grossi et al. (1989) provided further evidence for the inference that this patient had difficulty generating images in which parts have to be arranged properly. They gave him a task devised by Paivio (1975), which requires one to listen to specifications of two times (e.g., 12:05 and 3:40), and to visualize the corresponding clock faces; the subject is to decide which face would have hands that are spread further apart (3:40, in this case). This patient could perform this task relatively well when the clocks were actually presented (he was correct on about 87% of the trials), but was unable to perform it using imagery (he was correct on only about 47% of the trials, about what would result from guessing). Thus, he apparently could make the judgment (most of the time), but could not "supply" the internal stimulus in the imagery condition. Presumably, categorical spatial representations of the positions of the hands are used to generate the image, and his left-hemisphere lesion disrupted the processes used to place images of hands in the proper locations. However, the lesion was in the occipital-temporal area, which (if it was truly limited to this region, with no remote hypometabolism in the dorsal system) would imply that he had trouble imaging the parts per se, not arranging the parts using categorical spatial relations. But it seems unlikely that the functional effects of the lesion would be so confined. It would have been useful to test him explicitly on spatial relations tasks (see also Pena-Casanova et al. 1985).

Goldenberg and Artner (1991) also studied patients with lesions in the left hemisphere, and compared these patients' performance to that of patients with lesions in the right hemisphere and to normal control subjects. The subjects evaluated low-imagery or high-imagery statements (concerning shape or color); the high-imagery statements were presented with or without pictures of the objects that should have been imaged. Goldenberg and Artner only examined accuracy, and so the results are ambiguous (there could have been speed-accuracy trade-off and/or additional deficits evident in response times). Although the patients with lesions in the region of the left temporal-occipital area did make more errors than the two other groups on the high-imagery statements, they also were impaired when the pictures were available. If these patients had an image generation deficit, showing them pictures should have circumvented the problem and hence improved their performance. Thus, the results suggest that the patients had trouble interpreting objects in images (or in pictures), not just difficulty generating mental images. Of course, the patients could have had a problem both generating and interpreting images, as would presumably occur if the pattern activation subsystems were damaged severely enough. As expected, the normal control subjects and the patients with right-hemisphere damage did show improvement when pictures were available.

More detailed analyses revealed that some of the patients with posterior left-hemisphere damage did have an imagery deficit. Unlike the majority of patients with posterior left-hemisphere damage (12 of the 19), who did not show an imagery deficit as measured here, the patients with impaired imagery had damage in the regions served by the temporal-occipital branch of the posterior cerebral artery. The patients with damage to this region appeared to have impaired color imagery, but there was only a marginally significant deficit for the shape questions (however, this could reflect a lack of statistical power; see also Goldenberg, Artner, and Podreka 1991). The fact that only damage to this region was related to an imagery deficit may suggest that a region in the temporal lobe is critically involved in implementing the pattern activation subsystems, as I have suggested; when damaged, this region may send "noise" over the corpus callosum, which disrupts homologous processing on the other side. In addition, it is possible that the patients with apparently intact imagery did in fact have disrupted left-hemisphere-based imagery, but the "noise" sent over the callosum did not disrupt right-hemisphere processing—allowing them to accomplish the task using a right-hemisphere strategy. It would have been interesting to discover whether their images tended to be of specific exemplars rather than prototypes (see also Goldenberg, Artner, and Podreka 1991).

Farah (1986) reports a divided-visual-field study with normal subjects that appears to suggest a left-hemisphere basis for image generation. She found that imaging a letter facilitates encoding that letter better in the right visual field than the left. However, Sergent (1989) notes that these results may not reflect imagery processing, but may simply indicate that the left hemisphere can be primed better in this task. But even the latter would not be a trivial finding. In any case, the finding is difficult to interpret because Biggins, Turetsky, and Fein (1990) did not replicate it, using a similar methodology.

Cohen (1975) also describes evidence that subjects can generate images of letters better in the left hemisphere. She tested subjects in a Cooper and Shepard (1973) mental rotation task, in which letters were presented normally or mirror-reversed at different orientations about the circle. The subjects were to judge whether the letters faced normally, regardless of their tilt. Cohen lateralized the stimuli, and, prior to each stimulus told the subjects either nothing, the identity of the to-be-judged letter, or the identity of the letter along with information about its orientation. She found that subjects could use advance information more effectively when the stimuli were presented initially to the left hemisphere than to the right, which suggested to her that the left hemisphere could prepare by generating the image of the letter more effectively than the right hemisphere. However, there was no independent evidence that subjects actually generated images, as opposed to priming the visual representation of the letter (which facilitates encoding) or shifting attention to the location of the top of the letter (which might facilitate rotation).

Finally, it is worth noting that several studies of brain activation have suggested a left-hemisphere role in image generation. Goldenberg et al. (1987) asked one group of people to memorize concrete words, and another to use imagery to memorize such words. They found increased blood flow in the left hemisphere when imagery instructions were given; although such comparisons between subjects are difficult to make in these kinds of studies, the results are of interest nevertheless. (This finding is a little puzzling, however, given that Paivio [1971] provides evidence that subjects use imagery to memorize concrete words even without being asked to do so.) In a later study, Goldenberg, Podreka, Steiner, et al. (1989) found increased blood flow in the inferior portion of the left occipital lobe when subjects evaluated high-imagery statements, relative to low-imagery statements (but another, spatial, task did not produce such an asymmetry). It is important to note, however, that regions in the occipital and temporal lobes were active bilaterally in both studies, and hence one cannot use these results to conclude that imagery is solely the province of one hemisphere.

Right-Hemisphere Image Generation   Corballis and Sergent (1988) reported experiments like those of Farah et al. (1985) and Kosslyn et al. (1985), but with different results. They asked split-brain patient L. B. to observe uppercase letters, which were lateralized to the right or left visual field, and then to decide whether the corresponding lowercase letter was "short" or "tall." In addition, they showed L. B. digital clock times in either visual field, and asked him to decide whether the hands on an analog clock would subtend more or less than 90° at that particular time of day.

Counter to our earlier results, L. B. was *faster* when the stimuli were presented to the right hemisphere. Unfortunately, he also made more errors when stimuli were presented to this hemisphere. Thus, he exhibited a classic speed-accuracy trade-off, which makes the results difficult to interpret. The right hemisphere could have made more errors because it was responding too quickly, before it was ready. However, both hemispheres responded at better than chance levels of performance, which indicates that both were in fact able to form the images at least some of the time.

Sergent (1989) used the divided-visual-field technique to administer the same letter-height task to normal subjects. She found that they, like L. B., responded faster when the cues were presented initially to the right cerebral hemisphere. And in this case, there was no speed-accuracy trade-off. However, her subjects participated in over 500 trials, and it seems likely that they knew the answers by heart before too long (perhaps even memorizing the verbal responses after the 24 practice trials). Nevertheless, Kosslyn and Jacobs (summarized in Kosslyn 1987) found a similar result. We found that the left or right hemisphere could be faster in this task; indeed, which hemisphere was faster sometimes changed over blocks of trials. It is possible that subjects image the letters using one of two methods: They might rely on the exemplar pattern activation subsystem (which apparently is more effective in the right hemisphere) for the global shape and on coordinate spatial relations for high-resolution parts, or they might rely on the category pattern activation subsystem (which apparently is more effective in the left hemisphere) for the global shape and use categorical spatial relations to place high-resolution parts.

Indeed, Penfield and Rasmussen (1950) report that stimulating the right temporal lobe can produce the experience of visual mental imagery of specific instances. Similarly, Goldenberg, Podreka, Uhl, et al. (1989) found more blood flow in the right hemisphere, relative to a resting baseline, when subjects began to use imagery. The imagery tasks were relatively complex and could have been performed using a number of strategies. Paivio and te Linde (1982) summarize additional evidence that the right hemisphere is involved in imagery, at least in some circumstances.

Sergent (1990) acknowledged the possibility that either hemisphere might be involved in generating images, but was disturbed by the reports that only left-hemisphere damage leads to image generation deficits. Thus, Sergent critically reviewed the individual case studies that were included in Farah's (1984) analysis, and noted ambiguities and other problems of interpretation that weakened the original conclusions. Consistent with a review published by Ehrlichman and Barrett (1983), which focused in large part on EEG studies, the evidence as a whole seems most consistent with the theory that both cerebral hemispheres can generate visual mental images (see also Paivio and te Linde 1982).

Finally, Blanc-Garin, Faure, and Sabio (1993) described two experiments conducted with a partial split-brain patient (only the posterior portion of the corpus callosum was damaged by a stroke). In one, the patient was shown uppercase letters in the left or right visual field and was asked whether the corresponding lowercase letters were short or tall. Although this patient began by showing superiority for image generation in the left hemisphere, his right hemisphere improved dramatically with practice during each of the five testing sessions. Kosslyn et al. (1985) found a similar result with patient V. P., but found that patient J. W. improved in his right hemisphere only after he was explicitly trained to imagine "mentally drawing" the letters. The right-hemisphere improvement with practice in Blanc-Garin's patient was probably not due to learning; the patient did not receive feedback, and there was little carryover of the effects of practice between sessions. Rather, Blanc-Garin, Faure, and Sabio argue that the right hemisphere may simply have become more aroused over the course of practice; it is possible that the stroke reduced the activation levels in this hemisphere to the point where complex processing was not possible until a certain level of arousal was achieved (see chapter 2). In a second experiment, Blanc-Garin and colleagues asked their patient to use an object as a "standard," and then to look at pictures or names of common objects or animals and decide whether each was larger or smaller than the standard. The most interesting result for present purposes was that there was no difference between the left and right hemispheres with the picture stimuli, whereas the left hemisphere was clearly superior with the word stimuli. With words, the right hemisphere again improved with practice (except for an odd dip during the last session). These results suggest that this patient's right hemisphere had difficulty using names to access the appropriate representations in associative memory when generating images, but could perform the other component processes adequately.

Bilateral Processing One of the major advances of research in cognitive neuroscience is the decomposition of functions such as perception, memory, attention, and imagery into sets of component processes. And each component process might be implemented in a different place in the brain (cf. Allen 1983). Hence, it seems unlikely to me that the brain has only one way to accomplish any given task, or that the processing used to accomplish a given task will be localized to a single place in the brain. Different combinations of subsystems can be used to compose different strategies. As noted earlier, the theory I have developed here suggests that there are at least four ways to generate multipart images, which either involve shifting attention (and using either categorical or coordinate spatial relations to guide the shifts) and marking regions of the visual buffer, or involve activating visual memories (and using categorical or coordinate spatial relations to juxtapose parts). Depending on the method used, different parts of the brain will be involved.

Perhaps the strongest support for the claim that image generation is lateralized to a single hemisphere comes from single case reports. However, Sergent (1990) showed that the case reports are rarely precise enough to lead to firm conclusions. In addition, Goldenberg (1989) did not find consistent and general differences in the lateralization of brain damage for patients who had difficulty performing imagery tasks. Goldenberg's study is very impressive because he examined 195 patients. The patients had circumscribed lesions or Parkinson's disease, and control patients had disorders of the spine, peripheral nerves, or muscles. Goldenberg administered tasks that presumably tapped "visuospatial imagery" and "verbal" abilities. The visuospatial imagery tasks were: counting corners of imagined letters (a variant of the Brooks [1968] task), a task in which one imagines walking along an uppercase letter and indicates when one has to turn right or left, and a variant of the Podgorny and Shepard (1978) task. The verbal tasks consisted of learning pairs of words, which were abstract, concrete, or concrete with imagery instructions. Goldenberg also administered "visuospatial control tasks" that did not require image generation, namely Ratcliff's (1979) mental rotation task and a task requiring localization of a dot. In all cases, only measures of accuracy were collected.

Goldenberg computed the correlations among the performance measures for the different tasks and submitted these data to a multidimensional scaling analysis. The solutions revealed clear clusters, which were rather similar for the left-brain-damaged and right-brain-damaged patients. The scaling solutions for both groups included one cluster that contained the three visuospatial tasks and another that contained the three memory tasks. In both cases, the dot localization and rotation tasks were not included in any cluster. In addition, the results from patients with bilateral lesions displayed a similar pattern, with the same two clusters. In contrast, the solution for the control subjects included only a cluster for the verbal tasks. Brain damage clearly did not affect the use of imagery in memorizing words the same way that it affected the use of imagery in performing the visuospatial tasks.

These results can be understood if people use visual-memory-based imagery to memorize words but use attention-based imagery to perform the visuospatial tasks—and the damage selectively affected one or the other type of imagery. If so, then the results suggest that images could be formed by either hemisphere, given the similarity of the scaling solutions. In this case, differences in damage along the ventral/dorsal axis may have been more important than differences in damage along the left/right axis. Alternatively, one could argue that the results simply show a dissociation between tasks that require memorization and those that do not. These results are difficult to interpret because each task requires many different component processes, and response times were not taken (recording response times is critical if only to guard against speed-accuracy trade-offs).[8]

If images can in fact be generated by either hemisphere, why does it seem that patients with left-hemisphere damage appear to have an image generation deficit more often than patients with right-hemisphere damage? I have five responses to this question. First, at least in some cases patients with posterior damage to the left hemisphere do not have imagery deficits (e.g., Goldenberg and Artner 1991); these people may in fact be using right-hemisphere-based imagery. Second, some left-hemisphere-damaged patients may not use such right-hemisphere imagery because images of exemplars are more difficult to generate than are images of prototypes. And when left-hemisphere damage disrupts the ability to generate images of prototypes, it may also decrease activation levels to the point where images of exemplars cannot be activated (recall my arguments in chapter 2 about the relationship between brain damage and processing deficits). Third, for some types of materials, one may not have stored an image of an exemplar, and hence cannot use such imagery when the left-hemisphere-based system is disrupted. Fourth, it is also possible that the right-hemisphere pattern activation sub-system is implemented in a more compact neural network than the left (per-haps because it does not average over inputs to form representations of prototypes) or for some other reason is more vulnerable to damage, and hence damage tends to affect both its ability to activate images and to match input (cf., Sergent 1990); thus, one will be less likely to find a "pure" image genera-tion deficit (or to diagnose one, given that the patient cannot recognize objects using this system and so one cannot know whether he or she could visualize objects). Fifth, perhaps Corballis (1991) is correct, and the left hemi-sphere contains a subsystem that combines elements according to rules, a *generative assembly device* (GAD); this subsystem would perform some of the functions subsumed by the PUT process posited by Kosslyn (1980; which—as noted earlier—I now assume to be the province of several distinct sub-systems). When this mechanism was disconnected from the posterior regions, the image would not be formed.

In any event, there is now considerable evidence that both hemispheres can generate images (see also Deloche et al. 1987), and so the important issue is not whether, but how and when; given that good examples of left-hemisphere-based and right-hemisphere-based image generation exist, we are faced with the task of understanding how the hemispheres work to produce and use imagery.

Summary: Image Generation

Five classes of image generation abilities have been discussed in this section. First, an image of a single global shape is generated when a property lookup subsystem accesses a pattern code in associative memory and sends it to the pattern activation subsystems. The most-activated pattern activation subsystem in turn engenders a configuration of activity (an image) in the visual buffer. This kind of activation is an extreme form of priming, of the sort used when one expects to see a specific object or part during perception.

Second, if high-resolution parts are required, they are added to the global image by a set of processes that relies on subsystems that are also used in perceptual top-down hypothesis testing. These property lookup subsystems access a representation (in associative memory) of the location of the part and its relation to a "foundation part" (i.e., where the to-be-added part belongs). This representation is used by the attention-shifting subsystems to shift the attention window, just as during top-down hypothesis testing in perception proper. Once properly positioned, the imagery mapping function is altered to image a new part at the appropriate location and size.

I distinguished between two ways of generating such multipart images: Either coordinate spatial relations representations or categorical spatial relations representations could be used to position the parts. I assume that if coordinate spatial relations are used, the exemplar pattern activation subsystem typically is used to image the parts; in most cases, parts with specific shapes are needed if precise spatial relations are employed. Similarly, I assume that if categorical spatial relations are used, the category pattern activation subsystem typically is used to image the parts; in most cases, parts with prototypical shapes are most appropriate if "generic" spatial relations are employed.

Third, the three types of imagery noted so far all involve visual-memory-based imagery, but one can also generate attention-based imagery. Visual-memory-based imagery requires activating representations of object properties in the pattern activation subsystem. In contrast, attention-based imagery does not require activating visual memories. Rather, spatial relations (directly or via the categorical-coordinate conversion subsystem) in associative memory are sent to the attention-shifting subsystems, which move the attention window in the visual buffer. Attention is engaged at each successive location, forming a spatial image. I again distinguished two means whereby such images are formed, which depend on the use of categorical or coordinate spatial relations to shift the attention window.

In addition, I hypothesized that images of novel combinations of familiar parts, characteristics, or objects are formed in the same way as images of objects with high-resolution parts. In this case, spatial relations representations (either decoded from a verbal description or formulated elsewhere in the system) are used to arrange global images or images of parts or characteristics. To generate an image of a novel scene, the imagery mapping function is altered just as it is when a single object is augmented, and the images of objects are formed just as they are when they are visualized in isolation.

Finally, squiggles and other forms of novel patterns are formed using attention-based imagery, only now the attention window is shifted not from one discrete location to another, but incrementally. In this case, a path of activation is left in the wake of the attention window as it is shifted.

All of this sounds relatively complex, but my hunch is that it just scratches the surface. As we learn more about the mechanisms of perception, theories of imagery will no doubt become even more complex. Fortunately, an increasing array of tools allow us to test even complex theories of the sort offered here.

IMAGE MAINTENANCE

For many tasks, images must be retained over time to be useful. Imagining how to put luggage into one's trunk is a good example. If one cannot retain the images of the previously considered pieces, one will not be able to perform the task. At the end of chapters 4 and 5 I offered reasons why mental images fade quickly, and I suggested that image maintenance is a special case of image generation. This aspect of the theory can now be elaborated in the context of the more detailed theory of image generation. Once a visual-memory-based image has been generated, the mapping functions from the individual perceptual units in the pattern activation subsystems to the visual buffer are established. If so, then one should not need to engage the mechanisms used in top-down hypothesis testing to maintain an image; rather, one should simply reactivate the compressed image representations of the global image and the parts and characteristics that were added to it. Similarly, once an attention-based image has been generated, attention is fixated on the appropriate regions of the visual buffer. To retain this image, one need only keep attention focused on those regions. Both sorts of processes adapt rather quickly, which is one reason why images become increasingly hard to maintain as one holds them for longer spans.

Maintenance versus Generation

The theory posits that the mechanisms used in top-down hypothesis testing during perception are not used in image maintenance. Uhl et al. (1990) describe results that support this hypothesis. They asked subjects to visualize a face, a color, or a route on a previously memorized map, and recorded DC shifts before and after the stimulus was named (the subjects first saw a slide with the name of the condition, followed by a spoken name). The subjects were told to maintain the image until the end of the trial was announced. Frontal areas and retrorolandic regions (from scalp locations over posterior temporal, parietal, and occipital cortex) showed DC negativity shortly after the cue was heard; this activity presumably reflects image generation, and is consistent with the PET findings discussed earlier. In addition, the DC potentials shifted with time: Activity over the frontal regions ceased, leaving only activity over the retrorolandic regions. This is as expected if image maintenance processes do not require the mechanisms that are used to integrate parts into an image during image generation. Uhl et al. also found differences in the amount of negativity for the different materials (smallest for faces, in the middle for the colors, and greatest for the map), which may reflect the difficulty of retaining each type of image.

"Chunking" during Image Maintenance

In order to maintain an image of a novel object or scene, one must first encode the image into a pattern activation subsystem as a new representation, and then must activate this new representation. I assume that the amount of material one can hold in an image is limited by the number of stored units that can be activated at the same time, for the following reasons: Each unit is activated individually, and time is required for each operation. And as soon as a unit has been activated, the image begins to fade (recall that the visual buffer does not retain representations very long; this would be very nonadaptive during perception; see chapter 4). Thus, after a certain number of units are activated, the ones that were activated initially will have faded.

In chapter 5 I suggested that the preprocessing subsystem extracts non-accidental and signal properties, which then are entered into the pattern activation subsystems. Processing in the visual buffer reflexively organizes the input unit into perceptual units, as defined by edges and regions of the same color, texture, or intensity. These units may often be fragmentary (e.g., see Marr 1982), and need to be organized further to provide useful clues for recognition; nonaccidental and signal properties organize such units into sets, which delineate higher-order perceptual units. These perceptual units (e.g., defined by a symmetrical set of lines, a pattern of stripes, etc.) serve to activate stored representations of objects, parts, or characteristics. I argued in chapter 5 that the preprocessing subsystem extracts sets of properties in accordance with "hard-wired" principles and as a consequence of prior experience, which can build new "filters" that organize the input into useful units.

The preprocessing subsystem operates on whatever input it receives, and so should play the same role in imagery. If so, then the number of elements in the input should not be the critical determinant of how much information one can maintain in an image, but rather the way these elements are arranged. If a novel pattern has the proper juxtapositions among the elements, it will be encoded as relatively few units and hence will be easy to maintain. When arranged effectively, nonaccidental and signal properties will span individual elements, leading them to be encoded in larger (and fewer) units; but with other arrangements, the same number of elements will be difficult to maintain. Chunks can be formed in part by attending to selected elements of a pattern; for example, if one focuses on a symmetrical region of a larger pattern by properly positioning the attention window, that portion may be encoded as a unit. If one did not focus on it, however, it may have been organized with other portions of the pattern. Thus, factors that influence how one "looks at" a pattern should also influence how it is chunked.

The results of Bersted (1988) speak to this hypothesis. He asked subjects to visualize scenes that contained from 2 to 8 objects, and then asked whether a specific object was present. The subjects required comparable amounts of time for all set sizes to affirm that a specific object was indeed in the image. The details of this experiment will be considered in the following chapter when we discuss image inspection, but the point for now is simple: These results demonstrate that subjects could organize images of up to 8 objects into few enough chunks to be maintained in an image at the same time. Kirby and Kosslyn (as cited in Kirby and Kosslyn 1990) asked subjects to form a clear visual image of a brick, and then to add new bricks one at a time to the image until they added so many that not all of them could be "seen clearly" at the same time. Based on the subjects' reports, we estimated that they could maintain an average of 6.3 bricks (with individuals ranging from 4 to 9). Thus, the fact that Bersted's subjects showed no increase in times or errors for up to 8 objects is evidence that they did in fact chunk the objects into fewer units.

According to the present theory, the capacity limits of mental images should be determined by three kinds of factors: First, how effectively one can chunk a given sort of material. Second, how quickly each perceptual unit fades. And third, how quickly and how often one can refresh the image. Attneave and Curlee (1983) studied image maintenance for location, and provided an estimate of how many locations can be maintained in an image. They showed subjects matrices, which varied from 3×3 to 8×8. The subjects heard 12 directions, such as "up, left, down," and were to visualize a spot moving through the matrix. At the end of the series of instructions, the subjects pointed to the final position of the spot. Half of the subjects were told to mentally divide the larger matrices into smaller regions, and such hierarchical chunking generally improved the subjects' ability to remember the pathways. Attneave and Curlee found that the subjects performed more poorly with the larger matrices, but there was a particularly large decrement in performance when the matrix was expanded from 3×3 to 4×4. This result led them to infer that a 3×3 matrix was as large as one could maintain in an image.

Kerr (1987) followed up Attneave and Curlee's study by comparing how well subjects' could retain two- and three-dimensional imaged patterns. She asked subjects to form pathways through a two-dimensional array drawn on a piece of cardboard or through a set of cubes arranged into a large cube. Kerr found that subjects were markedly better in the three-dimensional case. Indeed, they could correctly visualize a path through a $3 \times 3 \times 3$ matrix 97% of the time. At least part of this advantage apparently was due to chunking; the subjects could organize the large cubes into three 3×3 arrays. In later experiments Kerr showed that the subjects performed better if the matrices were "structured" into subregions (by inserting heavy lines). Kerr suggested that subjects can encode three distinct locations in each direction, but that this limit applies to each "chunk." The three-dimensional objects apparently invited chunking, which is why they were easier to use.

However, in a later replication, Cornoldi, Cortesi, and Preti (1991) found that subjects recalled only 82% of pathways through a $3 \times 3 \times 3$ matrix, which is not as impressive as the near-perfect performance of Kerr's subjects. This decrement may suggest that chunking strategies are affected by differences in the instructions and/or that the tactual response used in the replication may have required more time than the pointing response used by Kerr, allowing more of the image to fade. The experimenters tested not only sighted people but also blind people, and found that the blind had more difficulty with the three-dimensional pathways than the sighted. This result implies that the task was not performed solely by recalling spatial information (using sequences of coordinate or categorical relations) but also involved visual-memory imagery; the chunking operation itself apparently took place on the image representation in the visual buffer. This finding is consistent with my earlier claim that chunking can be performed only during visual-memory-based imagery.

Imagery and "Working Memory"

Image maintenance lies at the heart of the use of imagery in reasoning; such tasks usually require at least a few seconds to perform—and hence if one cannot maintain the image, it is useless. For example, one might be told that "Sally is smarter than Sam," "Sam is dumber than Sheila," and "Sheila is dumber than Sally." If one images each person as a dot on a line, with the smarter people being further to the right (and can remember which name goes with which dot), it is easy to decide who is smartest, who is dumbest, and so forth. I think of this sort of imagery as one type of "mental model," of the sort discussed by Johnson-Laird (1983).

The role of imagery in reasoning relies on what Baddeley (1986, 1992) has called *working memory*. In my view image maintenance processes define key aspects of working memory (cf. Logie 1986; Logie and Baddeley 1990).[9] Working memory relies in part on short-term and long-term memory. *Short-term memory* occurs when a perceptual structure (such as the visual buffer) is used to represent information activated from long-term memory; such representations are transitory and require effort to maintain. Visual mental images are one form of short-term memory representation. In contrast, information in *long-term memory* is not necessarily transitory and does not require effort to maintain. These representations may be modality specific, such as the representations in the pattern activation subsystems, or may be amodal, in associative memory.

Working memory includes the information being held in the various short-term memory structures plus the information that is activated in the various long-term memory structures. In addition, it includes the "control processes" (including the property lookup subsystems) that activate information in long-term memory and maintain information in short-term memory. This conception implies a dynamic relation between the contents of short-term and long-term memory. The fact that one can have "unconscious priming" (the usual kind; see Schacter 1987), indicates that more information can be activated in long-term memory than is represented in short-term memory. Given the severe capacity limits of short-term memory (e.g., Miller 1956), more information often may be activated in long-term memory than can be represented in short-term memory. Thus, there often will be a complex "swapping" process between the two types of memory, which shuffles information in and out of short-term memory. I assume that the frontal lobes play a critical role in governing this swapping process, just as they do in selecting objects or parts to be attended to or imaged (e.g., see Damasio 1985a; Goldman-Rakic 1987).

Although at present I am focusing only on visual working memory, one could argue that corresponding processes take place in each sensory modality.

Summary: Image Maintenance

Visual-memory-based images are maintained by repeatedly activating a compressed image representation or set of such representations in a pattern activation subsystem. The amount of material that can be retained in an image depends on how effectively it can be organized into chunks, which is accomplished by the preprocessing subsystem; this process is also influenced by how one attends to local regions of a pattern. Attention-based images are maintained by continuing to engage attention at the same loci in the visual buffer. Finally, image maintenance processes play a key role in visual working memory.

CONCLUSIONS

Both image generation and image maintenance can be accomplished by mechanisms that are used in visual perception. Image generation is carried out by the subsystems that access information in associative memory, prime the pattern activation subsystems, and re-allocate attention during perceptual top-down hypothesis testing, and image maintenance is carried out by repeatedly reactivating representations in the pattern activation subsystems or by re-engaging attention. These accounts are not ad hoc insofar as the mechanisms were proposed for other reasons, as was shown in the previous chapters. Moreover, not only did these mechanisms lead to accounts of key findings in the literature, but results from a perception experiment allowed us to predict the pattern of neural activity—as assessed by PET scanning—when people visualized objects. Thus, the theory is more than a post hoc explanation of previous data.

This chapter takes us most of the way toward providing the remaining pieces needed to resolve the imagery debates. In the following chapter I show that the theory can in fact provide plausible accounts for two remaining classes of imagery phenomena, those pertaining to image inspection and image transformation.

10 Inspecting and Transforming Visual Images

The mechanisms underlying image inspection and transformation often work closely together. For example, if asked whether frogs have short stubby tails, many people report that they visualize a frog, "mentally rotate" it so that it is facing away from them, and then "zoom in" on its posterior quarters to "see" whether a tail is present. But the relation between the two abilities may be deeper than the fact that they often work together. In this chapter I will argue that some of the processes that generate images also play a role in image inspection and image transformation.

Once again, the properties of these imagery abilities arise directly out of properties of our visual perception system. This claim seems intuitively obvious for image inspection; that is why we call imagery "seeing with the mind's eye." But this claim is not obviously correct for image transformation abilities; at first glance, it might seem that mental image transformations are a unique imagery ability, which evolved in the service of reasoning, and are not intimately involved in perception. After all, mental imagery is useful not simply because it helps one to remember information but also because it plays a role in reasoning—and imagery would not be very useful in reasoning if objects and parts could not be rearranged and reinterpreted in various ways. However, results reviewed in chapter 5 demonstrated that visual perception utilizes powerful mechanisms that could also alter the size, location, and projected shape of visual mental images, and I will argue here that these mechanisms do in fact underlie image transformations.

IMAGE INSPECTION

As noted in chapter 3, many researchers have provided good evidence that imaged objects are interpreted using the same mechanisms as perceived objects. This discovery allows us to explain an enormous amount of data, given the present hypotheses about the nature of these mechanisms.

Imagery and Perception

In chapter 3 I briefly reviewed key behavioral results that indicate that imagery shares mechanisms with like-modality perception. I will now briefly return to those findings and indicate how the present theory accounts for them. The findings fall into three classes: interference, facilitation, and corresponding phenomena.

First, images interfere with perception when the imaged and to-be-detected stimuli are not very similar (e.g., Craver-Lemley and Reeves 1987; Peterson and Graham 1974; Segal and Fusella 1970). Such findings may reflect competition for the state of the visual buffer at a specific location, with information from a pattern activation subsystem trying to force it into one state and input from the eyes trying to force it into another. Indeed, Goldenberg et al. (1987) found that only some of the subjects who used imagery to learn words had greater blood flow in the inferior occipital lobe, and Farah and Peronnet (1989) recorded greater occipital ERPs from subjects who reported more vivid imagery. These results are easily interpreted if more vivid images are a consequence of greater neural activity in the visual buffer.[1]

Second, by the same token, if the imaged pattern and perceived pattern are the same, then imagery can facilitate visual encoding, not interfere with it (e.g., Farah 1985). This finding may be a consequence of priming in the visual buffer and in the pattern activation subsystems, which predisposes certain regions to represent certain patterns. In this view, the facilitation may result from (1) a lowering of thresholds for a specific shape in a specific region (which is consistent with the findings of Farah 1989b), or (2) increased sensitivity in the visual buffer or pattern activation subsystems for a specific shape (Farah 1985; Sanocki 1991; Spitzer, Desimone, and Moran 1988). I expect increased sensitivity when subjects must distinguish among similar stimuli (see Sanocki 1991) or when the task leads subjects to use attention-based imagery. Indeed, Heil, Rösler, and Hennighausen (in press) showed that subjects can detect dots better when they fall on the shape of an imaged letter, but that the effect decreases when the image is larger and is enhanced when it is more compact (see also Podgorny and Shepard 1983). They suggest that the image serves to focus attention, which causes figure-ground segregation. This view is consistent with the mechanisms I have proposed. Moreover, the scope-resolution trade-off observed by Heil, Rösler, and Hennighausen is consistent with the possibility that subjects used attention-based imagery in this task. Indeed, my colleagues and I have found evidence that such imagery is used by default when subjects are asked to image the kinds of stimuli used by Heil, Rösler, and Hennighausen (see chapter 9).

Third, if imagery and perception both rely on the same encoding mechanisms, then quirks in the operation of those mechanisms should often make themselves known in both cases. I do not expect every bottom-up perceptual phenomenon to be present in imagery, however, because mental images are a transient and "weaker" type of representation. Nevertheless, we find various perceptual aftereffects (see Finke 1985, 1986; Finke and Shepard 1986) and illusions (e.g., Berbaum and Chung 1981; Finke 1985; Okhuma 1986; Wallace 1984) in imagery. Moreover, as was briefly discussed in chapter 3, we find numerous parallels in the ease of inspecting imaged and perceived objects (e.g., Bagnara et al. 1988; Freyd and Finke 1984; Podgorny and Shepard 1978).

The assumption that imagery and perception share common mechanisms allows us to understand why brain damage can cause deficits in imagery like those found in perception (see chapter 3). For example, in chapter 3 I noted that patients can have difficulty encoding shape or location in images, and that these deficits appear to follow damage to the occipital-temporal and occipital-parietal regions, respectively. This result neatly parallels corresponding deficits seen in perception proper, as would be expected if subsystems in the ventral and dorsal systems have been damaged. Similarly, Mehta, Newcombe, and De Hann (1992) describe a patient who had difficulty identifying and imaging living things, compared to nonliving things; this difficulty could arise at the level of the pattern activation subsystems; living things have more similar nearest neighbors (i.e., most similar alternative members of the category) than nonliving things (see Gaffan and Heywood 1993), and brain damage may partially disrupt the winner-take-all mechanism that allows one representation to be matched during recognition or activated during imagery. However, their patient also had difficulty retrieving facts about living things from memory; for example, if asked what a giraffe is, he could not even state that it lives in Africa. The finding that identification, imagery, and fact retrieval were all impaired together is consistent with the inference that associative memory or processing within it was disrupted. In this case, the patient could not access the necessary representations to generate the image or identify the object during perception.

Intact Imagery and Impaired Perception   However, we must consider what at first blush appears to be an embarrassment for the present theory: Jankowiak et al. (1992) and Behrmann, Winocur, and Moscovitch (1992) report patients who had difficulty recognizing objects perceptually, but could perform mental imagery tasks. I have claimed that the same processes are used to inspect actual objects and imaged objects, so how could image inspection be intact when perception is disrupted? The patients were not suffering from a retinal disease and did not appear to have low-level visual impairments.

My account for the pattern of these patients' spared and impaired abilities hinges on a simple observation: Although imagery and perception rely on the same mechanisms, those mechanisms are not used identically in the two cases. In particular, images contain "previously digested" information; they are already organized into perceptual units that have been previously interpreted. In contrast, in perception one must organize the input from scratch and match it to stored representations; one does not know in advance what the object is likely to be. Thus, problems in perceptual organization or in matching input to stored representations in the pattern activation subsystems can impair perception but leave imagery relatively intact.

This is such an important hypothesis that it is worth reviewing the two case studies in detail. M. D., the patient studied by Jankowiak et al. (1992), had bilateral lesions in the occipital-temporal area, which apparently disrupted his ability to encode multiple nonaccidental and signal properties at the same time. This deficit alone would cause slow encoding over multiple attention fixations, but the material would eventually accumulate in the pattern activation subsystems. But M. D. made many errors; he did not eventually recognize objects. Thus, I am led to infer that the damage not only impaired his ability to organize visual input effectively but also disrupted his ability to accumulate information in the pattern activation subsystems. These deficits would affect his ability to recognize objects but not his ability to visualize them. This interpretation is consistent with the pattern of results in perceptual testing, as follows.

First, M. D. could identify only 50% of the black-and-white drawings of objects and only 50% of the symbols (such as $, %) he was shown; in contrast, he could identify 91% of actual objects. He identified all of the objects when he was allowed both to see and to feel them, which shows that information was intact in associative memory and also suggests that not enough information was reaching the pattern activation subsystems or associative memory via the visual modality alone—especially when only two-dimensional, black-and-white patterns were shown. His language skills generally were intact, if sometimes slow, and thus this deficit probably was not due to the difficulty of accessing names (he also failed to use gestures appropriately to identify the objects).

Second, he also had difficulty detecting hidden figures in relatively complex designs, and had difficulty on the Hooper Visual Organization Test. These tasks rely critically on the preprocessing subsystem. In contrast, he did not have difficulty with spatial tasks, such as judging line orientation or tracing a path through a maze. Similarly, M. D. could always determine whether two drawings of common objects were the same or different, when both were visible at the same time. In this task, he could encode a small amount at a time and compare the objects point-for-point (this process would be very time-consuming; the authors did not measure response times, unfortunately).

Third, M. D. also had great difficulty recognizing faces, and appeared to try to do so on the basis of individual features. For example, he not only failed to identify Sylvester Stallone, but inferred that he was a woman because he wore an earring. However, M. D. could name perfectly either the large composite letter or the small constituent letters in Navon (1977) figures; this result shows that his attention window could be adjusted to subsume material that subtended different visual angles. His superior ability identifying letters as opposed to symbols or objects could have arisen because less information is needed to discriminate among the highly overlearned letter representations.

Fourth, when objects were presented for brief periods of time, M. D. had particular problems drawing animals, but he could draw inanimate objects. This result suggests an encoding problem. Gaffan and Heywood (1993) showed that animals are more similar visually than members of other categories, which makes them more difficult to discriminate perceptually—and hence requires that more information be encoded in order to make such discriminations.

Fifth, when asked to copy drawings, he did so in a "slow, methodical, often laborious manner" (p. 123). But he did not draw in a piecemeal fashion; he noticed the overall proportions. His problem was not in the scope of the region he could encode, but rather in the sheer amount of information he could encode.

Sixth, when given verbal cues about the category of the to-be-seen object or about the specific object, his ability to identify drawings shown briefly improved, but never became very good. If the input itself was impoverished, such cues would be of limited use. In contrast, tactile cues (being able to feel the possible object) helped him considerably. In this case, the cue allowed him to identify the objects 65% of the time. I can only conjecture that the tactile cues often activated the corresponding representations in associative memory, which in turn primed the visual representations (as described earlier). Carr et al. (1982) found that picture primes activated semantic representations more effectively than words, and something similar may be occurring here with tactile primes.

Seventh, M. D. could classify whether stimuli were real objects or "pseudo-objects" much better than he could name them. Judging from the example in figure 7 of Jankowiak et al. 1992, this discrimination often could be accomplished by encoding the overall shape envelope, without needing to encode details. Similarly, he often could categorize the object correctly (i.e., discriminate among fruits, vegetables, insects, and animals). The investigators selected objects within each category that were "visually markedly different," so that details would not always be necessary to discriminate among them. Consistent with this interpretation, ten normal control subjects also categorized the stimuli more easily than they named them.

Although the present interpretation is consistent with the results, I also worried that such a pattern of results could occur if the patient had low-level visual deficits (e.g., problems encoding high spatial frequencies), but this did not appear to be the case (although the results of a formal low-level visual examination are not reported). In many ways, this patient appears to be similar to the one tested by Humphreys and Riddoch (1987; see chapter 5).

If M. D.'s deficit really was in organizing the input in the preprocessing subsystem and in accumulating inputs in the pattern activation subsystem, then one would not expect dramatic deficits in his ability to use visual mental imagery (although it would be surprising if he were completely normal, by dint of the fact that he does have a damaged brain). And in fact M. D. answered with equal levels of accuracy questions that Eddy and Glass (1981) had previously shown did or did not require imagery; indeed, M. D. was about as accurate as two control subjects (the number of control subjects leaves something to be desired). Thus, M. D. apparently could form images. However, again response times were not recorded, and so it is possible that M. D. did have a deficit in these tasks. If M. D.'s response times were in the normal range (relative to the nonimagery control items), this might imply that he could effectively visualize just the relevant portions of the imaged object. Because he would be "looking" for a specific previously encoded property, he would not need to reorganize the entire imaged pattern, and hence the deficit in preprocessing would not be relevant. In searching the object during perception he may often have had to scan and accumulate information in the pattern activation subsystem, which was not necessary during imagery.

M. D. also was virtually perfect when asked questions about relative size, but these questions may not have required visual imagery. The two examples were, "Which is longer, a screwdriver or a saw?", which is a large enough size disparity that imagery may not have been required (see chapter 9 of Kosslyn 1980), and "Which is thicker, a blanket or a sheet?", which could have been answered using tactile imagery. In addition, 95% of M. D.'s drawings were identified by a naive control subject, but he himself identified only 45%. If we assume (though there is no reason to do so) that imagery is used when drawing, then this too would support the putative distinction between M. D.'s recognition and imagery abilities.[2]

Behrmann, Winocur, and Moscovitch's (1992) patient, C. K., had a similar pattern of deficits but differed from M. D. in several interesting ways. This patient suffered a closed head injury, which resulted in a partial left homonymous hemianopia. However, no focal lesion was present in CT scanning or MRI, but there was "a suggestion of thinning of the occipital lobes bilaterally" (p. 636). C. K. was able to identify only 18 of 60 black-and-white line drawings (the norm is 57 of 60). Unlike M. D., his errors indicated that he proceeded in "a piecemeal fashion, reconstructing elements of the stimulus and then inferring the object's identity rather than recognizing the object as a meaningful whole" (p. 636). For example, C. K. named only 11 of 23 three-dimensional objects and called a saw a "knife," a padlock an "earring," and pliers a "clothes peg." In contrast, M. D. apparently encoded the global shape, but not the details. Indeed, the two patients also copied objects differently: Whereas M. D. drew the overall proportions, C. K. copied a segment at a time, drawing the parts in an unusual order.

The two patients may have adopted different strategies to deal with their limited abilities to encode visual information: M. D. allocated the attention window over a larger region to subsume the global shape, whereas C. K. allocated the attention window over smaller parts. M. D.'s strategy may have been dictated by his difficulty accumulating information in the pattern activation subsystems over time. Alternatively, C. K.'s left hemianopia could reflect posterior right-hemisphere damage that impaired his ability to encode global forms (see chapters 6 and 7). This deficit could be at the level of the preprocessing subsystem, forcing him to encode individual nonaccidental and signal properties, or at the level of matching in the pattern activation subsystems. This sort of deficit would affect encoding global shapes, not large-sized stimuli; C. K. did no better with very small (a few millimeters) stimuli than with larger ones (several centimeters).

Although C. K. could not identify letters visually, he could identify them perfectly if he traced them. Tracing not only would facilitate encoding the nonaccidental properties one at a time, but also might allow him to match the letters to motor memories. In addition, C. K. could name all objects when he touched and palpated them. He also could provide detailed descriptions of named objects. Thus, C. K. apparently had an intact associative memory.

In striking contrast to patient M. D., C. K. could identify faces. He had no trouble identifying pictures of famous faces, and was correct on 49 of 54 items in a difficult face-matching task (the norm for males is 46). His preprocessing subsystem may have been capable of organizing faces (either because of extensive learning or innate neural organization) into relatively few perceptual units, and hence they did not overload the pattern activation subsystems. That is, C. K.'s damage may have degraded the usual organizational abilities of the preprocessing subsystem (not eliminated these abilities altogether), and such degregation did not seriously disrupt very efficient "filters" (which were represented by many redundant connections in neural networks). Alternatively, this result may suggest that C. K. only had difficulty using the category pattern activation subsystem in recognition: specific faces presumably would be recognized using the exemplar pattern activation subsystem, whereas the category pattern activation subsystem would be used to recognize generic objects.

Although he had severe perceptual deficits, C. K. had excellent imagery abilities. He was perfectly able to decide from memory whether uppercase letters have any curved lines, and was perfectly able to name the characteristic colors of objects (colors that were not memorized using verbal associates, such as the inside color of a cantaloupe). He could also determine perfectly from memory which of two similar-sized objects (e.g., Popsicle and pack of cigarettes) was larger. Similarly, he answered perfectly when asked to decide whether animals have long tails (relative to their bodies) and when asked whether animals have floppy or upright ears. He also performed other imagery tasks, such as visualizing hand configurations on a clock face and deciding which would have the larger angle. Like M. D., C. K. could draw from memory, including objects that he failed to recognize, and was unable to identify his own drawings subsequently.

In short, C. K.'s pattern of spared and impaired abilities suggests that he could activate representations in the pattern activation subsystems top-down, forming an image, or bottom-up on the basis of limited input. The results are consistent with a problem in organizing input effectively in the preprocessing subsystems. However, this difficulty was different from that shown by M. D., who appeared to be limited by the sheer amount of material that could be organized rather than the relative scope of the material. The results are also consistent with a problem in matching input to representations in the pattern activation subsystems. Specifically, representations in the pattern activation subsystems may not have properly inhibited each other, so that representations of parts were not subsumed by representations of the whole (Gurd and

Marshall, 1992, offer a similar account of these results). Even geometric figures (such as a diamond) could be recognized as juxtaposed lines rather than as entire forms. Faces may be special in that the parts are more strongly inhibited by the representation of the whole, or the whole is organized into a more tightly defined unit.

Given that C. K. could generate images, he could easily perform the imagery tasks: Virtually all of them required attending only to one part of the object at a time. It is unfortunate that Behrmann and her co-workers apparently did not ask C. K. to perform the perceptual analogs of the imagery tasks; it is possible that he could have classified lines in letters, shapes of dog's ears, and so forth as easily when he saw them as when he visualized them. The imagery versions of these tasks may be easier, however, because one often can visualize just the relevant part or characteristic, thereby minimizing the load on the subsequent recognition process.

To sum up, rather than challenging the present theory, these results are easily explained within its framework; indeed, the theory presents alternative hypotheses that could be empirically investigated. In addition to showing that the theory can account for such counterintuitive findings, I have reviewed these studies in so much detail in order to make a more general point. I find it interesting to use the theory to provide accounts for individual case studies only when the imagery deficits were examined relatively thoroughly, and so numerous possible alternative accounts can be ruled out. Without having a thorough description of a patient's processing deficits and lesion constellation, it is simply too easy to explain the findings (or, often, their converse). The brain is a remarkably complex entity, and any reasonable theory of the brain will no doubt also be complicated. To make rigorous predictions, one must compare performance on sets of tasks that have been designed to tap specific underlying processes and have accurate neurologic assessments of both the structural and functional damage. If we have only partial knowledge about a case, the theory affords too many degrees of freedom; it is easy to find many possible accounts for the result.[3]

Imagery in the Blind   M. D. and C. K. had relatively mild perceptual problems, and hence it may not not surprising that they could use imagery. However, take this to the extreme, where the patient is blind. If the blindness is due to cortical damage to the visual buffer or other essential subsystems, the patient should not be able to use imagery. Thus at first blush it may be disturbing to learn that congenitally blind people require more time to scan farther distances over images, more time to rotate objects in images through larger arcs, and more time to evaluate smaller parts of objects (see Carpenter and Eisenberg 1978; Kerr 1983; Marmor and Zaback 1976). Indeed, Zimler and Keenan (1983) found that both blind and sighted people remember objects more poorly if they were imaged as concealed than if they were imaged as "visible" (see also Keenan and Moore [1979] and the dispute between Kerr and Neisser [1983] and Keenan [1983]).

However, such results are not troublesome in light of the proposed mechanisms underlying these phenomena. First, as I shall argue in the next part of this chapter, to scan, rotate, or "zoom in," one anticipates what one would see in those situations. There is no reason why one could not also anticipate what one would feel, resulting in a kind of tactile/kinesthetic imagery. In either kind of processing, the incremental processing is a consequence of constraints on the motor system: one must move through a trajectory. Similarly, the effects of concealing an object on later memory can be explained if the blind do not image "feeling" the concealed objects. Presumably, the imaged material is itself stored, enhancing later memory (see Paivio 1971, 1986); thus, imaging an object will result in better memory—no matter how it is imaged—than not imaging it (for a similar perspective, see Millar 1990).

This is not to say that visual mental imagery does not involve modality-specific processing. To address this issue, Arditi, Holtzman, and Kosslyn (1988) considered a visual property that could not easily be mimicked by processing in another modality, namely effects of perspective. We asked seeing and congenitally blind subjects to suppose that an object was in front of them and then to point to where its left and right side would be; we measured the angles they produced when pointing. The subjects were asked to image three objects that differed in size, a car, card table, and a typewriter—and were asked to image each one three times, as if it were 3, 10, or 30 feet away. All subjects produced larger angles for the larger objects. However, when the subjects imaged the objects farther away, we observed a striking difference in performance between the sighted and blind subjects. The sighted subjects produced smaller visual angles as the distance to the object increased, as one would expect due to perspective effects, but the blind subjects did not. The blind subjects appreciated the concept of spatial extent, which is applicable to tactile, kinesthetic, and auditory modalities, but they did not appreciate a uniquely visual property. Objects subtend progressively small visual angles when viewed from further distances (according to an arc tangent function).

Thus, if the PET results described in chapters 1 and 9 were not enough, these findings show that visual mental imagery does indeed involve modality-specific visual processing. Finally, in memory tasks the blind do not benefit from "high-imagery" words in the same way as sighted people (e.g., see De Beni and Cornoldi 1988), nor do they remember three-dimensional configurations the same way (Cornoldi, Cortesi, and Preti 1991). In short, although visual and tactile/kinesthetic images share certain properties, they are not entirely the same.

Geometric Representation

Perhaps the most basic property of visual mental imagery is that images make accessible the local geometry of objects. For example, one can determine from memory whether the tip of a racehorse's tail is above its rear knees, whether the uppercase version of the letter *a* contains an enclosed region, or whether a mug is taller than it is wide. The image depicts the spatial relations among portions of an object or scene, allowing one to interpret them in a novel way.

Such spatial configurations of activity would be useless if they could not be interpreted. Consider the old conundrum, would a tree falling make a sound if there was nobody there to hear it? Although intensity is a measure of physical energy, loudness is not. To hear a sound, there must be both a physical state and an observer; a person must be present to register loudness. So, the answer to the question is no. Similarly, we would not have the experience of imagery, and image representations would not be functional, if there were no way to interpret patterns in images.

I have argued throughout this book that imaged objects are interpreted using exactly the same mechanisms that are used to interpret objects during perception. Once a configuration of activity exists in the visual buffer, input is sent to the ventral and dorsal systems and is processed in the usual ways—regardless of whether the activity arose from immediate input from the eyes or from information stored in memory. This notion lies at the heart of the similarities found between imagery and perception (see chapter 3).

At first glance, these ideas seem inconsistent with a set of results reported by Chambers and Reisberg (1985). These researchers showed subjects ambiguous figures, such as the Necker cube and the duck/rabbit. After the subjects visualized a figure, they were asked to "reverse" it, "seeing" the alternative interpretation. The subjects could not do this; if they visualized the duck/rabbit as a duck, they could not then alter the image to "see" the rabbit. If images are spatial patterns, Chambers and Reisberg reasoned, then subjects should be able to reinterpret them. Their findings led them to suggest that images are not spatial patterns, but rather are interpretations that cannot be reorganized.

However, we should take pause before accepting these findings at face value. Chambers and Reisberg used rather complex stimuli in this research, and the subjects might have been unable to maintain their images long enough to reorganize the figure. The proper test of the hypothesis requires using simple stimuli, so that such capacity limitations would not be a problem. If subjects can reorganize any type of objects in mental images, this is good evidence that images are not simply interpretations (of the sort specified in a propositional representation); rather, they must specify geometric information in the way that perceptual representations do.

Finke, Pinker, and Farah (1989) report a better test of the hypothesis, with strikingly different results. They asked their subjects to close their eyes and juxtapose or superimpose mental images of familiar patterns, and then to describe the result, and then to draw the pattern in their image. For example, try this: Form an image of an uppercase *D*, mentally rotate it 90° counterclockwise, and then put an uppercase *J* directly beneath it. Can you "see" the resulting pattern? What object does it resemble? Subjects could in fact identify the result of such manipulations (an umbrella, in this case) at much better levels than would be expected by guessing. Similarly, Pinker and Finke (1980) found that subjects could imagine the appearance of a three-dimensional scene as viewed from a novel perspective, and Finke and Slayton (1988) showed that subjects could mentally arrange geometric patterns to form recognizable patterns that were not easily anticipated on the basis of the parts themselves. Indeed, many of these patterns were not anticipated in advance by the investigators. Anderson and Helstrup (1993) extended this line of research to show that subjects could use imagery to "see" the results of novel combinations of patterns as effectively as they could use drawings; drawings helped the subjects to produce more combinations of patterns, but not more recognizable or creative ones.

In addition, Brandimonte, Hitch, and Bishop (1992) showed that subjects can "mentally subtract" part of an imaged object and reinterpret the remaining portion. They presented two visual stimuli in succession, such as a complete jump rope and then just the rope, and asked the subjects to mentally subtract the second portion from the first; in this case, the subjects could "see" that the handles looked like ice cream cones. In my terms, the subjects would encode the input image of the first object, which is organized into perceptual units by processing in the visual buffer and in the preprocessing subsystem (see chapter 5). Given the nature of the task, the subjects would attend to individual parts, and store them along with the global shape in the exemplar pattern activation subsystem. When the second stimulus is presented, it is also encoded and stored. Provided that the images are not too complex (and these were not; see p. 158 of Brandimonte et al.), the encoded representations of the first object can later be activated and an image maintained. Following this, the subject visualizes the part over the image of the complete object, adjusting it until it matches a portion of the first imaged object; this process is the same as that used during perception, when a mental image completes an input image—only in this case one is superimposing two mental images. At each point where the image of the part covers the image of the object, the image is allowed to fade; this is accomplished by altering the mapping function from the pattern activation subsystems to the visual buffer so that portion is no longer regenerated (I will shortly have more to say about the method whereby this mapping function is altered). The resulting image is then "inspected" in the usual way. I assume that some type of reasoning system controls which units are activated into the image, in accordance with the task instructions (see chapters 6 and 9 of Kosslyn and Koenig 1992). Brandimonte and co-workers also asked another group of subjects to memorize the complete pictures beforehand, and then to perform the subtraction task on the basis of images that were generated from long-term memory. They found that these subjects performed the task better if they were prevented from "recoding the pictures into a phonological form" (i.e., naming them and subvocally rehearsing the names) during learning—which provides evidence that the task was performed using imagery per se.

Helstrup and Anderson (1991) present convergent evidence from a less structured decomposition task. They showed subjects simple shapes formed by juxtaposing letters, digits, and geometrical forms (two or three elements were joined per figure), and asked the subjects to mentally decompose these patterns into recognizable elements. Not only could the subjects perform this task at better than chance levels of performance, but they were equally accurate when they performed the decompositions "in their heads" and when they were allowed to use paper and pencil. Taken together, the evidence is strong that people can indeed reinterpret patterns in mental images (see also Finke 1990; Pinker and Finke 1980).

In a subsequent paper, Reisberg and Chambers (1991) themselves note, "It seems obvious that images can surprise or instruct us. If images are unambiguous embodiments of ideas we already have, how can new information or insights be gleaned from images?" (p. 337). Good point. In this paper Reisberg and Chambers respond to this question (prompted in part by Finke, Pinker, and Farah's findings) and modify their proposal. Their idea is that an image is perceptually organized in accordance with how the object is "understood." In some of their experiments, the subjects were led to understand a shape as a nonsense pattern, and then mentally rotated it so that the shape itself now depicted Texas; nevertheless, the subjects failed to "see" what the shape depicted. In my terms, the rotated shape was organized differently when it was initially encoded than it would have been in its normal upright position (see chapter 6); the viewpoint consistency constraint cannot match an input to a stored representation that is organized into different units, and orientation clearly affects how we perceptually organize a stimulus (e.g., see Rock 1973). However, if the subjects were asked not to rotate the image, but rather to "think of it as having a new top," many more of them were able to recognize the shape. In this case, the "hint" essentially instructed the subjects to try to reorganize the stimulus mentally, which is what is necessary if it is to be recognized. This mental reorganization process is no mean feat for a pattern as complex as Texas, and hence it is understandable that less than half the subjects were successful in this condition. Reisberg and Chambers's revised position appears to come down to the claim that one's understanding of a shape affects how it is perceptually organized, and its perceptual organization places constraints on how the shape can be interpreted in an image. These observations are entirely consistent with the present theory.

Subsequent research by Hyman and Neisser (1991) and by Peterson et al. (1992) showed that subjects can indeed reconstrue even relatively complex images if they understand how to reorganize the object. For example, over half of Hyman and Neisser's (1991) subjects could reverse the duck/rabbit ambiguous figure in an image if they were told that the front of the animal they were viewing should be regarded as the back of another animal. Similarly, in a series of elegant experiments Peterson et al. showed that a number of factors affect how easily subjects can reverse ambiguous figures in visual mental images. For example, if a front/back reversible figure was used as a demonstration figure, more subjects apparently hit on the strategy of reorganizing the figure along this axis when evaluating their images. In addition, Peterson et al. also showed subjects sets of "good" (natural) or "bad" (unnatural) parts of reversible figures, and found that the subjects could reorganize their images much better if they had received the good parts—as expected if the objects must be mentally reorganized into new perceptual units in order to be reinterpreted.

Finally, Brandimonte and Gerbino (1993) provide evidence that verbal encoding impairs one's ability to reorganize images. They first showed subjects the rat/man and young girl/old woman in practice trials to teach them how to reverse figures, and then asked them to memorize the duck/rabbit figure. The subjects either remained silent or said "la, la, la" at a rate of 3 to 4 *la*'s per second while studying the figure (this activity has been shown to disrupt verbal encoding; see Baddeley 1986). The subjects were then asked to image the figure and to try to reverse it, "seeing" another object. Both 10-year-olds and adults were much better at reversing the figure if they were prevented from verbally encoding it; in both age groups, 13 of 20 subjects reversed the figure, compared to only 5 of 20 when verbal encoding was possible. Simply saying "la, la, la" per se was not at the root of the effect; subjects were better in the imagery task if they repeated this during encoding, but not if they repeated it during the imagery task itself. Verbal coding may lead one to store descriptions of specific parts and properties in associative memory— which in turn are used to reactivate specific perceptual units during imagery maintenance—and thereby tends to preserve the initial perceptual organization of the image. Consistent with earlier findings noted above, Brandimonte and Gerbino also report that if subjects knew the category of the sought object (which presumably guided search and reorganization), they could reverse more of their images.

In short, the evidence is strongly in favor of the view that visual mental images are depictive representations that can be interpreted and manipulated in novel ways.

Imagery "Pop-Out"

Introspectively, I do not always have to scan an image in search of a part or characteristic; rather, I often seem to go right to the sought material. Bersted (1988) reports results that support this introspection. Bersted tested subjects in a variant of the Sternberg memory scanning task (Sternberg 1969). He asked subjects to remember lists that contained from 2 to 8 names of common objects, and instructed them to encode the items in different ways. The subjects were asked either to form an image of a scene containing the items on the list, to form such an image and then to describe it aloud, to formulate a story connecting the objects, or simply to rehearse the names by rote. The subjects then saw a word, and decided as quickly as possible whether that word was on the list. The striking finding was that response times for "yes" trials did not increase with longer lists when the subjects formed an image but did *not* describe it, whereas they did show the typical increase in time with increasing list length in all other conditions. Thus, the subjects did not have to scan the image to locate the sought part or characteristic; if they had, they would have required more time to scan over the objects in the image with more objects (see Kosslyn et al. 1978).

In a second experiment, Bersted asked a new group of subjects to use the imagery, imagery-plus-description, or story strategies (on different blocks of trials). Unlike the first experiment, the same subjects used all three strategies, which allows one to compare the results more precisely. The findings of his first experiment for "yes" probes were replicated, with essentially no increase in time for larger memory sets in the imagery condition, but an increase in the other two conditions. Bersted (1983) obtained similar results when set sizes varied from 1 to 4 items.

Results such as Bersted's are predicted by the present theory for the following reason.[4] When the probe word appears, associative memory should prime the pattern activation subsystem to facilitate encoding the object, just as would occur in perception. But now such priming enhances the appropriate part of the image, if it is present, making it sharper. This process would cause that part or object to provide stronger input to the pattern activation subsystem when the image is encoded, which would allow that object or part to win in the winner-take-all process. Hence, one can inspect the image for the sought object or property without having to scan it an item at a time. However, if the sought item does not "win," the sought part, characteristic, or object could be implicit in the image (i.e., organized into a larger perceptual unit), and hence the imaged pattern would be scanned. Such scanning is serial; only one thing is examined at time, which explains why response times did increase with memory set size for "no" trials, even in the imagery condition. When the subject encoded a description, a list was formed in associative memory, which could be searched serially at the same time that the image was being processed.[5]

These findings are important in part because they appear to resolve a contradiction in the literature. Seamon (1972) originally reported that the typical increase in response time for larger memory sets was eliminated when subjects used images of interacting objects, but Rothstein and Atkinson (1975) failed to replicate this result (see also Kerst 1976). A major difference in the experiments was that Rothstein and Atkinson asked the subjects to describe each image. The results from Bersted's second experiment provide hints about why describing the scene may have been the critical difference between the experiments. The response time function for the image-plus-description condition is decidedly nonlinear in both of his experiments: the subjects required progressively more time as the set sizes increased from 2 words to 5 or 6 words, but not for the largest set sizes. In the second experiment, where the same subjects used all three strategies, the function for the image-plus-description condition flattens out just at the point where it intersects the imagery function. That is, the subjects were faster in the image-plus-description condition than in the imagery condition for the smaller set sizes, but required about the same time in the two conditions for the larger sets; moreover, the functions for the story and image-plus-description conditions are very similar for the smaller set sizes.

The simplest account for these findings is that the image-plus-description condition engendered two types of representations, which were processed in parallel. One representation was a list of the items, which was stored in associative memory; such a list was also constructed in the story condition. These items had to be searched serially, and hence more time was required for longer lists. The other representation was a depictive image, as was generated in the imagery condition. Although the "pop-out" search process may have taken more time than scanning a short list in associative memory, such imagery search times did not increase with set size. Thus, for shorter lists, the serial search process in associative memory finished first, but for longer lists, the imagery process was faster. In short, whichever process allowed the items to be evaluated most quickly ended up producing the response.

Bersted (1983) also presented the probes in the left visual field or right visual field, and found that response times increased with set size—even for "yes" responses—when the probes were shown initially to the left hemisphere; there was no such increase when the probes were shown initially to the right hemisphere. This finding is consistent with the possibility that the left hemisphere incidentally encoded and searched descriptions even when the subject was not asked to do so, but these representations were not very strongly encoded. Thus, only when the stimuli were presented initially to the left hemisphere did such processing finish before imagery processing. Alternatively, it is possible that descriptions were encoded so effectively that imagery processing "outraced" serial processing of descriptions only when the input was presented initially to the right hemisphere, which more effectively encoded the images (in the exemplar pattern activation subsystem).

Imagery in Question-Answering

In earlier work, my colleagues and I found that people use imagery to compare from memory the sizes of similar-sized objects, but they do not use imagery to compare from memory the sizes of very different-sized objects. For example, they use imagery when deciding which is bigger, a hamster or a mouse, but not when deciding which is bigger, an elephant or a mouse (see chapter 9 of Kosslyn 1980). To document the use of imagery, we asked the subjects to begin by forming either a "normal-sized" or "tiny" image of one of the to-be-examined objects, and then presented the name of another object. We told the subjects to determine which object is larger as quickly as possible, and emphasized that they did not have to use the image to make the decision. In such experiments, we found that subjects compared objects more slowly when they started with a tiny image only if the actual (not imaged) sizes of the two objects were similar; the subjects apparently had to "expand" the image (using size scaling) or "move closer" (zoom in) to the object in a tiny image in order to "see" subtle differences in size between two imaged objects. We found no such effects when subjects compared objects of disparate sizes or when we taught the subjects distinctive size tags prior to the size-comparison task (see chapter 9 of Kosslyn 1980).

I compared several different classes of models for such phenomena, and found that a parallel search model provided the best fit to the data. This model posited that images are generated and compared at the same time that propositional information is retrieved and compared. As in the earlier version of the theory, I assume that one stores descriptions of categories (category "tags") with the representations of objects (in associative memory, according to the present theory). For example, a mouse and a hamster might be specified as "small" (relative to animals), whereas an elephant might be specified as "large." When later asked which is larger, these size tags will allow one to judge an elephant versus a mouse, but not a mouse versus a hamster. Thus, if the size tags are reasonably well learned, they may be retrieved and compared before images are completely generated and compared. In contrast, imagery will be used either if the tag retrieval and comparison process is slower than the image generation and comparison process, or if the category tags are not sufficient to make a judgment but the requisite visual information is stored in the pattern activation subsystems.

Similar processes can be used to make judgments about geographical position. For example, Maki (1981) and Wilton (1979) asked subjects to decide whether one town is north of another; these subjects responded faster when the towns were farther apart on a north-south axis, which is exactly the opposite of what we have found in image scanning experiments. These findings can also be explained if we adopt the mechanism I posited in the earlier version of the theory (chapter 9 of Kosslyn 1980), if we assume is that categories (e.g., "northwest England") describing geographical location are stored in memory. If so, then the farther apart are two towns, the more likely it is that the tags will not match and the decision can be made quickly, without using imagery. Note, however, that the tags must be relative to the same category. Both Maki (1981) and Wilton (1979) found that subjects could judge relative position more quickly if towns were in the same geographical unit (state for Maki, county for Wilton) than if they were in different units. Moreover, when towns are close together, and so an image is used, the "pop-out" phenomenon will result in their being highlighted on the image. In this case, one need not scan to find them, and the categorical spatial relations subsystem can encode their relation. This subsystem categorizes the objects faster when their positions are more distinct; indeed, it would produce the same results if a picture were shown as it would for an image (see chapter 7).

In addition, Wilton and Pidcock (1982) describe a task that I take to require an interesting mixture of imagery and nonimagery processes (although they did not interpret it this way). They asked people to memorize a map of Europe and then to decide whether an imaginary line that connected two towns would pass through a specific country. The towns were relatively close or relatively far apart, and the intersected country was relatively large or small. Let us see how the present theory accounts for three aspects of the results.

First, the subjects evaluated larger countries faster when the towns were farther apart than when they were closer together. I assume that the subjects stored category information about the locations of the towns and countries relative to the map as a whole. For example, when studying the map they may have encoded four categories along the horizontal dimension and four along the vertical dimension. When the towns are separated by a great distance, different category information is apt to be associated with each town and the probed country; and because the country is large, one need not be concerned (most of the time) with the details of its contour. Moreover, Wilton and Pidcock selected large countries that were long and narrow, and lines that typically passed through the long axis. Thus, if the country is vertically aligned, information about the horizontal positions of the towns and countries usually will allow one to solve the problem. By analogy, it is as if one were deciding whether a horse falls in size between a mouse and elephant; the tags alone can be used to make the judgment, without recourse to imagery.

In contrast, such a tag-comparison process is unlikely to succeed for short distances because at least one of the towns is more likely to share a category tag with the country. In this case, the subjects presumably visualized the map, the locations of the towns "popped out," and a line was visualized between them (no scanning is required, just imposing a line of the right length, orientation, and position). The subject then noted whether the line fell across the named country. This process requires more time than retrieving and comparing category tags, and hence the subjects were faster with towns that were farther apart.

Second, Wilton and Pidcock obtained the opposite result with small countries; the subjects were faster when the towns were closer together. An explanation for this effect flows naturally from the account just offered: The category tags specify rather large regions, and a small country is less likely than a large one to fill at least one of these regions; depending on its precise shape, a line passing through the region may or may not pass over the country. Thus, the category tags often would not be sufficient to make the judgment, and the subjects would visualize a line connecting the towns. Moreover, the line would need to be more precise when it was longer to ensure that it fell over the country; imagine performing the analogous task with a map in front of you—with a short distance, you would be less likely to need a ruler. Countries do not have perfectly regular shapes, and so one must "look" more carefully when the towns are farther apart.

Third, this account also explains why the subjects were generally slower with smaller countries. Not only is imagery always required, but more precise images of the map and lines are necessary than would be needed when imagery is used to evaluate large countries.

Although the present theory is consistent with the data, there is no independent evidence for it (unlike my inferences about size comparisons; see chapter 9 of Kosslyn 1980). However, it is easy to devise ways to study the role of imagery in this task. For example, if imagery were more important in evaluating small countries, then having the subjects begin with a small image of the map would have had greater effects for these probes. Or, patients with imagery deficits should have particular difficulty with the small countries and with the large countries when the towns were close, and so forth.

Scanning

My first imagery experiment (Kosslyn 1973) was an attempt to use image scanning to show that image representations embody spatial extent. As reviewed in chapter 1, many additional experiments followed, and there is no doubt that people can scan over objects in mental images. I suggested in chapter 4 that the attention window plays a role in some types of image scanning; I inferred that the attention window can be shifted in the visual buffer during perception (e.g., see Sperling 1960), and hence that the mechanism is available for doing the same thing in imagery. This notion would explain why Reed, Hock, and Lockhead (1983) found that subjects required more time to scan along a bent or curved trajectory than to scan the same distance along a straight line: When the path is straight, the attention-shifting subsystems do not need to be guided by feedback from the attention window. In contrast, when the path changes, one must encode its coordinates and use this information to alter the trajectory. The more often the attention-shifting subsystems must change the trajectory, the more computation will be required and the more time will be taken to scan.

However, this cannot be the entire account of image scanning. People can scan "off screen," to objects that were not initially "visible"—and they can do this as easily as scanning the equivalent distance between two objects that were initially "visible" (Kosslyn 1978, 1980). The attention window cannot be shifted to a region outside the visual buffer. Moreover, as noted in chapter 4, the visual buffer is neither homogeneous nor isotropic, and yet the time to scan over an imaged object increases linearly with the distance scanned over the object. Thus, some other mechanism must be at work. I will discuss details of the scanning mechanism in the following section; in addition, I will discuss how one "zooms in" on an object when a sought part or characteristic is not "visible" immediately in the image. It is clear that image transformation abilities work hand-in-glove with image inspection abilities.

Summary: Image Inspection

Objects in images are inspected using the same mechanisms that are used to encode and interpret objects during perception. When one seeks a specific object, part, or characteristic, its representation in the pattern activation subsystems is primed; if the object, part, or characteristic is depicted in the image, it will "pop out" if its representation is activated in the pattern activation subsystem. If the sought object, part, or characteristic is not detected, it may be implicit in the image, and one will scan the image in search of it. Image inspection will be used to access information in memory when the sought information is not represented propositionally and cannot be deduced from propositional information, or when the image generation and inspection process is faster than the process of retrieving and using propositional information.

Scanning is accomplished by shifting the attention window and by image transformation. Similarly, if the object subtends too small a visual angle, "zooming" will be necessary; this process is also a form of image transformation. Thus, a theory of image transformation is necessary to flesh out a theory of image inspection.

TRANSFORMING VISUAL IMAGES

The vast majority of studies in the literature on mental image transformations address mental rotation. I believe that this is in part a historical accident. Shepard and Metzler (1971), followed shortly by Cooper and Shepard (1973), had an enormous impact on the field. Not only were their data very systematic and straightforward, but also the results were surprising—and perhaps even paradoxical to some; it is not immediately obvious why an object in a mental image should require more time to rotate greater amounts, given that images are not constrained by the laws of physics to pass through a trajectory. Many researchers were intrigued, and an extensive literature has blossomed. Although I will not review the entire literature here, I will discuss representative examples of each type of research with normal and brain-damaged populations. (I will not discuss research on special populations, such as children, the elderly, or psychiatric patients.) In addition, we will briefly consider image scanning, zooming, and other sorts of image transformations.

I am led to infer that image transformation processes alter representations in the visual buffer itself. One could not visualize the results of the kinds of transformations people can perform (such as rotating, translating, scaling, bending, or folding objects), and reinterpret the transformed shape, unless representations that preserve the local geometry of the object are modified. This claim is consistent with the finding that the occipital lobe is activated during image rotation (Deutsch et al. 1988). Indeed, using functional MRI, Cohen, Kosslyn, Thompson, Breiter, DiGirolamo and Anderson have preliminary data that suggest increased activity in area V1 when people rotate Shepard and Metzler figures.

In a departure from my earlier work, I argue here that visual mental images are transformed in part via motor processes. This hypothesis first occurred to me when I saw a brain-damaged patient behaving oddly in a mental rotation task. We were fascinated to observe that when the stimulus appeared on the screen, she consistently reached up to the screen and pretended to twist the stimulus. Seeing this reminded me of something Jacky Metzler, then testing subjects for the now-classic mental rotation paper by Shepard and Metzler (1971), said when I was a graduate student. She commented that some of her subjects reported "kinesthetic imagery" in their hands while participating in this task. It is clear that spatial representations play a key role in motor control (e.g., see chapter 7 of Kosslyn and Koenig 1992), and such observations led me to conjecture that mental image transformations themselves may hinge on motor processes. As it happens, there is good support for the role of motor processes in mental image transformations, both from studies of animals and from studies of humans. Thus, the present theory of image transformations is quite different from that offered in Kosslyn (1980).

Motor Processes and Image Transformations

Georgopoulos et al. (1989) report compelling data that the monkey motor cortex is involved in at least one form of mental rotation. They showed a monkey a light in the center of a display, and trained it to move a handle toward the light. The center light was turned off after a variable period, and a second light was turned on. This second light appeared in one of eight locations. In addition, the light was dim or bright, which cued the monkey for the specific task. When dim, the monkey was to move the handle to the light; when bright, it was to move the handle counterclockwise to a position that was perpendicular to the light. Thus, when the light was bright, the animal had to perform a kind of mental extrapolation.

Georgopoulos et al. recorded from neurons in the primary motor strip while the animal performed this task. They compared activity before the light changed with activity afterward, and found that the activity of individual neurons varied when the arm was in different positions. The neurons were tuned for specific orientations (see Georgopoulos, Schwartz, and Kettner 1986), and Georgopoulos et al. discovered their tuning by observing activity during the trials with a dim light. These findings allowed them to interpret the pattern of neural activity during the mental rotation trials, which was also recorded. They found that neurons tuned for the starting arm position fired the most at the beginning of the trial, but then other neurons became more active. The neurons that were most active changed over time in a systematic way: Those that were tuned for positions along the trajectory were activated in turn, just as if the animal were rotating mentally through the intervening positions! This shift occurred within the first 225 ms or so after the light changed—before the actual movement began (about 260 ms after the light changed). The changes in neural activation mimicked a movement in a counterclockwise direction, which anticipated the actual motion.

These data are good evidence that at least one kind of mental rotation involves motor processing. However, we must interpret these findings with caution. First, this sort of mental rotation is intimately related to movement; the results may not generalize to rotation that is not used to compute a movement trajectory. And second, these results do not show that the rotation actually occurred in motor cortex. It is possible that the rotation operation actually took place in visual cortex, or somewhere else, and this operation in turn was driving motor cortex. Third, there is of course no guarantee that these results generalize to humans.

There is evidence, however, that the motor system is involved in image transformations when humans imagine making movements. This line of work began with a study reported by Cooper and Shepard (1975), who asked subjects to view hands and decide whether both were left or both were right hands. The hands were rotated and presented either palm-up or reversed. Not only did response times increase with greater rotation, but the relative difficulty of evaluating certain positions suggested that subjects were mimicking the actual movement of the hands. Later experiments by Parsons (1987a, b) showed that the process of mentally rotating one's hands and feet seems to simulate the process of actually moving them; subjects required more time to perform mental rotations that would have been physically awkward. Similarly, Sekiyama (1982) showed that subjects mentally rotate hands faster in the "manageable direction" (e.g., the left hand was rotated clockwise more easily than counterclockwise, and vice versa for the right hand). Sekiyama (1983) had subjects actually move their hands into the positions indicated by a picture, and then asked them to rate the difficulty of moving the hand to that position. These ratings lined up well with the response times she reported earlier. In addition, Sekiyama reports that the subjects almost always used the correct hand when matching the drawings, which suggests to me that they performed mental rotation before beginning to move. (Otherwise how could they know whether it was the right or left hand?) It would be of interest to measure the time that subjects require to initiate a movement in this task; if one really does mental rotation first, then one should require more time before beginning to move one's hand into a position that requires more rotation.

Cooper and Shepard (1975), Parsons (1987a, 1987b), and Sekiyama (1982, 1983) studied imaged transformations of body parts. One could ask, however, whether these results imply anything about how one mentally rotates other sorts of objects. Thus, it is important that other researchers have studied brain activation when humans perform mental rotation, and have found that parts of the brain that are involved in motor programming are activated during mental rotation even when the rotation is not used to compute a movement trajectory. In particular, Deutsch et al. (1988) used the ^{133}Xe technique to observe brain activity while subjects performed Shepard and Metzler's (1971) mental rotation task. Deutsch et al. found selective activation of portions of frontal and parietal cortex that are clearly involved in programming and executing actions (see chapter 7 of Kosslyn and Koenig 1992). Similarly, using the same technique, Decety, Philippon, and Ingvar (1988) found that the prefrontal cortex, supplementary motor cortex, and parts of the cerebellum were activated when subjects actually wrote letters and when they simply imagined that they were writing them.

The proposal that the motor system is intimately involved in imagery is not new (e.g., see Annett 1990; Finke 1979; Johnson 1982; Weimer 1977). However, most of the findings in the literature are consistent with the view that the motor system is slaved to the visual system, not that the motor system alters visual representations.[6] For example, Finke (1979) showed that imagery can substitute for visual feedback in biasing the motor system. In one type of perceptual-motor adaptation experiment subjects wear prisms that displace the world to one side; the subjects monitor the position of their arms when pointing. They then remove the prisms and point, and typically now have a bias to point as if they were still compensating for the effects of the prism. Finke showed that this effect occurs even if subjects merely visualize seeing their arms being displaced, instead of actually seeing them displaced.

In addition, there is a literature that imaging practicing can actually improve performance in some situations, provided that imaged practice is intermixed with actual practice (for reviews, see Corbin 1972; Goss et al. 1986; McBride and Rothstein 1979; Richardson 1967). Kohl and Roenker (1983) argue that proprioceptive feedback from the periphery is not responsible for the role of imagery in motor learning. Rather, they claim that the motor programs that are set up during imagery are themselves the basis for later improvement when the task is actually performed (compared to when no such imagery practice occurred; see Kosslyn and Koenig 1992, chapter 7). One prediction of this hypothesis is that imagining practicing a rotary pursuit task with one hand should enhance one's ability to perform the task with either hand—which was in fact true. However, more transfer occurred when the task was actually practiced, and this transfer was greatest to the same hand. These findings suggest that imagery only activates relatively "high level" aspects of the motor system (see also Johnson 1982).[7]

Other findings suggest that the motor system is not passively slaved to the visual system in imagery. For example, Quinn and Ralston (1986) report that motor movements selectively interfered with visual mental imagery. They asked subjects to listen to digits and to mentally place them in specific cells of an array. The subjects listened to these stimuli in four conditions: while keeping their hands in front of them, while tracing out the pattern formed by the digits, while moving their hands through the matrix in a simple pattern that had nothing to do with the digits, or while tapping. Incompatible movements disrupted memory (relative to the first condition), whereas compatible movements or tapping did not.[8] Logie and Marchetti (1991) showed that one's ability to retain such information in memory can also be disrupted by unseen arm movements; but other findings suggest that motor movements will only disrupt image retention if the subject is "rehearsing" an imaged sequence (see Quinn 1991; Smythe and Pendleton 1989).

Such findings are consistent with my proposal that the rotation process can be guided by input from the motor system. However, it is clear that the rotation operation itself involves visual mechanisms. For example, consider the results of Corballis and McLaren (1982). They showed subjects a rotating textured disk prior to presenting letters in a mental rotation task, and found that subjects tended to prefer to mentally rotate the letters in the opposite direction of the disk—apparently being influenced by motion aftereffects from the disk. Subjects appeared to rotate their images more slowly when the motion aftereffect was in the opposite direction as the direction of mental rotation, and seemed to rotate their images faster when the image moved in the same direction as the aftereffect (see Corballis 1986a). However, it is not clear that the aftereffect really influenced the rate of rotation per se, rather than simply biasing the subjects toward rotation in a particular direction; if the subjects sometimes rotated the "long way around" to the standard upright, this would give the appearance of slowed rate (for additional discussion and related evidence, see Corballis and Blackman 1990). In either case, such effects are evidence for visual processing in mental rotation.

Jolicoeur and Cavanagh (1992) used a different technique to study the interaction between image rotation and perceived rotation. They presented letters at various tilts and asked the subjects to determine whether the letter faced normally or was mirror-reversed. The letter itself actually rotated, or the background rotated. They found interference if the letter physically rotated the opposite way as the mental image (i.e., the "long way around"), but not if the background rotated. In addition, the shape of the letter was defined by a difference in luminance, color, texture, relative motion, or binocular disparity. Similar results were obtained in all conditions; this is good evidence that mental rotation operates on a relatively high-level representation, which is produced in common by the different stimulus conditions.

Shepard and Judd (1976) also present evidence that mental rotation relies on visual processes. Using the Shepard and Metzler (1971) stimuli, Shepard and Judd found that longer interstimulus intervals (ISIs) were required to produce good apparent motion when the stimuli had greater angular disparities. These findings were qualitatively similar to those reported by Shepard and Metzler in their mental rotation task; in both cases, more time is required when objects are "seen" to be rotating greater amounts. Such findings led Shepard and his colleagues to suppose that the rotation is accomplished by purely perceptual processes.

However, given Jolicoeur and Cavanagh's findings, it seems unlikely that low-level visual processes are used in mental rotation per se. I worry that Shepard and Judd's study rests on a correlational logic; the fact that angular disparity had similar effects in the two tasks does not necessarily show that common processes were at work. Indeed, subsequent work has shown that apparent motion is determined by the angular disparity of the stimuli and by the ISI, but that mental image rotation is determined by a host of factors. For example, Friedman and Harding (1990) found that subjects had more difficulty mentally rotating stimuli around an oblique axis than a vertical one—but found it equally easy to see apparent motion in the two cases. Indeed, Parsons (1987c) found large variations in the speed of mental rotation depending on the axis of the orientational difference between two members of a pair (of Shepard-Metzler stimuli). It is tempting to suspect that oblique mental rotations are more difficult in part because it is harder to "get a grasp" on the objects. In fact, in Friedman and Harding's study, the slopes of the rotation functions for vertical and oblique axes are very similar, but the oblique rotations require more time overall—just as would occur if it takes one longer to "set up" the process. Parsons's results are more complex, and he suggests that the results for the different axes reflect differences in the type of rotation (shortest-path or "spin-precession"), the rate of rotation, and the time to initiate the rotation process. These findings may reflect a complex mixture of motoric and visual processing; it would be of interest to observe people with actual models of the forms and measure the time to perform the corresponding physical transformations.

Motion-Encoded versus Motion-Added Transformations

On the face of things, it seems plausible that two general methods could be used to visualize moving objects. First, stored representations of moving objects could be activated. The claim that motion relations are extracted and stored during perception suggests that in some cases moving mental images can be created simply by activating stored representations. For example, if one views a running horse, one later may be able to visualize it. I call this a *motion-encoded* transformation. Second, one can visualize an object that was previously viewed in a static situation, and imagine its appearance as it rotates, is stretched, breaks into pieces, and so forth. In this case, one is not simply "playing back" previously encoded memories. I call this a *motion-added* transformation.

Both types of transformations may involve an interplay between motoric and visual processing. First, let us consider the claim that motor processes may be involved even in motion-encoded transformations. The scope-resolution trade-off implies that one must add parts or characteristics to an image to have a high-resolution image of the object. This is a special problem if the object was moving. In this situation, the location of the "foundation part" (on the global shape) must be encoded at a specific point in time, and the encoding of the part or characteristic may have occurred subsequently. Because the object was moving, portions of it must have been encoded over a period of time, and hence a number of eye movements were made. The eye movement patterns could be used to index when a given encoding was made, and these eye movement patterns could be stored (see Noton and Stark 1971). If so, then it makes sense that eye movements would be executed when the image is generated. In such imagery, I suggest that the position of the eyes is itself a cue that is used to access the next image in the sequence, and also indexes which representations of parts and characteristics are appropriate at a given location at that point in the sequence.

Indeed, Stark and Ellis (1981) summarize evidence that subjects make similar eye movements when they recognize a pattern to those they made when they initially encoded it. Stark and Ellis want to infer that the pattern of eye movements itself is stored, but one could argue that these results indicate that the same perceptual factors that dictated the initial pattern of eye movements dictate the subsequent pattern of eye movements. Nevertheless, Brandt et al. (1989), de Groot (1965), and Gopher (1973) find that subjects make systematic eye movements while they are recalling spatial information or using it to solve problems; these eye movements, at least in some cases, appear to reflect the spatial structure of the object or scene (I too collected such data but never published them). These findings lead me to suspect that motor programs are also executed when one reconstructs a memory of a moving object in an image.

Eye movements need not be the only type of motor information used to recall images. For example, Conway et al. (1991) report that subjects can visualize familiar routines, such as making a cup of tea. In such cases, arm movements and the like may index visual memories instead of, or in addition to, eye movements.

Consider now motion-added transformations, which occur when one causes an imaged object to move in a way it was not moving when the representation was initially encoded. For example, if one has seen a letter only in its standard upright orientation, visualizing it rotating requires adding movement to a pattern that was not moving when it was encoded. This sort of imaged motion underlies the kind of processing that Lowe posited: When imagery feedback augments an input, the mapping is altered until the feedback maximally "covers" the shape in the visual buffer—one does not simply activate a previously stored motion sequence. This second kind of imaged motion could be produced by incrementally altering the mapping function from the pattern activation subsystem to the visual buffer. Such moving images are a kind of "mental simulation" of what would happen if one moved or manipulated an object in a specific way.

According to the present theory, orientation is not represented explicitly in the pattern activation subsystems; rather, this spatial property is encoded in the dorsal system. Thus, to transform the orientation, size, or location of an imaged object using a motion-added image transformation, one first alters representations in the spatiotopic mapping subsystem, and then modulates the mapping function from the pattern activation subsystems to the visual buffer so that the image is consistent with the modified spatial properties. As the representations of an object's spatial properties are altered, the visual angle, orientation, or shape of the image must be modified.

In my view, the motor system plays a role in motion-added image transformations by altering an object's representation in the spatiotopic mapping subsystem, and thereby guiding the transformation itself. My hypothesis is that *one actively anticipates what one will see when one makes a movement*, and this anticipation not only primes representations of object properties in the pattern activation subsystems (as was discussed in chapters 7 and 9), but also alters representations of spatial properties in the spatiotopic mapping subsystem. In perception, if one anticipates manipulating an object, the appropriate representations in the pattern activation and spatiotopic mapping subsystems are primed. In imagery, the priming processes are so strong that a mental image is generated, and this image moves through the sequence one anticipates seeing.[9]

Many others have suggested that one's expectations about the consequences of acting in a particular way affect one's perception (for a brief review and evidence that motor processes affect the perception of visual illusions, see Coren 1986). For example, Muensterberg (1914) claimed, "We all perceive the world just as far as we are prepared to react to it" (p. 141). And many others have suggested that imagery arises when one anticipates perceptual events (e.g., see Hochberg 1981, 1982; Neisser 1976; Shepard 1984). My proposal appears especially similar to that of Droulez and Berthoz (1990), who note that the maximal speed that one can rotate mental images is "of the same order" as the maximal speed that one can make orienting movements. This observation leads them to suggest that mental rotations are computed on the basis of a "simulated oriented movement"; they argue that the process that produces such simulated movements is used in actual motor control.

Without question, the processes that program the motor system interact intimately with those that subserve visual perception. For example, Prablanc, Pelisson, and Goodale (1986) showed that people can reach about three times more accurately if they can see the target throughout the entire reaching movement than if the target is removed shortly after the reach is initiated; this finding shows that the action is not entirely "open-loop," but rather vision is used to correct it on-line. Neurons in the posterior parietal lobe appear to play a special role in this process (e.g., see Kalaska and Crammond 1992; Taira et al. 1990; Sakata et al. in press). Moreover, connections exist between regions of the parietal lobe and frontal lobe that are involved in motor control and the regions of the frontal lobe and inferior temporal lobe that presumably implement the pattern activation subsystems (e.g., see Felleman and Van Essen 1991). And in fact, damage to the posterior parietal lobe can cause human patients (Perenin and Vighetto 1983) or monkeys (Lamotte and Acuna 1978) to have trouble anticipating the consequences of reaching, which results in their needing to guide reaching very carefully under visual control; such deficits can result from unilateral lesions and be restricted to one visual hemifield (sometimes with either hand when it reaches into that hemifield). Goodale, Pelisson, and Prablanc (1986) showed that when a target changes position in the middle of a reach toward it, normal people can correct the trajectory of the limb even if they cannot see their hand.

At first glance, the role of vision in guiding movement again might appear to imply merely that motor activity is slaved to vision. However, this correction process is very fast, which suggests a rather tight linkage between what one expects to see as a consequence of making the movement and an error-correction motor output system (for relevant computational models, see Mel 1991; Reeke et al. 1989; for a review of other such models, see Kosslyn and Koenig 1992, chapter 7). Andersen (1989) concludes that neurons in the posterior parietal lobe, an area that brain scanning has shown to be active during image transformations, "generally have both sensory and movement-related responses. Cells responding to reaching behavior also have somatosensory inputs, and cells responding to smooth pursuit, saccades, or fixations also respond to visual stimuli" (pp. 397–398). Thus, these cells could participate in priming the visual system so that one can more easily encode anticipated visual feedback.

Freyd (1987, 1993) summarizes a series of findings that suggest that one actually stores the anticipated visual consequences of an action or event. She and her colleagues have documented a phenomenon they call "representational momentum." When one sees a sequence of static images that progress along a trajectory (such as a person in the act of jumping off a wall, beginning to fall, falling farther, etc.), one is likely to misremember the final member of the sequence as being farther along the trajectory than it actually was. Similarly, as one begins to copy a pattern, but does not complete the drawing, one later remembers having produced more than one actually did produce. Such findings suggest that subjects extrapolate the progression and store the end result of this anticipation. Indeed, Finke and Shyi (1988) found that memory shifts are highly correlated with the actual rate at which implied motion is extrapolated along a trajectory. Such results are consistent with the claim that representations of anticipated impending events are primed.[10]

If images are formed by mechanisms used to prime what one anticipates seeing after an action is performed, then we can understand a fascinating result reported by Meador et al. (1987). Meador et al. studied three patients who had right parietal lesions and accompanying unilateral neglect. As was reported by Bisiach and his colleagues (see chapter 3), Meador et al. found that the patients not only ignored objects to their left in perception but also neglected objects to the left in their mental images (see also Bisiach and Berti 1988). But Meador et al. introduced a twist into the testing: They asked one of the patients to move his head and eyes so that he actually looked into the left half of space when recalling objects from mental images—and found that this instruction markedly improved his ability to "see" objects on the left side of his images![11] By anticipating what he would see, he apparently was able to shift the previously neglected material into regions of the visual buffer that could be selected by the attention window.

The two types of image transformations may often work together. Perception is not like a camera, even a movie camera. One's attention wanders, and one often does not study an object carefully. Thus, one may not have encoded all of a pattern of movement, or very much of it over a length of time. Rather, one may have encoded a succession of images (as the philosopher Bergson [1954] seems to have suggested). In this case, motion-added imagery will supplement motion-encoded imagery.

Shape Shift Subsystem

Image transformations require that spatial representations and the image mapping function be altered in tandem. The computations underlying this process are distinct from the others considered so far; hence, I am led to hypothesize another subsystem. Once an image is formed (in the usual ways), the *shape shift subsystem* receives input (often from motor programming subsystems) and alters representations in the spatiotopic mapping subsystem; it then modulates the mapping function from the pattern activation subsystems to the visual buffer so that the image will be consistent with the modified spatial properties. Thus, the shape shift subsystem causes the configuration of activity in the visual buffer to shift. This subsystem is also used in perception to anticipate the visual feedback that would be produced by executing a motor program. I conjecture that this subsystem can also be programmed on the basis of anticipated interactions among objects, using information in associative memory, but the details of such processing are an open question.

Incremental Transformations, Reconsidered

In *Image and Mind* I suggested that mental image transformations might occur in small steps because the representations specify individual parts, which are transformed separately. Because the system is noisy (as are all physical systems), each part would be shifted a different amount, and error would be proportional to the size of the increment. Thus, imaged objects would tend to become scrambled and need to be realigned. At the core of this hypothesis was the idea that if the increments were too large, the scrambling would be too severe to realign using "dumb" local computations—and thus one transforms imaged objects in small steps.

One problem with this theory is that individual parts may not always be specified explicitly in the representations of shapes, as was discussed in chapter 6. Another is that even single-part shapes, such as a straw, tend to be mentally rotated incrementally—not in a single leap, using what I called a *blink transformation*: letting the initial image fade and generating a new one in a different location, size, or orientation. If rotation were incremental because parts otherwise become scrambled, one would not expect such processing when only a single component was present.[12]

An alternative account follows from the notion that motion-added image transformations rely on anticipated consequences of actions. Because objects move through trajectories, we typically anticipate seeing them—and visualize seeing them—move in such a manner. And so, we transform objects in small increments.[13] Indeed, we can transform imaged objects in ways analogous to how we can manipulate them; years ago I performed (but never published) experiments that showed that people can perform even very novel image transformations, such as "seeing" a rolled-up carpet unfurling and estimating how long it would be, "seeing" a hinge opening and assessing how far it would extend, and so on.

The present theory is a departure from the earlier version of the theory in another important way. The earlier version posited that image transformations operate on the surface image itself (the representation in the visual buffer), whereas the new theory posits that transformations occur by altering the mapping function from the pattern activation subsystems to the visual buffer. This feature of the new theory grew out of the function of image transformations in perception (see chapter 5), which is most effectively accomplished if images are transformed by altering the mapping function directly. I no longer see the necessity for positing that image transformations are actually performed in the visual buffer, as opposed to the results of such transformations merely being "displayed" there.

This development is fortunate, given the findings of Corballis (1986b). Corballis measured mental rotation slopes when subjects rotate letters with no memory load, when they rotate while simultaneously remembering 8 numbers, or when they rotate while simultaneously remembering a random-dot pattern containing 8 dots. The slopes were the same in all three conditions, although the subjects required more time overall (i.e., the functions had higher intercepts) with the memory loads. This finding suggests that attention does not play a critical role in the rotation process itself (although it is used to "set up" the rotation process, as witnessed by the different intercepts of the functions). These results are counter to what the earlier version of my theory would have predicted, given that I posited that we rotate images by attending to each part and shifting the location of the part in the visual buffer.

Probably the strongest evidence that images are transformed in the visual buffer is that found by Shwartz (1981). Shwartz showed his subjects a series of trials with pairs of Attneave random polygons (angular bloblike shapes); the polygons were relatively large or small. He asked the subjects to rotate the first member of a pair to a specific orientation; they pressed a button when it was fully rotated, and then a second polygon appeared. The subjects decided whether the first and second polygons were identical, regardless of their relative orientations. Shwartz not only found that subjects required more time to rotate the stimuli progressively farther from the standard upright, but he also found a sharper increase in time per degree of rotation for larger stimuli. This finding suggested to Shwartz and me that more time was required to process a larger region of the visual buffer when one rotated the large stimulus each increment, and these times compounded so that the large stimuli had steeper rotation slopes than the small stimuli.

Unfortunately, the effect of size on rotation time was not replicated with different materials, either in my laboratory or in other laboratories (Suzuki and Nakata 1988). The key property of Shwartz's random-polygon stimuli may have been that all the information that was required for the subjects to judge same/different was at the edges, and hence the subjects may have scanned around the edges as they were rotating the figures, augmenting their global images with details about local portions (generating these images using the processes described in the previous chapter). If so, then the subjects would have required increased times for larger stimuli because they had to scan greater distances; I assume that the subjects scanned over the entire contour after shifting the image a set amount (to keep it refreshed), and therefore required progressively more time to rotate larger images greater amounts. (Note that this account still hinges on properties of depictive images, and hence the finding can still be taken as evidence for such representations.)

Consistent with this hypothesis, Suzuki and Nakata (1988) found that neither the objective nor retinal size consistently affected the rate of mental rotation of Shepard-and-Metzler-like figures. In some conditions, however, the retinal size of the stimuli did affect mental rotation rates—but in the opposite direction to what Shwartz found. When the room was lit (so that size and distance cues would be more accessible), the subjects rotated the smaller figures in "same" pairs relatively more slowly than the larger ones. Unlike most such studies, Suzuki and Nakata (1988) found no evidence that the subjects rotated the stimuli in "different" pairs. This result suggests that the different stimuli were quite distinct, and could be discriminated purely on the basis of bottom-up matching in the pattern activation subsystem. If so, then the subjects presumably rotated the "same" pairs because they feared that the members of at least some "different" pairs were subtly different, and hence allowed the imagery feedback process to be completed. This process helped them to compare the figures carefully, which required more precise inspection of the corresponding portions of the small figures at each increment than was necessary for the larger figures (the small figures subtended 2.9° of visual angle, compared to 5.7° and 11.5° for the medium and large sizes).

The scanning hypothesis allows us to explain why more complex stimuli require longer to rotate in three circumstances: when the stimuli are relatively unfamiliar (Bethell-Fox and Shepard 1988); when the subjects adopt a part-by-part strategy (Bethell-Fox and Shepard 1988; see also Paquet 1991); and when the subjects rotate in preparation for making a subtle discrimination between the shape and a similar distractor (Folk and Luce 1987).[14] In all of these circumstances, the subjects may scan local details to augment the global image during the rotation process. If so, then it may not be the rotation operation itself that is affected by stimulus complexity, but rather the process of scanning to ensure that local portions of the contour are present (and generating portions of the image, if need be) that requires more time for more complex shapes. In fact, Kosslyn, Ball, and Reiser (1978) found that an increment of time was required for each item that one scanned over in an image; thus, scanning more complex shapes may require more time than scanning simpler shapes, provided that one must keep the local details sharp. If the figure is scanned at each increment of rotation, then we expect an interaction between complexity and amount of rotation: The overall difference will compound as the figure is scanned more times in the course of larger rotations.

Indeed, Yuille and Steiger (1982) found that more complex Shepard-Metzler stimuli require more time to rotate mentally, provided that the subjects do in fact rotate the entire figure; presumably, they scan over it to ensure that all of its parts and characteristics are present. When the subjects were told that they could perform the task by rotating only part of the figure, their rotation speed increased. Moreover, when the stimuli were very complex, some subjects spontaneously discovered ways of only rotating part of the patterns. In contrast, if none of the three conditions noted above obtains, and hence subjects are not encouraged to scan the contours to retain high-resolution images of the components as they rotate, then subjects can rotate complex shapes as easily as simpler ones (Cooper and Podgorny 1976).[15]

In addition, Jolicoeur et al. (1985) found that people can mentally rotate two-dimensional objects in images faster than very similar planar projections of three-dimensional objects, which also suggests that the previous theory was too simple: Jolicoeur et al. ensured that the planar projections of three-dimensional objects occupied the same region of the visual buffer as the two-dimensional objects, and so the difference in rotation rates probably did not reflect processing material in the visual buffer itself. Similarly, the two types of objects had similar amounts of internal structure, and hence differences in complexity per se cannot explain the results. In the spirit of Tye's (1991) ideas about an augmented representation in the visual buffer, and the claim that image representations are like Marr's (1982) 2.5 D sketches, I posit that there is more information at each point (specifying depth) when one has an image of a three-dimensional object. But this will not solve the problem: even for two-dimensional figures, information about depth must be specified at each point. Rather, the key may be that the mapping function from the pattern activation subsystem to the visual buffer is more complex for three-dimensional objects. If an object varies in the third dimension, the rotation must take into account hidden-line removal, changes in perspective, and so forth. Hence, more time will be required to update the mapping function when a three-dimensional object is rotated through each increment than is required when a corresponding two-dimensional pattern is rotated.

However, I must note that S. Shepard and D. Metzler (1988) argued that two- and three-dimensional objects (Attneave random polygons versus Shepard-Metzler figures) are rotated at equivalent rates. Unfortunately, this conclusion was not warranted by their data. Not only did the three-dimensional forms require more time in general (which they attribute to differences in encoding the stimuli), but S. Shepard and D. Metzler did in fact find an interaction between dimensionality and rotation rate (with steeper slopes for the three-dimensional figures). But these results are difficult to interpret; as noted by S. Shepard and D. Metzler, the two- and three-dimensional stimuli were not equated for psychological complexity (the two-dimensional form was very complex; the three-dimensional form was not), and the two-dimensional form was rotated in the picture plane whereas the three-dimensional one was rotated in depth. Jolicoeur and Bauer (in preparation) note other problems with this study.

Finally, the mechanisms proposed here could explain why Jolicoeur (1990b) found that subjects can identify misoriented letters more quickly if they are presented with another letter in the same orientation than if they are presented with another letter in a different orientation. He suggested that a "pattern rotation process" can itself be primed; in my terms, this finding is analogous to performing the same action twice in a row. Altering the mapping function the same way twice in a row probably is easier than setting it two different ways in succession. Alternatively, this finding may not reflect mental rotation, but instead may bear on perceptual organization: to recognize misoriented letters, one may need to perceptually organize them so that they have the same internal structure that they would have if seen upright (and hence will match the organization of stored representations of the letters). Hence, one seeks the top of the letters and organizes them accordingly. Presumably, the letter was not recognized immediately, but could be identified well enough to determine where its top should be. And once one has found the top of one letter, it is easier to find the top of another letter in the corresponding location than if it is in a different location.

Two Types of Motion-Added Transformation

The system I have described offers two ways to add motion to an image of an object or part. First, if one can recognize the object, one then can activate the previously stored representation in a pattern activation subsystem. This image would then be altered as one anticipates what one would see if the object were manipulated in a specific way. Second, if the stimulus has not previously been stored, one would need to encode it and store it in the pattern activation subsystems—and only then would an image be projected back into the visual buffer and altered. In the first case, the image will seem independent of the stimulus, whereas in the second case the subjective experience will be that the image seems to spring from the stimulus, moving from it.

I have argued that left-right orientation is not accessible in the pattern activation subsystems (see chapter 5). Thus, to rotate the imaged object to make a mirror-reversal judgment, one would be forced to encode the object anew on each trial. Indeed, in this situation one would need to encode the object a part at a time in order to preserve the organization among the parts. And in fact, Just and Carpenter (1976) and Carpenter and Just (1978) found that subjects moved their eyes back and forth between corresponding parts of objects when one was being rotated into congruence with the other; indeed, subjects made more such comparisons when more rotation was necessary. Carpenter and Just referred to this as the "search and confirmation" stage, which they distinguished from a "transformation stage" in which the individual parts are rotated.

If one is forced to encode the object at the time of rotation, and to preserve enough information to distinguish left-right orientation, this should require more time than if one can form an image based on prior encodings. Steiger and Yuille (1983) report results that speak directly to this issue. They compared performance in the standard Shepard and Metzler (1971) task, where two stimuli were present simultaneously, to performance when the subjects had memorized the "standard" versions of the figures in advance and were shown only a single probe and asked whether it was identical to one of the memorized figures. They found that subjects could rotate the images about five times faster in the single-probe version of the task. Jolicoeur et al. (1985) report comparable findings when the two versions of the task are compared, but found only a 1.5-fold difference in rotation rates between the conditions. Similarly, S. Shepard and D. Metzler (1988) essentially replicated this result, but found that subjects could rotate images about 2.7 times faster in the single-probe version of the task.

Steiger and Yuille's subjects may have rotated the sequential images exceptionally fast because they had very good representations of the stimuli (including descriptions of how the parts were arranged). The subjects saw only a single test shape (presented in different orientations), which they studied, along with its mirror image, extensively during training. In addition, they participated in a relatively large number of trials (the subjects evaluated 8 blocks of trials with 36 trials in each). Given such extensive exposure to the stimuli, the subjects may have learned that the normal mirror-reversed discrimination could be accomplished by inspecting the bottom half of the stimulus (e.g., learning that when the bottom leg is toward the front, it points to the right in the standard and to the left in the mirror version; see p. 386 of

Steiger and Yuille 1983). If so, then these subjects may have been able to judge the stimuli without using imagery on some trials, which artificially reduced the estimate of the rotation rate. Indeed, when another group of subjects did not see the mirror image stimulus during training, the subsequent rotation times were slower. Jolicoeur et al. (1985) did not use such extensive training.

The finding that subjects are faster in the single-probe condition makes sense because they could not check back and forth between the stimuli, and hence may have engaged in less scanning as they rotated than they did in the simultaneous condition. In addition, the subjects presumably rotated images in the single-probe condition based on previously stored information, and had good representations of the figures; in the simultaneous condition, they may not have encoded the probe figures as well, and hence spent more time checking them as they rotated. Jolicoeur (1990a) argues that for the first presentation of a stimulus, the slopes are the same for naming (presumably after rotating) misoriented pictures and single-object mental rotation (using a left/right discrimination) within the range of 0° to 120°. This finding is consistent with the view that subjects are using stored information to aid rotation of individual familiar objects.

There is a potential problem with this account, however: I earlier inferred that left-right orientation information is not available in the ventral system; input is matched to stored representations in accordance with the viewpoint consistency constraint, which ignores such differences in the positions of portions of objects. Hence, how could a shape be encoded and then used to rotate the image, preserving left-right orientation? The same problem arises when imagery is used during recognition; in order to match the image in the visual buffer, the mapping from the stored compressed image representation must capture the proper left-right orientation. This mapping could be established by matching portions of the stored image to parts of the input image. Alternatively, just as the image is rotated, scaled for size, and translated to find the best match, it can also be "flipped." In any case, once this mapping is established, it can be altered to change the orientation of the imaged object.[16]

Rotation and Reference Frames

Mental rotation typically is employed when one cannot identify a property of a misoriented object. The classic case is left-right orientation, which requires running a visual routine (Ullman 1984) to check the spatial relations among specific parts. As discussed in chapter 7, a visual routine corresponds to a way of shifting the attention window to classify a stimulus in some way; I earlier discussed how such routines could be used to compute a categorical spatial relation between two parts of an object. Such routines may be defined relative to a standard orientation of an object; if so, then the object must be rotated to this orientation before the routine can be used. For example, to determine whether an F faces normally or is mirror-reversed, one might locate the bottom of the vertical line, and then trace it up until a horizontal line is found; if this line extends to the right, the letter faces normally, otherwise it is mirror-reversed. Note that this routine cannot operate unless "bottom," "vertical," "left," and so on, are properly assigned. Given that we do not often distinguish left-right orientation, it is likely that the heuristics we use are defined relative to the standard upright. However, if one is very familiar with a set of stimuli, one can devise strategies that obviate the need to mentally rotate the stimulus to the upright prior to using such routines (for a similar view, see Steiger and Yuille 1983). For example, Hinton and Parsons (1981) showed that such strategies can be engendered by properties of the set of stimuli. They showed subjects the letters F, G, L, and R. Half of the time the letter was normal and half the time it was mirror reversed, and letters were presented at different degrees of rotation. The "front" of each of these letters faces to the right, and is signaled by an open region on the right relative to a line on the left. The subjects were given advance information about the orientation of the stimuli, and could use this to prepare to judge the letters in a way that obviated mental rotation. In this case, they presumably used the cue to attend to the region of space where the line on the left should be, and prepared to note whether the open region was to its left or right.

This effect may be analogous to one found in blind subjects who performed a haptic mental rotation task; the effect of orientation depended in part on the position of the hand that touched the letter (Carpenter and Eisenberg 1978). Only the "hand" is one's attention, which allows one to "grasp" (i.e., run a visual routine on) the letter immediately when it appears at the expected orientation and compare two segments to make the judgment. Such a strategy will not succeed if the visual routine will not classify all stimuli correctly. For example, Hinton and Parsons found that when subjects judged the stimuli F, R, J, and 7 (half of which face right and half of which face left), advance information about orientation (without the identity of the upcoming letter) did not eliminate the need to perform mental rotation. The same results were reported by Cooper and Shepard (1973), who found that mental rotation was required unless both the identity and the orientation of an upcoming stimulus were provided in advance; their stimulus set contained letters and digits that faced in different directions, and so without knowing the identity of the character the subjects could not prepare to make the judgment at the expected orientation. If all of the members of a set do not face the same way, a single visual routine cannot be used.

Shifting the attention window could play two roles in such tasks. Not only does this prepare one to categorize a specific spatial relation, such as that used to distinguish normal and mirror-reversed directions, but it also may help one to organize the stimulus differently. As discussed in chapter 6, Rock (1973) and others showed that stimuli are perceptually organized differently when they are seen at different orientations. I argued that this fact places a major constraint on the operation of the viewpoint consistency constraint; if some different perceptual units are encoded when a stimulus is presented at different orientations, then a new encoding of the stimulus cannot be completely matched to a stored representation of the stimulus as seen in a different orientation. In such circumstances, mental rotation is used, which allows one to reorganize the figure and match it to stored information (for a similar view, see Jolicoeur 1990a).

A number of factors affect how a stimulus will be organized with respect to its perceived orientation. When subjects perform a standard mental rotation task with their heads tilted, Corballis and his colleagues (see Corballis, Nagourney, Shetzer, and Stefanatos, 1978; Corballis, Zbrodoff, and Roldan 1976) found that the gravitational upright was most important, but that there was also some contribution of retinal orientation. However, Humphreys (1983) showed that objects that have strong intrinsic axes, such as oblong shapes, are represented relative to their intrinsic upright even when they are tilted. In addition, McMullen and Jolicoeur (1990) tilted subjects' heads in a naming task and two different mental rotation tasks (with objects or letters as stimuli), and found that the environmental frame of reference was more important for mental rotation, but that a retinal frame was more important for naming objects. They concluded that the nature of the task, and not stimulus factors, play the major role in determining how subjects will align the frame of reference. Thus, at least three frames of reference appear to affect how we perceptually organize stimuli—environmental, retinal, and intrinsic—and their relative contributions may depend on the precise task demands.

The fact that objects with no strong intrinsic axis are organized differently at different orientations illuminates a puzzling facet of the literature: numerous researchers have found that subjects judge rotated figures faster than expected for angles under 60° (e.g., Cooper and Shepard 1973; Hock and Tromley 1978; Koriat and Norman 1985). Steiger and Yuille (1983) present good evidence that the subjective upright, what they call the *fold point* (the angle at which subjects take the least amount of time to evaluate the figure), does not always correspond to the actual upright. Steiger and Yuille could account for .913 of the variance in mental rotation times (with Shepard-Metzler type figures) if the fold point was treated as the baseline "vertical" orientation (compared to .782 if the standard upright was used). The subjects varied considerably in the location of the fold point, which was located from 0° to 90° from the standard upright. However, the subjects were remarkably consistent in where they assigned the fold point, with an intersession correlation of .88. Damos (1990) found that subjects assigned different fold points for the standard and mirror versions of stimuli (cf. Koriat and Norman 1985).

Even something as seemingly perceptual as a fold point may arise in part because of motor processes. The fold point may be determined in part by where one visualizes "grasping" an object prior to rotating it. This process would require some effort, and hence it is of interest that the mental rotation slopes became more linear when subjects simultaneously held eight digits or an eight-dot random pattern in memory (Corballis 1988b). In these conditions, the usual flattening of the slope from 0° to 60° appeared to be eliminated; this flattening may reflect the range of values that subjects can see as "upright," if they organize the figure appropriately. Alternatively, the effort required to perform the simultaneous memory task may have discouraged subjects from using special-purpose visual routines that allow them to judge stimuli in non-standard orientations.

Indeed, the properties of these routines may play a major role in determining how far one must rotate a figure. For example, Hock and Tromley (1978) demonstrated that the top of a figure must be at the top of the picture plane before the direction of the figure can be categorized. For example, subjects did not appear to mentally rotate the letters *L* and *J* until they were at least 72° from the standard upright, whereas the subjects rotated *e* and *G* when they were as little as 36° from the upright (the smallest deviation examined). It would be of interest to repeat this experiment with a memory load, and discover whether subjects now use a different, less sensitive (but perhaps less effortful), procedure for categorizing direction.

Two Strategies: Rotation versus Attention Shifting

My account of Hinton and Parsons's (1981) findings suggests that people may sometimes have a choice about whether to use mental rotation or shift attention to the appropriate location and execute the appropriate visual routine. This choice is apparently heavily influenced by task demands. In experiments that demonstrate the role of such factors, researchers examine rotation effects relative to the angular deviation from the upright (ADU) and relative to the angular deviation of the preceding (ADP) stimulus. For example, Koriat and Norman (1984) found the usual large effects of angular deviation from the upright, but also reported small effects relative to the orientation of the previous stimulus. In an effort to study the basis of this small ADP effect, Robertson, Palmer and Gomez (1987) presented subjects with four copies of a letter in a 2 × 2 table, and the table was either presented 90° rotated to the left or to the right; the subjects decided whether the letters faced normally or were mirror-reversed. Following this, a single character appeared, and the subjects decided whether it faced normally or was mirror-reversed. The experimenters found that the time to evaluate the single character was influenced by the orientation of the previous ones, for both normal and reflected stimuli. These results suggested to Robertson, Palmer, and Gomez that people can alter the frame of reference in which they encode stimuli—an idea that is consistent with Hinton and Parsons's (1981) findings. I interpret "frame of reference" to mean how the attention window is positioned, which can help or hinder one's execution of the visual routine used to evaluate the stimulus.

This proposal may also help to explain the complex set of findings reported by Koriat and Norman (1988). In one experiment, they found that the ADP effect was almost completely confined to pairs of trials where the same character had been repeated, particularly when both trials were reflected. In a second experiment, they found that the identity of the prior letter was less important than the direction in which it faced: The ADP effect was largest when the present stimulus and prior stimulus were both reflected. Indeed, the ADP effect occurred when two different letters appeared in sequence, provided that they both were reflected (but only for the error rate data in experiment

2, not the response times; however, a similar result was reported in experiment 4 for response times and error rates). Over the course of all of their experiments, Koriat and Norman found that the ADP effect increased with increasing angular disparity from the standard upright. However, they sometimes found effects of angular disparity from the previous stimulus even when the stimuli were presented at their standard upright! Finally, similar increases in time were found for increasing ADP and ADU.

Koriat and Norman hypothesize a race between two processes, one that rotates an object to the standard upright and one that uses "backward alignment" to rotate the figure to the orientation of the prior figure. However, this account does not appear to explain why there is an effect of ADP when the letter is upright and no mental rotation is required. More fundamentally, it is not clear what would be gained by rotating an image to the position of the prior image—one presumably did not represent the left-right orientation of that figure in visual memory; if one had, mental rotation would not have been necessary in the first place. Koriat and Norman (p. 97) appear to assume that the left-right orientation of the previous figure is actually stored, along with its angular orientation. Furthermore, rotating a letter into congruence with a different letter does not seem likely to help one decide whether the current letter is facing normally or is reflected.

Koriat and Norman's findings appear to be consistent with the hypothesis that after subjects categorize a letter, they use one of two strategies for the next letter (Robertson, Palmer, and Gomez [1987] develop a related idea). On some proportion of the trials, the subjects use a standard rotation strategy, rotating the image to the upright. On other trials, they prepare for the next stimulus by shifting their attention to the location of a diagnostic portion of the previous letter at its previous orientation (e.g., where the top horizontal segment meets the vertical one at the left of an uppercase F), and prepare to run a visual routine to categorize the direction of the upcoming letter. Parsons (1988) showed that examination of a property at a specific location on one stimulus—imaged or perceived—can guide examination of that feature on a subsequent stimulus, but that such a guide is less useful if the properties are arranged differently. According to this theory, an ADP effect occurs when one must shift attention further from the location of a diagnostic portion of the previous letter at its previous orientation. The fact that there is a larger effect of ADP for mirror-reversed images may suggest that one "looks" for normally facing letters, and if one does not find the expected spatial relation among the parts, one "looks again" to confirm that the letter is mirror-reversed (in general, more time is required to categorize letters as mirror-reversed in these kinds of mental rotation tasks). If so, then categorizing mirror-reversed stimuli requires a more complex process, and subjects may be inclined to want to repeat this process once it is primed. Thus, they would be more likely to adopt the attention-shifting strategy on these trials.[17] Moreover, the visual routines are fairly general, provided that the characters all face the same way, and so it would be the direction of the previous stimulus, and not its identity, that is critical in determining whether an ADP effect is present. This hypothesis predicts that ADP effects will be weaker (if present at all) if characters on successive trials face in opposite directions (e.g., 5 and G).[18]

After formulating this account, I discovered an often-overlooked paper by Roldan and Phillips (1980) that presents somewhat complex findings. I was pleased to find that the mechanisms I hypothesized, for different reasons, also can explain these results. Roldan and Phillips used the Cooper and Shepard (1973) paradigm in which the subjects see a cue prior to a probe; the cue specified both the identity and orientation of the upcoming character. The character then was presented in the expected orientation or in a different orientation, and the subjects had to decide whether it faced normally or was mirror-reversed. When the image was prepared at the standard upright orientation, Roldan and Phillips obtained the usual mental rotation results; the subjects required the most time when the letter was 180° from the upright, and progressively less time as less rotation was required to bring it to the standard upright. In contrast, when the subjects prepared by forming an upside-down image, Roldan and Phillips did not find the typical mental rotation function. Although the subjects evaluated upside-down characters fastest, they also evaluated upright characters faster than expected if they had to rotate their images 180° from the expected orientation. Indeed, the response times showed two peaks, one at 45° and one at 315°.

These findings can be explained exactly the way I explained the fact that both ADP and ADU effects occur. First, consider the results with upside-down cues. Because the identity of the character is given in advance, the subject can retrieve the proper visual routine for evaluating its direction (the stimuli included letters and digits, which face in different directions; hence their identity is necessary to evaluate the direction of a stimulus). The probe appeared at the cued orientation on 72% of the trials, and appeared at one of the other seven orientations on the remaining trials. Given these odds, it paid the subjects to prepare to execute the visual routine on a noncued orientation some of the time. On most of the trials, the subjects prepared to evaluate an upside-down letter, and this is why they were fastest for these probes. But on other trials, they prepared to evaluate an upright letter; this is the default for the visual routine, and hence is easiest to execute and splits the difference with the other orientations, minimizing the average rotation that will be needed. According to this account, the subjects never prepared to evaluate an intermediate orientation, and so rotation was always required for these orientations—and hence the subjects responded most slowly for these orientations. The fact that the peak response times in the upside-down cue condition were not midway between upright and upside down suggests that the subjects did in fact prepare at the upside-down position more often than at the upright position.

Now consider the upright cues. In this case, I assume that the subjects allocated attention to all the other orientations the same proportion of the time; no other orientation was particularly easy to evaluate, and so no other position was privileged. Indeed, because the standard upright is so easy to evaluate, they may have focused on this cued orientation more often than they focused on the upside-down cued orientation. This conjecture would explain why the subjects were generally faster when the cue and probe were upright than when they were upside down. Alternatively, the visual routine may simply be easier to execute when it is has been set up for the upright position—perhaps because this is the default orientation for it or because the to-be-sought parts are easier to locate when their orientations are normal with respect to the gravitational axis.

In another experiment Roldan and Phillips (1980) probed only five orientations: the cued orientation, 20° to either side of it, and 40° to either side of it. Critically, each orientation was probed equally often. Because each location was equally likely to be probed, the subjects were equally likely to attend to any of these locations. And in fact, as expected by the account offered above, the trends for upright and upside-down cues now were the same. Indeed, the subjects now evaluated all probe orientations equally easily—as expected if the equal probe probabilities led them to attend to each orientation equally often.

In their final experiment, Roldan and Phillips probed a wider spread of orientations; now the cued orientation, 40° to either side, and 80° to either side were probed. Again, the orientations were probed equally often. They again found the same pattern of times for the upright and upside-down cues, but now the subjects were faster for the cued orientation and progressively slower for larger angular disparities. Furthermore, the subjects apparently rotated more slowly when they began with an upside-down image.[19]

Roldan and Phillips point out that over the set of their four experiments a pattern emerges: The larger the range of probe orientations, relative to the cued orientation, the slower rotation appeared to be for probes 45° or 40° from the cued orientation when the subjects prepared by forming upside-down images. This pattern is just what one would expect if subjects "gambled" more often by shifting attention to noncued orientations when they were relatively close to the cued orientation; but if the angular deviations were large enough, the costs of guessing wrong and focusing attention on the wrong orientation became much higher—and so subjects tended to allocate attention more often at the cued orientation. The subjects were very practiced and probably had a good sense of the probe probabilities.

Region-Bounded and Field-General Transformations

In the earlier version of the theory, I distinguished between two kinds of image transformations, *region bounded* and *field general*. Region-bounded transformations are defined over a specific portion of the visual buffer, whereas field-general transformations alter the entire contents at once. The revised theory preserves this distinction in the following way: Region-bounded transformations occur when one anticipates the consequences of operating on a single part or object in a scene, whereas field-general transformations occur when one anticipates the consequences of moving relative to a scene.

Field-general transformations are used when one scans relatively large distances across an imaged object or scene or when one zooms in or pans back from an imaged object or scene, as is discussed below.

Image Scanning

I argued earlier that not all scanning is accomplished by shifting the attention window (as also noted by Pinker 1980); if it were, subjects would have difficulty scanning "off screen"—but they do not (Kosslyn 1978, 1980). One way to explain this finding rests on the idea that image scanning involves a type of image transformation. The imaged pattern is slid across the visual buffer, with material being deleted at the trailing edge and introduced at the leading edge. In this case, scanning would be like an image on a television screen as the camera scans across a scene.

How is this kind of image transformation actually accomplished? Brandt et al. (1989) report that subjects make systematic eye movements when they visualize objects. These eye movements may reflect either type of image transformation, motion encoded (when one replays a stored memory of a moving object), or motion added (when one anticipates the results of making a specific movement). In a motion-encoded transformation, the eye movements would index visual memories that were encoded at specific locations. In this case, the eye movements would cue one to generate a sequence of images, which would be representations of what was seen while one scanned over an object or scene. In this sort of scanning, it should be easiest to scan an image in the same way that one scanned the actual object; this prediction has not been tested.

It seems unlikely that most image scanning consists of recalling what one saw when actually scanning along an object, but such processing may be more common than one might suspect; people usually have the opportunity to scan an object at the time that it is initially perceived. But at least in some cases, people scan objects in images in novel ways. Indeed, Denis and Cocude (1989), Kosslyn et al. (1983), and Kosslyn et al. (1984) found that subjects could visualize scenes that were described to them, and then could scan over the scene in various ways. Such scanning cannot be a replay of perceptual encodings, given that the subjects never actually saw the scenes. Thus, at least some scanning is of the motion-added variety. In such situations, eye movements would reflect altered representations in the spatiotopic mapping subsystem, which would register where one is "looking" at each point in time; with each new spatial representation, a different portion of the object would be primed in the pattern activation subsystems, and a new image created.

And in fact, Brandt et al. (1989) provided evidence that subjects tend to move their eyes when scanning visual mental images internally. In 1973 I also collected data that suggested that subjects move their eyes in the same direction that they scan a mental image. (I never published these results because they relied on the Haidinger's Brush technique in a somewhat uncontrolled group testing setting.)

The image scanning discussed so far would be akin to imaged saccades. But the time to scan typically increases linearly with the distance scanned, which suggests a more continuous process. It is possible that such image scanning can result if one uses a field-general transformation. That is, one anticipates what one would see not when moving the eyes, but when rotating the head or body. This process is presumably relatively fast, so that the speed of the mechanism that shifts the attention window may be the rate-limiting factor. If so, then it makes sense that the scan rates are about the same when one scans between two visible locations or between a visible and an initially invisible location.[20]

In short, image scanning may involve two mechanisms: one that shifts the attention window and one that transforms the contents of the visual buffer. This latter mechanism may rely on motor programs that ordinarily move the eyes, head, or body; in imagery, these programs may have the effect of replacing the contents of the visual buffer with a new representation of material that is contiguous to that in the previous representation. In this case the image would "slide" (either continuously or in discrete jumps) across the visual buffer.

The present theory can also explain why Finke and Pinker (1983) and Wilton (1979) could eliminate scanning in a specific situation. In Finke and Pinker's task, the subjects visualized a pattern of dots and then saw an arrow; they decided whether the arrow would point to one of the dots if the dots were physically present. If the subjects knew the location of the arrow in advance, they could make this judgment equally easily no matter how far away it was from a target dot. In this case, the subjects could fixate attention on the location where the arrow would appear, and this location would define the "origin" of the spatiotopic map. I assume that one can assign the origin of a reference space to one's body, a body part, or an object, and the locations of all other objects are specified relative to that origin. If the origin is the arrow, then it is easy to determine whether the arrow points to a dot without using imagery. One merely looks at the "tail" of the arrow and specifies the angle of the head relative to the tail (using polar coordinates), which allows one to determine where the arrow points. One then merely needs to discover whether any dot has the same angle coordinate; if so, the arrow points to it. In contrast, if the origin is not the arrow, then it is difficult to compute the relative locations of the arrows and dots without using imagery. And in fact, Finke and Pinker (1982, 1983) and Pinker, Choate, and Finke (1984) found that image scanning is required in this task when the subjects do not know the location of the arrow in advance.[21]

In addition, if scanning is accomplished in part by a motion-added image transformation, then the present theory leads us to expect that one can vary the rate of scanning (just as one can vary one's rate of reaching). And in fact, Intons-Peterson and Roskos-Ewoldsen (1989) found that subjects imagined themselves moving along a pathway more slowly when they imagined carrying a heavier weight (a 3-oz balloon, a 3-lb ball, or a 30-lb cannonball, all imaged with a 3-inch diameter). Moreover, the subjects scanned an imaged map more slowly than a picture of the map, which apparently occurred because the subjects embellished their images (partly via associations to familiar locations on the map), so that more material had to be scanned over (see their experiment 2). As demonstrated by Kosslyn, Ball, and Reiser (1978), subjects require more time to scan over more items—presumably because they "inspect" each one as they scan over it. I expect knowledge and belief often to affect image transformation processes; the anticipated consequence of a manipulation may often depend on information in associative memory. One of the main uses of imagery, after all, is as a "mental simulation" of the consequences of specific actions or events (e.g., see Kosslyn 1981). Hence, I find it odd to read that evidence of such effects challenges the claim that depictive images are scanned.

Finally, Charlot et al. (1992) found that "high imagers" (selected using spatial tasks) showed greater right-posterior activity during image scanning than did "low imagers." Specifically, they tested two groups of subjects, who were selected to be in the top or bottom third on two spatial tests (the Minnesota Paper Form Board and a mental rotation test); both tests require mentally manipulating patterns. The subjects' brain activity was monitored in three conditions: while they rested with eyes closed in a dimly lit room "without any precise instruction except to relax"; while they performed a verbal task (silently conjugating abstract verbs); and while they performed an imagery task (visualizing a map of an island and scanning between pairs of named locations; this task was based on that of Kosslyn et al. 1978). It is unfortunate that Charlot et al. did not select the subjects using tests that depended on the same processes used in the experiment, and that their resting baseline task may have also inadvertently induced imagery (the conditions were certainly conducive to daydreaming). Moreover, the authors comment that "the resolution of our SPECT machine does not allow us to discriminate between motor, premotor, or Broca's area increases" (p. 578); these are large spatial differences. Nevertheless, Charlot et al. did find that low imagers showed greater whole-brain activity in both cognitive tasks, whereas the high imagers showed greater activity in the "right association unimodal cortex." Given their poor spatial resolution, it is difficult to know the source of this activation (it could have corresponded to the locus where associative memory or the spatiotopic mapping, coordinate spatial relations encoding, or shape shift subsystems are putatively implemented). The authors also found activation in some other areas the theory would predict, such as left dorsolateral prefrontal cortex (but not in primary visual cortex, which may reflect their choice of a baseline condition or the technique's poor signal-to-noise resolution).

Zooming

People can "zoom in" on an imaged object, which allows them to "see" additional details (see Kosslyn 1980). For example, if you visualize seeing a bee on a flower that is three feet away, it would take you longer to report the color of the bee's head than if you started off seeing the bee very close up. Subjects in these kinds of experiments typically report that they "zoom in" on the object until the sought part or characteristic is clearly visible. I assume that the visual buffer has only limited resolution (see Finke and Kosslyn 1980, but also see Intons-Peterson 1983 for possible methodological problems, and the reply in Jolicoeur and Kosslyn 1985), and I assume that these resolution limits are a consequence of its anatomical substrate. Specifically, I suggested earlier that spatial summation, which is evident in vision, also constrains imagery. If so, then if an object is imaged in a relatively small region of the visual buffer, more of its parts and characteristics will be obscured than if it is visualized in a larger region (just as occurs on a television screen). Zooming involves changing the parameter values of the function that maps the stored visual information (in a pattern activation subsystem) into the visual buffer. This operation apparently alters the image incrementally; Kosslyn (1975) asked subjects to visualize objects at one of four sizes, and found that they required progressively more time to "see" properties of objects that were visualized at smaller sizes.

This conceptualization explains why zooming is sometimes necessary, but it does not explain why zooming is incremental: Introspectively, it feels as if one moves closer to the object gradually. According to the present theory, one typically would use a kind of field-general motion-added imagery to anticipate what one would see if one were to move closer to an object. Movements are constrained to follow a trajectory, and hence one would see a looming image. In situations where one uses motion-encoded imagery, one would recall what such a looming image looked like when one actually moved closer to the stimulus, and hence here too the image should change visual angle incrementally.

According to the present theory, when one searches for a specific part or characteristic, one primes its representation in the pattern activation subsystems. Hence, if the part or characteristic is present in the image, it "pops out." However, if it is not initially present because of resolution limits, it will "pop into view" as soon as the image is at the right level of resolution. The priming process completes parts or characteristics that may be only implicitly depicted in the global image. This operation is identical to the "vector completion" process used during recognition (see chapter 5).

Malmstrom et al. (1980) found that the accommodation of the eye actually changes when people are asked to image objects at different distances— which is exactly as expected if zooming is accomplished by a mechanism used to anticipate visual input. However, although Hubbard and Baird (1988) found that more time is required to visualize oneself moving progressively closer to an object, such times did not increase linearly with distance. This finding may suggest that one changes zooming rate for very large zooms or that with a large distance one sometimes performs a blink transformation, deleting the initial image and replacing it with a second one that is formed at a new size. Hubbard and Baird note that subjects sometimes reported using such strategies (see also Finke and Shepard 1986).

Finally, zooming is distinct from the kind of size scaling that I discussed in chapter 5. In size scaling one alters the perceived size, not the distance, of a stimulus. At least in some cases, size scaling is a field-general transformation; the entire contents of an image are altered. Such scaling can be accomplished by altering the mapping function from the pattern activation subsystem to the visual buffer. However, in other cases, size scaling is a region-bounded transformation; only one object in an image is altered. If one wants to scale up or down the visual angle of a single imaged object in a scene, this can be accomplished in two steps. First, the relevant region of the visual buffer is selected; and second, the mapping function from the pattern activation subsystem to the visual buffer is altered, changing the size scale.

This hypothesis predicts that it should be much easier to alter the scale of an object or part that is represented by a distinct perceptual unit than to alter an arbitrary portion. For an object or part, the "pop-out" phenomenon allows one to accomplish the first step of the process, and the second step involves a relatively simple parameter change. In contrast, to alter the size of an arbitrarily defined portion, the first step requires one to shift the attention window to encompass the to-be-altered region so that input to the pattern activation subsystems delineates portions of compressed image representations. The second step requires one to activate those representations and to alter the mapping function for each in a different way—inhibiting some portions while changing the parameter values for other portions.

Transforming Color

The present theory also allows us to account for other sorts of image transformations, which do not involve altering shape or viewpoint. For example, Watkins and Schiano (1982) not only provided good evidence that people can mentally "paint" a form with color, but also that the colored shape is then encoded into memory. They showed subjects black-and-white drawings of familiar objects and abstract shapes. The subjects visualized the drawings as if they were filled in with a specific color, and indicated how difficult this was for each drawing. Watkins and Schiano later surprised the subjects by showing them pictures and asking which ones had been seen initially; these test stimuli were either the color that was imaged or a different color. The subjects recognized the drawings better when they were presented in the color previously imaged—even though they were told to disregard the color when making their judgments.

In another experiment, the subjects saw the test drawings along with the name of a color and the actual color. The name or color could match the previously imaged color, and the subjects were told to make recognition judgments solely on the basis of form, but that either the name or the color could help. The subjects did better when the color matched the imaged color than when the name matched the imaged color, which suggests that they were not simply associating a verbal label with the object. Indeed, when only the name matched the imaged color, the subjects did no better than when neither the name nor the color corresponded to the imaged color. In short, the imaged color apparently was integrated into the representation of shape and later stored in the pattern activation subsystem with the shape.

Such transformations also presumably involve modifying the mapping function from the pattern activation subsystem to the visual buffer. In addition to evoking a configuration of activity in the visual buffer for the shape, each point is also assigned a color value. It is clear that color is specified in at least some of the retinotopically mapped areas in the monkey (such as V1, V2, and V4), and many nonshape properties are presumably associated with local properties of shape per se (cf. Tye 1991).

Combining Transformations

If transformations mimic what one would see after moving or manipulating an object in some way, it should be possible to perform more than one transformation at a time. Thus, at first glance it is surprising that Sekuler and Nash (1972) and Bundesen, Larsen, and Farrell (1981) found that rotation and size transformations are additive. Such additive effects probably imply that the two operations were performed sequentially. (Smythe and Lockhart [1989] also attribute this result to studies reported by Besner [1983], Besner and Coltheart [1976], and Bundesen and Larsen [1975]. However, the subjects in these experiments judged whether the stimuli were upside down, and it is not clear that they actually had to perform mental rotation to do so.) Although Kubovy and Podgorny (1981) found no effect of size when size and orientation were varied, Larsen (1985) did find linear and additive effects of the two variables with the same type of random polygon stimuli (unless the subjects were highly overtrained, in which case there was no effect of size). Smythe and Lockhart (1989) found very complex results when a variety of transformations were combined.

In addition, McCormick and Jolicoeur (1991) report evidence that a "zoom lens" operator is used when one traces a curve when trying to determine whether two dots lie on the same segment of a complex pattern. They found that if distractor curves are placed so that one can filter them out relatively easily, subjects can attend to large stretches of curvature without having to scan. If the distractors are close to target curves, however, subjects apparently "zoom in" and scan along the target curve. This "zoom" operator (which mimics moving closer to or away from the figure) apparently operates at the same time as a scanning operator.

These somewhat contradictory results may be interpreted as follows. There is no hard-and-fast constraint on the system to perform more than one transformation at the same time any more than one must twist one's hand while moving it away from one as opposed to performing the movements one at a time. A person always can perform the transformations sequentially, and so they would have additive effects. But one cannot always perform transformations simultaneously: Capacity limitations would serve to constrain how many transformations can be performed at the same time. And even if one *can* perform transformations in parallel, if one believes that it would be easier to perform them sequentially, one may do so. Thus, there is a large strategic element to how transformations are combined, which is essentially what Smythe and Lockhart demonstrated. Oddly enough, they seem to feel that this finding runs counter to the earlier version of my theory, but I cannot see why: If one could not voluntarily control such processes, imagery would have limited use as a way of anticipating the consequence of actions or as an aid to reasoning.[22]

Anatomical Localization

The shape shift subsystem appears to rely on the posterior parietal lobes and the frontal lobes. For example, as discussed previously, Deutsch et al. (1988) asked subjects to rotate objects mentally while their brains were being scanned (using the ^{133}Xe regional cerebral blood flow technique), and found selective activity in the occipital lobe, parietal lobe, and frontal lobe (particularly in the right hemisphere). These results are consistent with the present idea that motor activity plays an important role in image transformations; the parietal and frontal lobes play key roles in programming and monitoring movements (for a review, see chapter 7 of Kosslyn and Koenig 1992).

Most of the literature on the neural basis of image transformations focuses on the relative contributions of the cerebral hemispheres. This literature is complex, and simple conclusions are not forthcoming. One reason for the complexity may be that mental image transformations are carried out by a number of processing subsystems. Not only are the shape shift, spatiotopic mapping, and pattern activation subsystems involved, but so are subsystems that provide input to them. Depending on the task, the prowess of any of the individual subsystems may play a critical role in determining overall performance; for example, if precise transformations are required, the ability of the spatiotopic mapping subsystem to represent precise locations will be more important than if less precise transformations are required. And hence the efficacy of a subsystem that is more effective in the right cerebral hemisphere may contribute greatly to the quality of the performance in one task, but not in another. Depending on how the various contributing subsystems are implemented in the brain, then, performance of the task as a whole may appear to rely to a greater or lesser degree on processes in the left or right hemisphere. Moreover, the situation is further complicated because there may be more than one way to transform objects in images. For example, one could transform an imaged object a part at a time, or alter the global image and add parts or characteristics only if they are needed later. Depending on the strategy one adopts, each hemisphere may contribute more or less to processing and hence to the observed behavior (for a related perspective, see Fischer and Pellegrino 1988). In addition, people may vary widely in their processing abilities, and such individual differences may also underlie some of the variability in this literature.

It is clear, however, that one or more subsystems that are more effective (in typical right-handed males) in the right hemisphere play a special role in image transformations. For example, Corballis and Sergent (1988) tested the split-brain patient L. B. in a variant of the mental rotation task developed by Cooper and Shepard (1973). The patient was shown letters at different orientations, and was to mentally rotate each one to its standard upright position and decide whether it faced normally or was mirror-reversed. L. B. made this evaluation faster and more accurately when the rotated letter appeared in the left visual field and so was presented to the right hemisphere, than when it appeared in the right visual field and was seen by the left hemisphere. By the final three sessions L. B. was able to mentally rotate stimuli presented to his left hemisphere, but he was slower and made more errors than when stimuli were presented to his right hemisphere. Sergent and Corballis (1991) showed that this left-hemisphere deficit could not be attributed to a problem in identifying the letters or in making the normal/mirror-reversed judgment. These findings dovetail nicely with those reported by LeDoux, Wilson, and Gazzaniga (1977) with another split-brain patient. This patient had great difficulty using his left hemisphere to arrange fragments to form a specified pattern, which presumably involves mental rotations and translations of the sort used in packing luggage into one's trunk.

Such a right-hemisphere superiority for mental image rotation is consistent with results from studies of focal-lesion patients reported by Butters, Barton, and Brody (1970), Ditunno and Mann (1990), Layman and Greene (1988; although they did not conceive of their task this way) and Ratcliff (1979). For example, Ditunno and Mann (1990) found that right-hemisphere-damaged patients made more errors and took longer to evaluate Shepard-and-Metzler-like rotated stimuli than did left-hemisphere damaged patients. All of these researchers not only found that right-hemisphere damage disrupted performance in a mental rotation task more than left-hemisphere damage, but also report that the patients had lesions in parietal cortex. This reliance on the right parietal lobe could reflect the importance of the spatiotopic mapping subsystem in carrying out motion-added image transformations. Alternatively, it could indicate that the shape shift transformation process itself relies on this tissue.

But the picture is more complicated than this. For example, Mehta and Newcombe (1991) showed that left-hemisphere-damaged patients have a deficit in rotating the Shepard and Metzler (1971) three-dimensional objects. These results were complicated by the finding that only the left-hemisphere-damaged patients with above-average intelligence had a deficit. This finding may indicate that these patients were devising an ineffective strategy, perhaps trying (ineffectively) to use categorical spatial relations representations to describe the figures and compare them a part at a time (Mehta and Newcombe suggest something similar, based on the earlier version of the present theory). Alternatively, the left frontal lobe apparently has a critical role in motor programming (e.g., see Kimura 1977), which may be used to direct the shape shift subsystem. Even though all of the patients had posterior lesions, some may have had functional impairments in more anterior locations (recall the discussion in chapters 2 and 8 about indirect effects of lesions).

This possibility is consistent with results reported by Kim et al. (1984), who compared the performance of brain-damaged patients on five "visuoperceptual tasks" and five corresponding "visuomotor tasks." The patients fell into four groups, defined by whether the lesion was in the left or right hemisphere and, within the hemisphere, was anterior or posterior. The visuoperceptual tasks (VP) and corresponding visuomotor tasks (VM) were as follows: (1) VP: the subjects saw two cards with crosses on them and indicated whether the crosses were in the same locations; VM: the subjects saw a cross on one card and drew a cross on a blank card in the same location; (2) VP: the subjects were shown a line at an angle and pointed to the corresponding angle in an array of lines; VM: the subjects saw an oriented line and drew it on another card; (3) VP: the subjects saw a tilted *H* on two cards and decided whether the second orientation could be achieved by rotating the first 90° clockwise; VM: the subjects saw the first figure and drew it on another card at that orientation; (4) VP: the subjects saw two human figures, which were depicted at different orientations and from the front or back; the figures each held up a disk in one hand, and the subject had to say whether it was the same hand in each figure; VM: the visuomotor task was the same except that one of the figures had nothing in its hands and the subject had to draw the disk in the same hand as was illustrated in the first figure; (5) VP: a geometric figure was presented along with four pairs of fragments, and the subject had to indicate which pair could be assembled to form the figure; VM: the subject saw a geometric figure and was given two cardboard pieces and was asked to assemble them to make the geometric figure.

When all ten tests were compared, only four of them "significantly discriminated" between the right-hemisphere-damaged and left-hemisphere-damaged patients in general: namely, both versions of the cross task (number 1 above) and both versions of the form assembly task (number 5). The cross task relies on coordinate spatial relations encoding, and hence it is not surprising that the right-hemisphere-damaged patients performed more poorly than the left-hemisphere-damaged patients. Similarly, the form assembly task requires novel image transformations, which also apparently rely on right-hemisphere functions. The authors note that the other laterality effects revealed an interaction between hemisphere and caudal position: The patients with posterior lesions in the right hemisphere were worse than those with anterior lesions, but vice versa for patients with lesions in the left hemisphere. Although the results are not presented in this way, the data illustrated in graphs show that the right-posterior-damaged patients performed more poorly than the left-posterior-damaged patients on all but the visuoperceptual version of the *H* task (number 3 above, which was relatively easy). The theory leads us to expect posterior right-hemisphere damage to disrupt any task in which precise spatial properties must be encoded. However, the left-anterior-damaged patients appear worse than the right-anterior-damaged patients on the visuomotor version of both rotation tasks, but only on the corresponding visuoperceptual *H* task.

The functions of the right posterior cortex have been discussed above, but what about the left frontal lobe? Following Luria (1980), Kim et al. (1984) suggest that the frontal lesions may have disrupted scanning ability. It is possible that the left frontal lobe plays a special role in the scanning process that I suggest is sometimes used to augment portions of figures during image transformations (perhaps because the scanning is directed by accessing stored categorical spatial relations representations). Alternatively, as noted earlier, it is possible that the left frontal lobe plays a special role in setting up movement sequences, which are used to program the shape shift subsystem. I was struck by the close correspondence between performance in the visuoperceptual and visuomotor variants of the tasks—which is of course exactly as expected if imagery transformations often rely on motor processing anyway. It is unfortunate that the authors did not report correlations of performance scores on the two types of tasks.[23]

A cornerstone of the present theory is that multiple subsystems are used to carry out any task. Thus, one must take care in drawing inferences about the lateralization of a single subsystem on the basis of overall task performance. This point was driven home by a result reported by Sergent and Corballis (1991). They tested split-brain patient L. B. with a stimulus made up of a long arm and a short arm; the short arm had an arrow, which pointed either to the left or right. L. B. had to indicate which direction the arrow pointed. In this task, L. B. performed almost perfectly in his left hemisphere, but only at chance levels in his right hemisphere. Given that he performed other mental rotation tasks better in his right hemisphere, this result probably does not reflect the operation of the shape shift subsystem per se. Rather, as Sergent and Corballis suggest, the problem may reflect the fact that this task required encoding a categorical spatial relation (see also Sergent and Corballis 1989a). This was particularly difficult because the stimulus did not have a strong intrinsic "reference frame" that could be used to describe the relations of its parts. Hence, it is possible that L. B.'s right hemisphere could rotate images but was unable effectively to encode the categorical relations among the parts of this stimulus when it was tilted.

A number of researchers have also investigated mental rotation in divided-visual-field studies with normal subjects. The results are ambiguous. Some researchers (e.g., Cohen 1975; Ditunno and Mann 1990) report faster processing when stimuli are presented initially to the right hemisphere (but Cohen did not find a difference in rotation slopes per se), whereas others (e.g., Fischer and Pellegrino 1988) report faster processing when the stimuli are presented initially to the left hemisphere (but show no evidence that this faster processing was due to rotation per se, as opposed to encoding operations; see also Corballis and Sergent 1989b). Others have reported no hemispheric differences (e.g., Corballis, Macadie, and Beale 1985; Corballis et al. 1985; Corballis and McLaren 1984; Jones and Anuza 1982; Simion et al. 1980; Uecker and Obrzut 1993; Van Strien and Bouma 1990).[24]

It is difficult to interpret a null finding, of course, but when so many of them are reported (and who knows how many others never made it to publication), one must take pause. The stimuli and task are complex, which implies that many subsystems are likely to contribute to processing—and hence laterality differences may be obscured. For example, letters and numbers might be encoded better by the left hemisphere, which could obscure a right-hemisphere advantage; some subjects may engage in part-by-part rotation and others may operate on each stimulus as a single chunk; the parafoveal presentation may have degraded the stimuli, which would put a premium on effective encoding processes, and so on. As noted earlier, task demands can alter the relative importance of processes that are performed more effectively in one or the other hemisphere. In addition, Kim and Levine (1992) report large individual differences in perceptual asymmetries, which would introduce variance into any study that uses relatively small numbers of subjects (see also Kim and Levine 1991; Kosslyn 1987).

Summary: Image Transformations

Image transformations are not accomplished by a single process. Motion-encoded transformations occur when one activates a representation of an object that was encoded while it was moving, which produces a moving image. Motion-added transformations occur when an imaged object is made to move in a novel way. Motion-added transformations are accomplished by the shape shift subsystem, which often receives input from motor programming subsystems. During perception, the shape shift subsystem systematically alters representations in the spatiotopic mapping subsystem and alters the imagery mapping function while the pattern activation subsystems are primed (in the usual way), which helps one to encode the expected consequences of performing a specific action. During imagery, the priming causes an image to form, and as the shape shift subsystem alters spatial representations it also alters the mapping function from the pattern activation subsystem to the visual buffer to be consistent with the new spatial properties. The resulting image transformations are continuous if the anticipated perceptual input is continuous.

Although the shape shift subsystem may primarily receive input from motor programming subsystems, it also receives input from more complex processes that allow one to predict how events will unfold. Thus, the shape shift subsystem not only allows one to visualize what one expects to see when one manipulates an object, it also allows one to visualize what one expects to see when objects interact in some way—the key is that one anticipates what one would see if a specific sequence occurred. Thus, one can visualize seeing the results of a tank hitting the side of a house. The process of predicting the sequence of events, which directs the shape shift subsystem, clearly involves stored knowledge and undoubtedly is very complex.

Finally, one can transform either the entire field (e.g., by anticipating what one would see as one turned one's head in a room), or a selected object, part, or characteristic (by surrounding it with the attention window and altering the mapping function to that object or part). In some circumstances one can transform objects by allowing one image to fade and generating a new one that is altered in the specified way.

CONCLUSIONS

According to the present theory, image inspection and image transformation both rely in large part on processing subsystems that contribute to other abilities; this is an example of "weak modularity," as described in chapter 2. Indeed, I needed to posit only one additional subsystem to understand image inspection and image transformation. It is clear that a theory of imagery gains enormous leverage from the assumption that imagery draws on the same processes used in high-level perception. Indeed, this premise not only allowed us to understand image inspection, but also allowed us to address the deepest puzzle about mental rotation, namely why it occurs at all; images are not constrained to move along a trajectory by the laws of physics.

I distinguished between two major classes of image transformations. The simplest type is a "replay" of a stored transformation; such objects changed over time when viewed, and hence the subsequent mental image also changes over time. The other type consists of transforming an object in a novel way, not merely replaying a previously encoded transformation. According to the theory, novel transformations rely on a shape shift subsystem, which alters the representation of an object's spatial properties and alters the imagery mapping function while the pattern activation subsystems are primed to encode a sequence of stimuli. In perception, this process is used to prepare one to encode what one would see as one performs an action or witnesses an event unfold. In imagery, priming is carried to such an extreme that an image arises; one visualizes what one would expect to see if an object were manipulated or otherwise acted upon in some way. The shape-shift process has the effect of modulating the mapping function from the pattern activation subsystems to the visual buffer, so that the imaged object or scene is transformed.

In a sense, this theory makes contact with Shepard's (1987) idea that the brain has internalized some of the laws of physics via the process of evolution. If image transformations are evoked by motor processes, and the brain is wired so that one anticipates what one will see as one moves, then something like what Shepard believes will result: The brain will respect the laws of physics that govern movements, and images will be transformed continuously. Similarly, because objects in the world are constrained to move along trajectories, if one anticipates how an event will unfold, this too will result in a continuously changing image.

This chapter again illustrates that there is nothing mystical or paradoxical about depictive mental images; a brain-based, mechanistic theory can address the key aspects of the phenomena. This chapter adds to my case that the "imagery debates" are for all intents and purposes settled.

11 Visual Mental Images in the Brain

The theory of imagery developed here grew naturally out of a theory of high-level visual perception. I have claimed that the same mechanisms underlie both abilities, and that imagery plays a key role in normal perception. Nevertheless, it will be helpful to focus on the theory of imagery itself and to consider the claims about the role of each subsystem in imagery in their own right. Although the imagery theory is motivated by the theory of perception, it must be evaluated on its own merits. In this chapter I illustrate how the subsystems work together to confer our major imagery abilities, and then show how they map onto the component processes posited in the earlier version of the theory (Kosslyn 1980). This is important because the previous version had considerable explanatory power, which is inherited by the present theory to the extent that it preserves the distinctions that did the work in the earlier version. I then turn to a test of the assumptions about how the subsystems work together; this test centers on whether individual differences in imagery can be understood in terms of independent variations in the efficacy of the subsystems. Finally, I consider the computational utility of the proposed mechanisms, and put the theory in a broader context.

The functions and tentative anatomical localization of each subsystem are summarized in table 11.1 and the entire system is illustrated in figure 11.1. When a subsystem is characterized as being lateralized to one cerebral hemisphere, this should be taken as a matter of degree; I assume that it also is implemented in the other hemisphere but does not operate as effectively there.

ACCOUNTS OF MAJOR IMAGERY ABILITIES

The theory of high-level visual perception was guided by the taxonomy of visual abilities developed in chapter 3. The theory was designed with an eye toward explaining these (coarsely characterized) abilities, and hence the accounts are to some extent post hoc (but not entirely so; see chapter 8). Of more interest, I feel, are the accounts for the four major imagery abilities; these accounts are rooted in the theory of perception—not in a theory that was designed from the start to explain them.

Table 11.1 Subsystems posited by the theory

Subsystem	Input	Operation	Output	Localization?
Visual buffer	Images produced by low-level vision subsystems or via priming in the pattern activation subsystems	Retinotopic representation of perceptual image; topographic representation of mental image; organize into units bottom-up	Edges indicated; regions of common color, texture defined; geometric properties explicit	Occipital lobe
Attention window	Images in visual buffer	Selects region for further processing	Pattern in a region sent to dorsal and ventral systems	Occipital lobe
Stimulus-based attention shifting	Change in stimulus value	Shifts body, head, eyes, attention window to location of change; scales size of attention window	New pattern surrounded by attention window	Superior colliculus
Pre-processing	Pattern from attention window	Extracts nonaccidental and signal properties; organizes image into learned units	Nonaccidental and signal properties, organized image	Occipital-temporal cortex
Motion relations encoding	Pattern of movement in visual buffer	Detects motion patterns	Motion-pattern code to pattern activation subsystems and spatiotopic mapping subsystem	Circumstriate occipital-temporal cortex
Category pattern activation	Nonaccidental and signal properties, input image plus motion pattern code; pattern code from property lookup subsystems; 3D and spatial properties from spatiotopic mapping subsystem; priming and mapping function from shape shift subsystem	Matches input properties to those of stored prototypes of shapes; if poor match, then generates image into visual buffer; generates image of prototype when receives pattern code; stores new "compressed images"	Pattern code, plus goodness-of-match index, when matching shapes; mental image when activated by pattern code	Middle temporal and/or fusiform gyri (stronger in left hemisphere)

Exemplar pattern activation	Nonaccidental and signal properties, input image plus motion pattern code; pattern code from property lookup sub-systems; 3D and spatial properties from spatiotopic mapping subsystem; priming and mapping function from shape shift subsystem	Matches input properties to those of stored exemplars of shapes; if poor match, then generates image into visual buffer; generates image of exemplar when receives pattern code; stores new "compressed images"	Pattern code, plus goodness-of-match index, when matching shapes; mental image when activated by pattern code	Middle temporal and/or fusiform gyri (stronger in right hemisphere)
Spatiotopic mapping	Location of perceptual units in visual buffer, attention window, eyes, head, body; motion pattern; transformation specification from shape shift system	Produces a representation of locations of perceptual units, size, and orientation of units	Map of locations with sizes and orientations of units specified	Posterior parietal lobes (stronger in right hemisphere)
Coordinate spatial relations encoding	Locations of two perceptual units in space	Computes motor-based coordinates of one unit relative to another, also encodes size and orientation	Motor-based coordinates, metric size, orientation	Posterior parietal lobe (stronger in right hemisphere)
Categorical spatial relations encoding	Locations of two perceptual units in space	Computes categorical relation between units, also categorizes size and orientation	Categorical spatial relation, size, and orientation category	Posterior parietal lobe (stronger in left hemisphere)
Associative memory	Pattern codes, categorical and coordinate spatial relations representations	Activates object representation that is most consistent with input; activates associated representations	Information associated with object activated	Posterior superior temporal cortex; temporal-occipital-parietal junction
Coordinate property lookup	Instruction to look up information associated with a salient part or characteristic	Accesses pattern code and coordinates of part or characteristic in associative memory	Pattern code sent to pattern activation subsystems and spatial information sent to attention-shifting subsystems	Dorsolateral prefrontal cortex (stronger in right hemisphere)

Table 11.1 (continued)

Subsystem	Input	Operation	Output	Localization?
Categorical property lookup	Instruction to look up information associated with a salient part or characteristic	Accesses pattern code and categorical relation of part or characteristic in associative memory	Pattern code sent to pattern activation subsystem and spatial information sent to categorical–coordinate conversion subsystem	Dorsolateral prefrontal cortex (stronger in left hemisphere)
Categorical–coordinate conversion	Categorical spatial representation from categorical property lookup, and size and orientation of object from coordinate property lookup	Converts categorical spatial representation to range of coordinates	Range of coordinates sent to attention-shifting subsystems	Posterior parietal lobes??
Attention shifting	Coordinates of a perceptual unit	Disengages attention from previous location, shifts to a new location by moving attention window, eye, head, and/or body, and then engages attention window at new location and size	New pattern surrounded by attention window	Posterior parietal cortex, superior colliculus, thalamus, anterior cingulate, frontal eye fields
Shape shift	Output from motor programming system, or other transformation specification	Alters representation in spatiotopic mapping subsystem, alters mapping function from pattern activation subsystems to visual buffer	Priming to encode a changing stimulus or an image of a transformed object	Posterior parietal cortex (stronger in right hemisphere)

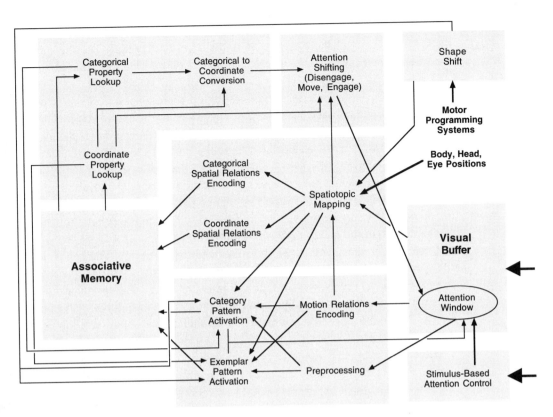

Figure 11.1 The architecture of visual mental imagery.

In this section I summarize how the subsystems work together to confer our major imagery abilities. Consider again the example of preparing to pack camping gear into a trunk by generating an image of one item, "looking for" the best location for it, maintaining this image while the backpacks, tent, and so on are added, and "moving" the objects around to find the best way to arrange them.

Image Generation

Single Part During perception, one can attend to an entire shape (albeit with relatively low resolution), and this shape can be stored in the pattern activation subsystems. It can be stored as a particular exemplar or as a member of a shape category. These representations later can be activated to form an image of a single global shape. To generate an image of a specific piece of gear, a property lookup subsystem accesses a pattern code in associative memory that is associated with that object, and sends this code to the pattern activation subsystems. The code can specify a prototype or a specific exemplar, which will correspond best to a representation in one of the two pattern activation subsystems. In this case, it is an exemplar of your tent (when it is packed into a sack), and so the exemplar pattern activation subsystem is most activated—which in turn engenders a configuration of activity (an image) in the visual buffer. Such activation is an extreme form of "priming," of the sort used when one expects to see a specific object or part during perception.

Multiple Part   In some tasks, high-resolution representations of parts or characteristics (e.g., surface markings) must be added to the global image. This process draws on subsystems that are also used in perceptual top-down hypothesis testing. To flesh out an image, the property lookup subsystems access representations of parts or characteristics that are associated with the object in associative memory. These representations specify the location and size of each part or characteristic and its relation to a "foundation part" (where the to-be-added part belongs). For example, in visualizing a duffel bag, the representation of the handle may be the strongest representation, so it "wins," and that part or characteristic will be added next to the image. The handle is at a specific location on the bag. If the part or characteristic is associated with a coordinate spatial representation (one is forming an image of a specific exemplar that was examined carefully during encoding), then this representation is sent to the attention-shifting subsystems to shift the attention window to that part of the global image, just as during top-down hypothesis testing in perception proper. If the part or characteristic is associated with a categorical spatial representation, the location of the foundation part is looked up (e.g., the handle might be "at the top"). The location of this part or characteristic is sent to the categorical-conversion subsystem, which computes the "top" of the object (which probably involves numerous heuristics, such as the fact that this object is wider than it is high), and then it sends these coordinates to the attention-shifting subsystem. These coordinates would indicate the location of the part relative to the foundation part. Once the attention window is properly positioned, the pattern code is sent to the pattern activation subsystems and the mapping function is adjusted so that the additional part or characteristic (the handle) is imaged at the appropriate location and size (see pp. 291–293 for additional details).

According to the theory, multipart images can be generated in the following ways. One can form two types of visual-memory-based images. These images are formed by activating representations of parts or characteristics in the pattern activation subsystems. Such images can be generated by using either coordinate spatial relations representations or categorical spatial relations representations to position the parts or characteristics. I assume that if coordinate spatial relations are used, then representations in the exemplar pattern activation subsystem typically are used to visualize the individual components; parts or characteristics with specific shapes usually are required if precise spatial relations are employed. In contrast, if categorical spatial relations are used, then representations in the category pattern activation subsystem typically are used to visualize the parts or characteristics; parts or characteristics with prototypical shapes usually are most appropriate if "generic" spatial relations are employed. In addition, in some cases it is possible that both sorts of representations are used to form an image; for example, if one did not notice the shape of a handle on a particular piece of luggage, the exemplar image might be augmented by a prototypical handle placed in the typical location.

One can visualize novel combinations of familiar objects using the same processes that generate images of objects with high-resolution parts or characteristics. For example, a helpful relative might suggest that one pack all of the large items at the back of the trunk, side by side, and the small ones up front. To form such an image, spatial relations representations (either decoded from a verbal description or formulated elsewhere in the system) are used to arrange global images (or, subsequently, images of parts or characteristics). The attention window is shifted successively just as it is when a single object is augmented, and images are generated just as they are when the objects are visualized in isolation.

I also argued that attention-based images can be generated in two ways. The kinds of visual-memory-based images discussed so far require activating representations of object properties in a pattern activation subsystem. In contrast, attention-based images do not require activating such modality-specifc visual memories. Rather, after the attention window has been properly positioned in the visual buffer (as described above), attention is engaged at that location. For example, such images occur if one looks at a regular pattern of dots (as on a peg board) and "sees" the dots organized into geometric forms. After one attends to a specific location, attention is not disengaged when one shifts to another location—and so a spatial image is built up as one attends to successive locations. Such images can be formed using either categorical or coordinate spatial relations to shift the attention window.

Mental Drawing   Finally, one can mentally draw by using a special type of attention-based imagery. In such cases, one can imagine arbitrary patterns of lines by shifting the attention window not from one discrete location to another, but incrementally. As the attention window is moved, a path of activation is left in its wake. For example, one might visualize tying the camping equipment on a roof rack, and "seeing" where rope should go to secure the lot.

Image Inspection

One inspects objects in images using the same mechanisms that are used to encode and interpret objects during perception.

Object Properties   As one visualizes packing camping gear into the trunk, one will "look" for likely places for specific items. If one "looks at" an imaged object or scene with no expectations about its parts or characteristics (including its color and texture), the attention window would surround the portion of the image in the central, high-resolution region of the visual buffer, non-accidental and signal properties are extracted from the image in the preprocessing subsystem, and these properties are matched to stored representations in the pattern activation subsystems. At the same time, motion relations are encoded, as are three-dimensional and spatial properties (via the spatiotopic mapping subsystem). Recognition occurs when the input matches the properties of a representation stored in either the category or exemplar pattern activation subsystem. The pattern code associated with this representation, along with a measure of goodness of match, is sent to associative memory (at which point a name, category, or other associate can be accessed). For example, one might notice that one of the backpacks has long rods protruding from the top (which one had forgotten, at the level of explicit representations in associative memory). These rods would get in the way if the backpack were positioned against the spare tire, and so one will not want to put it there.

If one is seeking a specific object, part, or property, its representation in associative memory is accessed by the property lookup subsystems, and its pattern code is sent to the pattern activation subsystems. These subsystems are primed for the corresponding representation to the extent that the pattern code activates a stored representation. If the object, part, or property is depicted in the image, the input from the pattern activation subsystem will cause it to "pop out" in the image.

Spatial Properties   Subsystems in the dorsal system are used when one encodes spatial properties, such as the relative sizes of two pieces of luggage or whether one piece of luggage is in front of another or six inches from another. The categorical spatial relations subsystem is used to categorize spatial properties of objects or their spatial relations, whereas the coordinate spatial relations encoding subsystem is used to estimate metric properties or distances between objects or properties. If the input is too complex, a visual routine may be used for these purposes. Such routines consist of instructions in associative memory about how to shift the attention window over an image (see Ullman 1984); if the instructions can be carried out successfully, a particular pattern or sought property is present. For example, if one wants to know whether two line fragments are connected, one can trace along the line from one to the other; if this is possible, then they are in fact connected.

Scanning and Zooming   If a sought part or characteristic is not found, the attention window may not be focused on the appropriate portion of the object and/or the object may be at the wrong level of resolution. Scanning short distances can be achieved by shifting the attention window; scanning longer distances requires an image transformation. When longer distances are scanned, one visualizes what one would see if one shifted one's eyes, head, or body in a certain way. In so doing, the shape shift subsystem alters the spatial properties represented in the spatiotopic mapping subsystem and alters the mapping function from the pattern activation subsystems to the visual buffer. Similarly, if the object subtends too small a visual angle, "zooming" will be necessary; this process is also a form of image transformation. To "zoom in," one visualizes what one would see if one moved closer to the object in the image, which also involves altering the representations of spatial properties and changing the mapping function from the pattern activation subsystems to the visual buffer so that the image is consistent with the new spatial properties. As the resolution improves, parts and characteristics that are implicit on the global image are fleshed out via a process of vector completion, which is also used during perception proper.

Image Maintenance

In my example, as one visualizes additional pieces of camping equipment, images of the previous pieces must be maintained. Visual-memory-based images are retained over time by repeatedly activating the appropriate representation or representations in a pattern activation subsystem. The amount of material that can be retained in an image depends on how effectively it can be organized into chunks, which is accomplished by the preprocessing subsystem (and can be promoted by adjusting the attention window to encode to-be-chunked material at the same time). In contrast, attention-based images are retained over time by continuing to engage attention to the same loci in the visual buffer.

Image Transformations

Motion Encoded   Motion-encoded transformations arise when one generates an image of a previously seen moving object or scene. In such cases, different representations in a pattern activation subsystem may have been stored at different points in time. Hence, one activates a series of moving images. Associative memory may contain representations of where the eyes were looking at each point in time, and these representations are used to activate the appropriate images in sequence.

Motion Added   Motion-added transformations arise when one alters an imaged object in a novel way. For example, one can imagine sliding baggage around in the trunk, rotating it, flipping it over, or even squishing it together. The shape shift subsystem modifies spatial representations in the spatiotopic mapping subsystem and makes corresponding changes to the mapping function from a pattern activation subsystem to the visual buffer. At the same time, the pattern activation subsystem is primed. The instructions for the shape shift subsystem often come from motor programming subsystems; this process prepares one to encode the input that results from an action. In some cases, one may actually imagine carrying out a movement in order to transform an imaged object; for example, to visualize a duffel bag with the ends pushed together, one may program the relevant movement and imagine performing that action on the luggage, which will change the image accordingly. Such motor-initiated processing causes image transformations to occur in small increments. Such seemingly continuous *shift transformations* are to be distinguished from *blink transformations*. Objects sometimes can be transformed by allowing one image to fade and generating a new one that is altered in the specified way; objects transformed in this may do not appear to move through intermediate positions.

Field-General versus Region-Bounded   In addition, one can transform either the entire field (e.g., by anticipating what one would see as one moved closer to the trunk), or a selected object, part, or portion (by surrounding it with the attention window and altering the mapping function to that region).

Transformation Locus   Finally, if a visible object is familiar, one can recognize it and generate the image, which is transformed. This image appears distinct from the object. But if the object is not familiar, or if task requirements (e.g., having to distinguish left from right, which is not preserved in the pattern activation subsystems) preclude generating an image from memory, then the stimulus is encoded anew and an image is formed on the basis of that representation. In this case, the image seems to spring from the object.

In summary, the present theory offers concise accounts for our major imagery abilities. These accounts follow naturally from mechanisms that were hypothesized for other reasons. Thus, the theory has some measure of what I called "explanatory adequacy," by analogy to Chomsky's ideas (see chapter 5 of Kosslyn 1980).

RELATION TO THE PREVIOUS VERSION OF THE THEORY

The present theory is an extension of the one I offered in 1980; except as noted, the previously inferred mechanisms have not been rejected but rather have been recast and further articulated. Because the key distinctions drawn in the previous version of the theory are preserved here, the phenomena that the previous version accounted for can also be accounted for by the present one. And because the new version of the theory offers additional distinctions, it can account for phenomena that were not addressed by the previous one. Rather than review the literature prior to 1980 again (Kosslyn 1980 contains an extensive and detailed literature review), I will point out the correspondences between previous constructs and the present ones, and explain how the operation of the previously formulated components is captured by the present theory. Table 11.2 summarizes the subsystems posited by the previous version of the theory (from Kosslyn 1980). Let us consider each subsystem in turn.

Visual Buffer

The visual buffer in the previous version of the theory was modeled by an array in a computer, which was anisotropic but homogeneous. The present conception is that the visual buffer corresponds to a set of topographically mapped visual areas in cortex, which are anisotropic and nonhomogeneous; resolution is greatest in the center and decreases toward the periphery. The areas works together to implement a multiscaled structure, and images are represented at different spatial scales within this structure. In addition, the visual buffer in the previous version of the theory was a passive receptacle of information, whereas it plays a much more active role in the present theory. The visual buffer actively fills in missing information, growing regions of homogeneous color and texture, and completing edges. In addition, the Spitzer, Desimone, and Moran (1988) findings indicate that task demands affect the sensitivity of neurons in at least some of the areas that compose the visual buffer. Thus, unlike the fixed-resolution array posited by the previous version of the theory, it is possible that the resolution of the visual buffer may change, within limits, depending on task requirements. In all other respects, the visual buffer plays the same role in both versions of the theory.

The PICTURE Process

The PICTURE process is equivalent to the process whereby information in a pattern activation subsystem is activated so much that it forces a new configuration of activation in the visual buffer. In addition, I now distinguish between this kind of visual-memory-based imagery and attention-based imagery, which is engendered by the pulvinar (and perhaps other nuclei of the thalamus). Attention-based images consist of a configuration of regions in the visual buffer that are attended to; these configurations do not specify object-property values, such as color or texture.

The FIND Process

The FIND process is equivalent to the joint operation of several subsystems. First, in the earlier theory it looked up a description of a part; this is now accomplished by the property lookup subsystems. Second, it looked up procedures (the equivalent of visual routines) that corresponded to the description. According to the revised theory, the property lookup subsystems can access stored descriptions of how to shift the attention window (i.e., visual routines). Such descriptions consist of sets of instructions about how to search for specific patterns or properties (see chapter 7). Third, the FIND process executed procedures in the visual buffer. In the revised theory, the attention-shifting subsystems execute visual routines. The revised theory also posits two other processes that are used when the FIND process was used previously. (1) The property lookup subsystems access a pattern code and prime the corresponding representation in a pattern activation subsystem, which prepares one to encode a sought part, characteristic, or object; when this representation is primed during image inspection, the sought pattern "pops out." This same process is used during perception to fill in a noisy input image; in this case, if the input image can be completed properly, one has located the sought part, characteristic, or object. (2) In addition, if one is seeking a specific spatial configuration, the spatial relations subsystems can be primed. Finally, the revised theory also accounts for bottom-up inspection, whereas the previous version only addressed top-down inspection.

Table 11.2 Outline of the theory-relevant processes posited by Kosslyn (1980)

Name	Type[a]	Input[b]	Operation	Output
PICTURE	P	r, θ file [size, location, orientation]	Maps points into surface matrix; mapping function may be adjusted to vary size, location, and/or orientation.	Configuration of points depicting contents of an IMG file (produces new format; if mapping function adjusted also produces new content).
FIND	C	Name of sought part	Looks up description; looks up procedures specified in description; executes procedures on surface matrix.	Passes back Locate/Not Locate; if Locate, passes back Cartesian coordinates of part.
PUT	P	Name of to-be-placed part	Looks up name of image file, location relation, and foundation part; looks up description of foundation part and relation; calls FIND to locate foundation part; adjusts mapping function; calls PICTURE.	Part integrated into image (produces new content).
IMAGE	P	Name of to-be-imaged object(s) [size, location, orientation, level of detail]	Locates IMG file; calls PICTURE [if size, location, or orientation specified, adjusts mapping function; if detail required, searches for HASA entries, calls PUT].	Detailed or skeletal image at specified or default size, location, and/or orientation (produces new content with different format, organization).
RESOLUTION	P	Surface image	Computes density of points in image.	A number indicating dot density of image (produces new format).
REGENERATE	A	Surface image	Works over surface matrix, refreshing most-faded parts first until all parts are refreshed.	Image reactivated, with sharpness relations among parts altered (alters content).

LOOKFOR	P	Command to find a named part or property on an image	Calls REGENERATE; looks up description and size of part; calls RESOLUTION; if density not optimal calls ZOOM or PAN; checks whether image overflows in direction of part, if so calls SCAN; calls FIND; if part not located searches for relevant HASA entries, calls PUT to insert regions, calls FIND.	Found/Not Found response.
SCAN	A	Image, direction of required shift [rate]	Moves all points in surface matrix along vector; fills in new material at leading edge via inverse mapping function.	Image repositioned (alters content).
ZOOM	A	Surface image, target resolution [rate]	Moves all points in surface matrix out from the center; fills in new material via inverse mapping function; calls RESOLUTION; calls PUT to insert new parts as resolution allows.	Scale change in image, higher resolution, and new parts (alters content).
PAN	A	Surface image, target resolution [rate]	Moves all points in surface matrix in from the center.	Scale change in image, lower resolution (alters content).
ROTATE	A	Image, angle, and direction [rate]	Moves all points in bounded region in specified direction around a pivot.	Reorients image (alters content).

[a] A indicates alteration transformations, which alter the initial data structure; P indicates production transformations that do not alter the initial data structure but produce a new one from it; C indicates comparison operations that compare two data structures or parts thereof.

[b] Optional input is indicated in brackets.

Reprinted from Kosslyn (1980) with permission.

The PUT Process

The PUT process served to coordinate the FIND and PICTURE processes. These functions are now performed locally, by the subsystems that accomplish the PICTURE and FIND operations. The use of parallel search through associative memory and winner-take-all networks obviates the need for a distinct control subsystem like PUT.

The IMAGE Process

The IMAGE process initiated the PICTURE process, searched for representations of stored properties, and called the PUT process if there were any parts to be added to the image. In the revised version of the theory, the IMAGE process is replaced by one that sends the name of the to-be-imaged object and the command to form an image to the property lookup subsystems. I assume that this "command" subsystem is part of a more general reasoning system, as sketched out in chapter 9 of Kosslyn and Koenig (1992). According to the revised theory, all other processing occurs because of local interactions among subsystems; no executive is necessary to coordinate them. Kosslyn, Flynn, and Amsterdam (1987, unpublished) programmed a model of an earlier version of the present imagery theory (which was missing the two types of pattern activation subsystems and the motion encoding subsystem, and included one additional subsystem), and demonstrated that it could indeed simulate image generation and inspection without needing any central control.

The RESOLUTION Process

The RESOLUTION process was used to determine whether one needed to zoom in or out in order to locate a sought part or characteristic. The revised theory posits that zooming is accomplished by the shape shift subsystem, which is often directed by subsystems used to program actions; these subsystems make use of information in associative memory. I assume that associative memory contains information about the relative sizes of parts and properties, and also contains information from the ventral and dorsal systems about the present contents of the visual buffer. If the sought part is smaller than the parts currently being attended to, then zooming in is necessary; if it is larger, then zooming out is necessary. Information in associative memory clearly plays a role in programming actions (see chapter 7 of Kosslyn and Koenig 1992), and one such role is determining whether one needs to move closer to or farther from an object to see a sought part or characteristic.

The RESOLUTION process was also used when subjects had to determine when an image matched a previous image that was at a specific level of resolution (as was necessary to perform some of the tasks used by Kosslyn et al. 1984). The revised theory posits that this function is accomplished by the exemplar pattern activation subsystem, which stores a representation of an object as it appeared at a specific time and place.

The REGENERATE Process

The earlier version of the theory posited that a distinct subsystem regenerates images. According to the present version, an image is regenerated by re-activating the appropriate representation or representations in the pattern activation subsystems. If a multipart image has been formed, then each of the underlying representations is reactivated individually, using the same parameter values on the mapping function to the visual buffer (so that the part, characteristic, or object appears at the appropriate location).

The LOOKFOR Process

LOOKFOR was another executive process, which coordinated a number of separate activities. First, the image was always regenerated prior to being inspected. In the present theory one cannot activate a representation to form an image at precisely the same time that the representation is used to match an input. Thus, if the image is to be regenerated, this must be done before or after it is inspected—and it makes more sense to regenerate the image before "looking" at it. According to the revised version of the theory, the regeneration process is more selective than was previously assumed. One primes the representation of the sought object, characteristic, or part prior to looking for it; this priming has the added benefit of making the target seem to jump into relief on the image, if it is present, which eliminates the need for exhaustive scanning.

Second, the LOOKFOR process accessed a representation of the size of the part, which I now claim is accomplished by the property lookup subsystems. Third, if the resolution was incorrect, the ZOOM or PAN process (which accomplished zooming in and out, respectively) was called into play. In the present theory, if the sought part or characteristic is the same size as "visible" details but is not currently evident, then the attention window is adjusted to a specific location and size via the attention-shifting subsystems which receives coordinates from the coordinate property lookup subsystem or the categorical–coordinate conversion subsystem. If the sought part or characteristic is the wrong size to be evident in the image, the shape shift subsystem alters the spatial properties of the representation and makes the corresponding changes in the mapping function from a pattern activation subsystem to the visual buffer—creating the impression of zooming in on or panning back from the imaged object.

Fourth, the LOOKFOR process also recruited the SCAN process, if scanning was necessary. In the revised theory, I posit that scanning is accomplished by shifting the attention window in the appropriate direction (using the same mechanisms that direct it during image generation). In addition, the image is shifted so that new portions "come into view." This shifting process is accomplished in the same way as zooming. Fifth, after scanning, the LOOKFOR process called the FIND process. According to the present theory, images can be inspected using "bottom-up" processing; input is encoded by the ventral and dorsal systems, as occurs in perception. Thus, one does not need to call a separate process whenever one is inspecting an imaged pattern, and one can notice unanticipated objects, parts, or characteristics in an image. When one is searching for a specific object, part, or characteristic, the pattern activation subsystems are primed to help one recognize the sought pattern—which can cause a sought part to "pop out," obviating the need for serial scanning.

Sixth, if the part or property was not found, the LOOKFOR process searched memory for descriptions of parts, which were sent to the PUT process and the image was augmented. According to the revised theory, one primes the representation of a sought part or property in the pattern activation subsystems, which causes it to "pop into view" as soon as the image is at the right level of resolution. The priming process not only highlights parts that are clearly evident in the image but also completes parts that may be only implicitly or partially depicted in the global image.

The SCAN, ZOOM, PAN, and ROTATE Processes

The SCAN, ZOOM, PAN, and ROTATE processes accomplished distinct image transformations. The present theory has replaced all of them with more general image transformation processes, as summarized earlier.

The ANSWERIF Process

Finally, the previous version of the theory accounted for considerable amounts of data on the role of imagery in fact retrieval and question answering. The ANSWERIF process mimicked a parallel search process that looks up stored propositional information at the same time as it generates and inspects images. According to the present theory, the property lookup subsystems are also used to search associative memory for propositions when one is trying to answer a question (see chapter 10; see also chapters 4 and 6 of Kosslyn and Koenig 1992). These subsystems will initially access a representation of the entire object (or scene, part, or characteristic—but I focus on objects here), and the pattern code associated with this representation addresses a global image representation in the pattern activation subsystems. While the global image is being generated, properties that are associated with the object can be accessed—either to add parts to an image or to use them to answer a question. Thus, the present theory also assumes that an image is generated and inspected at the same as propositional representations are being accessed. As before, whichever process operates most quickly will produce the response.[1]

Summary: Mapping to the Previous Version of the Theory

The revised theory is in fact able to mimic the operation of the mechanisms proposed previously. This is desirable because the previous version of the theory was able to account for virtually all of the relevant findings in the literature. If one were so inclined, one could now go through the literature review in *Image and Mind* and substitute the functions described here for those posited previously. The present theory accounts for all of the subtle effects that were previously explained, particularly in chapters 6, 7, 8, and 9 of Kosslyn (1980), which were entitled "Generating Visual Images," "Inspecting Visual Images," "Transforming Visual Images," and "Using Visual Images to Answer Questions," respectively.[2]

TESTING THE THEORY AS A WHOLE: INDIVIDUAL DIFFERENCES AND TASK ANALYSES

The present theory is relatively complex for a psychological theory. This does not worry me; the brain is a very complex machine. Indeed, as I noted previously I have exactly the opposite concern: The theory is relatively simple for a description of a complex mechanism—even one as complex as a personal computer. The brain is arguably the most complex structure in the known universe (see Fischbach 1992). Thus any viable theory of the brain will not be simple. However, this complexity is also a potential pitfall; it affords a great deal of leeway for explaining empirical results. Thus it becomes critical to test not only the assumptions about individual subsystems but also the claims about how the subsystems work together.

Brain-scanning studies are one way to perform such overall tests, but these studies rely in part on assumptions about anatomical localization. Such assumptions could be awry, even if the functional decomposition is correct. Hence, we need a test of the overall theory that focuses on the claims about function, independently of the claims about localization. In this section I summarize one such investigation.

I expect some readers to have had difficulty with some of the imagery examples provided earlier in the book; it has long been known that people differ widely in their ability to use visual mental imagery. Indeed, Galton's (1883) work on this topic was one of the foundations on which scientifc psychology was built. Intuitively, it seems clear that individual differences in imagery have important ramifcations for how well one could perform specifc tasks. For example, if a person had no imagery whatsoever, it seems unlikely that that person could be a successful architect or be adept at packing equipment efficiently into helicopter loading bays. But it may not be intuitively obvious how to extend the theory developed in this book to this topic. In fact, the study of individual differences in imagery is one way to investigate the theory taken as a whole.

Kosslyn et al. (1984) and Kosslyn, Van Kleeck and Kirby (1990) asked whether individual differences in imagery are to be understood at the level of a single overarching ability, or whether people differ at a finer level of analysis, that is, at the level of individual subsystems. Logically, there are three alternative conceptions of individual differences in imagery. At one extreme, a person could simply be relatively good or bad at imagery in general; in this case, imagery ability would have the status of a trait. At another extreme, each imagery task could be accomplished by a distinct skill; in this case, a person's performance on one task might have no bearing on his or her performance on another. A third possibility is suggested by the present theory. This conception lies between these two extremes, and posits that imagery involves a relatively small number of processing subsystems that are drawn upon in different combinations for different tasks. If this conception is correct, then the similarity of performance between two tasks should depend on which processing subsystems are used in each of them; performance levels should be more similar when more of the same subsystems are used to perform two tasks. However, some processes are more important for a given task than others, and this consideration must also be taken into account.

Kosslyn et al. (1984) reported evidence that this third possibility is correct. We designed a battery of imagery tasks and gave them to 50 people; these people were recruited through an advertisement in the *Boston Globe*, and varied widely with respect to numerous variables (including age, education, and socioeconomic status). We first simply correlated the ranked performance measures for each task. If the first possibility were correct, and imagery ability is a trait, then we would expect high correlations for all pairs of tasks. If a person was poor at one task, he or she should have been poor at them all; if he or she was good at one task, he or she should have been good at them all. (We did not expect perfect correlations, of course, because of measurement error; but we did expect correlations as high as the split-half reliability of the measures.) If the second possibility were correct, and imagery corresponded to a set of task-specific independent skills, then we would expect correlations of essentially zero. Performance on each task should not have predicted performance on another. Finally, if people differed in the efficacy of individual processing subsystems, which are shared to greater or lesser degrees by different pairs of tasks, then we would expect a wide range of correlations. And in fact, the correlations ranged from −.44 to .79, and more than twice as many were significant than would be expected merely due to chance.

Similar results were reported by Poltrock and Brown (1984), who compared the performance of 77 subjects on 15 imagery measures that were designed to assess image generation, interpretation, and transformation. The correlations among their measures ranged from −.76 to .93, but in general the measures were only weakly related, which is of interest because many of the tasks intuitively appeared to tap different aspects of imagery processing. Poltrock and Brown interpreted their results in terms of the earlier version of the present theory, and found that the theory provided qualitative insights into the patterns of correlations among their imagery measures. Poltrock and Brown also examined the usefulness of traditional self-report and questionnaire methods, but I will forgo discussion of such findings (which have many potential pitfalls; e.g., see Kaufmann 1981, 1983; Marks 1983; Poltrock and Brown 1984).

Comparing Tasks

Intuitively, it might seem that the sheer number of processing subsystems that are shared by two tasks should predict the similarity in performance by a given individual. But, on reflection, it seems that the situation is not so straightforward: some subsystems will be more important than others, if only because a given dependent measure is more sensitive to some aspects of performance than to others. If so, then the efficacy of these subsystems will contribute disproportionately to measures of task similarity. Thus, my colleagues and I "weight" some subsystems more than others when we compare performance on tasks. In order to do so, we must not only determine which subsystems are likely to be recruited in each task, but also must determine which subsystems contribute most to the dependent measure.

However, one need not determine the entire set of subsystems that will be used for a specific task. To do so, one would have to predict which strategy most people will be likely to adopt; depending on the strategy, different combinations of processing subsystems will be recruited. But even if the tasks were designed so that a specific strategy was optimal, there is no way to ensure that subjects will necessarily use that strategy. Instead, we designed each of our tasks so that it would be very difficult unless the subjects used a particular class of strategies—which were characterized by the use of certain critical subsystems. For example, in a mental rotation task in which we measured the time to evaluate forms presented at different angular disparities from the standard upright, the task would be very difficult to perform without using the shape shift subsystem. Because the tasks were designed to strongly encourage use of these critical subsystems (if the subject was to perform them even moderately well), we focused our analysis on them.

The procedure Kosslyn, Van Kleeck, and Kirby (1990) devised for weighting subsystems is as follows: To determine which subsystems should be weighted for a given task, we (1) hypothesized which subsystems the subjects would need to use to perform the task with any relatively efficient strategy, (2) identified the dependent measure, and (3) selected the "key" subsystems, namely those that were the "rate-limiting" aspect of processing. Specifcally, we determined *which subsystems, if they were more effective, would result in improved scores on the dependent measure.* These subsystems were weighted in subsequent analyses. It is important to note that subsystems can vary in their speed, capacity, sensitivity, or accuracy, and differences in these characteristics will affect performance—but will be evident only if the characteristic affects the dependent measure. For example, if one is measuring only accuracy, the speed of processing will be irrelevant. The other subsystems, which are not rate-limiting, need only perform at a bare minimum for the task to be accomplished at near-maximal performance. Provided that they operate at all, greater efficacy of such subsystems will have only a slight influence, if any, on the assessed performance. Thus, we ignored these subsystems, given that individual differences in their efficacy will not contribute substantially to individual differences in performance on a task.

Another way to conceptualize the weighting criteria is as follows: As a task becomes more difficult (as assessed by the dependent measure of interest), some subsystems will have to "work harder" than others. For example, in a mental rotation task the shape shift subsystem must work harder (i.e., over a longer period) when the stimulus is tilted farther from the standard upright (and more rotation is required). It is these subsystems that should be weighted in subsequent analyses. Only if these "stressed" subsystems are efficacious will a subject be able to perform a task well as it becomes more difficult.

Thus, we identified the weighted subsystems that should be used in each task, and compared the number that were shared by every possible pair of tasks. This matrix of numbers was then correlated with the observed correlations among tasks. The earlier version of the theory did reasonably well in characterizing the underlying pattern of the correlations in task performance; the pattern of similarities we expected based on the models was correlated with the observed similiarities $r = .56$ with the actual pattern of correlations.

The earlier version of the theory was developed on the basis of a combination of behavioral data and computational reasoning. I made no attempt to consider properties of the brain, in part because relatively few relevant facts about neural information processing were then available. Indeed, most of the major discoveries about the brain that I have found so useful in this book were published after I developed the earlier version of the theory (e.g., Goldman-Rakic 1987; Moran and Desimone 1985; Ungerleider and Mishkin 1982; Van Essen and Maunsell 1983). This information not only has helped to make the theory more rigorous but also has helped me to articulate it further.

If the theory developed in this book is really an advance over the earlier one, then it should do at least as well in accounting for these data. The present theory was not developed with individual differences in mind, and makes contact with a wider range of phenomena than did the earlier one (which did not address neuropsychological findings). Kosslyn, Van Kleeck, and Kirby (1990) reanalyzed the individual differences data using a variant of the present theory. We found that task similarity based on this theory did indeed account for variation in the actual correlations, with $r = .63$ (for the comparison of predicted and observed correlations). This correlation is marginally higher than that obtained using the Kosslyn (1980) theory, and rested on fewer parameters (11 here, versus 13 before). Thus, we have some evidence that the theory as a whole can be taken seriously.

Wallace and Hofelich (1992) report another way to test our method of task analysis. Using the earlier version of the theory, they examined whether "improvement in one process, due to practice in a task weighted in that process, would lead to a generalized improvement in the process and be demonstrated in other tasks also weighted in that process" (p. 696). They examined two processes, FIND and REGENERATE. In one experiment, Wallace and Hofelich assigned the subjects to one of four practice groups. One group performed a standard mental rotation task (using angular nonsense figures, in the paradigm of Cooper 1975). According to the previous theory, the FIND process was used to monitor the rotation and was part of the process that realigned scrambled parts; the shape shift subsystem obviates the need for this process, and would be used instead of FIND. Subjects memorized six such figures in their standard upright orientations, and later determined whether they were normal or mirror-reflected; the figures were presented at different angular disparities from the upright. The subjects performed this task "until a ceiling on improvement was established." A second group was taught how to visualize line segments end to end, forming a pathway, when given a series of directions (e.g., "north," "northwest," etc.); this was one of the tasks used by Kosslyn et al. (1984), adapted from Bower (1972). This task clearly requires maintaining images over time. After visualizing a two- to six-segment sequence, the subjects were asked to determine whether the end point was above or below the start point (the responses were timed), and then were asked to draw the configuration. They repeated this task until they reached ceiling levels of performance. A third group was a "time control group." These subjects simply rested for about the amount of time required by subjects in the other groups. A fourth group was given visual distractor tasks that did not rely upon the critical processes.

Before and after each of these conditions, the subjects were given half of the "geometric analogies task" (see Novick and Tversky 1987). In this test, the subjects see three parts of a four-part geometric analogy on one page, and then turn the page to select which of five alternatives completes the analogy. The subjects must perform two image transformations in order to complete the analogy, and hence the processes used to transform images are critical in this task.

As expected, practice at mental rotation improved performance on the geometric analogies task, relative to the control conditions. Moreover, performance on the two tasks was significantly correlated. I now attribute this practice to improvement in the shape shift subsystem (see chapter 10). In contrast, practice at the line-drawing task did not improve performance on the geometric analogies task; this finding was also expected, given that the two tasks do not share weighted subsystems.

In a second experiment, Wallace and Hofelich reversed the roles of the mental rotation and geometric analogies tasks, now investigating whether practice at geometric analogies transfers to mental rotation. As expected, practice also transferred in this experiment. But again, there was no transfer from line drawing performance to mental rotation.

In a third experiment, Wallace and Hofelich examined process-specific transfer based on the REGENERATE process. They adapted a task developed by Kosslyn (1975). They had subjects visualize animals as if they were superimposed upon a 16-cell matrix. The subjects were then asked to find named parts of the animal, or to place the parts on the animal even if they were not present; they were then to indicate whether each part was appropriate for the animal, and to indicate where it was located in the image. The subjects learned to assign a number to each cell of the matrix, and used these numbers to specify the locations. Both the response times and the accuracy of the locations were measured. The line-drawing task was now used for pre- and posttesting.

As expected, performance on the line-drawing task improved after subjects practiced holding complex images (animals against matrices) in mind. Moreover, performance on the two tasks was highly correlated. In contrast, practice in mental rotation did not affect performance on the line-drawing task.

In short, Wallace and Hofelich provide good evidence for the independence of at least two processes used in imagery, one involved in transforming imaged objects and one involved in maintaining them in images. Their technique is very promising, and can be used to investigate virtually all of the distinctions I have drawn.

Accounting for Missing Variance in Individual Differences

Although the present theory accounted for the results reasonably well, it is worth keeping in mind that it accounted for only a bit more than 40% of the total variance in individual differences. Much of the missing variance was probably due to measurement error; the average split-half reliability was $r = .77$, and in this light the correlation of $r = .66$ between the predicted and observed similarities was rather good. However, at least some of the unexplained variance must be due to other factors. One problem may be in the rules we developed to determine when specific subsystems will be used; table 11.3 summarizes the rules we developed for assigning subsystems, and table 11.4 summarizes the weighting rules (both tables are modfied from the original to fit the present version of the theory[3]). These rules are formulated as if the effects of the systems are completely additive, but as was discussed in chapter 2, this is unlikely to be correct; I have repeatedly relied on the idea that subsystems prime subsystems earlier in the flow of information, which will surely produce various sorts of interdependencies among subsystems that result in nonlinear interactions. In addition, although we designed the tasks so that there was a "best" type of strategy, it seems unlikely that all subjects used this strategy. Some of the missing variance may reflect differences in cognitive styles, which lead subjects to select certain types of strategies even if they are not particularly effective for a given task (cf. Eley 1981; MacLeod, Hunt, and Mathews 1978; Mathews, Hunt, and MacLeod 1980).

At least three factors seem necessary to explain individual differences. First, differences in the efficacy of individual subsystems is clearly important. Second, people develop preferred strategies for a number of reasons, not all of which are based on how useful the strategy is. If one hits upon a way to solve a specific type of problem, one may stick with this method in the future simply because it is familiar. These strategies can differ in subtle but important ways, such as the kind of reference system the subject imposes on an object when performing a specific task (see Just and Carpenter 1985). And third, people also differ in a number of parameters that are likely to cut across the operation of individual subsystems and to place constraints on which strategies they are likely to adopt. For example, people vary in their overall speed of processing, capacity of short-term memory, and so on. These factors will interact with

Table 11.3 Subsystem assignment rules (adapted from Kosslyn, Van Kleeck, and Kirby 1990). The visual buffer and attention window are used in all tasks

Generation

These subsystems are used whenever images are formed. They are also used if one expects to see a specific type of stimulus, in which case they prime the pattern activation subsystems.

Single-unit patterns: associative memory, categorical or coordinate property lookup subsystem, category or exemplar pattern activation subsystem.[a]

Multi-unit patterns: (1) For mutable objects when named spatial relations are adequate for positioning parts: associative memory, categorical property lookup, category pattern activation subsystem, categorical–coordinate conversion, attention shifting, spatiotopic mapping, categorical spatial relations encoding. (2) For specific exemplars when precise metric positioning is required: associative memory, coordinate property lookup, exemplar pattern activation subsystem, attention shifting, spatiotopic mapping, coordinate spatial relations encoding.

Inspection

These subsystems are used whenever imagery is used or one is encoding a stimulus perceptually.

Object-properties encoding or shape identification: (1) normal viewpoint, small visual angle (4° or less), highly familiar shape configuration: preprocessing, category or exemplar pattern activation, associative memory; (2) not highly familiar shape configuration: preprocessing, category or exemplar pattern activation, associative memory, spatiotopic mapping, categorical spatial relations encoding, categorical property lookup, categorical–coordinate conversion, attention shifting; (3) unusual viewpoint or viewed at a large visual angle or in arbitrary portions: same as (2) but coordinate spatial relations encoding used to integrate over successive encodings; (4) specific exemplar must be identified, familiar shape and viewpoint, small visual angle: preprocessing, exemplar pattern activation, associative memory; (5) specific exemplar must be identified when viewed at a large visual angle or from unusual viewpoint: preprocessing, exemplar pattern activation, associative memory, spatiotopic mapping, coordinate spatial relations encoding, coordinate property lookup, attention shifting. In all cases, the motion relations encoding subsystem is also used if the object is moving and one is inspecting movement patterns.

Color or texture identification

(1) The preprocessing, exemplar pattern activation, and associative memory subsystems are used when one must encode precise information about color or texture; (2) the preprocessing, category pattern activation, and associative memory subsystems are used when one must encode categorical information about color or texture.

Spatial relations identification

Categorical spatial relations: Spatiotopic mapping, categorical spatial relations encoding, associative memory

Coordinate spatial relations: Spatiotopic mapping, coordinate spatial relations encoding, associative memory

Image maintenance

These subsystems are used whenever a mental image must be retained for more than 1 second.

Associative memory, categorical property lookup or coordinate property lookup, preprocessing, category or exemplar pattern activation.

Table 11.3 (continued)

Image transformation

These subsystems are used whenever one expects to see specific consequences after performing an action or after an imaged object is transformed.[b]

Motion encoded: When one is recalling a moving image: Multiunit patterns: (1) For mutable objects when named spatial relations are adequate for positioning parts: associative memory, categorical property lookup, category pattern activation categorical–coordinate conversion, attention shifting, spatiotopic mapping, categorical spatial relations encoding, motion relations encoding. (2) For specific exemplars when precise metric positioning is required: associative memory, coordinate property lookup, exemplar pattern activation subsystem, attention shifting, spatiotopic mapping, coordinate spatial relations encoding, motion relations encoding.

Motion-added: When one is visualizing an object being transformed in a novel way: shape shift subsystem, spatiotopic mapping, category or exemplar pattern activation, coordinate spatial relations encoding, motion relations encoding, associative memory, coordinate property lookup (if feedback is sent to the motor programming system).

---

[a] The category pattern activation subsystem is used whenever the categorical property lookup subsystem is used, and the exemplar pattern activation subsystem is used whenever the coordinate property lookup subsystem is used.

[b] If an imaged object must be transformed a large amount, the image may be allowed to fade and a new one generated (this is a *blink transformation*).

Table 11.4 Rules for weighting the subsystems (adapted from Kosslyn, Van Kleeck, and Kirby 1990).

Preprocessing

Response time: (1) Objects or parts must be recognized from unusual viewpoints; (2) a task involves figure/ground segregation or perceptual organization.

Accuracy: A figure is camouflaged or partially occluded.

Motion relations encoding

Response time: (1) One must classify a pattern of motion; (2) one must use a pattern of motion to recognize a stimulus.

Accuracy: (1) Distinctive motion patterns are very similar to other familiar motion patterns; (2) motion is obscured by moving background.

Category pattern activation

Response time: (1) Objects or parts are recognized as members of a category on the basis of their shapes; (2) images of prototypical shapes are generated.

Accuracy: (1) One must maintain in an image more than about four perceptual units; (2) one must maintain in an image a single perceptual unit for more than its fade time (about 1 second).

Exemplar pattern activation

Response time: (1) One assesses shape, texture or color precisely; (2) one images a specific exemplar.

Accuracy: (1) Precise shape, color, or texture is used to guide processing; (2) a precise judgment of shape, color, or texture is required; (3) one must maintain in an image more than about four perceptual units; (4) one must maintain in an image a single perceptual unit for more than its fade time (about 1 second).

Spatiotopic Mapping

Response time: (1) The categorical or coordinate spatial relations encoding subsystems are weighted.

Accuracy: (1) The categorical or coordinate spatial relations encoding subsystems are weighted.

Categorical spaiial relations encoding

Response time: (1) Categorical spatial properties of or between parts or objects must be reported or evaluated; (2) the parts of an imaged object must be positioned during image generation and the parts are arranged using categorical relations.

Accuracy: A very subtle categorical discrimination is required.

Coordinate spatial relations encoding

Response time: (1) Precise metric spatial properties of or between parts or objects must be reported or evaluated; (2) the parts of an imaged object must be positioned precisely during image generation.

Accuracy: Precise metric positioning or evaluation of objects or parts is required.

Categorical property lookup

Response time: (1) An image of a multipart object is generated or inspected, and recall of nameable spatial relations is adequate for positioning or location parts.

Accuracy: This subsystem is not weighted.

Coordinate property lookup

Response time: An image of a multipart object is generated or inspected, and recall of precise spatial relations is necessary to position or locate parts.

Accuracy: This subsystem is not weighted.

Categorical–coordinate conversion

Response time: The categorical property lookup subsystem is weighted.

Accuracy: This subsystem is not weighted.

Attention shifting

Response time: (1) The task requires shifting attention across or between objects or parts; (2) the task requires changing the resolution of the image.

Accuracy: This subsystem is not weighted.

Shape shift

Response time: An object must be rotated, translated, scaled, or scanned more than about 10° of visual angle in a novel way (and hence one cannot recall a moving image or simply shift the attention window, but rather must use motion-added processes to translate the imaged pattern in addition to shifting the attention window).

Accuracy: Precise metric relations are required to rotate, translate, scale, or scan an object more than about 10° of visual angle.

differences in the efficacies of individual subsystems. For example, if two processes are working in parallel, the probability that either will finish first may increase if both operate very quickly and often nearly "tie" each other than if they operate relatively slowly. The speeds of the two subsystems could differ by the same percentage, but if the actual means are very low, variability might alter the distributions of the outcomes (assuming that variability is not a simple function of the means). Similarly, these factors will place constraints on which strategies one adopts; for example, if one is relatively slow, strategies with relatively few steps might be desirable.

But even so, we should not neglect the fact that the glass is half (well, say 40%) full, and not simply half-empty. The fact that the present theory, which was not designed with individual differences in mind, could predict the structure underlying the set of data as well as it did is unlikely to be due to chance. I am optimistic that more sophisticated modeling in the future will allow us to examine nonlinear effects that arise when subsystems interact, and I trust that we eventually will devise ways to assess cognitive styles. Such an effort could have wide-ranging consequences (e.g., see Strosahl and Ascough 1981).

NEXT STEPS

The theory developed in this book focuses on architecture, that is, on delineating the components of the imagery processing system. This theory sets the stage for asking many interesting questions about imagery, particularly those about its role in mental life. In *Image and Mind* I discussed at length the role of imagery in memory retrieval, and it is also clear that imagery plays a critical role in many types of reasoning (e.g., see Shepard and Cooper 1982). Detailed theories of the role of imagery in reasoning can easily be built on the foundations of the present theory. Pylyshyn (1981) seemed to feel that depictive images would have little or no computational utility, even if they were computationally tractable. But in fact, Funt (1976, 1977) had already shown that such representations were useful in a computer system that solved complex problems, such as anticipating how a pile of tumbling, irregularly shaped blocks would settle. More recently, Gardin and Meltzer (1989) found that analogical models helped a computer program to solve certain types of "naive physics" problems. These models were represented by sets of pixels in an array, and had a "structural similarity" to the objects that were being modeled. This approached proved to be useful in predicting the behavior of flexible objects, such as strings, and of liquids. Particularly interesting, I found, was the report that once the program could simulate the behavior of strings, the researchers were able to use it to solve mazes—it simply found a pathway between the initial and terminal locations that respected the continuity constraints between each pair of points along a string. Thus, the program did not simply provide an ad hoc account of certain phenomena, but demonstrated genuine computational utility. Similarly, Glasgow, Fortier, and Allen (1992) have found an imagery-based system useful for determining crystal and molecular structure, and Stein (in press) finds it useful to endow a navigating robot with depictive imagery. Baron (1985) and Julstrom and Baron (1985) also describe computational models of imagery that rely on depictive representations, as well as mechanisms that produce and interpret such representations. Indeed, theories of the general sort I have proposed seem to be cropping up with increased frequency (e.g., see also Lindsay 1988; Omori 1992), for good reason (see the discussion surrounding Glasgow's [in press] argument that imagery is an alternative to exclusively proposition-based reasoning in AI).

In addition, imagery appears to play a special role in representing emotionally charged material (e.g., see Aylwin 1990; Horowitz 1983; Martin and Williams 1990). I suggest that the present theory can be viewed as providing constraints on theories of such phenomena. Some of the brain loci that play key roles in imagery have connections (direct and indirect) to areas of the brain that are known to be critical for emotion, such as the amygdala (e.g., see Aggleton 1992). By understanding the functions of these areas, we can begin to formulate specific hypotheses about the role of imagery in emotion. Moreover, once we know the fundamentals about what a mental image is, how it arises, and how it is used, this will provide hints about why imagery "feels" the way it does. For example, if image transformations depend in part on motor processing, this will say a lot about why people sometimes feel as if they are physically manipulating objects. Hampson and Morris (1990) provide a theory that shows how consciousness can be addressed in the context of facts about the role of imagery in information processing. More recently, Horne (1993) suggests that a "sensory-perceptual loop" lies at the heart of one's experience of imagery; this idea appears to make contact with the role of imagery in vector completion and as a form of cooperative computation, as developed in the present theory.

Rather than speculating further about such processes (in this already, perhaps, too-speculative book), I will only note that we are now in a good position to address such topics. With luck, future research can build on our understanding of basic imagery processes, showing how they shape the contributions of imagery to mental life more generally.

THE RESOLUTION OF THE IMAGERY DEBATES

Although we do not fully understand the mechanisms underlying imagery, I believe that we now know enough to assert that the "imagery debates" have been resolved. Recall that there were two central issues. First, we needed to specify what an image is: do images rely, at least in part, on depictive representations, or are the depictive aspects evident to introspection merely epiphenomenal concomitants of propositional processing? Addressing this issue turned out to be remarkably straightforward, once we knew that human visual cortex includes topographically mapped areas. Given that the size of an imaged object shifts the pattern of activity in at least one such area (identified as area 17 by the Talairach and Tournoux [1988] atlas), we have good evidence that image representations are depictive. This inference is further buttressed by the results of studies of brain-damaged patients. For example, Farah, Soso, and Dasheiff (1992) found that a patient who had her occipital lobe resected in one hemisphere could image objects over only about half the horizontal visual angle that she could prior to the surgery. Thus, it is very difficult to argue that the depictive representations in the occipital lobe play a merely epiphenomenal role in imagery.

Second, to resolve the debates we needed to know what "looks" at patterns in images and how images are generated and transformed. Does the claim that image representations are depictive imply various paradoxes and incoherencies, as suggested by Pylyshyn (1973, 1981)? Addressing this set of issues was no mean task. My strategy was to take advantage of the abundant evidence that imagery and perception share common mechanisms, and to build a theory of imagery piggybacked upon a theory of high-level visual perception. This approach allowed my colleagues and I to develop theories of specific processing subsystems, and helped us to hypothesize where these subsystems are implemented in the brain. The results from PET studies summarized in chapters 8 and 9 supported the proposed decomposition of high-level visual processing, and demonstrated that imagery does indeed rely on many of the same mechanisms used in top-down hypothesis testing during perception. Furthermore, the theory of processing subsystems that was developed to account for our perceptual abilities also accounted for our imagery abilities and provided insight into the nature of individual differences in imagery. Given that this theory has been simulated in a computer model (see Kosslyn 1987; Kosslyn et al. 1990), one cannot complain that the theory trades on vague constructs or on ambiguities inherent in the English language.

In short, we now have strong evidence in favor of depictive representations, and a reasonably clear picture of the mechanisms that generate, interpret, and use imagery in information processing. One cannot object to the claim that images are depictive by asserting that there are various paradoxes associated with the very idea. Rather, the mechanisms underlying imagery seem no more mysterious than those underlying visual perception—which is not surprising, since many of the same mechanisms underlie both abilities. I am not claiming that all of the puzzles surrounding imagery have now been solved; far from it. But I am claiming that we can stop debating about the fundamentals, and can address additional questions within a general framework. In my view, the fact that many issues are left open is not a weakness of the present project, but a strength: these issues clearly are empirically tractable, and research designed to address them will only further illuminate our understanding of visual mental imagery.

Although I have focused on imagery in this book, I hope that it makes a much more general point. Let me illustrate this point with an anecdote. Some years ago I discovered a text file buried in my word processing program. It recounted the history of the program, explaining how many of its features seemed interesting but not very practical when the program was first written. But then "a miracle" occurred: The first laser printer was released. Suddenly, all those "extra" features became relevant, and desktop publishing was on its way. In a sense, the theory and methods developed by cognitive psychologists are like the original program; they have been lying in wait of something to make the field really take off. The connection to the brain appears to have been that extra something, allowing us to learn more from what we do best: designing tasks that require specific types of information processing. When behavioral data alone are not sufficient to resolve an issue, the tasks designed by experimental psychologists can be used to selectively activate specific brain systems while neural activity is being monitored and to study the consequences of brain damage—and these additional data can settle many issues.

I can now envision a research program that extends from the genetics of the brain systems that underlie imagery all the way to the behavioral consequences of imagery, which would have been impossible just a few years ago. It is clear that there are well-defined individual differences in imagery ability, and at least some of these differences may run in families (I have anecdotal evidence favoring this possibility). If so, then we may be able to discover which genes are responsible for variations in the properties of the brain (connection densities, transmitter availability, etc.) that give rise to variations in specific imagery abilities. In the near future we should have a reasonably clear idea about which parts of the brain are involved in specific aspects of imagery processing, and will know where to look for effects of genetic variation. Such a research program would map behavior into the mind, the mind into processing subsystems implemented in specific regions of the brain, those brain regions into circuits and transmitter systems, and so forth, all the way down to the genes. This sort of project would allow psychology to take advantage of the rich harvest of other fields, ranging from biology to molecular genetics. And to think that 100 years ago psychologists had barely discovered how to use behavior to assess cognitive function.

Notes

CHAPTER 1

1 Let me qualify this: I fully expect philosophers to continue to debate the matter; after all, that is their business. But I believe that enough is now known to begin to build on and accumulate theory. Philosophers are still arguing about the status of basic constructs in physics (e.g., Davies and Brown 1986) and biology (e.g., Sober 1984), but that has not gotten in the way of genuine progress in those fields. I do not mean to imply that philosophers have not played a useful role in the past or that they shall never do so again. For a recent example, Tye (1991) is not only helping to clarify key concepts but is also generating some stimulating new ideas that can be put to empirical test.

2 The material in this section was adapted from Kosslyn (1984) and Marsolek and Kosslyn (1992).

3 A depictive representation typically corresponds to a planar projection of an object, and hence each part of the representation corresponds to a part of the object as viewed from a specific perspective. However, this need not be so; a depictive representation could be fully three-dimensional and object-centered—analogous to a statue seen from God's eyes.

4 Note that distance per se is not explicitly represented in a depiction, as it is in a mileage chart. Rather, it is an emergent property of specifying values of locations in a space, which cannot be avoided if depictive representations are used.

5 This was, I must confess, a rather heavy-handed manipulation, and I apologized to the experimenter for it afterward. I assured him that I would never release his identity, or make him look silly, and I don't mean to be doing that here. Laboratory assistants do aim to please, but there are limits to what they can do—or (fortunately!)—are willing to do.

6 I use the term "approximately correct" because I do not believe that any current theory of mental events will prove entirely accurate. But that does not worry me; biology, physics, and chemistry have done reasonably well in spite of this condition. As long as a reasonably narrow class of theories can be delimited, researchers can begin to build on them even if the details have yet to be worked out.

7 Anderson's actual proof shows that if a particular theory is available, one can always formulate a less parsimonious alternative. This is not very interesting in and of itself. However, he pointed out that in many cases, such as the examples I've provided here, it is not clear whether one alternative is less parsimonious than the other.

8 Anderson's paper appeared irrelevant for at least two different reasons. One tradition in experimental psychology (the direct descendant of the behaviorist tradition leads researchers not be interested in specifying the nature of internal representations, only the effects of using them. In contrast, from another perspective the mere fact that two theories could produce

the same input/output relations is uninteresting. In this case, the question is whether the theories are equally "explanatory"; one theory might be based on straightforward principles, whereas the other rests on convoluted principles or vague, ill-defined ideas.

9 The distortions are probably not arbitrary. For example, Johnston (1986) argues that some aspects of the distortions help one to compute shape constancy.

10 I will not review in detail the electroencephalography (EEG) or event-related potential (ERP) studies of imagery in this book. EEG and ERP appear to be exquisitely sensitive to a wide range of variables, and hence the results in imagery studies are often inconsistent (e.g., see Ehrlichman and Barrett 1983). Although I have no doubt that many of the EEG and ERP findings are invaluable, I lack the technical expertise to evaluate specific studies. Thus, as a general rule I have focused on other techniques.

11 In fact, of the 16 subjects we tested, 3 did not show this difference. When the PET results were analyzed without the data from these subjects, we found greater differences between the large and small image conditions (although the difference was still statistically significant when all data were analyzed). I will discuss the reason why people require more time to inspect objects imaged at a small size than at a large size in chapter 10.

12 Several other areas were also affected by image size; these areas are discussed later in the book.

13 From here on the term "image" will refer to a depictive representation.

CHAPTER 2

1 To my knowledge, no one knows exactly which aspects of the networks are responsible for their brainlike properties. Two candidates are the use of gradient descent during training and the logistic accumulation function.

2 Kosslyn and Koenig (1992) posited a principle of "opportunistic processing." Any given task typically can be performed in many different ways. Particularly when the input is impoverished, people will try to make do with the available information by devising novel strategies, using information in unusual ways. For example, spatial information can be used to encode the shape of an object (e.g., by registering the width of an object at different heights), even though spatial information is used primarily for other purposes. I do not treat this as a separate characteristic, however, because it appears to be an emergent property of the others, specifically of concurrent processing and cooperative computation.

3 Skinner (1978) appears to have been confused about these points when he denigrated "cognitivism." He asks, rightly, what is gained by simply moving behavior into the head? Given that there are an infinite number of potential behaviors, such a direct mapping gives one reason to pause from the start. The present goal is not to move behaviors into the head, but to delineate the underlying mechanisms that give rise to them.

4 The principle of division of labor presumably came about in part as a consequence of natural selection. This raises a cautionary note: Many of the activities currently performed by the brain (such as the one you are engaged in right now) are not evolutionary "adaptations" in their own right. At least some of these activities may not be performed very efficiently from a computational point of view. Moreover, even when an activity is "basic" (i.e., was present during the periods when our ancestors were evolving), it need not have been organized very effectively. Some activities are parasitic upon others, and what is good for one may not be good for another. Imagery is a case in point; for example, it would be better for imagery if images did not fade so quickly, but this property appears to be useful in vision. If it had been important enough, a separate "mode" presumably could have evolved to retain images longer—but apparently did not. Thus, the principle of division of labor is merely one of many principles that must be taken together to describe the properties of neural information processing.

5 Many of these ideas were developed in collaboration with Vera Maljkovic, and were discussed more fully in a jointly authored paper (Kosslyn and Maljkovic 1990).

6 I thank Michael Tye for pointing out this perspective to me.

7 This is a methodological point. After one understands how a system operates, one might be able to formulate a sharp distinction between a what/how level—without representations—and an algorithmic level. My argument is that such a sharp distinction is not very useful when one is studying a system, trying to understand it.

8 Kosslyn and Koenig (1992) used the term *behavior* instead of *abilities* in part to emphasize that we ultimately are trying to explain what people can *do* and why. This term has led to confusion among some readers of that book, and so I've changed it here. However, in my view, a theory of processing is a theory of the underlying basis of observable behavior. Others (e.g., linguists) may disagree, preferring to focus on characterizing the nature of knowledge for its own sake. Depending on the question one asks, different things count as answers.

CHAPTER 3

1 In chapter 9 I summarize recent PET research that strongly supports this claim.

2 In this book I will not address reading per se, which appears to share some—but not all—of the processes used in object recognition and identification. This topic is considered in chapter 5 of Kosslyn and Koenig 1992.

3 In my earlier work (Kosslyn 1987), I stressed the "hierarchical decomposition constraint," which states that further subdivisions should not violate the boundaries among subsystems delineated at a coarser level of analysis. This was an idealization, given that some fine-grained subsystems can participate in carrying out the operations performed by more than one coarsely characterized subsystem (see the discussion of weak modularity in chapter 2). Although processing subsystems can often be organized into nested set, they are not fully independent.

4 Knierim and Van Essen (1992) report that there are some exceptions to this pattern among areas in the temporal lobe (see also Webster, Ungerleider, and Bachevalier 1991): although areas TF, TH, and 35 project to area TE, they do not receive reciprocal connections from it. In addition, these areas, plus TG and 36, send information to area TEO but do not receive information directly from it. Knierim and Van Essen conclude, "Thus, top-down influences arising from high-level areas in the cortical hierarchy may have direct access to inferotemporal areas where visual memories are thought to be stored" (p. 150). In the following chapter I will discuss evidence that specific regions of the inferior temporal lobe store visual memories.

5 As will be discussed in chapter 11, the ventral system serves as the repository of the "literal files" posited by Kosslyn (1980), which stored modality-specific representations, and associative memory serves as the repository of the "propositional files" I posited earlier, which are used to position the parts appropriately. The top-down search processes access the proper information, shift attention to the proper location, and insert the images of parts or characteristics (e.g., a surface deformation) as necessary.

CHAPTER 4

1 Thus, the networks did not optimize their solutions to the problem; if they had, they should have developed separate streams for identity and location. One can think of the networks as having fallen prey to local minima (for additional discussion, see Rueckl, Cave, and Kosslyn 1989).

2 Biederman (personal communication) suggests that one reason for this difference may be that there are fewer possible locations that one can encode than possible shapes. If location is

specified in terms of rather large regions relative to the body, this suggestion may be correct; but location can be specified very precisely and relative to extrapersonal landmarks, which introduces the possibility that we can store as many locations as shapes.

3 Computation of depth is clearly a complex process (e.g., see Cavanagh 1987), and I will sidestep the details of this and all other low-level processing in this book.

4 My conception of the visual buffer in many ways resembles that of Tye (1991).

5 Even very low-level areas may be influenced by feedback loops, so that the effect of the input on higher-level areas in turn affects them; there are reciprocal connections from cortex to the LGN and even earlier in the system. To be classified "low-level," however, knowledge cannot modulate an area's processing. To understand this distinction, consider the fact that no matter how well one knows that the two lines in a Muller-Lyer illusion are the same length, one cannot see them as being the same. This fact shows that the illusion is produced by low-level vision processes.

6 Sperling did not specify the visual angles of the arrays, but rather provided the approximate heights of the letters and the viewing distances. Based on the samples in his figure 2, I estimated the maximal width of the displays and computed the visual angle, but this was by necessity only an approximation.

7 Other researchers, however, have not found evidence of a serial shifting of attention (e.g., Eriksen and Spencer 1969; Kinchla 1974; Shiffrin and Gardner 1972; Shiffrin, McKay, and Shaffer 1976). In some of these experiments, methodological problems appear to have allowed the subjects to avoid shifting attention to perform the task (e.g., see the discussion of Shiffrin, McKay, and Shaffer 1976, in Keren and Skelton 1976). In others, the task requirements may have allowed the subjects to encode the stimulus on the basis of preattentive processing, or the dependent measures may have been insensitive (as is discussed by Eriksen and St. James 1986). In yet other experiments, the task requirements may have allowed the attention window to be expanded to cover the entire field, which would allow encoding without shifting attention.

8 I assume that the rectangle itself could be identified very quickly, so that this processing did not interfere with encoding the picture.

9 Cavanagh (1992) has recently argued that attention can in fact be split to noncontiguous regions. I do not find this argument conclusive because it is very difficult to distinguish such processing from two alternatives: Either the attention window could be shifted back and forth rapidly ("time sharing") between two loci, or it could be adjusted very large, allowing one to register stimuli over a wide region. Given the weight of evidence suggesting that one can only attend to a single location, I have adopted that assumption here.

10 Downing and Pinker also showed that the attention window not only can select a region in the plane for further processing, but it also can select a region at a particular distance from the viewer. I assume that representations of depth in the dorsal system are used by processes that adjust the eyes to register stimuli at different distances from one. I also assume that such representations can be associated with stored information and used to visualize objects at different distances from the viewer; the processes that use such stored information to generate images are discussed in chapter 9, and the processes that use such information to transform objects in images are discussed in chapter 10.

11 Moran and Desimone (1985) found that cells also respond to stimuli outside their "classical receptive fields," but this is probably a "preattentive" response (for a model, see Olshausen, Anderson, and Van Essen 1992). The attention window provides high-resolution input, but apparently relatively low-resolution input can reach the ventral system even if the attention window is not properly positioned. This sort of information is not fully processed, however (for a classic discussion of preattentive processing, see Neisser 1967).

12 I assume that the visual buffer is structurally organized to represent inputs at multiple scales of resolution. However, this property would also arise if the attention window selects outputs from a fixed number of neurons: If the attention window selects outputs of neurons that have relatively separated receptive fields, a wider region will be sampled but with poorer resolution than if it selects outputs of neurons that have relatively close together receptive fields.

13 As Shulman and Wilson point out, the results could be understood in terms of selecting different spatial frequency channels. This interpretation, however, is predicated on the notion that spatial frequency channels exist. As has been argued elsewhere in the literature (e.g., Marr 1982), this notion has limited utility; the representation of shape formed by such a system is too sensitive to differences in visual angle (as an object moves away, the lower frequencies shift up and the higher ones are lost) and viewing position (an object seen from a different point of view may have a very different spectrum). Thus, although I cannot rule out such an interpretation on the basis of the results, this alternative is not compatible with the purposes of the system. My goal is not to explain the data in their own right, but to use them to select among plausible mechanisms.

14 Jolicoeur and Ingleton (1991) and McCormick and Jolicoeur (1991) manipulated the distance between dots on curved lines, keeping Euclidean distance constant; to increase the curved distance, the line had to be more convoluted—and hence higher resolution presumably was necessary to trace along it.

15 In the earlier version of the theory I assumed that the resolution of the visual buffer could not change. This and all additional revisions to the earlier version are summarized in chapter 11.

CHAPTER 5

1 In the computer simulation reported by Kosslyn et al. (1990), asterisks were placed on edges that corresponded to such properties. According to the theory we implemented there, the extraction process was entirely stimulus driven; it was accomplished purely on the basis of properties of the input, before the input was identified. (Note that much other preprocessing probably occurs prior to extracting these properties, but I assume that such processing is the province of low-level vision and hence discuss it no further here.)

2 In some situations, low-level processing may actually complete fragments to form "virtual lines"(see Kellman and Shipley 1991). It is not clear to me, however, how much of such completion is a *consequence* of higher-level perceptual organization rather than a prelude to it; it is possible that feedback from higher-level areas plays a role in at least some of the visual completion processes documented by Kellman and Shipley (1991).

3 This extraction process may rely on a competitive algorithm in which each edge is classified using a set of contrasts: it is registered as being straight or curved; edges are parallel or not; and so on. Hummel and Biederman's (1992) model relies on such processing.

4 Biederman (personal communication) believes that the critical factor is not the deletion of nonaccidental properties per se, but rather the deletion of recognizable parts of the object. The issue is whether the nonaccidental properties are used to address volumetric primitives that represent parts prior to recognition of the object. I will address this issue in more detail shortly.

5 Note that not all prosopagnosics need have this underlying deficit; there are probably multiple causes of this disorder (see chapter 3 of Kosslyn and Koenig 1992).

6 Although Schwartz (1984) argues that the log polar coordinates of striate cortex contribute to shape constancy, Cavanagh (1984) argues against this view and claims that local computations in striate cortex can accomplish these ends. Both approaches are based on variants of a Fourier analysis scheme, which I have not adopted (for reasons articulated by Olshausen, Anderson, and Van Essen 1992, and Marr 1982). My approach is quite similar to that of

Olshausen, Anderson, and Van Essen, which may be of interest given that the two efforts were independent (but this could simply mean that we are both responding to the same fashions, rather than converging on deep underlying truths!).

7 In a sense, the operations accomplished by the preprocessing subsystem are a continuation of the perceptual organizational processes that take place in the visual buffer; this is an example of the type of incremental transitions discussed in chapter 2. But the visual buffer uses only local information to delineate edges and regions, whereas the preprocessing subsystem uses more abstract properties to specify nonaccidental and signal properties. In addition, as is discussed shortly, the preprocessing subsystem can be trained to encode new types of units, but the visual buffer cannot.

8 Kosslyn (1987) sketches out an algorithm that could produce such perceptual learning, and Jacobs, Jordan, and Barto (1991) describe a sophisticated variant of such an algorithm that appears to produce the sort of learning by feedback that is described here.

9 Such signal properties would also allow one to categorize an object along multiple dimensions. Etcoff and Magee (1992) present a particularly striking example of such categorization. They showed subjects computer-generated faces that had expressions varying in equal increments between two emotions (or from an emotional expression to a neutral expression). The subjects were able to discriminate faces across categories better than those within categories, even though the faces differed by equal physical amounts. This result may suggest that the preprocessing subsystem is analogous to an auditory preprocessing subsystem that organizes speech into discrete phonemes (see chapter 6 of Kosslyn and Koenig 1992).

10 Note that in order for the viewpoint consistency constraint to operate properly, the relative positions must be specified over the course of separate eye movements. In the following chapter I argue that information from the dorsal system is in fact provided to the ventral system for this purpose.

11 I do not mean to imply that Lowe has solved all of the problems of computer vision. His system does not fare well when curved lines are present, and may break down if too many different objects are present. However, I suspect that he is on the right track, and that some of the limitations of his program have more to do with the implementation (which does not involve parallel distributed processing networks) than with the underlying conceptual foundations.

12 Neural networks blur the distinction between an address and the content of a representation. Nonaccidental and signal properties not only correspond to patterns across an input vector, but also are captured by patterns of weights in the network. These weights are part of the content of the representation and are the address for the appropriate output.

13 However, neurons need not code only abstract properties. For example, neurons have been described that appear to be coding specific features of the faces (e.g., see Perrett, Smith, Potter 1985). Indeed, Young and Yamane (1992) found that they could "read" the configuration of activity of neurons in the anterior inferior temporal lobe well enough to predict properties of the face being viewed.

14 This process also underlies object-based attention: Attention is the selective aspect of information processing. According to the present theory, the attention window selects a specific region of the visual buffer for further processing, and the processing in the pattern activation subsystem selects an object or part for further processing. Thus, attention is not solely space-based or object-based, but involves both sorts of processing at different levels of the system. For further discussion of these issues, see Cave and Kosslyn (1989).

15 Note that in such tasks one must know how a stimulus is oriented prior to knowing its identity; if one did not know its orientation, one would not be able to rotate the figure the "shortest way around" (see chapter 8 of Kosslyn 1980). Hochberg and Gellman (1977), Tarr and Pinker (1991), Ullman (1989), and others suggest that one finds a "landmark" that would allow one to establish orientation. The processes that allow one to recognize parts, as discussed in the

following chapter, could play this role. And in fact, Corballis and Cullen (1986) found that subjects could determine whether an asterisk was at the top or bottom of a rotated letter without needing to mentally rotate the letter.

16 Besner based his conclusions purely on whether or not there was an interaction in an analysis of variance between response and size disparity; he included means from three same-size pairs along with means from the three pairs where the sizes were different. I computed the slopes for the different-size pairs and, as Besner describes, found comparable slopes for both of the "same" judgments and for the upside-down distractors, but a shallower slope for different-stimuli distractors. However, I cannot determine with confidence whether this difference is significant. I will assume that it is, but may in fact just be describing the underlying basis of a trend.

17 Edelman and Bulthoff (1991) and Bulthoff and Edelman (1992) only examined error rates; without also having response times, we cannot know whether there were speed-accuracy trade-offs nor can we discern whether there was evidence for explicit interpolation, simple generalization, or mental rotation. In any event, the result stands as evidence that people can recognize objects from unfamiliar points of view.

18 There are "face cells" in the lower and upper banks of STS. Ones in the upper bank are not in IT cortex; rather, they appear to be in the superior temporal polysensory (STP) area.

19 Although these findings are widely interpreted as indicating that viewer-centered representations are used in object recognition, note that this inference does not necessarily follow from the results; it is possible that Perrett et al. recorded from an area that is used to direct action. Area STP has rich interconnections to the parietal lobe. This portion of the parietal lobe has a role in directing action (Andersen 1987; Harries and Perrett [1991] appear to adopt a similar perspective). Viewer-centered information clearly is necessary to guide reaching and other movements. There is no evidence, to my knowledge, that these cells are involved in recognition per se. Thus, it is important that there are other sources of evidence that viewer-centered representations are used in recognition, as is discussed shortly.

20 Performance in discrimination tasks is heavily influenced by the nature of the distractors. It would have been easy to make these recognition tasks more difficult by including similar distractors. However, I suspect (for what it's worth) that in actual recognition we rarely are called upon to make subtle discriminations; depending on the context, some objects are likely and others are not. I will discuss such context effects in chapters 7 and 8.

21 Johnson (1991) points out that there is a small residual effect of orientation after practice, and Tarr and Pinker (1991) note that this effect could reflect the operation of an "axis/feature finding" mechanism (which is required prior to rotation, in order to know which way to rotate) or could indicate that subjects used rotation on a small proportion of the trials (see Corballis 1988a, Corballis, Zbrodoff, Shetzer, and Butler 1978).

22 Kraft and Jenkins (1977) showed that subjects can remember the left-right orientation of pictures of scenes well if they are embedded in a story, so left-right differences could be related to the action. Such memory presumably does not involve modality-specific visual representations, but rather depends on representations in associative memory. Kosslyn, LeSueur, Dror, and Gazzaniga (1993) found that both hemispheres of a split-brain patient could recognize mirror-reversed stimuli very well, and so this ability cannot depend on the hemispheres' having distinct representations (as suggested by Corballis and Beale 1976). Rather, we proposed that the representation and/or matching process does not respect left-right orientation, and that special representations (e.g., an explicit description in associative memory) must be encoded to store such information.

23 Each of the different factors may be more or less important in a given task; I will not delve into the variables that influence the relative weighting of these factors.

24 Tarr and Pinker (1990) hypothesize that object-centered representations can be encoded, but only along a single dimension. This conjecture was based on their finding that subjects could identify patterns whose features differed along a single dimension equally easily in all orientations. For their ideogram-like abstract stimuli, subjects may have adopted a strategy of identifying the major axis and scanning along it, encoding the ordering of features. The features would be stored in associative memory as an ordered list, and in this sense an object-centered representation would have been encoded; the visual representation itself would not be object-centered. McMullen and Farah (1991) assume that the lack of effects of orientation on naming times for symmetrical objects reflects a similar process. I have offered an alternative account for their findings above; the data do not distinguish between the two accounts. However, the persistent effects of orientation on the time to name asymmetrical objects suggest that subjects do not reorganize and encode them at different orientations, perhaps because the rotation process requires less effort (on a single trial—in the long run, it might be more efficient to reorganize and re-encode the figures, but humans are not known for their ability to make such long-range projections).

25 Tarr and Pinker (1989) suggest that the subjects encode a new viewer-centered representation of the objects at each orientation. My view differs from theirs in that I do not assume that the orientation of objects is stored in the ventral system; rather, orientation affects the representations of shape by influencing how the shape is organized into perceptual units. Tarr and Pinker do not conceptualize the matching process as involving the viewpoint consistency constraint; if such a process is assumed, then their theory cannot account for the results.

26 The perceptual units of symmetrical objects may often be organized along a strong axis, and if so they would be more likely to be preserved when the object is seen upside down. This notion would explain why McMullen and Farah (1991) found that subjects named upside-down symmetrical objects faster than asymmetrical ones.

27 Weiskrantz and Saunders did include a control condition that was designed to equate the difficulty of the transform and nontransform trials: The animals also had to distinguish the target from five novel foils on each trial. However, this control does not speak to the possibility raised here. In addition, I must note that Holmes and Gross (1984) did not find that IT lesions disrupt transfer of discriminations to targets that were of different sizes or orientations (provided that the orientations were greater than 60°; see also Cowey and Gross 1970; Eacott and Gaffan 1991). However, they used only two objects, and had many training trials; thus it is possible that the animals used dorsal processing to discover distinctive spatial properties of the stimuli. I shall discuss such processing at the end of chapter 8.

28 Indeed, Gross (1978) found that these lesioned animals could discriminate 90° and 180° rotations almost as well as control animals. However, when the angular difference was down to 60° in other studies, the animals failed (e.g., Cowey and Gross 1970; Eacott and Gaffan 1991). Gross suggests that the animals may have been able to use body posture as a cue with larger angles, but could not do so when the angle was too small. I am puzzled why the animals should have had difficulty with the more subtle angles, if the dorsal system was intact. One possibility is that brain damage of any kind makes difficult tasks more difficult to perform; another possibility is that the preprocessing subsystem is necessary to extract subtle orientations; yet another possibility is that differences in perceptual organization that occur with different orientations are used as cues for small angular discriminations. In addition, Gross (1978) found that animals with IT lesions were deficient in discriminating among rotated striped patterns, which makes sense if these patterns are encoded as patterns rather than as oriented lines.

29 Dean (1976) reviews inconclusive or negative findings and provides a methodological critique of this sort of lesion research; even when a deficit is found following IT lesions, it is important to document the cause of this deficit (attention, visual discrimination, memory, etc.). In a subsequent, thoughtful review, Dean (1982) raises a number of alternative interpretations of the deficits following IT lesions. However, this review was written prior to the development

of the distinction between habit and cognitive learning (discussed shortly), and many of the problems in interpretation noted by Dean fall into place in this newer context.

30 Cirillo et al. (1989) report other work that is partially inconsistent with this hypothesis. Although they found that cooling IT during the recall phase severely impairs visual memory, in some conditions recall was better than chance even when IT was cooled. This finding could indicate that uncooled parts of IT were able to encode partial information (the cryodes did not cover all of IT, and could only be so cold without causing tissue damage). In addition, it is of course possible that cooling interacted with the role of the "habit" system, allowing it to govern behavior (albeit perhaps with incomplete habits) in some cases. The cooling method they used is apt to produce complex changes in neural dynamics, perhaps even more complex than those that occur following damage (see chapter 2).

31 Sergent et al. (1992) suggest that the middle temporal gyrus is not involved in recognition per se, but rather in naming. This suggestion was based in part on their finding activation in the middle temporal gyrus during the object-categorization task only when activation from the letter-spatial task was subtracted. They argue that this result may have occurred because the pictures evoked a name whereas the letters did not. Even though the subjects were not asked to name stimuli in any of their tasks, it seems reasonable that subjects may have spontaneously named the objects. But it seems equally reasonable that they would spontaneously name the letters. Moreover, the passive fixation point presumably did not evoke a name, and hence the middle-temporal activation should have been evident following that subtraction if subjects named the drawings spontaneously. In addition, Sergent et al. cite results indicating that lesions of the left middle temporal gyrus do not disrupt recognition but do impair naming. I have two responses to this argument: First, in my view, recognition can occur in either temporal lobe (but I will suggest in the following chapter that recognition of visual categories is better in the left hemisphere than in the right, which is consistent with the left-hemisphere activation found here); careful response time studies would be necessary to detect a deficit due to such a unilateral lesion (see chapter 8). Second, it is unlikely that the effects of lesions were restricted just to the left middle temporal area (see chapters 2 and 8); they could have indirectly affected any number of left-hemisphere regions involved in speech production. The specific role of the middle temporal gyrus, as I see it, is open; nevertheless, it does seem clear that visual memories involve structures in the ventral portions of the temporal lobe.

32 I also should note that Zeki and Shipp suggest that the efferent connections do not excite cells in lower areas so much as modulate them; other findings, such as those of Haenny, Maunsell, and Schiller (1984) lead me to suspect that the function of these connections depends very much on the task—and Zeki and Shipp did not consider tasks that are likely to elicit priming or imagery.

33 Such coding schemes also throw away information about spectral composition, which is one reason television, color film, and so forth can fool our eyes so easily. Nevertheless, they can support a very large number of discriminations, and visual mental imagery is not perfectly accurate.

34 As discussed when I considered Besner's (1983) results, imagery is more likely to be invoked during the recognition process when similar distractors are used. If so, then the process of activating an image may contribute to the kind of increased sensitivity documented by Sanocki (1991) when subtly different forms had to be discriminated.

CHAPTER 6

1 This subsystem probably can be divided into finer-grade subsystems. For example, Cavanagh (1992) demonstrated that motion is encoded via two systems, one that is low-level and automatic and one that depends on attention. The low-level component may best be regarded as part of the dorsal system; many of the relevant anatomical areas are often treated as part of that system (see figures 3.3 and 3.4).

2 Knierim and Van Essen (1992) caution against identifying the areas activated in the human brain by motion with area MT in monkeys; they suggest that the area activated in PET might include MT and other areas as well. For example, area MST has been subdivided, and neurons in these regions also respond to motion. They make a similar argument concerning equating regions of the human brain that are found to be activated during PET studies of color perception with area V4 of the monkey brain.

3 A host of different cues may influence how an object is organized into parts, many pertaining to "high-information" locations on contours—for example, see Attneave (1954); Braunstein, Hoffman, and Saidpour (1989); Kennedy and Domander (1985); Leeuwenberg and van der Helm (1991); and Palmer (1992). Leeuwenberg and van der Helm (1991) appear to be describing how patterns are organized, but sometimes seem to address how objects are recognized as well. If so, then their "minimum principle" (patterns are organized into the simplest representations) conflicts with my idea that the pattern activation subsystem attempts to account for as much variance in the input as possible. As far as I can tell, there is no strong evidence one way or the other.

4 The concept of size is complex. In a sense, size is implicit in the ventral system if part-whole relations are represented, as discussed earlier. However, relative size could be derived from such representations only for parts of the same object, and metric size information would not be represented at all.

5 Only 5 of their 7 patients had been diagnosed as having parietal damage; one was not diagnosed at all, and one had frontal and temporal damage. I assume that the results were due to direct or indirect disruption of parietal functioning (see chapters 2 and 8).

6 Rizzolatti and Berti (1990) argue that the parietal lobes play a special role in consciousness (see also Bisiach, Meregalli, and Berti 1990). I will avoid discussing the nature of consciousness in this book (for a brief treatment, see chapter 9 of Kosslyn and Koenig 1992).

7 This literature is not clear-cut; some researchers report no evidence for hemispheric specialization (for a review, see De Renzi 1982). If the spatiotopic mapping subsystem is highly localized, it need not be affected by all posterior right hemisphere lesions. Moreover, lesions in the left hemisphere could have indirect effects that alter processing in the right (see chapters 2 and 8).

8 Our predictions were also based on the roles of different sorts of spatial relations representations, as will be discussed in the following chapter. I again want to emphasize that I assume that the hemispheres differ in degree, not absolute specialization. I expect all subsystems to be implemented bilaterally, but to differ in their relative efficacy in each hemisphere.

9 I say "initially presented" to remind the reader that these are not split-brain patients. Although the stimuli are presented in one visual field for less time than is necessary to move one's eyes, processing of the stimulus is not restricted to one hemisphere; after 15 ms or so, information crosses to the other side (see chapter 2 for further discussion of the logic underlying this methodology).

CHAPTER 7

1 In general, I treat parts as a special case of a characteristic, such as an oddly shaped blotch on a dog's head. However, parts play a critical role in delineating the structure of an object, and hence are worth considering in their own right.

2 There has been some confusion about the nature of this claim (e.g., see Kosslyn et al., 1992; Sergent, 1991a), so let me try to be absolutely unambiguous: The claim is not that the hemispheres have absolute specializations, with one encoding categorical and the other encoding coordinate spatial representations. Rather, the claim is that the hemispheres differ in their relative efficacy of encoding the different sorts of representations. I assume that both hemispheres implement both sorts of spatial relations encoding subsystems. Throughout this book,

hemispheric specialization is assumed to be quantitative—a matter of degree—not qualitative. Kosslyn, Sokolov, and Chen (1989) used computer simulations to illustrate ways in which such relative differences could arise.

3 The actual motivation for the laterality predictions was more subtle than this, but this brief summary provides the essence of the idea; for more details, see Kosslyn (1987).

4 Kosslyn et al. (1992) present a meta-analysis of the efficacy of the two types of judgments in the two hemispheres, which allows one to consider whether nonsignificant trends taken together are in fact significant. This analysis revealed that the slight left-hemisphere advantage for categorical spatial relations encoding should be taken seriously.

5 Laeng's study required the subjects to hold in memory the first stimulus of each pair. Thus, they could have performed poorly because they failed to encode the spatial relations of the first stimulus and/or the second—which probably provided added power to the test.

6 In addition, in another experiment the rectangles were presented at 45° and 30° to the left and right of vertical. There was no hemispheric difference here, which is as expected if the 45° stimuli were more effectively encoded by the left hemisphere and the 30° stimuli were more effectively encoded by the right hemisphere.

7 The difference between the right-hemisphere-damaged patients and the control subjects did not reach significance with a two-tailed test; given the strong prediction made here, a one-tailed test seems appropriate.

8 As discussed in chapter 6, this hemispheric difference may also explain why Mehta and Newcombe's left-hemisphere-damaged patients had difficulty comparing four-segment Shepard-Metzler shapes in a same/different task. When these shapes differed, only the direction of the top or bottom segment was changed. These changes were rather small, and required the subject to encode parts. As discussed in chapter 6, left-hemisphere-damaged patients often have deficits when parts must be encoded.

9 Rybash and Hoyer (1992) also found evidence that males have greater functional asymmetries than females in encoding the two types of spatial relations. Males tended to perform better than females on the coordinate tasks, and vice versa on the categorical tasks. I will not speculate about the underlying causes for such gender differences. However, it is worth noting that this dissociation is one more piece of evidence in favor of the distinction. In addition, although the means are not presented, it appears that Rybash and Hoyer found a right-hemisphere superiority for yet another coordinate task, which required the subjects to determine whether a line would fit between two dots that were immediately above it.

10 Recall the caveats about split-brain research in chapter 2. In addition, other factors would also have conspired against obtaining evidence for hemispheric specialization in these experiments. Sergent (1991b) showed the split-brain subjects a circle in which a dot could appear in one of nine locations along the diagonal axes. In different conditions, the subjects were to categorize whether the dot was exactly in the center, was near the center (in one of the four locations closest to the center) or far from the center, above or below the center, or left or right of the center. These tasks do not lend themselves to the mechanisms described above. The wide range of dot locations along the diagonals would make it difficult to define discrete bins of space if neurons with small receptive fields were monitored, and it was not clear how critical metric information was in Sergent's tasks. Sergent (1991a) administered these same tasks to normal subjects (with high levels of illumination), and not surprisingly failed to find evidence of hemispheric specialization.

11 Much of the literature characterizes visual hemispheric differences in terms of differences in spatial frequencies that are encoded (e.g., see Christman, Kitterle, and Hellige 1991; Kitterle 1991; Kitterle, Christman, and Hellige 1990; Sergent 1987; for a review, see Brown and Kosslyn, in press). The results of Kosslyn, Anderson, Hamilton, and Hillger's (in press) experiments indicate that hemispheric differences in visual encoding do not arise because spatial

frequencies per se are encoded: the line segments had the same spatial frequencies, and the sequential presentation prevented any differences in spatial frequency per se. All of the data that can be explained by positing that spatial frequencies are encoded can also be explained by positing that neurons with different-sized receptive fields are monitored—but not vice versa.

12 However, I expect that this attentional bias can be overcome by task demands, which would alter the relative efficacy of the subsystems. Such a sensitivity to task demands might help to explain the variability in the literature in this area (for a review, see Van Kleeck 1989) and perhaps in divided-visual-field experiments more generally (e.g., White 1969). In addition, this notion would help to explain a striking finding with split-brain patient J. W. He evaluated whether a dot was above a bar faster and more accurately in his *right* hemisphere than in his left hemisphere, and evaluated the distance of a dot from a bar faster and more accurately in his *left* hemisphere than in his right hemisphere (Kosslyn, Koenig, Brown, and Gazzaniga, in preparation). To investigate whether his hemispheres differed in the sizes of regions they encoded, we asked J. W. to study pictures of common objects that contained easily identifiable parts; he studied a picture for 4 seconds and was then asked to decide whether a lateralized test stimulus was the same object or was a part of that object. We orthogonally varied whether the test stimulus was a whole or a part and whether it appeared at a large or small size; whole objects could be scaled down to the size of a part, and parts could be scaled up to the size of a whole. Thus, the experiment was designed to determine whether the hemispheres are specialized for wholes versus parts or for different-sized stimuli (which usually is confounded with wholes versus parts). The results indicated that the hemispheres differed in the sizes of the stimuli they evaluated fastest, and not according to whether the stimulus was a part or whole per se. Moreover, the left hemisphere responded faster for large stimuli than for small stimuli and vice versa for the right hemisphere. Thus, J. W. showed the exact opposite pattern of hemispheric dissociation than was hypothesized based on our research with normal subjects. These findings are consistent with Fendrich and Gazzaniga's (1990) finding that J. W.'s left hemisphere was better at encoding low-spatial-frequency gratings than high-spatial-frequency gratings, and vice versa for his right hemisphere. In short, the hemisphere that appeared to monitor outputs from neurons with relatively small receptive fields was also better at encoding categorical spatial relations, and that the hemisphere that appeared to monitor outputs from neurons with relatively large receptive fields was also better at encoding coordinate spatial relations—but we were very surprised that the roles of the left and right hemispheres were opposite of those found in divided-visual-field studies with normal subjects. Solely on the basis of these data, we cannot know whether the normal subjects and J. W. simply allocated attention differently in the tasks or whether J. W.'s brain is organized unusually.

13 Our original motivation for suspecting hemispheric differences for spatial relations encoding did not hinge on receptive field properties. Rather, we suspected that left hemisphere use in language might promote the development of the categorical spatial relations encoding subsystem, and right hemisphere use in navigation might promote the development of the coordinate spatial relations encoding subsystem. This idea may help answer the question of why the right hemisphere tends to monitor larger fields than the left instead of the other way around: Categorical spatial relations are useful for language, and one often focuses on objects when naming them, and coordinate spatial relations are useful for navigation, and one usually focuses on rather large regions when navigating. An alternative account rests on three observations: (1) The right cerebral hemisphere is more mature at birth (Taylor 1969); (2) a young infant relies primarily on preattentive processes to guide visual attention; for reasons noted above, using such processes to locate points of interest is more effective if large receptive fields are monitored; (3) because the right hemisphere is more mature, it is initially used often for this purpose, and becomes automated for such processing. Thus, when the left hemisphere matures, it is used to guide focal attention, which is typically more effective if smaller receptive fields are monitored. This line of reasoning is based on proposals of de Schonen and Mathivet, 1989; Hellige 1989; and Sergent 1988).

14 Although the ventral system cannot represent explicit spatial relations, it must be able to represent implicit spatial relations; such relations are inherent in any pattern. For example, a representation of a face by necessity includes implicit information about the locations of the parts and the distances among them. However, such spatial representations are embedded in the pattern itself; they cannot be used in any other context.

15 Sergent et al. did not find such results when activation was compared to activation in a passive fixation condition. As noted in the previous chapter, they also failed to find activation in the middle temporal gyrus in an object-categorization task when the fixation baseline was used, but did find such activation when the object-categorization task was compared to the task described here. It is not obvious what the subjects could have been doing during the passive fixation condition to produce these null results; as usual, null results are difficult to interpret. In addition, Sergent et al. found greater activation in the right inferior gyrus of prefrontal cortex when subjects categorized the directions of letters, which might reflect the operation of subsystems that direct the "visual routines" used to categorize the positions of the segments. Alternatively, this area might be involved in executing automatized "habits" that direct attention systematically during reading. The effect apparently had something to do with encoding letters per se; it was not present when activation from a letter-rhyming task was subtracted from activation in the directions task (both tasks used the same letters as stimuli). This result is consistent with the fact that split-brain patient L. B. was more accurate in his right hemisphere when asked to decide whether letters faced normally or were mirror-reversed (although there was no difference in response times and the left hemisphere was accurate on 85% of the trials; see Sergent and Corballis 1991).

16 Under some circumstances, this binding process can go awry, and subjects will fail to realize that two examples of the same object appeared or will fail to conjoin properties of an object properly (e.g., see Kanwisher 1987, 1991; Treisman and Schmidt 1982).

17 I also assume that the same types of structures can form hierarchical representations of large-scale environments. Such representations could consist of representations of the spatial relations among relatively close objects, and additional representations would in turn specify how these bundles of information are related. McNamara (1986) finds evidence for such hierarchical representations of large-scale space. In some cases, coordinate spatial relations may be more likely to be encoded among relatively close objects (because such representations are useful for guiding movements among them), whereas categorical relations may be more likely to be encoded among the clusters of objects (which are treated as units when one relates them—but because they are heterogeneous, no single metric relation is sufficient).

18 In contrast, Holmes and Gross (1984) found that monkeys with IT lesions generalized to stimuli when the size or orientation was altered. However, in these experiments only a single discrimination (between J versus the Greek letter pi in one experiment, and P versus T in the other) was required. It is possible that the monkeys were able to use spatial relations representations to make these discriminations, and hence relied on dorsal processing. This notion is supported by the fact that when two-dimensional versions of the letters were used, rather than three-dimensional shapes, the animals with lesions in IT were unable to transfer from the cut-out versions used during training. If the animals were encoding parts of the letters as locations that could be reached to, they would not transfer to two-dimensional versions, which do not define such locations.

19 This theory predicts that the "entry level" should become more subordinate as one becomes more expert in a domain, drawing more distinctions and learning more information that applies only to specific cases. Tanaka and Taylor (1991) present evidence that supports this prediction.

20 This is the traditional view, which I find compelling. Nevertheless, some researchers have argued recently that in certain circumstances attention can split; see note 9 of chapter 4.

21 An alternative mechanism would have the attention-shifting subsystem respond only to the strongest output, and not have the lookup subsystems inhibit each other. However, I will shortly argue that the lookup subsystems also send information about the expected property to prime the pattern activation subsystems—and this information must be consistent with the location information sent to the attention-shifting subsystem. It seems computationally easier to nip in the bud the problem of potentially incompatible location specifications and shape primes (coming from different lookup subsystems), but this is in fact an empirical issue.

22 Nakayama and Mackeben (1989) distinguish between a transient and a sustained attentional process. According to the present theory, the transient process is subserved by the stimulus-based attention control subsystem (which is driven purely by properties of the input), whereas the sustained process is carried out by the attention-shifting subsystem (which is under the control of "voluntary" instructions).

23 The differences in the conclusions reached by Irwin (1991) and Hayhoe, Lachter, and Feldman (1991) probably reflect the nature of their tasks and stimulus materials. Irwin required subjects to judge successive random patterns of eight dots, which are not the sort of stimuli that would be easily encoded in the ventral system as I have characterized it; thus it is not surprising that he found that people had difficulty integrating such patterns over multiple eye fixations. Hayhoe, Lachter, and Feldman required subjects to encode three dots, and were interested in the shape of the triangle thereby specified—and this information was integrated relatively well over successive fixations.

CHAPTER 8

1 In addition to not including the motion relations encoding subsystem, the model included another subsystem called the *feature detection subsystem*. As the work progressed, it became clear that the functions of this subsystem were not distinct from those of the preprocessing and pattern activation subsystems, and so it was eliminated from the theory.

2 We also found greater activation in several areas in the baseline task than in the picture evaluation task, which is further evidence that the baseline task was less than ideal.

3 This section is based on the article by Kosslyn and Chabris (1990).

4 This increase in time need not imply that the different properties are encoded serially; they could be encoded in parallel, but with a limited "capacity" (e.g., see Townsend 1974).

5 The damage was on the left side, which may have directly affected the category pattern activation subsystem. Even though the stimuli were exemplars, I expect both pattern activation subsystems to encode them temporarily. I assume that the two subsystems differ in the types of information that are stored structurally in a long-term form, but that both store all inputs (although perhaps not equally well) for brief periods.

6 If both pattern activation subsystems usually operate in parallel, they would be in a "race." If the speed of each is distributed normally, one of two processes will generally finish before only a single process. By analogy, if two randomly selected horses are running, chances are that one will be faster than if only a single randomly selected horse is running (see Luce 1986; Townsend 1974). Thus, if one pattern activation subsystem is impaired, I expect the entire system to operate more slowly than when both are intact.

CHAPTER 9

1 Hoffmann, Denis, and Ziessler did not contrast the entry level and the basic level; the present theory predicts that one should visualize entry-level items faster than items at other levels. Hoffman, Denis, and Ziessler et al. also asked people to decide whether pictured objects were of the same type as the image, and found the usual effect of basic level (see chapter 8).

Unfortunately, they only report response times from conditions in which the image matched the picture, and so we cannot tell whether imagery selectively primed the perceptual encoding of objects that were similar to the imaged objects.

2 The present theory also leads us to expect such a correlation if the same representation in the pattern activation subsystems was used in recognition and image generation. However, such correlational results cannot tell us whether precisely the same visual representations were used to activate the mental images as were used to name the pictures. In particular, the images may have included parts and other characteristics that were not evident in the pictures; the processes used to add such additional information are described below.

3 I have stopped using the term *skeletal image* because it suggested to some a framework of bones. What I have in mind is a low-spatial-frequency image of the object, which I now call a global image.

4 Although the noncanonical-canonical results are similar in figures 8.2 and 9.2, they are not identical. Some of the disparities may reflect individual differences, and some may reflect the relatively low statistical power in the experiment described here (only six subjects were tested). Moreover, it is not always clear when two loci are in fact from distinct areas. In any case, both sets of results support the general conclusions offered here, which are at a relatively coarse level of analysis.

5 However, contrary to our expectations, simple standard letters showed a greater effect of probe distance than complex standard letters—but this finding was apparently due to a speed-accuracy trade-off.

6 These subjects made more errors in general for the logos, but were faster in general for logos. However, there was no trade-off between error rates and response times for simple versus complex stimuli, belying a speed-accuracy trade-off as an account for this aspect of the data.

7 Richardson (1990) provides an excellent review of the effects of brain damage on the role of imagery in learning and memory. Although some of these deficits could reflect problems in image generation, I have not discussed these findings here because they could also reflect problems in storing new memories or accessing previously stored memories per se.

8 Goldenberg (1989) tested only four patients with left-sided temporal-occipital damage and one patient with right-sided temporal-occipital damage. The results for these individuals were mixed, but there was a hint that the patients with left-sided damage had difficulty using imagery to remember concrete words. The n's were too small to permit statistical analyses of these data, but they cannot be taken as strong disconfirmation of any hypothesis about the effects of temporal-occipital lesions on image generation ability.

9 Much of the research on the "visuospatial sketch pad" hinges on factors that affect learning. I have not addressed such research in this book.

CHAPTER 10

1 This sort of imagery-perception interference should be distinguished from the fact that one may not remember accurately whether one saw or visualized a stimulus (e.g., Finke, Johnson, and Shyi 1988; Intraub and Hoffman 1992; Johnson and Raye 1981); if information about context was not stored in associative memory, memory confusions will arise because the same type of representation is stored in the pattern activation subsystems when one encodes visualized and perceived objects.

2 Trojano and Grossi (1992) note: "After having generated a mental image one probably must decide which element to draw first, where, and with how much accuracy, and then must draw other elements in correct relation to each other. Failure in these intermediate processes between imagery and graphic realization might lead to a different functional impairment in which

Notes to Pages 291–332

patients can generate a model of the object to be drawn but cannot draw a recognizable picture.... Furthermore, drawing from memory is not the mere copying of mental images because the actual graphic output receives further specifications from other nonvisual information." (pp. 341–342; for support and an unusually sophisticated analysis of the processing underlying drawing, see van Sommers 1989). Trojano and Grossi describe an agnosic patient who could recognize some objects, but could not draw objects from memory—even those he could recognize—although he could copy them. He could generate images of letters and clock faces, and mentally rotate the letter L. However, he refused even to attempt to use imagery to decide whether named objects have specific properties, are larger or smaller than other objects, or whether animals have long or short tails. Given his likely imagery deficit with complex naturalistic material, his pattern of spared and impaired abilities could simply have reflected the relative difficulty of the tasks (see chapter 2). Nevertheless, van Sommers (1989, pp. 144–146) describes a patient who could visualize much better than he could draw. In contrast, Kosslyn et al. (1985) found that split-brain patient J. W.'s right hemisphere could draw letters even when it could not visualize them, and Basso, Bisiach, and Luzzatti (1980) describe a stroke patient who could at least sometimes draw recognizable objects that he could not visualize.

3 I have not reviewed the literature on reports of imagery deficits in individual cases because most of them are not well characterized. Moreover, many of these studies are methodologically flawed (e.g., see Sergent [1990] for a critique of many of them). For example, imagery deficits often were not measured rigorously, the supposedly intact abilities were not thoroughly assessed, and the different types of stimuli often differed in familiarity and complexity. Furthermore, different patients typically were given different sets of tasks. Goldenberg (1993) provides a scholarly review of reports of patients who purportedly had imagery deficits following brain damage. On the basis of these reports, he argues that there are at least five types of imagery that can be affected independently, namely imagery for forms of objects, colors of objects, faces, letters, and spatial relationships. The present theory can easily explain these dissociations if one assumes that different subsystems (e.g., the exemplar pattern activation subsystem for faces) or channels within subsystems (e.g., for color) are critical for the different abilities.

4 This prediction also represents a departure from the previous version of the theory (see p. 252 of Kosslyn 1980). In the earlier theory images had to be scanned whenever they were inspected; the bottom-up perceptual encoding mechanisms posited in the present theory obviates this requirement.

5 It is tempting to suggest that pop-out phenomena in perception, such as those discussed by Treisman and Gelade (1980), also reflect such a mechanism. However, such perceptual pop-out probably also relies in part on the stimulus-based attention-shifting subsystem, which would not affect the corresponding imagery processing in this task.

6 There is also a body of research on imagery for motor movements per se, which is not directly relevant to the question of whether visual imagery depends on motor processes. For example, Annett (1985) provided evidence that motor processes are used in some image transformation tasks (such as imagining how to tie a bow), Decety, Jeannerod, and Prablanc (1989) found that people require very similar amounts of time to imagine walking to a target and actually to walk to the target, and Anderson (1984) found that people have difficulty remembering whether they actually performed a simple action or imagined performing it. For a review and stimulating discussion of the possible neurological bases of motor imagery and its role in planning and movement control, see Jeannerod (in press).

7 Consistent with this proposal, numerous other studies have shown that imagery can affect heart rate and other autonomic functions (e.g., see Beyer et al. 1990; Decety, Jeannerod, Germain, and Pastene 1991; Deschaumes-Molinaro, Dittmar, and Vernet-Maury 1992; Jowdy and Harris 1990). However, this sort of motor interface is outside the scope of the present book.

8 Quinn and Ralston (1986) also report an experiment in which the subjects moved their hands or their hands were moved by the experimenters. They found that even passive movements interfered with memory when they were incompatible with the imaged pattern. I was surprised

by this finding because the present theory predicts that when movement interferes with imagery, it is because the motor programming systems (via another subsystem, as will be discussed shortly) alter the spatial representations in ways that are incompatible with the image. It is possible that the subjects cooperated with the experimenter, and actively moved their arms in the to-be-moved direction; alternatively, in the passive movement condition, the subjects may have visualized their arms moving—which interfered with imagery for the digits more when the movements were incompatible with "movement" through the array of digits. It is also possible that kinesthetic feedback from movement primes the visual system, in addition to collateral input from the motor command.

9 Information in associative memory must be used to anticipate the results of a manipulation; I assume that the motor programming system uses this information, but so must systems used in reasoning. In addition, the present proposal should be distinguished from the claim that one often has corresponding imagery in different modalities, which may also be true. For example, Klatzky, Lederman, and Matula (1991) report that when subjects judge the roughness, hardness, temperature, or weight of objects from memory, or compare objects along such dimensions, many spontaneously report visual mental imagery at the same time that they imagine touching the object. However, visual imagery also sometimes occurred even when the subjects did not report haptic imagery, particularly when shape and size were judged.

10 As expected if perceptual anticipations are stored, Foster, Castro, and McNaughton (1989) report that neurons in the hippocampus respond to the "motor set" of an animal when it is prepared to move in a specific way (see also Evarts, Shinoda, and Wise 1984). It has long been known that some neurons in the hippocampus selectively discharge when the animal is in a specific location; these neurons have been called "place cells" (see O'Keefe and Nadel 1978). Foster et al. suggest that place cells are in fact encoding information related to the movements necessary to get from one location to another. They found that when the animal was snugly wrapped in towels so that it could not move, the "place cells" tuned for that location virtually ceased firing. The activity seemed related to the animal's anticipating moving, not to the fact that it was in a specific location per se. The hippocampus receives input from all sensory modalities, and appears to play a critical role in setting up associations in memory (see Kosslyn and Koenig 1992, chapter 8); if so, then it would not be surprising if the motor set also were accompanied by a visual set, but this has yet to be tested.

11 This finding might help to explain why Sunderland's (1990) neglect patients did not ignore one half of imaged clocks. He asked them to imagine that a specific time was displayed, and to indicate what number the minute hand pointed at (e.g., the 9 at 12:45). The relative response times did not differ from those of a control group. It is possible that the patients shifted their heads or eyes to "look" at the relevant part of the imagined clock, which allowed them to retrieve the information. In addition, as Sunderland points out, this task could have been performed using a verbal strategy, which led the neglect subjects to make errors based on the similarity of the description of the time rather than on the proximity of numbers (as occurred for the control subjects). This issue cannot be resolved on the basis of what is currently known about neglect (see also Mesulam, 1985).

12 I earlier argued (Kosslyn 1987) that a *position alteration* and a *part realignment* subsystem transform images, and that these subsystems work closely with the subsystems that direct the attention window. In the revised theory, the shape shift subsystem performs the functions accomplished by the position alteration subsystem, but in a different way (it does not operate on the material in the visual buffer directly, but rather alters the mapping function from the pattern activation subsystems to the visual buffer)—and hence I have renamed it. In addition, the part realignment subsystem has been eliminated in the revised theory; this subsystem is only necessary if parts become misaligned during rotation, and there is no good evidence that this actually occurs. In the earlier version of the theory I hypothesized that faces are difficult to rotate because the parts become scrambled, but it is not clear why stored spatial relations representations could not be used to realign them. It is clear, however, that imaged faces cannot

be effectively rotated; for example, people have a very difficult time encoding an upside-down face, rotating the image, and then recognizing the face (e.g., see Yin 1969). According to the present version of the theory, faces are difficult to rotate effectively for two reasons. First, faces—like a picture of the state of Texas—are difficult to reorganize after being rotated. Hence, it is difficult to encode a picture of an upside-down face, mentally rotate it, and recognize the face. Second, faces have many components, which would be difficult to augment as the image is rotated because the components initially may not be organized in a way that allows them to activate the corresponding representation in a pattern activation subsystem (and hence to allow an image to be formed). Finally, the present claim that rotation is accomplished by altering the mapping function from the pattern activation subsystems to the visual buffer suggests that attention may play a role in monitoring the transformation, not in the actual transformation process itself. The revised theory predicts that subjects can transform imaged objects even if they are forced to maintain an attentional fixation in the center of the object, or next to the object.

13 Funt (1983) describes a parallel processing algorithm that rotates imaged objects incrementally. This algorithm operates purely on visual representations within an array-like structure, and rests in part on the assumption that computational elements communicate via short connections; and in fact, most connections in topographically mapped areas are short. It is possible that factors like this constrain the ways in which images can be manipulated, but I argue here that the primary reason image transformations are incremental rests on constraints on the processes that direct the transformation—namely that actual movements must pass through a trajectory. Many other sorts of theories have been offered for mental rotation, including ones that do not rely on depictive representations (e.g., Morgan 1983; Palmer 1975), but I usually have difficulty discovering what new predictions follow from such theories. The present view, whatever its faults, makes many new predictions (e.g., about the relation between subjects who have deficits in programming hand motions and their ability to mentally rotate hands, about which areas of the brain should be active during rotation, about possible interference between actual and imagined movement, etc.).

14 All three of these conditions apply to the complex novel three-dimensional wire objects used by Rock, Wheeler, and Tudor (1989), who found that subjects could not anticipate what the objects would look like from a different perspective. Moreover, the figures may have been too complex to represent and rotate reliably. On the basis of these results, the authors suggest that mental rotation may not occur at all, but rather findings in mental rotation experiments may simply reflect the difficulty of making comparisons between misoriented figures. This hypothesis fails to explain one of the most fundamental results in the literature: Cooper (1976) measured rotation rates and then asked subjects to begin rotating a figure; she then presented a to-be-evaluated version of that figure either at the expected orientation of the image (based on the estimate of rotation rate) or at another orientation. Cooper was able to "catch the image on the fly"; subjects were fastest when their image was congruent with the physical stimulus, and progressively slower when there was a greater angular disparity between the presumed present orientation of the image and the stimulus. Rock et al. discuss this result in a footnote (p. 209), which ends with the statement, "This critical experiment should be repeated preferably with a large number of less practiced subjects." Metzler (1973) performed the three-dimensional analog of this task as part of her Ph.D. thesis and obtained comparable results, and we have obtained similar results with a variant of the paradigm.

15 As is discussed in chapter 8 of Kosslyn (1980), the literature on effects of complexity on rotation times is somewhat messy. The present approach can explain this because it is up to the subject to adopt the strategy of augmenting local regions; depending on the precise task demands, subjects may or may not be led to engage in such processing.

16 Alternatively, the mapping could be established "automatically" by the vector-completion process itself.

17 Koriat and Norman estimate that there were similar rates of increased time with ADP and ADU. This may suggest that the speed of attention shifting and mental rotation reflect a deeper underlying principle of neural information processing, such as the speed with which neurons can be inhibited or excited.

18 Scanning to augment the object during mental rotation must be distinguished from the kind of attention shifting used when one prepares to execute a visual routine. The theory predicts that more complex patterns will require more time to rotate if the parts are scanned and augmented, but also predicts that more complex patterns will not necessarily require more time to evaluate if a visual routine is executed at a selected location (this depends on the difficult of finding the location). For example, Robertson and Palmer (1983) found that subjects could apparently rotate local and global levels as quickly as when only one level had to be rotated when Navon (1977) figures were used as stimuli. But, as Robertson and Palmer point out, in their task the subjects could have rotated a "frame of reference" instead of the image. The mechanism I propose to account for Koriat and Norman's "backwards alignment" data can also explain these findings.

19 I do not want to press this account, given that the authors did not report the details of the statistical analyses that would strongly support their conclusions. For example, although there was no interaction between the cue type and orientation, or between cue type, orientation, and response in their experiment 4, they nevertheless discuss selected comparisons they apparently performed among specific data points—but no F or t values are noted for these comparisons, and no mention is made as to whether the p values were Bonferroni corrected. Nevertheless, the means illustrated in the graphs appear orderly, and I am persuaded by the general thrust of their arguments that the slopes do vary depending on the range of the alternative orientations.

20 Note that this process is not the same as the one that controls smooth-pursuit eye movements. Not only are such eye movements stimulus driven, but the speed of shifting the attention window, in the 30–50 ms range (see chapter 4), would require a very fast smooth-pursuit system—faster than is likely to be used when controlling the eyes.

21 At first glance it might be tempting to invoke category tags to explain these results, but such tags cannot specify arbitrary relative positions (as defined by the way the arrow points); they are stored in memory relative to a previously defined frame of reference. Such tags could be used to help one decide whether one location is above or below another, left or right of another, and so on, but only if the judgments are all relative to the same frame of reference and subjects had previously encoded such categorical information relative to this frame of reference.

22 The shape shift subsystem can allow one to "see" the consequences of a wide range of activities, such as flipping an object over. Subjects may sometimes mentally "flip" an object when it is presented upside down, which may require less time than rotating it the full distance—which might be another account of why subjects can name objects faster when they are upside down than when they are tilted 120° (Jolicoeur 1990a; see also Just and Carpenter 1985; Koriat, Norman, and Kimchi 1991).

23 Kosslyn, Berndt, and Doyle (1985) found that two patients with left-hemisphere damage had difficulty mentally rotating two-dimensional nonsense forms. One of these patients was a classic Broca's aphasic, with anterior damage, and one was a Wernicke's aphasic, with posterior damage. In both cases, the deficit was most evident in the mental rotation rates—as assessed by response times, which are not typically measured by neuropsychologists. Thus, it is possible that the left posterior part of the brain does play a role in mental rotation; for example, perhaps it encodes categorical spatial relations among portions of the figure, which are used to guide the scanning-and-augmenting process. Alternatively, the posterior left-hemisphere damage may have indirectly disrupted some aspects of left frontal function (see chapter 2).

24 To complicate matters further, Vauclair, Fagot, and Hopkins (1993) found a left-hemisphere superiority in mental rotation in baboons. This finding dovetails with previous reports of

superior visual-spatial processing in the left hemispheres of nonhuman primates (e.g., see Hamilton and Vermeire 1991). It is possible that one or more portions of the left hemisphere are genetically endowed with greater computational capacity than the right, and hence this tissue assumes the most "important" type of processing for the animal. In any event, such findings are an additional warning against uncritical generalization from animal models to humans.

CHAPTER 11

1 The previous model also included a COMPARE process, which was used solely when one compared an attribute of two objects (e.g., their size) from memory. According to the revised version of the theory, two objects can be compared by encoding their object and spatial properties successively and then comparing the appropriate representations in associative memory or by determining whether the second representation matches the first in the pattern activation or spatial relations encoding subsystems, depending on the task. The precise method used will depend on factors such as the interstimulus interval (subjects should rely on associative memory more when longer intervals are used). In addition, Kosslyn, Brunn, Cave, and Wallach (1984) posited a LOAD subsystem, which was used to retain on-line perceptual input. In the revised version of the theory, the priming mechanisms that activate stored representations in the pattern activation subsystems will also keep recently encoded representations activated. Furthermore, Kosslyn et al. (1984) posited a PARSE subsystem, which refreshed selected segments in an image to create new units; this process is now subserved by the attention window (which selects portions of an image) and the shape shift subsystem (which alters the mapping function from the pattern activation subsystems to the visual buffer; for constraints on the ease of such processing, see p. 370). Finally, Kosslyn et al. (1984) posited a special TRANSLATE subsystem, which is now subsumed by the shape shift subsystem.

2 In Kosslyn (1980) I developed a taxonomy for classifying results. The more interesting types of data either disconfirmed the theory or could be explained in more than one way (and hence were an impetus for further research). Although I have not used this taxonomy here, I have tried to point out alternative explanations when they are open invitations to additional research.

3 The present version of the theory differs from the one used by Kosslyn, Van Kleeck, and Kirby (1990) in three ways: (1) the "feature detection" subsystem turned out to be superfluous, once the theory of the exemplar pattern activation subsystem was formulated and supported by the results of Marsolek et al. (1992). The exemplar pattern activation subsystem is narrowly tuned, and so could encode the kinds of information needed for sharp texture and shape discriminations. In addition, the spatiotopic mapping and stimulus-based attention-shifting subsystems play the role in preattentive processing that was previously ascribed to the feature detection subsystem. (2) The motion relations encoding subsystem was added to the theory only in Kosslyn (1991). (3) The exemplar pattern activation subsystem was added to the theory only in this book.

References

Adelson, E. H., C. H. Anderson, J. R. Bergen, P. J. Burt, and J. M. Ogden. 1984. Pyramid methods in image processing. *RCA Engineer* 29:33–41.

Aggleton, J. P., ed. 1992. *The amygdala: Neurobiological aspects of emotion, memory, and mental dysfunction*. New York: Wiley-Liss.

Albright, T. D. 1992. Form-cue invariant motion processing in primate visual cortex. *Science* 255:1141–1143.

Allen, M. 1983. Models of hemispheric specialization. *Psychological Bulletin* 93:73–104.

Allman, J. M., and J. H. Kaas. 1971. A representation of the visual field in the caudal third of the middle temporal gyrus of the owl monkey (*Aotus trivirgatus*). *Brain Research* 31:85–105.

Allman, J. M., and J. H. Kaas. 1976. Representation of the visual field on the medial wall of occipital-parietal cortex in the owl monkey. *Science* 191:572–575.

Allman, J. M., F. Miezin, and E. McGuinness. 1985. Stimulus specific responses from beyond the classical receptive field: Neurophysiological mechanisms for local-global comparisons in visual neurons. *Annual Review of Neuroscience* 8:407–430.

Andersen, R. A. 1987. Inferior parietal lobule function in spatial perception and visuomotor integration. In *Handbook of physiology*, Section 1: *The nervous system*, Volume 5: *Higher functions of the brain*, edited by F. Plum and V. B. Mountcastle, 483–518. Bethesda, Md.: American Physiological Society.

Andersen, R. A., 1989. Visual and eye movement functions of the posterior parietal cortex. *Annual Review of Neuroscience* 12:377–403.

Andersen, R. A., G. K. Essick, and R. M. Siegel. 1985. Encoding of spatial location by posterior parietal neurons. *Science* 230:456–458.

Andersen, R. A., and D. Zipser. 1988. The role of the posterior parietal cortex in coordinate transformations for visual-motor integration. *Canadian Journal of Physiology and Pharmacology* 66:488–501.

Anderson, C. H., and D. C. Van Essen. 1987. Shifter circuits: A computational strategy for dynamic aspects of visual processing. *Proceedings of the National Academy of Sciences of the United States of America* 84:6297–6301.

Anderson, J. A., A. Pellionisz, and E. Rosenfeld, ed. 1990. *Neurocomputing 2: Directions for research*. Cambridge, Mass.: MIT Press.

Anderson, J. R. 1978. Arguments concerning representations for mental imagery. *Psychological Review* 85:249–277.

Anderson, J. R., and G. H. Bower. 1973. *Human associative memory*. New York: Winston.

Anderson, R. E. 1984. Did I do it or only imagine doing it? *Journal of Experimental Psychology: General* 113:594–613.

Anderson, R. E., and T. Helstrup. 1993. Visual discovery in mind and on paper. *Memory and Cognition* 21:283–293.

Annett, J. 1985. Motor learning: A review. In *Motor behavior: Programming, control and acquisition*, edited by H. Heuer, U. Kleinbeck, and K.-H. Schmitt, 187–212. Berlin: Springer-Verlag.

Annett, J. 1986. On knowing how to do things. In *Generation and modulation of action patterns*, edited by H. Heuer and C. Fromm, 187–200. Berlin: Springer-Verlag.

Annett, J. 1990. Relations between verbal and gestural explanations. In *Cerebral control of speech and limb movements*, edited by G. E. Hammond, 327–346. Amsterdam: Elsevier Science Publishers B.V.

Antrobus, J. 1987. Cortical hemisphere asymmetry and sleep mentation. *Psychological Review* 94:359–368.

Arditi, A., J. D. Holtzman, and S. M. Kosslyn. 1988. Mental imagery and sensory experience in congenital blindness. *Neuropsychologia* 26:1–12.

Atkinson, J., and O. J. Braddick. 1989. "Where" and "what" in visual search. *Perception* 18:181–189.

Attneave, F. 1954. Some informational aspects of visual perception. *Psychological Review* 61:183–193.

Attneave, F. 1974. How do you know? *American Psychologist* 29:493–499.

Attneave, F., and T. E. Curlee. 1983. Locational representation in imagery: A moving spot task. *Journal of Experimental Psychology: Human Perception and Performance* 9:20–30.

Aylwin, S. 1990. Imagery and affect: Big questions, little answers. In *Imagery: Current developments*, edited by P. J. Hampson, D. F. Marks, and J. T. E. Richardson, 247–267. London: Routledge.

Bachevalier, J., and M. Mishkin. 1986. Visual recognition impairment follows ventromedial but not dorsolateral prefrontal lesions in monkeys. *Behavioural Brain Research* 20:249–261.

Baddeley, A. D. 1976. *The psychology of memory*. New York: Basic Books.

Baddeley, A. D. 1986. *Working memory*. Oxford: Oxford University Press.

Baddeley, A. D. 1992. Working memory. *Science* 255:556–559.

Bagnara, S., F. Simion, M. E. Tagliabue, and C. Umilta. 1988. Comparison processes on visual mental images. *Memory and Cognition* 16:138–146.

Bain, A. 1855/1977. The senses and the intellect. In *Significant contributions to the history of psychology: 1750–1920*, edited by D. N. Robinson. Washington, D.C.: University Publishers of America.

Baizer, J. S., L. G. Ungerleider, and R. Desimone. 1991. Organization of visual inputs to the inferior temporal and posterior parietal cortex in macaques. *The Journal of Neuroscience* 11:168–190.

Baron, R. J. 1985. Visual memories and mental images. *International Journal of Man-Machine Studies* 23:275–311.

Bartram, D. 1974. The role of visual and semantic codes in picture naming. *Cognitive Psychology* 6:325–335.

Basso, A., E. Bisiach, and C. Luzzatti. 1980. Loss of mental imagery: A case study. *Neuropsychologia* 18:435–442.

Baylis, G. C., E. T. Rolls, and C. M. Leonard. 1987. Functional subdivisions of the temporal lobe neocortex. *Journal of Neuroscience* 7:330–342.

Baylor, G. W. 1971. A treatise on mind's eye. Ph.D. dissertation, Carnegie Mellon University.

Beaumont, J. G., ed. 1982. *Divided visual field studies of cerebral organization*. New York: Academic Press.

Beauvois, M. F., and B. Saillant. 1985. Optic aphasia for colours and colour agnosia: A distinction between visual and visuo-verbal impairments in the processing of colours. *Cognitive Neuropsychology* 2:1–48.

Beck, J., and B. Ambler. 1973. The effects of concentrated and distributed attention on peripheral acuity. *Perception and Psychophysics* 14: 225–230.

Behrmann, M., G. Winocur, and M. Moscovitch. 1992. Dissociation between mental imagery and object recognition in a brain-damaged patient. *Nature* 359:636–637.

Benevento, L. A., and M. Rezak. 1976. The cortical projections of the inferior pulvinar and adjacent lateral pulvinar in the Rhesus monkey: An autoradiographic study. *Brain Research* 108:1–24.

Benton, A. L., N. R. Varney, and K. Hamsher. 1987. Visuospatial judgment: A clinical test. *Archives of Neurology* 35:364–367.

Berbaum, K., and C. S. Chung. 1981. Muller-Lyer illusion induced by imagination. *Journal of Mental Imagery* 5:125–128.

Bergson, H. 1954. *Creative evolution*. London: Macmillan.

Bersted, C. T. 1983. Memory scanning of described images and undescribed images: Hemispheric differences. *Memory and Cognition* 11:129–136.

Bersted, C. T. 1988. Flexibility in scanning described images. *Journal of Experimental Psychology: Learning, Memory, and Cognition* 14:121–125.

Berti, A., and G. Rizzolatti. 1992. Visual processing without awareness: Evidence from unilateral neglect. *Journal of Cognitive Neuroscience* 4:345–351.

Bertram, D. J. 1974. The role of visual and semantic codes in object naming. *Cognitive Psychology* 6:325–356.

Besner, D. 1983. Visual pattern recognition: Size preprocessing re-examined. *Quarterly Journal of Experimental Psychology* 35A:209–216.

Besner, D., and M. Coltheart. 1976. Mental size scaling examined. *Memory and Cognition* 4:525–531.

Bethell-Fox, C. E., and R. N. Shepard. 1988. Mental rotation: Effects of stimulus complexity and familiarity. *Journal of Experimental Psychology: Human Perception and Performance* 14:12–23.

Beyer, L., T. Weiss, E. Hansen, and A. Wolf. 1990. Dynamics of central nervous activation during motor imagination. *International Journal of Psychophysiology* 9:75–80.

Biederman, I. 1985. Human image understanding: Recent research and a theory. *Computer Vision, Graphics, and Image Processing* 32:29–73.

Biederman, I. 1987. Recognition-by-components: A theory of human image understanding. *Psychological Review* 94:115–147.

Biederman, I., E. Beiring, G. Ju, and T. Blickle. 1985. A comparison of the perception of partial vs. degraded objects. Manuscript, State University of New York at Buffalo, Image Interpretation Laboratory.

Biederman, I., E. Beiring, G. Ju, T. W. Blickle, D. Gagnon, and H. J. Hilton. 1987. A comparison of the perception of partial vs degraded objects. Manuscript, State University of New York at Buffalo, Image Interpretation Laboratory.

Biederman, I., and T. W. Blickle. 1985. The perception of objects with degraded contours. Manuscript, State University of New York at Buffalo, Image Interpretation Laboratory.

Biederman, I., T. W. Blickle, R. C. Teitelbaum, and G. J. Klatsky. 1988. Object search in nonscene displays. *Journal of Experimental Psychology: Learning, Memory and Cognition* 14:456–467.

Biederman, I., and E. E. Cooper. 1991a. Priming contour-deleted images: Evidence for intermediate representations in visual object recognition. *Cognitive Psychology* 23:393–419.

Biederman, I., and E. E. Cooper. 1991b. Object recognition and laterality: Null effects. *Neuropsychologia* 29:685–694.

Biederman, I., and E. E. Cooper. 1991c. Evidence for complete transformational and reflectional invariance in visual object priming. *Perception* 20:585–593.

Biederman, I., and E. E. Cooper. 1992. Size invariance in visual object priming. *Journal of Experimental Psychology: Human Perception and Performance* 18:121–133.

Biederman, I., P. C. Gerhardstein, E. E. Cooper, and C. A. Nelson. 1992. High-level shape recognition without inferior temporal lobe. *33rd Annual Meeting of The Psychonomic Society.*

Biederman, I., and H. J. Hilton. 1987. Recognition of objects that require texture specification. Manuscript, State University of New York at Buffalo, Image Interpretation Laboratory.

Biederman, I., and G. Ju. 1988. Surface versus edge-based determinants of visual recognition. *Cognitive Psychology* 20:38–64.

Biederman, I., R. J. Mezzanotte, and J. C. Rabinowitz. 1982. Scene perception: Detecting and judging objects undergoing relational violations. *Cognitive Psychology* 14:143–177.

Biederman, I., and M. Shiffrar. 1987. Sexing day-old chicks: A case study and expert sytems analysis of a difficult perceptual-learning task. *Journal of Experimental Psychology: Learning, Memory, and Cognition* 13:640–645.

Biggins, C. A., B. Turetsky, and G. Fein. 1990. The cerebral laterality of mental image generation in normal subjects. *Psychophysiology* 27:57–67.

Bisiach, E., and A. Berti. 1988. Hemineglect and mental representation. In *Cognitive and neuropsychological approaches to mental imagery*, edited by M. Denis, J. Engelkamp, and J. T. E. Richardson. Dordrecht: Martinus Nijhoff.

Bisiach, E., E. Capitani, and E. Porta. 1985. Two basic properties of space representation in the brain: Evidence from unilateral neglect. *Journal of Neurology* 48:141–144.

Bisiach, E., and C. Luzzatti. 1978. Unilateral neglect of representational space. *Cortex* 14:129–133.

Bisiach, E., C. Luzzatti, and D. Perani. 1979. Unilateral neglect, representational schema, and consciousness. *Brain* 102:609–618.

Bisiach, E., S. Meregalli, and A. Berti. 1990. Mechanisms of production control and belief fixation in human visuospatial processing: Clinical evidence from unilateral neglect and misrepresentation. In *Quantitative analyses of behavior: Computational and clinical approaches to pattern recognition and concept formation*, edited by M. L. Commons, R. J. Herrnstein, S. M. Kosslyn, and D. B. Mumford, 3–21. Hillsdale, N.J.: Erlbaum.

Blanc-Garin, J., S. Faure, and P. Sabio. 1993. Right hemisphere performance and competence in processing mental images, in a case of partial interhemispheric disconnection. *Brain and Cognition* 22:118–133.

Block, N., ed. 1981. *Imagery*. Cambridge, Mass.: MIT Press.

Blum, H. 1973. Biological shape and visual science (part 1). *Journal of Theoretical Biology* 38: 205–287.

Boer, L. C., and P. J. G. Keuss. 1982. Global precedence as a postperceptual effect: An analysis of speed-accuracy trade-off functions. *Perception and Psychophysics* 31:358–366.

Bogousslavsky, J., J. Miklossy, P. Deruaz, G. Assal, and F. Regli. 1987. Lingual and fusiform gyri in visual processing: A clinicopathologic study of altitudinal hemianopia. *Journal of Neurology, Neurosurgery, and Psychiatry* 50:607–614.

Boring, E. G. 1950. *A history of experimental psychology.* New York: Appleton-Century-Crofts.

Boussaoud, D., R. Desimone, and L. G. Ungerleider. 1991. Visual topography of area TEO in the macaque. *The Journal of Comparative Neurology* 306:554–575.

Boussaoud, D., L. G. Ungerleider, and R. Desimone. 1990. Pathways for motion analysis: Cortical connections of the medial superior temporal and fundus of the superior temporal visual areas in the macaque. *Journal of Comparative Neurology* 296:462–495.

Bower, G. H. 1972. Mental imagery and associative learning. In *Cognition in learning and memory,* edited by L. Gregg, 51–88. New York: Wiley.

Bower, G. H., and A. L. Glass. 1976. Structural units and the reintegrative power of picture fragments. *Journal of Experimental Psychology: Human Learning and Memory* 2:456–466.

Boyce, S. J., A. Pollatsek, and K. Rayner. 1989. Effect of background information on object identification. *Journal of Experimental Psychology: Human Perception and Performance* 15:556–566.

Bradshaw, J., D. Bradley, and K. Patterson. 1976. The perception and identification of mirror-reversed patterns. *Quarterly Journal of Experimental Psychology* 28:221–246.

Bradshaw, J. L., and N. C. Nettleton. 1981. The nature of hemispheric specialization in man. *Behavioral and Brain Sciences* 4:51–91.

Brandimonte, M. A., and W. Gerbino. 1993. Mental image reversal and verbal recoding: When ducks become rabbits. *Memory and Cognition* 21:23–33.

Brandimonte, M. A., G. J. Hitch, and D. V. M. Bishop. 1992. Influence of short-term memory codes on visual image processing: Evidence from image transformation tasks. *Journal of Experimental Psychology: Learning, Memory, and Cognition* 18:157–165.

Brandt, S. A., L. W. Stark, S. Hacisalihzade, J. Allen, and G. Tharp. 1989. Experimental evidence for scanpath eye movements during visual imagery. *Proceedings of the 11th IEEE Conference on Engineering, Medicine, and Biology.*

Braunstein, M. L., D. D. Hoffman, and A. Saidpour. 1989. Parts of visual objects: An experimental test of the minima rule. *Perception* 18:817–826.

Brody, B. A., and K. H. Pribram. 1978. The role of frontal and parietal cortex in cognitive processing: Tests of spatial and sequence functions. *Brain* 101:607–633.

Broerse, J. 1981. Misinterpretation of imagery induced McCullough effect: A reply to Finke. *Perception and Psychophysics* 30:96–98.

Broerse, J., and B. Crassini. 1980. The influence of imagery ability on color aftereffects produced by physically present and imagined induction stimuli. *Perception and Psychophysics* 28:560–568.

Brooks, L. R. 1968. Spatial and verbal components of the act of recall. *Canadian Journal of Psychology* 22:349–368.

Brooks, R. A. 1981. Symbolic reasoning among 3-D models and 2-D images. *Artifical Intelligence* 17:205–244.

Brown, H. D., and S. M. Kosslyn. In press. Hemispheric differences in visual object processing: Part/whole relations? In *Brain asymmetry*, edited by R. Davidson and K. Hugdahl. Cambridge, Mass.: MIT Press.

Bruce, C. J., R. Desimone, and C. G. Gross. 1981. Visual properties of neurons in a polysensory area in superior temporal sulcus of the macaque. *Journal of Neurophysiology* 46:369–384.

Bruce, C. J., R. Desimone, and C. G. Gross. 1986. Both striate cortex and superior colliculus contribute to visual properties of neurons in superior temporal polysensory area of macaque monkey. *Journal of Neurophysiology* 55:1057–1075.

Bryden, M. P. 1976. Response bias and hemispheric differences in dot localization. *Perception and Psychophysics* 19:23–28.

Bryden, M. P. 1982. *Laterality: Functional asymmetry in the intact brain*. New York: Academic Press.

Bryden, M. P., and F. Allard. 1976. Visual hemifield differences depend on typeface. *Brain and Language* 3:191–200.

Bulthoff, H. H., and S. Edelman. 1992. Psychophysical support for a two-dimensional view interpolation theory of object recognition. *Proceedings of the National Academy of Sciences of the United States of America* 89:60–64.

Bundesen, C., and A. Larsen. 1975. Visual transformation of size. *Journal of Experimental Psychology: Human Perception and Performance* 1:214–220.

Bundesen, C., A. Larsen, and J. E. Farrell, 1981. Mental transformations of size and orientation. In *Attention and performance IX*, edited by A. Baddeley and J. Long, 279–294. Hillsdale, N.J.: Erlbaum.

Burt, P. J., and E. H. Adelson. 1983. The Laplacian pyramid as a compact image code. *IEEE Transactions on Communications* COM-31:532–540.

Bushnell, M. C., M. E. Goldberg, and L. L. Robinson. 1981. Behavioral enhancement of visual responses in monkey cerebral cortex. 1. Modulation in posterior parietal cortex related to selective visual attention. *Journal of Neurophysiology* 46:755–772.

Butter, C. M., and W. L. Gekoski. 1966. Alterations in pattern equivalence following inferotemporal and lateral striate lesions in rhesus monkeys. *Journal of Comparative and Physiological Psychology* 61:309–312.

Butters, N., M. Barton, and B. Brody. 1970. Role of the right parietal lobe in the mediation of cross-modal associations and reversible operations in space. *Cortex* 6:174–190.

Butters, N., C. Soeldner, and P. Fedio. 1972. Comparison of parietal and frontal lobe spatial deficits in man: Extrapersonal vs personal (egocentric) space. *Perceptual and Motor Skills* 34:27–34.

Caplan, D. 1981. On the cerebral localization of linguistic functions: Logical and empirical issues surrounding deficit analysis and functional localization. *Brain and Language* 14:120–137.

Caramazza, A. 1984. The logic of neuropsychological research and the problem of patient classification in aphasia. *Brain and Language* 21:9–20.

Caramazza, A. 1986. On drawing inferences about the structure of normal cognitive systems from the analysis of patterns of impaired performance: The case for single-patient studies. *Brain and Cognition* 5:41–66.

Caramazza, A. 1992. Is cognitive neuropsychology possible? *Journal of Cognitive Neuroscience* 4:80–95.

Carmon, A., and H. P. Bechtoldt. 1969. Dominance of the right cerebral hemisphere for stereopsis. *Neuropsychologia* 7:29–40.

Carroll, J. B., and M. N. White. 1973. Word frequency and age of acquisition as determiners of picture-naming latency. *Quarterly Journal of Experimental Psychology* 25:85–95.

Carpenter, G. A., S. Grossberg, and C. Mehanian. 1989. Invariant recognition of cluttered scenes by a self-organizing ART architecture: CORT-X boundary segmentation. *Neural Networks* 2:169–181.

Carpenter, P. A., and P. Eisenberg. 1978. Mental rotation and the frame of reference in blind and sighted individuals. *Perception and Psychophysics* 23:117–124.

Carpenter, P. A., and M. A. Just. 1978. Eye fixations during mental rotation. In *Eye movements and psychological processes II*, edited by J. Sendes, R. Monty, and D. Fisher, Hillsdale, N.J.: Erlbaum.

Carr, T. H., C. McCauley, R. D. Sperber, and C. M. Parmelee. 1982. Words, pictures, and priming: On semantic activation, conscious identification, and the automaticity of information processing. *Journal of Experimental Psychology: Human Perception and Performance* 8:757–777.

Cavanagh, P. 1981. Size invariance: Reply to Schwartz. *Perception* 10:469–474.

Cavanagh, P. 1982. Functional size invariance is not provided by the cortical magnification factor. *Vision Research* 22:1409–1412.

Cavanagh, P. 1984. Image transforms in the visual system. In *Figural synthesis*, edited by P. C. Dodwell and T. Caelli, 185–218. Hillsdale, N.J.: Erlbaum.

Cavanagh, P. 1987. Reconstructing the third dimension: Interactions between color, texture, motion, binocular disparity, and shape. *Computer Vision, Graphics, and Image Processing* 37:171–195.

Cavanagh, P. 1992. Attention-based motion perception. *Science* 257:1563–1565.

Cave, C. B., and S. M. Kosslyn. 1993. The role of parts and spatial relations in object identification. *Perception* 22:229–248.

Cave, C. B., and L. R. Squire. 1992. Intact and long-lasting repetition priming in amnesia. *Journal of Experimental Psychology: Learning, Memory and Cognition* 18:509–520.

Cave, K. R., and S. M. Kosslyn. 1989. Varieties of size-specific visual selection. *Journal of Experimental Psychology: General* 148–164.

Chambers, D., and D. Reisberg. 1985. Can mental images be ambiguous? *Journal of Experimental Psychology: Human Perception and Performance* 11:317–328.

Charlot, V., M. Tzourio, M. Zilbovicius, B. Mazoyer, and M. Denis. 1992. Different mental imagery abilities result in different regional cerebral blood flow activation patterns during cognitive tasks. *Neuropsychologia* 30:565–580.

Cherniak, C. 1990. The bounded brain: Toward quantitative neuroanatomy. *Journal of Cognitive Neuroscience* 2:58–68.

Chomsky, N. 1965. *Aspects of the theory of syntax*. Cambridge, Mass: MIT Press.

Christman, S., F. L. Kitterle, and J. Hellige. 1991. Hemispheric asymmetry in the processing of absolute versus relative spatial frequency. *Brain and Cognition* 16:62–73.

Churchland, P. S., and T. J. Sejnowski. 1992. *The computational brain*. Cambridge, Mass.: MIT Press.

Cirillo, R. A., P. J. George, J. A. Horel, and C. Martin-Elkins. 1989. An experimental test of the theory that visual information is stored in the inferotemporal cortex. *Behavioural Brain Research* 34:43–53.

Clark, H. H. and H. H. Brownell. 1975. Judging up and down. *Journal of Experimental Psychology: Human Perception and Performance* 1:339–352.

Cohen, G. 1975. Hemispheric differences in the utilization of advance information. In *Attention and Performance*, edited by P. M. A. Rabbitt and S. Dornic, 20–32. New York: Academic Press.

Colby, C. L., and E. K. Miller. 1986. Eye movement related responses of neurons in superior temporal polysensory area of macaque. *Neuroscience Abstracts* 12:1184.

Conway, M. A., H. Kahney, K. Bruce, and H. Duce. 1991. Imaging objects, routines, and locations. In *Mental images in human cognition*, edited by R. H. Logie and M. Denis, 171–182. Amsterdam: North-Holland.

Cooper, L. A. 1975. Mental rotation of random two-dimensional shapes. *Cognitive Psychology* 7:20–43.

Cooper, L. A. 1976. Demonstration of a mental analog of an external rotation. *Perception and Psychophysics* 19:296–302.

Cooper, L. A., and P. Podgorny. 1976. Mental transformations and visual comparison processes: Effects of complexity and similarity. *Journal of Experimental Psychology: Human Perception and Performance* 2:503–514.

Cooper, L. A., and D. L. Schacter. 1992. Dissociations between structural and episodic representations of visual objects. *Current Directions in Psychological Science* 1:141–146.

Cooper, L. A., D. L. Schacter, S. Ballesteros, and C. Moore. 1992. Priming and recognition of transformed three-dimensional objects: Effects of size and reflection. *Journal of Experimental Psychology: Learning, Memory, and Cognition* 18:43–57.

Cooper, L. A., D. L. Schacter, and C. Moore. 1991. Orientation affects both structural and episodic representations of 3-D objects. In *Annual Meeting of the Psychonomic Society*, San Francisco, Calif.

Cooper, L. A., and R. N. Shepard. 1973. Chronometric studies of the rotation of mental images. In *Visual information processing*, edited by W. G. Chase, 76–176. New York: Academic Press.

Cooper, L. A., and R. N. Shepard. 1975. Mental transformations in the identification of left and right hands. *Journal of Experimental Psychology: Human Perception and Performance* 1:48–56.

Corballis, M. C. 1986a. On imagined revolutions. In *Theories of image formation*, edited by D. F. Marks, 151–168. New York: Brandon House.

Corballis, M. C. 1986b. Is mental rotation controlled or automatic? *Memory and Cognition* 14:124–128.

Corballis, M. C. 1988a. Recognition of disoriented shapes. *Psychological Review* 95:115–123.

Corballis, M. C. 1988b. Distinguishing clockwise from counterclockwise: Does it require mental rotation? *Memory and Cognition* 16:567–578.

Corballis, M. C. 1991. *The lopsided ape: Evolution of the generative mind*. New York: Oxford University Press.

Corballis, M. C., and I. L. Beale. 1976. *The psychology of left and right*. Hillsdale, N.J.: Erlbaum.

Corballis, M. C., and I. L. Beale. 1983. *The ambivalent mind: The neuropsychology of left and right*. Chicago: Nelson-Hall.

Corballis, M. C., and A. R. Blackman. 1990. The effect of apparent movement on mental rotation. *Memory and Cognition* 18:551–555.

Corballis, M. C., and S. Cullen. 1986. Decisions about the axes of disoriented shapes. *Memory and Cognition* 14:27–38.

Corballis, M. C., L. Macadie, and I. L. Beale. 1985. Mental rotation and visual laterality in normal and reading disabled children. *Cortex* 21:225–236.

Corballis, M. C., L. Macadie, A. Crotty, and I. Beale. 1985. The naming of disoriented letters by normal and reading disabled children. *Journal of Child Psychology and Psychiatry* 26:929–938.

Corballis, M. C., and R. McLaren. 1982. Interactions between perceived and imagined rotation. *Journal of Experimental Psychology: Human Perception and Performance* 8:215–224.

Corballis, M. C., and R. McLaren. 1984. Winding one's P's and Q's: Mental rotation and mirror image discrimination. *Journal of Experimental Psychology. Human Perception and Performance* 10: 318–327.

Corballis, M. C., and B. A. Nagourney. 1978. Latency to categorize alphanumeric characters as letters or digits. *Canadian Journal of Psychology* 32:186–188.

Corballis, M. C., B. A. Nagourney, L. I. Shetzer, and G. Stefanatos. 1978. Mental rotation under head tilt: Factors influencing the location of the subjective reference frame. *Perception and Psychophysics* 24:263–273.

Corballis, M. C., and J. Sergent. 1988. Imagery in a commissurotomized patient. *Neuropsychologia* 26:13–26.

Corballis, M. C., and J. Sergent. 1989a. Mental rotation in a commissurotomized subject. *Neuropsychologia* 27:585–597.

Corballis, M. C., and J. Sergent. 1989b. Hemispheric specialization for mental rotation. *Cortex* 25:15–25.

Corballis, M. C., N. J. Zbrodoff, and C. E. Roldan. 1976. What's up in mental rotation? *Perception and Psychophysics* 19:525–530.

Corballis, M. C., N. J. Zbrodoff, L. I. Shetzer, and P. B. Butler. 1978. Decisions about identity and orientation of rotated letters and digits. *Memory and Cognition* 6:98–107.

Corbetta, M. C., F. M. Miezin, S. Dobmeyer, G. L. Shulman, and S. E. Petersen. 1990. Attentional modulation of neural processing of shape, color, and velocity in humans. *Science* 248: 1556–1559.

Corbetta, M., F. M. Miezin, S. Dobmeyer, G. L. Shulman, and S. E. Petersen 1991. Selective and divided attention during visual discriminations of shape, color, and speed: Functional anatomy by positron emission tomography. *Journal of Neuroscience* 11:2383–2402.

Corbetta, M., F. M. Miezen, G. L. Schulman, and S. E. Petersen. 1993. A PET study of visuospatial attention. *Journal of Neuroscience* 13:1202–1226.

Corbin, C. B. 1972. Mental practice. In *Ergogenic aids and muscular performance*, edited by W. P. Morgan, 94–118. London: Academic Press.

Coren, S. 1986. An efferent component in the visual perception of direction and extent. *Psychological Review* 93:391–410.

Corkin, S. 1979. Hidden-figures test performance: Lasting effects of unilateral penetrating head injury and transient effects of bilateral cingulotomy. *Neuropsychologia* 17:585–605.

Cornoldi, C., A. Cortesi, and D. Preti. 1991. Individual differences in the capacity limitations of visuospatial short-term memory: Research on sighted and totally congenitally blind people. *Memory and Cognition* 19:459–468.

Cornoldi, C., R. De Beni, and A. Pra Baldi. 1989. Generation and retrieval of general, specific and autobiographic images representing concrete nouns. *Acta Psychologica* 72:25–39.

Coslett, H. B. 1988. Dissociation of attentional mechanisms in vision: Evidence from neglect. *International Neuropsychological Society Abstracts.*

Cowey, A. 1985. Aspects of cortical organization related to selective attention and selective impairments of visual perception: A tutorial review. In *Attention and performance XI*, edited by M. S. Posner and O. S. Marin. Hillsdale, N.J.: Erlbaum.

Cowey, A., and C. G. Gross. 1970. Effects of foveal prestriate and inferotemporal lesions on visual discrimination by rhesus monkeys. *Experimental Brain Research* 11:128–144.

Craver-Lemley, C., and A. Reeves. 1987. Visual imagery selectively reduces vernier acuity. *Perception* 16:533–614.

Crick, F., and C. Koch. 1990. Towards a neurobiological theory of consciousness. *Seminars in the Neurosciences* 2:263–275.

Critchley, M. 1953. *The parietal lobes.* New York: Hafner.

Crowne, D. P. 1983. The frontal eye field and attention. *Psychological Bulletin* 93:232–260.

Cutting, J. 1990. *The right cerebral hemisphere and psychiatric disorders.* Oxford: Oxford University Press.

Cutting, J. E. 1978. Generation of synthetic male and female walkers through manipulation of a biomechanical invariant. *Perception* 1:393–405.

Cutting, J. E. 1982. Blowing in the wind: Perceiving structure in trees and bushes. *Cognition* 12:25–44.

Cutting, J. E., and L. T. Kozlowski. 1977. Recognizing friends by their walk: Gait perception without familiarity. *Bulletin of the Psychonomic Society* 9:353–356.

Cutting, J. E., and D. R. Proffitt. 1981. Gait perception as an example of how we may perceive events. In *Intersensory perception and sensory integration,* edited by R. D. Walk and H. L. Pick, 249–273. New York: Plenum.

Damasio, A. R. 1985a. The frontal lobes. In *Clinical neuropsychology,* edited by K. M. Heilman and E. Valenstein, 339–402. New York: Oxford University Press.

Damasio, A. R. 1985b. Disorders of complex visual processing: Agnosias, achromatopsia, Balint's syndrome, and related difficulties of orientation and construction. In *Principles of behavioral neurology,* edited by M.-M. Mesulam, 259–288. Philadelphia: F. A. Davis.

Damasio, A. R. 1989. Time-locked multiregional retroactivation: A systems-level proposal for the neural substrates of recall and recognition. *Cognition* 33:25–62.

Damasio, A. R. 1990. Category-related recognition defects as a clue to the neural substrates of knowledge. *Trends in Neurosciences* 13:95–98.

Damasio, A. R., H. Damasio, D. Tranel, and J. P. Brandt. 1990. Neural regionalization of knowledge access: Preliminary evidence. *Cold Spring Harbor Symposia on Quantitative Biology* 55:1039–1047.

Damasio, A. R., H. Damasio, and G. W. Van Hoesen. 1982. Prosopagnosia: Anatomic basis and behavioral mechanisms. *Neurology* 32:331–341.

Damasio, A. R., T. Yamada, H. Damasio, J. Corbett, and J. McKee. 1980. Central achromatopsia: Behavioral, anatomic and physiologic aspects. *Neurology* 30:1064–1071.

Damos, D. L. 1990. Using the fold point to analyze mental rotation data: A second look. *Bulletin of the Psychonomic Society* 28:23–26.

Daniel, P. M., and D. Whitteridge. 1961. The representation of the visual field on the cerebral cortex in monkeys. *Journal of Physiology* 159:203–221.

Darwin, C. 1859. *The origin of species.* Reprinted 1993, New York: Random House.

David, A. S., and J. C. Cutting. 1992. Categorical-semantic and spatial-imagery judgements of non-verbal stimuli in the cerebral hemispheres. *Cortex* 28:39–51.

Davidoff, J. 1982. Studies with non-verval stimuli. In *Divided visual field studies of cerebral organization,* edited by J. G. Buamont, 29–55. London: Academic Press.

Davidoff, J. B., and A. L. Ostergaard. 1984. Colour anomia resulting from weakened short-term colour memory: A case study. *Brain* 107:415–431.

Davies, P. C. W., and J. R. Brown. 1986. *The ghost in the atom: A discussion of the mysteries of quantum physics*. Cambridge: Cambridge University Press.

Dawkins, R. 1987. *The blind watchmaker: The evidence of evolution reveals a universe without design*. New York: Norton.

Dean, P. 1976. Effects of inferotemporal lesions on the behaviour of monkeys. *Psychological Bulletin* 83:41–71.

Dean, P. 1982. Visual behavior in monkeys with inferotemporal lesions. In *Analysis of visual behavior*, edited by D. J. Ingle, M. A. Goodale, and R. J. W. Mansfield, 587–628. Cambridge, Mass.: MIT Press.

Dean, P., and L. Weiskrantz. 1974. Loss of preoperative habits in rhesus monkeys with inferotemporal lesions: Recognition failure or relearning deficit? *Neuropsychologia* 12:299–311.

De Beni, R., and C. Cornoldi. 1988. Imagery limitations in totally congenitally blind subjects. *Journal of Experimental Psychology: Learning, Memory, and Cognition* 14:650–655.

Decety, J., B. Philippon, and D. H. Ingvar. 1988. rCBF landscapes during motor performance and motor ideation of a graphic gesture. *European Archives of Psychiatry and Neurological Sciences* 238:33–38.

Decety, J., M. Jeannerod, and C. Prablanc. 1989. The timing of mentally represented actions. *Behavioural Brain Research* 34:35–42.

Decety, J., M. Jeannerod, M. Germain, and J. Pastene. 1991. Vegetative response during imagined movement is proportional to mental effort. *Behavioural Brain Research* 42:1–5.

de Groot, A. D. 1965. *Thought and choice in chess*. The Hague: Mouton.

Deleval, J., J. De Mol, and J. Noterman. 1983. La perte des images souvenirs. *Acta Neurologica Belgica* 83:61–79.

Delis, D. C., J. H. Kramer, and M. G. Kiefner. 1988. Visuospatial functioning before and after commissurotomy: Disconnection in hierarchical processing. *Archives of Neurology* 45:462–465.

Delis, D. C., L. C. Robertson, and R. Efron. 1986. Hemispheric specialization of memory for visual hierarchical stimuli. *Neuropsychologia* 24:205–214.

Deloche, G., X. Seron, G. Scius, and J. Segui. 1987. Right hemisphere language processing: Lateral differences with imageable and nonimageable ambiguous words. *Brain and Language* 30:197–205.

Denis, M., and M. Carfantan. 1985. People's knowledge about images. *Cognition* 20:49–60.

Denis, M., and M. Cocude. 1989. Scanning visual images generated from verbal descriptions. *European Journal of Cognitive Psychology* 1:293–307.

Denis, M., and M. Cocude. 1992. Structural properties of visual images constructed from poorly or well-structured verbal descriptions. *Memory and Cognition* 20:497–506.

De Renzi, E. 1982. *Disorders of space exploration and cognition*. New York: Wiley.

De Renzi, E., P. Faglioni, and G. Scotti. 1971. Judgment of spatial orientation in patients with focal brain damage. *Journal of Neurology, Neurosurgery, and Psychiatry* 34: 489–495.

De Renzi, E., G. Scotti, and H. Spinnler. 1969. Perceptual and associative disorders of visual recognition. *Neurology* 19:634.

De Renzi, E., and H. Spinnler. 1966. Visual recognition in patients with unilateral cerebral disease. *Journal of Nervous Mental Disorders* 142:515–525.

De Renzi, E., and H. Spinnler. 1967. Impaired performance on color tasks in patients with hemispheric damage. *Cortex* 3:194–217.

Deschaumes-Molinaro, C., A. Dittmar, and E. Vernet-Maury. 1992. Automatic nervous system response patterns correlate with mental imagery. *Physiology and Behavior* 51:1021–1027.

De Schonen, S., and E. Mathivet. 1989. First come, first served: A scenario about the development of hemispheric specialization in face recognition during infancy. *European Bulletin of Cognitive Psychology* 1:3–44.

Desimone, R. 1992. Neural circuits for visual attention in the primate brain. In *Neural networks for vision and image processing*, edited by G. A. Carpenter and S. Grossberg, 343–364. Cambridge, Mass.: MIT Press.

Desimone, R., T. D. Albright, C. G. Gross, and C. Bruce. 1984. Stimulus-selective properties of inferior temporal neurons in the macaque. *Journal of Neuroscience* 8:2051–2062.

Desimone, R., and S. J. Schein. 1987. Visual properties of neurons in area V4 of the macaque: Sensitivity to stimulus form. *Journal of Neurophysiology* 57:835–868.

Desimone, R., S. J. Schein, J. Moran, and L. G. Ungerleider. 1985. Contour, color and shape analysis beyond the striate cortex. *Vision Research* 25:441–452.

Desimone, R., and L. G. Ungerleider. 1989. Neural mechanisms of visual processing in monkeys. In *Handbook of neuropsychology*, edited by F. Boller and J. Grafman, 267–299. Amsterdam: Elsevier.

Desimone, R., M. Wessinger, L. Thomas, and W. Schneider. 1989. Effects of deactivation of lateral pulvinar or superior colliculus on the ability to selectively attend to a visual stimulus. *Society for Neuroscience Abstracts* 15:162.

Desimone, R., M. Wessinger, L. Thomas, and W. Schneider. 1990. Attentional control of visual perception: Cortical and subcortical mechanisms. *Cold Spring Harbor Symposia on Quantitative Biology* 55:963–971.

Deutsch, G., W. T. Bourbon, A. C. Papanicolaou, and H. M. Eisenberg. 1988. Visuospatial experiments compared via activation of regional cerebral blood flow. *Neuropsychologia* 26:445–452.

De Valois, R. L., and K. K. De Valois. 1988. *Spatial vision*. New York: Oxford University Press.

De Valois, R. L., H. C. Morgan, M. C. Polson, W. R. Mead, and E. M. Hull. 1974. Psychophysical studies of monkey vision, I: Macaque luminosity and color vision tests. *Vision Research* 14:53–67.

De Valois, R. L., H. Morgan, and D. M. Snodderly. 1974. Psychophysical studies of monkey vision, III: Spatial luminance contrast tests of macaque and human observers. *Vision Research* 14:75–81.

DeYoe, E. A., and D. C. Van Essen. 1988. Concurrent processing streams in monkey visual cortex. *Trends in Neurosciences* 11:219–226.

Distler, C., D. Boussaoud, R. Desimone, and L. G. Ungerleider. 1993. Cortical connections of inferior temporal area TEO in Macaque monkeys. *Journal of Comparative Neurology* 334:125–150.

Ditchburn, R. W., and B. L. Ginsborg. 1952. Vision with a stabilized retinal image. *Nature* 170:36–37.

Ditunno, P. L., and V. A. Mann. 1990. Right hemisphere specialization for mental rotation in normals and brain damaged subjects. *Cortex* 26:177–188.

Dobbins, A., S. W. Zucker, and M. S. Cynader. 1987. Endstopped neurons in the visual cortex as a substrate for calculating curvature. *Nature* 329:438–441.

Douglas, K. L., and K. S. Rockland. 1992. Extensive visual feedback connections from ventral inferotemporal cortex. *Society of Neuroscience Abstracts* 18:390.

Dow, B. M. 1974. Functional classes of cells and their laminar distribution in monkey visual cortex. *Journal of Neurophysiology* 37:927–946.

Dowling, J. 1987. *The retina: An approachable part of the brain.* Cambridge, Mass.: Harvard University Press.

Downing, C. J., and S. Pinker. 1985. The spatial structure of visual attention. In *Attention and performance XI*, edited by M. I. Posner and O. S. M. Marin, 171–187. Hillsdale, N.J.: Erlbaum.

Dreyfus, H. L. 1979. *What computers can't do.* New York: Harper Colophon.

Droulez, J., and A. Berthoz. 1990. The concept of dynamic memory in sensorimotor control. In *Freedom to move: Dissolving boundaries in motor control*, edited by D. R. Humphrey and H. J. Freund, 137–161. Chichester, England: Wiley.

Dubner, R., and S. M. Zeki. 1971. Response properties and receptive fields of cells in an anatomically defined region of the superior temporal sulcus in the monkey. *Brain Research* 35:528–532.

Durnford, M., and D. Kimura. 1971. Right hemisphere specialization for depth perception reflected in visual field differences. *Nature* 231:394–395.

Durso, F. T., and M. K. Johnson. 1980. The effects of orienting tasks on recognition, recall, and modality confusion of pictures and words. *Journal of Verbal Language and Verbal Behavior* 19: 416–429.

Eacott, M. J., and D. Gaffan. 1991. The role of monkey inferior parietal cortex in visual discriminations of identity and orientation of shapes. *Behavioural Brain Research* 46:95–98.

Earhard, B. 1990. The generality of outside-in processing routines in the analysis of form. *Canadian Journal of Psychology* 44:14–29.

Eddy, J. K., and A. L. Glass. 1981. Reading and listening to high and low imagery sentences. *Journal of Verbal Learning and Verbal Behaviour* 20:333–345.

Edelman, S., and H. H. Bulthoff. 1991. Generalization of object recognition in human vision across stimulus transformations and deformations. In *Artificial intelligence and computer vision*, edited by Y. A. Feldman and A. Bruckstein, 475–483. Amsterdam: Elsevier.

Edelman, S., S. Ullman, and T. Flash. 1990. Reading cursive handwriting by alignment of letter prototypes. *International Journal of Computer Vision* 5:303–331.

Egeth, H. 1977. Attention and preattention. In *The psychology of learning and motivation*, edited by G. H. Bower, 277–320. New York: Academic Press.

Ehrlichman, H., and J. Barrett. 1983. Right hemispheric specialization for mental imagery: A review of the evidence. *Brain and Cognition* 2:55–76.

Eley, M. G. 1981. Distinguishing imagery from propositional recoding processes in sentence-picture verification tasks. *Canadian Journal of Psychology* 35:254–269.

Ellis, R., D. A. Allport, G. W. Humphreys, and J. Collis. 1989. Varieties of object constancy. *Quarterly Journal of Experimental Psychology* 41:775–796.

Eriksen, C. W., and J. E. Hoffman. 1974. Selective attention: Noise suppression or signal enhancement? *Bulletin of the Psychonomic Society* 4:587–589.

Eriksen, C. W., and J. D. St. James. 1986. Visual attention within and around the field of focal attention: A zoom lens model. *Perception and Psychophysics* 40:225–240.

Eriksen, C. W., and T. Spencer. 1969. Rate of information processing in visual perception: Some results and methodological considerations. *Journal of Experimental Psychology Monograph* 79:1–16.

Eriksen, C. W., and Y.-Y. Yeh. 1985. Allocation of attention in the visual field. *Journal of Experimental Psychology: Human Perception and Performance* 11:583–597.

Etcoff, N. L., and J. J. Magee. 1992. Categorical perception of facial expressions. *Cognition* 44:227–240.

Evarts, E. V., Y. Shinoda, and S. P. Wise. 1984. *Neurophysiological approaches to higher brain functions.* New York: Wiley.

Farah, M. J. 1984. The neurological basis of mental imagery: A componential analysis. *Cognition* 18:245–272.

Farah, M. J. 1985. Psychophysical evidence for a shared representational medium for visual images and percepts. *Journal of Experimental Psychology: General* 114:91–103.

Farah, M. J. 1986. The laterality of mental image generation: A test with normal subjects. *Neuropsychologia* 24:541–551.

Farah, M. J. 1988. Is visual imagery really visual? Overlooked evidence from neuropsychology. *Psychological Review* 95:307–317.

Farah, M. J. 1989a. The neural basis of mental imagery. *Trends in Neurosciences* 12:395–399.

Farah, M. J. 1989b. Mechanisms of imagery-perception interaction. *Journal of Experimental Psychology: Human Perception and Performance* 15:203–211.

Farah, M. J. 1990. *Visual agnosia: Disorders of object recognition and what they tell us about normal vision.* Cambridge, Mass.: MIT Press.

Farah, M. J. In press. Neuropsychological inference with an interactive brain: A critique of the "locality assumption." *Behavioral and Brain Sciences*

Farah, M. J., M. S. Gazzaniga, J. D. Holzman, and S. M. Kosslyn. 1985. A left hemisphere basis for visual mental imagery? *Neuropsychologia* 23:115–118.

Farah, M. J., and K. M. Hammond. 1988. Mental rotation and orientation-invariant object recognition: Dissociable processes. *Cognition* 29:29–46.

Farah, M. J., K. M. Hammond, D. N. Levine, and R. Calvanio. 1988. Visual and spatial mental imagery: Dissociable systems of representation. *Cognitive Psychology* 20:439–462.

Farah, M. J., D. N. Levine, and R. Calvanio. 1988. A case study of mental imagery deficit. *Brain and Cognition* 8:147–164.

Farah, M. J., and J. L. McClelland. 1991. A computational model of semantic memory impairment: Modality specificity and emergent category specificity. *Journal of Experimental Psychology: General* 120:339–357.

Farah, M. J., P. A. McMullen, and M. M. Meyer. 1991. Can recognition of living things be selectively impaired? *Neuropsychologia* 29:185–193.

Farah, M. J., and F. Peronnet. 1989. Event-related potentials in the study of mental imagery. *Journal of Psychophysics* 3:99–109.

Farah, M. J., F. Peronnet, M. A. Gonon, and M. H. Girard. 1988. Electrophysiological evidence for a shared representational medium for visual images and visual percepts. *Journal of Experimental Psychology: General* 117:248–257.

Farah, M. J., M. J. Soso, and R. M. Dasheiff. 1992. Visual angle of the mind's eye before and after unilateral occipital lobectomy. *Journal of Experimental Psychology: Human Perception and Performance* 18:241–246.

Farley, A. M. 1974. VIPS: A visual imagery and perception system; the result of protocol analysis. Ph.D. dissertation, Carnegie Mellon University.

Feldman, J. A. 1985. Four frames suffice: A provisional model of vision and space. *Behavioral and Brain Sciences* 8:265–289.

Felleman, D. J., and D. C. Van Essen. 1991. Distributed hierarchical processing in the primate cerebral cortex. *Cerebral Cortex* 1:1–47.

Fendrich, R., and M. Gazzaniga. 1990. Hemispheric processing of spatial frequencies in two commissurotomy patients. *Neuropsychologia* 28:657–663.

Festinger, L., H. Ono, C. A. Burnham, and D. Bamber. 1967. Efference and the conscious experience of perception. *Journal of Psychology Monographs* 74:1–36.

Feyerabend, P. K. 1962. Problems of microphysics. In *Frontiers of science and philosophy*, edited by R. G. Colodny. Pittsburgh: University of Pittsburgh Press.

Finke, R. A. 1979. The functional equivalance of mental images and errors of movement. *Cognitive Psychology* 11:235–264.

Finke, R. A. 1981. Interpretations of imagery-induced McCollough effects. *Perception and Psychophysics* 30:94–95

Finke, R. A. 1985. Theories relating mental imagery to perception. *Psychological Bulletin* 98:236–259.

Finke, R. A. 1986. Mental imagery and the visual system. *Scientific American* 254:88–95.

Finke, R. A. 1989. *Principles of mental imagery*. Cambridge, Mass.: MIT Press.

Finke, R. A. 1990. *Creative imagery: Discoveries and inventions in visualization*. Hillsdale, N.J.: Erlbaum.

Finke, R. A., M. K. Johnson, and G. C.-W. Shyi. 1988. Memory confusions for real and imagined completions of symmetrical visual patterns. *Memory and Cognition* 16:133–137.

Finke, R. A., and S. M. Kosslyn. 1980. Mental imagery acuity in the peripheral visual field. *Journal of Experimental Psychology: Human Perception and Performance* 6:126–139.

Finke, R. A., and S. Pinker. 1982. Spontaneous imagery scanning in mental extrapolation. *Journal of Experimental Psychology: Learning, Memory, and Cognition* 8:142–147.

Finke, R. A., and S. Pinker. 1983. Directional scanning of remembered visual patterns. *Journal of Experimental Psychology: Learning, Memory, and Cognition* 9:398–410.

Finke, R. A., S. Pinker, and M. Farah. 1989. Reinterpreting visual patterns in mental imagery. *Cognitive Science* 13:51–78.

Finke, R. A., and M. J. Schmidt. 1977. Orientation-specific color aftereffects following imagination. *Journal of Experimental Psychology: Human Perception and Performance* 3:599–606.

Finke, R. A., and M. J. Schmidt. 1978. The quantitative measure of pattern representation in images using orientation-specific color aftereffects. *Perception and Psychophysics* 23:515–520.

Finke, R. A., and R. N. Shepard. 1986. Visual functions of mental imagery. In *Handbook of perception and human performance*, edited by K. R. Boff, L. Kaufman, and J. P. Thomas, 37-1–37-55. New York: Wiley-Interscience.

Finke, R. A., and G. C.-W. Shyi. 1988. Mental extrapolation and representational momentum for complex implied motions. *Journal of Experimental Psychology: Learning, Memory, and Cognition* 14:112–120.

Finke, R. A., and K. Slayton. 1988. Explorations of creative visual synthesis in mental imagery. *Memory and Cognition* 16:252–257.

Fischbach, G. D. 1992. Mind and brain. *Scientific American* 267:48–57.

Fischer, S. C., and J. W. Pellegrino. 1988. Hemispheric differences for components of mental rotation. *Brain and Cognition* 7:1–15.

Fisher, B., B. Bridgeman, and I. Biederman. 1990. Task differences in visual search: Does attention aid detection? In *Annual Meeting of the Association for Research in Vision and Ophthalmology*, Sarasota, FL.

Fisk, J. D., and M. A. Goodale. 1988. The effects of unilateral brain damage on visually guided reaching: Hemispheric differences in the nature of the deficit. *Experimental Brain Research* 72:425–435.

Fodor, J. A. 1968. *Psychological explanation: An introduction to the philosophy of psychology.* New York: Random House.

Fodor, J. A. 1975. *The language of thought.* New York: Crowell.

Fodor, J. A. 1983. *Modularity of mind: An essay on faculty psychology.* Cambridge, Mass.: MIT Press.

Folk, M. D., and R. D. Luce. 1987. Effects of stimulus complexity on mental rotation rate of polygons. *Journal of Experimental Psychology: Human Perception and Performance* 13:395–404.

Foster, T. C., C. A. Castro, and B. L. McNaughton. 1989. Spatial selectivity of rat hippocampal neurons: Dependence on preparedness for movement. *Science* 244:1580–1581.

Fox, P. T., F. M. Miezin, J. M. Allman, D. C. Van Essen, and M. E. Raichle. 1987. Retinotopic organization of human visual cortex mapped with positron-emission tomography. *Journal of Neuroscience* 7:913–922.

Fox, P. T., M. A. Mintun, M. E. Raichle, F. M. Miezin, J. M. Allman, and D. C. Van Essen. 1986. Mapping human visual cortex with positron emission tomography. *Nature* 323:806–809.

Franklin, N., and B. Tversky. 1990. Searching imagined environments. *Journal of Experimental Psychology: General* 119:63–76.

Frederickson, R. E., and J. C. Bartlett. 1987. Cognitive impenetrability of memory for orientation. *Journal of Experimental Psychology: Learning, Memory and Cognition* 13:269–277.

Freyd, J. J. 1987. Dynamic mental representations. *Psychological Review* 94:427–438.

Freyd, J. J. 1993. Five hunches about perceptual processes and dynamic representations. In *Attention and performance XIV: Synergies in experimental psychology, artificial intelligence, and cognitive neuroscience*, edited by D. E. Meyer and S. Kornblum, 99–119. Cambridge, Mass.: MIT Press.

Freyd, J. J., and R. A. Finke. 1984. Facilitation of length discrimination using real and imaged context frames. *American Journal of Psychology* 97:323–341.

Friedman, A., and C. A. Harding. 1990. Seeing versus imagining movement in depth. *Canadian Journal of Psychology* 44:371–383.

Fujita, I., K. Tanaka, M. Ito, and K. Cheng. 1992. Columns for visual features of objects in monkey inferotemporal cortex. *Nature* 360:343–346.

Funt, B. V. 1976. WHISPER: A computer implementation using analogues in reasoning. Ph.D. dissertation, University of Biritish Columbia.

Funt, B. V. 1977. WHISPER: A problem solving system utilizing diagrams and a parallel processing retina. *Proceedings IJCAI-77:* 459–464.

Funt, B. V. 1983. A parallel-process model of mental rotation. *Cognitive Science* 7:67–93.

Fuster, J. M. 1990. Inferotemporal units in selective visual attention and short-term memory. *Journal of Neurophysiology* 64:681–697.

Fuster, J. M., and J. P. Jervey. 1982. Neuronal firing in the inferotemporal cortex of the monkey in a visual memory task. *Journal of Neuroscience* 2:361−375.

Gaffan, D., S. Harrison, and E. A. Gaffan. 1986. Visual identification following inferotemporal ablation in the monkey. *Quarterly Journal of Experimental Psychology* 38B:5−30.

Gaffan, D., and C. A. Heywood. 1993. A spurious category-specific visual agnosia for living things in normal human and nonhuman primates. *Journal of Cognitive Neuroscience* 5:118−128.

Gaffan, E. A., S. Harrison, and D. Gaffan. 1986. Single and concurrent discrimination learning by monkeys after lesions of inferotemporal cortex. *Quarterly Journal of Experimental Psychology* 38B:31−51.

Gallant, J. L., J. Braun, and D. C. Van Essen. 1993. Selectivity for polar, hyperbolic, and Cartesian gratings in macaque visual cortex. *Science* 259:100−104.

Galton, F. 1883. *Inquiries into human faculty and its development.* London: Macmillan.

Gardin, F., and B. Meltzer. 1989. Analogical representations of naive physics. *Artifical Intelligence* 38:139−159.

Gardner, H. 1985. *The mind's new science: A history of the cognitive revolution.* New York: Basic Books.

Gentilucci, M., C. Scandolara, I. N. Pigarev, and G. Rizzolatti. 1983. Visual responses in the postarcuate cortex (area 6) of the monkey that are independent of eye position. *Experimental Brain Research* 50:464−468.

Georgopoulos, A. P., J. T. Lurito, M. Petrides, A. B. Schwartz, and J. T. Massey. 1989. Mental rotation of the neuronal population vector. *Science* 243:234−236.

Georgopoulos, A. P., A. B. Schwartz, and R. E. Kettner. 1986. Neural population coding of movement direction. *Science* 233:1416−1419.

Gibson, J. J. 1950. *The perception of the visual world.* Boston: Houghton Mifflin.

Gibson, J. J. 1966. *The senses considered as perceptual systems.* Boston: Houghton Mifflin.

Gibson, J. J. 1979. *The ecological approach to visual perception.* Boston: Houghton Mifflin.

Glasgow, J. I. In press. The imagery debate revisited: A computational perspective. *Computational Intelligence*

Glasgow, J. I., S. Fortier, and F. H. Allen. 1992. Molecular scene analysis: Crystal structure determination through imagery. In *Artifical intelligence and molecular biology,* edited by L. Hunter, 433−458. Cambridge, Mass.: MIT Press.

Glassman, R. B. 1978. The logic of the lesion experiment and its role in the neural sciences. In *Recovery from brain damage: Research and theory,* edited by S. Finger. New York: Plenum.

Glushko, R. J., and L. A. Cooper. 1978. Spatial comprehension and comparison processes in verification tasks. *Cognitive Psychology* 10:391−421.

Gnadt, J. W., and R. A. Andersen. 1988. Memory related motor planning activity in posterior parietal cortex of macaque. *Experimental Brain Research* 70:216−220.

Goldberg, M. E., and C. L. Colby. 1989. The neurophysiology of spatial vision. In *Handbook of neuropsychology,* edited by F. Boller and J. Grafman, 301−316. Amsterdam: Elsevier.

Goldenberg, G. 1989. The ability of patients with brain damage to generate mental visual images. *Brain* 112:305−325.

Goldenberg, G. 1993. The neural basis of mental imagery. *Bailliére's Clinical Neurology* 2:265−286.

Goldenberg, G., and C. Artner. 1991. Visual imagery and knowledge about the visual appearance of objects in patients with posterior cerebral artery lesions. *Brain and Cognition* 15:160–186.

Goldenberg, G., C. Artner, and I. Podreka. 1991. Image generation and the territory of the left posterior cerebral artery. In *Mental images in human cognition*, edited by R. H. Logie and M. Denis, 383–395. Amsterdam: North-Holland.

Goldenberg, G., I. Podreka, M. Steiner, and K. Willmes. 1987. Patterns of regional cerebral blood flow related to memorizing of high and low imagery words: An emission computer tomography study. *Neuropsychologia* 25:473–485.

Goldenberg, G., I. Podreka, M. Steiner, K. Willmes, E. Suess, and L. Deecke. 1989. Regional cerebral blood flow patterns in visual imagery. *Neuropsychologia* 27:641–664.

Goldenberg, G., I. Podreka, F. Uhl, M. Steiner, K. Willmes, and L. Deecke. 1989. Cerebral correlates of imaging colours, faces, and a map, I: SPECT of regional cerebral blood flow. *Neuropsychologia* 27:1315–1328.

Goldman-Rakic, P. S. 1987. Circuitry of primate prefrontal cortex and regulation of behavior by representational knowledge. In *Handbook of physiology*, Section 1: *The nervous system*, Volume 5: *Higher functions of the brain*, edited by F. Plum and V. B. Mountcastle, 373–417. Bethesda, Md.: American Physiological Society.

Goldman-Rakic, P. S. 1992. Working memory and the mind. *Scientific American* 267:110–117.

Goldston, D. B., J. V. Hinrichs, and C. L. Richman. 1985. Subjects' expectations, individual variability, and the scanning of mental images. *Memory and Cognition* 13:365–370.

Goodale, M. A. 1988. Hemispheric differences in motor control. *Behavioural Brain Research* 30:203–214.

Goodale, M. A., and A. D. Milner. 1992. Separate visual pathways for perception and action. *Trends in Neurosciences* 15:20–25.

Goodale, M. A., A. D. Milner, L. S. Jakobson, and D. P. Carey. 1991. A neurological dissociation between perceiving objects and grasping them. *Nature* 349:154–156.

Goodale, M. A., D. Pelisson, and C. Prablanc. 1986. Large adjustments in visually guided reaching do not depend on vision of the hand or perception of target displacement. *Nature* 320:748–750.

Goodman, N. 1968. *Languages of art*. Indianapolis: Bobbs-Merrill.

Goodman, N. 1983. *Fact, fiction, and forecast, 4th edition*. Cambridge, Mass.: Harvard University Press.

Goodman, S. J., and R. A. Andersen. 1989. Microstimulation of a neural-network model for visually guided saccades. *Journal of Cognitive Neuroscience* 4:317–326.

Gopher, D. 1973. Eye-movement patterns in selective listening tasks of focused attention. *Perception and Psychophysics* 14:259–263.

Goss, S., C. Hall, E. Buckolz, and G. Fishburne. 1986. Imagery ability and the acquisition and retention of movements. *Memory and Cognition* 14:469–477.

Graf, P., A. P. Shimamura, and L. R. Squire. 1985. Priming across modalities and priming across category levels: Extending the domain of preserved function in amnesia. *Journal of Experimental Psychology: Learning, Memory, and Cognition* 11:385–395.

Gray, C. M., A. K. Engel, P. König, and W. Singer. 1990. Stimulus-dependent neuronal oscillations in cat visual cortex: Receptive field properties and feature dependence. *European Journal of Neuroscience* 2:607–619.

Gray, C. M., P. König, A. K. Engel, and W. Singer. 1989. Oscillatory responses in cat visual cortex exhibit inter-columnar synchronization which reflects global stimulus properties. *Nature* 338:334–337.

Gray, C. M., and W. Singer. 1989. Stimulus-specific neuronal oscillations in orientation columns of cat visual cortex. *Proceedings of the National Academy of Sciences of the United States of America* 86:1698–1702.

Graziano, M. S., and C. G. Gross. 1992a. Coding of extrapersonal visual space in body-part centered coordinates. *Neuroscience Abstracts* 18:593.

Graziano, M. S., and C. G. Gross. 1992b. Somatotopically organized maps of near visual space exist. *Behavioral and Brain Sciences* 15:750.

Gregory, R. L. 1961. The brain as an engineering problem. In *Current problems in animal behaviour*, edited by W. H. Thorpe and O. L. Zangwill. Cambridge: Cambridge University Press.

Gregory, R. L. 1966. *Eye and brain*. New York: McGraw-Hill.

Gregory, R. L. 1970. *The intelligent eye*. London: Weidenfeld and Nicholson.

Gross, C. G. 1973. Inferotemporal cortex and vision. In *Progress in physiological psychology*, edited by E. Stellar and J. M. Sprague, 77–123. New York: Academic Press.

Gross, C. G. 1978. Inferior temporal lesions do not impair discrimination of rotated patterns in monkeys. *Journal of Comparative and Physiological Psychology* 92:1095–1109.

Gross, C. G., and M. H. Bornstein. 1978. Left and right in science and art. *Leonardo* 11:29–38.

Gross, C. G., C. J. Bruce, R. Desimone, J. Fleming, and R. Gattass. 1981. Cortical visual areas of the temporal lobe. In *Cortical sensory organization II: Multiple visual areas*, edited by C. N. Woolsey. Clifton, N.J.: Humana Press.

Gross, C. G., R. Desimone, T. D. Albright, and E. L. Schwartz. 1984. Inferior temporal cortex as a visual integration area. In *Cortical integration*, edited by F. Reisnoso-Suarez and C. Ajmone-Marsan, New York: Raven.

Gross, C. G., and M. Mishkin. 1977. The neural basis of stimulus equivalence across retinal translation. In *Lateralization in the nervous system*, edited by S. Harnad, R. Doty, J. Jaynes, L. Goldstein, and G. Krauthamer. New York: Academic Press.

Grossberg, S., ed. 1988. *Neural networks and natural intelligence*. Cambridge, Mass.: MIT Press.

Grossi, D., A. Modafferi, L. Pelosi, and L. Trojano. 1989. On the different roles of the cerebral hemispheres in mental imagery: The "O'Clock Test" in two clinical cases. *Brain and Cognition* 10:18–27.

Grossi, D., A. Orsini, and A. Modafferi. 1986. Visuoimaginal constructional apraxia: On a case of selective deficit of imagery. *Brain and Cognition* 5:255–267.

Guariglia, C., A. Padovani, P. Pantano, and L. Pizzamiglio. 1993. Unilateral neglect restricted to visual imagery. *Nature* 364:235–237.

Gurd, J., and J. Marshall. 1992. Drawing upon the mind's eye. *Nature* 359:590–591.

Haenny, P. E., J. H. R. Maunsell, and P. H. Schiller. 1988. State dependent activity in monkey visual cortex. *Experimental Brain Research* 69:245–259.

Hamilton, C. R., and B. A. Vermeire. 1991. Functional lateralization in monkeys. In *Cerebral laterality: Theory and research*, edited by F. L. Kitterle. Hillsdale, N.J.: Erlbaum.

Hampson, P. J., and P. E. Morris. 1990. Imagery, consciousness, and cognitive control: The BOSS model reviewed. In *Imagery: Current developments*, edited by P. J. Hampson, D. F. Marks, and J. T. E. Richardson, 78–102. London: Routledge.

Hannay, H. J., N. R. Varney, and A. L. Benton. 1976. Visual localization in patients with unilateral brain disease. *Journal of Neurology, Neurosurgery and Psychiatry* 39:307–313.

Harries, M. H., and D. I. Perrett. 1991. Visual processing of faces in temporal cortex: Physiological evidence for a modular organization and possible anatomical correlates. *Journal of Cognitive Neuroscience* 3:9–24.

Hart, J., R. S. Berndt, and A. Caramazza. 1985. Category-specific naming deficit following cerebral infarction. *Nature* 316:439–440.

Harth, E., K. P. Unnikrishnan, and A. A. Pandya. 1987. The inversion of sensory processing by feedback pathways: A model of visual cognitive functions. *Science* 237:184–187.

Hasselmo, M. E., E. T. Rolls, and G. C. Baylis. 1989. The role of expression and identity in the face-selective responses of neurons in the temporal visual cortex of the monkey. *Behavioural Brain Research* 32:203–218.

Hasselmo, M. E., E. T. Rolls, G. C. Baylis, and V. Nalwa. 1989. Object-centered encoding by face-selective neurons in the cortex in the superior temporal sulcus of the monkey. *Experimental Brain Research* 75:417–429.

Hatta, T. 1977. Functional hemisphere asymmetries in an inferential thought task. *Psychologia* 20:145–150.

Haxby, J. V., C. L. Grady, B. Horwitz, L. G. Ungerleider, M. Mishkin, R. E. Carson, P. Herscovitch, M. B. Schapiro, and S. I. Rapoport. 1991. Dissociation of object and spatial visual processing pathways in human extrastriate cortex. *Proceedings of the National Academy of Sciences of the United States of America* 88:1621–1625.

Hayes-Roth, F. 1979. Distinguishing theories of representation: A critique of Anderson's "Arguments concerning mental imagery." *Psychological Review* 86:376–392.

Hayhoe, M., J. Lachter, and J. Feldman. 1991. Integration of form across saccadic eye movements. *Perception* 20:393–402.

Hebb, D. O. 1968. Concerning imagery. *Psychological Review* 75: 466–477.

Hecaen, H., and M. L. Albert. 1978. *Human neuropsychology*. New York: Wiley.

Heil, M., F. Rösler, and E. Hennighausen. In press. Imagery-perception interaction depends on the shape of the image: A reply to Farah (1989). *Journal of Experimental Psychology: Human Perception and Performance*

Hellige, J. B., ed. 1983. *Cerebral hemisphere asymmetry*. New York: Praeger.

Hillige, J. B. 1989. Endogenous and experimental determinants of cerebral laterality: What develops? *European Bulletin of Cognitive Psychology* 1:85–89.

Hellige, J. B., and C. Michimata, 1989. Categorization versus distance: Hemispheric differences for processing spatial information. *Memory and Cognition* 17:770–776.

Hellige, J. B., and J. Sergent. 1986. Role of task factors in visual field asymmetries. *Brain and Cognition* 5:200–222.

Hellige, J. B., and R. Webster. 1979. Right hemisphere superiority for initial stages of letter processing. *Neuropsychologia* 17:653–660.

Helstrup, T., and R. E. Anderson. 1991. Imagery in mental construction and decomposition tasks. In *Mental images in human cognition*, edited by R. H. Logie and M. Denis, 229–240. Amsterdam: Elsevier.

Henderson, J. M., A. Pollatsek, and K. Rayner. 1987. Effects of foveal priming and extrafoveal preview on object identification. *Journal of Experimental Psychology: Human Perception and Performance* 13:449–463.

Henderson, J. M., A. Pollatsek, and K. Rayner. 1989. Covert visual attention and extrafoveal information use during object identification. *Perception and Psychophysics* 45:196–208.

Henle, N. 1969. A study of the semantics of animal terms. *Journal of Verbal Behavior* 8:176–184.

Heywood, C. A., and A. Cowey. 1987. On the role of cortical area V4 in the discrimination of hue and pattern in macaque monkeys. *Journal of Neuroscience* 7:2601–2617.

Heywood, C. A., and A. Cowey. 1992. The role of the "face-cell" area in the discrimination and recognition of faces by monkeys. *Philosophical Transactions of the Royal Society of London* 335: 31–38.

Hikosaka, K., E. Iwai, H. A. Saito, and K. Tanaka. 1988. Polysensory properties of neurons in the anterior bank of the caudal superior temporal sulcus of the macaque monkey. *Journal of Neurophysiology* 60:1615–1637.

Hinton, G. 1979. Some demonstrations of the effects of structural descriptions in mental imagery. *Cognitive Science* 3:231–250.

Hinton, G. E. 1981. A parallel computation that assigns canonical object-based frames of reference. *Proceedings of the Seventh International Joint Conference on Artificial Intelligence* 2:683–685.

Hinton, G. E., J. L. McClelland, and D. E. Rumelhart. 1986. Distributed processing. In *Parallel distributed processing: Explorations in the microstructure of cognition*, Volume 1: *Foundations*, edited by D. E. Rumelhart and J. L. McClelland, 77–109. Cambridge, Mass.: MIT Press.

Hinton, G. E., and L. M. Parsons. 1981. Frames of reference in mental imagery. In *Attention and performance IX*, edited by J. Long and A. Baddeley, 261–277. Hillsdale, N.J.: Earlbaum.

Hinton, G. E., and L. M. Parsons. 1988. Scene-based and viewer-centered representations for comparing shapes. *Cognition* 30:1–35.

Hinton, G. E., and T. J. Sejnowski. 1986. Learning and relearning in Boltzmann machines. In *Parallel distributed processing: Explorations in the microstructure of cognition*, Vol. 1: *Foundations*, edited by D. E. Rumelhart and J. L. McClelland, Cambridge, Mass.: MIT Press.

Hintzman, D., C. O'Dell, and D. Arndt. 1981. Orientation in cognitive maps. *Cognitive Psychology* 13:149–206.

Hochberg, J. 1968. In the mind's eye. In *Contemporary theory and research in visual perception*, edited by R. N. Haber, 309–331. New York: Holt, Rinehart, and Winston.

Hochberg, J. 1978. *Perception.* Englewood Cliffs, N.J.: Prentice-Hall.

Hochberg, J. 1981. On cognition in perception: Perceptual coupling and unconscious inference. *Cognition* 10:127–134.

Hochberg, J. 1982. How big is a stimulus? In *Organization and representation in perception*, edited by J. Beck, 191–217. Hillsdale, N.J.: Erlbaum.

Hochberg, J., and L. Gellman. 1977. The effect of landmark features on "mental rotation" times. *Memory and Cognition* 5: 23–26.

Hock, H., C. Kronseder, and S. Sissons. 1981. Hemispheric asymmetry: The effect of orientation on same-different comparison. *Neuropsychologia* 19:723–727.

Hock, H. S., and C. L. Tromley. 1978. Mental rotation and perceptual uprightness. *Perception and Psychophysics* 24:529–533.

Hoekstra, J., D. P. J. van der Goot, G. van der Brink, and F. Bilsen. 1974. The influence of the number of cycles upon the visual contrast threshold for spatial sine wave patterns. *Vision Research* 14:365–368.

Hoffman, D. D., and W. Richards. 1985. Parts of recognition. *Cognition* 18:65–96.

Hoffman, J., M. Denis, and M. Ziessler. 1983. Figurative features and the construction of visual images. *Psychological Research* 45:39–54.

Hoffman, J. E. 1979. A two-stage model of visual search. *Perception and Psychophysics* 25:319–327.

Hoffman, J. E. 1980. Interaction between global and local levels of a form. *Journal of Experimental Psychology: Human Perception and Performance* 6:222–234.

Hoffman, J. E. and B. Nelson. 1981. Spatial selectivity in visual search. *Perception and Psychophysics* 30:283–290.

Holmes, E. J., and C. G. Gross. 1984. Stimulus equivalence after inferior temporal lesions in monkeys. *Behavioral Neuroscience* 98:898–901.

Hooper, S. L., and M. Moulins. 1989. Switching of a neuron from one network to another by sensory-induced changes in membrane properties. *Science* 244:1587–1589.

Horne, P. V. 1993. The nature of imagery. *Consciousness and Cognition* 2:58–82.

Horowitz, M. J. 1983. *Image formation and psychotherapy.* New York: Jason Aronson.

Horwitz, B., C. I. Grady, J. V. Haxby, M. B. Schapiro, S. I. Rapoport, L. G. Ungerleider, and M. Mishkin. 1992. Functional associations among human posterior extrastriate brain regions during object and spatial vision. *Journal of Cognitive Neuroscience* 4:311–322.

Howard, I. P. 1982. *Human visual orientation.* New York: Wiley.

Howard, J. H., and S. M. Kerst. 1978. Directional effects of size changes on the comparison of visual shapes. *American Journal of Psychology* 91:491–199.

Hubbard, T. L., and J. C. Baird. 1988. Overflow, first-sight, and vanishing point distances in visual imagery. *Journal of Experimental Psychology* 14:641–649.

Hubbard, T. L., D. Kall, and J. C. Baird. 1989. Imagery, memory, and size-distance invariance. *Memory and Cognition* 17:87–94.

Hubel, D. H., and T. N. Wiesel. 1962. Receptive fields, binocular interaction and functional architecture in the cat's visual cortex. *Journal of Physiology* 160:106–154.

Hubel, D. H., and T. N. Wiesel. 1968. Receptive fields and functional architecture of monkey striate cortex. *Journal of Physiology* 195:215–243.

Hughes, H. C., W. M. Layton, J. C. Baird, and L. S. Lester. 1984. Global precedence in visual pattern recognition. *Perception and Psychophysics* 35:361–371.

Hughes, H. C., and L. D. Zimba. 1985. Spatial maps of directed visual attention. *Journal of Experimental Psychology: Human Perception and Performance* 11:409–430.

Hughes, H. C., and L. D. Zimba. 1987. Natural boundaries for the spatial spread of directed visual attention. *Neuropsychologia* 25:5–18.

Hummel, J. E., and I. Biederman. 1992. Dynamic binding in a neural network for shape recognition. *Psychological Review* 99: 480–517.

Humphrey, G. K., and P. Jolicoeur. 1988. Visual object identification: Some effects of image foreshortening and monocular depth cues. In *Computational processes in human vision: An interdisciplinary perspective,* edited by Z. W. Pylyshyn, 429–442. Norwood, N.J.: Ablex.

Humphrey, N. K., and L. Weiskrantz. 1969. Size constancy in monkeys with inferotemporal lesions. *Quarterly Journal of Experimental Psychology* 21:225–238.

Humphreys, G. W. 1983. Reference frames and shape perception. *Cognitive Psychology* 15:151–196.

Humphreys, G. W. 1984. Shape constancy: The effects of changing shape orientation and the effects of changing the position of focal features. *Perception and Psychophysics* 36:50–64.

Humphreys, G. W., and P. T. Quinlan. 1987. Normal and pathological processes in visual object constancy. In *Visual object processing: A cognitive neuropsychological approach*, edited by G. W. Humphreys and M. J. Riddoch, 43–105. London: Erlbaum.

Humphreys, G. W., and P. T. Quinlan. 1988. Priming effects between two-dimensional shapes. *Journal of Experimental Psychology: Human Perception and Performance* 14:203–220.

Humphreys, G. W., and M. J. Riddoch. 1987. *To see but not to see: A case study of visual agnosia.* Hillsdale, N.J.: Erlbaum.

Humphreys, G. W., M. J. Riddoch, and P. T. Quinlan. 1988. Cascade processes in picture identification. *Cognitive Neuropsychology* 5:67–104.

Huttenlocher, D. P., and S. Ullman. 1987. Object recognition using alignment. *Proceedings of the First International Conference on Computer Vision* 102–111.

Hyman, I. E., and U. Neisser. 1991. *Reconstruing mental images: Problems of method.* Emory Cognition Project Tech. Rep. No. 19, Emory University, Atlanta, Ga.

Hyvarinen, J. 1982. Posterior parietal lobe of the primate brain. *Physiological Review* 62:1060–1129.

Inhoff, A. W., A. Pollatsek, M. I. Posner, and K. Rayner. 1989. Covert attention and eye movements in reading. *Quarterly Journal of Experimental Psychology* 41A:63–89.

Intons-Peterson, M. J. 1981. Constructing and using unusual and common images. *Journal of Experimental Psychology: Human Learning and Memory* 7:133–144.

Intons-Peterson, M. J. 1983. Imagery paradigms: How vulnerable are they to experimenters' expectations? *Journal of Experimental Psychology: Human Perception and Performance* 9:394–412.

Intons-Peterson, M. J. 1984. Faces, rabbits, skunks, and ducks: Imaginal comparisons of similar and dissimilar items. *Journal of Experimental Psychology: Learning, Memory, and Cognition* 10:699–715.

Intons-Peterson, M. J., and B. B. Roskos-Ewoldsen. 1989. Sensory-perceptual qualities of images. *Journal of Experimental Psychology: Learning, Memory, and Cognition* 15:188–199.

Intraub, H., and J. E. Hoffman. 1992. Reading and visual memory: Remembering scenes that were never seen. *American Journal of Psychology* 105:101–114.

Irwin, D. E. 1991. Information integration across saccadic eye movements. *Cognitive Psychology* 23:420–456.

Iversen, S. D., and L. Weiskrantz. 1964. Temporal lobe lesions and memory in the monkey. *Nature* 201:740–742.

Iversen, S. D., and L. Weiskrantz. 1967. Perception of redundant cues by monkeys with inferotemporal lesions. *Nature* 214:241–243.

Iwai, E. 1985. Neuropsychological basis of pattern vision in macaque monkeys. *Vision Research* 25:425–439.

Iwata, M. 1989. Modular organization of visual thinking. *Behavioral Neurology* 2:153–165.

Jacobs, R. A., and M. I. Jordan. 1992. Computational consequences of a bias toward short connections. *Journal of Cognitive Neuroscience* 4:323–336.

Jacobs, R. A., M. I. Jordan, and A. G. Barto. 1991. Task decomposition through competition in a modular connectionist architecture: The what and where vision tasks. *Cognitive Science* 15:219–250.

Jacobs, R. A., and S. M. Kosslyn. In press. Encoding shape and spatial relations: The role of receptive field size in coordinating complementary representations. *Cognitive Science.*

Jacoby, L. L., and M. Dallas. 1981. On the relationship between autobiographical memory and perceptual learning. *Journal of Experimental Psychology: General* 110:306–340.

Janer, K. W., and J. Pardo. 1991. Deficits in selective attention following bilateral anterior cingulotomy. *Journal of Cognitive Neuroscience* 3:231–241.

Jankowiak, J., M. Kinsbourne, R. S. Shalev, and D. L. Bachman. 1992. Preserved visual imagery and categorization in a case of associative visual agnosia. *Journal of Cognitive Neuroscience* 4:119–131.

Jay, M. F., and D. L. Sparks. 1984. Auditory receptive fields in primate superior colliculus shift with changes in eye position. *Nature* 309:345–347.

Jeannerod, M. 1992. The where in the brain determines the when in the mind. *Behavioral and Brain Sciences* 15:212–213.

Job, R., R. Rumiati, and L. Lotto. 1992. The picture superiority effect in categorization: Visual or semantic? *Journal of Experimental Psychology: Learning, Memory, and Cognition* 18: 1019–1028.

Johansson, G. 1950. *Configurations in event perception.* Uppsala, Sweden: Almqvist and Wiksell.

Johansson, G. 1973. Visual perception of biological motion and a model for its analysis. *Perception and Psychophysics* 14:201–211.

Johansson, G. 1975. Visual motion perception. *Scientific American* 232:76–88.

Johnson, M. K., and C. L. Raye. 1981. Reality monitoring. *Psychological Review* 88:67–85.

Johnson, P. 1982. The functional equivalence of imagery and movement. *Quarterly Journal of Experimental Psychology* 34A:349–365.

Johnson, S. H. 1991. Commentary on Tarr and Pinker. *Psychological Science* 2:205–206.

Johnson-Laird, P. N. 1983. *Mental models.* Cambridge, Mass.: Harvard University Press.

Johnston, A. 1986. A spatial property of the retino-cortical mapping. *Spatial Vision* 1:319–331.

Jolicoeur, P. 1985. The time to name disoriented natural objects. *Memory and Cognition* 13:289–303.

Jolicoeur, P. 1987. A size-congruency effect in memory for visual shape. *Memory and Cognition* 15:531–543.

Jolicoeur, P. 1988. Mental rotation and the identification of disoriented objects. *Canadian Journal of Psychology* 42:461–478.

Jolicoeur, P. 1990a. Identification of disoriented objects: A dual-systems theory. *Mind and Language* 5:387–410.

Jolicoeur, P. 1990b. Orientation congruency effects on the identification of disoriented shapes. *Journal of Experimental Psychology: Human Perception and Performance* 16:351–364.

Jolicoeur, P., and P. Cavanagh. 1992. Mental rotation, physical rotation, and surface media. *Journal of Experimental Psychology: Human Perception and Performance* 18:371–384.

Jolicoeur, P., M. A. Gluck, and S. M. Kosslyn. 1984. Pictures and names: making the connection. *Cognitive Psychology* 16:243–275.

Jolicoeur, P., and M. Ingleton. 1991. Size invariance in curve tracing. *Memory and Cognition* 19:21–36.

Jolicoeur, P., and S. M. Kosslyn. 1983. Coordinate systems in the long-term memory representation of three-dimensional shapes. *Cognitive Psychology* 15:301–345.

Jolicoeur, P., and S. M. Kosslyn. 1985. Is time to scan visual images due to demand characteristics? *Memory and Cognition* 13:320–332.

Jolicoeur, P., and M. J. Landau. 1984. Effects of orientation on the identification of simple visual patterns. *Canadian Journal of Psychology* 38:80–93.

Jolicoeur, P., and B. Milliken. 1989. Identification of disoriented objects: Effects of context of prior presentation. *Journal of Experimental Psychology: Learning, Memory, and Cognition* 15:200–210.

Jolicoeur, P., S. Regehr, L. B. J. P. Smith, and G. N. Smith. 1985. Mental rotation of representations of two-dimensional and three-dimensional objects. *Canadian Journal of Psychology* 39:100–129.

Jolicoeur, P., S. Ullman, and M. MacKay. 1986. Curve tracing: A possible basic operation in the perception of spatial relations. *Memory and Cognition* 14:129–140.

Jolicoeur, P., S. Ullman, and M. MacKay. 1991. Visual curve tracing properties. *Journal of Experimental Psychology: Human Perception and Performance* 17:997–1022.

Jones, B., and T. Anuza. 1982. Effects of sex, handedness, stimulus, and visual field on "mental rotation." *Cortex* 18:501–514.

Jonides, J. 1980. Towards a model of the mind's eye. *Canadian Journal of Psychology* 34:103–112.

Jonides, J. 1983. Further toward a model of the mind's eye's movement. *Bulletin of the Psychonomic Society* 21: 247–250.

Jonides, J., E. E. Smith, R. A. Koeppe, E. Awh, S. Minoshima, and M. A. Mintun. 1993. Spatial working memory in humans as revealed by PET. *Nature* 363:623–625.

Jonsson, J. E., and J. B. Hellige. 1986. Lateralized effects of blurring: A test of the visual spatial frequency model of cerebral hemisphere asymmetry. *Neuropsychologia* 24:351–362.

Jowdy, D. P., and D. V. Harris. 1990. Muscular responses during mental imagery as a function of motor control. *Journal of Sport and Exercise Psychology* 12:191–201.

Julstrom, B. A., and R. J. Baron. 1985. A model of mental imagery. *International Journal of Man-Machine Studies* 23: 313–334.

Just, M. A., and P. A. Carpenter. 1976. Eye fixations and cognitive processes. *Cognitive Psychology* 8:441–480.

Just, M. A., and P. A. Carpenter. 1985. Cognitive coordinate systems: Accounts of mental rotation and individual differences in spatial ability. *Psychological Review* 92:137–172.

Kaas, J. H. 1986. The structural basis for information processing in the primate visual system. In *Visual Neuroscience*, edited by J. P. Pettigrew, K. J. Sanderson, and W. R. Levick, 315–340. Cambridge: Cambridge University Press.

Kaas, J. H., and M. F. Huerta. 1988. The subcortical visual system of primates. *Comparative Primate Biology* 4:327–391.

Kahneman, D., and A. Treisman. 1984. Changing views of attention and automaticity. In *Varieties of attention*, edited by R. Parasuraman and D. R. Davies, 29–61. New York: Academic Press.

Kahneman, D., A. Treisman, and B. J. Gibbs. 1992. The reviewing of object files: Object specific integration of information. *Cognitive Psychology* 24:175–219.

Kalaska, J. F., and D. J. Crammond. 1992. Cerebral cortical mechanisms of reaching movements. *Science* 255:1517–1522.

Kandel, E. R., J. H. Schwartz, and T. M. Jessell, ed. 1991. *Principles of neural science*, third ed. New York: Elsevier.

Kanwisher, N. 1987. Repetition blindness: Type recognition without token individuation. *Cognition* 27:117–143.

Kanwisher, N. 1991. Repetition blindness and illusory conjunctions: Errors in binding visual types with visual tokens. *Journal of Experimenal Psychology: Human Perception and Performance* 17:404–421.

Kaufman, J. H., J. G. May, and S. Kunen. 1981. Interocular transfer of orientation-contingent color aftereffects with external and internal adaptation. *Perception and Psychophysics* 30:547–551.

Kaufman, L. 1974. *Sight and mind: An introduction to visual perception.* New York: Oxford University Press.

Kaufmann, G. 1981. What is wrong with imagery questionnaires? *Scandinavian Journal of Psychology* 22:59–64.

Kaufmann, G. 1983. How good are imagery questionnaires? A rejoinder to David Marks. *Scandinavian Journal of Psychology* 24:247–249.

Keating, E. G., and S. G. Gooley. 1988. Disconnection of parietal and occipital access to the saccadic oculomotor system. *Experimental Brain Research* 70:385–398.

Keenan, J. M. 1983. Qualifications and clarifications of images of concealed objects: A reply to Kerr and Neisser. *Journal of Experimental Psychology: Learning, Memory, and Cognition* 9:222–230.

Keenan, J. M., and R. E. Moore. 1979. Memory for images of concealed objects: A reexamination of Neisser and Kerr. *Journal of Experimental Psychology: Human Learning and Memory* 5: 374–385.

Kelleman, P. J., and T. F. Shipley. 1991. A theory of visual interpolation in object perception. *Cognitive Psychology* 23:141–221.

Kennedy, J. M., and R. Domander. 1985. Shape and contour: The points of maximum change are least useful for recognition. *Perception* 14:367–370.

Keren, G., and J. Skelton. 1976. On selecting between theories of selective attention. *Perception and Psychophysics* 20:85–86.

Kerr, N. H. 1983. The role of vision in "visual imagery" experiments: Evidence from the congenitally blind. *Journal of Experimental Psychology: General* 112:265–277.

Kerr, N. H. 1987. Locational representation in imagery: The third dimension. *Memory and Cognition* 15:521–530.

Kerr, N. H., and U. Neisser. 1983. Mental images of concealed objects: New evidence. *Journal of Experimental Psychology: Learning, Memory, and Cognition* 9:212–221.

Kerst, S. M. 1976. Interactive visual imagery and memory search for words and pictures. *Memory and Cognition* 4:573–580.

Kim, H., and S. C. Levine. 1991. Sources of between-subjects variability in perceptual asymmetries: A meta-analytic review. *Neuropsychologia* 29:877–888.

Kim, H., and S. C. Levine. 1992. Variations in characteristic perceptual asymmetry: Modality specific and modality general components. *Brain and Cognition* 19:21–47.

Kim, Y., L. Morrow, D. Passafiume, and F. Boller. 1984. Visuoperceptual and visuomotor abilities and locus of lesion. *Neuropsychologia* 22:177–185.

Kimchi, R. 1992. Primacy of wholistic processing and global/local paradigm: A critical review. *Psychological Bulletin* 112:24–38.

Kimchi, R., and S. E. Palmer. 1985. Separability and integrality of global and local levels of hierarchical patterns. *Journal of Experimental Psychology: Human Perception and Performance* 11: 673–688.

Kimura, D. 1969. Spatial localization in left and right visual fields. *Canadian Journal of Psychology* 23: 445–458.

Kimura, D. 1977. Acquisition of a motor skill after left hemisphere damage. *Brain* 100:527–542.

Kinchla, R. A. 1974. Detecting target elements in multielement array: A confusability model. *Perception and Psychophysics* 15:149–158.

Kinchla, R. A., and J. Wolfe. 1979. The order of visual processing: "Top down," "bottom up," or "middle out." *Perception and Psychophysics* 25:225–231.

Kirby, K. N., and S. M. Kosslyn. 1990. Thinking visually. *Mind and Language* 5:324–341.

Kirsner, K., D. Milech, and P. Standen. 1983. Common and modality-specific processes in the mental lexicon. *Memory and Cognition* 11:621–630.

Kitterle, F. L., ed. 1991. *Cerebral laterality: Theory and research*. Hillsdale, N.J.: Erlbaum.

Kitterle, F. L., S. Christman, and J. B. Hellige. 1990. Hemispheric differences are found in the identification, but not the detection, of low versus high spatial frequencies. *Perception and Psychophysics* 48:297–306.

Kitterle, F. L., J. B. Hellige, and S. Christman. 1992. Visual hemispheric asymmetries depend on which spatial frequencies are task relevant. *Brain and Cognition* 20:308–314.

Kitterle, F. L., and L. Selig. 1991. Visual field effects in the discrimination of sine wave gratings. *Perception and Psychophysics* 50:15–18.

Klatzky, R. L., S. J. Lederman, and D. E. Matula. 1991. Imagined haptic exploration in judgments of object properties. *Journal of Experimental Psychology: Learning, Memory, and Cognition* 17:314–322.

Klatzky, R. L., and A. M. Stoy. 1974. Using visual codes for comparisons of pictures. *Memory and Cognition* 2:727–736.

Klein, R., and P. McCormick. 1989. Covert visual orienting: Hemifield-activation can be mimicked by zoom lens and midlocation placement strategies. *Acta Psychologica* 70:235–250.

Klopfer, D. S. 1985. Constructing mental representations of objects from successive views. *Journal of Experimental Psychology: Human Perception and Performance* 11:566–582.

Knierim, J. J., and D. C. Van Essen. 1992. Visual cortex: Cartography, connectivity, and concurrent processing. *Current Opinion in Neurobiology* 2:150–155.

Koch, C., and S. Ullman. 1985. Shifts in selective visual attention: Towards the underlying neural circuitry. *Human Neurobiology* 4:219–227.

Koenderink, J., and A. van Doorn. 1982. The shape of smooth objects and the way contours end. *Perception* 11:129–137.

Kohl, R. M., and D. L. Roenker. 1983. Mechanism involvement during skill imagery. *Journal of Motor Behavior* 15:179–190.

Kolb, B. 1990. Recovery from occipital stroke: A self-report and an inquiry into visual processes. *Canadian Journal of Psychology* 44:130–147.

Koriat, A., and J. Norman. 1984. What is rotated in mental rotation? *Journal of Experimental Psychology: Learning, Memory, and Cognition* 10:421–434.

Koriat, A., and J. Norman. 1985. Mental rotation and visual familiarity. *Perception and Psychophysics* 37:429–439.

Koriat, A., and J. Norman. 1988. Frames and images: Sequential effects in mental rotation. *Journal of Experimental Psychology: Learning, Memory, and Cognition* 14:93–111.

Koriat, A., J. Norman, and R. Kimchi. 1991. Recognition of rotated letters: Extracting invariance across successive and simultaneous stimuli. *Journal of Experimental Psychology: Human Perception and Performance* 17:444–457.

Kosslyn, S. M. 1973. Scanning visual images: Some structural implications. *Perception and Psychophysics* 14:90–94.

Kosslyn, S. M. 1974. Constructing visual images: An exercise in neo-mentalism. Ph.D. dissertation, Stanford University.

Kosslyn, S. M. 1975. Information representation in visual images. *Cognitive Psychology* 7:341–370.

Kosslyn, S. M. 1978. Measuring the visual angle of the mind's eye. *Cognitive Psychology* 10:356–389.

Kosslyn, S. M. 1980. *Image and mind.* Cambridge, Mass.: Harvard University Press.

Kosslyn, S. M. 1981. The medium and the message in mental imagery: A theory. *Psychological Review* 88:46–66.

Kosslyn, S. M. 1983. *Ghosts in the mind's machine.* New York: Norton.

Kosslyn, S. M. 1984. Mental representations. In *Tutorials in learning and memory: Essays in honor of Gordon Bower,* edited by J. R. Anderson and S. M. Kosslyn, New York: Freeman.

Kosslyn, S. M. 1987. Seeing and imagining in the cerebral hemispheres: A computational approach. *Psychological Review* 94:148–175.

Kosslyn, S. M. 1991. A cognitive neuroscience of visual cognition: Further developments. In *Mental images in human cognition,* edited by R. H. Logie and M. Denis, 351–381. Amsterdam: North-Holland.

Kosslyn, S. M., and S. N. Alper. 1977. On the pictorial properties of visual images: Effects of image size on memory for words. *Canadian Journal of Psychology* 31:32–40.

Kosslyn, S. M., N. M. Alpert, and W. L. Thompson. 1993. Visual mental imagery and visual perception: PET studies. In *Functional MRI of the brain: A workshop presented by the Society of Magnetic Resonance in Medicine and the Society for Magnetic Resonance Imaging,* 183–190. Arlington, Va.: Society of Magnetic Resonance in Medicine.

Kosslyn, S. M., N. M. Alpert, W. L. Thompson, C. F. Chabris, S. L. Rauch, and A. K. Anderson. 1993. Identifying objects seen from different viewpoints: A PET investigation. Manuscript, Harvard University.

Kosslyn, S. M., N. M. Alpert, W. L. Thompson, V. Maljkovic, S. B. Weise, C. F. Chabris, S. E. Hamilton, S. L. Rauch, and F. S. Buonanno. 1993. Visual mental imagery activates topographically organized visual cortex: PET investigations. *Journal of Cognitive Neuroscience* 5:263–287.

Kosslyn, S. M., A. K. Anderson, L. A. Hillger, and S. E. Hamilton. In press. Hemispheric differences in sizes of receptive fields or attentional biases? *Neuropsychology*

Kosslyn, S. M., T. M. Ball, and B. J. Reiser. 1978. Visual images preserve metric spatial information: Evidence from studies of image scanning. *Journal of Experimental Psychology: Human Perception and Performance* 4:47–60.

Kosslyn, S. M., R. S. Berndt, and T. J. Doyle. 1985. Imagery and language: A preliminary neuropsychological investigation. In *Attention and performance XI,* edited by M. S. Posner and O. S. Marin, Hillsdale, N.J.: Erlbaum.

Kosslyn, S. M., J. L. Brunn, K. R. Cave, and R. W. Wallach. 1984. Individual differences in mental imagery ability: A computational analysis. *Cognition* 18:195–243.

Kosslyn, S. M., C. B. Cave, D. Provost, and S. Von Gierke. 1988. Sequential processes in image generation. *Cognitive Psychology* 20:319–343.

Kosslyn, S. M., and C. F. Chabris. 1990. Naming pictures. *Journal of Visual Languages and Visual Computing* 1:77–95.

Kosslyn, S. M., C. F. Chabris, C. J. Marsolek, and O. Koenig. 1992. Categorical versus coordinate spatial representations: Computational analyses and computer simulations. *Journal of Experimental Psychology: Human Perception and Performance* 18:562–577.

Kosslyn, S. M., P. F. Daly, R. M. McPeek, N. M. Alpert, D. N. Kennedy, and V. S. Caviness, Jr. In press. Using locations to store shape: An indirect effect of a lesion. *Cerebral Cortex*

Kosslyn, S. M., R. A. Flynn, J. B. Amsterdam, and G. Wang. 1990. Components of high-level vision: A cognitive neuroscience analysis and accounts of neurological syndromes. *Cognition* 34:203–277.

Kosslyn, S. M., S. E. Hamilton, and J. H. Bernstein. 1993. The perception of curvature can be selectively disrupted in prosopagnosia. Manuscript, Harvard University.

Kosslyn, S. M., J. D. Holtzman, M. S. Gazzaniga, and M. J. Farah. 1985. A computational analysis of mental image generation: Evidence from functional dissociations in split-brain patients. *Journal of Experimental Psychology: General* 114:311–341.

Kosslyn, S. M., and G. Horwitz. 1993. The role of location information in object identification. Manuscript, Harvard University.

Kosslyn, S. M., and J. R. Intriligator. 1992. Is cognitive neuropsychology plausible? The perils of sitting on a one-legged stool. *Journal of Cognitive Neuroscience* 4:96–106.

Kosslyn, S. M., and R. A. Jacobs. In press. Encoding shape and spatial relations: A simple mechanism for coordinating complementary representations. In *Integrating symbol processors and connectionist networks in artificial intelligence*, edited by V. Honavar and L. Uhr, New York: Academic Press.

Kosslyn, S. M., and O. Koenig. 1992. *Wet mind: The new cognitive neuroscience.* New York: The Free Press.

Kosslyn, S. M., O. Koenig, A. Barrett, C. B. Cave, J. Tang, and J. D. E. Gabrieli. 1989. Evidence for two types of spatial representations: Hemispheric specialization for categorical and coordinate relations. *Journal of Experimental Psychology: Human Perception and Performance* 15:723–735.

Kosslyn, S. M., L. LeSueur, I. E. Dror, and M. S. Gazzaniga. 1993. The role of the corpus callosum in the representation of lateral orientation. *Neuropsychologia* 31:675–686.

Kosslyn, S. M., and V. Maljkovic. 1990. Marr's metatheory revisited. *Concepts in Neuroscience* 1:239–251.

Kosslyn, S. M., V. Maljkovic, S. E. Hamilton, W. L. Thompson, and G. Horwitz. In press. Two types of image generation: Evidence for left- and right-hemisphere processes. *Neuropsychologia.*

Kosslyn, S. M., G. L. Murphy, M. E. Bemesderfer, and K. J. Feinstein. 1977. Category and continuum in mental comparisons. *Journal of Experimental Psychology: General* 106:341–375.

Kosslyn, S. M., S. Pinker, G. E. Smith, and S. P. Shwartz. 1979. On the demystification of mental imagery. *Behavioral and Brain Sciences* 2:570–581.

Kosslyn, S. M., and J. R. Pomerantz. 1977. Imagery, propositions, and the form of internal representations. *Cognitive Psychology* 9:52–76.

Kosslyn, S. M., B. J. Reiser, M. J. Farah, and S. L. Fliegel. 1983. Generating visual images: Units and relations. *Journal of Experimental Psychology: General* 112:278–303.

Kosslyn, S. M., and L. M. Shin. In press. Visual mental images in the brain: Current issues. In *The neuropsychology of high-level vision: Collected tutorial essays*, edited by M. J. Farah and G. Ratcliff, Hillsdale, N.J.: Erlbaum.

Kosslyn, S. M., and S. P. Shwartz. 1977. A simulation of visual imagery. *Cognitive Science* 1:265–295.

Kosslyn, S. M., and S. P. Shwartz. 1978. Visual images as spatial representations in active memory. In *Computer vision systems*, edited by E. M. Riseman and A. R. Hanson. New York: Academic Press.

Kosslyn, S. M., M. A. Sokolov, and J. C. Chen. 1989. The lateralization of BRIAN: A computational theory and model of visual hemispheric specialization. In *Complex information processing comes of age: The impact of Herbert Simon*, edited by D. Klahr and K. Kotovsky. Hillsdale, N.J.: Erlbaum.

Kosslyn, S. M., and M. C. Van Kleeck. 1990. Broken brains and normal minds: Why Humpty-Dumpty needs a skeleton. In *Computational neuroscience*, edited by E. L. Schwartz, 390–402. Cambridge, Mass.: MIT Press.

Kosslyn, S. M., M. C. Van Kleeck, and K. N. Kirby. 1990. A neurologically plausible theory of individual differences in visual mental imagery. In *Advances in mental imagery*, edited by J. T. E. Richardson, P. Hampson, and D. Marks. London: Routledge.

Kraft, R. N., and J. J. Jenkins. 1977. Memory for lateral orientation of slides in picture stories. *Memory and Cognition* 5:397–403.

Kroll, J. F., and M. C. Potter. 1984. Recognizing words, pictures and concepts: A comparison of lexical, object and reality decisions. *Journal of Verbal Learning and Verbal Behavior* 23:39–66.

Krumhansl, C. L. 1984. Independent processing of visual form and motion. *Perception* 13:535–546.

Kubovy, M., and P. Podgorny. 1981. Does pattern matching require the normalization of size and orientation? *Perception and Psychophysics* 30:24–28.

Kunen, S., and J. G. May. 1980. Spatial frequency content of visual imagery. *Perception and Psychophysics* 28:555–559.

Kunzendorf, R. G. 1990. The causal efficacy of consciousness in general, imagery in particular: A materialist perspective. In *Mental imagery*, edited by R. G. Kunzendorf, 147–157. New York: Plenum.

LaBerge, D. 1983. Spatial extent of attention to letters in words. *Journal of Experimental Psychology: Human Perception and Performance* 9:371–379.

LaBerge, D., and V. Brown 1987. Variations in size of the visual field in which targets are presented: An attentional range effect. *Perception and Psychophysics* 40:188–200.

LaBerge, D., and M. S. Buchsbaum. 1990. Positron emission tomography measurements of pulvinar activity during an attention task. *Journal of Neuroscience* 10:613–619.

LaBerge, D., M. Carter, and V. Brown. 1992. A network simulation of thalamus circuit operations in selective attention. *Neural Computation* 4:318–331.

Lachman, R., J. L. Lachman, and E. C. Butterfield. 1979. *Cognitive psychology and information processing: An introduction*. Hillsdale, N.J.: Erlbaum.

Laeng, B. 1993. Lateralization of categorical and coordinate spatial functions. A study of unilateral stroke patients. Ph.D. dissertation, University of Michigan.

Lakoff, G. 1987. *Women, fire and dangerous things*. Chicago: University of Chicago Press.

Lamotte, R. H., and C. Acuna. 1978. Defects in accuracy of reaching after removal of posterior parietal cortex in monkeys. *Brain Research* 139:309–326.

Lansdell, H. 1968. Effect of extent of temporal lobe ablations on two lateralized deficits. *Physiology and Behavior* 3:271–273.

Larsen, A. 1985. Pattern matching: Effects of size ratio, angular difference in orientation, and familiarity. *Perception and Psychophysics* 38:63–68.

Larsen, A., and C. Bundesen. 1978. Size scaling in visual pattern recognition. *Journal of Experimental Psychology: Human Perception and Performance* 4:1–20.

Latto, A., D. Mumford, and J. Shah. 1984. The representation of shape. In *IEEE Workshop on Computer Vision.* Annapolis, Md.: IEEE.

Laursen, A. M. 1982. A lasting impairment in circle-ellipse discrimination after inferotemporal lesions in monkeys. *Behavioural Brain Research* 6:201–212.

Layman, S., and E. Greene. 1988. The effect of stroke on object recognition. *Brain and Cognition* 7:87–114.

Le Bihan, D., R. Turner, T. A. Zeffiro, C. A. Cuénod, P. Jezzard, and V. Bonnerot. 1993. Activation of human primary visual cortex during mental imagery. In *Functional MRI of the brain: A workshop presented by the Society of Magnetic Resonance in Medicine and the Society for Magnetic Resonance Imaging,* 191–196. Arlington, Va.: Society of Magnetic Resonance in Medicine, Inc.

LeDoux, J. E. 1992. Emotion and the amygdala. In *The amygdala,* edited by J. P. Aggleton. New York: Wiley-Liss.

LeDoux, J. E., D. H. Wilson, and M. S. Gazzaniga. 1977. Manipulo-spatial aspects of cerebral lateralization: Clues to the origin of lateralization. *Neuropsychologia* 15:743–750.

Leeuwenberg, E., and P. van der Helm. 1991. Unity and variety in visual form. *Perception* 20:595–622.

Lehky, S. R., and T. J. Sejnowski. 1988. Network model of shape-from-shading: Neural function arises from both receptive and projective fields. *Nature* 333:452–454.

Lenneberg, E. H. 1975. In search of a dynamic theory of aphasia. In *Foundations of language development: A multidisciplinary approach,* edited by E. H. Lenneberg and E. Lenneberg, 3–20. New York: Academic Press.

Lettvin, J. Y., H. R. Maturana, W. S. McCulloch, and W. H. Pitts. 1959. What the frog's eye tells the frog's brain. *Proceedings of the Institute of Radio Engineers* 47:1940–1951.

Levine, D. N. 1982. Visual agnosia in monkey and man. In *Analysis of visual behavior,* edited by D. J. Ingle, M. A. Goodale, and R. J. W. Mansfield, 629–670. Cambridge, Mass.: MIT Press.

Levine, D. N., and R. Calvanio. 1989. Prosopagnosia: A defect in visual configural processing. *Brain and Cognition* 10:149–170.

Levine, D. N., R. B. Mani, and R. Calvanio 1988. Pure agraphia and Gerstmann's syndrome as a visuospatial-language dissociation: An experimental case study. *Brain and Language* 35:172–196.

Levine, D. N., J. Warach, and M. J. Farah. 1985. Two visual systems in mental imagery: Dissociation of "what" and "where" in imagery disorders due to bilateral posterior cerebral lesions. *Neurology* 35:1010–1018.

Levy, J., W. Heller, M. T. Banich, and L. A. Burton. 1983. Are variations among right-handed individuals in perceptual asymmetries caused by characteristic arousal differences between hemispheres? *Journal of Experimental Psychology: Human Perception and Performance* 9:329–359.

Ley, R. G. 1979. Cerebral asymmetries, emotional experience, and imagery: Implications for psychotherapy. In *The potential of fantasy and imagination*, edited by A. A. Sheikh and J. T. Shaffer. New York: Brandon House.

Lindsay, R. K. 1988. Images and inference. *Cognition* 29:229–250.

Livingstone, M. S., and D. H. Hubel. 1987. Psychophysical evidence for separate channels for the perception of form, color, movement and depth. *Journal of Neuroscience* 7:3416–3468.

Livingstone, M. S., and D. H. Hubel. 1988. Segregation of form, color, movement, and depth: Anatomy, physiology, and perception. *Science* 240:740–749.

Loarer, E., and A. Savoyant. 1991. Visual imagery in locomotor movement without vision. In *Mental images in human cognition*, edited by R. H. Logie and M. Denis, 35–46. Amsterdam: North-Holland.

Loftus, E. F. 1979. *Eyewitness testimony*. Cambridge, Mass.: Harvard University Press.

Loftus, G. R. 1972. Eye fixations and recognition memory for pictures. *Cognitive Psychology* 3:525–551.

Loftus, G. R. 1983. Eye fixation on text and scenes. In *Eye movements in reading*, edited by K. Rayner, 359–376. New York: Academic Press.

Loftus, G. R., and N. H. Mackworth. 1978. Cognitive determinants of fixation location during picture viewing. *Journal of Experimental Psychology: Human Perception and Performance* 4:565–572.

Loftus, G. R., W. W. Nelson, and H. J. Kallman. 1983. Differential acquisition rates for different types of information from pictures. *Quarterly Journal of Experimental Psychology* 35A:187–198.

Logie, R. H. 1986. Visuo-spatial processing in working memory. *Quarterly Journal of Experimental Psychology* 38A:229–247.

Logie, R. H., and A. D. Baddeley. 1990. Imagery and working memory. In *Imagery: Current developments*, edited by P. J. Hampson, D. F. Marks, and J. Richardson, 103–128. London: Routledge.

Logie, R. H., and C. Marchetti. 1991. Visuo-spatial working memory: Visual, spatial or central executive? In *Mental images in human cognition*, edited by R. H. Logie and M. Denis, 105–115. Amsterdam: North-Holland.

Lowe, D. G. 1985. *Perceptual organization and visual recognition*. Boston: Kluwer.

Lowe, D. G. 1987a. Three-dimensional object recognition from single two-dimensional images. *Artificial Intelligence* 31:355–395.

Lowe, D. G. 1987b. The viewpoint consistency constraint. *International Journal of Computer Vision* 1:57–72.

Luce, R. D. 1986. *Response times: Their role in inferring elementary mental organization*. New York: Oxford University Press.

Luria, A. R. 1959. Disorders of "simultaneous perception" in a case of bilateral occipito-parietal brain injury. *Brain* 82:437–449.

Luria, A. R. 1973. *The working brain*. New York: Basic Books.

Luria, A. R. 1980. *Higher cortical functions in man*. New York: Basic Books.

Lynch, J. C., V. B. Mountcastle, W. H. Talbot, and T. C. T. Yin. 1977. Parietal lobe mechanisms for directed visual attention. *Journal of Neurophysiology* 40:362–389.

Lynch, J. C. 1980. The functional organization of posterior parietal association cortex. *Behavioral and Brain Sciences* 3:485–584.

MacLeod, C. M., E. B. Hunt, and N. N. Mathews. 1978. Individual differences in the verification of sentence-picture relationships. *Journal of Verbal Learning and Verbal Behavior* 17:493–507.

Madigan, S., and M. Rouse. 1974. Picture memory and visual-generation processes. *American Journal of Psychology* 87:151–158.

Maki, R. H. 1981. Categorization and distance effects with spatial linear orders. *Journal of Experimental Psychology: Human Learning and Memory* 7:15–32.

Maki, R. H. 1986. Naming and locating the tops of rotated pictures. *Canadian Journal of Psychology* 40:368–387.

Malamut, B. L., R. C. Saunders, and M. Mishkin. 1984. Monkeys with combined amygdalo-hippocampal lesions succeed in object discrimination learning despite 24-hour intertrial intervals. *Behavioral Neuroscience* 98:759–769.

Malmstrom, F. V., R. J. Randle, J. S. Bendix, and R. J. Weber. 1980. The visual accommodation response during concurrent mental activity. *Perception and Psychophysics* 28:440–448.

Malonek, D., and H. Spitzer. 1989. Response histogram shapes and tuning curves: The predicted responses of several cortical cell types to drifting gratings stimuli. *Biological Cybernetics* 60:469–475.

Marder, E. 1988. Modulating a neuronal network. *Nature* 335:296–297.

Marks, D. F. 1983. In defense of imagery questionnaires. *Scandinavian Journal of Psychology* 24:243–246.

Marmor, G. S., and L. A. Zaback. 1976. Mental rotation by the blind: Does mental rotation depend on visual imagery? *Journal of Experimental Psychology: Human Perception and Performance* 2:515–521.

Marr, D. 1982. *Vision: A computational investigation into the human representation and processing of visual information.* New York: Freeman.

Marr, D., and H. K. Nishihara. 1978. Representation and recognition of the spatial organization of three-dimensional shapes. *Proceedings of the Royal Society of London B* 200:269–294.

Marsolek, C. J. 1992. Visual form systems in the cerebral hemispheres. Ph.D. dissertation, Harvard University.

Marsolek, C. J., and S. M. Kosslyn. 1992. Mental imagery representation. In *Encyclopedia of artificial intelligence,* 2d Edition, edited by S. C. Shapiro, 928–931. New York: Wiley.

Marsolek, C. J., S. M. Kosslyn, and L. R. Squire. 1992. Form-specific visual priming in the right cerebral hemisphere. *Journal of Experimental Psychology: Learning, Memory, and Cognition* 18:492–508.

Martin, M., and R. Williams. 1990. Imagery and emotion: Clinical and experimental approaches. In *Imagery: Current developments,* edited by P. J. Hampson, D. F. Marks, and J. T. E. Richardson, 268–306. London: Routledge.

Martin-Elkins, C. L., P. George, and J. A. Horel. 1989. Retention deficits produced in monkeys with reversible cold lesions in the prestriate cortex. *Behavioural Brain Research* 32:219–230.

Mathews, N. N., E. B. Hunt, and C. M. MacLeod. 1980. Strategy choice and strategy training in sentence-picture verification. *Journal of Verbal Learning and Verbal Behavior* 19:531–548.

Maunsell, J. H. R., and W. T. Newsome. 1987. Visual processing in monkey extrastriate cortex. *Annual Review of Neuroscience* 10: 363–401.

McBride, E., and A. Rothstein. 1979. Mental and physical practice and the learning and retention of open and closed skills. *Perceptual and Motor Skills* 49:359–365.

McCann, J., R. Savoy, and J. Hall. 1978. Visibility of low-frequency sine-wave targets: Dependence on number of cycles and surround parameters. *Vision Research* 18:891–894.

McClelland, J. L. 1979. On the time-relations of mental processes: An examination of systems of processes in cascade. *Psychological Review* 86:287–330.

McClelland, J. L., and D. E. Rumelhart. 1981. An interactive activation model of context effects in letter perception: Part 1. An account of basic findings. *Psychological Review* 88:375–407.

McClelland, J. L., and D. E. Rumelhart. 1986. *Parallel distributed processing: Explorations in the microstructure of cognition*, vol. 2: *Psychological and biological models*. Cambridge, Mass.: MIT Press.

McCormick, P. A., and P. Jolicoeur. 1991. Predicting the shape of distance functions in curve tracing: Evidence for a zoom lens operator. *Memory and Cognition* 19:469–486.

McMullen, P. A., and M. J. Farah. 1991. Viewer-centered and object-centered representations in the recognition of naturalistic line drawings. *Psychological Science* 2:275–277.

McMullen, P. A., and P. Jolicoeur. 1990. The spatial frame of reference in object naming and discrimination of left-right reflections. *Memory and Cognition* 18:99–115.

McNamara, T. P. 1986. Mental representations of spatial relations. *Cognitive Psychology* 18:87–121.

Meador, K. J., D. W. Loring, D. Bowers, and K. M. Heilman. 1987. Remote memory and neglect syndrome. *Neurology* 37:522–526.

Mehta, Z., F. Newcombe, and E. De Haan. 1992. Selective loss of imagery in a case of visual agnosia. *Neuropsychologia* 30: 645–655.

Mehta, Z., and F. Newcombe. 1991. A role for the left hemisphere in spatial processing. *Cortex* 27:153–167.

Mehta, Z., F. Newcombe, and H. Damasio. 1987. A left hemisphere contribution to visuospatial processing. *Cortex* 23:447–461

Mel, B. W. 1991. A connectionist model may shed light on neural mechanisms for visually guided reaching. *Journal of Cognitive Neuroscience* 3:273–292.

Menon, R., S. Ogawa, D. W. Tank, J. Ellermann, H. Merkele, and K. Ugurbil. 1993. Visual mental imagery by functional brain MRI. In *Functional MRI of the brain: A workshop presented by the Society of Magnetic Resonance in Medicine and the Society for Magnetic Resonance Imaging*, 252. Arlington, Va.: Society of Magnetic Resonance in Medicine, Inc.

Merzenich, M. M., and J. H. Kaas. 1980. Principles of organization of sensory-perceptual systems in mammals. *Progress in Psychobiology and Physiological Psychology* 9:1–42.

Mesulam, M.-M. 1981. A cortical network for directed attention and unilateral neglect. *Annals of Neurology* 10:309–325.

Mesulam, M.-M., ed. 1982. *Tracing neural connections with horseradish peroxidase*. New York: Wiley.

Mesulam, M.-M., ed. 1985. *Principles of behavioral neurology*. Philadelphia: F.A. Davis.

Mesulam, M.-M. 1990. Large-scale neurocognitive networks and distributed processing for attention, language, and memory. *Annals of Neurology* 28: 597–613.

Metzler, J. 1973. Chronometric studies of cognitive analogues of the rotation of three-dimensional objects. Ph.D. dissertation, Stanford University.

Metzler, J., and R. N. Shepard. 1974. Transformational studies of the internal representation of three-dimensional objects. In *Theories of cognitive psychology: The Loyola symposium*, edited by R. L. Solso. Potomac, Md.: Erlbaum.

Michimata, C. and J. B. Hellige. 1987. Effects of blurring and stimulus size on the lateralized processing of nonverbal stimuli. *Neuropsychologia* 25:397–407.

Millar, S. 1990. Imagery and blindness. In *Imagery: Current developments*, edited by P. J. Hampson, D. F. Marks, and J. T. E. Richardson, 129–149. London: Routledge.

Miller, E. K., L. Li, and R. Desimone. 1991. A neural mechanism for working and recognition memory in inferior temporal cortex. *Science* 254:1377–1379.

Miller, G. A. 1956. The magical number seven, plus or minus two: Some limits on our capacity for processing information. *Psychological Review* 63:81–97.

Milliken, B., and P. Jolicoeur. 1992. Size effects in visual recognition memory are determined by perceived size. *Memory and Cognition* 20:83–95.

Milner, B. 1968. Visual recognition and recall after right temporal-lobe excision in man. *Neuropsychologia* 6:191–209.

Milner, B., S. Corkin, and H. L. Teuber. 1968. Further analysis of the hippocampal amnesic syndrome: 14 year followup study of H. M. *Neuropsychologia* 6:215–234.

Mishkin, M. 1972. Cortical visual areas and their interaction. In *Brain and human behavior*, edited by A. G. Karezmar and J. C. Eccles. New York: Springer-Verlag.

Mishkin, M., and T. Appenzeller. 1987. The anatomy of memory. *Scientific American* 256:80–89.

Mishkin, M., B. Malamut, and J. Bachevalier. 1984. Memories and habits: Two neural systems. In *Neurobiology of learning and memory*, edited by G. Lynch, J. L. McGaugh, and M. N. Weinberger, 65–77. New York: Guilford.

Mishkin, M., and L. G. Ungerleider. 1982. Contribution of striate inputs to the visuospatial functions of parieto-preoccipital cortex in monkeys. *Behavioural Brain Research* 6:57–77.

Mishkin, M., L. G. Ungerleider, and K. A. Macko. 1983. Object vision and spatial vision: Two cortical pathways. *Trends in Neurosciences* 6:414–417.

Mitchell, D. B., and C. L. Richman. 1980. Confirmed reservations: Mental travel. *Journal of Experimental Psychology: Human Perception and Performance* 6:58–66.

Miyashita, Y., and H. S. Chang. 1988. Neuronal correlate of pictorial short-term memory in the primate temporal cortex. *Nature* 331:68–70.

Monsell, S. 1991. The nature and locus of word frequency effects in reading. In *Basic processes in reading: Visual word recognition*, edited by D. Besner and G. W. Humphreys, 148–197. Hillsdale, N.J.: Erlbaum.

Moran, J., and R. Desimone. 1985. Selective attention gates visual processing in the extrastriate cortex. *Science* 229:782–784.

Moran, T. P. 1973. The symbolic imagery hypothesis: A production system model. Ph.D. dissertation, Carnegie-Mellon University.

Morgan, M. J. 1983. Mental rotation: A computationally plausible account of transformation through intermediate steps. *Perception* 12:203–211.

Morgan, M. J., J. M. Findlay, and R. J. Watt. 1982. Aperture viewing: A review and a synthesis. *Quarterly Journal of Experimental Psychology* 34A:211–233.

Morrison, C. M., A. W. Ellis, and P. T. Quinlan. 1992. Age of acquisition, not word frequency, affects object naming, not object recognition. *Memory and Cognition* 20:705–714.

Motter, B. C., and V. B. Mountcastle. 1981. The functional properties of the light-sensitive neurons of the posterior parietal cortex studied in waking monkeys: Foveal sparing and opponent vector organization. *Journal of Neuroscience* 1:3–26.

Mountcastle, V. B. 1978. Brain mechanisms for directed attention. *Journal of the Royal Society of Medicine* 71:14–28.

Mountcastle, V. B., J. C. Lynch, A. P. Georgopoulos, H. Sakata, and C. Acuna. 1975. Posterior parietal association cortex of the monkey: Command functions for operations within extrapersonal space. *Journal of Neurophysiology* 38:871–908.

Movshon, J. A., E. H. Adelson, M. S. Gizzi, and W. T. Newsome. 1986. The analysis of moving visual patterns. In *Pattern recognition mechanisms*, edited by C. Chagas, R. Gattass, and C. Gross, 117–151. Vatican City: Pontifical Academy of Sciences.

Muensterberg, H. 1914. *Psychology, general and applied*. New York: Appleton.

Mumford, D. 1991. On the computational architecture of the neocortex I. *Biological Cybernetics* 65:135–145.

Mumford, D. 1992. On the computational architecture of the neocortex II. *Biological Cybernetics* 66:241–251.

Mumford, D. In press. Pattern theory: A unifying perspective. In *Proceedings of the First European Congress of Mathematics*. Cambridge, MA: Birkhauser-Boston.

Mumford, D., S. M. Kosslyn, L. A. Hillger, and R. J. Herrnstein. 1987. Discriminating figure from ground: The role of edge detection and region growing. *Proceedings of the National Academy of Sciences of the United States of America* 84:7354–7358.

Murphy, G. L., and H. H. Brownell. 1985. Category differentiation in object recognition: Typicality constraints on the basic category advantage. *Journal of Experimental Psychology: Learning, Memory, and Cognition* 11:70–84.

Nakayama, K. 1985. Biological motion processing: A review. *Vision Research* 25:625–660.

Nakayama, K. 1990. The iconic bottleneck and the tenuous link between early visual processing and perception. In *Vision: Coding and efficiency*, edited by C. Blakemore, 411–422. Cambridge: Cambridge University Press.

Nakayama, K., and J. M. Loomis. 1974. Optical velocity patterns, velocity sensitive neurons and space perception: A hypothesis. *Perception* 3:63–80.

Nakayama, K., and M. Mackeben. 1989. Sustained and transient components of focal visual attention. *Vision Research* 29:1631–1647.

Navon, D. 1977. Forest before trees: The precedence of global features in visual perception. *Cognitive Psychology* 9:353–383.

Navon, D., and J. Norman. 1983. Does global precedence really depend on visual angle? *Journal of Experimental Psychology: Human Perception and Performance* 9:955–965.

Nebes, R. D. 1971. Superiority of the minor hemisphere in commissurotomized man for the perception of part-whole relations. *Cortex* 7:333–349.

Nebes, R. D. 1972. Dominance of the minor hemisphere in commissurotomized man on a test of figural unification. *Brain* 95:633–638.

Neisser, U. 1967. *Cognition psychology*. New York: Appleton-Century-Crofts.

Neisser, U. 1976. *Cognition and reality*. San Francisco: Freeman.

Nemire, K., and B. Bridgeman. 1987. Oculomotor and skeletal motor systems share one map of visual space. *Vision Research* 27: 393–400.

Newcombe, F., G. Ratcliff, and H. Damasio. 1987. Dissociable visual and spatial impairments following right posterior cerebral lesions: Clinical, neuropsychological and anatomical evidence. *Neuropsychologia* 25:149–161.

Newcombe, F., and W. R. Russell. 1969. Dissociated visual perceptual and spatial deficits in focal lesions of the right hemisphere. *Journal of Neurology, Neurosurgery, and Psychiatry* 32:73–81.

Newell, A. 1990. *Unified theories of cognition.* Cambridge, Mass.: Harvard University Press.

Newell, A., J. C. Shaw, and H. A. Simon. 1958. Elements of a theory of human problem solving. *Psychological Review* 65:151–166.

Newsome, W. T., R. H. Wurtz, M. R. Dursteler, and A. Mikami. 1985. Deficits in visual motion processing following ibotenic acid lesions in the middle temporal visual area of the macaque monkey. *Journal of Neuroscience* 5:825–840.

Nickerson, R. S., and M. J. Adams. 1979. Long-term memory for a common object. *Cognitive Psychology* 11:287–307.

Nickerson, R. S. 1965. Short-term memory for complex meaningful visual configurations: A demonstration of capacity. *Canadian Journal of Psychology* 19:155–160.

Nickerson, R. S. 1968. A note on long-term recognition memory for pictorial material. *Psychonomic Science* 11:58.

Nielsen, G. D., and E. E. Smith. 1973. Imaginal and verbal representations in short-term recognition of visual forms. *Journal of Experimental Psychology* 101:375–378.

Noton, D., and L. Stark. 1971. Scanpaths in saccadic eye movements while viewing and recognizing patterns. *Vision Research* 11:929–942.

Novick, L. R., and B. Tversky. 1987. Cognitive constraints on ordering operations: The case of geometric analogies. *Journal of Experimental Psychology: General* 116:50–67.

Ogren, M. P., and A. E. Hendrickson. 1977. The distribution of pulvinar terminals in visual areas 17 and 18 of the monkey. *Brain Research* 137:343–350.

O'Keefe, J., and L. Nadel. 1978. *The hippocampus as a cognitive map.* Oxford: Clarendon.

Okhuma, Y. 1986. A comparison of image-induced and perceived Muller-Lyer illusion. *Journal of Mental Imagery* 10:31–38.

Oldfield, R. C., and A. Wingfield. 1965. Response latencies in naming objects. *Quarterly Journal of Experimental Psychology* 17:273–281.

Olshausen, B., C. Anderson, and D. C. Van Essen. 1992. A neural model of visual attention and invariant pattern recognition. California Institute of Technology Computation and Neural Systems Program, Memo 18 .

Olson, D., and E. Bialystok. 1983. *Spatial cognition: The structure and development of mental representations of spatial relations.* Hillsdale, N.J.: Erlbaum.

Omori, T. 1992. Dual representation of image recognition process: Interaction of neural network and symbolic processing. *Proceedings of the International Symposium on Neural Information Processing,* 50–53.

Optican, L. M., and B. J. Richmond. 1987. Temporal encoding of two-dimensional patterns by single units in primate inferior temporal cortex III: Information theoretic analysis. *Journal of Neurophysiology* 57:162–178.

O'Reilly, R. C., S. M. Kosslyn, C. J. Marsolek, and C. F. Chabris. 1990. Receptive field characteristics that allow parietal lobe neurons to encode spatial properties of visual input: A computational analysis. *Journal of Cognitive Neuroscience* 2:141–155.

Ostergaard, A. L., and J. B. Davidoff. 1985. Some effects of color on naming and recognition of objects. *Journal of Experimental Psychology: Learning, Memory, and Cognition* 11:579–587.

Paivio, A. 1971. *Imagery and verbal processes*. New York: Holt, Rinehart, and Winston.

Paivio, A. 1975. Perceptual comparisons through the mind's eye. *Memory and Cognition* 3:635–648.

Paivio, A. 1986 *Mental representations*. New York: Oxford University Press.

Paivio, A. 1989. A dual coding perspective on imagery and the brain. In *Neuropsychology of visual perception*, edited by J. W. Brown. Hillsdale, N.J.: Erlbaum.

Paivio, A., J. M. Clark, N. Digdon, and T. Bons. 1989. Referential processing: Reciprocity and correlates of naming and imaging. *Memory and Cognition* 17:163–174.

Paivio, A., and J. te Linde. 1980. Symbolic comparisons of objects on color attributes. *Journal of Experimental Psychology: Human Perception and Performance* 6:652–661.

Paivio, A., and J. te Linde. 1982. Imagery, memory, and the brain. *Canadian Journal of Psychology* 36:243–272.

Palmer, S. E. 1975. Visual perception and world knowledge: Notes on a model of sensory-cognitive interaction. In *Explorations in cognition*, edited by D. A. Norman and D. E. Rumelhart, 279–307. San Francisco: Freeman.

Palmer, S. E. 1977. Hierarchical structure in perceptual representation. *Cognitive Psychology* 9:441–474.

Palmer, S. E. 1980. What makes triangles point: Local and global effects in configurations of ambiguous triangles. *Cognitive Psychology* 12:285–305.

Palmer, S. E. 1982. Symmetry, transformation and the structure of the perceptual system. In *Organization and representation in perception*, edited by J. Beck, 95–144. Hillsdale, N.J.: Erlbaum.

Palmer, S. E. 1983. The psychology of perceptual organization: A transformational approach. In *Human and machine vision*, edited by J. Beck, B. Hope, and A. Rosenfeld, 269–339. New York: Academic Press.

Palmer, S. E. 1985. The role of symmetry in shape perception. *Acta Psychologia* 59:67–90.

Palmer, S. E. 1992. Common region: A new principle of perceptual grouping. *Cognitive Psychology* 24:436–447.

Palmer, S. E., E. Rosch, and P. Chase. 1981. Canonical perspective and the perception of objects. In *Attention and Performance IX*, edited by J. Long and A. Baddeley, 135–151. Hillsdale, N.J.: Erlbaum.

Paquet, L. 1991. Mental rotation of compound stimuli: The effects of task demands, practice, and figural goodness. *Memory and Cognition* 19:558–567.

Pardo, J., P. T. Fox, and M. E. Raichle. 1991. Localization of a human system for sustained attention by positron emission tomography. *Nature* 349:61–64.

Park, S., and S. M. Kosslyn. 1990. Imagination. In *Reflections on "The Principles of Psychology": William James after a century*, edited by M. G. Johnson and T. B. Henley. Hillsdale, N.J.: Erlbaum.

Parker, D. E., R. L. Poston, and W. L. Gulledge. 1983. Spatial orientation: Visual-vestibular-somatic interaction. *Perception and Psychophysics* 33:139–146.

Parsons, L. M. 1987a. Imagined spatial transformations of one's body. *Journal of Experimental Psychology: General* 116:172–191.

Parsons, L. M. 1987b. Imagined spatial transformations of one's hands and feet. *Cognitive Psychology* 19:178–241.

Parsons, L. M. 1987c. Visual discrimination of abstract mirror-reflected three-dimensional objects at many orientations. *Perception and Psychophysics* 42:49–59.

Parsons, L. M. 1988. Serial search and comparison of features of imagined and perceived objects. *Memory and Cognition* 16:23–35.

Pena-Casanova, J., T. Roig-Rovira, A. Bermudez, and E. Tolosa-Sarro. 1985. Optic aphasia, optic apraxia, and loss of dreaming. *Brain and Language* 26:63–71.

Penfield, W., and T. Rasmussen. 1950. *The cerebral cortex of man: A clinical study of localization of function*. New York: Macmillan.

Pentland, A. P. 1986. Perceptual organization and the representation of natural form. *Artificial Intelligence* 28:293–331.

Pentland, A. P. 1987. Recognition by parts. *First International Conference on Computer Vision*, 612–621.

Pentland, A. P. 1989. Part segmentation for object recognition. *Neural Computation* 1:82–91.

Perenin, M. T., and A. Vighetto. 1983. Optic ataxia: A specific disorder in visuomotor coordination. In *Spatially oriented behavior*, edited by A. Hein and M. Jeannerod, 305–326. New York: Springer-Verlag.

Perky, C. W. 1910. An experimental study of imagination. *American Journal of Psychology* 21:422–452.

Perrett, D. I., M. H. Harries, R. Bevan, S. Thomas, P. J. Benson, A. J. Mistlin, A. J. Chitty, J. K. Hietanen, and J. E. Ortega. 1989. Frameworks of analysis for the neural representation of animate objects and actions. *Journal of Experimental Biology* 146:87–113.

Perrett, D. I., E. T. Rolls, and W. Caan. 1982. Visual neurons responsive to faces in the monkey temporal cortex. *Experimental Brain Research* 47:329–342.

Perrett, D. I., P. A. J. Smith, A. J. Mistlin, A. J. Chitty, A. S. Head, D. D. Potter, R. Broennimann, A. D. Milner, and M. A. Jeeves. 1985. Visual analysis of body movements by neurons in the temporal cortex of the macaque monkey: A preliminary report. *Behavioural Brain Research* 16:153–170.

Perrett, D. I., P. A. J. Smith, D. D. Potter, A. J. Mistlin, A. S. Head, A. D. Milner, and M. A. Jeeves. 1985. Visual cells in the temporal cortex sensitive to face view and gaze direction. *Proceedings of the Royal Society of London*. Series B. *Biological Sciences* 223:293–317.

Petersen, S. E., P. T. Fox, M. I. Posner, M. Mintun, and M. E. Raichle. 1988. Positron emission tomographic studies of the cortical anatomy of single-word processing. *Nature* 331:585–589.

Petersen, S. E., D. L. Robinson, and W. Keys. 1985. Pulvinar nuclei of the behaving rhesus monkey: Visual responses and their modulation. *Journal of Neurophysiology* 54:867–886.

Peterson, M. A., J. F. Kihlstrom, P. M. Rose, and M. L. Glisky. 1992. Mental images can be ambiguous: Reconstruals and reference-frame reversals. *Memory and Cognition* 20:107–123.

Peterson, M. J., and S. E. Graham. 1974. Visual detection and visual imagery. *Journal of Experimental Psychology* 103:509–514.

Peterzell, D. H., L. O. Harvey, C. D. Hardyck. 1989. Spatial frequencies and the cerebral hemispheres: Contrast sensitivity, visible persistence, and letter classification. *Perception and Psychophysics* 46:443–455.

Pinker, S. 1980. Mental imagery and the third dimension. *Journal of Experimental Psychology: General* 109:354–371.

Pinker, S. 1984. *Language Learnability and Language Development*. Cambridge, Mass.: Harvard University Press.

Pinker, S., P. Choate, and R. A. Finke. 1984. Mental extrapolation in patterns constructed from memory. *Memory and Cognition* 12:207–218.

Pinker, S., and R. A. Finke. 1980. Emergent two-dimensional patterns in images rotated in depth. *Journal of Experimental Psychology: Human Perception and Performance* 6:244–264.

Pinker, S., K. Stromswold, and L. Beck. 1984. Visualizing objects at prespecified orientations. In *Annual Meeting of the Psychonomics Society*, San Antonio, texi.

Podgorny, P., and R. N. Shepard. 1978. Functional representations common to visual perception and imagination. *Journal of Experimental Psychology: Human Perception and Performance* 4:21–35.

Podgorny, P., and R. N. Shepard. 1983. Distribution of visual attention over space. *Journal of Experimental Psychology: Human Perception and Performance* 9:380–393.

Pohl, W. 1973. Dissociation of spatial discrimination deficits following frontal and parietal lesions in monkeys. *Journal of Comparative and Physiological Psychology* 82:227–239.

Pollatsek, A., K. Rayner, and W. E. Collins. 1984. Integrating pictorial information across eye movements. *Journal of Experimental Psychology: General* 113:426–442.

Pollatsek, A., K. Rayner, and J. M. Henderson. 1990. Role of spatial location in integration of pictorial information across saccades. *Journal of Experimental Psychology: Human Perception and Performance* 16:199–210.

Poltrock, S. E., and P. Brown. 1984. Individual differences in visual imagery and spatial ability. *Intelligence* 8:93–138.

Polyak, S. 1957. *The vertebrate visual system*. Chicago: University of Chicago Press.

Pomerantz, J. R. 1983. Global and local precedence: Selective attention in form and motion perception. *Journal of Experimental Psychology: General* 112:516–540.

Popper, K. R., Sir. 1959. *The logic of scientific discovery*. New York: Basic Books.

Posner, M. I. 1978. *Chronometric explorations of mind*. Hillsdale, N.J.: Erlbaum.

Posner, M. I. 1988. Structures and functions of selective attention. In *Clinical neuropsychology and brain function: Research, measurement, and practice*, edited by T. Boll and B. K. Bryant, 169–202. Washington, D.C.: American Psychological Association.

Posner, M. I., and J. Driver. 1992. The neurobiology of selective attention. *Current Opinion in Neurobiology* 2:165–169.

Posner, M. I., A. W. Inhoff, F. J. Friedrich, and A. Cohen. 1987. Isolating attentional systems: A cognitive-anatomical analysis. *Psychobiology* 15:107–121.

Posner, M. I., M. J. Nissen, and W. C. Ogden. 1978. Attended and unattended processing modes: The role of set for spatial location. In *Modes of perceiving and processing information*, edited by H. L. Pick and I. J. Saltzman, 137–158. Hillsdale, N.J.: Erlbaum.

Posner, M. I., and S. E. Petersen. 1990. The attention system of the human brain. *Annual Review of Neuroscience.* 13:25–42.

Posner, M. I., S. E. Petersen, P. T. Fox, and M. E. Raichle. 1988. Localization of cognitive operations in the human brain. *Science* 240:1627–1631.

Posner, M. I., C. R. R. Snyder, and B. J. Davidson. 1980. Attention and the detection of signals. *Journal of Experimental Psychology: General* 109:160–174.

Posner, M. I., J. A. Walker, F. J. Friedrich, and R. D. Rafal. 1984. Effects of parietal lobe injury on covert orienting of visual attention. *Journal of Neuroscience* 4:1863–1874.

Potter, M. C. 1966. On perceptual recognition. In *Studies in cognitive growth*, edited by J. S. Bruner, R. R. Olver, and P. M. Greenfield, 103–134. New York: Wiley.

Prablanc, C., D. Pelisson, and M. A. Goodale. 1986. Visual control of reaching movements without vision of the limb. *Experimental Brain Research* 62:293–302.

Prinzmetal, W., and W. P. Banks. 1983. Perceptual capacity limits in visual detection and search. *Bulletin of the Psychonomic Society* 21:263–266.

Puff, C. R., ed. 1982. *Handbook of research methods in human memory and cognition.* New York: Academic Press.

Pylyshyn, Z. W. 1973. What the mind's eye tells the mind's brain: A critique of mental imagery. *Psychological Bulletin* 80:1–24.

Pylyshyn, Z. W. 1979. The rate of "mental rotation" of images: A test of a holistic analogue hypothesis. *Memory and Cognition* 7:19–28.

Pylyshyn, Z. W. 1981. The imagery debate: Analogue media versus tacit knowledge. *Psychological Review* 87:16–45.

Quinn, J. G. 1991. Encoding and maintenance of information in visual working memory. In *Mental images in human cognition,* edited by R. H. Logie and M. Denis, 95–104. Amsterdam: North-Holland.

Quinn, J. G., and G. E. Ralston. 1986. Movement and attention in visual working memory. *Quarterly Journal of Experimental Psychology* 38A:689–703.

Rademacher, J., V. S. Caviness, Jr., H. Steinmetz, and A. Galaburda. In press. Topographical variation of the human primary cortices: Implications for neuroimaging, brain mapping and neurobiology. *Cerebral Cortex.*

Rafal, R. D., J. Smith, J. Krantz, A. Cohen, and C. Brennan. 1990. Extrageniculate vision in hemianopic humans: Saccade inhibition by signals in the blind field. *Science* 250:118–121.

Ratcliff, G. 1979. Spatial thought, mental rotation and the right cerebral hemisphere. *Neuropsychologia* 17:49–54.

Ratcliff, G., and G. A. B. Davies-Jones. 1972. Defective visual localization in focal brain wounds. *Brain* 95:49–60.

Ratcliff, G., and F. Newcombe. 1973. Spatial orientation in man: Effects of left, right, and bilateral posterior cerebral lesions. *Journal of Neurology, Neurosurgery, and Psychiatry* 36:448–454.

Reed, S. K., H. S. Hock, and G. R. Lockhead. 1983. Tacit knowledge and the effect of pattern configuration on mental scanning. *Memory and Cognition* 11:137–143.

Reed, S. K., and J. A. Johnsen. 1975. Detection of parts in patterns and images. *Memory and Cognition* 3:569–575.

Reeke, G. N., Jr., L. H. Finkel, O. Sporns, and G. M. Edelman. 1989. Synthetic neural modeling: A multilevel approach to the analysis of brain complexity. In *Signal and sense: Local and global order in perceptual maps,* edited by G. M. Edelman, W. E. Gall, and W. M. Cowan. New York: Wiley.

Reisberg, D., and D. Chambers. 1991. Neither pictures nor propositions: What can we learn from a mental image? *Canadian Journal of Psychology* 45:336–352.

Reisberg, D., and A. Morris. 1985. Images contain what the imager put there: A non-replication of illusions in imagery. *Bulletin of the Psychonomic Society* 23:493–496.

Rezak, M., and L. A. Benevento. 1979. A comparison of the organization of the projections of the dorsal lateral geniculate nucleus, the inferior pulvinar and adjacent lateral pulvinar to primary visual cortex (area 17) in the macaque monkey. *Brain Research* 167:19–40.

Rhodes, G., and A. O'Leary. 1985. Imagery effects on early visual processing. *Perception and Psychophysics* 37:382–388.

Richardson, A. 1967. Mental practice: A review and discussion (Parts I and II). *Research Quarterly* 38:95–107, 263–273.

Richardson, A. 1969. *Mental imagery*. New York: Springer.

Richardson, J. T. E. 1990. Imagery and memory in brain-damaged patients. In *Imagery: Current developments*, edited by P. J. Hampson, D. F. Marks, and J. T. E. Richardson, 351–372. London: Routledge.

Richman, C. L., D. B. Mitchell, and J. S. Reznick. 1979. Mental travel: Some reservations. *Journal of Experimental Psychology: Human Perception and Performance* 5:13–18.

Riddoch, M. J. 1990. Loss of visual imagery: A generation deficit. *Cognitive Neuropsychology* 7:249–273.

Riddoch, M. J., and G. W. Humphreys. 1987. A case of integrative visual agnosia. *Brain*. 110:1431–1462.

Rieser, J. J., D. H. Ashmead, C. R. Talor, and G. A. Youngquist. 1990. Visual perception and the guidance of locomotion without vision to previously seen targets. *Perception* 19:675–689.

Riseman, E. M., and A. R. Hanson, ed. 1978. *Computer vision systems*. New York: Academic Press.

Rizzolatti, G., and A. Berti. 1990. Neglect as a neural representation deficit. *Revue Neurologique* (Paris) 146:626–634.

Rizzolatti, G., M. Gentilucci, and M. Matelli. 1985. Selective spatial attention: One center, one circuit, or many circuits? In *Attention and performance XI*, edited by M. I. Posner and O. S. M. Marin, Hillsdale N.J.: Erlbaum.

Rizzolatti, G., M. Matelli, and G. Pavesi. 1983. Deficits in attention and movement following the removal of postarcuate (area 6) and prearcuate (area 8) cortex in macaque monkeys. *Brain* 106:655–673.

Rizzolatti, G., C. Scandolara, M. Mattelli, and M. Gentilucci. 1981. Afferent properties of periarcuate neurons in macaque monkeys. II. Visual responses. *Behavioural Brain Research* 2: 147–163.

Robertson, L. C., and D. C. Delis. 1986. "Part-whole" processing in unilateral brain damaged patients: Dysfunction of hierarchical organization. *Neuropsychologia* 24:363–370.

Robertson, L. C., M. R. Lamb, and R. T. Knight. 1988. Effects of lesions of temporal-parietal junction on perceptual and attentional processing in humans. *Journal of Neuroscience* 8:3757–3769.

Robertson, L. C., and S. E. Palmer. 1983. Holistic processes in the perception and transformation of disoriented figures. *Journal of Experimental Psychology: Human Perception and Performance* 9: 203–214.

Robertson, L. C., S. E. Palmer, and L. M. Gomez. 1987. Reference frames in mental rotation. *Journal of Experimental Psychology: Learning, Memory, and Cognition* 13:368–379.

Robinson, D. A., and A. F. Fuchs. 1969. Eye movements evoked by stimulation of frontal eye fields. *Journal of Neurophysiology* 32:637–648.

Robinson, D. L., M. E. Goldberg, and G. B. Stanton. 1978. Parietal association cortex in the primate: Sensory mechanisms and behavioral modulations. *Journal of Neurophysiology* 41:910–932.

Robinson, D. L., and S. E. Petersen. 1992. The pulvinar and visual salience. *Trends in Neuroscience* 15:127–132.

Rock, I. 1973. *Orientation and form*. New York: Academic Press.

Rock, I. 1981. Anorthoscopic perception. *Scientific American* 244:145–153.

Rock, I., and J. DiVita. 1987. A case of viewer-centered object perception. *Cognitive Psychology* 19:280–293.

Rock, I., J. DiVita, and R. Barbeito. 1981. The effect on form perception of change of orientation in the third dimension. *Journal of Experimental Psychology: Human Perception and Performance* 7:719–732.

Rock, I., D. Wheeler, and L. Tudor. 1989. Can we imagine how objects look from other viewpoints? *Cognitive Psychology* 21:185–210.

Rockland, K. S. In press. The organization of feedback connections from area V2 (18) to area V1 (17). In *Cerebral Cortex*, vol. 10, edited by A. Peters and K. S. Rockland. New York: Plenum.

Rockland, K. S., and D. N. Pandya. 1979. Laminar origins and terminations of cortical connections of the occipital lobe in the rhesus monkey. *Brain Research* 179:3–20.

Rockland, K. S., K. S. Saleem, and K. Tanaka. 1992. Widespread feedback connections from areas V4 and TEO. *Society for Neuroscience Abstracts* 18:390.

Rockland, K. S., and A. Virga. 1989. Terminal arbors of individual "feedback" axons projecting from area V2 to V1 in the macaque monkey: A study using immunohistochemistry of anterogradely transported phaseolus vulgaris-leucoagglutinin. *Journal of Comparative Neurology* 285:54–72.

Roediger, H. L., and T. A. Blaxton. 1987. Effects of varying modality, surface features, and retention interval on priming in word-fragment completion. *Memory and Cognition* 15:379–388.

Roland, P. E., and L. Friberg. 1985. Localization of cortical areas activated by thinking. *Journal of Neurophysiology* 53:1219–1243.

Roldan, C. E., and W. A. Phillips. 1980. Functional differences between upright and rotated images. *Quarterly Journal of Experimental Psychology* 32:397–412.

Rollins, M. 1989. *Mental imagery: On the limits of cognitive science.* New Haven, Conn.: Yale University Press.

Rolls, E. T. 1987. Information representation, processing, and storage in the brain: Analysis at the single neuron level. In *The neural and molecular bases of learning*, edited by J.-P. Changeux and M. Konishi, 503–539. New York: Wiley.

Rolls, E. T., and G. C. Baylis. 1986. Size and contrast have only small effects on the responses to faces of neurons in the cortex of the superior temporal sulcus of the monkey. *Experimental Brain Research* 65:38–48.

Rolls, E. T., G. C. Baylis, M. E. Hasselmo, and V. Nalwa. 1989. The effect of learning on the face selective responses of neurons in the cortex in the superior temporal sulcus of the monkey. *Experimental Brain Research* 76:153–164.

Rosch, E. 1975. The nature of mental codes for color categories. *Journal of Experimental Psychology: Human Perception and Performance* 1:303–322.

Rosch, E., C. B. Mervis, W. D. Gray, D. M. Johnson, and P. Boyes-Braem. 1976. Basic objects in natural categories. *Cognitive Psychology* 8:382–439.

Rosenfeld, A. 1985. Pyramid algorithms. In *Vision: Coding and efficiency*, edited by C. Blakemore, 423–430. Cambridge: Cambridge University Press.

Rosenthal, R. 1976. *Experimenter effects in behavioral research.* New York: Irvington.

Rosenthal, R., and L. Jacobson. 1992. *Pygmalion in the classroom: Teacher expectancy and pupils' intellectual development.* New York: Irvington.

Roth, J. R., and S. M. Kosslyn. 1988. Construction of the third dimension in mental imagery. *Cognitive Psychology* 20:344–361.

Rothstein, L. D., and R. C. Atkinson. 1975. Memory scanning for words in visual images. *Memory and Cognition* 3:541–544.

Rueckl, J. G., K. R. Cave, and S. M. Kosslyn. 1989. Why are "what" and "where" processed by separate cortical visual systems? A computational investigation. *Journal of Cognitive Neuroscience* 1:171–186

Rumelhart, D. E., and J. L. McClelland, ed. 1986. *Parallel distributed processing: Explorations in the microstructure of cognition*, vol. 1: *Foundations*. Cambridge, Mass.: MIT Press.

Russo, M., and L. A. Vignolo. 1967. Visual figure-ground discrimination in patients with unilateral cerebral disease. *Cortex* 3:113–127.

Rybash, J. M., and W. J. Hoyer. 1992. Hemispheric specialization for categorical and coordinate spatial representations: A reappraisal. *Memory and Cognition* 20:271–276.

Saarinen, J., and B. Julesz. 1991. The speed of attentional shifts in the visual field. *Proceedings of the National Academy of Sciences of the United States of America* 88:1812–1814.

Sagi, D., and B. Julesz. 1985. "Where" and "what" in vision. *Science* 228:1217–1219.

Saint-Cyr, J. A., L. G. Ungerleider, and R. Desimone. 1990. Organization of visual cortical inputs to the striatum and subsequent outputs to the pallido-nigral complex in the monkey. *Journal of Comparative Neurology* 298:129–156.

Saito, H., M. Yukio, K. Tanaka, K. Hikosaka, Y. Fukada, and E. Iwai. 1986. Integration of direction signals of image motion in the superior temporal sulcus of the macaque monkey. *Journal of Neuroscience* 6:145–157.

Sakai, K., and Y. Miyashita. 1991. Neural organization for the long-term memory of paired associates. *Nature* 354:152–155.

Sakata, H., and M. Kusunoki. 1992. Organization of space perception: Neural representation of three-dimensional space in the posterior parietal cortex. *Current Opinion in Neurobiology* 2:170–174.

Sakata, H., H. Shibutani, and K. Kawano. 1983. Functional properties of visual tracking neurons in posterior parietal association cortex of the monkey. *Journal of Neurophysiology* 49:1364–1380.

Sakata, H., M. Taira, S. Mine, and A. Murata. In press. The hand-movement-related neurons of the posterier parietal cortex of the monkey: Their role in the visual guidance of hand movement. *Experimental Brain Research [Suppl]*

Sakitt, B., and H. B. Barlow. 1982. A model for the economical encoding of the visual image in cerebral cortex. *Biological Cybernetics* 43:97–108.

Sandell, J. H., and P. H. Schiller. 1982. Effect of cooling area 18 on striate cortex cells in the squirrel monkey. *Journal of Neurophysiology* 48:38–48.

Sanocki, R. 1991. Effects of early common features on form perception. *Perception and Psychophysics* 50:490–497.

Sato, T. 1988. Effects of attention and stimulus interaction on visual responses of inferior temporal neurons in macaque. *Journal of Neurophysiology* 60:344–364.

Savoy, R., and J. McCann. 1975. Visibility of low-spatial-frequency sine-wave targets: Dependence on number of cycles. *Journal of the Optical Society of America* 65:343–350.

Schacter, D. L. 1987. Implicit memory: History and current status. *Journal of Experimental Psychology: Learning, Memory, and Cognition* 13:501–518.

Schacter, D. L., C.-Y. Chiu, and K. N. Ochsner. 1993. Implicit memory: A selective review. *Annual Review of Neuroscience* 16:159–182.

Schacter, D. L., L. A. Cooper, and S. M. Delaney. 1990. Implicit memory for unfamiliar objects depends on access to structural descriptions. *Journal of Experimental Psychology: General* 119:5–24.

Schacter, D. L., L. A. Cooper, S. M. Delaney, M. A. Peterson, and M. Tharan. 1991. Implicit memory for possible and impossible objects: Constraints on the construction of structural descriptions. *Journal of Experimental Psychology: Learning, Memory, and Cognition* 17:3–19.

Schacter, D. L., J. L. Harbluk, and D. R. McLachlan. 1984. Retrieval without recollection: An experimental analysis of source amnesia. *Journal of Verbal Learning and Verbal Behavior* 23:593–611.

Schiffman, H. R. 1982. *Sensation and perception.* New York: Wiley.

Schiller, P. H., and N. K. Logothetis. 1990. The color-opponent and broad-band channels of the primate visual system. *Trends in Neuroscience* 13:392–398.

Schiller, P. H., N. K. Logothetis, and E. R. Charles. 1990a. Functions of the colour-opponent and broad-band channels of the visual system. *Nature* 343:68–70.

Schiller, P. H., N. K. Logothetis, and E. R. Charles. 1990b. Role of the color-opponent and broad-band channels in vision. *Visual Neuroscience* 5:321–346.

Schiller, P. H., J. H. Sandell, and J. H. Maunsell. 1987. The effect of frontal eye field and superior colliculus lesions on saccadic latencies in the rhesus monkey. *Journal of Neurophysiology* 57:1033–1049.

Schneider, G. E. 1967. Contrasting visuomotor functions of tectum and cortex in the golden hamster. *Psychologische Forschung* 31:52–62.

Schneider, G. E. 1969. Two visual systems. *Science* 163:895–902.

Schwartz, E. L. 1977. Spatial mapping in the primate visual cortex: Analytic structure and relevance to perception. *Biological Cybernetics* 25:181–194.

Schwartz, E. L. 1980a. Computational anatomy and functional architecture of striate cortex: A spatial mapping approach to perceptual coding. *Vision Research* 20:645–669.

Schwartz, E. L. 1980b. A quantitative model of the functional architecture of human striate cortex with application to visual illusion and cortical texture analysis. *Biological Cybernetics* 37:63–76.

Schwartz, E. L. 1984. Anatomical and physiological correlates of visual computation from striate to infero-temporal cortex. *IEEE Transactions on Systems, Man, and Cybernetics* SMC–14:257–271.

Schwartz, E. L., R. Desimone, T. D. Albright, and C. G. Gross. 1983. Shape recognition and inferior temporal neurons. *Proceedings of the National Academy of Sciences of the United States of America* 80:5776–5778.

Schwartz, S., and K. Kirsner. 1982. Laterality effects in visual information processing: Hemispheric specialisation or the orienting of attention? *Quarterly Journal of Experimental Psychology* 34A:61–77.

Seamon, J. G. 1972. Imagery codes and human information retrieval. *Journal of Experimental Psychology* 96:468–470.

Segal, S. J., and V. Fusella. 1970. Influence of imaged pictures and sounds on detection of visual and auditory signals. *Journal of Experimental Psychology* 83:458–464.

Sekiyama, K. 1982. Kinesthetic aspects of mental representations in the identification of left and right hands. *Perception and Psychophysics* 32:89–95.

Sekiyama, K. 1983. Mental and physical movements of hands: Kinesthetic information preserved in representational systems. *Japanese Psychological Research* 25:95–102.

Sekuler, R., and D. Nash. 1972. Speed of size scaling in human vision. *Psychonomic Science* 27:93–94.

Selfridge, O. G. 1959. Pandemonium: A paradigm for learning. In *The mechanisation of thought processes: Proceedings of a symposium held at the National Physical Laboratory, November, 1958*, London: H.M. Stationery Office.

Sereno, A. B., and S. M. Kosslyn. 1991. Discrimination within and between hemifields: A new constraint on theories of attention. *Neuropsychologia* 29:659–675.

Sergent, J. 1982a. The cerebral balance of power: Confrontation or cooperation? *Journal of Experimental Psychology: Human Perception and Performance* 8:253–272.

Sergent, J. 1982b. Theoretical and methodological consequences of variations in exposure duration in visual laterality studies. *Perception and Psychophysics* 31:451–461.

Sergent, J. 1984. Inferences from unilateral brain damage about normal hemispheric functions in visual pattern recognition. *Psychological Bulletin* 96:99–115.

Sergent, J. 1987. Failures to confirm the spatial-frequency hypothesis: Fatal blow or healthy complication? *Canadian Journal of Psychology* 41:412–428.

Sergent, J. 1988. Face perception and the right hemisphere. In *Thought without language*, edited by L. Weiskrantz, 108–131. Oxford: Oxford University Press.

Sergent, J. 1989. Image generation and processing of generated images in the cerebral hemispheres. *Journal of Experimental Psychology: Human Perception and Performance* 15:170–178.

Sergent, J. 1990. The neuropsychology of visual image generation: Data, method, and theory. *Brain and Cognition* 13:98–129.

Sergent, J. 1991a. Judgments of relative position and distance on representations of spatial relations. *Journal of Experimental Psychology: Human Perception and Performance* 91:762–780.

Sergent, J. 1991b. Processing of spatial relations within and between the disconnected cerebral hemispheres. *Brain* 114:1025–1043.

Sergent, J., and M. C. Corballis. 1991. Ups and downs in cerebral lateralization. In *Cerebral laterality: Theory and research*, edited by F. L. Kitterle, 175–200. Hillsdale, N.J.: Erlbaum.

Sergent, J., and J. B. Hellige. 1986. Role of input factors in visual-field asymmetries. *Brain and Cognition* 5:174–199.

Sergent, J., and E. Lorber. 1983. Perceptual categorization in the cerebral hemispheres. *Brain and Cognition* 2:39–54.

Sergent, J., S. Ohta, and B. MacDonald. 1992. Functional neuroanatomy of face and object processing: A positron emission tomography study. *Brain* 115:15–36.

Sergent, J., E. Zuck, M. Lévesque, and B. MacDonald. 1992. Positron emission tomography study of letter and object processing: Empirical findings and methodological considerations. *Cerebral Cortex* 2:68–80.

Servos, P., and M. Peters. 1990. A clear left hemisphere advantage for visuo-spatially based verbal categorization. *Neuropsychologia* 28:1251–1260.

Seymour, P. H. K. 1979. *Human visual cognition*. London: Collier Macmillan.

Shallice, T., ed. 1988. *From neuropsychology to mental structure*. Cambridge: Cambridge University Press.

Shepard, R. N. 1967. Recognition memory for words, sentences, and pictures. *Journal of Verbal Learning and Verbal Behavior* 6:156–163.

Shepard, R. N. 1980. Multidimensional scaling, tree-fitting, and clustering. *Science* 210:390–398.

Shepard, R. N. 1984. Ecological constraints on internal representation: Resonant kinematics of perceiving, imagining, thinking, and dreaming. *Psychological Review* 91:417–447.

Shepard, R. N. 1987. Evolution of a mesh between principles of the mind and regularities in the world. In *The latest on the best: Essays on evolution and optimality*, edited by J. Dupre, 251–275. Cambridge, Mass.: MIT Press.

Shepard, R. N., and L. A. Cooper. 1982. *Mental images and their transformations*. Cambridge Mass.: MIT Press.

Shepard, R. N., and C. Feng. 1972. A chronometric study of mental paper folding. *Cognitive Psychology* 3:228–243.

Shepard, R. N., and S. A. Judd. 1976. Perceptual illusion of rotation of three-dimensional objects. *Science* 191:952–954.

Shepard, R. N., and J. Metzler. 1971. Mental rotation of three-dimensional objects. *Science* 171:701–703.

Shepard, S., and D. Metzler. 1988. Mental rotation: Effects of dimensionality of objects and type of task. *Journal of Experimental Psychology: Human Perception and Performance* 14:3–11.

Shepherd, G. M. 1988. *Neurobiology*. Oxford: Oxford University Press.

Shiffrin, R. M., and G. T. Gardiner. 1972. Visual processing capacity and attentional control. *Journal of Experimental Psychology* 93:72–82.

Shiffrin, R. M., D. P. McKay, and W. D. Shaffer. 1976. Attending to forty-nine spatial positions at once. *Journal of Experimental Psychology: Human Perception and Performance* 2:14–22.

Shimojo, S., and W. Richards. 1986. "Seeing" shapes that are almost totally occluded: A new look at Park's camel. *Perception and Psychophysics* 39:418–426.

Shulman, G. L., R. W. Remington, and J. P. McLean. 1979. Moving attention through visual space. *Journal of Experimental Psychology: Human Perception and Performance* 5:522–526.

Shulman, G. L., M. A. Sullivan, K. Gish, and W. J. Sakoda. 1986. The role of spatial-frequency channels in the perception of local and global structure. *Perception* 15:259–273.

Shulman, G. L., and J. Wilson. 1987. Spatial frequency and selective attention to local and global information. *Perception* 16:89–101.

Shuttleworth, E. C., V. Syring, and N. Allen. 1982. Further observations on the nature of prosopagnosia. *Brain and Cognition* 1:302–332.

Shwartz, S. P. 1981. The perception of disoriented complex objects. Manuscript, Yale University.

Simion, F., S. Bagnara, P. Bisiacchi, S. Roncato, and C. Umilta. 1980. Laterality effects, levels of processing, and stimulus properties. *Journal of Experimental Psychology: Human Perception and Performance* 6:184–195.

Simon, H. A. 1981. *The sciences of the artificial*. Cambridge, Mass.: MIT Press.

Skinner, B. F. 1978. *Reflections on behaviorism and society*. Englewood Cliffs, N.J.: Prentice-Hall.

Smith, E. E., and D. L. Medin. 1981. *Categories and concepts*. Cambridge, Mass.: Harvard University Press.

Smith, E. E., C. J. Balzano, and J. H. Walker. 1978. Nominal and semantic process in picture categorization. In *Semantic factors in cognition*, edited by J. Cotton and R. Klatzky, 137–168. Potomac, Md: Erlbaum.

Smythe, M. M., and L. L. Pendleton. 1989. Working memory for movements. *Quarterly Journal of Experimental Psychology* 41A:235–250.

Smythe, W. E., and R. S. Lockhart. 1989. The composition of imaginal transformations. *Canadian Journal of Psychology* 43:13–44.

Snodgrass, J. G., and B. McCullough. 1986. The role of visual similarity in picture categorization. *Journal of Experimental Psychology: Learning, Memory, and Cognition* 12:147–154.

Snowden, R. J. 1992. The perception of visual motion. *Current Opinion in Neurobiology* 2:175–179.

Sorber, E., ed. 1984. *Conceptual issues in evolutionary biology: An anthology*. Cambridge, Mass.: MIT Press.

Sperling, G. 1960. The information available in brief visual presentations. *Psychological Monographs: General and Applied* 74:74.

Spitzer, H., R. Desimone, and J. Moran. 1988. Increased attention enhances both behavioral and neuronal performance. *Science* 240:338–340.

Sprague, J. M. 1991. The role of the superior colliculus in facilitating visual attention and form perception. *Proceedings of the National Academy of Sciences of the United States of America* 88:1286–1290.

Springer, S. P., and G. Deutsch. 1985. *Left brain, right brain*. New York: Freeman.

Squire, L. R. 1987. *Memory and brain*. New York: Oxford University Press.

Squire, L. R., B. Knowlton, and G. Musen. 1993. The structure and organization of memory. *Annual Review of Psychology* 44:453–495.

Standing, L. 1973. Learning 10,000 pictures. *Quarterly Journal of Experimental Psychology* 25:207–222.

Standing, L., J. Conezio, and R. N. Haber. 1970. Perception and memory for pictures: Single-trial learning of 2500 visual stimuli. *Psychonomic Science* 19:73–74.

Stark, L., and S. Ellis. 1981. Scanpaths revisited: Cognitive models direct active looking. In *Cognition and visual perception*, edited by D. Fisher, R. Monty, and J. Senders, 193–226. Hillsdale, N.J.: Erlbaum.

Steiger, J. H., and J. C. Yuille. 1983. Long-term memory and mental rotation. *Canadian Journal of Psychology* 37:367–389.

Stein, L. A. In press. Imagination and situated cognition. *Journal of Experimental and Theoretical Intelligence*

Steinmetz, M. A., C. E. Connor, and K. M. MacLeod. 1992. Focal spatial attention suppresses responses of visual neurons in monkey posterior parietal cortex. *Society for Neuroscience Abstracts* 18:148.

Sternberg, S. 1969. Memory scanning: Mental processes revealed by reaction-time experiments. *American Scientist* 57:421–457.

Stevens, A., and P. Coupe. 1978. Distortions in judged spatial relations. *Cognitive Psychology* 10:422–437.

Strosahl, K. D., and J. C. Ascough. 1981. Clinical uses of mental imagery: Experimental foundations, theoretical misconceptions, and research issues. *Psychological Bulletin* 89:422–438.

Stucki, D. J., and J. B. Pollack. 1992. Fractal (reconstructive analogue) memory. *Proceedings of the 14th Annual Conference of the Cognitive Science Society*. Hillsdale, N.J.: Erlbaum.

Sunderland, A. 1990. The bisected image? Visual memory in patients with visual neglect. In *Imagery: Current developments*, edited by P. J. Hampson, D. F. Marks, and J. T. E. Richardson, 333–350. London: Routledge.

Suzuki, K., and Y. Nakata. 1988. Does the size of figures affect the rate of mental rotation? *Perception and Psychophysics* 44:76–80.

Taira, M., S. Mine, A. P. Georgopoulos, A. Murata, and H. Sakata. 1990. Parietal cortex neurons of the monkey related to the visual guidance of hand movement. *Experimental Brain Research* 83:29–36.

Takano, Y. 1989. Perception of rotated forms: A theory of information types. *Cognitive Psychology* 21:1–59.

Talairach, J., and D. P. Tournoux. 1988. *Coplanar stereotaxic atlas of the human brain*. New York: Thieme.

Tanaka, J. W., and M. Taylor. 1991. Object categories and expertise: Is the basic level in the eye of the beholder? *Cognitive Psychology* 23:457–482.

Tanaka, K., H. Saito, Y. Fukada, and M. Moriya. 1991. Coding visual images of objects in the inferotemporal cortex of the macaque monkey. *Journal of Neurophysiology* 66:170–189.

Tarr, M. J., and S. Pinker. 1989. Mental rotation and orientation-dependence in shape recognition. *Cognitive Pychology* 21:233–282.

Tarr, M. J., and S. Pinker. 1990. When does human object recognition use a viewer-centered reference frame? *Psychological Science* 1:253–256.

Tarr, M. J., and S. Pinker. 1991. Orientation-dependent mechanisms in shape recognition: Further issues. *Psychological Science* 2:207–209.

Taylor, A. M., and E. K. Warrington. 1973. Visual discrimination in patients with localized brain lesions. *Cortex* 9:82–93.

Taylor, D. C. 1969. Differential rates of cerebral maturation between sexes and between hemispheres. *Lancet* 2:140–148.

Templeton, W. B. 1973. The role of gravitational cues in the judgment of visual orientation. *Perception and Psychophysics* 14: 451–457.

Teuber, H. L. 1955. Physiological psychology. *Annual Review of Psychology* 6:267–296.

Teuber, H. L., and S. Weinstein. 1956. Ability to discover hidden figures after cerebral lesions. *Archives of Neurology and Psychiatry* 76:369–379.

Tigges, J., W. B. Spatz, and M. Tigges. 1973. Reciprocal point-to-point connections between parastriate and striate cortex in the squirrel monkey (*Saimiri*). *Journal of Comparative Neurology* 148:481–490.

Tippett, L. 1992. The generation of visual images: A review of neuropsychological research and theory. *Psychological Bulletin* 112:415–432.

Tolman, E. C. 1948. Cognitive maps in rats and men. *Psychological Review* 55:189–208.

Tootell, R. B. H., M. S. Silverman, E. Switkes, and R. L. De Valois. 1982. Deoxyglucose analysis of retinotopic organization in primate striate cortex. *Science* 218:902–904.

Townsend, J. T. 1974. Issues and models concerning the processing of a finite number of inputs. In *Human information processing: Tutorials in performance and cognition*, edited by B. H. Kantrowitz, 133–185. New York: Wiley.

Treisman, A. M. 1969. Strategies and models of selective attention. *Psychological Review* 76: 282–299.

Treisman, A. M., and G. Gelade. 1980. A feature integration theory of attention. *Cognitive Psychology* 12:97–136.

Treisman, A. M., and S. Gormican. 1988. Feature analysis in early vision: Evidence from search asymmetries. *Psychological Review* 95:15–48.

Treisman, A. M., and H. Schmidt. 1982. Illusory conjunctions in the perception of objects. *Cognitive Psychology* 14:107–141.

Treisman, A. M., and J. Souther. 1985. Search asymmetry: A diagnostic for preattentive processing of separable features. *Journal of Experimental Psychology: General* 114:285–310.

Trojano, L., and D. Grossi. 1992. Impaired drawing from memory in a visual agnosic patient. *Brain and Cognition* 20:327–344.

Tsal, Y. 1983. Movements of attention across the visual field. *Journal of Experimental Pscychology: Human Perception and Performance* 9:523–530.

Tulving, E., and D. L. Schacter. 1990. Priming and human memory systems. *Science* 247:301–396.

Tye, M. 1991. *The imagery debate*. Cambridge, Mass.: The MIT Press.

Tyler, H. R. 1969. Disorders of visual scanning with frontal lobe lesions. In *Modern neurology*, edited by S. Locke, 381–393. Boston: Little, Brown.

Uecker, A., and J. E. Obrzut. 1993. Hemisphere and gender differences in mental rotation. *Brain and Cognition* 22:42–50.

Uhl, F., G. Goldenberg, W. Lang, G. Lindinger, M. Steiner, and L. Deecke. 1990. Cerebral correlates of imagining colours, faces and a map-II. Negative cortical DC potentials. *Neuropsychologia* 28:81–93.

Ullman, S. 1979. *The interpretation of visual motion*. Cambridge, Mass.: MIT Press.

Ullman, S. 1984. Visual routines. *Cognition* 18:97–159.

Ullman, S. 1989. Aligning pictorial descriptions: An approach to object recognition. *Cognition* 32:193–254.

Ullman, S., and R. Barsi. 1990. *Recognition by linear combinations of models*. A.I. Memo No. 1152, Artifical Intelligence Laboratory, MIT.

Umilta, C., G. Rizzolatti, C. A. Marzi, G. Zamboni, C. Franzini, R. Camarda, and G. Berlucchi. 1974. Hemispheric differences in the discrimination of line orientation. *Neuropsychologia* 12: 165–174.

Umilta, C., D. Sava, and D. Salmaso. 1980. Hemispheric asymmetries in a letter classification task with different typefaces. *Brain and Language* 9:171–181.

Ungerleider, L. G., L. Ganz, and K. H. Pribram. 1977. Size constancy in rhesus monkeys: Effects of pulvinar, prestriate, and inferotemporal lesions. *Experimental Brain Research* 27:251–269.

Ungerleider, L. G., and M. Mishkin. 1982. Two cortical visual systems. In *Analysis of visual behavior*, edited by D. J. Ingle, M. A. Goodale, and R. J. W. Mansfield, 549–586. Cambridge, Mass.: MIT Press.

Vaina, L. M. 1989. Selective impairment of visual motion interpretation following lesions of the right occipito-parietal area in humans. *Biological Cybernetics* 61: 347–359.

Vaina, L. M., and S. D. Zlateva. 1990. The largest convex patches: A boundary-based method for obtaining object parts. *Biological Cybernetics* 62:225–236.

Valiant, L. G. 1988. Functionality in neural nets. *Proceedings of the American Association for Artificial Intelligence*, 629–634. Los Altos, Calif. Morgan Kaufmann.

Van Essen, D. C. 1985. Functional organization of primate visual cortex. In *Cerebral Cortex*, vol. 3, edited by A. Peters and E. G. Jones, 259–329. New York: Plenum.

Van Essen, D. C. 1987. Visual cortex, extrastriate. In *Encyclopedia of neuroscience, Vol. II*, edited by G. Adelman, 1271–1273. Boston: Birkhauser.

Van Essen, D. C., C. H. Anderson, and D. J. Felleman. 1992. Information processing in the primate visual system: An integrated systems perspective. *Science* 255:419–423.

Van Essen, D. C., D. J. Felleman, E. A. DeYoe, J. Olavarria, and J. Knierim. 1990. Modular and hierarchical organization of extrastriate visual cortex in the macaque monkey. *Cold Spring Harbor Symposia on Quantitative Biology* 55:679–696.

Van Essen, D. C., and J. H. Maunsell. 1983. Hierarchical organization and functional streams in the visual cortex. *Trends in Neurosciences* 6:370–375.

Van Essen, D. C., W. T. Newsome, and H. R. Maunsell. 1984. The visual field representation in striate cortex of the macaque monkey: Asymmetries, anisotropies, and individual variability. *Vision Research* 24:429–448.

Van Kleeck, M. H. 1989. Hemispheric differences in global versus local processing of hierarchical visual stimuli by normal subjects: New data and a meta-analysis of previous studies. *Neuropsychologia* 27:1165–1178.

Van Kleeck, M. H., and S. M. Kosslyn. 1989. Gestalt laws of perceptual organization in an embedded figures task: Evidence for hemispheric specialization. *Neuropsychologia* 27:1179–1186.

Van Sommers, P. 1989. A system for drawing and drawing-related neuropsychology. *Cognitive Neuropsychology* 6:117–164.

Van Strien, J. W., and A. Bouma. 1990. Mental rotation of laterally presented random shapes in males and females. *Brain and Cognition* 12:297–303.

Vauclair, J., J. Fagot, and W. Hopkins. 1993. Rotation of mental images in baboons when the visual input is directed to the left cerebral hemisphere. *Psychological Science* 4:99–103.

Vitkovitch, M., and G. Underwood. 1991. Hemispheric differences in the processing of pictures of typical and atypical semantic category members. *Cortex* 27:475–480.

Vitkovitch, M., and G. Underwood. 1992. Visual field differences in an object decision task. *Brain and Cognition* 19:195–207.

Von Eckardt Klein, B. 1978. Inferring functional localization from neurological evidence. In *Explorations in the biology of language*, edited by E. Walker, 27–66. Montgomery, Vt.: Bradford.

Von Monakow, C. 1914/1969. Diaschisis. (Excerpt from "Die Lokalisation Im Grosshirm Und Der Abbau Der Funktion Durch Kortikale Herde" by J. F. Bergmann, Wiesbaden, 1914. Translated by G. Harris). In *Brain and Behavior*: vol. 1: *Mood, states, and mind*, edited by K. H. Pribram. Baltimore: Penguin.

Wallace, B. 1984. Apparent equivalence between perception and imagery in the production of various visual illusions. *Memory and Cognition* 12:156–162.

Wallace, B., and B. G. Hofelich. 1992. Process generalization and the prediction of performance on mental imagery tasks. *Memory and Cognition* 20:695–704.

Wang, J., T. Aigner, and M. Mishkin. 1990. Effects of neostriatal lesions on visual habit formation in rhesus monkeys. *Neuroscience Abstracts* 16:617.

Ward, L. M. 1982. Determinants of attention to local and global features of visual forms. *Journal of Experimental Psychology: Human Perception and Performance* 8:562–581.

Warrington, E. K., and M. James. 1967. Disorders of visual perception in patients with localised cerebral lesions. *Neuropsychologia* 5:253–266.

Warrington, E. K., and M. James. 1986. Visual object recognition in patients with right-hemisphere lesions: Axes or features? *Perception* 15:355–366.

Warrington, E. K., and M. James. 1988. Visual apperceptive agnosia: A clinico-anatomical study of three cases. *Cortex* 24:13–32.

Warrington, E. K., and M. James. 1991. A new test of object decision: 2D silhouettes featuring a minimal view. *Cortex* 27:377–383.

Warrington, E. K., and P. Rabin. 1970. Perceptual matching in patients with cerebral lesions. *Neuropsychologia* 8:475–487.

Warrington, E. K., and T. Shallice. 1984. Category specific semantic impairments. *Brain* 107: 829–853.

Warrington, E. K., and A. M. Taylor. 1973. The contribution of the right parietal lobe to object recognition. *Cortex* 9: 152–164.

Warrington, E. K., and A. M. Taylor. 1978. Two categorical stages of object recognition. *Perception* 7:695–705.

Watkins, M. J., and D. J. Schiano. 1982. Chromatic imaging: An effect of mental colouring on recognition memory. *Canadian Journal of Psychology* 36:291–299.

Webster, M. J., L. G. Ungerleider, and J. Bachevalier. 1991. Connections of inferior temporal-lobe areas TE and TEO with medial temporal-lobe structures in infant and adult monkeys. *Journal of Neuroscience* 11:1095–1116.

Weimer, W. B. 1977. A conceptual framework for cognitive psychology: Motor theories of the mind. In *Perceiving, acting and knowing: Toward an ecological psychology*, edited by R. Shaw and J. Bransford, 267–311. Hillsdale, N.J.: Erlbaum.

Weiskrantz, L. 1968. Some traps and pontifications. In *Analysis of behavioral change*, edited by L. Weiskrantz. New York: Harper and Row.

Weiskrantz, L. 1986. *Blindsight: A case study and its implications.* New York: Oxford University Press.

Weiskrantz, L. 1990. Visual prototypes, memory, and the inferotemporal cortex. In *Vision, memory, and the temporal lobe*, edited by E. Iwai and M. Mishkin, 13–28. New York: Elsevier.

Weiskrantz, L., and R. C. Saunders. 1984. Impairments of visual object transforms in monkeys. *Brain* 107:1033–1072.

Weller, R. E., and J. H. Kaas. 1983. Retinotopic patterns of connections of area 17 with visual areas V-II and MT in macaque monkeys. *Journal of Comparative Neurology* 220: 253–279.

White, M. J. 1969. Laterality differences in perception: A review. *Psychological Bulletin* 72:387–405.

White, M. J. 1971. Visual hemifield differences in the perception of letter and contour orientation. *Canadian Journal of Psychology* 25:207–212.

White, M. J. 1972. Hemispheric asymmetries in tachistoscopic information-processing. *British Journal of Psychology* 63:497–508.

Wilson, F. A. W., S. P. O'Scalaidhe, and P. S. Goldman-Rakic. 1993. Dissociation of object and spatial processing domains in primate prefrontal cortex. *Science* 260:1955–1958.

Wilson, H. R., and J. R. Bergen. 1979. A four mechanism model for spatial vision. *Vision Research* 19:19–32.

Wilson, M., and H. M. Kaufman. 1969. Effect of inferotemporal lesions upon processing of visual information in monkeys. *Journal of Comparative and Physiological Psychology* 69:44–48.

Wilton, R. N. 1979. Knowledge of spatial relations: The specification of the information used in making inferences. *Quarterly Journal of Experimental Psychology* 31:133–146.

Wilton, R. N., and B. Pidcock. 1982. Knowledge of spatial relations: Varying the precision with which locations must be specified. *Quarterly Journal of Experimental Psychology* 34A:515–528.

Wingfield, A. 1968. Effects of frequency on identification and naming of objects. *The American Journal of Psychology* 81:226–234.

Winston, P. H., ed. 1975. *The Psychology of computer vision.* New York: McGraw-Hill.

Wittgenstein, L. 1953. *Philosophical investigations.* New York: Macmillan.

Wong-Riley, M. 1978. Reciprocal connections between striate and prestriate cortex in the squirrel monkey as demonstrated by combined peroxidase histochemistry and autoradiography. *Brain Research* 147:159–164.

Wood, C. C. 1982. Implications of simulated lesion experiments for the interpretation of lesions in real nervous systems. In *Neural models of language processes,* edited by M. A. Arbib, D. Caplan, and J. C. Marshall. New York: Academic Press.

Wurtz, R. H., M. E. Goldberg, and D. L. Robinson. 1980. Behavioral modulation of visual responses in the monkey: Stimulus selection for attention and movement. In *Progress in psychobiology and physiological psychology,* edited by J. M. Sprague and A. N. Epstein, 48–83. New York: Academic Press.

Wurtz, R. H., B. J. Richmond, and W. T. Newsome. 1984. Modulation of cortical visual processing by attention, perception, and movement. In *Dynamic aspects of neocortical function,* edited by G. M. Edelman, W. E. Gall, and W. M. Cowan, 195–217. New York: Wiley.

Yamane, S., S. Kaji, and K. Kawano. 1988. What facial features activate face neurons in the inferotemporal cortex of the monkey? *Experimental Brain Research* 73:209–214.

Yarbus, A. L. 1967. *Eye movements and vision.* New York: Plenum.

Yin, R. K. 1969. Looking at upside-down faces. *Journal of Experimental Psychology* 81:141–145.

Yin, T. C. T., and V. B. Mountcastle. 1977. Visual input to the visuomotor mechanisms of the monkey's parietal lobe. *Science* 197:1381–1383.

Young, A. W., and H. D. Ellis, ed. 1989. *Handbook of research on face processing.* Amsterdam: North-Holland.

Young, J. M., S. R. Palef, and G. D. Logan. 1980. The role of mental rotation in letter processing by children and adults. *Canadian Journal of Psychology* 34:265–269.

Young, M. P., and S. Yamane. 1992. Sparse population coding of faces in the inferotemporal cortex. *Science* 256:1327–1331.

Yuille, J. C., and J. H. Steiger. 1982. Nonholistic processing in mental rotation: Some suggestive evidence. *Perception and Psychophysics* 31:201–209.

Zeki, S. M. 1978. Functional specialization in the visual cortex of the rhesus monkey. *Nature* 274:423–428.

Zeki, S. M. 1983. The distribution of wavelength and orientation selective cells in different areas of monkey visual cortex. *Proceedings of the Royal Society of London.* Series B. *Biological Sciences* 217:449–470.

Zeki, S. M. 1992. The visual image in mind and brain. *Scientific American* 267:68–76.

Zeki, S. M., and S. Shipp. 1988. The functional logic of cortical connections. *Nature* 335:311–317.

Zeki, S. M., J. D. G. Watson, C. J. Lueck, K. J. Friston, C. Kennard, and R. S. J. Frackowiak. 1991. A direct demonstration of functional specialization in human visual cortex. *Journal of Neuroscience* 11:641–649.

Zemel, R. S., and G. E. Hinton. 1991. Discovering viewpoint-invariant relationships that characterize objects. In *Advances in neural information processing systems* vol. 3, edited by R. P. Lippman, J. E. Moody, and D. S. Touretzky, 299–305. San Mateo, Calif.: Morgan Kaufmann.

Zihl, D., D. Von Cramon, and N. Mai. 1983. Selective disturbance of movement vision after bilateral brain damage. *Brain* 106:311–340.

Zimler, J., and J. M. Keenan. 1983. Imagery in the congenitally blind: How visual are visual images? *Journal of Experimental Psychology: Learning, Memory, and Cognition* 9:269–282.

Zipser, D., and R. A. Andersen. 1988. A back-propagation programmed network that simulates response properties of a subset of posterior parietal neurons. *Nature* 331:679–684.

Author Index

Subject Index

Note: Page numbers followed by "f" represent figures; those followed by "t" represent tables.

Area V1, 65–67, 66f–68f, 254. *See also*
  Visual cortex; Area 17
  damage to, 44
  and visual angle, 310, 311
  motion encoding in, 155
  in visual buffer, 86
Area V2, 31. *See* Area 18
Area V4
  in color processing, 30, 31
  effect of attention on neuron sensitivity in,
    100
  feedback projections of, 146
  motion encoding in, 156
  in preprocessing subsystem, 116
  in visual buffer, 86, 87
Arguments, in propositional representation,
    5, 6
Arm movements
  in mental rotation, 346–348
  in visual memory, 350, 351
Arousal, cerebral, and attentional biases, 41
Artificial intelligence, and mental events, 2
Association(s), among brain damage deficits,
    42–45
Associationists, British, 1
Associative memory, 69f, 73, 75, 76, 118,
    120, 214–225, 215f, 249–251
  anatomical localization of, 223–225
  in basic visual abilities, 259, 260, 262, 263
  binding problem of, 218, 219
  brain activity in, 255
  characteristics of, 381t
  contents of, 215
  as distinct subsystem, 216–218
  in identifying contorted images, 214–225
  in image generation, 288–291, 383, 384
  in image inspection, 386
  and imagery, 242
  level of hierarchy in, 221, 222
  long-term, 224
  in naming time, 266, 269, 274
  processing in, 219–222
  in RESOLUTION process, 392
  schema in, 263
  structural description in, 216
"Assumptions" in theory of computation, 34
Attention
  anatomical bases of, 236–239
  changes in focus of. *See* Attention window
  covert, 89
  disengaged/shifted/engaged, 234
  effects of context on, 97
  in mental rotation, 355
  preattentive processes and, 91, 92

spatial selectivity of, 87, 91
theories about, 90, 91
top-down influences on, 225
Attentional biases
  in divided-visual-field studies, 41
  in spatial relations encoding, 207–209
  and structural lateralization, 184, 185
Attentional priming, 287
Attention-based imagery, 301–308, 303f,
    318, 321, 325, 387, 391
  in image generation, 385
  in image inspection, 328
  and mental drawing, 310
Attention shifting, 69f, 74, 75, 77, 88, 89
  anatomical localization of, 93
  in blindness, 92
  bottom-up, 92
  characteristics of, 382t
  in image inspection, 386
  in imagery vs. perception, 102, 103
  serial, in computing categorical spatial
    relations, 211
  stimulus-based, 92–94, 93f, 102–104, 247,
    259
  characteristics of, 380t
  in encoding parts, 167
Attention-shifting strategies, vs. mental
    rotation, in image
  transformation, 362–365
Attention-shifting subsystem, 230, 233–239,
    235f, 250
  decomposition of, 234
  in FIND process, 391
  finer-grained subsystems of, 234
  in image generation, 384
  in LOOKFOR process, 393
  weighting of, 403t
Attention window, 69f, 70, 76, 85, 87–92,
    93f, 247–251, 258
  anatomical localization of, 91
  characteristics of, 380t
  in image generation, 384, 385
  in image inspection, 385
  in imagery/perception, 101, 102
  in image scanning, 101, 344
  incremental adjustment in scope of, 94, 95,
    124
  operation of, 89
  strategic control of, 158
  position of. *See* Reference frame
  scope-resolution trade-off of, 96–98, 101,
    104
  and selection of level of scale, 95–98
  shifting of. *See* Attention shifting

Auditory imagery/verbal task
  cerebral blood flow in, 59
Autobiographical images, 308

Basic level in hierarchy, 222, 272
Basic-level representation, 273, 287, 289
Behavioral dysfunction, in brain-damaged
  subjects, 42–45
Behavioral neurological approach to brain
  damage, 42
Behavioral studies, of imagery and
  perception, 54–58
Best-matching representations, 120–122
  in parts recognition, 157, 158
Bias, attentional. *See* Attentional biases
Binding of objects, 214
Binding problem in associative memory, 218
Blindness
  color, 116
  congenital, imagery in, 334
  damage to geniculostriate pathway and, 92
  mental rotation in, 360
  in one visual field, 92
  three-dimensional imaging in, 323
Blind spot, 13
Blink scan, 150
Blink transformation, 100, 354, 369, 387,
  402t
Blob structure, damage to, 44
Blood flow, cerebral. *See* Cerebral blood flow
Body-centered coordinates, 168, 170, 233
Bottom-up attention shifting, 92
Bottom-up processing, 119, 121, 124, 151,
  152
  left hemisphere in, 206
  in LOOKFOR process, 393
  in parts recognition, 159, 160
  testing predictions about, 256
Brain ablation studies, 49
Brain activity
  in brain-damaged subjects, 43
  cerebral lateralization in. *See* Cerebral
    lateralization; Hemispheric specialization
  during color perception, 116
  excitatory vs. inhibitory, 27
  in image maintenance, 321
  during imagery, 13–20
    2-deoxyglucose uptake for, 13, 14f
    magnetic resonance imaging for, 19
    positron emission tomography for, 13, 16f
    retinotopic mapping for, 13–15, 14f, 16f
  in input/output mappings, 25–28
  during mental rotation, 346, 347

methods for studying, 45–49
techniques for measuring, 45–49
testing predictions about, 251–258, 253f,
  254f, 256f
  in image generation, 298–301, 300f
  during visual perception, 17
Brain damage
  attention shifting in, 92
  and color blindness, 116
  and drawing from memory, 313
  dysfunction after (case history), 276–283
  effect on color perception, 59, 113
  effect on imagery and perception, 59, 329
  imagery deficits in, 329
  image transformation in, 373–375
  and motion deficits, 156
  patterns of deficits in, 42–45
  and preprocessing deficits, 112, 113
  spatiotopic mapping subsystem in, 171
  studies of processing in, 41–45
  visual angle in, 310, 311
Brain scanning. *See* Scanning
British Associationists, 1
Broca, 42
Buffer, visual, 69f, 70, 74–76

Canonical view of object, 270
  subsystem processing in, testing of,
    252–255, 254f, 256f
Carbon monoxide poisoning, ventral
  damage in, 214
Cartesian coordinates, 169, 171
Cascades in visual processing, 32, 148,
  263
Categorical-coordinate conversion
  subsystem, 231–233, 232f, 250
  damage to, 244
  in image generation, 385
  in LOOKFOR process, 393
Categorical judgment, cerebral blood flow in,
  198
Categorical property lookup subsystem,
  230, 231, 232f, 250
  characteristics of, 382t
  weighting of, 403t
Categorical spatial relations, 193, 231, 232
  effect of practice on, 202, 203
  in image generation, 295–298, 297f,
    309, 384
  rules in, 401t
  serial vs. reflexive computations of,
    210–212
  vs. metric spatial relations, 193, 194

Computational utility of images, 404
Computer analogy
  for mental representations, 4, 8
  for visual processing, 25
Computer models
  of imagery, 4, 8, 147, 392, 404–406
  of spatial relations encoding subsystems,
    203–206
  of visual memory structure, 182–187, 183f,
    187f
Computer vision system (Lowe's), 108
Conceptual information, in associative
    memory, 73
Concurrent learning, 140
Configural processing, 113
Connectionist systems. *See* Neural networks
Constancies, perceptual, 61
Constraint satisfaction process, 26, 32, 38, 39
  in figure-ground segregation, 159, 160f
  in pattern activation subsystem, 120, 151,
    153
Context, 249
  in associative memory, 221
  and attentional bias, 235
  in naming time, 271
Contorted objects, identification of, 191–
    245. *See also* Object identification, in
    contorted objects
Contours of image
  degraded, and naming time, 265
  deletion of, 110, 111f
    vs. part deletion, 161–163, 162f
Contractive affine transforms, 147
Convergence zones in neural networks, 31
Cooperative computation, 32, 51, 121, 148,
    263, 405
Coordinate mapping, 228
Coordinate property lookup subsystem,
    226–230, 229f, 250
  anatomical localization of, 228
  characteristics of, 382t
  deficit in, 244
  weighting of, 403t
Coordinate representations, 195, 227, 228,
    236
  in right-hemisphere damage, 199–202
Coordinates
  body-centered, 233
  as derived from categorical spatial relation,
    231–233
  head-centered, 233
  motor-based, 227, 233
  object-centered, 150

spatial, 227
  in spatiotopic mapping, 168–178
  viewer-centered, 149, 234
Coordinate spatial relations, 262
  in action control, 204
  in image generation, 295–298, 297f, 384
  rules in, 401t
Coordinate spatial relations encoding
    subsystem, 192–214, 249, 262
  anatomical localization of, 213, 214
  in associative memory, 222
  characteristics of, 381t
  computer models of, 203–206
  convergent evidence for, 198–202
  dorsal and ventral representations in, 209,
    210
  effect of practice on, 202, 203
  empirical tests of, 194–203, 196f–198f
  in image inspection, 386
  output from, 219
  potential paradox in, 212, 213
  testing a prediction from, 206–209, 207f,
    209f
  weighting of, 403t
Coordinate transformations, 234
Corpus callosum
  "noise" over, 314
  in retinal processing, 40
Cortex, visual. *See* Visual cortex
Cortical activity. *See* Brain activity
Cortical connections, length of, 30, 31
Cortico-cortical connections, 147, 148
Covert attention, 89
Craniotopic coordinates, 169, 171, 233
Crystal structure, imagery-based system in,
    404
Cuneus, 304
Curved objects, encoding of, 28, 83
  deficit in, 113
Curvilinearity of image, 108, 109f

DC potential shift in image maintenance, 321
Decomposable subsystems, 29
Deep representation, 146
Degraded contours, and naming time, 265
Degraded images, identification of, 153–189.
    See also Object identification, in degraded
    images
Degraded input, 32, 62, 126, 260–262
2-Deoxyglucose uptake
  in retinotopic mapping, 13, 14f
  in studies of brain activation, 46
Depictive images, utility of, 404–406

Grain, in visual buffer, 99, 100
Gravitational upright, 133, 360, 361

Habit system, vs. cognitive system, 140–142
Hand movements, in mental rotation, 347
Head-centered coordinates, 169, 171, 233
Hemianopia, homonymous, 92, 332
Hemispheric specialization. *See also* Cerebral
 lateralization
 in categorical vs. coordinate spatial
  relations, 195
 in image generation, 295–298, 297f
 size of receptive field in, 204–206, 207f,
  209f
 in spatial relations processing
  computer models of, 203–206
  empirical evidence of, 194–203, 196f–
   198f
  testing prediction of, 206–209, 207f, 209f
Hidden units, 27, 28
 as "feature detectors," 83, 88
 receptive and projective fields of, 82–84,
  177
Hierarchical structure of objects, 157, 221
 differences in, 272
Hippocampus, in memory, 214, 223
Homology, cross-species, 49, 50, 257
Homonymous hemianopia, 92, 332
Hooper Visual Organization Test, 330

Identification, vs. recognition, 72
Identity of object. *See* Object identification
Illusions, perceptual, imagery and, 57
Image(s). *See also* Object(s); Representation(s)
 autobiographical, 308
 capacity limits of, 323, 336
 compressed, 119, 151
  matching of, 126
 computational utility of, 404
 contorted. *See* Object identification, in
  contorted images
 contours of, deleted, 110, 111f
 conversion to standard representation of,
  79, 80
 curved, 28
 decay of, 101
 degraded. *See* Object identification, in
  degraded images
 depictive, 404–406
 distorted, visual buffer inhomogeneities
  and, 114
 fast fading of, 74–76, 101, 150, 323
 general vs. specific, 308
 global, 292

high-resolution, generation of, 310
interpretation of, infinite regress in, 21
large vs. small, differences in cortical
 activity for, 18, 18f
mental drawing of, 286
mental subtraction of, 337
mirror, 270
multipart, generation of, 291–295, 317
nonaccidental properties of, 108–114, 109f,
 111f
novel combinations of, 286
occluded, 62
prototypical, 308, 319
recall of, eye movements in, 350
reinterpretation of, 327, 336
reorganization of, 338
represented at different scales, 95–98
reversible, 338
saccadic suppression of, 101
single-part, generation of, 287–291
skeletal, 292
storage of, 79, 80
stored. *See* Representation(s), stored
as template, 69, 121
vanishing point of, 100
visual angle and. *See* Visual angle(s)
vividness of, 129, 328
vs. percepts, 74, 102–104
Image activation, 146–149
Image-based matching, 120–122
Imaged object. *See* Object(s)
Imaged practice, 348
Image generation, 75, 285–321, 383–385
 anatomical localization of, 311–319
  bilateral processing in, 317–319
  in left hemisphere, 312–315
  in right hemisphere, 315–317
 associative memory in, 288–291
 attention-based imagery in, 301–308, 303f,
  387
 brain activity in
  and commonalities between imagery and
   perception, 298–301, 300f
  testing predictions of, 298–301, 300f
 categorical and coordinate spatial relations
  in, 295–298, 297f
 deficits in, right and left hemispheres in,
  312–319
 dorsal and ventral imagery in, 301–308,
  303f, 306f
 eye movements in, 101
 hemispheric lateralization in, 295–298, 297f
 of multipart images, 291–295, 317, 384
 multiscaled representation in, 310

Input averaging by neurons, 99
Input/output mappings
  in attention-shifting subsystem, 234
  categorical vs. coordinate, 228
  computations in, 25, 26
  conflation of, 31, 32
  consistency of, 32
  cooperative computation in, 32
  division of labor in, 80, 105, 106
  in encoding object identity and location,
    80–85, 81f
  in identifying objects from different
    vantage points, 105–107
  neural network models for, 26–28
  processing of, 25–28. *See also* Visual
    processing subsystems
  recurrent feedback in, 32
  spatiotopic mapping subsystem in, 170
Input properties. *See* Object properties
Input units, 27, 28
Inspection of image. *See* Image inspection
Integrative agnosia, 112
Interblob structure, damage to, 44
Interference, in image inspection, 328
"Internal eyeball," 97
Internal representations. *See* Image(s);
    Representation(s)
Introspection, 7, 305, 339
Iterative processing, 294

James, William, 1, 21, 54

Kinesthetic imagery, 335, 345

Language
  comprehension, 179
    Wernicke's area in, 223
  processing of, 194
  production, 179
  programming, and propositional
    representations, 8
Lateral geniculate nucleus, 65, 67f
Lateralization, cerebral. *See* Cerebral
    lateralization
Law of common fate (Gestalt), 153, 155
Laws of physics, 345, 377
Learning
  concurrent, 140
  imagery in, 285
  motor, imagery in, 348
Left hemisphere
  in bottom-up processing, 206
  in categorical spatial relations, 202, 203

damage to
  and image generation deficits, 312–319
  and mental rotation, 373–375
  and parts encoding, 186
  and spatial relations processing, 199–202
  in image generation, 295–298, 297f, 311–
    315
  language processing in, 194
  in spatial relations encoding, 252, 253
  in visual memory
    computer models of, 182–187
    empirical evidence of, 179–182
Left-hemisphere imagery, 312–315
Left-right orientation
  differences in, and naming time, 270
  mental rotation and, 358–360, 363
Left-right orientation, memory for, 131,
    138
Left/right task in spatial relations testing,
    197, 197f
Limbic system, in memory, 214, 218
Line drawings, processing of, 112
Line-drawing task, to test imagery theory,
    399
Linguistics, Chomskian, 2
LISP, 8
List search operation, 8, 12
Literal files, 146, 294
Local coordinates, 169, 185
Location, memory for, 218
Location discrimination, in parietal lobe
    damage, 71
Location of objects
  coarse coding in, 177
  differences in, and naming time, 269
  processing of, 60, 71, 80–85, 81f, 258
  spatiotopic mapping system for, 168–178,
    169f
  transformation of, 351
Location representations, 227
LOOKFOR process, 390t, 393
Lookup, information, 69f, 73, 75, 76
Lookup subsystems
  in ANSWERIF process, 394
  categorical, 230, 231, 232f
  coordinate, 226–230, 229f
  and FIND process, 391
  in frontal lobe damage, 251
  in image generation, 294
  in image inspection, 386
  left hemisphere in, 252, 253
  in LOOKFOR process, 393
Lowe's computer vision system, 108

Lowe's nonaccidental properties, 108–114, 109f, 111f

Macular stimulation, cortical response to, 16f
Magnetic resonance imaging
  functional, 47
  during imagery, 19
Magnetoencephalography, strengths and
    weaknesses of, 45, 47–49
Magnocellular ganglion cells, 64, 65
Marr's principle of least commitment, 86,
    118
Marr's theory of algorithm, 35–37
Marr's theory of computation, 33–35
Marr's theory of edge detection, 34, 37, 95
Matching, image-based, 120–122
McCullough effect, 56, 57
M cells, 64, 65
Memory
  associative. *See* Associative memory
  autobiographical, 308
  drawing from, 313
  long-term, in image maintenance, 324
  semantic, 113
  short-term, 286
    in image maintenance, 324
  swapping process in, 324
  visual. *See* Visual memory
  "working," 143, 324
Memory deficit, after right temporal
    lobectomy, 180
Memory shifts, and anticipated motion of
    object, 353
Mental decomposition of patterns, 337, 338
Mental drawing, 286, 310, 385
"Mental flipping," 134
Mentalistic psychology, 2
Mental representations. *See* Image(s);
    Representation(s)
Mental rotation, 3, 9, 130, 267
  attention in, 355
  in blindness, 360
  in image transformation, 345
    and reference frames, 359–362
  left-right orientation in, 358–360, 363
  low-level visual processes in, 349
  mental aftereffects in, 348
  in mirror-reversed judgments, 135
  motor processes in, 346
  neural activity in, 346, 372–376
  oblique, 349
  right hemisphere in, 373
  size of objects and, 355
  of three-dimensional objects, 356

time required for, 355–357
  for upside-down pictures, 134
  vs. attention-shifting strategies, 362–365
Mental scanning. *See* Scanning
Mental sentence, 5
Mental subtraction of images, 337
Metabolism, cerebral, studies of, 46
Metric judgment, cerebral blood flow in, 198
Metric representations, in right-hemisphere
    damage, 199–202
Metric spatial relations
  encoding of, 192
  representations of, 193
  vs. categorical, 193, 194, 262
Minimalist theory of imagery, 64
Minnesota Paper Form Board test, 368
Mirror images, 270
  mental rotation and, 358
Mirror-reversed image, 131, 138, 359, 360
Mirror-reversed/normal judgment, 135
Modularity of visual system components, 29
Molecular structure, imagery-based system
    in, 404
Momentum, representational, 352
Monkey, retinotopic mapping in, 13, 14f
Monkey brain, as human homolog, 49, 50,
    257
Motion-added image transformation, 350–
    353, 376, 387
  eye movements in, 366
  rules in, 402t
  for scanning, 367
Motion aftereffects in mental rotation, 348
Motion cues, 261
  to delineate object, 153
  to identify object, 154
Motion-encoded image transformation
  eye movements in, 366
  rules in, 402t
  types of, 357–359
  vs. motion-added transformation, 350–353,
    376, 387
  zooming in, 369
Motion fields, properties of, 154
Motion of objects, 153–157, 155f
  neurons encoding, 155
Motion perception deficits, in brain damage,
    156
Motion relations encoding subsystem, 154–
    157, 155f, 248, 261
  characteristics of, 380t
  in image inspection, 386
  weighting of, 402t
Motion sensors, to track objects, 30

Motion vectors, 154
Motor activity. *See also* Movement(s)
  in image transformations, 372
Motor-based coordinates, 227, 233
Motor learning, imagery in, 348
Motor processing, 213
  in image transformation, 346–349
Movement(s)
  anticipated, 351–353
  laws of physics in, 377
  simulated, 352
  visually guided, 352
Movement control, 213
Moving objects, image transformation in, 350–353
MRI. *See* Magnetic resonance imaging
Muller-Lyer illusion, 57
Multiple objects, identification of
  automatic, 64, 263
  in single fixation, 63, 64, 263
Multiscaled representations, 95–98

Name frequency, differences in, 274
Name of object
  accessing, 264, 274–276
  assigning of, 264, 271–274
  difference in age-of-acquisition of, 275
  familiarity with, 275
  superordinate vs. subordinate, 273, 274
Naming of object
  in priming, 287, 289
  time required for, 258, 264–276
Navigation
  right hemisphere in, 179
Navigation, right hemisphere in, 194
Near-space mapping, 171
Neglect, visual. *See* Visual neglect
Neostriatum, 140, 141
Networks, neural. *See* Neural networks
Neural activity. *See* Brain activity
Neural basis of image transformation, 372–376
Neural computation, 25–28, 32, 51
  theories of, 33–37, 51
Neural information processing. *See also* Visual processing
  assumptions about, 25–32, 51
  theories of, 35–39
Neural networks
  bidirectional structure of, 243
  convergence zones in, 31
  diffuse activation of, 31
  formalisms in, 54
  hidden units in, 81f, 82–84

input and output units in, 27, 28, 81f, 81–84
interdigitated, 31
models of
  to encode object identity and location, 80–85, 81f
  in input/output mapping, 26–28
  split vs. unsplit, 82–84, 182
  in visual processing subsystems, 25–28
  "winner-take-all," 119, 150
Neuroanatomical constraints on visual system protomodel, 64–67, 66f–68f
Neurology, behavioral, 42
Neuromodulatory events, in visual processing, 32, 51
Neuron(s)
  input averaging by, 99
  multiple operations of, 31
  in parietal lobe, 72
  receptive fields of, in high-level vision, 67
  in registering motion, 155
  in temporal lobe, 71
  visual-somatosensory, 171
Neuronal connections
  feedback of, 146
  in figure-ground segregation, 30
  interaction time of, 30, 31
Neuron sensitivity
  effect of attention on, 97, 100
Neuropsychological studies of imagery and perception, 58–60
Noise
  over corpus callosum, 314
  visual, 55
Nonaccidental properties, 108–114, 109f, 111f, 248
  in basic visual abilities, 258–261, 263
  clinical evidence for, 112–114
  concept of, 108–110, 109f, 114
  deletion of, 110
  experimental evidence for use of, 110–112, 111f
  extraction of, 108, 109, 114
  limitations on, 112
  in image inspection, 385
  in image maintenance, 322
  insufficient, 119, 120
  and naming time, 268
  in parts recognition, 160, 161
  psychological reality of, 110, 111f
  vs. signal properties, 114
Novel combinations of objects, 286, 308–310, 385

Novel patterns, visualization of, 286, 310, 321

Object(s). *See also* Image(s)
binding of, 214
categorization of. *See* Category pattern activation subsystem
close, identification of, 63, 261
curved, visual processing of, 28
decay of, 101
degraded. *See* Object identification, in degraded images
distinctive properties of, 221, 226, 227, 230, 252
encoding of, ventral system in, 265–271
familiar, and naming time, 275
fixation on, 85, 89, 92, 93
foreshortened, and naming time, 270
geometry of, 335–339
hierarchical structure of, 157
high-information parts of, 225, 226
impossible, 132
inspection of. *See* Image inspection
location of, spatiotopic mapping subsystem in, 168–178, 169f
mental rotation of. *See* Mental rotation
motion of, 153–157, 155f
moving, image transformation in, 350–353
multiple, identification of, 63, 64, 263
naming of, processes in, 258, 264–276
nonaccidental properties of. *See* Nonaccidental properties
novel combinations of, 286
occluded, identification of, 62, 261
orientation of
disparity in, 125
spatiotopic mapping subsystem in, 168, 172
storage of, 130–135
overflow of, 99, 100
parts of. *See* Parts of objects
recall of, 286
scale of, selection of, 95–98
size of
disparity in, 95, 124, 125
spatiotopic mapping subsystem in, 168, 172
specific, identification of, 63, 262
stored properties of, 220, 227
symmetrical, 132
viewed parafoveally, 89
visual angle subtended by. *See* Visual angle(s)
visual tracking of, 30

Object-categorization task, 144
Object-centered coordinates, 150, 169
Object-centered representations, 127, 135, 149
Object files, 216
Object identification
abilities required for, 60–64, 61f, 258–264
at basic vs. entry level, 222, 272
in brain damage. *See also* Brain damage
case history, 276–283
in contorted objects, 191–245
associative memory in, 214–225, 215f. *See also* Associative memory
categorical vs. coordinate spatial relations in, 192–214
constraints in ventral system and, 239–241
coordinate spatial relations in, 192–214
and imagery/perception, 242–244
summary of, 241
top-down hypothesis testing in, 192, 225–239
in degraded images, 32, 62, 126, 153–189, 260–262
category pattern activation subsystem in, 178–188
exemplar pattern activation subsystem in, 178–188, 260
motion and, 153–157, 155f, 261
parts/wholes and, 157–167, 160f, 162f, 164f–167f, 261
spatial properties and, 168–178. *See also* Spatial properties
visual memory structures and, 178–188
at different distances, 60, 94–98, 259
context effects in, 97
incremental adjustment of attention window for, 94, 95
multiple eye movements in, 98
multiscaled representation in, 95–98
scope-resolution trade-off in, 96–98, 101, 104
at different positions in visual field, 60, 79–94, 258
attention shifting in, 92–94, 93f, 259
attention window in, 85, 87–92, 93f
division of labor in, 80–85, 81f
input/output mapping in, 80–85, 81f
neural network models in, 80–85, 81f
nonaccidental properties and, 114
summary of, 94
temporal and parietal lobes in, 80
visual buffer in, 85–87, 93f

Parts of objects
  complementary vs. identical, 162f, 163
  disrupted, 163–166, 164f–167f
    and naming time, 265
  disrupted spatial relations among, and
    naming time, 265
  high-information, 225, 226
  matching of, 163, 166
  metric spatial relations among, 193
  missing, and naming time, 265
  optional, 62, 260
  recognition of, 157–167, 160f, 162f, 164f–
    167f
  role of in recognition, 161–168, 162f,
    164f–167f
  scrambled, 163–166, 164f–167f
    and naming time, 265
  shape variations in, 62, 259
  storage of, 161
  varied spatial relations of, 62, 260. *See also*
    Object identification, in contorted
    objects
Parvocellular ganglion cells, 64, 65
Pattern activation subsystem(s), 117–145,
    118f, 122f, 123f, 248, 254
  and accumulation of visual input, 240
  in attention, 239
  in basic visual abilities, 258–263
  category. *See* Category pattern activation
    subsystem
  exemplar. *See* Exemplar pattern activation
    subsystem
  in FIND process, 391
  in image generation, 289, 293, 294, 383,
    384
  in image inspection, 386
  in image transformation, 387
  in LOOKFOR process, 393, 394
  in naming time, 266, 271, 272, 275
  output of, 117
  and PICTURE process, 391
  priming in, 236
  in REGENERATE process, 393
  storage of motion in, 154
  winner-take-all mechanism in, 119, 150
Pattern codes, 117, 219, 222, 236, 250
  in ANSWERIF process, 394
  in image generation, 292, 384
  in image inspection, 386
  and imagery, 242
  in lookup subsystems, 391
  in priming, 287
P cells, 64, 65

Percepts
  persistence of, 103
  vs. images, 74, 102–104
Perceptual abilities, 379
  basic, 60–64, 61f, 258–264
  at different locations/distances (visual
    angles), 60, 258, 259
  impoverished output, 62, 260–262
  in object identification, 60–64, 61f. *See also*
    Object identification
  objects and scenes, 63, 262–264
  shape variations, 61, 259, 260
  specific instances, 63, 262
Perceptual aftereffects, in imagery, 328
Perceptual category, 202
Perceptual constancies, 61
Perceptual illusions, induced by imagery, 57
Perceptual input, degraded vs. strong, 126
Perceptual parsing, 158–167, 160f, 162f,
    164f–167f
Perceptual representation systems, 118
Perceptual units, 107, 115
  in image inspection, 329
  individual, visualization of, 287
  integration of, 291–295
  marked by preprocessing system, 114,
    115
  organization of, 322
  in organizing input, 132, 133
Perspective, differences in, and naming time,
    270
PET. *See* Positron emission tomography
Physics, laws of, 345, 377
Picture(s). *See* Depictive representations
PICTURE process, 294, 389t, 391
Planar orientation, memory for, 131
"Pop-out" phenomenon, 342, 344, 369, 370,
    386
"Pop-out" search process
  in image inspection, 339–341, 391
Population codes, storage of, 118
Positron emission tomography
  in imagery vs. perception tasks, 302–305,
    303f
  to measure cerebral blood flow, 14, 16f
  pitfalls of, 19
  with small vs. large images, 17, 18, 18f
  in retinotopic mapping, 13, 14, 15f, 16f
  strengths and weaknesses of, 46–49
  in testing imagery theory predictions,
    252–258, 253f, 254f, 256f
Posner orienting task, 234
Practice, imaged, 348

Practice effect
and naming time, 268
in spatial relations encoding, 202, 203
in split-brain studies, 317
Preattentive processes, 91, 92, 173
Preattentive processing, 249
in controlling actions, 205
Predicate, in propositional representation, 5, 6
Prefrontal cortex
in image generation, 300, 300f, 304
lookup subsystems in, 228, 229, 231
Prefrontal lobe, in spatial relations encoding, 253
Preprocessing subsystem, 107f, 107–117, 109f, 111f, 248
and accumulation of visual input, 241
in attention, 239
in basic visual abilities, 258, 259
in brain damage, 330–333
characteristics of, 380t
damage to, 112, 113
in image inspection, 385
in image maintenance, 322, 387
mechanisms for shape recognition in, 113
weighting of, 402t
Preverbal representations, 202
Preview effect, 89
Primary visual cortex. *See* Visual cortex; Area 17; Area V1
Primate studies
neuroanatomical, 39, 49, 50
strengths and weaknesses of, 49, 50
Priming
attentional, 235, 238, 287
in attention-shifting subsystem, 235
and encoding facilitation, 328
in image generation, 287–289
imagery vs. nonimagery, 289
for impossible objects, 132
in LOOKFOR process, 394
mechanisms underlying, in imagery, 287–289
naming of objects in, 287, 289
in naming times, 266, 268, 269
in object recognition, 110, 111, 120, 148
tactile, 331
"unconscious," 324
via episodic relatedness, 263, 264
Priming paradigm, word stem-completion, 179
Principle of least commitment (Marr), 86, 118
Projective fields, analysis of, 82–84

Property lookup subsystems. *See* Lookup subsystems
Propositional files, 294
Propositional representations, 5–9, 12, 194
in ANSWERIF process, 394
definition of, 5
and priming, 289
vs. depictive, 405
Prosopagnosia, 113
Prothetic scales, 228
Protomodel of visual system, 64–76
associative memory in, 69f, 73, 75, 76
attention shifting in, 69f, 74, 75, 77
attention window in, 69f, 70, 76
dorsal system in, 68f, 69f, 71–73, 76
in imagery, 74–76
information lookup in, 69f, 73, 75, 76
neuroanatomical constraints on, 64–67, 66f–68f
in object identification, 69f, 69–74
subsystems of, 68–76, 69f
ventral system in, 67f–69f, 70, 72, 76
visual buffer in, 69f, 70, 74–76
Prototypical images, 308, 319
Proximity, Gestalt law of, 11
Psychological approach to imagery, 1–3
Pulvinar
in attention, 237, 238
in image generation, 304, 305, 310
in spatial attention, 91, 92
PUT process, 294, 319, 389t, 392
in split-brain studies, 312

Quadrant-depletion theory of attention, 90
Question-answering, 394
image inspection in, 341–343

Radical behaviorism, 2
Radioactive water
in retinotopic mapping, 13, 14
in studies of brain activation, 46
Radiolabeled sugar. *See* 2-Deoxyglucose
Reaching behavior, 352
Reality monitoring, 55
Reasoning, imagery in, 285, 324, 327, 404
Recall
eye movements in, 350
in image generation, 286
immediate, 129
Receptive field(s)
analysis of, 82–84
in area IT vs. area 7a, 176–178
in computing spatial relations, 204–206
in encoding shapes, 210

of hidden unit, 177
large vs. small, 182
and hemispheric lateralization, 204–206, 207f, 209f
tactile, 171
visual, 171
Receptive field hypothesis, 185
Recognition, vs. identification, 72
Reference frame, 231, 270
alteration of, 362
environmental, 361
in image transformation, 359–362
intrinsic, 361, 375
retinal, 361
Reference systems in object location, 168–170
Referential processing factor, 291
REGENERATE process, 389t, 393
Region-bounded image transformation, 365, 370, 388
Relatedness, episodic, 263, 264
Repetition priming paradigm, 110, 111, 120
Representation(s)
2, 2.5, and 3-dimensional, 169
alternative types of, 4–9
basic-level, 273, 287, 289
best matching of, 120–122
category. *See* Category representations
classes vs. individuals, 221
coordinate. *See* Coordinate representations
deep vs. surface, 146
depictive. *See* Depictive representations
entry-level, 273, 274, 289, 290
exemplar. *See* Exemplar representations
frame-independent, 130
generic, 289, 290
geometric, 335–339
inhibition of, 119, 121
of locations, 227
multiscaled, 95–98
of overall shape, 167
preverbal, 202
properties of, 4, 11
propositional, 5–9, 12, 194, 394, 405
retention of, 138
of spatial relations, metric vs. categorical, 193
stored, 79, 80
deformed, 126
object-centered, 127, 135
in object identification, 150
pattern activation subsystem and, 117–122

resolution of, 104
viewer-centered, 127–135
surface, 146
tokens of, 216, 217, 223
Representational momentum, 352
Resolution
of object
and size of region attended to, 96
in spatiotopic mapping, 172–174
trade-off with scope of view, 96
in visual buffer, 99
scales of. *See* Scale of object
of stored representation, 104
RESOLUTION process, 389t, 392
Response time studies, 27, 39, 40
Retention interval, 138, 139
Retention of image. *See* Image maintenance
Retina
projection of image on, 60, 61, 259
role in vision, 64, 67, 67f
Retinal cones, coarse coding by, 177
Retinal frame of reference, 361
Retinal input, processing of, hemispheric specialization and, 195–198, 196f–198f
Retinal stimulus, projection of to cerebral hemispheres, 40–42
Retinal translation, stimulus equivalence across, 61, 87
Retinotopic coordinates in visual buffer, 168, 170
Retinotopic mapping, 13–15, 14f, 16f, 67
Retinotopic mapping experiments, 13, 14, 15f, 16f
Retrorolandic regions of brain, in image maintenance, 321
Right hemisphere
in associative memory, 255
damage to
and global shape encoding, 186
and image generation deficits, 314–319
and mental rotation, 373–375
and spatial relations processing, 199–202
in image generation, 295–298, 297f, 311, 312, 315–317
in image rotation, 373
and navigation, 194
in visual memory
computer models of, 182–187
empirical evidence of, 179–182
Right-hemisphere imagery, 311, 315–317
ROTATE process, 390t, 394
Rotation, mental. *See* Mental rotation

Saccadic eye movements, 174
  area 8 in, 229
  area STP and, 223
Saccadic suppression of input, 75, 101
Scale
  prothetic, 228
  spatial, 212
Scale of object
  resolution of
    hemispheric lateralization in, 186
    in image generation, 310
  selection of, 95–98
  in spatiotopic mapping, 172–174
Scaling, size, 370
Scalp electrodes to detect brain activity, 45
Scan, blink, 150
Scanning
  attention window in, 101
  in image generation, 309
  in image inspection, 340, 344
  in image transformation, 345, 366–368
  incremental, 12
  in LOOKFOR process, 393
  "off-screen," 102
  of trajectory, 344
Scanning experiments, 7, 8
  constraints of, 11
  depictive vs. propositional representations
    in, 12
  dummy nodes in, 8, 12
  effect of experimenter expectancy on, 10,
    11
  effect of task demands on, 9
SCAN process, 390t, 394
Schema, in associative memory, 263
Scope of attention window, adjustment of,
  94, 95
Scope-resolution trade-off, 96–98, 101, 104
  in encoding moving objects, 350
  in image generation, 292
  in motion encoding, 158
Scrambled parts of objects, 163–166, 164f–
  167f
Selfridge Pandemonium model, 230
Semantic fields, 275
Semantic memory, 113
Semantic similarity, 271
Sensory-perceptual loop, 405
Serial scanning in image inspection, 340, 341
Shape(s)
  computation of, 28
  contorted, 62, 260. See also Object
    identification, in contorted images
  differences in, and naming time, 265

as feature vectors, 147
global. See Global shapes
hierarchical decomposition of, 157
internal structure of, 167
processing of, 31, 44, 61, 62, 80–85, 81f,
  92
  in different vantage points, 62, 259
  with parts missing or added, 62, 260
  when parts vary, 62, 259
  when spatial relations between parts vary,
    62, 260
reorganization of, 338
stored model of, 69
Shape, alphabet of, 161
Shape categories, encoding of, 210
Shape exemplars, encoding of, 210
Shape identification, rules in, 401t
Shape overlap, 272
Shape shift subsystem, 353, 372, 376, 377
  characteristics of, 382t
  in image transformation, 387
  in LOOKFOR process, 393
  in RESOLUTION process, 392
  weighting of, 403t
Shift transformations, 387
Signal detection methodology, in perception
  studies, 55
Signal properties, 114, 115, 248
  in basic visual abilities, 258, 259, 261
  in image inspection, 385
  in image maintenance, 322
  and naming time, 268
Simon's nearly decomposable subsystems, 29
Single photon emission tomography
  during imagery, 17
  in imagery/perception studies, 58
  strengths and weaknesses of, 45, 47–49
Size constancy, encoding of, 219
Size of objects
  comparisons of, 341
  differences in
    and naming time, 268
  processing of, 71
  and rotation time, 355
  spatiotopic mapping subsystem in, 168, 172
  transformation of, 351
Size scaling, 341, 370
Size tags, 341, 342
Skeletal image, 292, 294
Source amnesia, 225
Spatial codes, 194, 219, 236
  and imagery, 242
Spatial constraints of visual buffer, 291
Spatial coordinates, 227

Spatial extent concept, 344
  in blindness, 335
Spatial frequency, 212
Spatial imagery task, cerebral blood flow in, 59
Spatial information
  in identifying contorted objects, 191–214. *See also* Categorical spatial relations; Coordinate spatial relations
  in image generation, 291
  recall of, eye movements in, 350
Spatial localization deficit, 175
Spatial organization of visual buffer, 70, 85, 86, 153
Spatial orientation, tectopulvinar pathway in, 65
Spatial properties
  alteration of, 351
  in associative memory, 219–222
  encoding of, 250
    brain activity in, 256
  in image generation, 301, 302
  stored
    accessing of, 227, 228
Spatial properties of objects. *See also* Spatiotopic mapping subsystem
  to identify degraded image, 168–178
  processing of, 71, 80, 84, 88
    motion in, 156
Spatial relations
  categorical. *See* Categorical spatial relations
  coarse coding in, 204–206
  in contorted objects, computation of, 191, 192
  in depictive representations, 5, 7, 11
  disrupted, and naming time, 265
  hemispheric processing of, 194–203, 196f–198f
    in brain damage, 199–202
  identifying specific, 63, 262
  in image generation, 291, 292, 295–298, 297f
  metric, 192–194
  receptive fields in, 204–206
  rules in, 401t
  topological, 194
  variations in, 62, 260
Spatial relations encoding subsystems, 259
  categorical vs. coordinate, 192–214
  in FIND process, 391
  in image inspection, 243
Spatial representations, 210
  reconstruction of, 147

Spatial resolution, P cells in, 65
Spatial scale, 212
Spatial selectivity, of attention window, 87, 90
Spatial summation, 99
Spatiotopic coordinates, 168–170
Spatiotopic mapping subsystem, 168–178, 169f, 249
  and accumulation of visual input, 240
  anatomical localization of, 174–176
  in basic visual abilities, 258, 259, 262
  brain activity in, 254
  categorical vs. coordinate, 192–194, 195f
  characteristics of, 381t
  disruption of, 176
  distinctiveness of, 170–172
  in image inspection, 386
  in image transformation, 387
  levels of resolution in, 172–174
  location/size/orientation in, 172
  in motion-added image transformation, 351
  in near and far space, 171
  reference systems in, 168–170
  weighting of, 403t
Specific exemplars, 178, 183f
Specific images, 308
SPECT. *See* Single photon emission tomography
Speed-accuracy trade-off, 134, 135
  in lateralized lesion, 314, 316
Split-brain studies, 41, 311, 316, 317
  mental rotation in, 373, 375
Spotlight theory of attention, 90, 95
Sternberg memory scanning task, 339
Stimulus-based attention shifting. *See* Attention shifting, stimulus-based
Stimulus equivalence across retinal translation, 61, 87
Stimulus-specific habituation, 139
Storage-processing trade-off, 136
Stored properties of objects, 220, 227
Stored representations. *See* Representation(s), stored
Streams of processing subsystems, 32
Striate cortex. *See* Visual cortex
Structural description, 216, 263, 320
Structure, in mental representations, 12
Structure-process trade-offs, 40
  in imagery theories, 12
Subordinate level of object naming, 273, 274, 289
Subtraction, mental, 337

Subtraction methodologies in brain scanning, 48
Sulcus(i)
  studying electrical events in, 45
  superior temporal, 128, 141, 142
Superior colliculus, 93, 103
Superior temporal sulcus, 128, 141, 142
Superordinate level of object naming, 273, 274, 287, 289
Surface properties, distinction of, 114
Surface representation, 146
Symbols, in propositional representation, 5, 6
Symmetrical figures, encoding of, 133
Symmetry of image, 108, 109f
Synaptic strengths, changes in, 266
Syntactic classes, 194

Tactile/kinesthetic imagery, 335
Tags
  category, 342
  neural, 219
  size, 341, 342
Task demands
  effect on attentional biases, 41
  in scanning experiments, 9
Tectopulvinar (tectofugal) pathway, 65, 171
  in attention shifting, 93
  in orientation processing, 92
Template, deformable, 126
Template matching, 69, 121
Temporal gyri, in face recognition, 143, 144
Temporal lobe. See also Ventral system
  activity in, during imagery/perception studies, 58, 59
  in associative memory, 223–225
  damage to, 137, 138
    effect on discrimination task, 71, 72
  in image generation, 289, 305
  motion encoding in, 154–156
  neurons in, 71
  pattern activation subsystems in, 136–145, 187
  in preprocessing subsystem, 116
  receptive fields of, 137
  specialization of, 80, 84
  and visual memory, 117, 180
Texture, differences in, and naming time, 266
Texture gradients, distinction of, 114
Texture identification, rules in, 401t
Thalamus
  in attention, 237, 238
  connections to visual areas, 147, 148
  in image activation, 147, 148
  in image generation, 300

Theory of computation (Marr), 33–35
Theory of edge detection, 34, 37, 95
Theory of perceptual representation systems, 118
Three-dimensional images, chunking of, 323
Three-dimensional objects, mental rotation of, 356, 357
Three-dimensional representations, 169, 176
Tokens of representations, 216, 217, 223
Top-down control strategies, 226
Top-down hypothesis testing, 192, 225–239
  attention shifting subsystem in, 230, 233–239, 235f
  in basic visual abilities, 259–262
  categorical-coordinate conversion subsystem in, 231–233, 232f
  categorical property lookup subsystem in, 230, 231, 232f
  coordinate property lookup subsystem in, 226–230, 229f
  in image generation, 299–301, 384
  PET scanning in, 252–258, 253f, 254f, 256f
  priming in, 235, 236
Trajectory scanning, 344
  mental rotation in, 346
Transformation
  blink, 354, 369, 387, 402t
  of image. See Image transformation
  shift, 387
Transformation locus, 388
Transformation stage, 358
Two-dimensional objects, mental rotation of, 356, 357
Two-dimensional representations, 169, 176
Typicality of object, differences in, and naming time, 271

Upright
  gravitational vs. subjective, 361
  standard, 360, 364
Upright cues, 364, 365
Upside-down cues, 364
Upside-down stimulus, 133, 134

Vanishing point of image, 100
Vector completion, 121, 126, 163, 369, 405
Ventral imagery function, vs. dorsal imagery function, 305–308, 306f
Ventral system, 67f–69f, 70, 72, 76, 248–250
  accumulation of constraints in, 239–241
  activity in, 254
  damage to, 214
  encoding motion in, 156